Organizational Capability and Competitive Advantage

The International Library of Critical Writings in Business History

Series Editor: Geoffrey Jones
Professor of Business History,
University of Reading

1. The Growth of Multinationals
   Mira Wilkins

2. Government and Business
   Steven W. Tolliday

3. Mergers and Acquisitions
   Gregory P. Marchildon

4. Antitrust and Regulation
   Giles H. Burgess Jr

5. The Rise of Big Business
   Barry E. Supple

6. Marketing (Volumes I and II)
   Stanley C. Hollander and Kathleen M. Rassuli

7. Coalitions and Collaboration in International Business
   Geoffrey Jones

8. Business Elites
   Youssef Cassis

9. Technology Transfer and Business Enterprise
   David J. Jeremy

10. Big Business in Mining and Petroleum
    Christopher Schmitz

11. Organizational Capability and Competitive Advantage
    William Lazonick and William Mass

Future titles will include:

Family Business
Mary B. Rose

Entrepreneurship and the Growth of Firms
Harold Livesay

Women in Business
Mary A. Yeager

The Rise and Fall of Mass Production
Steven W. Tolliday

Industrial Research and Innovation in Business
David Edgerton

Organizational Capability and Competitive Advantage

Debates, Dynamics and Policy

Edited by

William Lazonick

University Professor of Policy and Planning
University of Massachusetts Lowell, US

and

William Mass

Interim Dean of Graduate Programs
College of Management
University of Massachusetts Lowell, US

THE INTERNATIONAL LIBRARY OF CRITICAL WRITINGS IN BUSINESS HISTORY

An Elgar Reference Collection

Published by
Edward Elgar Publishing Limited
Gower House
Croft Road
Aldershot
Hants GU11 3HR
England

Edward Elgar Publishing Company
Old Post Road
Brookfield
Vermont 05036
USA

British Library Cataloguing in Publication Data
Organizational Capability and Competitive
Advantage. – (International Library of
Critical Writings in Business History;
Vol. 11)
    I. Lazonick, William   II. Mass, William
    III. Series
    338.6

Library of Congress Cataloguing in Publication Data
Organizational capability and competitive advantage / edited by
    William Lazonick and William Mass.
        p. cm. — (The international library of critical writings in
    business history; 11) (An Elgar reference collection)
        1. Organizational effectiveness. 2. Competition. 3. Industrial
    management. I. Lazonick, William. II. Mass, William, 1949–
    III. Series. IV. Series: An Elgar reference collection.
    HD58.9.07325 1995
    338.6'048—dc20   94–44343
                                                                                  CIP

ISBN 1 85278 776 7

Printed in Great Britain by Galliard (Printers) Ltd, Great Yarmouth

Contents

Acknowledgements   ix
Introduction   xi

PART I   HISTORICAL DEBATES
1.   Alfred Marshall (1961), Chapters X and XI of *Principles of
     Economics*, London: Macmillan, 267–90   3
2.   Allyn A. Young (1928), 'Increasing Returns and Economic
     Progress', *Economic Journal*, **XXXVIII** (152), December,
     527–42   27
3.   Joseph A. Schumpeter (1947), 'The Creative Response in
     Economic History', *Journal of Economic History*, **VII** (2),
     November, 149–59   43
4.   Edith Tilton Penrose (1952), 'Biological Analogies in the
     Theory of the Firm', *American Economic Review*, **XLII** (5),
     December, 804–19   54

PART II   CONTEMPORARY DEBATES
5.   Louis Galambos (1983), 'Technology, Political Economy, and
     Professionalization: Central Themes of the Organizational
     Synthesis', *Business History Review*, **57** (4), Winter, 471–93   73
6.   Alfred D. Chandler, Jr. (1992), 'Managerial Enterprise and
     Competitive Capabilities', *Business History*, **34** (1), January,
     11–41   96
7.   Roy Church, Albert Fishlow, Neil Fligstein, Thomas Hughes,
     Jürgen Kocka, Hidemasa Morikawa and Frederic M. Scherer
     (1990), '*Scale and Scope*: A Review Colloquium', *Business
     History Review*, **64** (3), Autumn, 690–735   127
8.   Michael E. Porter (1990), 'The Competitive Advantage of
     Nations', *Harvard Business Review*, No. 2, March–April, 73–93   173
9.   Richard R. Nelson (1991), 'Why Do Firms Differ, and How
     Does it Matter?', *Strategic Management Journal*, **12**, 61–74   194
10. Dorothy Leonard-Barton (1992), 'Core Capabilities and Core
     Rigidities: A Paradox in Managing New Product Develoment',
     Strategic Management Journal, **13**, 111–25   208
11. Sebastiano Brusco (1982), 'The Emilian Model: Productive
     Decentralisation and Social Integration', *Cambridge Journal of
     Economics*, **6** (2), June, 167–84   223
12. Ronald Dore (1983), 'Goodwill and the Spirit of Market Capitalism',
     The British Journal of Sociology, **XXXIV** (4), December, 459–82   241

13. William Lazonick (1990), 'Organizational Capabilities in
     American Industry: The Rise and Decline of Managerial
     Capitalism', *Business and Economic History*, second series, **19**,
     35–54   265

PART III THE DYNAMICS OF SUCCESS
14. William Mass (1989), 'Mechanical and Organizational
     Innovation: The Drapers and the Automatic Loom', *Business
     History Review*, **63** (4), Winter, 876–929   287
15. David A. Hounshell (1992), 'Continuity and Change in the
     Management of Industrial Research: The Du Pont Company,
     1902–1980' Chapter 8 in Giovanni Dosi, Renato Giannetti and
     Pier Angelo Toninelli (eds), *Technology and Enterprise in a
     Historical Perspective*, Oxford: Clarendon Press, 231–60   341
16. Edith T. Penrose (1960), 'The Growth of the Firm – A Case
     Study: The Hercules Powder Company', *Business History
     Review*, **34**, Spring, 1–23   371
17. Louis Ferleger and William Lazonick (1993), 'The Managerial
     Revolution and the Developmental State: The Case of U.S.
     Agriculture', *Business and Economic History*, **22** (2), Winter,
     67–98   394
18. Takeshi Abe (1992), 'The Development of the Producing-Center
     Cotton Textile Industry in Japan between the Two World Wars',
     Japanese Yearbook on Business History, **9**, 3–27   426
19. Kazuo Wada (1991), 'The Development of Tiered Inter-firm
     Relationships in the Automobile Industry: A Case Study of
     Toyota Motor Corporation', *Japanese Yearbook on Business
     History*, **8**, 23–47   451
20. Richard Florida and Martin Kenney (1991), 'Transplanted
     Organizations: The Transfer of Japanese Industrial Organization
     to the U.S.', *American Sociological Review*, **56** (3), June,
     381–98   476
21. Richard N. Langlois (1992), 'External Economies and Economic
     Progress: The Case of the Microcomputer Industry', *Business
     History Review*, **66** (1), Spring, 1–50   494
22. AnnaLee Saxenian (1991), 'Institutions and the Growth of
     Silicon Valley', *Berkeley Planning Journal*, **6**, 36–57   544

PART IV POLICY PERSPECTIVES
23. Michael L. Dertouzos, Richard K. Lester and Robert M. Solow
     (1989), 'Imperatives for a More Productive America', Chapter
     10 of *Made in America: Regaining the Productive Edge*,
     Cambridge and London: MIT Press, 129–46   569
24. Robert B. Reich (1990), 'Who is Us?', *Harvard Business
     Review*, No. 1, January–February, 53–64   587

25. Laura D'Andrea Tyson (1991), 'They Are Not Us: Why American Ownership Still Matters', and Robert B. Reich (1991), 'Who Do We Think They Are?', *The American Prospect*, No. 4, Winter, 37–53   599
26. William Lazonick (1993), 'Industry Clusters versus Global Webs: Organizational Capabilities in the American Economy', *Industrial and Corporate Change*, **2** (1), 1–24   616

Name Index   641

Acknowledgements

The editors and publishers wish to thank the following who have kindly given permission for the use of copyright material.

Academic Press Ltd for article: Sebastiano Brusco (1982), 'The Emilian Model: Productive Decentralisation and Social Integration', *Cambridge Journal of Economics*, **6** (2), June, 167–84.

American Economic Association for article: Edith Tilton Penrose (1952), 'Biological Analogies in the Theory of the Firm', *American Economic Review*, **XLII** (5), December, 804–19.

American Prospect for article: Laura D'Andrea Tyson (1991), 'They Are Not Us: Why American Ownership Still Matters' and Robert B. Reich (1991), 'Who Do We Think They Are?', *American Prospect*, No. 4, Winter, 37–53.

American Sociological Association for article: Richard Florida and Martin Kenney (1991), 'Transplanted Organizations: The Transfer of Japanese Industrial Organization to the U.S.', *American Sociological Review*, **56** (3), June, 381–98.

Berkeley Planning Journal for article: AnnaLee Saxenian (1991), 'Institutions and the Growth of Silicon Valley', *Berkeley Planning Journal*, **6**, 36–57.

Business and Economic History for articles: William Lazonick (1990), 'Organizational Capabilities in American Industry: The Rise and Decline of Managerial Capitalism', *Business and Economic History*, **19**, 35–54; Louis Ferleger and William Lazonick (1993), 'The Managerial Revolution and the Developmental State: The Case of U.S. Agriculture', *Business and Economic History*, **22** (2), Winter, 67–98.

Cambridge University Press for article: Joseph A. Schumpeter (1947), 'The Creative Response in Economic History', *Journal of Economic History*, **VII** (2), November, 149–59.

Frank Cass & Co. Ltd for article: Alfred Chandler, Jr. (1992), 'Managerial Enterprise and Competitive Capabilities', *Business History*, **34** (1), January, 11–41.

Harvard Business School for articles: Edith T. Penrose (1960), 'The Growth of the Firm – A Case Study: The Hercules Powder Company', *Business History Review*, **34**, Spring, 1–23; Louis Galambos (1983), 'Technology, Political Economy, and Professionalization: Central Themes of the Organizational Synthesis', *Business History Review*, **57** (4), Winter, 471–93;

William Mass (1989), 'Mechanical and Organizational Innovation: The Drapers and the Automatic Loom', *Business History Review*, **63** (4), Winter, 876–929; Michael E. Porter (1990), 'The Competitive Advantage of Nations', *Harvard Business Review*, No. 2, March–April, 73–93; Robert B. Reich (1990), 'Who is Us?', *Harvard Business Review*, No. 1, January–February, 53–64; Roy Church, Albert Fishlow, Neil Fligstein, Thomas Hughes, Jürgen Kocka, Hidemasa Morikawa and Frederic M. Scherer (1990), '*Scale and Scope*: A Review Colloquium', *Business History Review*, **64** (3), Autumn, 690–735; Richard N. Langlois (1992), 'External Economics and Economic Progress: The Case of the Microcomputer Industry', *Business History Review*, **66** (1), Spring, 1–50.

John Wiley & Sons, Ltd for article: Richard R. Nelson (1991), 'Why Do Firms Differ, and How Does it Matter?', *Strategic Management Journal*, **12**, 61–74; Dorothy Leonard-Barton (1992), 'Core Capabilities and Core Rigidities: A Paradox in Managing New Product Development', *Strategic Management Journal*, **13**, 111–25.

Macmillan Press Ltd for excerpt: Alfred Marshall (1961), Chapters X and XI, *Principles of Economics*, 267–90.

MIT Press for excerpt: Michael L. Dertouzos, Richard K. Lester and Robert M. Solow (1989), 'Imperatives for a More Productive America', Chapter 10 of *Made in America: Regaining the Productive Edge*, 129–46.

Nagoya City University, Kazuo Wada and Takeshi Abe for articles: Kazuo Wada (1991), 'The Development of Tiered Inter-firm Relationships in the Automobile Industry: A Case Study of Toyota Motor Corporation', *Japanese Yearbook on Business History*, **8**, 23–47; Takeshi Abe (1992), 'The Development of the Producing-Center Cotton Textile Industry in Japan between the Two World Wars', *Japanese Yearbook on Business History*, **9**, 3–27.

Oxford University Press for excerpt and article: David A. Hounshell (1992), 'Continuity and Change in the Management of Industrial Research: The Du Pont Company, 1902–1980' in Giovanni Dosi, Renato Giannetti and Pier Angelo Toninelli (eds), *Technology and Enterprise in a Historical Perspective*, 231–60; William Lazonick (1993), 'Industry Clusters versus Global Webs: Organizational Capabilities in the American Economy', *Industrial and Corporate Change*, **2** (1), 1–24.

Routledge and the *British Journal of Sociology* for article: Ronald Dore (1983), 'Goodwill and the Spirit of Market Capitalism', *British Journal of Sociology*, **XXXIV** (4), 459–82.

Every effort has been made to trace all the copyright holders but if any have been inadvertently overlooked the publishers will be pleased to make the necessary arrangement at the first opportunity.

In addition the publishers wish to thank the Library of the London School of Economics and Political Science, the Marshall Library of Economics, Cambridge University and the Photographic Unit of the University of London Library for their assistance in obtaining these articles.

Introduction

Organizational Capability

Why do some enterprises do better than others in competition for product markets? What are the sources of competitive advantage? To what extent does the competitive advantage of the enterprise depend on its own strategy and structure, and to what extent on the institutional environment in which it operates? And how do the sources of competitive advantage vary across different industries over time?

These are critical questions for understanding how businesses and economies operate, and call for nothing less than a comprehensive theory of the competitive advantage of enterprises, regions and nations. Over the last decade or so, many academics concerned with business performance have begun to focus on 'organizational capability' as a prime determinant of competitive advantage. Organizational capability represents the power of a specialized division of labour that is planned and coordinated to achieve strategic goals. Through planned coordination, an organization can combine and integrate the various types of knowledge needed to develop new products and processes. Through planned coordination, an organization can speed the flow of work from purchased inputs to sold output, thereby enabling it to achieve lower unit costs. Through planned coordination, the specialized productive activities of numerous individuals can coalesce into a coherent collective force. When the technological and organizational requirements of the productive transformation are complex, the planned coordination of the specialized division of labour makes it possible to develop and utilize productive resources in ways that would not otherwise be possible.

To recognize the role of organizational capability in technological progress and business performance is to acknowledge that attaining and sustaining competitive advantage is a collective endeavour. A contrasting perspective – and one that has many adherents – is that business performance depends on the vision and knowledge of those strategic decision makers at the top of the business enterprise. Neglected in this perspective is the role of the organization – planned and coordinated productive relationships among numerous individuals – in implementing a competitive strategy. In a world of complex technology and intense competition, central to any theory of competitive advantage is the dynamic relationship between investment strategy and organizational structure.

The responsibility for formulating investment strategy may be at the level of the enterprise, the region or the nation. The investment strategy of an enterprise is constrained (to an extent that varies by industry, across nations and over time) by the social environment in which it operates, as well as by the organizational structure that it has inherited from the past. Nevertheless, in many of the more capital- and research-intensive industries, a characteristic feature of advanced industrial economies has been the emergence of strong industrial corporations that possess sufficient resources and market power to transform their organizational structures in order to implement innovative investment strategies.

It is the rule rather than the exception that manufacturing industries characterized by a preponderance of smaller firms rely heavily on geographic concentration for the development and utilization of technology. In many industries in which dominant enterprises have not emerged, interventions by government bodies and trade associations have helped to transform the organizational structures of regional industrial sectors in ways that permit the implementation of innovative investment strategies across a large number of small enterprises. Indeed, there are cases – agriculture, medical equipment and armaments being prominent in the US (see Kash 1989; Ferleger and Lazonick: Chapter 17 in this volume) – in which innovative investment strategies have been implemented by building an organizational structure that transforms the industry throughout an entire national economy.

The focus on organizational capability as a source of competitive advantage implies that it is the productive relationships among those who must implement an investment strategy that determine how the enterprise, region or nation performs in market competition. From the organizational-capability perspective, moreover, enterprise strategy entails both choices of markets in which to compete and investments in the productive capabilities of members of the enterprise so that these capabilities are enhanced as a collective force. Furthermore, because effective organizational capabilities must be built up over prolonged periods of time, the existing capabilities of the enterprise can have a significant constraining influence on the types of investment strategies that top managers choose. In the evolution of the enterprise, strategy and structure are integrally related.

Our perspective on organizational capability builds on, and elaborates, Alfred Chandler's (1962) strategy-structure approach to business history. In his two more recent books (Chandler 1977 and 1990), however, Chandler's analysis of the relation between strategy and structure has not progressed beyond the notion that structure *follows* strategy. He has not analysed either how structure constrains strategy or the conditions under which strategic managers decide to confront structural constraints for the purpose of transforming them. He does not ask why some companies undertake and implement strategies that change structures, while others in the same industries do not.

If Chandler contends that structure follows strategy, Richard Nelson and Sidney Winter (1982) have in effect proposed that strategy flows from structure. In their influential book, *An Evolutionary Theory of Economic Change*, Nelson and Winter argued that what differentiates firms are organizational capabilities based on tacit knowledge and organizational routines. Unlike machines and blueprints, tacit knowledge and organizational routines cannot easily be transferred to other enterprises; indeed, they can exist and create value only in the companies in which they have evolved. From this perspective, even investment strategies become organizational routines that derive from the tacit knowledge of strategic decision makers.

From our perspective, the activities and relationships that determine organizational capabilities generate the tacit knowledge and organizational routines that enable the enterprise to function as a coherent, cohesive and, hence, productive system. A focus on organizational capability as a prime determinant of competitive advantage must ask where (within the specialized division of labour) this tacit knowledge resides and who (within the specialized division of labour) is able and willing to participate in organizational routines. Our focus also asks why and under what conditions strategic decision makers might choose to engage in innovative investment strategies that confront and alter organizational routines, for example by extending the right to possess and utilize tacit knowledge from the managerial level to shop-floor employees and suppliers. The intellectual challenge is to construct a theory of competitive advantage that can analyse the dynamic interaction of organization and technology.

The Six Ms of Enterprise

Under what circumstances does organizational capability result in enhanced performance? To answer this question, we require an understanding of how the planned coordination of the specialized division of labour results in higher quality products at lower unit costs.

When the technological and organizational requirements of the productive transformation are complex, the planned coordination of the specialized division of labour makes it possible to develop and utilize productive resources in ways that would not otherwise be possible. By collectivizing the activities of numerous specialists, organizational capability can generate superior products and processes. The combined knowledge of numerous individuals can be systematically planned, and their various interdependent productive activities systematically coordinated. When the complexity of developing and utilizing new technology demands such interdependency, specialized producers who decide and act independently of one another will not generate innovations. It is the role of the organization to make the decisions and actions of individuals interdependent, thereby transforming the capabilities of numerous individuals into an organizational capability.

Where is organizational capability located within an enterprise, region or nation, and how does it work to foster innovation? Organizational capability shapes the ways in which an investment strategy allocates *money*; it determines how *management* plans and co-ordinates the specialized division of labour; how the factors of production – *manpower*, *machinery* and *materials* – are developed and combined to form new processes and products, and how enterprises gain access to *markets*. The potential contribution of organizational capability to innovation in each of these six Ms demonstrates how it can become deeply rooted in the enterprise.

Money, or finance, plays a critical role in the innovation process because those who control money get to choose what type of strategy an enterprise will pursue. An innovative strategy inherently entails fixed costs because expenditures have to be made on 'machinery' (that is, plant and equipment) and certain types of 'manpower' (including those people who inhabit the managerial structure) with a time lag before the receipt of returns. These fixed costs are high not only because of the scale of investments, but also the developmental period that by definition must occur before the investments that entail fixed costs can generate returns.

Those who control money may or may not make strategic decisions that entail innovation; they may or may not act as entrepreneurs. Strategic decision makers can, and often do, decide not to be innovative but rather to produce on the basis of resources that already exist within the company or that can be readily purchased on factor markets. This can be labeled an adaptive strategy (see Lazonick 1991: ch. 3). A necessary condition for innovation is that those who control financial resources choose innovative rather than adaptive investment strategies.

They must, moreover, keep financial resources committed to the innovative strategy until the products and processes are sufficiently developed and utilized so that they generate returns. A failure to generate returns at any point may be a manifestation, not of a failed strategy, but of the need to commit even more financial resources to an ongoing learning process

(Lazonick 1992). To keep money committed to the innovative investment strategy, those who control money must either have intimate knowledge of its problems and possibilities, or else entrust their money to strategic managers who have such knowledge.

Management must plan and coordinate the development of the specialized division of labour and the integration of the specialized productive activities so that innovation can emerge. The innovative efforts necessary for economic development invariably involve continuous, cumulative and collective learning. Continuous learning results in the improvement of skills without which acquired capabilities atrophy. Cumulative learning permits the use of acquired technological capabilities as the basis for acquiring new complex capabilities. Collective learning enables the planned coordination of specialized divisions of labour to develop complex technology and generate productivity. Without collective learning, planned coordination is an economic burden rather than an economic benefit. Management's role is to ensure the continuity, cumulativity, and collectivity of the learning process.

Manpower (or labour power, to be gender neutral) is the one factor in the innovation process with the potential to learn. But because of the continuous, cumulative and collective character of the learning process, individuals' learning cannot be random. Central to the innovative strategy is investment in the capabilities of those people who comprise the specialized division of labour that management must plan and coordinate. Strategic decision makers ('money') do not invest in everyone they employ, but only in those whom they expect to participate in the collective learning process. Strategic decision makers do not want to invest in people who may exit the enterprise, taking with them their human assets (unless they enter an industry-wide pool of skilled labour to which the enterprise maintains access). Nor do they want to invest in those who may use their voice within the enterprise to subvert rather than support the process of innovation.

Machines combine with manpower to transform materials into products. Innovation in machinery is both skill-displacing and skill-augmenting. It is skill-displacing because certain productive capabilities that used to reside in manpower can now more effectively be performed by machines. It is skill-augmenting because innovation in machinery requires the application of new knowledge to develop the machinery and utilize it effectively in the production process. Machines can affect the productivity and quality of a given product. There is generally an intricate relation between innovation in materials and innovation in machines. Innovation in machines and materials both in turn depend on the complementary skills of manpower.

Materials are the substance that people as labour power transform into products. As such, materials become embodied in work-in-process – components, parts and intermediate goods. An understanding of the character of these materials in their raw and semi-processed states is critical for the innovation process to proceed. A key innovation may entail the creation of new materials through chemistry or the blend of existing materials that enter the production process. The quality of materials and semi-processed inventories will affect not only the quality of the product, but also the ways in which machines and manpower are developed and utilized. In particular, high-throughput production processes require 'high-throughput' materials – that is, materials that do not cause machine stoppages and costly downtime. Similarly, costs are increased by the wastage of materials due to inadequate skills and inferior machinery in the production process. The combination of manpower, machines and materials constitutes the enterprise's technology.

Markets provide the opportunity to generate returns on the investment in innovation.

Management's role is to ensure not only the transformation of inputs into outputs, but also the production of goods that buyers both want and can afford. Identification of markets, actual or potential, that can be served by the enterprise's technological capabilities is critical to the strategic decision-making process, while gaining access to new markets is central to the actual innovation process.

Competitive Advantage of Enterprises

Why are some enterprises more effective than others in generating innovation? To answer this question requires a recognition that, holding industry and institutional environments constant, the organizational capabilities of an enterprise reflect its own unique evolutionary pattern of growth. That pattern depends on the dynamic interaction of investment strategy ('money'), organizational structure ('management'), technological development (the combination of 'manpower', 'machines' and 'materials') and competitive outcomes ('markets') often over a prolonged period of time. Building a theory to explain how some enterprises establish a dynamic that yields competitive advantage requires a research programme involving comparative case studies. Through such case studies, we can discover how and under what circumstances the dynamic interaction of strategy, structure, technology and markets permits some enterprises to outperform others over a sustained period of time.

Such a research programme can be built around what we call the organizational integration hypothesis (for an elaboration, see Lazonick and West forthcoming). Organizational integration exists when the relationships among participants in a specialized division of labour allow their activities to be planned and coordinated to achieve specific goals. These participants may be employees within one enterprise, or they may be members of legally distinct enterprises. What matters are the actual relationships that integrate the specialized division of labour where such integration is required for learning to occur. These integrative relationships are not necessarily limited by the 'boundaries of the firm'.

By this definition, organizational integration is the social substance of organizational capability. The activities that must be organizationally integrated to attain competitive advantage depend on the technologies to be developed and utilized, and hence on the industry in which the enterprise is competing and the stage of technological development that the particular industry has attained. Depending on the industry, critical relationships that must be organizationally integrated might include the following: shop-floor workers and production engineers, development personnel and production engineers, sales and development personnel, strategic decision makers in a main company and in its supplier companies, researchers who work in different companies that compete in the same industry or in technologically related industries. These relationships may also be used by the enterprise to transfer technology from an industry in which it already possesses substantial market share to a newer, but technologically related, industry. A central task of the research agenda embodied in the organizational integration hypothesis is to discover which relationships are critical for attaining competitive advantage in which industries at which points in time.

Whatever the critical relationships, for the business enterprise engaged in competition for product markets, organizational integration permits the specialized division of labour to generate higher-quality and/or lower-cost products than the enterprise had previously been capable of producing. Organizational integration provides the capability to learn as an enterprise (and often as a group of enterprises) and the potential to innovate in market competition.

At the same time, organizational integration is a costly process. It requires substantial commitments of resources over sustained periods of time to build the relationships among participants in the specialized division of labour that permit organizational integration. The building of these relationships will place the enterprise at a competitive disadvantage until such time as the learning process that these relationships generate yields returns. The prospects of returns, moreover, are always highly uncertain, in part because the expected learning may not occur and in part because, even when it does, this learning may not be sufficient to meet the challenge of more innovative competitors (see Lazonick 1991: chs 3 and 6).

The building of the relationships that constitute organizational integration must therefore be strategic. The strategy to invest in organizational integration must be appropriate to the technological possibilities in the particular industry, given the stage of development and utilization of technology at any point in time. The evolution of technology means that relationships that generate competitive advantage at one point in time would not necessarily have done so earlier or later.

The Competitive Advantage of Regions and Nations

Thus far, we have discussed organizational capability primarily in terms of the strategies and structures of business enterprises. In the advanced industrial nations, a relatively small number of major business enterprises have driven the growth of the economy (see Chandler 1990). At the same time, however, these enterprises operate within what some have called 'national innovation systems' (see Nelson 1993) in which the strategy and structure of educational, financial and legal institutions promote and limit certain technological and economic outcomes. Moreover, in some industries, the formulation of investment strategy and the implementation of organizational structure may be undertaken by 'intermediate organizations' – industry and regional associations (both private sector and public sector) that influence the access of regional enterprises to money, manpower, machines, materials and markets (Mass and Miyajima 1993). The theory of competitive advantage must extend beyond the enterprise to consider how organizational capability at the levels of the region and the nation affects the competitive advantage of enterprises that operate within them. Specifically, how and under what conditions can enterprises within a region or nation act collectively to generate competitive advantage in ways that each of the enterprises acting individually could not?

The organizational integration hypothesis mandates a research agenda to identify the types of productive relationships that generate technological innovation in different industries and give competitive advantage to particular enterprises. The hypothesis also permits us to ask to what extent national institutions influence the ability of enterprises based in the nation, or a region of a nation, to put in place the types of organizational integration required to innovate. By doing so, we can seek to explain why certain regions and nations gain competitive advantage in some industries rather than others.

Take, for example, the shift in competitive advantage across many industries from the United States to Japan over the past few decades. To test the organizational integration hypothesis as an explanation for US decline in global competition, we must first derive from the study of the American economy as a whole a model of organizational integration that represents a norm for American business enterprises in general for the 1950s and 1960s – the period when American industry was dominant and before the full thrust of the Japanese competitive challenges began to be felt. We must then show how this American norm of organizational integration differs from that which characterizes those Japanese companies that have most successfully challenged the Americans.

In the decades after World War II, both the Japanese and Americans possessed organizationally integrated managerial structures. Both societies had undergone thoroughgoing managerial revolutions during the first half of the 20th century. Coming into the second half of the century, however, organizational integration in Japan differed from that in the US along three key dimensions. First, in contrast to American companies, Japanese enterprises included shop-floor workers in the process of planned coordination, investing in their skills and extending to them permanent employment status. Second, also in contrast to American companies, Japanese enterprises developed long-term relations with other firms that supplied them with inputs so that (as with Japanese shop-floor workers) these firms were able to participate in an organizationally integrated learning process. Third, again in sharp contrast with American practice in which cooperation among competing firms is often illegal, competing Japanese enterprises, with the encouragement of the government, integrate their financial resources and research capabilities to generate new technologies.

The organizational integration hypothesis predicts that Japanese enterprises gained competitive advantage over the Americans in those industries – steel, consumer electronics and automobiles are three striking examples – in which the organizational integration of the managerial structure (including technical specialists) was critical for product innovation, but also those in which the evolution of process technology made organizational integration of shop-floor workers and suppliers of central importance for process innovation. In industries in which, from the 1960s, an organizationally integrated managerial structure alone continued to suffice in global competition – industries such as pharmaceuticals and chemicals – the Americans continued to be leading innovators, with Japanese companies thus far being unable to mount an effective competitive challenge.

The organizational integration hypothesis also predicts that, within industries in which the American model of organizational integration no longer sufficed to generate competitive advantage, those American companies that, for whatever historical reasons, were able to confront the Japanese competitive challenge with a *Japanese* model of organizational integration responded more quickly and effectively to Japanese competition. Similarly, the hypothesis predicts that those American companies that, after an initial period of inadequate response to the Japanese challenge because of insufficient organizational integration, were ultimately able to meet that challenge did so by integrating shop-floor workers and/or suppliers into the process of planned coordination. By the same token, the hypothesis predicts that such companies that failed to alter their organizational structures remained unable to respond effectively to the Japanese challenge.

Research on organizational capability and competitive advantage requires an understanding of the dynamics of industrial development and the relation of these dynamics to the social context of the region and nation in which they occur. In other words, one must analyse the process of industrial change as a social phenomenon. This research agenda entails (1) a focus on the organization as the unit of analysis, where the firm or enterprise may or may not be the relevant organizational unit, (2) an analysis of how organizational capabilities are influenced by the institutional environment in which they evolve, and (3) a theory of how organizational capabilities generate competitive advantage or disadvantage.

The Selections in this Volume

In carrying out this research agenda, it must be recognized that, first and foremost, we are analysing the process of industrial change. To analyse change means to capture the essence of historical processes in a theory that can be tested, amended and elaborated in terms of the ongoing process of change as it occurs in different times and places. The purpose of the set of readings in this volume is to root this research agenda respectively in (I) historical debates, (II) contemporary debates, (III) studies of the dynamics of success, and (IV) some of the implications for business and government policy. Space limitations precluded us from including a section on the dynamics of failure or decline (for examples, see Elbaum and Lazonick 1986).

The historical debates revolve around the great British economist, Alfred Marshall's 19th-century distinction between external and internal economies of scale, a distinction that prompted investigation into whether the process of industrial development would be characterized by industry dominated by a few large firms or populated by many small ones (see Chapter 1). Many followers of Marshall forgot that, in raising this critical issue of industrial organization, their teacher was focused on questions of the dynamics of industrial development rather than the statics of constrained optimization (see Lazonick 1991: ch. 5). Meanwhile, by the 1910s the reality of industrial development was the rise of big business (what we now know as the 'managerial revolution') as the dominant institutional characteristic of the most successful economies.

In the late 1920s, the American economist, Allyn Young, reminded his English colleagues that what was at issue was Adam Smith's inquiry into the nature and causes of the wealth of nations. With scant evidence, however, Young asserted that the process of 'increasing returns' would be driven by legions of small firms that, organized in what Marshall called 'industrial districts', would generate external economies of scale (Chapter 2). Young failed to notice how an organizational revolution in the planning and coordination of economic activity was even then altering the industrial landscape.

Another economist, Joseph Schumpeter, did take notice. In his earlier work, the Austrian-born Schumpeter had viewed entrepreneurship as the activity of individuals who, through some acute perceptions, were able to bring 'new combinations', or innovations, into the industrial sphere. By the 1940s, however, Schumpeter, then a professor at Harvard University, recognized that entrepreneurship had increasingly become a collective endeavour. He also recognized that, as an historical process, 'the creative response', once set in motion, need not inevitably be sustained. Economic actors could adapt to their social environment – that is, accept their environment as a constraint – rather than innovate to transform it.

As Schumpeter studied the process of industrial development, he became convinced that the most important skill that an economist could acquire was what he called 'historical experience' – the ability to analyse the process of historical change (see Chapter 3). Yet, even as Schumpeter wrote, the mainstream of the American economics profession was constructing a theory of the market economy that shunned any analysis of the process of change, historical or otherwise. Some of those economists who did try to understand change did so by constructing biological analogies rather than, as Schumpeter was advising, by building a theory of history. In the early 1950s, Edith Penrose raised a warning against biological analogies by insisting, as in Chapter 4, that economics had to be a social science, Penrose did not, at the time, have an historically relevant theory of the firm to offer the profession. But as her book, *The Theory of the Growth of the Firm*, published in 1958, would prove, she was working on one.

To understand organizations, one has to study them, and for the past few decades some academics have taken the study of business organizations as a major challenge. The articles in the 'contemporary debates' in Part II of this volume raise critical issues for understanding just what organizational capabilities are, how they evolve and why they may result in competitive advantage.

Louis Galambos's presentation of the 'central themes of the organizational synthesis' in Chapter 5 makes clear that the study of business organizations is not merely 'business history'. Because business organizations – both large-scale enterprises and trade associations – are so pivotal to the operation of the American economy, organizational history must comprehend technological change as the source of long-term economic growth, political change as the conflicts and compromises over which groups in society control that growth, and social change as the realignment of the interests of social groups arising from the occupational demands of economic growth.

At the heart of such an ambitious, but essential, research agenda are the strategy and structure of business organizations. This research programme was put on the map, so to speak, by the pathbreaking, and relentless, work of Alfred D. Chandler, Jr. In three monumental books – *Strategy and Structure* (1962), *The Visible Hand* (1977) and *Scale and Scope* (1990) – Chandler documented what he has called 'the collective history' of large-scale business organization, first in the US and, more recently, in comparison with Germany and Britain. Any analysis of the relation between organizational capability and competitive advantage must make reference to the wealth of data and the hypotheses, explicit and implicit, that Chandler has set before us (as in Chapter 6).

So focused is Chandler's own work on the relation between organization and technology in the business enterprise that it risks excluding the influence of political and social structures on both business organization and business performance. At the same time, despite the comparative dimension that Chandler added in *Scale and Scope*, his approach lacks a theory of competitive advantage or even a research agenda for constructing such a theory.

Many of the strengths and weaknesses in Chandler's work are outlined in the special symposium on *Scale and Scope*, compiled by *Business History Review* (see Chapter 7). F.M. Scherer, an industrial economist, correctly points out that, in analysing economies of scale, Chandler fails to distinguish between a shift in the cost curve that derives from new investment and a movement down the cost curve that derives from the utilization of this investment. Scherer might also have recognized that the critical role of organization is indeed to shape new cost curves in order to transform the high fixed costs of innovation into low unit costs, a process that by no means comes automatically from the act of investing (for an extended discussion of this organizational theory of competitive advantage, see Lazonick 1991: ch. 3 and Lazonick 1993).

Thomas Hughes, an historian of technology, criticizes Chandler for focusing exclusively on the firm rather than on the networks of enterprises required to put a whole industry in place. It is indeed critical to show how and to what extent the strategies and structures of technologically related business enterprises coalesce to generate a dynamic industrial economy. Roy Church, a British business historian, claims that Chandler adduces the competitive weaknesses of 'personal capitalism' from limited, and by implication biased, evidence, and cites arguments that 'managerial capitalism' is not inherently dynamic. But Church does not outline a framework for understanding when and under what conditions personal capitalism outperforms managerial capitalism, or vice versa.

Jürgen Kocka, a German business historian, quite rightly claims that in *Scale and Scope* 'the real working of the managerial structures remains something of a "black box"'. In apparent contradiction to Kocka's statement, Hidemasa Morikawa, a Japanese business historian, argues that 'the core concept of Chandler's new framework is "organizational capabilities"' in which 'human skills are the decisive element'. Later in his review, however, Morikawa laments that 'in *Scale and Scope*, Chandler's definition of "managerial enterprise" has become more vague', apparently for lack of an adequate definition of organizational capabilities.

Albert Fishlow, an economic historian, voices the objections of a neoclassical economist that market concentration and managerial power should weaken, not strengthen, the forces for economic growth; he goes on to argue that these problems are particularly applicable to developing economies. Finally, Neil Fligstein, a sociologist, questions whether the very organizational forms that Chandler claims made American enterprises dominant in the past might not pose barriers to remaining competitive 'because their previous success has locked them into organizational forms that will not readily change'.

Many of these criticisms are well-founded. Chandler is able to focus relentlessly on the evolution of the organizational forms of dominant business enterprises precisely because he ignores a thorough exploration of the social substance of interpersonal relationships in and across enterprises that transforms organizational structure into organizational capabilities. Chandler's spirited response to these reviews (not reprinted in this volume) reflects less a refutation of the alleged weaknesses of his perspective than a reiteration of the central, if restricted, theme that his work pursues.

If the inner workings of the corporate organization represent, as Kocka argues, a 'black box' in Chandler's work, such is even more the case in that of Michael Porter. Trained as an industrial-organization economist, Porter transforms the economist's notion of barriers to entry from being monopolistic practices to sources of competitive advantage. In 'The Competitive Advantage of Nations' (Chapter 8 – a summary article of his book of the same name), Porter recognizes the importance of what he calls 'factor creation' for competitive advantage, but has little to say about how decisions to invest in factor creation are made or the extent to which the factor-creation process is an organizational rather than an individual phenomenon.

In 'Why Do Firms Differ, and How Does it Matter?' (Chapter 9), Richard Nelson, one of the pioneers in the use of the 'organizational capabilities' concept, contends that, in contrast to the neoclassical theory of the firm, real-world enterprises that evolve over time do so by engaging in 'discretionary' behaviour. This enables them to influence the environment in which they operate and differentiate themselves from other firms against which they compete. If the strategy inherent in this discretionary behaviour is 'coherent', it enables the firm to put in place 'dynamic capabilities' that give them competitive advantage over other firms.

Nelson's integration of some recent literature into an evolutionary perspective certainly points scholars in the right direction. But what makes a strategy, and a structure, 'coherent'? And why are some organizations dynamic and others static? Is it not possible that a firm may have a coherent strategy, but fail to put in place dynamic capabilities?

Dorothy Leonard-Barton's distinction in Chapter 10 between 'core capabilities' and 'core rigidities' provides insights into these questions. Because innovation by definition involves something new, existing capabilities can form a base, or pose a barrier, for doing something new. Summarizing a number of case studies of product and process development, she argues that the job of the project manager is to challenge existing organizational values to ensure that the core capabilities of the enterprise provide a platform for the organizational learning that is the essence of continuous innovation.

Much contemporary scholarship has recognized that dynamic organizational capabilities need not reside within the firm. An important case is the 'Third Italy' where, in certain industries such as furniture and ceramic tiles, networks of small firms have provided the productive capabilities to be successful in global markets. In his pioneering article, 'The Emilian Model: Productive Decentralisation and Social Integration' (Chapter 11), Sebastiano Brusco shows that the success of the 'industrial districts' in the region of Emilia-Romagna is not based on networks of small firms alone, but also on the presence of some larger enterprises that take the lead in pursuing innovation. In addition, local and regional governments subsidize, and in some cases organize, critical financial, technological and marketing infrastructures that enable the small firms to participate in the innovation process.

In 'Goodwill and the Spirit of Market Capitalism', Ronald Dore draws on his research of the Japanese economy and society to explore the sociological foundations of what he calls 'relational contracting': a willingness of participants in the economy to forego short-term opportunities for gain that the market offers for the sake of maintaining long-term relationships with other participants. Dore's point in Chapter 12 is that, in comparison with the classic Smithian prescription of individualistic market capitalism, a form of capitalism in which short-term advantage is systematically eschewed is not only morally but also economically superior.

William Lazonick concludes this section by arguing that the collectivist form of capitalism for which Japan has become known is not unique to that society. Organizational capabilities embodied in managerial structures were central to the rise of American capitalism to international dominance during the first half of the 20th century. Rather than build more powerful organizational capabilities in response to the Japanese challenge, Lazonick argues that over the past few decades the American economy has become more reliant on market relations that actually erode the organizational capabilities built up in the past.

The nine chapters gathered together in Part III on 'the dynamics of success' provide case studies of how particular regional industries or particular firms developed and utilized the organizational capabilities that gave them competitive advantage. All of the examples are drawn from the experiences of the US and Japan, primarily because our own recent work has focused on competition between American and Japanese industry.

In 'Mechanical and Organizational Innovation: The Drapers and the Automatic Loom', William Mass documents the importance of investment in research and development in the late 19th and early 20th centuries even in an industrial sector – cotton textiles – that is associated with the machine-based 'first' industrial revolution rather than with the science-based 'second'. Mass also analyses how, once it had achieved dominance in the textile machinery industry, the Draper Company turned from innovation to adaptation, being content thereafter to live off its past success.

In another penetrating history of corporate R&D, this time in a key science-based industry, David Hounshell details how strategy and structure at Du Pont Chemical interacted to generate new knowledge that the company could commercialize. In Chapter 15, Hounshell shows how the company was largely justified in maintaining its 'faith' in the benefits of R&D over a period of eight decades. By definition, the benefits of investment in innovation are not calculable a priori, so that only a belief in its value by those with financial control can sustain it. Nevertheless, over an extended period of time, Du Pont's belief in the value of R&D was based on the successful commercialization of prior investments in innovation.

Such a sustained belief in innovation is a necessary condition for the long-run growth of an enterprise, as is borne out in Edith Penrose's case study of the Hercules Powder Company. This study was to have been included in Penrose's classic book, *The Theory of the Growth of the Firm*, but was omitted (in our view, unwisely) for reasons of space. In Chapter 16, Penrose begins with a summary of the main conclusions of her book, thus exposing the reader to the integral relation between theoretical and empirical work that inspired her unique insights into the growth of the firm. 'The Hercules story,' Penrose argues, 'illustrates the crucial role of changing knowledge about its own resources in the determination of a firm's course of expansion; at the same time it illustrates the restraining influence of a firm's existing areas of specialization, in particular its technological bases.'

As we have already emphasized, the 'firm' need not be the only relevant unit of analysis. In studying 'The Case of U.S. Agriculture' in Chapter 17, Louis Ferleger and William Lazonick document a public-sector managerial revolution that by the mid-20th century had developed new technologies for, and permitted their diffusion to, millions of small enterprises. What they call 'the managerial revolution in the developmental state' extended from the US Department of Agriculture at the federal level to experiment stations and public universities at the state level to extension services at the county level. This permitted millions of American farmers to gain access to yield-enhancing innovations that dramatically raised productivity, as well as stabilizing financial arrangements that enabled them to invest in best-practice technologies. In essence, the US Department of Agriculture supported the development of numerous agricultural districts, akin to the industrial districts of Emilia-Romagna, throughout the country.

In Chapter 18 on the Japanese cotton textile industry in the interwar period, Takeshi Abe provides an analysis of how, in certain regions characterized by small- and medium-sized enterprises, industry associations (and the industrial laboratories or extension centres that these associations set up) enabled textile producers to become integrated into a dynamic, export-oriented growth process that had previously been the preserve of large integrated (spinning and weaving) companies. These 'producing-centers', as Abe calls them, remained successful for decades (and indeed provide the empirical foundations for Dore's arguments about relational contracting in Chapter 12). In some other regions characterized by dominant weaving enterprises, however, the leading companies themselves reorganized the district to produce for export markets, often with the assistance of the large integrated companies that supplied them with yarn. Depending on prior development and market segment, even in the same national industry very different organizational structures yielded competitive success.

In 'The Development of Tiered Inter-firm Relationships in the Automobile Industry: A

Case Study of Toyota Motor Corporation', Kazuo Wada details how this leading car company built its (now-famous) vertical keiretsu structure in the decades after World War II. In particular, he shows how Toyota used this structure to learn about high-quality production and to diffuse new standards to its suppliers. Significantly, Wada reveals that the major impetus to the development and diffusion of a 'purchasing control guidance' system and new forms of supplier relations stemmed from a federal government programme put in place during World War II. After the war, it took several decades of persistent investigation and investment for Toyota to develop a smoothly functioning multi-tiered supplier system – a system in which, as he puts it, 'close cooperative relationships in themselves contain the means for preventing the occurrence of opportunism'.

In 'Transplanted Organizations: The Transfer of Japanese Industrial Organization to the U.S.', Richard Florida and Martin Kenney confront the issue of the cultural specificity of the organizational capabilities that underlie the successful Japanese challenge. They show that sufficient and systematic investments in organization in a foreign environment permit the emergence of both capabilities and performance at levels that approach those already achieved in Japan.

Quite a different perspective on the evolution of capabilities is provided by Richard Langlois in his analysis of the rise of the personal computer industry in the United States (Chapter 21). Langlois contends that relatively small, highly specialized enterprises linked by market relations underlay the emergence and success of this industry. Even if, as argued by Alfred Chandler, large-scale enterprise organization was responsible for US competitive advantage in other industries and at other times, the personal computer industry illustrated the possibility of a market-coordinated industry in which dominant enterprises have a limited and even inconsequential role. The reason, Langlois argues, is the ability to 'modularize' technology, thus allowing many different niche enterprises to choose where they want to compete in the modular chain.

In our view, Langlois places too much faith in market coordination to generate innovation; his analysis inadequately acknowledges both the role of interfirm social relationships that make innovation possible and the role of dominant enterprises. These relationships are the subject of AnnaLee Saxenian's arguments in 'Institutions and the Growth of Silicon Valley' concerning the regional determinants of industrial success. She argues in Chapter 22 that collaborative and cooperative networks of enterprises and individuals (who often move from one enterprise to another) characterize Silicon Valley and are responsible for its high levels of innovation and growth. There are a number of dominant enterprises in Silicon Valley including Hewlett-Packard, Apple and Intel; unlike Route 128 in Massachusetts (see Saxenian 1994), however, these enterprises have apparently helped to create conditions that encourage high levels of innovation by smaller and younger firms as well.

The final section of the volume deals with some of the policy implications that flow from the recognition of the importance of organizational capability for competitive advantage. The first selection is from the policy chapter of *Made in America: Regaining the Productive Edge*, written by the MIT Commission on Industrial Productivity. The MIT Commission investigated the competitive fate of eight major US industries in the 1970s and 1980s, some of which (such as automobiles, consumer electronics and machine tools) had lost substantial market share to the Japanese, while others (such as chemicals and commercial aircraft) continued to dominate in global competition. For the US to become more productive, the Commission argues, industry, government, labour and educators must pursue five interlinked 'imperatives': (1) focus on the new fundamentals of manufacturing, (2) cultivate a new economic citizenship in the work force, (3) blend cooperation and individualism, (4) learn to live in the world economy, and (5) provide for the future. The *Made in America* perspective relies deeply on the relation between organizational capabilities and productivity. Yet the book lacks perspectives on how the organizational capabilities that reap competitive advantage have changed over time and why superior capabilities emerge in some regions and nations rather than in others. As a result, the policy recommendations in *Made in America* fail to address the social complexities of institutional and organizational transformation.

In his well-known and provocative paper, 'Who is Us?' (Chapter 24), Robert Reich in effect avoids the issue of the competitive advantage of regions and nations by arguing that productive investment is no longer national, and hence the ownership of companies is of no concern to national industrial policy. Rather, national policy should focus on ensuring that the labour force is highly skilled because it is precisely such a skill base that attracts international investment. Laura Tyson's reply to Reich is that 'countryless' capital remains an emerging trend, and that national policy can still be used to exert direct influence over home-grown corporations to invest more at home than abroad. Reich responds by arguing that the trend towards globalization of investment is faster than Tyson thinks: 'American firms aren't exactly abandoning America; it is more accurate to say that they are joining the world, and spreading their production across many global continents, as they become truly global firms.'

The volume concludes with William Lazonick's 'Industry Clusters versus Global Webs'. Here he contends that Reich's arguments ignore the facts that major American corporations have for decades been characterized by the separation of asset ownership from strategic control, have long been 'truly global', and are pivotal actors in pursuing strategies and implementing structures that result in skill formation and competitive advantage. National policy is important because, through legislation and social relationships, nations can determine how corporations that operate within their boundaries are governed. Lazonick argues that 'Reich's vision of "global webs" of investment creates an excuse for ignoring corporate governance in the United States'. Companies cannot even begin to think about building organizational capabilities for competitive advantage unless the strategic decision makers who control corporate resources have an interest in making the necessary long-term collective commitments.

References

Chandler Jr, Alfred D. (1962), *Strategy and Structure: Chapters in the History of the American Industrial Enterprise*, MIT Press.

Chandler Jr, Alfred D. (1977), *The Visible Hand: The Managerial Revolution in American Business*, Harvard University Press.

Chandler Jr, Alfred D. (1990), *Scale and Scope: The Dynamics of Industrial Capitalism*, Harvard University Press.

Elbaum, Bernard and William Lazonick (eds) (1986), *The Decline of the British Economy*, Oxford University Press.

Kash, Don (1989), *Perpetual Innovation*, Basic Books.

Lazonick, William (1991), *Business Organization and the Myth of the Market Economy*, Cambridge University Press.

Lazonick, William (1992), 'Controlling the Market for Corporate Control: The Historical Significance of Managerial Capitalism', *Industrial and Corporate Change*, 1, 445–87.

Lazonick, William (1993), 'Learning and the Dynamics of International Competitive Advantage' in Ross Thomson (ed.), *Learning and Technological Change*, Macmillan.

Lazonick, William and Jonathan West (forthcoming), 'Organizational Integration and Competitive Advantage: Explaining Strategy and Performance in the American Economy', *Industrial and Corporate Change*.

Mass, William and Hideaki Miyajima (1993), 'Technology Transfer, Diffusion, and Development: Fostering Private Capabilities and the Roots of the Japanese "Economic Miracle"', *Business and Economic History*, second series, 22.

Nelson, Richard R. (ed.) (1993), *National Innovation Systems*, Oxford University Press.

Nelson, Richard R. and Sidney Winter (1982), *An Evolutionary Theory of Economic Change*, Harvard University Press.

Saxenian, AnnaLee (1994), *Regional Advantage*, Harvard University Press.

Part I
Historical Debates

[1]

INDUSTRIAL ORGANIZATION, CONTINUED. THE CONCENTRATION OF SPECIALIZED INDUSTRIES IN PARTICULAR LOCALITIES.

§ 1. IN an early stage of civilization every place had to depend on its own resources for most of the heavy wares which it consumed; unless indeed it happened to have special facilities for water carriage. But wants and customs changed slowly: and this made it easy for producers to meet the wants even of consumers with whom they had little communication; and it enabled comparatively poor people to buy a few expensive goods from a distance, in the security that they would add to the pleasure of festivals and holidays during a life-time, or perhaps even during two or three lifetimes. Consequently the lighter and more expensive articles of dress and personal adornment, together with spices and some kinds of metal implements used by all classes, and many other things for the special use of the rich, often came from astonishing distances. Some of these were produced only in a few places, or even only in one place; and they were diffused all over Europe partly by the agency of fairs[1] and professional pedlers, and partly by the producers themselves, who would vary their work by travelling on foot for many thousand miles to sell their goods and see the world. These sturdy travellers took on themselves the risks of their little

IV, x, 1.

Even in early stages of civilization the production of some light and valuable wares has been localized.

---

[1] Thus in the records of the Stourbridge Fair held near Cambridge we find an endless variety of light and precious goods from the older seats of civilization in the East and on the Mediterranean; some having been brought in Italian ships, and others having travelled by land as far as the shores of the North Sea.

IV, x, 2. businesses; they enabled the production of certain classes of goods to be kept on the right track for satisfying the needs of purchasers far away; and they created new wants among consumers, by showing them at fairs or at their own houses new goods from distant lands. An industry concentrated in certain localities is commonly, though perhaps not quite accurately, described as a localized industry[1].

This elementary localization of industry gradually prepared the way for many of the modern developments of division of labour in the mechanical arts and in the task of business management. Even now we find industries of a primitive fashion localized in retired villages of central Europe, and sending their simple wares even to the busiest haunts of modern industry. In Russia the expansion of a family group into a village has often been the cause of a localized industry; and there are an immense number of villages each of which carries on only one branch of production, or even only a part of one[2].

The various origins of localized industries; physical conditions;

§ 2. Many various causes have led to the localization of industries; but the chief causes have been physical conditions; such as the character of the climate and the soil, the existence of mines and quarries in the neighbourhood, or within easy access by land or water. Thus metallic industries have generally been either near mines or in places where fuel was cheap. The iron industries in England first sought those districts in which charcoal was plentiful, and

---

[1] Not very long ago travellers in western Tyrol could find a strange and characteristic relic of this habit in a village called Imst. The villagers had somehow acquired a special art in breeding canaries: and their young men started for a tour to distant parts of Europe each with about fifty small cages hung from a pole over his shoulder, and walked on till they had sold all.

[2] There are for instance over 500 villages devoted to various branches of woodwork; one village makes nothing but spokes for the wheels of vehicles, another nothing but the bodies and so on; and indications of a like state of things are found in the histories of oriental civilizations and in the chronicles of mediæval Europe. Thus for instance we read (Rogers' *Six Centuries of Work and Wages*, ch. IV.) of a lawyer's handy book written about 1250, which makes note of scarlet at Lincoln; blanket at Bligh; burnet at Beverley; russet at Colchester; linen fabrics at Shaftesbury, Lewes, and Aylsham; cord at Warwick and Bridport; knives at Marstead; needles at Wilton; razors at Leicester; soap at Coventry; horse girths at Doncaster; skins and furs at Chester and Shrewsbury and so on.

The localization of trades in England at the beginning of the eighteenth century is well described by Defoe, *Plan of English Commerce*, 85–7; *English Tradesman*, II. 282–3.

afterwards they went to the neighbourhood of collieries[1]. IV, x, 2.
Staffordshire makes many kinds of pottery, all the materials
of which are imported from a long distance; but she has
cheap coal and excellent clay for making the heavy "seggars"
or boxes in which the pottery is placed while being fired.
Straw plaiting has its chief home in Bedfordshire, where
straw has just the right proportion of silex to give strength
without brittleness; and Buckinghamshire beeches have
afforded the material for the Wycombe chairmaking. The
Sheffield cutlery trade is due chiefly to the excellent grit of
which its grindstones are made.

Another chief cause has been the patronage of a court. the
The rich fold there assembled make a demand for goods of patronage of courts;
specially high quality, and this attracts skilled workmen
from a distance, and educates those on the spot. When an
Eastern potentate changed his residence—and, partly for
sanitary reasons, this was constantly done—the deserted
town was apt to take refuge in the development of a
specialized industry, which had owed its origin to the presence of the court. But very often the rulers deliberately the
invited artisans from a distance and settled them in a group deliberate invitation
together. Thus the mechanical faculty of Lancashire is said of rulers.
to be due to the influence of Norman smiths who were
settled at Warrington by Hugo de Lupus in William the
Conqueror's time. And the greater part of England's manufacturing industry before the era of cotton and steam had
its course directed by settlements of Flemish and other
artisans; many of which were made under the immediate
direction of Plantagenet and Tudor kings. These immigrants
taught us how to weave woollen and worsted stuffs, though
for a long time we sent our cloths to the Netherlands to be
fulled and dyed. They taught us how to cure herrings, how
to manufacture silk, how to make lace, glass, and paper, and
to provide for many other of our wants[2].

[1] The later wanderings of the iron industry from Wales, Staffordshire and
Shropshire to Scotland and the North of England are well shown in the tables
submitted by Sir Lowthian Bell to the recent Commission on the Depression of
Trade and Industry. See their Second Report, Part I. p. 320.
[2] Fuller says that Flemings started manufactures of cloths and fustians in
Norwich, of baizes in Sudbury, of serges in Colchester and Taunton, of cloths in

270   LOCALIZED INDUSTRIES

IV, x, 3.

The industrial development of nations waits upon opportunities and upon character.

But how did these immigrants learn their skill? Their ancestors had no doubt profited by the traditional arts of earlier civilizations on the shores of the Mediterranean and in the far East: for nearly all important knowledge has long deep roots stretching downwards to distant times; and so widely spread have been these roots, so ready to send up shoots of vigorous life, that there is perhaps no part of the old world in which there might not long ago have flourished many beautiful and highly skilled industries, if their growth had been favoured by the character of the people, and by their social and political institutions. This accident or that may have determined whether any particular industry flourished in any one town; the industrial character of a whole country even may have been largely influenced by the richness of her soil and her mines, and her facilities for commerce. Such natural advantages may themselves have stimulated free industry and enterprise: but it is the existence of these last, by whatever means they may have been promoted, which has been the supreme condition for the growth of noble forms of the arts of life. In sketching the history of free industry and enterprise we have already incidentally traced the outlines of the causes which have localized the industrial leadership of the world now in this country and now in that. We have seen how physical nature acts on man's energies, how he is stimulated by an invigorating climate, and how he is encouraged to bold ventures by the opening out of rich fields for his work: but we have also seen how the use he makes of these advantages depends on his ideals of life, and how inextricably therefore the religious, political and economic threads of the world's history are interwoven; while together they have been bent this way or that by great political events and the influence of the strong personalities of individuals.

The causes which determine the economic progress of nations belong to the study of international trade and therefore lie outside of our present view. But for the present we

Kent, Gloucestershire, Worcestershire, Westmorland, Yorkshire, Hants, Berks and Sussex, of kerseys in Devonshire and of Levant cottons in Lancashire. Smiles' *Huguenots in England and Ireland*, p. 109. See also Lecky's *History of England in the eighteenth century*, ch. II.

must turn aside from these broader movements of the locali- IV, x, 3.
zation of industry, and follow the fortunes of groups of skilled
workers who are gathered within the narrow boundaries of
a manufacturing town or a thickly peopled industrial district.

§ 3. When an industry has thus chosen a locality for The
itself, it is likely to stay there long: so great are the ad- advantages of localized
vantages which people following the same skilled trade get industries; hereditary
from near neighbourhood to one another. The mysteries of skill;
the trade become no mysteries; but are as it were in the
air, and children learn many of them unconsciously. Good
work is rightly appreciated, inventions and improvements in
machinery, in processes and the general organization of the
business have their merits promptly discussed: if one man
starts a new idea, it is taken up by others and combined
with suggestions of their own; and thus it becomes the
source of further new ideas. And presently subsidiary trades the
grow up in the neighbourhood, supplying it with implements subsidiary trades;
and materials, organizing its traffic, and in many ways trades;
conducing to the economy of its material.

Again, the economic use of expensive machinery can the use
sometimes be attained in a very high degree in a district in specialized
which there is a large aggregate production of the same machinery;
kind, even though no individual capital employed in the
trade be very large. For subsidiary industries devoting themselves each to one small branch of the process of production,
and working it for a great many of their neighbours, are
able to keep in constant use machinery of the most highly
specialized character, and to make it pay its expenses, though
its original cost may have been high, and its rate of depreciation very rapid.

Again, in all but the earliest stages of economic develop- a local
ment a localized industry gains a great advantage from the special
fact that it offers a constant market for skill. Employers skill.
are apt to resort to any place where they are likely to find
a good choice of workers with the special skill which they
require; while men seeking employment naturally go to
places where there are many employers who need such skill
as theirs and where therefore it is likely to find a good market.
The owner of an isolated factory, even if he has access to

272   LOCALIZED INDUSTRIES

IV, x, 3. a plentiful supply of general labour, is often put to great shifts for want of some special skilled labour; and a skilled workman, when thrown out of employment in it, has no easy refuge. Social forces here co-operate with economic: there are often strong friendships between employers and employed: but neither side likes to feel that in case of any disagreeable incident happening between them, they must go on rubbing against one another: both sides like to be able easily to break off old associations should they become irksome. These difficulties are still a great obstacle to the success of any business in which special skill is needed, but which is not in the neighbourhood of others like it: they are however being diminished by the railway, the printing-press and the telegraph.

Sometimes however a localized industry makes too extensive demands for one kind of labour. On the other hand a localized industry has some disadvantages as a market for labour if the work done in it is chiefly of one kind, such for instance as can be done only by strong men. In those iron districts in which there are no textile or other factories to give employment to women and children, wages are high and the cost of labour dear to the employer, while the average money earnings of each family are low. But the remedy for this evil is obvious, and is found in the growth in the same neighbourhood of industries of a supplementary character. Thus textile industries are constantly found congregated in the neighbourhood of mining and engineering industries, in some cases having been attracted by almost imperceptible steps; in others, as for instance at Barrow, having been started deliberately on a large scale in order to give variety of employment in a place where previously there had been but little demand for the work of women and children.

The advantages of variety of employment are combined with those of localized industries in some of our manufacturing towns, and this is a chief cause of their continued growth. But on the other hand the value which the central sites of a large town have for trading purposes, enables them to command much higher ground-rents than the situations are worth for factories, even when account is taken of this combination of advantages: and there is a similar competition for dwelling space between the employees of the trading

houses and the factory workers. The result is that factories IV, x, 4.
now congregate in the outskirts of large towns and in manufacturing districts in their neighbourhood rather than in the
towns themselves[1].

A district which is dependent chiefly on one industry is Different
liable to extreme depression, in case of a falling-off in the industries
demand for its produce, or of a failure in the supply of the neighbour-
raw material which it uses. This evil again is in a great gate each
measure avoided by those large towns or large industrial pressions.
districts in which several distinct industries are strongly
developed. If one of them fails for a time, the others are
likely to support it indirectly; and they enable local shopkeepers to continue their assistance to workpeople in it.

So far we have discussed localization from the point Localiza-
of view of the economy of production. But there is also the shops.
convenience of the customer to be considered. He will go
to the nearest shop for a trifling purchase; but for an
important purchase he will take the trouble of visiting any
part of the town where he knows that there are specially
good shops for his purpose. Consequently shops which deal
in expensive and choice objects tend to congregate together;
and those which supply ordinary domestic needs do not[2].

§ 4. Every cheapening of the means of communication, The in-
every new facility for the free interchange of ideas between improved
distant places alters the action of the forces which tend to means of
localize industries. Speaking generally we must say that a cation on
lowering of tariffs, or of freights for the transport of goods, graphical
tends to make each locality buy more largely from a dis- tion of
tance what it requires; and thus tends to concentrate parti- industries.
cular industries in special localities: but on the other hand
everything that increases people's readiness to migrate from
one place to another tends to bring skilled artisans to ply

---

[1] The movement has been specially conspicuous in the case of the textile
manufacturers. Manchester, Leeds and Lyons are still chief centres of the trade
in cotton, woollen and silk stuffs, but they do not now themselves produce any
great part of the goods to which they owe their chief fame. On the other hand
London and Paris retain their positions as the two largest manufacturing towns
of the world, Philadelphia coming third. The mutual influences of the localization
of industry, the growth of towns and habits of town life, and the development of
machinery are well discussed in Hobson's *Evolution of Capitalism*.

[2] Comp. Hobson, *l. c.* p. 114.

IV, x, 4. their crafts near to the consumers who will purchase their wares. These two opposing tendencies are well illustrated by the recent history of the English people.

Illustration from the recent history of England.

On the one hand the steady cheapening of freights, the opening of railways from the agricultural districts of America and India to the sea-board, and the adoption by England of a free-trade policy, have led to a great increase in her importation of raw produce. But on the other hand the growing cheapness, rapidity and comfort of foreign travel, are inducing her trained business men and her skilled artisans to pioneer the way for new industries in other lands, and to help them to manufacture for themselves goods which they have been wont to buy from England. English mechanics have taught people in almost every part of the world how to use English machinery, and even how to make similar machinery; and English miners have opened out mines of ore which have diminished the foreign demand for many of England's products.

One of the most striking movements towards the specialization of a country's industries, which history records, is the rapid increase of the non-agricultural population of England in recent times. The exact nature of this change is however liable to be misunderstood; and its interest is so great, both for its own sake, and on account of the illustrations it affords of the general principles which we have been discussing in the preceding chapter and in this, that we may with advantage pause here to consider it a little.

The diminution of her agricultural population is less than at first sight appears.

In the first place, the real diminution of England's agricultural industries is not so great as at first sight appears. It is true that in the Middle Ages three-fourths of the people were reckoned as agriculturists; that only one in nine was returned to the last census as engaged in agriculture, and that perhaps not more than one in twelve will be so returned at the next census. But it must be remembered that the so-called agricultural population of the Middle Ages were not exclusively occupied with agriculture; they did for themselves a great part of the work that is now done by brewers and bakers, by spinners and weavers, by bricklayers and carpenters, by dressmakers and tailors and by many other trades. These self-sufficing habits died slowly; but most of them had nearly disappeared by the beginning of the last century; and

it is probable that the labour spent on the land at this time IV, x, 4.
was not a much less part of the whole industry of the country
than in the Middle Ages: for, in spite of her ceasing to export
wool and wheat, there was so great an increase in the produce
forced from her soil, that the rapid improvement in the arts
of her agriculturists scarcely availed to hold in check the
action of the law of diminishing return. But gradually a
great deal of labour has been diverted from the fields to
making expensive machinery for agricultural purposes. This
change did not exert its full influence upon the numbers of
those who were reckoned as agriculturists so long as the
machinery was drawn by horses: for the work of tending
them and supplying them with food was regarded as agricultural. But in recent years a rapid growth of the use of
steam power in the fields has coincided with the increased
importation of farm produce. The coal-miners who supply
these steam-engines with fuel, and the mechanics who make
them and manage them in the fields are not reckoned as
occupied on the land, though the ultimate aim of their labour
is to promote its cultivation. The real diminution then of
England's agriculture is not so great as at first sight appears;
but there has been a change in its distribution. Many tasks
which used once to be performed by agricultural labourers
are now done by specialized workers who are classed as in the
building, or road-making industries, as carriers and so on.
And, partly for this reason the number of people who reside
in purely agricultural districts has seldom diminished fast;
and has often increased, even though the number of those
engaged in agriculture has been diminishing rapidly.

Attention has already been called to the influence which Changes in the distri-
the importation of agricultural produce exerts in altering the bution of
relative values of different soils: those falling most in value the agri-cultural
which depended chiefly on their wheat crops, and which were population within the
not naturally fertile, though they were capable of being made country.
to yield fairly good crops by expensive methods of cultivation.
Districts in which such soils predominate, have contributed
more than their share to the crowds of agricultural labourers
who have migrated to the large towns; and thus the
geographical distribution of industries within the country has

IV, x, 4. been still further altered. A striking instance of the influence of the new means of transport is seen in those
pastoral districts in the remoter parts of the United Kingdom, which send dairy products by special express trains to
London and other large towns, meanwhile drawing their own
supplies of wheat from the further shores of the Atlantic or
even the Pacific Ocean.

Those set free from agriculture have gone not to manufactures But next, the changes of recent years have not, as would
at first sight appear probable, increased the proportion of the
English people who are occupied in manufactures. The output of England's manufactures is certainly many times as
great now as it was at the middle of the last century; but
those occupied in manufacture of every kind were as large a
percentage of the population in 1851 as in 1901; although
those who make the machinery and implements which do a
great part of the work of English agriculture, swell the
numbers of the manufacturers.

but chiefly to industries in which there has been no great increase in the efficiency of labour. The chief explanation of this result lies in the wonderful
increase in recent years of the power of machinery. This
has enabled us to produce ever increasing supplies of manufactures of almost every kind both for our own use and for
exportation without requiring any considerable increase in
the number of people who tend the machines. And therefore we have been able to devote the labour set free from
agriculture chiefly to supplying those wants in regard to
which the improvements of machinery help us but little: the
efficiency of machinery has prevented the industries localized
in England from becoming as exclusively mechanical as they
otherwise would. Prominent among the occupations which
have increased rapidly since 1851 in England at the expense
of agriculture are the service of Government, central and
local; education of all grades; medical service; musical,
theatrical and other entertainments, besides mining, building,
dealing and transport by road and railway. In none of these
is very much direct help got from new inventions: man's
labour is not much more efficient in them now than it was a
century ago: and therefore if the wants for which they make
provision increase in proportion to our general wealth, it is
only to be expected that they should absorb a constantly
growing proportion of the industrial population. Domestic

servants increased rapidly for some years; and the total amount of work which used to fall to them is now increasing faster than ever. But much of it is now done, often with the aid of machinery, by persons in the employment of clothiers of all kinds, of hotel proprietors, confectioners, and even by various messengers from grocers, fishmongers and others who call for orders, unless they are sent by telephone. These changes have tended to increase the specialization and the localization of industries.

IV, x, 4.

Passing away from this illustration of the action of modern forces on the geographical distribution of industries, we will resume our inquiry as to how far the full economies of division of labour can be obtained by the concentration of large numbers of small businesses of a similar kind in the same locality; and how far they are attainable only by the aggregation of a large part of the business of the country into the hands of a comparatively small number of rich and powerful firms, or, as is commonly said, by production on a large scale; or, in other words, how far the economies of production on a large scale must needs be *internal*, and how far they can be *external*[1].

Transition to the subject of the next chapter.

---

[1] The percentage of the population occupied in the textile industries in the United Kingdom fell from 3·13 in 1881 to 2·43 in 1901; partly because much of the work done by them has been rendered so simple by semi-automatic machinery that it can be done fairly well by peoples that are in a relatively backward industrial condition; and partly because the chief textile goods retain nearly the same simple character as they had thirty or even three thousand years ago. On the other hand manufactures of iron and steel (including shipbuilding) have increased so greatly in complexity as well as in volume of output, that the percentage of the population occupied in them rose from 2·39 in 1881 to 3·01 in 1901; although much greater advance has been meanwhile made in the machinery and methods employed in them than in the textile group. The remaining manufacturing industries employed about the same percentage of the people in 1901 as in 1881. In the same time the tonnage of British shipping cleared from British ports increased by one half; and the number of dock labourers doubled, but that of seamen has slightly diminished. These facts are to be explained partly by vast improvements in the construction of ships and all appliances connected with them, and partly by the transference to dock labourers of nearly all tasks connected with handling the cargo some of which were even recently performed by the crew. Another marked change is the increased aggregate occupation of women in manufactures, though that of married women appears to have diminished, and that of children has certainly diminished greatly.

The Summary Tables of the Census of 1911, published in 1915, show so many changes in classification since 1901 that no general view of recent developments can be safely made. But Table 64 of that *Report* and Prof. D. Caradog Jones' paper read before the Royal Statistical Society in December 1914 show that the developments of 1901–1911 differ from their predecessors in detail rather than in general character.

INDUSTRIAL ORGANIZATION, CONTINUED. PRODUCTION ON A LARGE SCALE.

IV, xi, 1.

The typical industries for our present purpose are those engaged in manufacture.

§ 1. THE advantages of production on a large scale are best shown in manufacture; under which head we may include all businesses engaged in working up material into forms in which it will be adapted for sale in distant markets. The characteristic of manufacturing industries which makes them offer generally the best illustrations of the advantages of production on a large scale, is their power of choosing freely the locality in which they will do their work. They are thus contrasted on the one hand with agriculture and other extractive industries (mining, quarrying, fishing, etc.), the geographical distribution of which is determined by nature; and on the other hand with industries that make or repair things to suit the special needs of individual consumers, from whom they cannot be far removed, at all events without great loss[1].

The economy of material.

The chief advantages of production on a large scale are economy of skill, economy of machinery and economy of materials: but the last of these is rapidly losing importance relatively to the other two. It is true that an isolated workman often throws away a number of small things which would have been collected and turned to good account in a factory[2];

---

[1] "Manufacture" is a term which has long lost any connection with its original use: and is now applied to those branches of production where machine and not hand work is most prominent. Roscher made the attempt to bring it back nearer to its old use by applying it to domestic as opposed to factory industries: but it is too late to do this now.

[2] See Babbage's instance of the manufacture of horn. *Economy of Manufactures*, ch. XXII.

THE ECONOMY OF MATERIAL 279

but waste of this kind can scarcely occur in a localized manu- IV, xi, 2.
facture even if it is in the hands of small men; and there is not
very much of it in any branch of industry in modern England,
except agriculture and domestic cooking. No doubt many
of the most important advances of recent years have been
due to the utilizing of what had been a waste product; but
this has been generally due to a distinct invention, either
chemical or mechanical, the use of which has been indeed
promoted by minute subdivision of labour, but has not been
directly dependent on it[1].

Again, it is true that when a hundred sets of furniture,
or of clothing, have to be cut out on exactly the same
pattern, it is worth while to spend great care on so planning
the cutting out of the boards or the cloth, that only a few
small pieces are wasted. But this is properly an economy of
skill; one planning is made to suffice for many tasks, and
therefore can be done well and carefully. We may pass then
to the economy of machinery.

§ 2. In spite of the aid which subsidiary industries can The
give to small manufactures, where many in the same branch advantages
of trade are collected in one neighbourhood[2], they are still of a large
placed under a great disadvantage by the growing variety factory
and expensiveness of machinery. For in a large establish- as regards
ment there are often many expensive machines each made the use of
specially for one small use. Each of them requires space specialized
in a good light, and thus stands for something considerable machinery.
in the rent and general expenses of the factory; and independently of interest and the expense of keeping it in repair,
a heavy allowance must be made for depreciation in consequence of its being probably improved upon before long[3].

---

[1] Instances are the utilization of the waste from cotton, wool, silk and other
textile materials; and of the by-products in the metallurgical industries, in the
manufacture of soda and gas, and in the American mineral oil and meat packing
industries.

[2] See the preceding chapter, § 3.

[3] The average time which a machine will last before being superseded is in
many trades not more than fifteen years, while in some it is ten years or even
less. There is often a loss on the use of a machine unless it earns every year
twenty per cent. on its cost; and when the operation performed by such a machine
costing £500 adds only a hundredth part to the value of the material that passes
through it—and this is not an extreme case—there will be a loss on its use unless
it can be applied in producing at least £10,000 worth of goods annually.

280   PRODUCTION ON A LARGE SCALE

IV, xi, 2.   A small manufacturer must therefore have many things done
——   by hand or by imperfect machinery, though he knows how to
              have them done better and cheaper by special machinery, if
              only he could find constant employment for it.

Advan-   But next, a small manufacturer may not always be
tages with
regard to   acquainted with the best machinery for his purpose. It is
the inven-   true that if the industry in which he is engaged has been
tion of
improved   long established on a large scale, his machinery will be well
machinery.   up to the mark, provided he can afford to buy the best
              in the market. In agriculture and the cotton industries, for
              instance, improvements in machinery are devised almost
              exclusively by machine makers; and they are accessible to
              all, at any rate on the payment of a royalty for patent right.
              But this is not the case in industries that are as yet in an
              early stage of development or are rapidly changing their
              form; such as the chemical industries, the watchmaking
              industry and some branches of the jute and silk manufac-
              tures; and in a host of trades that are constantly springing
              up to supply some new want or to work up some new
              material.

The small   In all such trades new machinery and new processes are
manufac-
turer   for the greater part devised by manufacturers for their own
cannot   use. Each new departure is an experiment which may fail;
often
afford to   those which succeed must pay for themselves and for the
experi-   failure of others; and though a small manufacturer may think
ment.
              he sees his way to an improvement, he must reckon on having
              to work it out tentatively, at considerable risk and expense
              and with much interruption to his other work: and even if he
              should be able to perfect it, he is not likely to be able to make
              the most of it. For instance, he may have devised a new
              speciality, which would get a large sale if it could be brought
              under general notice: but to do this would perhaps cost
              many thousand pounds; and, if so, he will probably have to
              turn his back on it. For it is almost impossible for him to
              discharge, what Roscher calls a characteristic task of the
              modern manufacturer, that of creating new wants by showing
              people something which they had never thought of having
              before; but which they want to have as soon as the notion
              is suggested to them: in the pottery trade for example the

ADVANTAGES IN THE USE OF MACHINERY   281

small manufacturer cannot afford even to make experiments _{IV, xi, 2.} with new patterns and designs except in a very tentative way. His chance is better with regard to an improvement in making things for which there is already a good market. But even here he cannot get the full benefit of his invention unless he patents it; and sells the right to use it; or borrows some capital and extends his business; or lastly changes the character of his business and devotes his capital to that particular stage of the manufacture to which his improvement applies. But after all such cases are exceptional: the growth of machinery in variety and expensiveness presses hard on the small manufacturer everywhere. It has already driven him completely out of some trades and is fast driving him out of others[1].

There are however some trades in which the advantages *But in some trades a factory of moderate size can have the best machinery.* which a large factory derives from the economy of machinery almost vanish as soon as a moderate size has been reached. For instance in cotton spinning, and calico weaving, a comparatively small factory will hold its own and give constant employment to the best known machines for every process: so that a large factory is only several parallel smaller factories under one roof; and indeed some cotton-spinners, when enlarging their works, think it best to add a weaving department. In such cases the large business gains little or no economy in machinery; and even then it generally saves something in building, particularly as regards chimneys, and

---

[1] In many businesses only a small percentage of improvements are patented. They consist of many small steps, which it would not be worth while to patent one at a time. Or their chief point lies in noticing that a certain thing ought to be done; and to patent one way of doing it, is only to set other people to work to find out other ways of doing it against which the patent cannot guard. If one patent is taken out, it is often necessary to "block" it, by patenting other methods of arriving at the same result; the patentee does not expect to use them himself, but he wants to prevent others from using them. All this involves worry and loss of time and money: and the large manufacturer prefers to keep his improvement to himself and get what benefit he can by using it. While if the small manufacturer takes out a patent, he is likely to be harassed by infringements: and even though he may win "with costs" the actions in which he tries to defend himself, he is sure to be ruined by them if they are numerous. It is generally in the public interest that an improvement should be published, even though it is at the same time patented. But if it is patented in England and not in other countries, as is often the case, English manufacturers may not use it, even though they were just on the point of finding it out for themselves before it was patented; while foreign manufacturers learn all about it and can use it freely.

IV, xi, 2. in the economy of steam power, and in the management and repairs of engines and machinery. Large soft-goods factories have carpenters' and mechanics' shops, which diminish the cost of repairs, and prevent delays from accidents to the plant[1].

Advantages of a large business, or of associated groups of businesses, in buying and selling.

Akin to these last, there are a great many advantages which a large factory, or indeed a large business of almost any kind, nearly always has over a small one. A large business buys in great quantities and therefore cheaply; it pays low freights and saves on carriage in many ways, particularly if it has a railway siding. It often sells in large quantities, and thus saves itself trouble; and yet at the same time it gets a good price, because it offers conveniences to the customer by having a large stock from which he can select and at once fill up a varied order; while its reputation gives him confidence. It can spend large sums on advertising by commercial travellers and in other ways; its agents give it trustworthy information on trade and personal matters in distant places, and its own goods advertise one another.

The economies of highly organized buying and selling are among the chief causes of the present tendency towards the fusion of many businesses in the same industry or trade into single huge aggregates; and also of trading federations of various kinds, including German cartels and centralized co-operative associations. They have also always promoted the concentration of business risks in the hands of large capitalists who put out the work to be done by smaller men[2].

---

[1] It is a remarkable fact that cotton and some other textile factories form an exception to the general rule that the capital required per head of the workers is generally greater in a large factory than in a small one. The reason is that in most other businesses the large factory has many things done by expensive machines which are done by hand in a small factory; so that while the wages bill is less in proportion to the output in a large factory than in a small one, the value of the machinery and the factory space occupied by the machinery is much greater. But in the simpler branches of the textile trades, small works have the same machinery as large works have; and since small steam-engines, etc. are proportionately more expensive than large ones, they require a greater fixed capital in proportion to their output than larger factories do; and they are likely to require a floating capital also rather greater in proportion.

[2] See below IV. xii. 3.

§ 3. Next, with regard to the economy of skill. Every- IV, xi, 3.
thing that has been said with regard to the advantages *Advan-*
which a large establishment has in being able to afford *tages of*
a large
highly specialized machinery applies equally with regard *factory as*
regards
to highly specialized skill. It can contrive to keep each of *specialized*
its employees constantly engaged in the most difficult work *skill,*
of which he is capable, and yet so to narrow the range of his
work that he can attain that facility and excellence which
come from long-continued practice. But enough has already
been said on the advantage of division of labour: and we
may pass to an important though indirect advantage which
a manufacturer derives from having a great many men in
his employment.

The large manufacturer has a much better chance than *the*
selection
a small one has, of getting hold of men with exceptional *of leading*
natural abilities, to do the most difficult part of his work— *men, etc.*
that on which the reputation of his establishment chiefly
depends. This is occasionally important as regards mere
handiwork in trades which require much taste and originality,
as for instance that of a house decorator, and in those which
require exceptionally fine workmanship, as for instance that
of a manufacturer of delicate mechanism[1]. But in most
businesses its chief importance lies in the facilities which
it gives to the employer for the selection of able and tried
men, men whom he trusts and who trust him, to be his
foremen and heads of departments. We are thus brought
to the central problem of the modern organization of industry, viz. that which relates to the advantages and
disadvantages of the subdivision of the work of business
management.

---

[1] Thus Boulton writing in 1770 when he had 700 or 800 persons employed
as metallic artists and workers in tortoiseshell, stones, glass, and enamel, says:—
"I have trained up many, and am training up more, plain country lads into good
workmen; and wherever I find indications of skill and ability, I encourage them.
I have likewise established correspondence with almost every mercantile town in
Europe, and am thus regularly supplied with orders for the grosser articles in
common demand, by which I am enabled to employ such a number of hands as to
provide me with an ample choice of artists for the finer branches of work: and I
am thus encouraged to erect and employ a more extensive apparatus than it would
be prudent to employ for the production of the finer articles only.", Smiles' *Life*
of Boulton, p. 128.

IV, xi, 4.

The subdivision of the work of business management: advantages of the large manufacturer;

§ 4. The head of a large business can reserve all his strength for the broadest and most fundamental problems of his trade: he must indeed assure himself that his managers, clerks and foremen are the right men for their work, and are doing their work well; but beyond this he need not trouble himself much about details. He can keep his mind fresh and clear for thinking out the most difficult and vital problems of his business; for studying the broader movements of the markets, the yet undeveloped results of current events at home and abroad; and for contriving how to improve the organization of the internal and external relations of his business.

For much of this work the small employer has not the time if he has the ability; he cannot take so broad a survey of his trade, or look so far ahead; he must often be content to follow the lead of others. And he must spend much of his time on work that is below him; for if he is to succeed at all, his mind must be in some respects of a high quality, and must have a good deal of originating and organizing force; and yet he must do much routine work.

those of the small manufacturer.

On the other hand the small employer has advantages of his own. The master's eye is everywhere; there is no shirking by his foremen or workmen, no divided responsibility, no sending half-understood messages backwards and forwards from one department to another. He saves much of the book-keeping, and nearly all of the cumbrous system of checks that are necessary in the business of a large firm; and the gain from this source is of very great importance in trades which use the more valuable metals and other expensive materials.

And though he must always remain at a great disadvantage in getting information and in making experiments, yet in this matter the general course of progress is on his side. For External economies are constantly growing in importance relatively to Internal in all matters of Trade-knowledge: newspapers, and trade and technical publications of all kinds are perpetually scouting for him and bringing him much of the knowledge he wants—knowledge which a little while ago would have been beyond the reach of anyone who

could not afford to have well-paid agents in many distant IV, xi, 5.
places. Again, it is to his interest also that the secrecy of
business is on the whole diminishing, and that the most
important improvements in method seldom remain secret for
long after they have passed from the experimental stage. It
is to his advantage that changes in manufacture depend less
on mere rules of thumb and more on broad developments of
scientific principle; and that many of these are made by
students in the pursuit of knowledge for its own sake, and
are promptly published in the general interest. Although
therefore the small manufacturer can seldom be in the front
of the race of progress, he need not be far from it, if he has
the time and the ability for availing himself of the modern
facilities for obtaining knowledge. But it is true that he
must be exceptionally strong if he can do this without neg-
lecting the minor but necessary details of the business.

§ 5. In agriculture and other trades in which a man *Rapid*
gains no very great new economics by increasing the scale of *growth of firms*
his production, it often happens that a business remains of *in some trades*
about the same size for many years, if not for many generations. *which offer*
But it is otherwise in trades in which a large business can *great economies*
command very important advantages, which are beyond the *to produc-*
reach of a small business. A new man, working his way *tion on a large scale.*
up in such a trade, has to set his energy and flexibility, his
industry and care for small details, against the broader
economies of his rivals with their larger capital, their higher
specialization of machinery and labour, and their larger trade
connection. If then he can double his production, and sell
at anything like his old rate, he will have more than doubled
his profits. This will raise his credit with bankers and other
shrewd lenders; and will enable him to increase his business
further, and to attain yet further economies, and yet higher
profits: and this again will increase his business and so on.
It seems at first that no point is marked out at which he
need stop. And it is true that, if, as his business increased,
his faculties adapted themselves to his larger sphere, as they
had done to his smaller; if he retained his originality, and
versatility and power of initiation, his perseverance, his tact
and his good luck for very many years together; he might

IV, xi, 5. then gather into his hands the whole volume of production in his branch of trade for his district. And if his goods were not very difficult of transport, nor of marketing, he might extend this district very wide, and attain something like a limited monopoly; that is, of a monopoly limited by the consideration that a very high price would bring rival producers into the field.

But long before this end is reached, his progress is likely to be arrested by the decay, if not of his faculties, yet of his liking for energetic work. The rise of his firm may be prolonged if he can hand down his business to a successor almost as energetic as himself[1]. But the continued very rapid growth of his firm requires the presence of two conditions which are seldom combined in the same industry. There are many trades in which an individual producer could secure much increased "internal" economies by a great increase of his output; and there are many in which he could market that output easily; yet there are few in which he could do both. And this is not an accidental, but almost a necessary result.

Where marketing is easy, the economies of production on a large scale are mostly open to firms of moderate size. For in most of those trades in which the economies of production on a large scale are of first-rate importance, marketing is difficult. There are, no doubt, important exceptions. A producer may, for instance, obtain access to the whole of a large market in the case of goods which are so simple and uniform that they can be sold wholesale in vast quantities. But, most goods of this kind are raw produce; and nearly all the rest are plain and common, such as steel rails or calico; and their production can be reduced to routine, for the very reason that they are plain and common. Therefore in the industries which produce them, no firm can hold its own at all unless equipped with expensive appliances of nearly the latest type for its main work; while subordinate operations can be performed by subsidiary industries; and in short there remains no very great difference between the economies available by a large and by a very large firm; and the tendency of large firms to drive out small ones has already gone so far as to exhaust most

---

[1] Means to this end and their practical limitations are discussed in the latter half of the following chapter.

LARGE AND SMALL TRADING ESTABLISHMENTS   **287**

of the strength of those forces by which it was originally IV, xi, 6.
promoted.

But many commodities with regard to which the tendency But in
to increasing return acts strongly are, more or less, specialities: specialities
some of them aim at creating a new want, or at meeting marketing
is difficult.
an old want in a new way. Some of them are adapted to
special tastes, and can never have a very large market; and
some have merits that are not easily tested, and must win
their way to general favour slowly. In all such cases the
sales of each business are limited, more or less according to
circumstances, to the particular market which it has slowly
and expensively acquired; and though the production itself
might be economically increased very fast, the sale could
not.

Lastly, the very conditions of an industry which enable a Causes
new firm to attain quickly command over new economies of which
enable
production, render that firm liable to be supplanted quickly firms
to rise
by still younger firms with yet newer methods. Especially quickly,
often
where the powerful economies of production on a large scale hasten
their fall.
are associated with the use of new appliances and new
methods, a firm which has lost the exceptional energy which
enabled it to rise, is likely ere long quickly to decay; and the
full life of a large firm seldom lasts very long.

§ 6. The advantages which a large business has over Advantages of
a small one are conspicuous in manufacture, because, as we large
have noticed, it has special facilities for concentrating a great businesses
of other
deal of work in a small area. But there is a strong tendency kinds.
for large establishments to drive out small ones in many
other industries. In particular the retail trade is being
transformed, the small shopkeeper is losing ground daily.

Let us look at the advantages which a large retail shop In retail
trade they
or store has in competing with its smaller neighbours. To are on the
increase
begin with, it can obviously buy on better terms, it can get
its goods carried more cheaply, and can offer a larger variety
to meet the taste of customers. Next, it has a great economy
of skill: the small shopkeeper, like the small manufacturer,
must spend much of his time in routine work that requires
no judgment: whereas the head of a large establishment,
and even in some cases his chief assistants, spend their whole

288   PRODUCTION ON A LARGE SCALE

IV, XI, 6. time in using their judgment. Until lately these advantages
have been generally outweighed by the greater facilities
which the small shopkeeper has for bringing his goods to
the door of his customers; for humouring their several
tastes; and for knowing enough of them individually to be
able safely to lend them capital, in the form of selling them
goods on credit.

owing to   But within recent years there have been many changes
the growth
of cash   all telling on the side of large establishments. The habit of
payments   buying on credit is passing away; and the personal relations
between shopkeeper and customer are becoming more distant.
The first change is a great step forwards: the second is on
some accounts to be regretted, but not on all; for it is partly
due to the fact that the increase of true self-respect among
the wealthier classes is making them no longer care for the
subservient personal attentions they used to require. Again,
the growing value of time makes people less willing than
they were to spend several hours in shopping; they now
often prefer to spend a few minutes in writing out a long
list of orders from a varied and detailed price-list; and this
they are enabled to do easily by the growing facilities for
ordering and receiving parcels by post and in other ways.
And when they do go shopping, tramcars and local trains are
often at hand to take them easily and cheaply to the large
central shops of a neighbouring town. All these changes
render it more difficult than it was for the small shopkeeper
to hold his own even in the provision trade, and others in
which no great variety of stock is required.

and the   But in many trades the ever-growing variety of commo-
increasing
variety of   dities, and those rapid changes of fashion which now extend
the goods   their baneful influence through almost every rank of society,
in common
demand.   weight the balance even more heavily against the small
dealer, for he cannot keep a sufficient stock to offer much
variety of choice, and if he tries to follow any movement of
fashion closely, a larger proportion of his stock will be left
stranded by the receding tide than in the case of a large
shopkeeper. Again, in some branches of the clothing and
furniture and other trades the increasing cheapness of
machine-made goods is leading people to buy ready-made

things from a large store instead of having them made to IV, xi, 7.
order by some small maker and dealer in their neighbourhood. Again, the large shopkeeper, not content with receiving travellers from the manufacturers, makes tours either
himself or by his agent in the most important manufacturing
districts at home and abroad; and he thus often dispenses
with middlemen between him and the manufacturer. A tailor
with moderate capital shows his customers specimens of
many hundreds of the newest cloths, and perhaps orders
by telegraph the selected cloth to be sent by parcels' post.
Again, ladies often buy their materials direct from the
manufacturer, and get them made up by dressmakers who
have scarcely any capital. Small shopkeepers seem likely
always to retain some hold of the minor repairing trades:
and they keep their own fairly well in the sale of perishable
food, especially to the working classes, partly in consequence
of their being able to sell goods on credit and to collect
small debts. In many trades however a firm with a large
capital prefers having many small shops to one large one.
Buying, and whatever production is desirable, is concentrated
under a central management; and exceptional demands are
met from a central reserve, so that each branch has large
resources, without the expense of keeping a large stock.
The branch manager has nothing to divert his attention
from his customers; and, if an active man, with direct
interest in the success of his branch, may prove himself
a formidable rival to the small shopkeeper; as has been
shown in many trades connected with clothing and food.

§ 7. We may next consider those industries whose geo- The
graphical position is determined by the nature of their work. carrying
trades.

Country carriers and a few cabmen are almost the only
survivals of small industry in the carrying trade. Railways
and tramways are constantly increasing in size, and the
capital required to work them is increasing at an even
greater rate. The growing intricacy and variety of commerce is adding to the advantages which a large fleet of
ships under one management derives from its power of
delivering goods promptly, and without breach of responsibility, in many different ports; and as regards the vessels

M.   10

IV, xi, 7. themselves time is on the side of large ships, especially in the passenger trade[1]. As a consequence the arguments in favour of the State's undertaking business are stronger in some branches of the carrying trade than in any other, except the allied undertakings of carrying away refuse, and bringing in water, gas, etc.[2]

Mines and quarries.

The contest between large and small mines and quarries has not so clearly marked a tendency. The history of the State management of mines is full of very dark shadows; for the business of mining depends too much on the probity of its managers and their energy and judgment in matters of detail as well as of general principle, to be well managed by State officials: and for the same reason the small mine or quarry may fairly be expected, other things being equal, to hold its own against the large one. But in some cases the cost of deep shafts, of machinery and of establishing means of communication, are too great to be borne by any but a very large business.

The case of agriculture is deferred.

In agriculture there is not much division of labour, and there is no production on a very large scale; for a so-called "large farm" does not employ a tenth part of the labour which is collected in a factory of moderate dimensions. This is partly due to natural causes, to the changes of the seasons and to the difficulty of concentrating a great deal of labour in any one place; but it is partly also due to causes connected with varieties of land tenure. And it will be best to postpone discussion of all of them till we come to study demand and supply in relation to land in the sixth Book.

---

[1] A ship's carrying power varies as the cube of her dimensions, while the resistance offered by the water increases only a little faster than the square of her dimensions; so that a large ship requires less coal in proportion to its tonnage than a small one. It also requires less labour, especially that of navigation: while to passengers it offers greater safety and comfort, more choice of company and better professional attendance. In short, the small ship has no chance of competing with the large ship between ports which large ships can easily enter, and between which the traffic is sufficient to enable them to fill up quickly.

[2] It is characteristic of the great economic change of the last hundred years that when the first railway bills were passed, provision was made for allowing private individuals to run their own conveyances on them, just as they do on a highway or a canal; and now we find it difficult to imagine how people could have expected, as they certainly did, that this plan would prove a practicable one

[2]

THE ECONOMIC JOURNAL

DECEMBER, 1928

INCREASING RETURNS AND ECONOMIC PROGRESS [1]

MY subject may appear alarmingly formidable, but I did not intend it to be so. The words economic progress, taken by themselves, would suggest the pursuit of some philosophy of history, of some way of appraising the results of past and possible future changes in forms of economic organisation and modes of economic activities. But as I have used them, joined to the other half of my title, they are meant merely to dispel apprehensions, by suggesting that I do not propose to discuss any of those alluring but highly technical questions relating to the precise way in which some sort of equilibrium of supply and demand is achieved in the market for the products of industries which can increase their output without increasing their costs proportionately, or to the possible advantages of fostering the development of such industries while putting a handicap upon industries whose output can be increased only at the expense of a more than proportionate increase of costs. I suspect, indeed, that the apparatus which economists have built up for dealing effectively with the range of questions to which I have just referred may stand in the way of a clear view of the more general or elementary aspects of the phenomena of increasing returns, such as I wish to comment upon in this paper.

Consider, for example, Alfred Marshall's fruitful distinction between the internal productive economies which a particular firm is able to secure as the growth of the market permits it to enlarge the scale of its operations and the economies external to the individual firm which show themselves only in changes of the organisation of the industry as a whole. This distinction has been useful in at least two different ways. In the first place it is, or ought to be, a safeguard against the common error of assuming that wherever increasing returns operate there is necessarily an effective tendency towards monopoly. In the second

[1] Presidential Address before Section F (Economic Science and Statistics) of the British Association for the Advancement of Science, Glasgow, September 10, 1928.

place it simplifies the analysis of the manner in which the prices
of commodities produced under conditions of increasing returns
are determined. A representative firm within the industry,
maintaining its own identity and devoting itself to a given range
of activities, is made to be the vehicle or medium through which
the economics achieved by the industry as a whole are transmitted
to the market and have their effect upon the price of the product.

The view of the nature of the processes of industrial progress
which is implied in the distinction between internal and external
economics is necessarily a partial view. Certain aspects of those
processes are illuminated, while, for that very reason, certain
other aspects, important in relation to other problems, are
obscured. This will be clear, I think, if we observe that, although
the internal economics of some firms producing, let us say,
materials or appliances may figure as the external economics of
other firms, not all of the economics which are properly to be
called external can be accounted for by adding up the internal
economics of all the separate firms. When we look at the internal
economics of a particular firm we envisage a condition of comparative stability. Year after year the firm, like its competitors,
is manufacturing a particular product or group of products, or is
confining itself to certain definite stages in the work of forwarding
the products towards their final form. Its operations change in
the sense that they are progressively adapted to an increasing
output, but they are kept within definitely circumscribed bounds.
Out beyond, in that obscurer field from which it derives its external
economics, changes of another order are occurring. New products are appearing, firms are assuming new tasks, and new industries are coming into being. In short, change in this external
field is qualitative as well as quantitative. No analysis of the
forces making for economic equilibrium, forces which we might
say are tangential at any moment of time, will serve to illumine
this field, for movements away from equilibrium, departures
from previous trends, are characteristic of it. Not much is to
be gained by probing into it to see how increasing returns show
themselves in the costs of individual firms and in the prices at
which they offer their products.

Instead, we have to go back to a simpler and more inclusive
view, such as some of the older economists took when they contrasted the increasing returns which they thought were characteristic of manufacturing industry taken as a whole with the
diminishing returns which they thought were dominant in agriculture because of an increasingly unfavourable proportioning

of labour and land. Most of them were disappointingly vague with respect to the origins and the precise nature of the " improvements " which they counted upon to retard somewhat the operation of the tendency towards diminishing returns in agriculture and to secure a progressively more effective use of labour in manufactures. Their opinions appear to have rested partly upon an empirical generalisation. Improvements had been made, they were still being made, and it might be assumed that they would continue to be made. If they had looked back they would have seen that there were centuries during which there were few significant changes in either agricultural or industrial methods. But they were living in an age when men had turned their faces in a new direction and when economic progress was not only consciously sought but seemed in some way to grow out of the nature of things. Improvements, then, were not something to be explained. They were natural phenomena, like the precession of the equinoxes.

There were certain important exceptions, however, to this incurious attitude towards what might seem to be one of the most important of all economic problems. Senior's positive doctrine is well known, and there were others who made note of the circumstance that with the growth of population and of markets new opportunities for the division of labour appear and new advantages attach to it. In this way, and in this way only, were the generally commonplace things which they said about " improvements " related to anything which could properly be called a doctrine of increasing returns. They added nothing to Adam Smith's famous theorem that the division of labour depends upon the extent of the market. That theorem, I have always thought, is one of the most illuminating and fruitful generalisations which can be found anywhere in the whole literature of economics. In fact, as I am bound to confess, I am taking it as the text of this paper, in much the way that some minor composer borrows a theme from one of the masters and adds certain developments or variations of his own. To-day, of course, we mean by the division of labour something much broader in scope than that splitting up of occupations and development of specialised crafts which Adam Smith mostly had in mind. No one, so far as I know, has tried to enumerate all of the different aspects of the division of labour, and I do not propose to undertake that task. I shall deal with two related aspects only : the growth of indirect or roundabout methods of production and the division of labour among industries.

N N 2

It is generally agreed that Adam Smith, when he suggested that the division of labour leads to inventions because workmen engaged in specialised routine operations come to see better ways of accomplishing the same results, missed the main point. The important thing, of course, is that with the division of labour a group of complex processes is transformed into a succession of simpler processes, some of which, at least, lend themselves to the use of machinery. In the use of machinery and the adoption of indirect processes there is a further division of labour, the economics of which are again limited by the extent of the market. It would be wasteful to make a hammer to drive a single nail; it would be better to use whatever awkward implement lies conveniently at hand. It would be wasteful to furnish a factory with an elaborate equipment of specially constructed jigs, gauges, lathes, drills, presses and conveyors to build a hundred automobiles; it would be better to rely mostly upon tools and machines of standard types, so as to make a relatively larger use of directly-applied and a relatively smaller use of indirectly-applied labour. Mr. Ford's methods would be absurdly uneconomical if his output were very small, and would be unprofitable even if his output were what many other manufacturers of automobiles would call large.

Then, of course, there are economies of what might be called a secondary order. How far it pays to go in equipping factories with special appliances for making hammers or for constructing specialised machinery for use in making different parts of automobiles depends again upon how many nails are to be driven and how many automobiles can be sold. In some instances, I suppose, these secondary economies, though real, have only a secondary importance. The derived demands for many types of specialised production appliances are inelastic over a fairly large range. If the benefits and the costs of using such appliances are spread over a relatively large volume of final products, their technical effectiveness is a larger factor in determining whether it is profitable to use them than any difference which producing them on a large or a small scale would commonly make in their costs. In other instances the demand for productive appliances is more elastic, and beyond a certain level of costs demand may fail completely. In such circumstances secondary economies may become highly important.

Doubtless, much of what I have said has been familiar and even elementary. I shall venture, nevertheless, to put further stress upon two points, which may be among those which have a familiar ring, but which appear sometimes to be in danger of being forgotten. (Otherwise, economists of standing could not have suggested that increasing returns may be altogether illusory, or have maintained that where they are present they must lead to monopoly.) The first point is that the principal economies which manifest themselves in increasing returns are the economies of capitalistic or roundabout methods of production. These economies, again, are largely identical with the economies of the division of labour in its most important modern forms. In fact, these economies lie under our eyes, but we may miss them if we try to make of *large-scale* production (in the sense of production by large firms or large industries), as contrasted with *large* production, any more than an incident in the general process by which increasing returns are secured and if accordingly we look too much at the individual firm or even, as I shall suggest presently, at the individual industry.

The second point is that the economies of roundabout methods, even more than the economies of other forms of the division of labour, depend upon the extent of the market—and that, of course, is why we discuss them under the head of increasing returns. It would hardly be necessary to stress this point, if it were not that the economies of large-scale operations and of " mass-production " are often referred to as though they could be had for the taking, by means of a " rational " reorganisation of industry. Now I grant that at any given time routine and inertia play a very large part in the organisation and conduct of industrial operations. Real leadership is no more common in industrial than in other pursuits. New catch-words or slogans like mass-production and rationalisation may operate as stimuli; they may rouse men from routine and lead them to scrutinise again the organisation and processes of industry and to try to discover particular ways in which they can be bettered. For example, no one can doubt that there are genuine economies to be achieved in the way of " simplification and standardisation," or that the securing of these economies requires that certain deeply rooted competitive wastes be extirpated. This last requires a definite concerted effort—precisely the kind of thing which ordinary competitive motives are often powerless to effect, but which might come more easily as the response to the dissemination of a new idea.

There is a danger, however, that we shall expect too much from these " rational " industrial reforms. Pressed beyond a certain point they become the reverse of rational. I have naturally been interested in British opinions respecting the reasons for the relatively high productivity (per labourer or per hour of labour) of representative American industries. The error of those who suggest that the explanation is to be found in the relatively high wages which prevail in America is not that they confuse cause and effect, but that they hold that what are really only two aspects of a single situation are, the one cause, and the other effect. Those who hold that American industry is managed better, that its leaders study its problems more intelligently and plan more courageously and more wisely can cite no facts in support of their opinion save the differences in the results achieved. Allowing for the circumstance that British industry, as a whole, has proved to be rather badly adjusted to the new post-war economic situation, I know of no facts which prove or even indicate that British industry, seen against the background of its own problems and its own possibilities, is less efficiently organised or less ably directed than American industry or the industry of any other country.

Sometimes the fact that the average American labourer works with the help of a larger supply of power-driven labour-saving machinery than the labourer of other countries is cited as evidence of the superior intelligence of the average American employer. But this will not do, for, as every economist knows, the greater the degree in which labour is productive or scarce—the words have the same meaning—the greater is the relative economy of using it in such indirect or roundabout ways as are technically advantageous, even though such procedure calls for larger advances of capital than simpler methods do.

It is encouraging to find that a fairly large number of commentators upon the volume of the American industrial product and the scale of American industrial organisation have come to surmise that the extent of the American domestic market, unimpeded by tariff barriers, may have something to do with the matter. This opinion seems even to be forced upon thoughtful observers by the general character of the facts, whether or no the observers think in terms of the economists' conception of increasing returns. In certain industries, although by no means in all, productive methods are economical and profitable in America which would not be profitable elsewhere. The importance of coal and iron and other natural resources needs no comment. Taking a country's economic endowment as given, however, the most important single factor in determining the effectiveness of its industry appears to be the size of the market. But just what constitutes a large market ?   Not area or population alone, but buying power, the capacity to absorb a large annual output of goods.   This trite observation, however, at once suggests another equally trite, namely, that capacity to buy depends upon capacity to produce.   In an inclusive view, considering the market not as an outlet for the products of a particular industry, and therefore external to that industry, but as the outlet for goods in general, the size of the market is determined and defined by the volume of production.   If this statement needs any qualification, it is that the conception of a market in this inclusive sense—an aggregate of productive activities, tied together by trade—carries with it the notion that there must be some sort of balance, that different productive activities must be proportioned one to another.

Modified, then, in the light of this broader conception of the market, Adam Smith's dictum amounts to the theorem that the division of labour depends in large part upon the division of labour.   This is more than mere tautology.   It means, if I read its significance rightly, that the counter forces which are continually defeating the forces which make for economic equilibrium are more pervasive and more deeply rooted in the constitution of the modern economic system than we commonly realise.   Not only new or adventitious elements, coming in from the outside, but elements which are permanent characteristics of the ways in which goods are produced make continuously for change.   Every important advance in the organisation of production, regardless of whether it is based upon anything which, in a narrow or technical sense, would be called a new " invention," or involves a fresh application of the fruits of scientific progress to industry, alters the conditions of industrial activity and initiates responses elsewhere in the industrial structure which in turn have a further unsettling effect.   Thus change becomes progressive and propagates itself in a cumulative way.

The apparatus which economists have built up for the analysis of supply and demand in their relations to prices does not seem to be particularly helpful for the purposes of an inquiry into these broader aspects of increasing returns.   In fact, as I have already suggested, reliance upon it may divert attention to incidental or partial aspects of a process which ought to be seen as a whole. If, nevertheless, one insists upon seeing just how far one can get into the problem by using the formulas of supply and demand, the simplest way, I suppose, is to begin by inquiring into the operations of reciprocal demand when the commodities exchanged are produced competitively under conditions of increasing returns and when the demand for each commodity is elastic, in the special sense that a small increase in its supply will be attended by an increase in the amounts of other commodities which can be had in exchange for it.[1] Under such conditions an increase in the supply of one commodity *is* an increase in the demand for other commodities, and it must be supposed that every increase in demand will evoke an increase in supply. The rate at which any one industry grows is conditioned by the rate at which other industries grow, but since the elasticities of demand and of supply will differ for different products, some industries will grow faster than others. Even with a stationary population and in the absence of new discoveries [2] in pure or applied science. there are no limits to the process of expansion except the limits beyond which demand is not elastic and returns do not increase.

If, under these hypothetical conditions, progress were un-impeded and frictionless, if it were not dependent in part upon a process of trial and error, if the organisation of industry were always such as, in relation to the immediate situation, is most economical, the realising of increasing returns might be progressive and continuous, although, for technical reasons, it could not always proceed at an even rate. But it would remain a process requiring time. An industrial dictator, with foresight and knowledge, could hasten the pace somewhat, but he could not achieve an Aladdin-like transformation of a country's industry, so as to reap the fruits of a half-century's ordinary progress in a few years. The obstacles are of two sorts. First, the human material which has to be used is resistant to change. New trades have to be learnt and new habits have to be acquired. There has to be a new geographical distribution of the population and established communal groups have to be broken up. Second, the accumulation of the necessary capital takes time, even though the process of accumulation is largely one of turning part of an increasing product into forms which will serve in securing a further increase of product. An acceleration of the rate of accumulation encounters increasing costs, into which both technical and psychological elements enter. One who likes

---

[1] If the circumstance that commodity *a* is produced under conditions of increasing returns is taken into account as a factor in the elasticity of demand for *b* in terms of *a*, elasticity of demand and elasticity of supply may be looked upon as different ways of expressing a single functional relation.

[2] As contrasted with such new ways of organising production and such new " inventions " as are merely adaptations of known ways of doing things, made practicable and economical by an enlarged scale of production.

to conceive of all economic processes in terms of tendencies towards an equilibrium might even maintain that increasing returns, so far as they depend upon the economics of indirect methods of production and the size of the market, are offset and negated by their costs, and that under such simplified conditions as I have dealt with the realising of increasing returns would be spread through time in such a way as to secure an equilibrium of costs and advantages. This would amount to saying that no real economic progress could come through the operation of forces engendered *within* the economic system—a conclusion repugnant to common sense. To deal with this point thoroughly would take us too far afield. I shall merely observe, first, that the appropriate conception is that of a *moving* equilibrium, and second, that the costs which (under increasing returns) grow less rapidly than the product are not the " costs " which figure in an " equilibrium of costs and advantages."

Moving away from these abstract considerations, so as to get closer to the complications of the real situation, account has to be taken, first, of various kinds of obstacles. The demand for some products is inelastic, or, with an increasing supply, soon becomes so. The producers of such commodities, however, often share in the advantages of the increase of the general scale of production in related industries, and so far as they do productive resources are released for other uses. Then there are natural scarcities, limitations or inelasticities of supply, such as effectively block the way to the securing of any important economies in the production of some commodities and which impair the effectiveness of the economies secured in the production of other commodities. In most fields, moreover, progress is not and cannot be continuous. The next important step forward is often initially costly, and cannot be taken until a certain quantum of prospective advantages has accumulated.

On the other side of the account are various factors which reinforce the influences which make for increasing returns. The discovery of new natural resources and of new uses for them and the growth of scientific knowledge are probably the most potent of such factors. The causal connections between the growth of industry and the progress of science run in both directions, but on which side the preponderant influence lies no one can say. At any rate, out of better knowledge of the materials and forces upon which men can lay their hands there come both new ways of producing familiar commodities and new products, and these last have a presumptive claim to be regarded as embodying more economical uses of productive resources than the uses which they displace. Some weight has to be given also to the way in which, with the advance of the scientific spirit, a new kind of interest—which might be described as a scientific interest conditioned by an economic interest—is beginning to infiltrate into industry. It is a point of controversy, but I venture to maintain that under most circumstances, though not in all, the growth of population still has to be counted a factor making for a larger *per capita* product—although even that cautious statement needs to be interpreted and qualified. But just as there may be population growth with no increase of the average *per capita* product, so also, as I have tried to suggest, markets may grow and increasing returns may be secured while the population remains stationary.

It is dangerous to assign to any single factor the leading rôle in that continuing economic revolution which has taken the modern world so far away from the world of a few hundred years ago. But is there any other factor which has a better claim to that rôle than the persisting search for markets? No other hypothesis so well unites economic history and economic theory. The Industrial Revolution of the eighteenth century has come to be generally regarded, not as a cataclysm brought about by certain inspired improvements in industrial technique, but as a series of changes related in an orderly way to prior changes in industrial organisation and to the enlargement of markets. It is sometimes said, however, that while in the Middle Ages and in the early modern period industry was the servant of commerce, since the rise of " industrial capitalism " the relation has been reversed, commerce being now merely an agent of industry. If this means that the finding of markets is one of the tasks of modern industry it is true. If it means that industry imposes its will upon the market, that whereas formerly the things which were produced were the things which could be sold, now the things which have to be sold are the things that are produced, it is not true.

The great change, I imagine, is in the new importance which the *potential market* has in the planning and management of large industries. The difference between the cost per unit of output in an industry or in an individual plant properly adapted to a given volume of output and in an industry or plant equally well adapted to an output five times as large is often much greater than one would infer from looking merely at the economies which may accrue as an existing establishment gradually extends the scale of its operations.   Potential demand, then, in the planning of industrial undertakings, has to be balanced against potential economies, elasticity of demand against decreasing costs.   The search for markets is not a matter of disposing of a "surplus product," in the Marxian sense, but of finding an outlet for a potential product.   Nor is it wholly a matter of multiplying profits by multiplying sales; it is partly a matter of augmenting profits by reducing costs.

Although the initial displacement may be considerable and the repercussions upon particular industries unfavourable, the enlarging of the market for any one commodity, produced under conditions of increasing returns, generally has the net effect, as I have tried to show, of enlarging the market for other commodities.   The business man's mercantilistic emphasis upon markets may have a sounder basis than the economist who thinks mostly in terms of economic statics is prone to admit.   How far "selling expenses," for example, are to be counted sheer economic waste depends upon their effects upon the aggregate product of industry, as distinguished from their effects upon the fortunes of particular undertakings.

Increasing returns are often spoken of as though they were attached always to the growth of "industries," and I have not tried to avoid that way of speaking of them, although I think that it may be a misleading way.   The point which I have in mind is something more than a quibble about the proper definition of an industry, for it involves a particular thesis with respect to the way in which increasing returns are reflected in changes in the organisation of industrial activities.   Much has been said about industrial integration as a concomitant or a natural result of an increasing industrial output.   It obviously is, under particular conditions, though I know of no satisfactory statement of just what those particular conditions are.   But the opposed process, industrial differentiation, has been and remains the type of change characteristically associated with the growth of production.   Notable as has been the increase in the complexity of the apparatus of living, as shown by the increase in the variety of goods offered in consumers' markets, the increase in the diversification of intermediate products and of industries manufacturing special products or groups of products has gone even further.

The successors of the early printers, it has often been observed, are not only the printers of to-day, with their own specialised establishments, but also the producers of wood pulp, of various

538   THE ECONOMIC JOURNAL   [DEC.

kinds of paper, of inks and their different ingredients, of type-metal and of type, the group of industries concerned with the technical parts of the producing of illustrations, and the manufacturers of specialised tools and machines for use in printing and in these various auxiliary industries. The list could be extended, both by enumerating other industries which are directly ancillary to the present printing trades and by going back to industries which, while supplying the industries which supply the printing trades, also supply other industries, concerned with preliminary stages in the making of final products other than printed books and newspapers. I do not think that the printing trades are an exceptional instance, but I shall not give other examples, for I do not want this paper to be too much like a primer of descriptive economics or an index to the reports of a census of production. It is sufficiently obvious, anyhow, that over a large part of the field of industry an increasingly intricate nexus of specialised undertakings has inserted itself between the producer of raw materials and the consumer of the final product.

With the extension of the division of labour among industries the representative firm, like the industry of which it is a part, loses its identity. Its internal economies dissolve into the internal and external economies of the more highly specialised undertakings which are its successors, and are supplemented by new economies. In so far as it is an adjustment to a new situation created by the growth of the market for the final products of industry the division of labour among industries is a vehicle of increasing returns. It is more than a change of form incidental to the full securing of the advantages of capitalistic methods of production—although it is largely that—for it has some advantages of its own which are independent of changes in productive technique. For example, it permits of a higher degree of specialisation in management, and the advantages of such specialisation are doubtless often real, though they may easily be given too much weight. Again, it lends itself to a better geographical distribution of industrial operations, and this advantage is unquestionably both real and important. Nearness to the source of supply of a particular raw material or to cheap power counts for most in one part of a series of industrial processes, nearness to other industries or to cheap transport in another part, and nearness to a larger centre of population in yet another. A better *combination* of advantages of location, with a smaller element of compromise, can be had by the more specialised industries. But the largest advantage secured by the division of labour among industries is the fuller realising of the economies of capitalistic or roundabout methods of production. This should be sufficiently obvious if we assume, as we must, that in most industries there are effective, though elastic, limits to the economical size of the individual firm. The output of the individual firm is generally a relatively small proportion of the aggregate output of an industry. The degree in which it can secure economies by making its own operations more roundabout is limited. But certain roundabout methods are fairly sure to become feasible and economical when their advantages can be spread over the output of the whole industry. These potential economies, then, are segregated and achieved by the operations of specialised undertakings which, taken together, constitute a new industry. It might conceivably be maintained that the *scale* upon which the firms in the new industry are able to operate is the secret of their ability to realise economies for industry as a whole, while presumably making profits for themselves. This is true in a way, but misleading. The scale of their operations (which is only incidentally or under special conditions a matter of the size of the individual firm) merely reflects the size of the market for the final products of the industry or industries to whose operations their own are ancillary. And the principal advantage of large-scale operation at this stage is that it again makes methods economical which would be uneconomical if their benefits could not be diffused over a large final product.

In recapitulation of these variations on a theme from Adam Smith there are three points to be stressed. First, the mechanism of increasing returns is not to be discerned adequately by observing the effects of variations in the size of an individual firm or of a particular industry, for the progressive division and specialisation of industries is an essential part of the process by which increasing returns are realised. What is required is that industrial operations be seen as an interrelated whole. Second, the securing of increasing returns depends upon the progressive division of labour, and the principal economies of the division of labour, in its modern forms, are the economies which are to be had by using labour in roundabout or indirect ways. Third, the division of labour depends upon the extent of the market, but the extent of the market also depends upon the division of labour. In this circumstance lies the possibility of economic progress, apart from the progress which comes as a result of the new knowledge which men are able to gain, whether in the pursuit of their economic or of their non-economic interests.

ALLYN A. YOUNG

NOTE

IN the accompanying construction (which owes much to Pareto), a collective indifference curve, *I*, is defined by the condition that, at equal cost, there would be no sufficient inducement for the community to alter an annual production of *x* units of one commodity and *y* units of another in order to secure the alternative combination of the two commodities indicated by any other point on the curve.[1] Each commodity might be taken as representative of a special class of commodities,

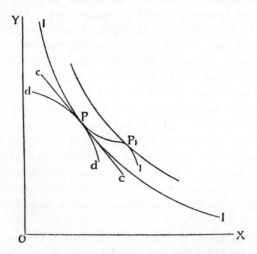

produced under generally similar conditions. Or one commodity might be made to represent " other goods in general," the annual outlay of productive exertions being regarded as constant. Alternatively, one commodity might represent " leisure " (as a collective name for all non-productive uses of time). The other would then represent the aggregate economic product.

There will be equilibrium (subject to instability of a kind which will be described presently) at a point *P*, if at that point a curve of equal costs, such as *d*, is tangent to the indifference curve. The curve of equal costs defines the terms upon which the community can exchange one commodity for the other by merely producing less of the one and more of the other (abstraction being made of any incidental costs of

---

[1] The collective indifference is to be taken as an expository device, not as a rigorous conception. The relative weights to be assigned to the individual indifference curves of which it is compounded will depend upon how the aggregate product is distributed, and this will not be the same for all positions of *P*.

change). Negative curvature, as in d, reflects a condition of decreasing returns, in the sense that more of either commodity can be had only by sacrificing progressively larger amounts of the other. Although a sufficient condition, the presence of decreasing returns is not a necessary condition of equilibrium. There would be a loss in moving away from P if equal costs were defined by the straight line c, which represents constant returns. Increasing returns, even, are consistent with equilibrium, provided that the degree of curvature of their graph is less than that of the indifference curve. It might happen, of course, that returns would decrease in one direction and increase in the other. Curve d, for example, might have a point of inflexion at or near P.

Consider now the conditions of departure from equilibrium. The curve i is drawn so as to represent *potential* increasing returns between P and P_1, which lies on a preferred indifference curve. If these increasing returns were to be had merely for the taking, if i were, for example, merely a continuation of the upper segment of d or c, P would not be a point even of unstable equilibrium. The advance from P to P_1 would be made by merely altering the proportions of the two commodities produced annually. To isolate the *problem* of increasing returns it is necessary to assume that P is a true point of equilibrium in the sense that it is determined by a curve of equal costs, such as d or c. The problem, then, has to do with the way in which the lower segment of d or c can be transformed into or replaced by such a curve as i. This requires, of course, that *additional* costs be incurred, of a kind which have not yet been taken into account. To diminish the amount of the one commodity which must be sacrificed for a given increment of the other, some of the labour hitherto devoted to its production must be used indirectly, so that the increase of the annual output of the one lags behind the curtailing of the output of the other.

This new element of cost might be taken into account by utilising a third dimension, but it is simpler to regard it as operating upon Δx, the increment in x accompanying the movement from P to P_1, so as to move the indifference curve upon which P_1 lies towards the left. It would be an error, however, to think that the combinations of x with y and $x +$ (Δx) with $y - \Delta y$ (where (Δx) is the contracted form of Δx) are themselves indifferent, so that P_1 is, in effect, brought over on to the original indifference curve, I, and no advantage is reaped. The path from P to P_1 is a *preferred* route, not merely a segment of an indifference curve. The cost of moving along that route is a function of the *rate* (in time) of the movement. An equilibrium rate (which need not be constant), such as would keep the movement from P to P_1 continuous and undeviating, would be determined by the condition, not that (Δx) and $- \Delta y$ should negate one another, but that either an acceleration or a retarding of the rate would be costly or disadvantageous. Because a mountain climber adjusts his pace to his physical powers and to the conditions of the ascent, it does not follow that he might as well have stayed at the foot. Or, alternatively but not inconsistently, the movement from P to P_1 may be conceived as made up of a series of small steps, each apparently yielding no more than a barely perceptible advantage, but only because the scale of reference for both costs and advantages depends at each step upon the position which has then been reached.

Several sets of circumstances will affect the amount and direction of the movement. (1) Even if i has no point of inflexion, such as has been indicated at P_1 (merely to simplify the first stages of this analysis), it will sooner or later (taking into account the "contraction" of Δx) become tangent to an indifference curve. In the absence of any other factor making for change, progress would then come to an end. (2) There may be another possible alternative path of increasing returns extending upwards from P and curving away from I. The most advantageous route will then be a compromise between (or a resultant of) the two limiting alternatives. In such circumstances the only effective limitation imposed upon the extent of the movement may come from the failure of elasticity of demand on one side or the other. (3) Successive indifference curves cannot be supposed to be symmetrical, in the sense that dy/dx remains the same function of y/x. If, for example, the slope of successive indifference curves at points corresponding to given values of y/x decreases (indicating that the demand for the commodity measured in units of y is relatively inelastic), freedom of movement in the direction of P_1 is reduced, while it becomes advantageous to move a little way in the opposite direction along even such a path as c or d. Under inverse conditions (with $-dy/dx$ increasing relatively to y/x for successive indifference curves) the extent of the possible movement in the direction of P_1 is increased. This conclusion amounts to no more than the obvious theorem that the degree in which the decreasing returns encountered in certain fields of economic activity operate as a drag upon the securing of increasing returns in other fields depends upon the relative elasticities of demand for the two types of products. But this consideration, like the others of which note has been made, serves to make clear the general nature of the reciprocal relation between increasing returns and the "extent of the market." (4) Discoveries of new supplies of natural resources or of *new* productive methods may have either or both of two kinds of effects. They may tilt the curves of equal cost and they may modify their curvature favourably. In either event a point such as P is moved to a higher indifference curve, and the paths along which further progress can be made are altered advantageously.

THE JOURNAL OF ECONOMIC HISTORY

VOL. VII   NOVEMBER 1947   NO. 2

The Creative Response in Economic History

I

ECONOMIC historians and economic theorists can make an interesting and socially valuable journey together, if they will. It would be an investigation into the sadly neglected area of economic change.

As anyone familiar with the history of economic thought will immediately recognize, practically all the economists of the nineteenth century and many of the twentieth have believed uncritically that all that is needed to explain a given historical development is to indicate conditioning or causal factors, such as an increase in population or the supply of capital. But this is sufficient only in the rarest of cases. As a rule, no factor acts in a uniquely determined way and, whenever it does not, the necessity arises of going into the details of its *modus operandi,* into the mechanisms through which it acts. Examples will illustrate this. Sometimes an increase in population actually has no other effect than that predicated by classical theory—a fall in per capita real income;[1] but, at other times, it may have an energizing effect that induces new developments with the result that per capita real income rises. Or a protective duty may have no other effect than to increase the price of the protected commodity and, in consequence, its output; but it may also induce a complete reorganization of the protected industry which eventually results in an increase in output so great as to reduce the price below its initial level.

What has not been adequately appreciated among theorists is the

---

[1] Even within the assumptions of classical theory this is not necessarily true; but we need not go into this.

distinction between different kinds of reaction to changes in "condition." Whenever an economy or a sector of an economy adapts itself to a change in its data in the way that traditional theory describes, whenever, that is, an economy reacts to an increase in population by simply adding the new brains and hands to the working force in the existing employments, or an industry reacts to a protective duty by expansion within its existing practice, we may speak of the development as *adaptive response*. And whenever the economy or an industry or some firms in an industry do something else, something that is outside of the range of existing practice, we may speak of *creative response*.

Creative response has at least three essential characteristics. First, from the standpoint of the observer who is in full possession of all relevant facts, it can always be understood *ex post*; but it can practically never be understood *ex ante*; that is to say, it cannot be predicted by applying the ordinary rules of inference from the pre-existing facts. This is why the "how" in what has been called above the "mechanisms" must be investigated in each case. Secondly, creative response shapes the whole course of subsequent events and their "long-run" outcome. It is not true that both types of responses dominate only what the economist loves to call "transitions," leaving the ultimate outcome to be determined by the initial data. Creative response changes social and economic situations for good, or, to put it differently, it creates situations from which there is no bridge to those situations that might have emerged in its absence. This is why creative response is an essential element in the historical process; no deterministic credo avails against this. Thirdly, creative response—the frequency of its occurrence in a group, its intensity and success or failure—has obviously something, be that much or little, to do (a) with quality of the personnel available in a society, (b) with relative quality of personnel, that is, with quality available to a particular field of activity relative to quality available, at the same time, to others, and (c) with individual decisions, actions, and patterns of behavior. Accordingly, a study of creative response in business becomes coterminous with a study of entrepreneurship. The mechanisms of economic change in capitalist society pivot on entrepreneurial activity.[2] Whether we emphasize opportunity or conditions, the responses of individuals or of groups, it is patently true that in capitalist society objective opportunities or conditions act through

---

[2] The function itself is not absent from other forms of society; but capitalist entrepreneurship is a sufficiently distinct phenomenon to be singled out.

The Creative Response in Economic History 151

entrepreneurial activity, analysis of which is at the very least a highly important avenue to the investigation of economic changes in the capitalist epoch.[3] This is compatible with widely different views about its importance as an "ultimate cause."

Seen in this light, the entrepreneur and his function are not difficult to conceptualize: the defining characteristic is simply the doing of new things or the doing of things that are already being done in a new way (innovation).[4] It is but natural, and in fact it is an advantage, that such a definition does not draw any sharp line between what is and what is not "enterprise." For actual life itself knows no such sharp division, though it shows up the type well enough. It should be observed at once that the "new thing" need not be spectacular or of historic importance. It need not be Bessemer steel or the explosion motor. It can be the Deerfoot sausage. To see the phenomenon even in the humblest levels of the business world is quite essential though it may be difficult to find the humble entrepreneurs historically.

Distinction from other functions with which enterpreneurship is frequently but not necessarily associated—just as "farmership" is frequently but not necessarily associated with the ownership of land and with the activity of a farm hand—does not present conceptual difficulties either. One necessary distinction is that between enterprise and management: evidently it is one thing to set up a concern embodying a new idea and another thing to head the administration of a going concern, however much the two may shade off into each other. Again, it is essential to note that the entrepreneurial function, though facilitated by the ownership of means, is not identical with that of the capitalist.[5] New light is urgently needed on the relation between the

---

[3] Arthur H. Cole has opened new vistas in this area in his presidential address before the Economic History Association, "An Approach to the Study of Entrepreneurship," THE TASKS OF ECONOMIC HISTORY (Supplemental Issue of THE JOURNAL OF ECONOMIC HISTORY), VI (1946), 1–15.

[4] An exact definition can be provided by means of the concept of production functions. On this, see Oscar Lange, "A Note on Innovations," *Review of Economic Statistics*, XXV (1943), 19–25.

[5] It is sometimes held that entrepreneurship, although it did not require antecedent ownership of capital (or very little of it) in the early days of capitalism, tends to become dependent upon it as time goes on, especially in the epoch of giant corporations. Nothing could be further from the truth. In the course of the nineteenth century, it became increasingly easier to obtain other people's money by methods other than the partnership, and in our own time promotion within the shell of existing corporations offers a much more convenient access to the entrepreneurial functions than existed in the world of owner-managed firms. Many a would-be entrepreneur of today does not found a firm, not because he could not do so, but simply because he prefers the other method.

two, especially because of the cant phrases that are current on this topic. In the third place, it is particularly important to distinguish the entrepreneur from the "inventor." Many inventors have become entrepreneurs and the relative frequency of this case is no doubt an interesting subject to investigate, but there is no necessary connection between the two functions. The inventor produces ideas, the entrepreneur "gets things done," which may but need not embody anything that is scientifically new. Moreover, an idea or scientific principle is not, by itself, of any importance for economic practice: the fact that Greek science had probably produced all that is necessary in order to construct a steam engine did not help the Greeks or Romans to build a steam engine; the fact that Leibnitz suggested the idea of the Suez Canal exerted no influence whatever on economic history for two hundred years. And as different as the functions are the two sociological and psychological types.[6] Finally, "getting new things done" is not only a distinct process but it is a process which produces consequences that are an essential part of capitalist reality. The whole economic history of capitalism would be different from what it is if new ideas had been currently and smoothly adopted, as a matter of course, by all firms to whose business they were relevant. But they were not. It is in most cases only one man or a few men who see the new possibility and are able to cope with the resistances and difficulties which action always meets with outside of the ruts of established practice. This accounts for the large gains that success often entails, as well as for the losses and vicissitudes of failure. These things are important. If, in every individual case, the difficulties may indeed be called transitional, they are transitional difficulties which are never absent in the economy as a whole and which dominate the atmosphere of capitalist life permanently. Hence it seems appropriate to keep "invention" distinct from "innovation."

The definition that equates enterprise to innovation is a very abstract one. Some classifications that are richer in content may be noticed because of their possible use in drawing up plans for specific pieces of research. There is the obvious classification—historical and systematic— of the phenomena of enterprise according to institutional forms, such as the medieval trading company, the later "chartered companies," the partnership, the modern "corporation," and the like, on all of which

---

[6] The relation between the two has attracted interest before. See, e.g., F. W. Taussig, *Inventors and Money-Makers* (New York: The Macmillan Company, 1915).

The Creative Response in Economic History   153

there exists a vast amount of historical work.[7] The interaction of institutional forms and entrepreneurial activity, the "shaping" influence of the former and the "bursting" influence of the latter, is, as has already been intimated, a major topic for further inquiry. Closely connected with this classification is the old one according to fields of activity—commerce, industry, finance [8]—which has been refined by the following distinctions: enterprise that introduces "new" commodities; enterprise that introduces technological novelties into the production of "old" commodities; enterprise that introduces new commercial combinations such as the opening up of new markets for products or new sources of supply of materials; enterprise that consists in reorganizing an industry, for instance, by making a monopoly out of it.[9]

But there are other classifications that may prove helpful. We may classify entrepreneurs according to origins and sociological types: feudal lords and aristocratic landowners, civil servants—particularly important, for instance, in Germany after the Thirty Years' War, especially in mining—farmers, workmen, artisans, members of the learned professions, all embarked upon enterprise as has often been noticed, and it is highly interesting from several points of view to clear up this matter. Or we may try to classify entrepreneurial performances according to the precise nature of the "function" filled and the aptitudes (some may even add motivation) involved. Since all this presumably changed significantly in the course of the capitalist epoch, economic historians are particularly qualified for work on this line.

Though the phrase "getting a new thing done" may be adequately comprehensive, it covers a great many different activities which, as the observer stresses one more than another or as his material displays one

---

[7] Gustav von Schmoller introduced the subject into his general treatise (*Grundriss*) of 1904. But the novelty consisted only in the systematic use he made of the result of historical research. Less systematically, the subject had entered general treatises before.

[8] Financial institutions and practices enter our circle of problems in three ways: they are "auxiliary and conditioning"; banking may be the object of entrepreneurial activity, that is to say, the introduction of new banking practices may constitute enterprise; and bankers (or other "financiers") may use the means at their command in order to embark upon commercial and industrial enterprise themselves (for example, John Law). See the recent book by Fritz Redlich, *The Molding of American Banking—Men and Ideas* (New York: Hafner Publishing Company, 1947).

[9] This case emphasizes the desirability, present also in others, of divesting our idea of entrepreneurial performance of any preconceived value judgment. Whether a given entrepreneurial success benefits or injures society or a particular group within society is a question that must be decided on the merits of each case. Enterprise that results in a monopoly position, even if undertaken for the sole purpose of securing monopoly gains, is not necessarily anti-social in its total effect although it often is.

more than another, may, locally, temporarily, or generally, lend different colors to entrepreneurship. In some cases, or to some observers, it may be the activity of "setting up" or "organizing" that stands out from the others; in other cases, or for other observers, it may be the breaking down of the resistances of the environment; in still other cases, or for still other observers, simply leadership or, again, salesmanship. Thus, it seems to me, there was a type of entrepreneur in early capitalist industry that is best described as a "fixer." Modern history furnishes many instances of entrepreneurship vested in a company promotor.[10] The typical industrial entrepreneur of the nineteenth century was perhaps the man who put into practice a novel method of production by embodying it in a new firm and who then settled down into a position of owner-manager of a company, if he was successful, or of stockholding president of a company, getting old and conservative in the process. In the large-scale corporation of today, the question that is never quite absent arises with a vengeance, namely, who should be considered as the entrepreneur. In a well-known book, R. A. Gordon has presented much interesting material bearing upon this question.[11]

II

The economic nature, amount, and distribution of the returns to entrepreneurial activity constitute another set of problems on which investigation may be expected to shed much-needed light. Conceptual difficulties confront us here even before we come up against the still more formidable difficulties of fact finding. For the "profit" of the English classics, which was analyzed by J. S. Mill into wages of management, premiums for risk, and interest on owned capital, was a return to normal business activity and something quite different from, though influenced by, the gain of successful enterprise in our sense of the term. What the latter is can best be explained by considering a special case. Suppose that a man, realizing the possibility of producing acceptable caviar from sawdust, sets up the Excelsior Caviar concern and makes it a success. If this concern is too small to influence the prices of either the product or the factors of production, he will sell the

---

[10] In a sense, the promotor who does nothing but "set up" new business concerns might be considered as the purest type of entrepreneur. Actually, he is mostly not more than a financial agent who has little, if any, title to entrepreneuriship—no more than the lawyer who does the legal work involved. But there are important exceptions to this.

[11] Robert A. Gordon, *Business Leadership in the Large Corporation* (Washington, D.C.: The Brookings Institution, 1945).

The Creative Response in Economic History   155

former and buy the latter at current prices. If, however, he turns out the unit of caviar more cheaply than his competitors, owing to his use of a much cheaper raw material, he will for a time, that is, until other firms copy his method, make (essentially temporary) surplus gains. These gains are attributable to personal exertion. Hence they might be called wages. They may with equal justice be attributed to the fact that, for a time, his method is exclusively his own. Hence they might also be called monopoly gains. But whether we elect to call them wages or monopoly gains, we must add immediately that they are a special kind of wages or monopoly gains that differ in important respects from what we usually mean to denote by these terms. And so we had better call them simply entrepreneurial gains or profit. However, it should be observed that if this venture means a "fortune," this fortune does not typically arise from the actual net receipts being saved up and invested in the same or some other business. Essentially, it emerges as a *capital* gain, that is, as the discounted value of the stream of prospective excess returns.

In this simple case, which, however, does constitute a type, the investigator is not confronted with difficulties other than those involved in fact finding. Also, it is clear what happens with that surplus gain: in this case the entrepreneurial gain goes to the entrepreneur,[12] and we can also see, if we have the facts, how, to use a current phrase, the "fruits of the progress involved are handed to consumers and workmen." The speed of this process of "handing on" varies widely, but it would always work, in isolated cases like the one under discussion, through a fall in the price of the product to the new level of costs, which is bound to occur whenever competition steps up to the successful concern. But even here we meet the practice of innovators striving to keep their returns alive by means of patents and in other ways. The gains described above shade off into gains from purposive restriction of competition and create difficulties of diagnosis that are sometimes insurmountable.[13] Cumulation of carefully analyzed historical cases is

---

[12] It should be obvious that this does not mean that the whole social gain resulting from the enterprise goes to the entrepreneur. But the question of appraisal of social gains from entrepreneurship, absolute and relative to the entrepreneurial shares in them, and of the social costs involved in a system that relies on business interests to carry out its innovations, is so complex and perhaps even hopeless that I beg to excuse myself from entering into it.

[13] Still more difficult is, of course, responsible appraisal, that is to say, appraisal that is not content with popular slogans. Measures to keep surplus gains alive no doubt slow up the process of "handing on the fruits of progress." But the knowledge that such measures are available may be necessary in order to induce anyone to embark upon certain ventures. There

the best means of shedding light on these things, of supplying the theorist with strategic assumptions, and banishing slogans.

If innovations are neither individually small nor isolated events, complications crowd upon us. Entrepreneurial activity then affects wage and interest rates from the outset and becomes a factor—the fundamental factor in my opinion—in booms and depressions. This is one reason, but not the only one, why entrepreneurial gains are not net returns (1) to the whole set of people who attempt entrepreneurial ventures, (2) to the industrial sector in which innovation occurs, (3) to the capitalist interests that finance entrepreneurial activity and to the capitalist class as a whole.

Concerning the first point, I might have made my special case more realistic by assuming that several or many people try their hands at producing that caviar but that all but one fail to produce a salable product before the success of this one presents an example to copy. The gains of the successful entrepreneur and of the capitalists who finance him—for whenever capital finances enterprise the interest is paid out of the entrepreneurial gains, a fact that is very important for our grasp of the interest phenomenon—should be related not to his effort and their loan but to the effort and the loans of all the entrepreneurs and capitalists who made attempts and lost. The presence of gains to enterprise so great as to impress us as spectacular and, from the standpoint of society, irrational is then seen to be compatible with a negative return to entrepreneurs and financing capitalists as a group.[14]

It is similarly clear that entrepreneurial gain is not a net accretion to the returns of the industrial sector in which it occurs. The impact of the new product or method spells losses to the "old" firms. The competition of the man with a significantly lower cost curve is, in fact, the really effective competition that in the end revolutionizes the industry. Detailed investigation of this process which may take many forms might teach us much about the actual working of capitalism that we are but dimly perceiving as yet.

---

also may be other compensating advantages to such measures, particularly where rapid introduction into general use of new methods would involve severe dislocations of labor, and where entrepreneurial gains are important sources of venture capital.

[14] Whether this actually is so in any particular case is, of course, extremely difficult to establish. The successes stand out, statistically and otherwise; the failures are apt to escape notice. This is one of the reasons why economists seem so much impressed by peak successes. Another reason for faulty appraisal is neglect of the fact that spectacular gains may stimulate more effectively than would the same sum if more equally distributed. This is a question that no speculation can decide. Only collection of facts can tell us how we are to frame our theory.

The Creative Response in Economic History 157

Concerning the third point, while we have a fair amount of information about how the working class fares in the process of economic change, in respect to both real wages and employment, we know much less about that elusive entity, capital, that is being incessantly destroyed and re-created. That the theorist's teaching, according to which capital "migrates" from declining to rising industries, is unrealistic is obvious: the capital "invested" in railroads does not migrate into trucking and air transportation but will perish in and with the railroads. Investigation into the histories of industries, concerns, and firms, including surveys of sectors in order to point out how long a typical firm stays in business and how and why it drops out, might dispel many a preconceived notion on this subject.

III

Finally, I should like to touch one more set of problems on which we may expect light from historical analysis, namely, the problems that come within the range of the question: does the importance of the entrepreneurial function decline as time goes on? There are serious reasons for believing that it does. The entrepreneurial performance involves, on the one hand, the ability to perceive new opportunities that cannot be proved at the moment at which action has to be taken, and, on the other hand, will power adequate to break down the resistance that the social environment offers to change. But the range of the provable expands, and action upon flashes or hunches is increasingly replaced by action that is based upon "figuring out." And modern milieus may offer less resistance to new methods and new goods than used to be the case. So far as this is so, the element of personal intuition and force would be less essential than it was: it could be expected to yield its place to the teamwork of specialists; in other words, improvement could be expected to become more and more automatic. Our impression to this effect is reinforced by parallel phenomena in other fields of activity. For instance, a modern commander no doubt means less in the outcome of a war than commanders meant of old, and for the same reasons; campaigns have become more calculable than they used to be and there is less scope for personal leadership.

But this is at present only an impression. It is for the historian to establish or to refute it. If, however, it should stand up under research, this would be a result of the utmost importance. We should be led to expect that the whole mechanism of economic development will change significantly. Among other things, the economy would progressively bureaucratize itself. There are, in fact, many symptoms of this. And consequences would extend far beyond the field of economic phenomena. Just as warrior classes have declined in importance ever since warfare—and especially the management of armies in the field—began to be increasingly "mechanized," so the business class may decline in importance, as its most vital figure, the entrepreneur, progressively loses his most essential function. This would mean a different social structure.

Therefore, the sociology of enterprise reaches much further than is implied in questions concerning the conditions that produce and shape, favor or inhibit entrepreneurial activity. It extends to the structure and the very foundations of, at least, capitalist society or the capitalist sector of any given society. The quickest way of showing this starts from recognition of the facts that, just as the rise of the bourgeois class as a whole is associated with success in commercial, industrial, and financial enterprise, so the rise of an individual family to "capitalist" status within that class is typically [15] associated with entrepreneurial success; and that the elimination of a family from the "capitalist" class is typically associated with the loss of those attitudes and aptitudes of industrial leadership or alertness that enter our picture of the entrepreneurial type of businessman.

Now these facts, if they are facts, might teach us a lot about such fundamental problems as the nature of the class structure of capitalist society; the sort of class civilization which it develops and which differs so characteristically from the class civilization of feudal society; its schema of values; its politics, especially its attitudes to state and church and war; its performance and failures; its degree of durability. But a great deal of work needs to be done in order to arrive at scientifically defensible opinions about all these and cognate things. First of all, these "facts" must be established. How far is it really true, for instance, that entrepreneurs, while not forming a social class themselves but originating in almost all existing strata, do "feed" or renew the capitalist stratum? To put it differently, does the latter recruit itself through entrepreneurial successes? Or, to put it still differently,

---

[15] That is to say, successful entrepreneurship is that method of rising in the social scale that is characteristic of the capitalist blueprint. It is, of course, not the only method. First, there are other possibilities within the economic sphere, such as possession of an appreciating natural agent (for example, urban land) or mere speculation or even, occasionally, success in mere administration that need not partake of the specifically entrepreneurial element. Secondly, there are possibilities outside the business sphere, for business success is no more the only method of rising in capitalist society than knightly service was in feudal society.

The Creative Response in Economic History   159

does the "typical" history of industrial families lead back to entrepreneurial performances that "created" a concern which then, for a time, yielded capitalistic surpluses by being merely "administrated" with more or less efficiency? How much statistical truth is there in the slogan: "Three generations from overalls to overalls"? Secondly, what is, as measured by observable results, the economic and cultural, also political, importance of the further fact that, though the entrepreneurial function cannot be transmitted by inheritance, except, possibly, by biological inheritance, the financial or industrial position that has been created can? How much truth is there in the contention that the industrial family interest is, in capitalist society, the guardian of the nation's economic future?

These questions, which could be readily multiplied, have often attracted attention. Every textbook of economic history contains some material about the origins of entrepreneurs of historical standing, and a number of studies have been inspired by full awareness of the importance of the answers for our understanding of capitalist society and of the ways in which it works.[16] But these studies are few and that attention has been desultory. We do not know enough in order to form valid generalizations or even enough to be sure whether there are any generalizations to form. As it is, most of us as economists have some opinions on these matters. But these opinions have more to do with our preconceived ideas or ideals than with solid fact, and our habit of illustrating them by stray instances that have come under our notice is obviously but a poor substitute for serious research. Veblen's—or, for that matter, Bucharin's—*Theory of the Leisure Class* exemplifies well what I mean. It is brilliant and suggestive. But it is an impressionistic essay that does not come to grips with the real problems involved. Yet there is plenty of material. A great and profitable task awaits those who undertake it.

Harvard University   JOSEPH A. SCHUMPETER

---

[16] An example is the study by F. J. Marquis and S. J. Chapman on the managerial stratum of the Lancashire cotton industry in the *Journal of the Royal Statistical Society*, LXXV, Pt. III (1912), 293–306.

[4]

BIOLOGICAL ANALOGIES IN THE THEORY OF THE FIRM[1]

By EDITH TILTON PENROSE*

Economics has always drawn heavily on the natural sciences for analogies designed to help in the understanding of economic phenomena. Biological analogies in particular have been widely used in discussions of the firm. Probably the best known and most common of these analogies is that of the *life cycle,* in which the appearance, growth and disappearance of firms is likened to the processes of birth, growth, and death of biological organisms. Marshall's reference to the rise and fall of the trees in the forest is an oft-quoted example of this type of analogy. Recently, two additional biological analogies have been presented —a natural selection analogy, dubbed by one writer *viability analysis,* and the *homeostasis* analogy designed to explain some aspects of the behavior of firms. The former, like the life cycle analogy, is for use in long-run analysis only. The latter is exclusively for short-run analysis. Both are supposed to represent improvements on the existing theory of the firm at the core of which lies the chief target of attack—the assumption that firms attempt to maximize profits.

The purpose of this paper is to examine critically all three types of reasoning and to show that they lead in most cases to a serious neglect of important aspects of the problem that do not fit the particular type of analogical reasoning employed. The chief danger of carrying sweeping analogies very far is that the problems they are designed to illuminate become framed in such a special way that significant matters are frequently inadvertently obscured. Biological analogies contribute little either to the theory of price or to the theory of growth and development of firms and in general tend to confuse the nature of the important issues.

The "Life Cycle" Theory of the Firm

Implicit in the notion that firms have a "life cycle" analogous to that of living organisms is the idea that there are "laws" governing the de-

* The author is research associate and lecturer in political economy in The Johns Hopkins University.

[1] This paper is a by-product of my work on the theory of the growth of the firm in connection with a project on firm growth directed by G. H. Evans, Jr., and Fritz Machlup, and financed by the Merrill Foundation for the Advancement of Financial Knowledge. I am particularly indebted to Professor Machlup for his careful criticism of the manuscript and for many valuable suggestions, and to Professor Bentley Glass for safeguarding my ventures into biology.

velopment of firms akin to the laws of nature in accordance with which living organisms appear to grow, and that the different stages of development are a function of age. Were this implication not present, then the life cycle concept would amount to little more than a statement that if we look at the past we find that all firms had some sort of a beginning, a period of existence and, if now extinct, an end. Even if a careful collection of the relevant facts about groups of firms in like circumstances should establish a statistical pattern in which some affinity in origin, regularity in development and similarity in disappearance could be discerned, it might be interesting history and might enable one to deduce a variety of *ad hoc* theories but it would not be a theory of development without the further generalizations about the principles according to which the life cycle proceeds.

Whatever superficial plausibility such a theory may have had in the days of the "family firm,"[2] it lost even that when the publicly held corporation became the dominant type of firm. Even Marshall, who was an early exponent in economics of this theory of the growth of the firm, was doubtful about its applicability to the joint-stock company, and I would not spend much time on it now had it not been recently adopted and put forward with vigor by one of America's foremost economists. Kenneth Boulding has virtually called for a "life cycle" theory of the firm[3] and has categorically insisted that there is an "inexorable and irre-

[2] In a paper published on the sizes of businesses in the textile industries in parts of England from 1884 to 1911, S. J. Chapman and T. S. Ashton came out rather wholeheartedly in favor of a life cycle interpretation of the development of firms: "Indeed the growth of a business and the volume and form which it ultimately assumes are apparently determined in somewhat the same fashion as the development of an organism in the animal or vegetable world. As there is a normal size and form for a man, so but less markedly, are there normal sizes and forms for businesses." "The Sizes of Businesses, Mainly in the Textile Industries," *Jour. Royal Stat. Soc.*, Apr. 1914, LXXVII, 512. In this article the analogy between the firm and the biological organism is carried very far, but in a "belated appendix" Professor Ashton, in his characteristically cautious way, very much qualifies the analogy: "The picture of the growth of an industry outlined here recalls a well-known passage in which Dr. Marshall compared business undertakings with the trees of the forest; and other biological analogies spring so readily to mind that it may be more useful to point out the differences, rather than the similarities, between the life-history of businesses and that of plants, or animals, or men. Businesses are by no means always small at birth; many are born of complete or almost complete stature. In their growth they obey no one law. A few apparently undergo a steady expansion. . . . With others, increase in size takes place by a sudden leap. . . . " "The Growth of Textile Businesses in the Oldham District, 1884-1924," *Jour. Royal Stat. Soc.*, May 1926, LXXXIX, 572. Professor Ashton attributes some of the differences between the development of firms in the earlier (1884-1914) and later (1918-1924) periods to the development of the joint-stock company.

[3] ". . . we must go on further to discuss the problem of what determines the 'optimum' or equilibrium balance sheet itself, as this is also to some extent under the control of the firm. This should bring us directly into 'life-cycle' theory, and indeed one would have expected Marshall's famous analogy of the trees of the forest again to have led economists to a discussion of the forces which determine the birth, growth, decline, and death of a

versible movement towards the equilibrium of death. Individual, family, firm, nation, and civilization all follow the same grim law, and the history of any organism is strikingly reminiscent of the rise and fall of populations on the road to extinction. . . ."[4]

The purposes a life cycle theory of the firm would serve are obvious, yet the theory as a bare undeveloped hypothesis has existed for a long time and nothing has been done to construct from it a consistent theoretical system with sufficient content to enable it to be used for any purpose whatsoever.[5] The basic hypothesis is not one from which significant logical consequences can be deduced, such as can be deduced,[6] for example, from the proposition that firms attempt to maximize profits. Supplementary hypotheses about the kind of organism the firm is and the nature of its life cycle are required. Although we have a respectable collection of information about firms, it has not stimulated economists even to suggest the further hypotheses necessary to the development of a life cycle theory of the firm. This, I think, is primarily because the available evidence does not support the theory that firms have a life cycle characterized by a consistent transition through recognizable stages of development similar to those of living organisms. Indeed, just the opposite conclusion must be drawn: the development of firms does not proceed according to the same "grim" laws as does that of living organisms. In the face of the evidence one is led to wonder why the analogy persists and why there is still a demand for a life cycle theory of the firm.

The purpose of analogical reasoning in which we consciously and

---

firm. In fact the theory of the firm, and of the economic organism in general, has not developed along these lines . . . much of the static theory of the firm can be salvaged . . . nevertheless, even when this has been done we still do not have a life-cycle theory. . . ." Kenneth E. Boulding, *A Reconstruction of Economics* (New York: Wiley & Sons, 1950), p. 34.

[4] *Ibid.*, p. 38.

[5] The idea that a firm's vigor declines with age, which follows naturally from the notion that firms have life cycles, did, however, enable Marshall to maintain the possibility of competitive equilibrium even when firms operated under increasing returns to scale. Growth takes time, and Marshall argued that before a business man got big enough to obtain a monopolistic position, his "progress is likely to be arrested by the decay, if not of his faculties, yet of his liking for energetic work." And if conditions in an industry were such that new firms could quickly master the economies of scale, then it would be likely that the established firms would be "supplanted quickly by still younger firms with yet newer methods." See Alfred Marshall, *Principles of Economics* (London: Macmillan, 1920, 8th ed.) pp. 286-87; also p. 808, footnote 2. The importance of this decline in a firm's luck or skill for the Marshallian use of the concept of the representative firm is clearly brought out by G. F. Shove in the symposium on "Increasing Returns and the Representative Firm," *Econ. Jour.*, Mar. 1930, XL, especially 109.

[6] Theoretical models of competition between "populations" or of the conditions of population equilibria do not require the assumption that individuals *develop* in accordance with life cycle patterns but merely that there exist "birth" and "death" rates.

systematically apply the explanation of one series of events to another very different series of events is to help us better to understand the nature of the latter, which presumably is less well understood than the former. If the analogy has really helpful explanatory value, there must be some reason for believing that the two series of events have enough in common for the explanation of one, *mutatis mutandis,* to provide at least a partial explanation of the other. This type of analogy must be distinguished from the purely metaphorical analogy in which the resemblances between two phenomena are used to add a picturesque note to an otherwise dull analysis and to help a reader to see more clearly the outlines of a process being described by enabling him to draw on what he knows in order to imagine the unknown. Analogies of this sort are not only useful but almost indispensable to human thought.

The biological analogies of the firm are not of this metaphorical type or there would be no call to push them into service to help *explain* the development of firms. They are clearly related to the whole family of analogies between biological organisms and social institutions that flourished in profusion during the 19th century[7] but which are, for the most part, no longer popular among social scientists, although curiously enough they are apparently still popular among some biologists.[8] In the notion that a firm is an organism akin to biological organisms, there is an implication that, since all such organisms have something in common, we can use our knowledge of biological organisms to gain more insight into the firm. It is not an easy task even for the biologist to state unambiguously what is meant by an organism[9] or what distinguishes the biological organism from non-living matter. But in principle it is characteristic of biological organisms that they reproduce and have an identifiable pattern of development that can be explained by the genetic nature of their constitution.[10] Furthermore, the particular pattern of

[7] These analogies are, as a matter of fact, very old and are found in classical literature. It is not even clear whether their first use was to help in explaining the nature of biological organisms by analogy with social institutions or in explaining the nature of social institutions by analogy with biological organisms. See Oswei Temkin, "Metaphors of Human Biology," in *Science and Civilization,* Robert C. Stauffer, editor (Madison: University of Wisconsin Press, 1949).

[8] See, for example, a series of papers published under the general title "Levels of Integration in Biological and Social Systems," *Biological Symposia,* 1942, VIII, in the introduction to which the editor stated: "What these papers seem to be saying, in most general terms, is this: The organism and the society are not merely analogues; they are varieties of something more general . . ." (p. 5).

[9] See J. H. Woodger, "The 'Concept of the Organism' and the Relation between Embryology and Genetics," *Quart. Rev. Biol.,* May 1930, V, 6 ff. It should be noted that the concept of "organism" as used in philosophy, notably by Alfred Whitehead, has no biological connotation.

[10] Moreover, biological organisms have a form in a sense in which societies (and firms) do not. This was one of the objections to the use of the economic analogy to explain bio-

development that is supposed to characterize firms—birth, youth, maturity, old age, death—is characteristic only of biological organisms that reproduce sexually. Organisms whose reproductive processes are primarily asexual have in general a very different pattern of development in which *death* plays no part,[11] and certainly the development of firms shows no pattern similar even to that of organisms that reproduce asexually. Clearly the one thing a firm does not have in common with biological organisms is a genetic constitution, and yet this is the one factor that determines the life cycle of biological organisms.

The characteristic use of biological analogies in economics is to suggest explanations of events that do not depend upon the conscious willed decisions of human beings. This is not, of course, characteristic of biology as such, for some branches of biology are concerned with learning processes and decision making, with purposive motivation and conscious choice in men as well as animals. In this, biology overlaps sociology and psychology and, in a sense, even economics. Information drawn from these branches of biology can be useful in helping us to understand the behavior of men and consequently of the institutions men create and operate. In using such information, however, we are not dealing with analogies at all, but with essentially the same problems on a more complex scale. But, paradoxically, where explicit biological analogies crop up in economics they are drawn exclusively from that aspect of biology which deals with the non-motivated behavior of organisms or in which motivation does not make any difference.

So it is with the life cycle analogy. We have no reason whatsoever for thinking that the growth pattern of a biological organism is *willed* by the organism itself. On the other hand, we have every reason for thinking that the growth of a firm is willed by those who make the decisions of the firm and are themselves part of the firm, and the proof of this lies in the fact that no one can describe the development of any given firm or explain how it came to be the size it is except in terms of decisions taken by individual men. Such decisions, to be sure, are constrained by the environment and by the capacity of the men who make them, but we know of no *general* "laws" predetermining men's choices, nor have we as yet any established basis for suspecting the existence of such laws. By contrast no one would seriously attempt to explain the transition from infancy to manhood or the normal processes of aging in terms of

logical facts: "The economic metaphors . . . do not account for the biological phenomenon of form." O. Temkin, *op. cit.*, p. 184.

[11] And yet Boulding points out that the chief difference between biological and social organisms is the absence of sexual reproduction and argues that the "genetic processes in the social system are perhaps somewhat more akin to asexual reproduction . . .", *op. cit.*, p. 7.

such decisions, for we have every reason for thinking that these matters are predetermined by the nature of the living organism.

There can be no doubt, I think, that to liken a firm to an organism and then attempt to explain its growth by reference to the laws of growth of biological organisms is an ill-founded procedure. If it were no more than this, one could still question whether one should take the trouble of seriously analyzing the analogy. But, besides being ill-founded, this type of reasoning about the firm obscures, if it does not implicitly deny, the fact that firms are institutions created by men to serve the purposes of men. It can be admitted that to some extent firms operate automatically in accordance with the principles governing the mechanism constructed,[12] but to abandon their development to the laws of nature diverts attention from the importance of human decisions and motives, and from problems of ethics and public policy, and surrounds the whole question of the growth of the firm with an aura of "natural-ness" and even inevitability.[13]

"Viability" Analysis

The second type of biological analogy I wish to discuss claims to have drawn on the principles of biological evolution and natural selection which were first put forth in a comprehensive form by Darwin. The discussion of the processes and progress of human society in terms of natural selection and evolution followed close on the introduction of these concepts into biology.[14] The analogy I am concerned with here avoids the crudities and attempts to avoid the value judgments that characterized the 19th century doctrines of Spencer and his followers in their application of these principles to society. It is very modern in its emphasis on uncertainty and statistical probabilities. Nevertheless, it

---

[12] See the discussion of homeostasis below. If analogies must be used, there is much to be said for comparing a firm to a machine that operates in accordance with the principles governing its physical organization, but the construction, evolution and uses of which are determined by a mechanic. However, neither type of analogical reasoning has much explanatory value.

[13] Not the least of the effects of this kind of reasoning is to bring "natural law" to the defense of the *status quo*. See the discussion in Richard Hofstadter, *Social Darwinism in American Thought* (Philadelphia: University of Pennsylvania Press, 1944) pp. 30 ff. and the quotation (p. 31) he gives from John D. Rockefeller: "The growth of a large business is merely a survival of the fittest. . . . The American Beauty rose can be produced in the splendor and fragrance which bring cheer to its beholder only by sacrificing the early buds which grow up around it. This is not an evil tendency in business. It is merely the work-ing out of a law of nature and a law of God."

[14] This subject was widely debated throughout the Western world and the literature is far too extensive to cite. For a useful, though limited, bibliography, see Hofstadter, *op. cit.* The idea of the survival of the fittest, however, was first suggested to Darwin by a work in the social sciences—Malthus on population.

is open to the same basic objections that in my opinion adhere to all such biological analogies.

The purpose of the theory is to get around a logical difficulty alleged to be inherent in the assumption that firms attempt to maximize profits in a world characterized by uncertainty about the future. If uncertainty exists, firms cannot know in advance the results of their actions. There is always a variety of possible outcomes, each of which is more or less probable. Hence the expected outcome of any action by a firm can only be viewed as a distribution of possible outcomes, and it is argued that while a firm can select those courses of action that have an optimum distribution of outcomes from its point of view, it makes no sense to say that the firm *maximizes* anything, since it is impossible to maximize a distribution. Hence profit maximization as a criterion for action is regarded as meaningless. According to the "viability analysis," however, this is not a serious difficulty for the economist if he draws on the principle of natural selection and considers the adaptation required of firms by their environment.

The argument, originally set forth by Armen A. Alchian,[15] is as follows: To survive firms must make positive profits. Hence positive profits can be treated as the criterion of natural selection—the firms that make profits are selected or "adopted" by the environment, others are rejected and disappear. This holds whether firms consciously try to make profits or not; even if the actions of firms were completely random and determined only by chance, the firms surviving, *i.e.*, adopted by the environment, would be those that happened to act appropriately and thus made profits. Hence "individual motivation and foresight, while sufficient, are not necessary,"[16] since the economist with his knowledge of the conditions of survival can, like the biologist, predict "the effects of environmental changes on the surviving class of living organisms."[17]

Alchian argues that the introduction of the supplementary and realistic assumption of purposive behavior by firms merely "expands" the model and also makes it useful in explaining the nature of purposive behavior under conditions of uncertainty.[18] If firms do try to make profits even though (because of uncertainty) they don't know how to do so, then clearly they will have a motive for imitating what appears to be

---

[15] Armen A. Alchian, "Uncertainty, Evolution, and Economic Theory," *Jour. Pol. Econ.*, June, 1950, LVIII.

[16] *Ibid.*, p. 217.

[17] *Ibid.*, p. 220.

[18] "It is not argued that there is no purposive, foresighted behavior present in reality. In adding this realistic element—adaptation by individuals with foresight and purposive motivation—we are expanding the preceding extreme model." *Ibid.*, p. 217.

PENROSE: BIOLOGICAL ANALOGIES—THEORY OF THE FIRM   811

successful action by other firms. This explains conventional rules of behavior (traditional markups, etc.) which can be looked on as "codified imitations of observed success."[19] This is the evolutionary aspect of the theory: successful innovations—regarded by analogy as "mutations"—are transmitted by imitation to other firms. Venturesome innovation and trial and error adaptation are also purposive acts which, if successful, are "adopted" by the environment. Thus "most conventional economic tools and concepts are still useful, although in a vastly different analytical framework—one which is closely akin to the theory of biological evolution. The economic counterparts of genetic heredity, mutations, and natural selection are imitation, innovation, and positive profits."[20]

In accepting and enlarging upon Alchian's argument Stephen Enke has argued that, if competition were so intense that zero profits would result in the long run, economists could make "aggregate predictions" *as if* every firm knew how to secure maximum long-run profits. For with intense competition only firms that succeeded in maximizing profits would survive.[21] But under these circumstances, Enke notes, the economist can use the traditional marginal analysis and his predictions will be the same as they would be if he employed the "viability analysis." Which of the two he uses however is not "immaterial," since "the language of the former method seems pedagogically and scientifically inferior because it attributes a quite unreasonable degree of omniscience and prescience to entrepreneurs."[22]

There is much to be said about this revival of an old approach to human affairs and about its relation to the traditional marginalist approach in economics, in particular as to whether the two approaches really answer the same types of questions about the effect of "environmental" changes on price and output. In this paper I am not so much concerned to present an analytical critique of the theory as to discuss the applicability of the biological analogy and the implications involved in its use. Again we find that the characteristic of the analogy employed

[19] *Ibid.*, p. 218.

[20] *Ibid.*, p. 219. It should be noted that the treatment of imitation as analogous to genetic heredity is essential to give the principle of natural selection any evolutionary significance. Natural selection has two meanings: "In a broad sense it covers all cases of differential survival: but from the evolutionary point of view it covers only the differential transmission of inheritable variations." See Julian Huxley, *Evolution, the Modern Synthesis* (London: Allen & Unwin, 1942), p. 16.

[21] Stephen Enke, "On Maximizing Profits: A Distinction between Chamberlin and Robinson." *Am. Econ. Rev.*, Sept., 1951, XLI. The assumption of intense competition is essential for the results claimed by the authors of this approach, as we shall see below.

[22] *Ibid.*, p. 573.

is to provide an explanation of human affairs that does not depend on human motives. The alleged superiority of "viability" over marginal analysis lies in the claim that it is valid even if men do not know what they are doing. No matter what men's motives are, the outcome is determined not by the individual participants, but by an environment beyond their control. Natural selection is substituted for purposive profit-maximizing behavior just as in biology natural selection replaced the concept of special creation of species.

In biology the theory of natural selection requires the postulate that competition—a struggle for existence—prevails, but it is a postulate that rests firmly on observed facts. Darwin deduced the struggle for existence from two empirical propositions: all organisms tend to increase in a geometrical ratio, and the numbers of any species remain more or less constant.[23] From this it follows that a struggle for existence must take place. Translated into economic terminology, the explanation of competition in nature is found in the rate of entry. The "excessive entry" is due to the nature of biological reproduction. But how shall we explain competition in economic affairs where there is no biological reproduction? The psychological assumption of the traditional economic theory that businessmen like to make money and strive to make as much as is practicable performs a function in economic analysis similar to that of the physiological assumption in the biological theory of natural selection that the reproduction of organisms is of a geometric type—it provides the explanation of competition (and in economics, incidentally, also of monopoly). To be sure, the two assumptions rest on vastly different factual foundations and should not be treated as analogous. We can only say that there is some evidence that such a psychological motivation is widely prevalent and that we have found we can obtain useful results by assuming it. If we abandon this assumption, and particularly if we assume that men act randomly, we cannot explain competition, for there is nothing in the reproductive processes of firms that would ensure that more firms would constantly be created than can survive; and certainly from observations of the real world we can hardly assume that competition is so intense that zero profits will result in the long run or that only the best adapted firms can survive.

Although insisting it is not necessary, Alchian is prepared to assume that firms do strive for positive profits.[24] But I cannot see that even this is sufficient to explain the existence of competition sufficiently intense to enable the economist to assume that only the "appropriately adapted"

---

[23] See Julian Huxley, *op. cit.*, p. 14.

[24] "The pursuit of profits, and not some hypothetical undefinable perfect situation, is the relevant objective whose fulfilment is rewarded with survival. Unfortunately, even this proximate objective is too high." *Op. cit.*, p. 218.

firms will survive. Even with this modification firms would still be affected by environmental changes only when these changes cause losses. When changes in the environment opened up new opportunities without acting adversely on the old, then, on the assumptions of this analysis, firms would not respond at all to the new conditions since profits would already be positive and firms are assumed to be uninterested in increasing their profits.[25]

Once motivation is introduced the usefulness of the model becomes even more questionable. Great emphasis is laid on the predictive power of the viability theory. Therefore the essence of the theory cannot be that those firms best adapted to the economic environment will survive; this could easily become a circular argument. Rather it is that the economist can know what the conditions of survival are and therefore can know the characteristics of firms that will be required by these conditions of survival. Now, apart from the pardonable notion that economists have a special knowledge denied to firms[26]—which is quite appropriate if firms (but not economists) are treated as non-motivated organisms—this would seem reasonable provided either that environmental conditions are identifiable and are independent of the actions of the firm or, if they are dependent on the actions of firms, that the economist can know how firms will, by their actions, change the environment.

Once human will and human motivation are recognized as important constituents of the situation, there is no *a priori* justification for assuming that firms, in their struggle for profits, will not attempt as much consciously to adapt the environment to their own purposes as to adapt

[25] Once we admit that when opportunities for making money arise, some firms will prefer to take a chance on making more money rather than to rest content with less, we might just as well assume that firms act *as if* they were attempting to maximize profits, since, for the purpose of detecting the direction of change, we get more useful results from using this assumption than from any other that has yet been devised. It should be obvious that for this purpose marginal movements are the significant ones, yet the viability approach leaves us no way of predicting marginal movements except under special conditions and leaves us completely helpless if there is a pronounced lag between the introduction of a given environmental change and the effect of the change on the birth and death rates of firms, for "these long-run forces of adjustment operate in the main through the effect of altered conditions of survival and the births and deaths of firms." Enke, *op. cit.*, p. 572.

[26] For the life of me I can't see why it is reasonable (on grounds other than professional pride) to endow the economist with this "unreasonable degree of omniscience and prescience" and not entrepreneurs. Although this is incidental to our discussion, it seems to me that the logic of the argument runs somewhat as follows: It is impossible to know in advance what actions will yield maximum profits. Therefore firms cannot know in advance what they should do to maximize their profits. If there is intense competition, zero profits will be maximum profits and firms making negative profits will fail. Economists can know the conditions of survival. Therefore economists can know what type of firm will escape negative profits. Therefore economists can know what firms must do to make zero or positive profits. Therefore economists can know how maximum profits can be obtained. Therefore it is *not* impossible to know in advance what actions will yield maximum profits.

One can only suggest that firms should hire economists!

themselves to the environment. After all, one of the chief characteristics of man that distinguishes him from other creatures is the remarkable range of his ability to alter his environment or to become independent of it. Underlying the viability analysis is the assumption that, even if firms can and do make more or less intelligent choices, they can do nothing in unpredictable ways to "force" the environment to "adopt," and thus make successful, the results of their action.

The concept of the environment of firms on which the economist using "viability" analysis bases his predictions is by no means clear. There is little doubt that there are parts of the external environment of firms which are identifiable and which for all practical purposes we can safely assume will not be quickly or unpredictably altered by firms—geographical factors, the conditions of transportation, established government policies. There are other aspects of the environment that can be altered within fairly narrow limits and in more or less predictable ways—the amount of natural resources, the state of employment. There are still other aspects of the environment, equally important for survival, which we cannot assume are beyond the influence of firms and which can be unpredictably altered by them in a large number of ways—the state of technology, the tastes of consumers.

It is these unpredictable possibilities of altering the environment by man that create difficulties in comparing the economist to the biologist observing the processes of natural selection and studying the nature of adaptation. Animals, too, alter their environment, but in a rather unconscious fashion without much deliberation about different probable outcomes of their actions. The possibilities open to animals of affecting their environment in a given period of time are so much more restricted than those open to men that the biologist has a very much easier task, for the relative consistency of animal behavior and the relatively narrow limits within which animals can act give him a more secure basis for prediction.[27] If firms can deliberate, if they can weigh the relative profitability of assaulting the environment itself and if they can act in ways unknown to the economist, what are the "realized requisites of survival" that can give the economist confidence in his predictions? Alchian has treated innovations as analogous to biological mutations. But mutations are "alterations in the substance of the hereditary constitution" of an organism,[28] while innovations, though they may consist of changes in the constitution of firms, more often than not are direct attempts by

[27] As a matter of fact, it is doubtful if many biologists would agree that their powers of prediction are as sweeping as are implied here, particularly if man is included among the organisms with respect to whom the effects of environmental change are predicted.

[28] Huxley, *op. cit.*, p. 18.

firms to alter their environment. In other words, innovations are directly related to the environment of firms whereas the biologists tell us that genetic mutations are apparently completely unrelated either to the environment or to the agent inducing the mutation. The biologist cannot explain why mutations take the course they do while the economist, if he can assume with some justification that the activity of firms is induced by a desire for profits, has a plausible partial explanation of innovation.

It is not possible to go very far with this aspect of the matter because the authors of the viability approach have given us no hint of what they mean by the environment. It is vaguely referred to as an "adoptive mechanism"[29] but in view of the enormous complexity of the interrelationships in the economy, a prediction of the types of organisms that will survive a given change in the environment involves the prediction of a new general equilibrium and does not seem to me to be an "intellectually more modest and realistic approach"[30] than any other. After all, even the most ardent proponent of the marginal analysis never claimed that his tools enabled him to make such sweeping predictions as are implied here. By its very nature a prediction of the kinds of firms that will survive in the long run must take account of all the reactions and interactions that a given change in the environment will induce. With our present knowledge this is impossible, and the assertion that "the economist, using the present analytical tools developed in the analysis of the firm under certainty, can predict the more adoptable or viable types of economic interrelationships that will be induced by environmental change even if individuals themselves are unable to ascertain them"[31] places the wrong interpretation on the kind of thing the economist can do. If he can predict the consequences of environmental changes, it is not because certain types of interrelationships are more "viable" in a long-run sense, but because he has an idea of how people will behave. He knows little about long-run viability since he knows very little about all of the secondary and tertiary reactions that will in the end determine the "conditions of survival"—at least he has as yet given little convincing evidence of such knowledge.

Alchian's central objective of exploring the "precise role and nature of purposive behavior in the presence of uncertainty and incomplete

---

[29] "The suggested approach embodies the principles of biological evolution and natural selection by interpreting the economic system as an adoptive mechanism which chooses among exploratory actions generated by the adaptive pursuit of 'success' or 'profits.'" Alchian, *op. cit.*, p. 211.

[30] *Ibid.*, p. 221.

[31] *Ibid.*, p. 220.

information" is important[32] but the biological framework in which he has cast his model has led him to underestimate the significance of the very thing he claims to be exploring. After all, one of the more powerful effects of uncertainty is to stimulate firms to take steps to reduce it by operating directly on the environmental conditions that cause it and men have a greater power consciously to change their environment than has any other organism. A direct approach, stripped of biological trappings, to the problem of what happens when men try to reach an objective but don't know the "best" route, would not lead to underemphasis on the significance of purposive activity on the part of men. It is by no means "straightforward" to assume non-motivation,[33] for without motivation economic competition, leading to the elimination of all but the best adapted within a community, cannot be assumed. Hence, if the operation of natural selection through competition is made the guiding principle of the analytical technique, then an assumption equivalent to profit maximization must be made and the professed *raison d'être* of the viability approach disappears.

Homeostasis of the Firm

A third biological concept that has appeared in one form or another in economic literature is the concept of homeostasis.[34] Organisms are so constructed that there is a certain "equilibrium" internal condition which their bodies are organized to maintain. Any disturbance of the equilibrium sets forces in motion that will restore it. Kenneth Boulding considers that "The simplest theory of the firm is to assume that there is a 'homeostasis of the balance sheet'—that there is some desired quantity of all the various items in the balance sheet, and that any disturbance of this structure immediately sets in motion forces which will restore the status quo."[35]

Once again we find the characteristic of the biological analogy—action taking place in human affairs without the intervention of human decisions based on deliberation and choice. But here it is applied to describe a characteristic of organized activity and a possible method by which men may achieve certain objectives. The notion of homeo-

[32] *Ibid.*, p. 221.

[33] "It is straightforward, if not heuristic, to start with complete uncertainty and non-motivation and then to add elements of foresight and motivation in the process of building an analytical model. The opposite approach, which starts with certainty and unique motivation, must abandon its basic principles as soon as uncertainty and mixed motivations are recognized." *Ibid.*, p. 221.

[34] C. Reinold Noyes, for example, who believes that "economics is fundamentally a biological science" uses the physiological concept of the homeostasis of the body in his discussion of consumers' wants. See *Economic Man* (New York: Columbia University Press, 1948), pp. 29 ff.

[35] *Op. cit.*, p. 27.

stasis, treated simply as a principle of organization, does not obscure the importance of purposive behavior in human affairs but rather emphasizes its significance and illuminates its rôle in a complex social framework. This analogy is of the helpful descriptive sort: it is not claimed that the principles of physiology can explain the working of a firm.

Indeed, one could legitimately object to the appropriateness of including the "homeostasis theory" of the firm among the biological theories. Homeostasis is a word drawn from physiology, but it describes a characteristic of any activity that takes place within a framework so constructed that certain types of action are automatically induced without any interference from whatever agency is responsible for the construction. This notion can be extended from the physio-chemical reactions which take place within a living organism in order to maintain a constant internal environment, to include the operation of a thermostatically controlled heating or air conditioning system[36] and even the conduct of a game of tag according to predetermined rules.

Thus the managers of a firm may lay down rules for the operation of the firm which are determined with reference to some "ideal" interrelationship of the parts of the firm. The desired ratio of assets to liabilities, of inventories to sales, of liquid assets to fixed assets, etc., may be determined in advance and an organization so constructed that any disturbance of the desired ratio automatically sets in motion a process to restore it. There can be little doubt that the more complex an organization becomes, the more necessary it is to establish areas of quasi-automatic operation. The importance of routine as a means of taking care of some aspects of life in order that others may be given more attention has frequently been stressed.[37] The fact that many business decisions are not "genuine decisions," but are quasi-automatic and made routinely in response to accepted signals without a consideration of alternative choices has misled many into attacking the assumption that firms try to make as much money as they can—particularly where it can be shown that the rules governing the routine actions are not fully consistent with profit maximization.

This whole area of the behavior of the firm is still not adequately explained. Imitation of apparent success may, as Alchian suggests, account for some habitual and apparently irrational behavior. The persistence of routine action after the conditions for which it was appropriate have passed may also account for some of it; other partial

[36] See Kenneth Boulding, "Implications for General Economics of More Realistic Theories of the Firm," *Am. Econ. Rev.*, (Papers and Proceedings), May, 1952, XLII, 37 ff.

[37] For a well-balanced discussion of the rôle of habitual behavior and routine decisions in business activity see George Katona, *Psychological Analysis of Economic Behavior* (New York: McGraw-Hill, 1951), especially pp. 229 ff.

explanations have been suggested.[38] The theory of homeostasis provides a formal framework of explanation into which many routine responses can be fitted, but it throws no light at all—nor does it claim to—on why and how the "ideal" relationships between the relevant variables which the firm is now attempting to maintain were originally established or on the conditions under which decisions may be made to alter them.[39] Strictly speaking, the basic principle is not a biological one at all in spite of the name given it. It is a general principle of organization, examples of which may be found in biology, in mechanics and in social organization, and if one chooses to introduce into economics another mysterious word borrowed from another science—well, that is a matter of taste.

*   *   *

The desire to draw biological concepts into the explanation of social affairs is hard to understand since for the most part they add to rather than subtract from the difficulties of understanding social institutions. The observed regularities and the postulated explanations of nonmotivated biological behavior are related to chemical processes, thermal reactions and the like; they are unrelated to conscious deliberation by the organism itself. The appeal of such biological analogies to the social scientist plainly springs from a persistent yearning to discover "laws" that determine the outcome of human actions, probably because the discovery of such laws would rid the social sciences of the uncertainties and complexities that arise from the apparent "free will" of man and would endow them with that more reliable power of prediction which for some is the essence of "science." It should be noted that the distinction to be made is not that between human and non-human beings but between actions that are in some degree bound up with and determined by a reasoning and choosing process, no matter how rudimentary, and actions that are, as it were, "built into" the organism, or into the relationship between the organism and its environment, and cannot be altered by conscious decision of the organism itself.

Our knowledge of why men do what they do is very imperfect, but there is considerable evidence that consciously formulated human values do affect men's actions, that many decisions are reached after a conscious consideration of alternatives, and that men have a wide range of genuine choices. The information that we possess about the behavior of firms, small as it is, does furnish us with some plausible explanations

---

[38] *Ibid.,* p. 230.

[39] The homeostasis principle ". . . says nothing about what determines the equilibrium state itself. In biology this can generally be assumed to be given by the genetic constitution: in social organisms, the equilibrium position of the organism itself is to a considerable degree under the control of the organism's director," Boulding, *Reconstruction of Economics,* pp. 33-34.

of what firms are trying to do and why.[40] Biological explanations reduce, if they do not destroy, the value of this information and put nothing in its place.[41]

To treat the growth of the firm as the unfolding of its genetic nature is downright obscurantism.[42] To treat innovations as chance mutations not only obscures their significance but leaves them essentially unexplained, while to treat them directly as purposive attempts of men to *do* something makes them far more understandable. To draw an analogy between genetic heredity and the purposive imitation of success is to imply that in biology the characteristics acquired by one generation in adapting to its environment will be transmitted to future generations. This is precisely what does *not* happen in biological evolution. Even as a metaphor it is badly chosen although in principle metaphorical illustrations are legitimate and useful.[43] But in seeking the fundamental explanations of economic and social phenomena in human affairs the economist, and the social scientist in general, would be well advised to attack his problems directly and in their own terms rather than indirectly by imposing sweeping biological models upon them.

[40] As Jacob Marschak observed, "It would be a pity if we should not avail ourselves of that type of hypothesis provided by our insight—however imperfect or ambiguous—in the behavior of our fellow-men. This is our only advantage against those who study genes or electrons: they are not themselves genes or electrons." "A Discussion on Methods in Economics," *Jour. Pol. Econ.*, June 1942, XLIX, 445.

[41] If one attempts to apply the biological evolutionary principle to human activity, one must first show that human activity does not differ in kind from that of other organisms, and the argument of one noted biologist must be shown to be invalid: "Man differs from any previous dominant type in that he can consciously formulate values. And the realization of these in relation to the priority determined by whatever scale of values is adopted, must accordingly be added to the criteria of biological progress, once advance has reached the human level." Huxley, *op. cit.*, p. 575.

[42] Boulding, for example, finds "mysterious" the "problem of death and decay" of firms and asserts that "the question as to whether death is inherent in the structure of organization itself, or whether it is an accident is one that must remain unanswered, especially in regard to the social organization." "Implications for General Economics of More Realistic Theories of the Firm," p. 40. It is surely unwarranted to confine the explanation of the disappearance of firms to some obscure thing, "inherent in the structure of organization itself" or to "accident," and it would not have been so confined if the very nature of the problem had not been prejudged and limited by the biological approach. I am not sure that there is any precise meaning at all in Boulding's statement and I suspect that this is the reason his question "must remain unanswered."

[43] But one should be discriminating in using them. The varieties of biological phenomena are so numerous that a parallel may be found somewhere for every conceivable type of social situation. There is even apparently a type of symbiotic growth among algae and fungi which combine to form characteristic lichens that can be compared to the growth of a firm by merger. Very curious "parallels" are sometimes drawn. For example, one biologist finds that "There is an interesting parallel in the need for salt by the organism and the epiorganism [*i.e.*, society]. The commodity is so important for the social group that it was one of the earliest and most prized objects traded . . ."| R. W. Gerard, *Biological Symposia, op. cit.*, pp. 77-78.

Part II
Contemporary Debates

[5]

Technology, Political Economy, and Professionalization: Central Themes of the Organizational Synthesis

LOUIS GALAMBOS

¶ In this suggestive essay, Professor Galambos surveys the large number of books and articles, published since 1970, that together point toward a new "organizational synthesis" in American history. Expanding upon an earlier, more tentative essay on the same subject published in the Autumn 1970 issue of the Business History Review, he contrasts the widely disparate postures adopted in recent years by historians studying organizational behavior. His survey reveals a rich diversity of opinion, less reliant than was previous scholarship upon abstractions drawn from the social sciences. This diversity of opinion, Galambos concludes, provides the organizational synthesis with much of its continued vitality, and makes possible "the kind of moral judgments that have always characterized the best historical scholarship."

Some years ago the Business History Review published an article on "The Emerging Organizational Synthesis in Modern American History." That piece focused on a new interpretational framework, a context that featured large-scale organizations as the centerpiece of recent U.S. history. Restructured along these lines, our history no longer stressed liberal-conservative political struggles leading to pulses of progressive reform; instead, the primary processes of change involved organization building, both public and private, and the creation of new and elaborate networks of formal, hierarchical structures of authority that gradually came to dominate our economy, polity, and culture. America's rendezvous was not with the liberal's good society. It was with bureaucracy.

In 1970 when that article appeared, the boundaries of the new school were still vague and its judgments contested, but the author confidently predicted "that more and more historians will explore the new field of organizational history in the years ahead."[1] Indeed they have. Scholars in a wide variety of subdisciplines and traditions in history have filled

LOUIS GALAMBOS is professor of history at the Johns Hopkins University. He is grateful to the American Telephone and Telegraph Company for financial support while he was researching and writing this article. He would also like to thank Bob Lewis, Bob Garnet, Glenn Porter, Sam Hayes, Joe Pratt, Tom Hughes, David Hounshell, Bill Leslie, Naomi Lamoreaux, Mary Schweitzer, Chris Tomlins, Tom McCraw, Bill Becker, Robert Kohler, Tom Haskell, Mark Kornbluh, Bob Cuff, Daun van Ee, and the several participants in seminars at which he presented early drafts of this article.
[1] Louis Galambos, "The Emerging Organizational Synthesis in Modern American History," Business History Review, 44 (Autumn 1970), 279–90: reprinted in Edwin J. Perkins, ed., Men and Organizations: The American Economy in the Twentieth Century (New York, 1977), 1–5.

out the synthesis, giving body and rich detail to this new intellectual construct.[2] To date, the important breakthroughs have not been produced by those authors who have engaged the synthesis en toto. Robert Wiebe, whose *Search for Order* had originally stimulated historical interest in modern organizations, published *The Segmented Society*, an overview that in essence left unchanged his seminal ideas about the modern (post-1877 or so) phase of organization building.[3] In similar fashion, Robert Berkhofer's important article on "The Organizational Interpretation of American History," surveyed in a new way the first three centuries of our nation's history but did not attempt to develop any original ideas about the modern era of large-scale organizations.[4]

The most significant innovations in the scholarship came from the monographic studies of particular types of organizations. Three areas of research and writing have been unusually fruitful in this regard, and the recent contributions in all three have been of such high quality that these subjects now dominate the organizational approach to American history.[5] The first of these is the study of technology and the corporation. The second concerns the development of a distinctive, twentieth-century brand of political economy in the United States. The third involves the emergence of the modern professions. These are today the three central pillars of the organizational synthesis.

TECHNOLOGY AND THE CORPORATION

No aspect of modern America has excited more concern in recent years than the rise of the large corporation and the special role that technology has played in that development. No scholar has done more to focus attention on that subject than Alfred D. Chandler, Jr. In the early seventies, Chandler's volume on *Strategy and Structure* encouraged scholars to produce a number of studies of diversification and corporate decentralization in the United States and abroad.[6] More

[2] See the following: Robert D. Cuff, "American Historians and the 'Organizational Factor,' " *Canadian Review of American Studies*, 4 (Spring 1973), 19–31; Tom G. Hall, "Agricultural History and the 'Organizational Synthesis': A Review Essay," *Agricultural History*, 48 (April 1974), 313–25; Robert F. Berkhofer, Jr., "The Organizational Interpretation of American History: A New Synthesis," *Prospects*, 4 (1979), 611–29.

[3] Robert Wiebe, *The Search for Order, 1877–1920* (New York, 1967); Robert Wiebe, *The Segmented Society: An Introduction to the Meaning of America* (New York, 1975). In the latter book, Wiebe offered a gloomier appraisal of organizational change than he had in 1967, and he tinkered with his chronology a bit; but for the most part, he left intact a synthesis stressing the manner in which modern bureaucratic organizations satisfied the need most Americans had for a new, legitimate order. Questions of power and wealth were still left subordinate to questions of value orientation and ideology.

[4] Berkhofer, "The Organizational Interpretation," 611–29. One other general treatment is my own — see Louis Galambos, *America at Middle Age: A New History of the United States in the Twentieth Century* (New York, 1982) — and I make use of that synthesis in the conclusion to this article.

[5] Some of this work was done by authors who explicitly placed their studies in an organizational context. But many of the historians — especially those dealing with political history and the history of technology — attached their work to other conceptual frameworks. I have lumped together these disparate analyses when they have, in my judgment, made important contributions to our understanding of the development of America's modern large-scale institutions.

[6] Alfred D. Chandler, Jr., *Strategy and Structure: Chapters in the History of the Industrial Enterprise*

recently, his Pulitzer Prize-winning *The Visible Hand: The Managerial Revolution in American Business* brought the corporation, technology, and innovations in management to the forefront of our nation's history in both the nineteenth and twentieth centuries.[7] *The Visible Hand* revitalized business history, in part by generating fruitful intersections between that subdiscipline and the history of technology,[8] the analysis of economic growth,[9] and the economics of the firm.[10]

The Visible Hand portrayed technology as the prime mover in the evolution of the giant firm. The traditional firm was supplanted when technological advances and a growing domestic market made mass production possible. The resulting multi-unit enterprises developed managerial hierarchies that enabled them to coordinate more efficiently than the market did the complex array of activities they controlled. Within these firms functional specialization took place at a rapid pace, and the techniques of control were greatly improved; at first the combines centralized authority, but then, after undertaking more diversified functions, they adopted a decentralized structure. "By the middle of the twentieth century," Chandler said, "the salaried managers of a relatively small number of large mass producing, large mass retailing, and large mass transporting enterprises coordinated current flows of goods through the processes of production and distribution in major sectors of the American economy. By then, the managerial revolution in American business had been carried out."[11]

While explicit value judgments did not play a role in Chandler's work, he left his readers with few doubts about the positive outcome of this corporate capitalist revolution. The diversified, decentralized firms were "dynamic"; they were administered efficiently (or they would not have survived); in recent years they "generated by far the largest share of nongovernment funds and provided most of the nongovernment personnel involved in industrial research and development. These same firms were the prime contractors used by the gov-

(Cambridge, 1962). For a few examples of the work related to this book see Jon Didricksen, "The Development of Diversified and Conglomerate Firms in the United States, 1920-1970," *Business History Review*, 46 (Summer 1972), 202–19; Derek F. Channon, *The Strategy and Structure of British Enterprise* (Boston, 1974); Richard P. Rumelt, *Strategy, Structure, and Economic Performance* (Boston, 1974); Harold F. Williamson, ed., *Evolution of International Management Structures* (Newark, 1975).

[7] Alfred D. Chandler, Jr., *The Visible Hand: The Managerial Revolution in American Business* (Cambridge, 1977).

[8] See, for instance, David A. Hounshell, "Commentary/On the Discipline of the History of American Technology," *Journal of American History*, 67 (March 1981), 854–65; and the same author's *From the American System to Mass Production: The Development of Manufacturing Technology in the United States, 1800–1932* (forthcoming, Johns Hopkins University Press).

[9] See Richard B. Du Boff, "Business Demand and the Development of the Telegraph in the United States, 1844–1860," *Business History Review*, 54 (Winter 1980), esp. 478–79.

[10] See Richard E. Caves, "Industrial Organization, Corporate Strategy and Structure," *Journal of Economic Literature*, 18 (March 1980), 64–92; and Oliver E. Williamson, "The Modern Corporation: Origins, Evolution, Attributes," *Journal of Economic Literature*, 19 (December 1981), 1537-68, for recent discussions of the literature and issues.

[11] Chandler, *The Visible Hand*, p. 11.

ernment in World War II and in the two decades of the cold war. They were the companies that provided the hardware for its atomic energy and space programs. They, too, were the same enterprises that continued to present the 'American challenge' to European and other businessmen overseas."[12] What more could one ask of a capitalist system that radical critics had long been describing as on the brink of total collapse?

Other scholars developed similar themes — each with distinctive characteristics, but each with an emphasis on the special role of technology in the emergence of America's modern corporate economy. In his perceptive biography of Elmer Sperry, Thomas Parke Hughes traced the activities of an "inventor-entrepreneur" whose career began in the age of the inspired individual (the 1880s) and ended in the era of organized corporate R&D (the 1920s). In effect, Sperry's career helped us see how distinct was the boundary that divided the modern setting of large-scale organizations from America's previous experience. Sperry was successful in both of these settings, but to do so, he had to have an unusual flair for entrepreneurship as well as a unique talent for solving engineering problems.[13]

This same transition from individual to institutionalized research was explored in Reese V. Jenkins's history of the American photographic industry from 1839 to 1925. Jenkins used the novel concept of "business-technological mind-sets," which he said characterized successive stages in the industry's development. Alterations in the mind-set were a product of "precedent-shattering technological change," which normally came from outside the industry. Each mind-set was defined by a dominant technology, and within the stages, the industry regularly evolved from imperfect competition, to perfect, and then to oligopolistic patterns of behavior.[14] Jenkins thus focused more attention than Chandler did on the modern corporation's security-seeking, risk-reducing aspect, a theme that an earlier generation of economists and historians had explored in great detail.[15] But neither Jenkins nor Chandler considered the search for stability as important a feature of business behavior as was technological innovation.

It is also interesting that neither Jenkins, nor Chandler, nor Hughes

12 *Ibid.*, pp. 474, 476, 483.

13 Thomas Park Hughes, *Elmer Sperry: Inventor and Engineer* (Baltimore, 1971).

14 Reese V. Jenkins, *Images and Enterprise: Technology and the American Photographic Industry, 1839 to 1925* (Baltimore, 1975). Both Hughes and Jenkins worked with Chandler, but they did not thereby come to a single overriding conclusion about technology as a causal factor. Jenkins gives more emphasis than Chandler does (in *The Visible Hand*) to the drive to stifle competition. Hughes looks more than Chandler does to the social and political environments as sources of change; see note 22 below.

15 See, for example, Arthur R. Burns, *The Decline of Competition: A Study of the Evolution of American Industry* (New York, 1936); Alfred S. Eichner, *The Emergence of Oligopoly: Sugar Refining as a Case Study* (Baltimore, 1969); and the literature discussed in Ellis W. Hawley, "Antitrust," in Glenn Porter, ed., *Encyclopedia of American Economic History*, vol. 2, 772–87.

wrote the history of a single business — in the style promoted some years ago by N.S.B. Gras.[16] The traditional sort of company history was fading into the intellectual background. The most significant work in this branch of the organizational synthesis was either problem-oriented, in the style of Hughes's biography, or aggregate in the style of Chandler (who studied the entire business system), of Jenkins (who looked at an entire industry), and of most of the materials cited in note 17 below. The works of this genre have thus recast business history along new lines, increasing the emphasis in the subdiscipline on careful analysis of the general institutional setting for technological change.

These volumes and numerous other publications in the years since 1970 have solidly established technological change and its related managerial innovations as a central feature in the history of America's modern corporate economy.[17] In an effort to determine with greater precision just how important technological factors have been, numerous scholars have begun to compare American economic institutions with those in other societies.[18] An ambitious survey appeared in Alfred D. Chandler, Jr., and Herman Daems, editors, *Managerial Hierarchies: Comparative Perspectives on the Rise of the Modern Industrial Enterprise*, which included essays on Great Britain, Germany, and France, as well as the United States.[19] In the very long run, this comparison suggested, the firms in each country tended to reach somewhat similar states of organizational development — a pattern consistent with the emphasis that the editors gave to technological considerations.[20] But the paths to these endpoints seemed — on the basis of

[16] Louis Galambos, *American Business History* (Washington, 1967).

[17] See, for example, Glenn Porter and Harold C. Livesay, *Merchants and Manufacturers: Studies in the Changing Structure of 19th Century Marketing* (Baltimore, 1971); Thomas G. Marx, "Technological Change and the Theory of the Firm: The American Locomotive Industry, 1920–1955," *Business History Review*, 50 (Spring 1976), 1–24; Michael Massouh, "Technological and Managerial Innovation: The Johnson Company, 1883–1898," *Business History Review*, 50 (Spring 1976), 46–68; William J. Abernathy, *The Productivity Dilemma: Roadblock to Innovation in the Automobile Industry* (Baltimore, 1978); Charles W. Cheape, *Moving the Masses: Urban Public Transit in New York, Boston and Philadelphia* (Cambridge, 1980). See also the literature cited in Thomas P. Hughes, "Emerging Themes in the History of Technology," *Technology and Culture*, 20 (October 1979), 697–711.

[18] See William N. Parker's discussion of this point in "American Capitalism: The Differentiation from European Origins" (Sapporo Cool Seminar on American Studies, Hokkaido University, 1981), esp. 22–24. An International Conference on Business History (the Fuji Conference) has been meeting since 1976 and regularly publishing comparative studies. See also Williamson, *Evolution of International Management Structures*; Rosamund Thomas, *The British Philosophy of Administration: A Comparison of British and American Ideas, 1900–1939* (New York, 1978). Many of the studies in Continental and British institutions have had a built-in comparative concept because they have followed the major analyses of the U.S. experience. See Channon, *The Strategy and Structure of British Enterprise;* Leslie Hannah, *The Rise of the Corporate Economy: The British Experience* (Baltimore, 1976); S. J. Prais, *The Evolution of Giant Firms in Britain* (Cambridge, 1976); John Zysman, *Political Strategies for Industrial Order: State, Market, and Industry in France* (Berkeley, 1977).

[19] Alfred D. Chandler, Jr., and Herman Daems, eds., *Managerial Hierarchies: Comparative Perspectives on the Rise of Modern Industrial Enterprise* (Cambridge, 1980).

[20] Herman Daems, "The Rise of the Modern Industrial Enterprise: A New Perspective," in *Managerial Hierarchies*, 203–23, provides the volume's comparative conclusion. He stresses the role of efficiency-producing technology as a common source of a common organizational form. For an earlier and slightly different interpretation see Daems's review of Derek F. Channon's book on British enterprise, *Business History Review*, 49 (Summer 1975), 280–81.

the evidence presented there — to have varied so considerably and to
have been shaped so substantially by complex political and social factors
that technological determinism provided an inadequate explanation of
what happened.[21]

Indeed, Thomas Parke Hughes's most recent book demonstrated
convincingly how technologies themselves have been altered by their
political, cultural, and economic settings. His careful comparison of the
early electrical systems of Great Britain, Germany, and the United
States revealed how differently each country applied the ideas originally developed by Thomas Edison. The contrasts between the lighting
systems that emerged in Berlin and London were for the most part a
result of political factors. As the networks in each country grew, they
acquired "a supportive context, or culture. . ." that gave "technological
momentum" to the nation's industry. Educational institutions, research
and development organizations, and engineering associations all
became part of a complex, socio-technological system that was particular to each city, region, and nation. A careful reading of Hughes's
book indicated that neither technology nor its corporate setting could
be understood without placing these phenomena in their social, political, and economic contexts.[22]

A similar conclusion could be drawn from the work done to date on
multinational corporations. Perforce, this research is comparative in
nature, and the companies examined seem to have adjusted in significantly different ways to their varied social and political environments
overseas. If technological imperatives alone had molded these giant
firms, then we would have expected to find more consistent patterns
of organizational behavior than have actually evolved.[23] Organizational
history along these lines seemed then to have acquired a particularistic
caste that it had lacked in 1970. The historical emphasis upon place
and time, the impact of a particular setting, have made inroads on the
sociological preference for universal patterns of action.

The synthesis has also acquired a rich moral emphasis — another
break with the sociological tradition. Scholars who stressed the causal
role of technology largely followed Chandler's lead and came to very
positive conclusions. Modern technology plus effective management

21 I dealt with this problem at greater length in my review of this book, *Science*, 208 (May 30, 1980),
1023–24.
22 Thomas Parke Hughes, *Networks of Power: Electrification in Western Society, 1880–1930* (Baltimore,
1983). See, as well, the following selections by Hughes: "Conservative and Radical Technologies," in Sven
B. Lundstedt and E. William Colglazier, Jr., eds., *Managing Innovation: The Social Dimensions of Creativity,
Invention and Technology* (New York, 1982), 31–44; "The Order of the Technological World," in A. Rupert
Hall and Norman Smith, eds., *History of Technology* (London, 1980), 1–16.
23 Raymond Vernon, *Sovereignty at Bay: The Multinational Spread of U.S. Enterprises* (New York, 1971),
and the same author's *Storm Over the Multinationals: The Real Issues* (Cambridge, 1977); Mira Wilkins, *The
Maturing of Multinational Enterprise: American Business Abroad from 1914 to 1970* (Cambridge, 1974).

equaled efficiency and economic growth. Market power should have caused no basic fears. A changing technology has always breached the walls of corporate strongholds, and besides, only the efficient firms have survived over the long run.

Other voices have been heard, however. Daniel J. Boorstin absorbed technology into the American democratic experience and then condemned its impact on the United States in the twentieth century.[24] Elting G. Morison portrayed our technology taking us *From Know-How to Nowhere*,[25] and his gloomy evaluation was seconded by those scholars who were opening the new field of environmental studies.[26] Robert L. Heilbroner saw our business civilization in decline, not triumph, as our technology encountered inevitable and unyielding ecological limits.[27] For labor, as well, all has not been so rosy in the past; the technological changes applauded by many business historians frequently eroded the workers' social and economic status. David Montgomery and Richard Edwards, who were critical of these developments, held sway in labor history, in part by default.[28] The historians of the corporation have for the most part ignored the labor force, perhaps assuming that the technological advances that were good for General Motors were equally good for the men who labored in GM's factories.

The history of corporate technology in modern America has thus acquired some intriguing characteristics. We have learned of late how particular these business institutions were to their American setting. We have found out, as well, that the drive for technical and organizational innovation — along with the security-seeking emphasized by a previous generation of scholars — has become a central feature of our new economic bureaucracies.[29] But we have not yet decided how to evaluate these changes, and thus a creative moral and ideological tension has been generated in organizational studies. Some have worried that our society is heading for a deep technological and economic crisis. More have concluded that the history of technology and the modern

[24] Daniel Boorstin, *The Americans: The Democratic Experience* (New York, 1973).

[25] Elting G. Morison, *From Know-How to Nowhere: The Development of American Technology* (New York, 1974).

[26] Joseph A. Pratt, "Growth or a Clean Environment? Responses to Petroleum-related Pollution in the Gulf Coast Refining Region," *Business History Review*, 52 (Spring 1978), 1–29; and the same author's "Letting the Grandchildren do it: Environmental Planning During the Ascent of Oil as a Major Energy Source," *The Public Historian*, 2 (Summer 1980), 28–61; Joseph Petulla, *American Environmental History* (San Francisco, 1977); Samuel P. Hays, "The Limits-to-Growth Issue: An Historical Perspective," in Chester L. Cooper, ed., *Growth in America* (Westport, 1976), 115–42.

[27] Robert L. Heilbroner, *Business Civilization in Decline* (New York, 1976).

[28] David Montgomery, *Workers' Control in America: Studies in the History of Work, Technology, and Labor Struggles* (Cambridge, 1979); Richard Edwards, *Contested Terrain: The Transformation of the Workplace in the Twentieth Century* (New York, 1979).

[29] Recent studies that presented relatively balanced accounts of these two major aspects of corporate development include Glenn Porter, *The Rise of Big Business, 1860–1910* (Arlington Heights, Illinois, 1973), and the books by Raymond Vernon, cited in note 23, above.

corporation is a study in progress. Recent events suggest that the positivists will become even more numerous in the years ahead. The current concern to improve the productivity of American enterprise, to copy those countries that now seem to be excelling in technological advances, to deregulate, to reindustrialize, to lower labor costs — all of these enthusiasms of the eighties will doubtless feed the interest in the history of technology and sustain a largely favorable evaluation of its role in our twentieth-century experience.

THE POLITICAL ECONOMY OF CORPORATE LIBERALISM

In the second major realm of organizational history, political economy, a sharply contrasting, negative evaluation of America's organizational society has emerged. For many decades this viewpoint was not popular. The dominant school of political history was the so-called progressive or liberal interpretation, which gave to the public sector a positive role in the nation's progress toward a more just and humane society; some historians today (and some very good ones, indeed) continue to espouse this reform-centered interpretation.[30] Others use the progressive synthesis as a foil, developing revisionist correctives that modify but do not really supplant the progressive vision of the active state in the good society.[31] But in the years since 1970, more and more scholars have advanced harsh and hostile analyses of the growth of the administrative state in America.

Some of the critics were conservatives who were chagrined, in particular, by the elaboration of regulatory measures in this century and by the inherent inefficiency of the nation's public bureaucracies. Albro Martin traced the beginnings of the decline of America's railroads to the strengthening of federal regulation by the Interstate Commerce Commission. The villains of his history were the Progressive reformers — not the Robber Barons. The liberals, the "archaic Progressives" to Martin, were both stubborn and shortsighted; they drove through the Act of 1910, "that unworkable piece of legislation which caused most of the trouble." For Martin, capitalism unfettered would have been the same sort of innovative system that was responsible for America's economic progress in the nineteenth century.[32]

[30] Alonzo L. Hamby, *Beyond the New Deal: Harry S. Truman and American Liberalism* (New York, 1973).

[31] James T. Patterson, *America in the Twentieth Century: A History* (New York, 1976) fits this mold, as does Robert F. Himmelberg, *The Origins of the National Recovery Administration: Business, Government and the Trade Association Issue, 1921–1933* (New York, 1976); see also Barry D. Karl's optimistic article on "Philanthropy, Policy Planning, and the Bureaucratization of the Democratic Ideal," *Daedalus* (Fall 1976), 129–49.

[32] Albro Martin, *Enterprise Denied: Origins of the Decline of American Railroads, 1897–1917* (New York, 1971), 359–60.

Jonathan R. T. Hughes, an eminent economic historian, has taken a similar stance in his several, recent publications. He has condemned *The Governmental Habit: Economic Controls from Colonial Times to the Present.*[33] In his presidential address to the Economic History Association in 1981, he offered "a little parable for our times," a description of the Bering Sea fishermen's strike against the salmon packers in 1951; the incident, he said, was "a microcosm of my larger results: regulatory agencies that finally became sponsors of monopoly pricing and output, some with falling or negative profits in older industries like railroads. Regulated results that clearly were not the intentions of those who had framed the original laws are the usual outcomes."[34] Others have joined Hughes in condemning liberal policies in our states[35] and the nation,[36] pointing frequently to the manner in which public bureaucrats have strengthened their own hands while ignoring the costs to the public (whose interests they were ostensibly protecting).

In the years to come, more is likely to be heard from the historians on the right, but to date theirs has been a minor attack on the American system of government compared to the full-scale reappraisal conducted by the scholars in the "corporate liberal" school of interpretation. The central idea in this critique of the U.S. polity is that organized interests — the corporate element — have meshed in various ways with public authority to develop a new, twentieth-century style of government; many of the changes have been introduced by reform-oriented leaders — the liberal element — who proclaimed that they had the public's welfare in mind. Frequently, however, the public interest yielded to private gain. In fact, so close were the relationships that it eventually became very difficult to distinguish what was public from what was private.[37] All that was clear was that the United States had acquired a formidable administrative state that either controlled directly or influenced in some fashion a substantial part of the income and wealth of this country.[38]

The changes in government took place at all levels — local, state, and national. In all three the same sort of functional specialization that

---

[33] Jonathan R.T. Hughes, *The Governmental Habit: Economic Controls from Colonial Times to the Present* (New York, 1977).

[34] Jonathan R.T. Hughes, "The Great Strike at Nushagak Station, 1951: Institutional Gridlock," *Journal of Economic History*, 42 (March 1982), 1–20.

[35] Peter D. McClelland and Alan L. Magdovitz, *Crisis in the Making: The Political Economy of New York State since 1945* (Cambridge, 1981).

[36] Carolyn L. Weaver, *Crisis in Social Security: Economic and Political Origins* (Durham, 1983).

[37] Ellis W. Hawley, "The Discovery and Study of a 'Corporate Liberalism,'" *Business History Review*, 52 (Autumn 1978), 319. All of the articles in this issue of the *Review* dealt with this theme. See also R. Jeffrey Lustig, *Corporate Liberalism: The Origins of Modern American Political Theory, 1890–1920* (Berkeley, 1982).

[38] See, for instance, Stephen Skowronek, *Building a New American State: The Expansion of National Administrative Capacity, 1877–1920* (Cambridge, 1982); see also James E. Hewes, Jr., *From Root to McNamara: Army Departmental Organization and Administration, 1900–1963* (Washington, D.C., 1975).

480   BUSINESS HISTORY REVIEW

characterized the evolution of the modern corporation took place within political organizations and among the institutions that sought to influence political decisions. Under the banner of liberal reform, municipal governments throughout the country were transformed along lines that appealed to the middle-class citizens who were organizing new sorts of business and professional associations to represent their occupational groups.[39] In city, state, and nation, political parties became less important as new functional groups and federations dramatically altered the political process.[40] The very large, very complex systems that emerged from this long-run transformation operated in ways that frequently baffled the nation's leaders and bewildered the citizens who wanted new government services but neither the increased taxes nor the periodic political crises that characterized the political economy of corporate liberalism.

There have been two distinct wings of corporate liberal analysis — one radical, with links to the New Left; the other moderate, with intellectual ties to the pluralists of political science. The cornerstone of the radical interpretation was a paradox: corporate capitalism, which has had overwhelming power in the twentieth-century United States and which has controlled most of our wealth, has nonetheless been a system on the brink of economic collapse.[41] To stave off failure the corporate leaders promoted an expansionary foreign policy. They organized effectively to push their program in government circles. Empire and influence — a private-public network — provided markets, sources of raw materials, and cheap labor.[42] But to protect this system, business leaders had continually to enlist the armed support of the state. Frequently they had to counter the forces of revolutionary change abroad, especially when those forces marched behind the banners of socialism or communism.[43]

---

[39] David B. Tyack, "City Schools: Centralization of Control at the Turn of the Century," in Jerry Israel, ed., *Building the Organizational Society: Essays on Associational Activities in Modern America* (New York, 1972); Samuel P. Hays, "The Politics of Reform in Municipal Government in the Progressive Era," *Pacific Northwest Quarterly*, 55 (October 1964), 157–69.

[40] Samuel P. Hays, "The New Organizational Society," in Jerry Israel, ed., *Building the Organizational Society*, 5–9.

[41] Gabriel Kolko, *Main Currents in Modern American History* (New York, 1976), 398, described the United States as "a society dangerously adrift and now locked into an enduring, permanent crisis at home and in the world. This increasingly violent experience, this absence of a hope of a better future, was the main heritage that American capitalism had at the end of its first hundred years bequeathed to its people and the international community. . . ."

[42] See, for example, Carle P. Parrini and Martin J. Sklar, "Periodization and History: The Corporate Reconstruction of American Society, 1896–1914" (a paper delivered at the Organization of American Historians, 1981). Burton I. Kaufman, "United States Trade and Latin America: The Wilson Years," *Journal of American History*, 57 (September 1971), 342–63; the same author's "The Organizational Dimension of United States Foreign Economic Policy, 1900–1920," *Business History Review*, 46 (Spring 1972), 17–44; and his *Efficiency and Expansion: Foreign Trade Organization in the Wilson Administration, 1913–1921* (Westport, 1974). Rodney Carlisle, "The 'American Century' Implemented: Stettinius and the Liberian Flag of Convenience," *Business History Review*, 54 (Summer 1980), 175–91.

[43] Robert Freeman Smith, *The United States and Revolutionary Nationalism in Mexico, 1916–1932* (Chicago, 1972); Jules Robert Benjamin, *The United States and Cuba: Hegemony and Dependent Develop-*

At home, corporate power was used to implement policies that directly benefited business and to thwart those reform measures that threatened business's interests. Much of this politicking was done in the name of liberal reform; these were the corporate leaders who graced the boards of liberal organizations and published articles espousing reform causes. Men like Owen D. Young of General Electric and Edward A. Filene of the Filene department stores filled the liberal ranks. These were the sorts of leaders who participated in the Commerce Department's Business Advisory and Planning Council and the Committee for Economic Development. The types of reform these business leaders promoted — the establishment in the 1930s of the National Recovery Administration, for example, or the development in the 1940s of a counter-cyclical fiscal policy — always profited corporate interests and consolidated business's political influence.[44]

The great combines that held sway in this version of our history were also those that Dwight D. Eisenhower had condemned as partners in the military-industrial complex. They were the businesses that profited most from war, either hot or cold. With their influence reaching deeply into the State Department and Defense Department, they could assure that America would stay prepared, poised on the edge of war, so that defense contracts would continue to be forthcoming. Debilitating at home and dangerous abroad, the public policies of corporate liberalism were only a holding action: intrinsic to this analysis was the assumption that ultimately this jerrybuilt system would have to collapse.[45]

Those scholars who espoused a more moderate version of this interpretation were of course less pessimistic about the future and more cautious about the past. Looking back to the origins and evolution of the regulatory commissions, such historians as Thomas K. McCraw, William Doezema, Donald A. Ritchie, William Graebner, and James P. Johnson found evidence of complex interactions between business and government.[46] At times the businesses had captured the regulators.

ment, *1880–1934* (Pittsburgh, 1977); see also Fred L. Block, *The Origins of International Economic Disorder: A Study of United States International Monetary Policy from World War II to the Present* (Berkeley, 1977).

[44] Kim McQuaid, "Corporate Liberalism in the American Business Community, 1920–1940," *Business History Review*, 52 (Autumn 1978), 342–68; and in the same issue, Robert M. Collins, "Positive Business Responses to the New Deal: The Roots of the Committee for Economic Development, 1933–1942," 369–91; see also McQuaid's *Big Business and Presidential Power: From FDR to Reagan* (New York, 1981); and Michael E. Parrish, *Securities Regulation and the New Deal* (New Haven, 1970).

[45] Carroll W. Pursell, Jr., ed., *The Military-Industrial Complex* (New York, 1972); and Paul A. C. Koistinen, *The Military-Industrial Complex: A Historical Perspective* (New York, 1980). Gabriel Kolko, *Main Currents*, 337–47; see also Richard Barnet, *Roots of War* (New York, 1972), 137–238, on "The Political Economy of Expansionism."

[46] Thomas K. McCraw, *TVA and the Power Fight, 1933–1939* (Philadelphia, 1971); and, also by McCraw, "Regulation in America: A Review Article," *Business History Review*, 49 (Summer 1975), 159–83, and "Rethinking the Trust Question," in Thomas K. McCraw, ed., *Regulation in Perspective: Historical Essays* (Cambridge, 1981), 1–55; William R. Doezema, "Railroad Management and the Interplay of Federal and State Regulation, 1885–1916," *Business History Review*, 50 (Summer 1976), 153–78; Donald A. Ritchie, *James M. Landis: Dean of the Regulators* (Cambridge, 1980); William Graebner, "Great Expectations: The

But frequently, the commissions heeded many interests and sought diverse ends, as did the ICC in the years following 1910. The simple idea that the commissions sought to further the public interest would not encompass all of these experiences — nor would the equally simple idea of "capture."[47] Neither in their origins nor their subsequent behavior, James Q. Wilson said, could the commissions be explained as merely "industry-serving"; in his view the commissions themselves had to be seen as "coalitions of diverse participants who have somewhat different motives." The "careerists," the "politicians," and the "professionals" were different sorts of regulators who performed their regulatory functions in different ways.[48] The "professionals" seemed, for instance, to have played an especially important role in the early activities of the Securities and Exchange Commission, an agency whose history well illustrated the complexity that the moderate branch of this school stressed. The SEC could not be analyzed only in terms of corporate objectives and corporate power; professional accountants — operating from a different organizational base than business — interacted with government officials, politicians, and corporate leaders to shape the activities of the SEC.[49]

What emerged from this literature was an historical perspective that emphasized the coalescence of organized interests — some public, some private — and the interaction of various political coalitions that shifted over time and normally settled for some sort of compromise. Coalition-building was the heart of the political process at all levels of government. Neither businessmen nor public officials nor the other interests involved were ever completely successful in achieving their objectives. As Mansel G. Blackford found in his study of the political economy of one state, "businessmen achieved only partial success. They failed to grasp the full meaning of the changes occurring around them and so were never totally effective in dealing with them."[50] Gone from this synthesis was the periodicity of reform history. Thus, Ellis W. Hawley's work converted the 1920s from an interlude between surges of reform to a decade of important innovations in the public

Search for Order in Bituminous Coal, 1890–1917," *Business History Review*, 48 (Spring 1974), 49–72, and *Coal-Mining Safety in the Progressive Period: The Political Economy of Reform* (Lexington, 1976); also see James P. Johnson, *The Politics of Soft Coal: The Bituminous Industry from World War I through the New Deal* (Urbana, 1979).

[47] Thomas K. McCraw, "Regulation in America," 160–71, makes this point very effectively.

[48] "The Politics of Regulation," in James Q. Wilson, ed., *The Politics of Regulation* (New York, 1980), 372–82; see also Samuel P. Hays's penetrating essay on "Political Choice in Regulatory Administration," in Thomas K. McCraw, ed., *Regulation in Perspective*, 124–54.

[49] Thomas K. McCraw, "With Consent of the Governed: SEC's Formative Years," *Journal of Policy Analysis and Management*, 1, no. 3 (1982), 346–70. See also McCraw, ed., *Regulation in Perspective*.

[50] Mansel G. Blackford, *The Politics of Business in California, 1890–1920* (Columbus, 1977), 171; also see Jonathan Lurie, *The Chicago Board of Trade, 1859–1905: The Dynamics of Self-Regulation* (Urbana, 1979).

realm; private groups developed such strong ties to government that Hawley labeled the combination an "associational state."[51]

The moderate style of corporate liberal interpretation also eschewed the relatively simple concept of causation that has characterized the radical view. For instance, Robert D. Cuff offered an organizational perspective on the military-industrial complex; he emphasized the complex, shifting coalitions and high degree of discontinuity in this aspect of institutional evolution. He concluded that in the defense realm in the years following World War II, the traditional distinctions between public and private activities, between business and government, and finally between the individual and the state were no longer very useful in understanding what was happening. For his part he offered a synthesis that stressed bureaucratic structure and the "politics of administration," categories that he hoped would transform the subject from one of intense ideological concern to one of intense scholarly analysis.[52]

In a similar manner, Robert M. Collins saw in *The Business Response to Keynes, 1929-1964* a "conscious effort to build a corporatist sociopolitical order that would avoid the dangers of both statist regimentation and laissez-faire waste and social tension." Both government leaders and businessmen worked toward this common goal; both of the major political parties made contributions to this effort. The corporatist vision, Collins said, "commingled with the value systems of liberals and conservatives and with the nation's democratic traditions to influence the modern American political economy."[53] According to Collins, and to Robert Griffith and Allen J. Matusow as well, presidents as different in style as Dwight David Eisenhower and John F. Kennedy could best be understood from this particular vantage point.[54]

In foreign as well as domestic policy, the moderates broke with the simple radical view stressing big business's dominant position. In the

[51] For Hawley's ideas see the following: "Herbert Hoover, The Commerce Secretariat, and the Vision of an Associative State," *Journal of American History,* 61 (June 1974), 116–40; "Secretary Hoover and the Changing Framework of New Era Historiography," and "Herbert Hoover and Economic Stabilization, 1921–22," both in Ellis W. Hawley, ed., *Herbert Hoover as Secretary of Commerce: Studies in New Era Thought and Practice* (Iowa City, 1981), 1–16, 43–79; "Three Facets of Hooverian Associationalism: Lumber, Aviation, and Movies, 1921–1930," in Thomas K. McCraw, ed., *Regulation in Perspective,* 95–123; see also Guy Alchon, "Technocratic Social Science and the Rise of Managed Capitalism, 1910–1933" (Ph.D. dissertation, University of Iowa, 1982).

[52] Robert D. Cuff, "An Organizational Perspective on the Military-Industrial Complex," *Business History Review,* 52 (Summer 1978), 250–67; see also Cuff's *The War Industries Board: Business-Government Relations During World War I* (Baltimore, 1973); and "Antitrust Adjourned: Mobilizations and the Rise of the National Security State," in *National Competition Policy: Historians' Perspective on Antitrust and Government-Business Relations in the United States* (Washington, D.C., 1981), 208–59; also see Donald J. Mrozek, "The Truman Administration and the Enlistment of the Aviation Industry in Postwar Defense," *Business History Review,* 48 (Spring 1974), 72–94; and Benjamin Franklin Cooling, ed., *War, Business, and American Society: Historical Perspectives on the Military-Industrial Complex* (Port Washington, 1977).

[53] Robert M. Collins, *The Business Response to Keynes, 1929–1964* (New York, 1981), 204–5.

[54] Robert Griffith, "Dwight D. Eisenhower and the Corporate Commonwealth," *American Historical Review,* 87 (February 1982), 87–122. Allen J. Matusow, "The Unravelling of America: A History of Liberalism in the 1960s" (forthcoming, Harper & Row), ch. 2.

moderate perspective there was still plenty of business input to policy: International Telephone and Telegraph had a great deal to do with U.S. policy toward Spain in the twenties and thirties.[55] But in this instance and others, businessmen seldom got exactly what they wanted. The State Department often dominated the businessmen, and policy was more often a product of muddling than of conspiracy. William H. Becker's recent book on the relations between the government and manufacturers seeking to promote exports demonstrated how important bureaucratic struggles within the government and congressional politics were in shaping national policies.[56] Becker's version of the mainsprings of U.S. foreign economic policies was similar to that of Michael J. Hogan, author of *Informal Entente: The Private Structure of Cooperation in Anglo-American Economic Diplomacy.*[57] For both Becker and Hogan, the crucial determinants of foreign policy were shifting alliances of public and private interests engaged in the politics of "cooperative competition."[58]

The corporate-liberal school — whether moderate or radical in orientation — has thus provided a very broad context for reinterpreting the dramatic organizational developments that have occurred in American government in this century. These historians have begun to describe government itself as a crucial actor in shaping America's development. Stationed around every government agency, every legislator, every executive and court have been organized interests seeking to shape public policy to their own ends. The corporate-liberal analysis focused attention on these interactions; organizational relationships have, in this new perspective, supplanted party politics as the driving force of political history. The scholars building the corporate liberal synthesis have looked beyond manifest political events — those events that were obvious to the participants — and studied latent or underlying factors of which the participants were unaware or only partially aware.[59] The resulting view of our history has in essence been critical. The analysts writing in this tradition were much more pessimistic about the nation's accomplishments than were the historians of technological change. The corporate commonwealth they described may indeed have

[55] Douglas J. Little, "Twenty Years of Turmoil: ITT, the State Department, and Spain, 1924–1944," *Business History Review*, 52 (Winter 1979), 449–72.

[56] William H. Becker, *The Dynamics of Business-Government Relations: Industry and Exports, 1893–1921* (Chicago, 1982).

[57] Michael J. Hogan, *Informal Entente: The Private Struture of Cooperation in Anglo-American Economic Diplomacy* (New York, 1977).

[58] The expression is Hogan's. See also Joan Hoff Wilson, *American Business and Foreign Policy, 1920–1933* (Lexington, 1971); Richard Hume Werking, *The Master Architects: Building the United States Foreign Service, 1890–1913* (Lexington, 1977); Irvine H. Anderson, *The Standard-Vacuum Oil Company and United States East Asian Policy, 1933–1941* (Princeton, 1975); Frederick C. Adams, *Economic Diplomacy: The Export-Import Bank and American Foreign Policy, 1934–1939* (New York, 1976).

[59] See Bernard Bailyn, "The Challenge of Modern Historiography," *American Historical Review*, 87 (February 1982), 9–11.

been productive, but its record was blemished by economic crises, fierce internal struggles, frequent political stalemates, and a skewed distribution of wealth and power.

In my view, the historians of corporate liberalism have been too harsh in evaluating America's domestic policies, leaving out of their purview, for example, government's rather remarkable contributions to technical and organizational change in this century. Concentrating almost exclusively on security-seeking, risk-reducing activities, they have largely ignored the massive subsidies our states have given to university-centered research and to the tasks of training personnel for research (they have thus written a lopsided history, as have those students of technology and the corporation who leave out business's search for security). The federal government has pumped billions of dollars of direct outlays into research and development. Defense-related expenditures have also stimulated research in many of our most advanced industries.[60] America's modern administrative state has been heavily involved in promoting innovation, as well as economic security, and we should take both functions into consideration, acknowledging how closely related are the developments in corporate technology and the corporate-liberal state.

That accomplished, the historical evaluation of our political system is still likely to be primarily negative, concerned more with the problems Americans have encountered at home and abroad than with the technical and administrative virtuosity they have achieved. Unless our government agencies and legislatures experience a sudden transformation, unless our executive officers become more prescient than they have been in recent years, unless our interest groups become less shortsighted or more public-minded than they are today, the corporate liberal vision will continue to be primarily a critique of the American past.

The Emergence of the Modern Professions

The organizational synthesis has thus acquired a strong moral flavor in recent years. The two contrasting ideologies at work are the negative evaluation of the corporate-liberal school and the positive viewpoint characteristic of the historians of technological and managerial innovation. Elements of both interpretations can be found in the third

[60] See, for example, John S. Brubacker and Willis Rudy, *Higher Education in Transition: A History of American Colleges and Universities, 1636–1976* (New York, 1976), 256–60, 378, 380–82, 400–4, 415–16; Joseph Ben-David, *American Higher Education* (New York, 1972), 1–2, 42–47, 87–109; J. Stefan Dupré and Stanford A. Lakoff, *Science and the Nation* (Englewood Cliffs, N.J., 1962), 9–19; National Science Foundation, "Report 62–37," in William R. Nelson, ed., *The Politics of Science* (London, 1968), 55–69.

major area of organizational research: the emergence of the modern professions.

Here there is no dominant mode of evaluation, no central pattern of analysis. In part this probably reflects the fact that historical interest in the professions is a relatively recent phenomenon. Moreover, generalization has been stymied by the great diversity in the organizations, intellectual traditions, political activities, elites, and social values of the various professions. One can excuse scholars for being hesitant about advancing interpretations that would have to stretch from such older, traditional professions as law and medicine to the new entries, which include occupations as diverse as nuclear chemistry, museum management, and history itself. Including the quasi-professions — advertising, for instance, or undertaking, or beauty culture — would make the task even more strenuous.

Historians of professionalization have, nevertheless, discovered some general processes of institutional change that characterized a wide range of these occupations and that were, incidentally, similar to those that took place during the last century in the nation's business system and its polity. The essence of professionalization was of course a special form of functional specialization similar to that which occurred in the corporation and in the state in the modern era. In the past one hundred years, thousands of new professions have emerged. Many of them supplied the employees that the newly differentiated corporations needed. Others were oriented to government and to the educational institutions that were experiencing a similar trend toward specialization. Each of these new specialties has created a system of governance to specify and control its boundaries and to define and achieve its professional goals. Normally, one of the major goals of the profession involved innovation, the ongoing process of improving the body of knowledge that each practitioner was supposed to understand better than the layperson. But professionals were also usually interested in exercising power so as to achieve a measure of security — that is, risk-reduction — by controlling their self-defined turf. Quite often they have used the power of the administrative state to satisfy that need.

Those historians who have been primarily interested in the process of intellectual innovation and in the professional networks and values that have contributed to order, efficiency, and systematic social change have for the most part written favorable accounts of the professions. Robert Wiebe — in *The Segmented Society* as in *The Search for Order* — found that the new professional organizations, their codes of conduct, and systems of socialization, all reflected a new set of social values stressing rationalization and order. The common and cooperative elements that drew specialists together were those that Wiebe emphasized when he reviewed the tremendous growth of professional organizations in turn-of-the-century America. While Wiebe did not explicitly evaluate these developments, his synthesis threw a very favorable light on the professions. After all, they symbolized reason and order. Who could find disfavor with these values?

Even historians who gave more attention than Wiebe did to the conflict arising in professionalization have frequently stressed the positive intellectual results of this social process. One of the most broad-gauged studies in this genre was sponsored by the American Academy of Arts and Sciences, which directed its attention to the development of scientific and scholarly institutions in the United States between 1860 and 1920.[61] All of the essays in the resulting volume did not fit a single pattern, but most of them analyzed the creation of an organized, unitary specialty out of diverse and often poorly coordinated beginnings; most treated conflict within the discipline; and most either discovered that progress was achieved or assumed that the evidence on this point spoke for itself.[62]

Thomas L. Haskell advanced a similar interpretation in *The Emergence of Professional Social Science*, but he placed his case study of the American Social Science Association — a transitional, semiprofessional institution — in an intellectual rather than a sociological context. The ASSA, he found, provided scholars with a new mode of inquiry at a time (1865–1909) when the traditional forms of explanation were losing respect. Having made its contribution, the ASSA gave way to more specialized groups which offered more "disciplined, intensive communities of inquiry."[63] Professionalization of this sort, Haskell later explained, "ought to be understood as a serious cultural reform movement. . . ."[64]

There were, however, scholars who were less certain than Haskell was that the benefits of professionalization clearly outweighed the costs. Burton J. Bledstein acknowledged that "the culture of professionalism

[61] Alexandra Oleson and John Voss, eds., *The Organization of Knowledge in Modern America, 1860–1920* (Baltimore, 1976); see also Charles E. Rosenberg, "Science in American Society: A Generation of Historical Debate" (Unpublished lecture, 1982).

[62] The editors explained that the diverse institutional structure created by 1920 "would provide the United States with the ability to achieve, within the next generation, a position of eminence in the intellectual world." *Ibid.*, vii. On page xix, they note that "American institutions of learning, like industrial corporations, also have been seen as part of a trend toward nationally oriented, impersonal, hierarchical organizations." See the review essay by Thomas L. Haskell, "Are Professors Professional?" in *Journal of Social History*, 14 (Spring 1981), 485–93; see also Bruce Sinclair, *A Centennial History of the American Society of Mechanical Engineers, 1880–1980* (Toronto, 1980).

[63] Thomas L. Haskell, *The Emergence of Professional Social Science: The American Social Science Association and the Nineteenth-Century Crisis of Authority* (Urbana, 1977).

[64] Thomas L. Haskell, "Professionalization as Cultural Reform," *Humanities in Society*, 1 (Spring 1978), 103–14. John W. Servos has reminded us that specialization has not always been successful: "A Disciplinary Program That Failed: Wilder D. Bancroft and the *Journal of Physical Chemistry*, 1896–1933," *Isis*, 73 (267), 207–32.

has allowed Americans to achieve educated expressions of freedom and self-realization, . . ." but he worried because "it has also allowed them to perfect educated techniques of fraudulence and deceit."[65] Mary O. Furner was similarly ambivalent. She described the struggle in social science between the advocates of social reform and the spokesmen for a science-bred quest for objectivity. The victory of the forces of objectivity "promoted caution, self-scrutiny, care with sources and methods, and a generally heightened rationalism." But the price was high. "Only rarely did professional social scientists do what no one else was better qualified to do: bring expert skill and knowledge to bear on cosmic questions pertaining to the society as a whole."[66] Furner's critique was a gentle reminder that organizational historians, like their progressive predecessors, could find themselves in an uncomfortable trap if they adopted uncritically the values of their subjects.

There was no threat of that if they followed the lead of Jerold S. Auerbach or the other scholars who have dealt primarily with professionalization as an exercise in power. Auerbach studied the legal profession and its encounters with social change in the past century. He treated, critically, the institutional aspects of professionalization, looking, for instance, at the growth in bar associations (from 16 in 1880 to over 600 in 1916!), the rise of the corporate law firms, and the assumption by law schools of a dominant position in legal education. These changes, Auerbach contended, did not improve conditions. The result was a profession virtually controlled by a WASP elite, which used its power and status to ward off threats from liberal reformers and the country's new immigrants. For Auerbach, the central features of the profession were its elitist institutions and a system that exercised power in order to impede social change.[67]

The modern history of the medical profession has also been in part a study of conflict over boundaries and the drive for professional autonomy. Having achieved a high degree of autonomy in regard to their own activities, medical doctors fought a long-term battle against the osteopaths and others who sought similar (and, not incidentally, competing) positions of power. There was no creative, intellectual interaction between the professions. Only a vicious struggle for control. Ultimately state governments decided the issues, for the most part

---

[65] *The Culture of Professionalism: The Middle Class and the Development of Higher Education in America* (New York, 1976), 334.
[66] Mary O. Furner, *Advocacy and Objectivity: A Crisis in the Professionalization of American Social Science, 1868–1905* (Lexington, Mass., 1975), 323–24.
[67] *Unequal Justice: Lawyers and Social Change in Modern America* (London, 1976); see also Stephen Botein's review essay, "Professional History Reconsidered," *American Journal of Legal History,* 21 (January 1977), 60–79. The essays in Thomas L. Haskell, ed., *The Authority of Experts: Historical and Theoretical Essays* (ms.) are for the most part highly critical of their subjects. Haskell sees in the 1970s a "crisis of the professions."

leaving the doctors to regulate themselves but at the same time protecting the rivals they wanted to define out of medicine.[68]

David F. Noble and E. Richard Brown were also interested almost exclusively in power, but in their viewpoint the professions and professional schools were dominated by corporate capital. According to Noble's *America by Design*, the scientific and engineering professions, the educational institutions that sustained them and their research, and the government that issued patent rights to protect the fruits of that research were all "merely a means to corporate ends. . . ."[69] Brown found more evidence of professional autonomy, but he concluded that America's great corporate combines worked through their foundations, the government, and the professional associations to exercise a substantial degree of control over medicine in this country.[70] In this radical perspective, the power and wealth of big business imposed hierarchical order on all of the professional institutions that mattered and controlled all of the scientific and technical advances that promised to yield profits to the corporation.

The idea of consensus by corporate command has, however, won few adherents among the historians of professionalization. Judging from the work done by those historians who have studied professionals engaged in research and engineering within the large firm, the radical interpretation was like one of those formal organizational charts that tell you much about the goals of planners and very little about how an organization actually works. Instead of a simple hierarchy, these scholars found tension between competing centers of power and value systems. Edwin T. Layton, Jr., stressed this theme in *The Revolt of the Engineers*, as did Leonard S. Reich, who analyzed the research and development conducted by the American Telephone & Telegraph Company.[71] Reich concluded that initially AT&T's concern for market control dominated its desire for science-based innovation; as the firm and Bell Labs matured, however, the R&D organization and the professions had an important impact on the company's leaders, who were thus

---

[68] James Gordon Burrow, *Organized Medicine in the Progressive Era: The Move Toward Monopoly* (Baltimore, 1977); Norman Gevitz, *The D.O.'s: Osteopathic Medicine in America* (Baltimore, 1982).

[69] *America by Design: Science, Technology, and the Rise of Corporate Capitalism* (Oxford, 1977), 321.

[70] E. Richard Brown, *Rockefeller Medicine Men: Medicine and Capitalism in America* (Berkeley, 1979). For a more moderate approach see Robert E. Kohler, "The Management of Science: The Experience of Warren Weaver and the Rockefeller Foundation Programme in Molecular Biology," *Minerva*, 14 (Autumn 1976), 279–306; and "A Policy for the Advancement of Science: The Rockefeller Foundation, 1924–29," *Minerva*, 16 (Winter 1978), 480–515.

[71] Edwin T. Layton, Jr., *The Revolt of the Engineers: Social Responsibility and the American Engineering Profession* (Cleveland, 1971); Leonard S. Reich, "Research, Patents, and the Struggle to Control Radio: A Study of Big Business and the Uses of Industrial Research," *Business History Review* 51 (Summer 1977), 208–35; and the same author's "Industrial Research and the Pursuit of Corporate Security: The Early Years of Bell Labs," *Business History Review*, 54 (Winter 1980), 504–29; and "Irving Langmuir and the Pursuit of Science and Technology in the Corporate Environment," *Technology and Culture*, 24 (April 1983), 199–221; also see John W. Servos, "The Industrial Relations of Science: Chemical Engineering at MIT, 1900–1939," *Isis*, 71 (no. 259), 531–49.

encouraged to develop a strong interest in scientific and technological innovation. Stuart W. Leslie's work on General Motors pointed to similar conclusions. There was tension between the goals and values of the scientific professions and the firms that employed their practitioners. While corporate objectives were normally overriding, compromises were reached and policies framed to appeal to both the business and the professional systems.[72] For Layton, Reich, Leslie, and others, there was no doubt that the two systems were in large part independent sources of authority. Even on the corporation's home turf, America's new scientific and engineering professions made their influence felt.

The history of accounting, a profession that has had a very close symbiotic relationship with business, also suggested that lines of authority in America's organizational society were tangled in ways that a radical perspective will not help us understand. Advances in corporate management have clearly spurred innovations in the field of accounting;[73] but in many cases large corporate clients have also prevented accountants from adopting the standard principles promoted by their professional associations. Over time, however, the increasing complexity of the business environment, the new role played by government regulators, and the development of new interests (e.g., investment groups) with a stake in standardization have increased the profession's autonomy.[74] Again, more than one center of power was involved — there were several in business; one in the public sector; another in the profession itself.

These historical studies have indicated that many highly organized networks — not one — have emerged in the past century. This is a subject dealt with explicitly by Hugh G. J. Aitken, author of the pathbreaking *Syntony and Spark — The Origins of Radio.*[75] Aitken explored the relationships between science and technology. In his conceptual framework, there were crucial boundaries between the scientific, technological, and economic systems; at these frontiers, he found some very unusual individuals — Heinrich Hertz, Oliver Lodge, and Guglielmo Marconi — men who functioned as "translators." When they were successful, the three systems were able to interact in a creative fashion, producing those innovations that have played such a crucial role in our economy in this century.

[72] Stuart W. Leslie, "Charles F. Kettering and the Copper-cooled Engine," *Technology and Culture*, 20 (October 1979), 752–76; Stuart W. Leslie, "Thomas Midgley and the Politics of Industrial Research," *Business History Review*, 54 (Winter 1980), 480–503; Stuart W. Leslie, *Boss Kettering* (New York, 1983).
[73] H. Thomas Johnson, "Management Accounting in an Early Multidivisional Organization: General Motors in the 1920s," *Business History Review*, 52 (Winter 1978), 490–517.
[74] Stephen A. Zeff, *Forging Accounting Principles in Five Countries: A History and an Analysis of Trends* (Champaign, 1972).
[75] Hugh G. J. Aitken, *Syntony and Spark — The Origins of Radio* (New York, 1976).

Aitken's framework helped us see how closely linked were the organizational changes taking place in business, in government, and in the professions — a theme that was also skillfully developed in Robert E. Kohler's *From Medical Chemistry to Biochemistry: The Making of a Biochemical Discipline.* Kohler compared the evolution of this discipline in Germany, Great Britain, and the United States. The distinctive American institutions — organs of governance as well as systems of scientific ideas — were shaped to a great extent by political and economic factors. His "political economy of science" provided a model that should help other historians of the professions explain the particular paths that innovation followed and the manner in which these paths related to the need for "institutional consolidation," that is, the quest for power and security.[76]

The history of the professions has thus provided an intellectual bridge between the work being done on technology and the modern corporation and the research directed at America's emerging corporate liberal state. Whether in the future the historical evaluation is primarily favorable toward or critical of the professions will not, I think, be as important as the manner in which this scholarship has already demonstrated the high degree of interdependence between the basic institutions of the organizational society. One of the most significant results of the reorganization of America has been the emergence of a set of professional institutions highly particular to the United States. They have helped a large and important part of middle-class America achieve a good measure of security and at the same time promote technical and organizational innovation. Neither these two goals nor the professions themselves were of special importance to the United States before the great reorganization took place. Now they play a crucial role both in our society and in the organizational synthesis.

The Organizational Synthesis Today

What then does the organizational synthesis look like today? Have we learned anything that we did not already know in 1970? We have of course learned more about the emergence of the professions, the development of the corporate liberal state, and the evolution of a technologically oriented business system. But what in general does this tell us about modern America?

---

[76] Robert E. Kohler, *From Medical Chemistry to Biochemistry: The Making of a Biochemical Discipline* (Cambridge, 1982); see also Kohler's "Medical Reform and Biomedical Science: Biochemistry — a Case Study," in Morris J. Vogel and Charles E. Rosenberg, eds., *The Therapeutic Revolution* (Philadelphia, 1979), 27–66.

The literature reviewed here suggests several answers to this question, one of which deals with the degree of change. Organizational historians have, in my judgment, established the revolutionary nature of the changes that have taken place in America's institutions in the past century. The changes have taken place across a very broad front and have penetrated deeply into the society. They have involved our most important institutions and have created a new economy, polity, and culture. All Americans have to some degree been touched by the manner in which this nation has been reorganized.

We can now recognize several general patterns of organizational change: one was that of functional specialization within and between organizations. Another involved the centralization of authority and the development of elaborate managerial hierarchies to coordinate and control our new, large-scale institutions. While these organizations did a multitude of specific tasks, they performed two general functions that were of overriding importance in modern America. They used their power to protect themselves, reducing risks by bringing under control the relevant parts of their environment; they also promoted technical and organizational innovation in a systematic fashion.[77] Where these two functions — the search for security and the drive to innovate — came into conflict, American institutions developed deep fault lines — alternating, for example, between centralized and decentralized structures in an effort to achieve a satisfactory balance between the need for flexibility and the powerful drive for stability.

Organization-building diffused power and tangled lines of authority in America. The changes were of such breadth and complexity that they were to my mind beyond the control of any group or any coherent social class. This was true even though many of the most fundamental transformations were closely interrelated. The technological innovations associated with the modern corporation were, for instance, linked to the development of our modern professions. Both were tied in numerous ways to the emerging administrative state. But functional specialization sliced across class lines. Organization-building generated intraclass conflict and social tension even when the outcome was a consensus within and between the new institutions. Consensus was not achieved by accident. The politics of institutional change involved above all the engineering of consensus and coalitions by organized interests which developed over the years elaborate networks to protect their interests.

---

[77] These two themes provide an opportunity for organizational historians to draw upon some recent developments in personality theory, a subdiscipline which has to date produced few concepts that historians have been comfortable using. See Robert Hogan, "A Socioanalytic Theory of Personality," in *Nebraska Symposium on Motivation*, 1982 (Lincoln, 1983), 55–89.

While we have thus found out a great deal about the process and the implications of organizational change, we know all too little about the general sources of these broad alterations in our society. In my own view, the crucial synthetic principle is provided by the fundamental transitions that began to take place in America's economy, geopolity, and demography around the end of the nineteenth century. Then, a fast-growing "extensive" economy gave way to a slower-growing "intensive" system. Population growth slowed. The nation's frontiers stabilized. These conditions created a need for new institutions that would provide Americans with a greater measure of security and with the kinds of ongoing technical and organizational innovations essential to our economic success over the long run. The result was America's organizational revolution.[78]

In analyzing that transformation organizational historians have gone beyond the sociological theory of bureaucracy which was such an important influence in 1970. The theory highlighted universal patterns of social change. But comparative research to date has emphasized the differences, not the similarities, between America's modern organizations and those in other countries. Historians have also broken with the sociological tradition by bringing the creative individual — the leader of an organization with substantial discretionary power, for instance, or the "translators" who moved across institutional boundaries — back into history.[79] Historians have as well parted ways with modern social science by infusing the organizational synthesis with the kind of moral judgments that have always characterized the best historical scholarship.[80] As yet, these moral questions are far from settled; no single, dominant interpretation has emerged. But in the meantime, ideological debate has blended with behavioral analysis and detailed historical research to make the organizational school one of the most interesting, vital fields of historical scholarship in the United States today.

---

[78] I have developed these ideas more fully in *America at Middle Age*.
[79] See *ibid.*; Harold C. Livesay, "Entrepreneurial Persistence Through the Bureaucratic Age," *Business History Review*, 51 (Winter 1977), 415–43; Hugh G. J. Aitken, *Syntony and Spark*, esp. 327–36.
[80] Gordan Wright, "History as a Moral Science," *American Historical Review*, 81 (February 1976), 1–11.

[6]

Managerial Enterprise and Competitive Capabilities

ALFRED D. CHANDLER, JR.
Harvard Business School

For the past century large managerial enterprises have been engines of economic growth and transformation in modern economies. These enterprises were created and continued to grow in much the same ways; and that pattern of creation and growth was based on a powerful economic logic. By following the logic of that dynamic, the decisions of entrepreneurs and managers helped to make Germany Europe's most powerful industrial nation before World War I, the United States the most productive in the world from the 1920s to the 1960s, and since the 1960s Japan their most successful competitor.

Departure from the dynamic – the ignoring of its logic – has been equally significant: since the 1960s, it has been largely responsible for the loss of competitive capabilities in such vital American industries as semiconductors, machine tools and consumer electronics and for the weakening of competitive abilities in metals and in machinery, including electrical equipment. On the other hand, in other industries, particularly computers and chemicals, managers sticking to that logic have maintained their competitive power at home and abroad. Finally, individual companies in machinery and metals, by staying with the logic or returning to it, have been able to maintain or retain their competitive strength.

This article begins by reviewing the pattern of the creation and evolution of managerial industrial enterprises and the logic behind that pattern. It then examines specific historical developments in the industries most critical to the growth of modern industrial economies – chemicals, electrical equipment, machinery (light and heavy), metals, motor vehicles and computers. In all of these managers followed the logic of the pattern outlined. It next looks at the competitive performance – success and failure – in those same industries in the past quarter of a century. Its conclusion suggests the long-term implications of the dynamic and the deviations from its logic for maintaining the competitive capabilities of vital American industries.

12 ORGANISATIONAL CAPABILITY & COMPETITIVE ADVANTAGE

The New Institution

By managerial enterprise I mean simply those industrial concerns where decisions as to current production and distribution and those involving investments in facilities and personnel for future production and distribution are made by a hierarchy of lower, middle and top salaried managers. Although such hierarchical organisations were common in military, government, and religious institutions in earlier centuries, they did not appear in commerce and industry until the coming of the railroads in the United States and Europe in the mid-nineteenth century. Before that time owners of business enterprise managed and managers owned.

Such managerial enterprises appeared in production and distribution shortly after they did in transportation and communication. In production they came suddenly in the 1880s and 1890s. From then on they continued to cluster in new capital-intensive industries with similar characteristics. And they were born and grew in much the same manner. From the start such hierarchies of salaried managers were governed by a board of directors consisting of inside directors – full-time senior managers – and outside directors – usually part-time representatives of owners.

Tables 1 and 2 indicate the industries in which large managerial firms have always clustered. Table 1 gives the location country by country and industry by industry in 1973 for all enterprises employing more than 20,000 persons. Seventy per cent of these enterprises clustered in seven of 20 manufacturing groups of the US Standard Industrial Classification – in food, chemicals, oil, primary metals and the three machinery groups. Just over 24 per cent of these were in subcategories of six other two-digit industries which had the same capital-intensive characteristics – cigarettes in tobacco, tires in rubber, newsprint in paper, plate and flat glass in stone, clay and glass, cans and razor blades in fabricated metals, mass-produced cameras in instruments. Only just over five per cent were in the more labour intensive industries – apparel, textiles, lumber, furniture, publishing and printing, leather, and miscellaneous. Table 2 shows that the pattern of concentration was much the same in the United States throughout the twentieth century. This, too, was the case for the 200 largest enterprises in the same years in Great Britain, Germany, France and Japan.

As the Nobel Prize winner, Simon Kuznets, emphasized in his *Economic Growth of Nations*, these capital-intensive industries in which the large firms clustered were the fastest growing of their day; while the labour intensive ones in which few such firms appeared were, in Kuznets'

MANAGERIAL ENTERPRISE AND COMPETITION   13

TABLE 1

DISTRIBUTION OF WORLD'S LARGEST INDUSTRIAL ENTERPRISES WITH MORE
THAN 20,000 EMPLOYEES, BY INDUSTRY AND COUNTRY, 1973ᵃ

Group	Industry	United States	Outside United States	Great Britain	West Germany	Japan	France	Others	Total
20	Food	22	17	13	0	1	1	2	39
21	Tobacco	3	4	3	1	0	0	0	7
22	Textiles	7	6	3	0	2	1	0	13
23	Apparel	6	0	0	0	0	0	0	6
24	Lumber	4	2	0	0	0	0	2	6
25	Furniture	0	0	0	0	0	0	0	0
26	Paper	7	3	3	0	0	0	0	10
27	Printing and publishing	0	0	0	0	0	0	0	0
28	Chemicals	24	28	4	5	3	6	10	52
29	Petroleum	14	12	2	0	0	2	8	26
30	Rubber	5	5	1	1	1	1	1	10
31	Leather	2	0	0	0	0	0	0	2
32	Stone, clay and glass	7	8	3	0	0	3	2	15
33	Primary metals	13	35	2	9	5	4	15	48
34	Fabricated metals	8	6	5	1	0	0	0	14
35	Machinery	22	12	2	3	2	0	5	34
36	Electrical machinery	20	25	4	5	7	2	7	45
37	Transportation equipment	22	23	3	3	7	4	6	45
38	Instrumentsᵇ	4	1	0	0	0	0	0	5
39	Miscellaneous	2	0	0	0	0	0	0	2
—	Conglomerate	19	3	2	1	0	0	0	22
	Total	211	190	50	29	28	24	59	401

Notes: a. The *Fortune* lists include enterprises of non-communist countries only.
            b. Medical equipment and supplies, photographic equipment and supplies,
            and watches and clocks.
Sources: Compiled from 'The Fortune Directory of the 500 Largest Industrial
            Corporations', *Fortune* (May 1974), pp.230–57: 'The Fortune Directory of
            the 300 Largest Industrial Corporations outside the US', *Fortune* (August
            1974), pp.174–81.

words, 'lagging industries'. In the economies of the United States, Great
Britain, and Germany these capital-intensive industries, in turn, made
manufacturing the fastest growing subdivision of the industrial sector
which also included mining, construction, utilities, and transportation
and communication. In the three economies the industrial sector, in its
turn, grew faster than either the agricultural or service sectors. And these
three economies until the 1930s accounted for close to two-thirds of the
world's industrial output. In this sense large managerial enterprises have
been primary engines of economic growth for the past century.[1]

Why, then, did these enterprises appear suddenly in the 1880s and
1890s in capital-intensive high-growth industries? They did so because

14 ORGANISATIONAL CAPABILITY & COMPETITIVE ADVANTAGE

in those industries such enterprises enjoyed the cost advantages of the economies of scale and scope. In those industries larger plants had significant cost advantages over smaller ones in producing a single line of products. The cost per unit dropped much more quickly as volume of output increased than was the case in the labour-intensive industries. Besides such economies of scale large works also often utilised the economies of scope – those that resulted from making different products in one factory using much the same raw and semifinished materials and the same intermediate processes of production.[2]

Such potential cost advantages of scale and scope, however, could only be fully realized if a constant flow of materials was maintained to assure capacity utilisation. If the volume of flow fell below rated capacity, then the actual cost per unit quickly rose. It did so because fixed costs remained high and sunk costs – the original capital investment – were larger than they were in the more labour-intensive industries.

TABLE 2

DISTRIBUTION OF THE 200 LARGEST INDUSTRIAL ENTERPRISES IN THE UNITED STATES, BY INDUSTRY, 1917–73[a]

Group	Industry	1917	1930	1948	1973
20	Food	29	31	27	22
21	Tobacco	6	5	5	3
22	Textiles	6	4	8	3
23	Apparel	3	0	0	0
24	Lumber	3	4	2	4
25	Furniture	0	1	1	0
26	Paper	5	8	6	9
27	Printing and publishing	2	2	2	1
28	Chemicals	20	20	23	28
29	Petroleum	22	26	22	22
30	Rubber	5	5	5	5
31	Leather	4	2	2	0
32	Stone, clay and glass	5	8	6	7
33	Primary metals	31	23	23	19
34	Fabricated metals	11	10	6	5
35	Machinery	17	19	23	16
36	Electrical machinery	5	5	7	13
37	Transportation equipment	24	23	29	19
38	Instruments	1	2	1	4
39	Miscellaneous	1	2	2	1
—	Conglomerate	0	0	0	19
	Total	200	200	200	200

Note: a. See Table 1 notes.
Sources: Appendixes A.1–A.3 for 1917, 1930, and 1948 from Chandler, *Scale and Scope*; figures for 1973 compiled from *Fortune* (May 1974), pp.230–57.

MANAGERIAL ENTERPRISE AND COMPETITION   **15**

The advantages of the economies of scale and scope can be illustrated by cost figures of more than a century ago – those from two of the very first modern managerial industrial enterprises – the Standard Oil Co. (its successor, Exxon, is still the world's largest oil company) and the oldest and still the world's largest chemical companies – the German firms, Bayer, BASF and Hoechst. John D. Rockefeller built the world's largest refinery in Cleveland only a few years after oil was discovered in north-eastern Pennsylvania. By increasing capacity from 500 barrels a day to over 1,500 barrels his enterprise reduced the cost of making a gallon of kerosene from 5¢ in 1870 to 2.5¢ in 1879. In 1881 Rockefeller's Standard Oil and allied companies formed the Standard Oil Trust. Their aim was not to obtain a monopoly. Linked by financial ties, they already controlled close to 90 per cent of the kerosene produced in the United States. Instead, the Trust was formed to provide the legal instrument that permitted the refining facilities of the many companies to be placed under a single management. The new enterprise quickly concentrated close to a quarter of the world's production into three 6,000 barrel refineries, resulting in economies of scale which helped the enterprise to reduce its unit cost per gallon to 0.534¢ in 1884 and to 0.425¢ in 1885. At the same time profit per gallon rose from 0.0534¢ in 1884 to 1.004¢ in 1885. At that cost Standard Oil's American-made kerosene was able to undersell that made from Russian oil in Europe and that made from South-east Asian oil in China, and also to produce profits that created at least three of the world's largest industrial fortunes.

When the three German companies began production of a new-man-made dye, red alizarin, its price was close to 200 marks per kilo. By 1878 the price had fallen to 23 marks per kilo, and by 1886 it had dropped to nine marks. Comparable price reductions were made in other dyes. The addition of new dyes and then pharmaceuticals added little cost to the production of each item and the additions permitted a reduction in the total unit cost of the others. By the 1880s a large German plant was producing more than 500 different dyes and pharmaceuticals at unit costs far below that of smaller competitors.

The story of oil and chemicals was repeated in the same years in other industries using new capital-intensive technologies of production including steel, copper, aluminium, glass, rubber, branded packaged food and drug products, and a wide variety of machinery. And they suddenly appeared in the 1880s and the 1890s because the completion and integration of modern transportation and communication networks – the railroad, the telegraph, the steamship, and the cable – made possible for the first time in history the high-volume, high-speed, flow of goods and messages without which substantial economies of scale and scope

16 ORGANISATIONAL CAPABILITY & COMPETITIVE ADVANTAGE

could not be realized. Transportation that depended on the power of animals, wind, and current was too slow and too uncertain to maintain the level of flow necessary to achieve the potential cost advantages of the new technologies.

In all these industries, however, the new large plants were able to maintain the cost advantages of scale and scope only if the entrepreneurs who built them made two other sets of investments. They had to create a national and then international marketing and distributing organisation, and they had to recruit teams of lower and middle managers to co-ordinate the flow of products through the processes of production and distribution and top managers to coordinate and monitor current operations and to plan and allocate resources for future activities. The first to make such a three-pronged set of investments in manufacturing, marketing, and management essential to exploit fully the economies of scale and scope quickly dominated their industries and continued to do so for decades.

It is important here to distinguish between the *inventors* of a product or process, the *pioneers* who first commercialise such an innovation, and the *first movers* who made the three-pronged investment essential to exploit fully the economies of scale or scope. For example, in mainframe computers several pioneers made investments large enough to market the innovation on a national scale. But it was IBM's massive investments in the production, distribution and management of its System 360 that made it the first mover in the industry. And what IBM did in computers, Rockefeller did in oil and the three German companies in chemicals.

The tripartite investment gave the first movers powerful advantages; to benefit from comparable costs, challengers had to construct plants of comparable size, and to do so after the first movers had already begun to work out the bugs in the new production processes. The challengers had to create distribution and selling organisations to capture markets where first movers were already established. They had to recruit management teams to compete with those already well down the learning curve in their specialised activities of production, distribution, and (in technologically advanced industries) research and development. Challengers did appear, but they were only a few.

The three-pronged investment by the first movers (as in the case of German chemicals there were often more than one) transformed the structure of industries. The new capital-intensive industries were quickly dominated by a small number of large managerial enterprises which competed for market share and profit in a new oligopolistic manner. Price remained a significant competitive weapon, but these firms competed more forcefully through functional and strategic efficiency; that is, by carrying out processes of production and distribution more capably by improving both product and process through systematical research and development, by locating more suitable sources of supply, by providing more effective marketing services, by product differentiation (in branded packaged products primarily through advertising), and finally by moving more quickly into expanding markets and out of declining ones. The test of such competition was changing market share, and in the new oligopolistic industries market share and profits changed constantly.

Such oligopolistic competition sharpened the product-specific capabilities of workers and managers. Such capabilities, plus the retained earnings from profits of the new capital-intensive technologies, became the basis for the continuing growth of these managerial enterprises. Firms did grow by combining with competitors (horizontal combination) or by moving backward to control materials and forward to control outlets (vertical integration), but they took these routes usually in response to specific situations. For most, the continuing long-term strategy of growth was expansion into new markets – either into new geographical areas or into related product markets. The move into geographically distant markets was normally based on competitive advantage of organisational capabilities developed from exploiting economies of scale. Moves into related industries rested more on those advantages developed from the exploitation of the economies of scope. Such organizational capabilities honed by oligopolistic competition provided the dynamic for the continuing growth of such firms, of the industries which they dominated, and of the national economies in which they operated.

The Historical Experience to World War II

Of all the new capital-intensive industries in what historians have properly called the Second Industrial Revolution – those that permitted the exploitation of the cost advantages of scale and scope – the chemical industry was the most technologically advanced and provided the widest range of new industrial and consumer products including man-made dyes, medicines, fertilizers, textiles, film, and other materials. The first major products of the new industry were synthetic dyes.

Here the British entrepreneurs were the pioneers. An Englishman, William Perkin, invented the first such dyes. The world's largest market for man-made dyes remained until after World War II the huge British textile industry. Dyes were made from coal, and Britain had the largest supplies of high quality coal in Europe. In the 1870s, Britain had almost every comparative advantage in the new dye industry. It lacked only

18   ORGANISATIONAL CAPABILITY & COMPETITIVE ADVANTAGE

experienced chemists, and British entrepreneurs had little difficulty in hiring trained German chemists to their factories. By any economic criteria the British entrepreneurs should have quickly dominated the world in this new industry. But they failed to make the essential investments in production, distribution and management. Instead the Germans – Bayer, BASF, and Hoesch and three smaller enterprises – made the first mover investments.[3]

The Bayer experience makes the point. In the 1880s Frederick Bayer & Co. was a relatively small pioneer. In that decade under the guidance of a young chemist, Carl Duisburg, still in his twenties, the company, exploiting economies of scope, developed new dyes and then pharmaceuticals. In 1891 it decided to expand by purchasing a dye maker on the Rhine near Cologne – a better location for receiving high movements of supplies into and finished goods out of the works than the original works at Eberfeld. At first the plan was to enlarge the Leverkusen plant, but then Duisburg convinced his colleagues to scrap its existing facilities and build a giant new works that would meet the company's needs for the next half-century.

Duisburg designed the new works to assure a steady flow of materials from their arrival at the works through the processes of production to storage and shipment of the final products. There were to be five processing departments, a sixth department consisting of the many workshops and offices required to service the processing plants, and Department VII, Central Administration. Department I, which included raw-material storage and the pump house and concentrated on the production of inorganic chemicals, was situated along the Rhine wharf. Separated from it by a street 120 feet wide (such streets separated all the departments) was Department II, which produced the organic intermediates. Then came Department III, making alizarin and azo dye stuffs. Department IV produced aniline dyes. Department V made pharmaceuticals. The last row back from the river consisted of the grinding and mixing plants, the refrigeration facilities, the power station, and the packaging and other works that made up Department VI. Along the wide streets ran the canals to supply the water needed in processing, the gas and electric lines, and 40 miles of railway tracks.

By this plan each of the five production departments was to have its own laboratories and engineering staff, for Duisberg thought it essential 'to place all chemists working in the same area in a common laboratory, so as to make possible a common working of various people, and encourage each individual by mutual stimulation'. The offices of the production engineers were to be close to the chemical laboratories so 'that works chemists can at any time get into direct communication

MANAGERIAL ENTERPRISE AND COMPETITION   19

with the works engineers'.[4] When completed the works covered 760 acres, and employed close to 8,000 workers. There was no comparable chemical establishment anywhere in the world except those of BASF and Hoechst. Today Leverkusen is still one of the most efficient chemical works in the world. Its laboratories became and remained amongst the most innovative in the world, producing a stream of new dyes, pharmaceuticals, films, fertilizers, varnishes, resins, and other chemical products.

By the time the Leverkusen works was in operation, Bayer's global sales force of experienced chemists were contacting and working with more than 20,000 customers; for every user of dyes in cloth, leather, paper, and other materials had to be taught how to apply the new products that had very different properties from natural dyes. And by the turn of the century Bayer and the other German chemical leaders had created the largest and most carefully defined managerial hierarchies the world had yet seen.

As might be expected, the resulting German competitive advantages quickly demolished Britain's economic comparative advantages. In 1913 160,000 tons of dyes were produced. Of these the German firms made 140,000 tons (72 per cent being produced by the Big Three); 10,000 more were produced by Swiss neighbours up the Rhine.[5] Total British production was 4,400 tons. The story was much the same for pharmaceuticals, films, agricultural chemicals, and electro-chemicals.

The electrical equipment industry, while employing a smaller number of professionally trained technicians and scientists, was even more of a transformer of economic life than chemicals. Not only did the new industry provide new sources of light and power that so altered urban living and transportation, but it changed the ways of the working place. Moreover, a new electrolytic process transformed and greatly reduced costs of producing copper, aluminum, and several chemicals. In this industry British pioneers were as active as those in Germany and the United States. But within a decade after the establishment by Thomas Edison of the first central power station (it was in New York City) two first movers in the United States – General Electric and Westinghouse – and two in Germany – Siemens and AEG – had made the investments in production and distribution necessary to exploit the economies of scale and scope.

Again, the German story is illustrative. In 1903, after merging with a major competitor, Siemens embarked on a ten year plan of systematising and rationalising production by concentrating production in what became the world's largest industrial complex under a single management. Where Bayer had built a single giant works, Siemens

20   ORGANISATIONAL CAPABILITY & COMPETITIVE ADVANTAGE

constructed several – one employing more than 8,000 workers for telecommunication equipment and instruments, and somewhat smaller ones for large machinery, small motors, dynamos, electrochemicals, and cables. Employing more than 20,000 workers and covering several square miles, the district of Berlin which this complex dominated soon became officially designated as Siemensstadt. As in the case of Bayer this massive investment in production was financed primarily from retained earnings. In these same years, its rival AEG built a comparable though somewhat less massive set of works only a few miles away. Nothing comparable occurred in Britain, even though Sir William Mather, senior partner of Mather & Platt, one of the largest British textile machinery manufacturers, had obtained the Edison patents at the same time as had Rathenau at AEG.

As a result, by 1913 two-thirds of the electrical equipment machinery made in British factories by British labour was produced by subsidiaries of General Electric, Westinghouse and Siemens. AEG sold more products in Britain than did the largest British firm. Mather & Platt had become a minor producer of electrical equipment for factories. From the 1890s on continuing research and development to improve existing products and develop new ones was carried out in Schenectady, Pittsburgh and Berlin, but not in Britain.

What was true of chemicals was also true of steel, copper and other metals, and in heavy and light machinery. In metals, the British pioneered, but the Germans and Americans made the necessary investments that quickly drove the British from international markets. In machinery, the British did not even try. The Germans quickly dominated the production of heavy processing machinery and equipment for the new industries of the Second Industrial Revolution, and for many of the old; while the Americans acquired a near global monopoly in machinery which was produced in volume by fabricating and assembling standardised parts, a process that by the 1880s was already known as 'the American system of manufacturing'.[6]

In office machinery, such first movers as Burroughs Adding Machine, National Cash Register, the Remington Typewriter Co., and the Computing-Tabulating-Recording Co. (later renamed International Business Machines) all dominated their industries world wide until well after World War II. In sewing machines the Singer Sewing Machine and in agricultural equipment McCormick Harvesting Machine were world leaders. Indeed in 1913 the two largest commercial enterprises in imperial Russia were Singer and International Harvester. (The latter was a 1902 merger in which the McCormick company was the major player.) By then Singer produced 79,000 machines annually in

MANAGERIAL ENTERPRISE AND COMPETITION   21

its Moscow factory with a work force of 2,500 wage earners and 300 salaried employees; while its sales force of more than 25,000 workers covered the vast territory from the Sea of Japan to the Baltic. For both companies their Russian operations were smaller than those of their other European business based on Singer's large factories in Scotland and Germany and Harvester's major plant in Germany. By World War I, American firms had achieved comparable global competitive power in the production of elevators (Otis Elevator), pumps (Worthington Pump), boilers (Babcock & Wilcox), printing presses (Merganthaler Linotype) and heating equipment (American Radiator). On the other hand, American machine tool makers which provided much of the equipment used by these companies in their processes of production, did not make large investments in production, distribution, and management. That industry continued to consist of a sizable number of small, mostly family-owned firms.[7]

In the inter-war years chemical, electrical equipment and machinery industries continued to be major drivers of economic growth. As late as 1946, 45 per cent of scientific personnel in American industry were employed in the first two of these industries – 30 per cent in chemicals, and 15 per cent in electrical equipment.[8] The chemical industry in the United States prospered as such pre-World War I firms as Du Pont, Dow, Monsanto, and two major mergers (Union Carbide in 1917 and Allied Chemical in 1920) expanded into new markets based on the organisational capabilities they had developed in the exploitation of scale and scope. So, too, in Britain formation of Imperial Chemical Industries in 1925 permitted the British industry to begin to challenge the Germans. But in other key industries – electrical equipment, heavy industrial and light mass produced machinery – British enterprises never became major contenders.

After World War I, the automobile industry surpassed all others as the prime source of economic growth and transformation. By 1908, less than a decade after the automobile was first sold commercially, the world's two largest automobile companies were the Ford Motor Co. and General Motors. It was Ford which made the first mover investments. With the building of the Highland Park factory where the moving assembly line was adopted in 1913, the creation of a national and international marketing organisation, and the recruitment of a team of excellent managers, Ford had even a stronger world-wide monopoly of low priced cars than did the American light machinery makers in their industries. Comparable investments in middle priced and high priced automobiles were made in the 1920s by General Motors and then by Chrysler. Both soon successfully challenged Ford in the low price range

22   ORGANISATIONAL CAPABILITY & COMPETITIVE ADVANTAGE

– GM with Chevrolet and Chrysler with Plymouth. By developing a full line of cars (and so to benefit more extensively from the economies of scale) both were able to remain profitable when the drastic drop in demand in the 1930s meant that the smaller middle priced manufacturers could no longer remain viable as automobile makers, with only Willys (it became American Motors) surviving beyond the early 1950s (thanks to its production of the military Jeep). By 1929 the United States produced 85 per cent of the world's automobiles and much of the remaining 15 per cent were produced by subsidiaries of American companies abroad. Ford and General Motors were among the leading car producers in Britain and Germany. In 1928 all but 347 of the 25,000 automobiles produced in Japan were assembled by General Motors and Ford.[9]

In automobiles, functional and strategic competition led to rapid shifts in market share and profits. Henry Ford destroyed his first mover advantages by firing his most effective executives (several went to General Motors), and his company's share of the market dropped from 55 per cent in 1921 to 19 per cent in 1940; while General Motors' share rose from 11 per cent to 45 per cent and Chrysler, after acquiring Dodge in 1925, from four per cent to 24 per cent in 1940. From 1927 until 1937 Ford's loses were about $100 million. In the same depression years General Motors profits after taxes were just under $2 billion! (In the early 1930s annual GNP dropped to below $100 billion.) Only after Henry Ford died and after his son hired a group of General Motors managers to restructure his company did Ford begin to regain competitive strength and profits.

Historical Experience Following World War II

In the years after World War II, as the information revolution transformed industries and economies, the computer industry took on the role that the automobile had had in the 1920s and the chemical, electrical and machinery industries in the years before World War I. The beginnings and the processes of growth of the leaders in this industry were similar to those of earlier industries with one striking different – most pioneers were not, as they had been in the past, entrepreneurs. Instead they were long-established managerial enterprises in closely related industries.

The first to appreciate the opportunities for the commercial application of the giant costly computers initially developed for scientific and military purposes were American business machine companies. In 1950 Remington Rand, the nation's leading typewriter company, began to develop UNIVAC, the first computer designed for business uses. (In 1955 Remington Rand merged with Sperry, a large defence contractor, to

MANAGERIAL ENTERPRISE AND COMPETITION   23

form Sperry Rand in order to obtain greater capabilities in research and production of electronic products.) Other leading business machinery firms – IBM, Burroughs Adding Machine, National Cash Register, and Honeywell – quickly followed. (Honeywell, a maker of heat control systems, had in 1934 challenged IBM by acquiring a small tabulating computing company.) Other pioneers were large established enterprises with electronic capabilities – Raytheon, General Electric, RCA, and Philco. The only new firm to compete with the pioneering mainframe producers was Control Data. All these pioneers made substantial investments in producing and distributing the new machine.[10]

But IBM was the first pioneer to make the investments that transformed it into the industry's first mover, much as Ford, Rockefeller and the leading American and German chemical, machinery and metal companies had done in earlier years. The strategy of IBM's top managers, particularly Thomas Watson, Jr., was to reach as wide a commercial market as possible by utilising the cost advantages of the economies of scale. This called for all-purpose machines, whose development demanded not only the standardisation of machines and components but also compatibility between different closely related products. Several years of intensive investment in research and then in production led in 1964 to the marketing of the System 360, a broad line of compatible mainframe computers with peripherals for a wide range of uses. The massive investment in research and production, the swift expansion of the company's international marketing organisation, and the impressive increase in the size of its management gave IBM the dominance in the industry that it retains today.[11]

With the one exception of Control Data, IBM's successful competitors continued to be business machine companies. Like Remington Rand, these three each acquired electronic companies in order to improve their production and research competences. On the other hand, the electronic companies dropped out. Raytheon and General Electric sold their operations to Honeywell, RCA's computer activities were acquired by Sperry Rand, and Philco dropped its computer operations soon after it was taken over by the Ford Motor Co.

In mini- and micro-computers, entrepreneurial firms played a greater role, for while the established business machinery firms were concentrating on developing the capabilities of the mainframe, other opportunities emerged for machines using different technologies for different markets. In minicomputers – low cost machines for specific purposes, particularly scientific and academic – the first mover was Ken Olsen's Digital Equipment (DEC), which after several years of development, began volume production of the PDP-8 line in 1965.

24 ORGANISATIONAL CAPABILITY & COMPETITIVE ADVANTAGE

Again, heavy investment in production was accompanied by the creation of a world-wide marketing network and a comparable increase in the size of management. In 1968 Edson de Castro, the engineer who headed the design team for the PDP-8, left DEC to form Data General and made a comparable set of investments. However, a third pioneer, Scientific Data Systems (SDS), failed to do so. After it was taken over by Xerox in 1969, it soon disappeared from the scene.

The most successful challengers to DEC and Data General were not entrepreneurial enterprises but established managerial ones. By 1980 DEC ranked second and Data General fourth in revenues generated. IBM was first, Burroughs third, and Hewlett Packard, an established producer of electronic measuring and testing instruments, fifth. The sixth was Wang Laboratories, a first mover with a new product for a different market – word processing and office systems. And these six accounted for 75 per cent of revenues generated in the minicomputer branch of the industry.[12]

The pattern is much the same in personal (micro) computers. These machines employed a still different architecture for a still different market – the individual user. The first entrepreneurial firms to make extensive three-pronged inter-related investments – Apple Computer, Tandy (Radio Shack), and Commodore – accounted by 1980 for 72 per cent of dollar sales in the United States. By then, three pioneers which together in 1976 accounted for 50 per cent of sales, but which failed to make such investments, had already dropped by the wayside. Two years later, however, three established firms – IBM, the Nippon Electric Co. (NEC) of Tokyo and Hewlett Packard – moved in. By 1982 they accounted for 35 per cent of sales; driving the market share of the three entrepreneurial first movers down to 48 per cent.[13]

Like the American machinery firms of earlier years, these computer companies quickly moved abroad. IBM almost immediately became the leading producer of mainframe computers in Europe. DEC led in microcomputers. By the mid-1980s Apple, IBM and NEC produced half the world's output of personal computers. All but one of the successful European or Japanese competitors were created by long-established enterprises. True to form, British pioneers failed to make the necessary investments. So by 1974 only a little over a quarter of all installations in Britain were from British producers.[14]

This brief review of the patterns of growth of the managerial enterprises that dominated the past century's most vital industries demonstrates the logic behind these patterns by emphasising three points.

First, unless the necessary investments in production, marketing, and management were made to exploit fully the cost advantages of scale and scope, neither the enterprises nor the industries in which they operated became competitive in national and international markets. To remain competitive, entrepreneurs in a new capital-intensive industry had to create enterprises administered by teams of lower, middle, and top managers.

The second point is that the opportunity to make such investments and to create such organisations was short-lived. Once the opportunity was lost, it was difficult for an enterprise and its national industry to regain competitive capabilities, even in its own domestic market. The British created such capabilities in chemicals with the formation of ICI, but they never developed a strong competitive edge in electrical equipment, heavy and light machinery, automobiles, and computers. Nor did they in steel, copper, or other metals.

The third point is that the first movers and the few successful challengers continued to grow by moving abroad and into related industries. The Americans became multinational in light machinery, automobiles, and computers using capabilities based on the economies of scale. The German and American electrical companies and the German and then American chemical companies also became multi-industrial by moving into related product markets based on the capabilities developed in using the economies of scope. These patterns of growth, based on organisational capabilities developed by exploiting the cost advantages of scale and scope, intensified inter-firm competition. The full impact of international and inter-industry competition created by such growth, however, was held back by world events. World War I and the massive inflation and military occupation of the Ruhr and the Rhineland that followed kept German companies out of international markets for almost a decade. They returned with impressive strength between 1925 and 1929, only to be reined in again by the coming of the Great Depression, then Hitler's command economy and the disastrous Second World War. Depression, global war and post-war recovery also dampened or redirected the growth of American enterprises and those of the smaller number of managerial enterprises in European nations other than Germany. It was not, therefore, until the 1960s, after the economic health of the European nations had been fully restored, and after Japan, following a massive transfer of technology, began to industrialise rapidly, that the international competition which had been developing before 1914 became a full-fledged reality. In the same post-World War II years, unprecedented investments in research and

26   ORGANISATIONAL CAPABILITY & COMPETITIVE ADVANTAGE

development intensified inter-industry competition in the United States
and Europe.

The American Response to Intensified Competition

Because American enterprises had become so numerous in the capital-
intensive industries at home, as well as abroad (Table 1) and because the
American market was the world's largest and richest, the new competition provided many American enterprises in these industries with the
greatest challenge that they had to face since their establishment decades
earlier. The challenge was unexpected, as the American economy of
the 1960s was prosperous. Even so, markets became saturated. With
capacity underutilised, costs rose.

Many American managers responded as they had in the past, and as
the office machinery firms did in the 1960s, by re-investing to improve
their capabilities in their own and closely related industries. Many others, however, began to grow by moving for the first time into industries
where their enterprise had no particular competitive advantage. These
companies were cash-laden precisely because the post-war years of
American hegemony had been so prosperous. Moreover, because they
had had little competition abroad since well before World War II, and
because they were being told by academic practitioners of management
science that management was a general skill, many – but certainly not
all – had come to believe that if they were successful managers in their
own industries, they could be just as successful in others. So they sought
to invest retained earnings in industries that appeared to show a greater
or even potential than their own, even though those industries were only
distantly related or even unrelated to their companies' core capabilities.
Because of their lack of knowledge of the operations of their target
industries, they obtained facilities and personnel through acquisitions or
occasionally merger rather than, as had been the case in earlier moves
into related industries, through direct investment, that is by building
of their own factories and hiring or transferring their own workers and
managers.

By the late 1960s, the drive for growth through acquisition and merger
had become almost a mania. The number of acquisitions and mergers
rose from just over 2,000 in 1965 to over 6,000 in 1969, dropping back
to 2,861 by 1974. During the period 1963–72 close to three-quarters
of the assets acquired were for product diversification. Half of these
were in unrelated product lines. In the years 1973–77 half of all assets
acquired through merger and acquisition came from those in unrelated
industries.[15]

Such unprecedented diversification led to another new phenomenon. That was the separation between top management at the corporate office – the executives responsible for co-ordinating, managing, and planning and allocating resources for the enterprise as a whole – and the middle managers responsible for maintaining the competitive capabilities of the operating divisions in the battle for market share and profits.

Massive diversification led to such separation for two reasons. First, the top managers often had little specific knowledge of, and experience with, the technological processes and markets of many of the divisions or subsidiaries they had acquired. The second was simply that the large number of different businesses acquired created an extraordinary overload in decision-making at the corporate office. Whereas before World War II the corporate office of large diversified international enterprises rarely managed more than ten divisions and only the largest as many as 25, by 1969 numerous companies were operating from 40 to 70 divisions and a few had even more.[16]

Because few senior executives had the training or experience necessary to evaluate the proposals and monitor the performance of so many divisions in so many different activities, they had to rely more and more on impersonal statistics. As Thomas Johnson and Robert Kaplan point out in *Relevance Lost: The Rise and Fall of Managerial Accounting*, such data were becoming increasingly less pertinent to controlling costs realistically and understanding the complexities of competitive battles.[17]

Managerial weaknesses resulting from the separation of top and operating management quickly led to another new phenomenon – the selling off of operating units in unheard-of numbers. Before the mid-1960s, divestitures were rare. By the early 1970s they had become commonplace. In 1965 there was only one divestiture for every 11 mergers; in 1969, at the height of the merger boom, the ratio was 1 to 8; by 1970, 1 to 2.4; and then, for the four years 1974 to 1977, the ratio was close to or even under 1 to 2.[18]

The unprecedented number of mergers and acquisitions followed so shortly by an unprecedented number of divestitures helped to bring into being another new phenomenon – the buying and selling of corporations as an established business, and a most lucrative one at that. Although the industrialists pioneered this business, the financial community prospered from it. This brand-new business was further stimulated by an unprecedented change in the nature of 'ownership' of American industrial companies, that is in the holders, buyers, and sellers of their shares. Before World War II the majority of securities were held by relatively wealthy individuals and families. Even as late as 1952 only 4.2 per cent of the United States population held corporate

28   ORGANISATIONAL CAPABILITY & COMPETITIVE ADVANTAGE

securities – a figure which included owners of mutual funds.[19] The major institutional investors were insurance companies and trust departments of banks. Such institutional investors, like wealthy individuals, normally invested for the long-term – for growth and assets rather than current dividends.

After World War II, increasingly large amounts of the voting shares of American industrial enterprises were held in the portfolios of pension and mutual funds. These funds had their beginnings in the 1920s, but grew little in the depressed years of the 1930s. By the 1960s, however, they had come into their own. The success of the managers of these funds was measured by their ability to have the value (dividends and appreciation) of their portfolios outperform the Standard & Poor index of the value of 500 companies. To perform satisfactorily they had constantly to buy and sell securities – transactions made more on the basis of short-term performance than on long-term potential. As time passed these portfolio managers – the new owners of American industry – increasingly traded securities in large blocks of 10,000 shares or more.

As the number of such funds and the volume of the securities they individually traded increased, both block sales and the turnover of securities traded rose rapidly. The proportion of the volume of shares traded annually on the New York Stock Exchange to total shares listed grew from 12 per cent and 16 per cent in the early 1960s to over 50 per cent by the 1980s. Block trading accounted for only 3.1 per cent of total sales on the New York Stock Exchange in 1965. By 1985 it accounted for 51 per cent of sales. In those years, too, the volume of total transactions rose on the Exchange rose from close to half a billion shares annually in the early 1950s to three billion at the end of the decade and to 27.5 billion by 1985.[20]

The great increase in the total volume of transactions, the rise in the turnover rate, and the growth of block sales made possible still another new phenomenon – the coming of an institutionalised market for corporate control. For the first time individuals, groups, and companies could obtain control of well-established enterprises in industries in which the buyers had no previous connection simply by purchasing their shares on the stock exchange. Large blocks of stock were being traded regularly; and buyers had little difficulty in raising funds for these purchases from financial institutions and financiers.

Thus the diversification of the 1960s, the divestitures of the 1970s, the business of buying and selling corporations stimulated by the shift in ownership, and finally the coming of the market for corporate control greatly facilitated the ease in which the modern managerial enterprise could be restructured. Such firms could now be bought, sold, split up, and recombined in ways that would have been impossible before the acquisition wave of the 1960s.

By the mid-1970s the intensified competition which had led to a rejection of the logic behind the dynamic of growth demanded extensive re-investment in reshaping and rationalising product-specific facilities and skills if industries were to maintain and regain competitiveness. At the same time this deviation made necessary the restructuring of enterprises which had grown so large and unwieldy through unbridled diversification. But the return to the logic through restructuring of enterprises and of industries was now clearly affected by the desires of investment banks and other financial institutions to maintain the new and profitable business of buying and selling companies and the needs for pension and mutual fund managers to maintain the current value of their portfolios.

Competitive Performance since the 1960s

What impact did the new developments have on the competitive performance of industries which were central to economic growth and competition in modern industrial urban economies? What relationships did they have to the ability of the chemical and computer industries to retain their competitive capabilities; to the abilities of the automobile and lesser extent metal industries to restore theirs, and to the failure of such industries as semiconductors (so closely allied to computers) and machine tools (so closely allied to the machinery industry) to maintain theirs? Answers to these questions are particularly important, as all these industries faced the same external environment – inflation and oil shocks in the 1970s, rising costs of capital, the fluctuating dollar, and anti-trust and other government regulatory legislation.

The American computer industry remains strong and competitive. The major players have changed little in the past decade. Of the 20 largest producers of hardware in 1987, only two had been founded in the 1980s. One, Compaq (ranked 14) was the single successful challenger in existing sectors (in this case microcomputers). It announced in its first annual report a strategy of 'thinking of itself as a major company in its formative stage rather than a small company with big plans'. It has invested accordingly. The other, Sun Microsystems, number 20 in size (and like one smaller competitor, Apollo) followed the pattern of entrepreneurial start-ups in the past, developing a new architecture for a new market – in this case workstations.[21]

Business machinery firms still dominate mainframe production and have major positions in the other two major sectors of the industry:

30 ORGANISATIONAL CAPABILITY & COMPETITIVE ADVANTAGE

Sperry Rand and Burroughs in 1986 merged to form UNISYS making it the second largest computer producer in the United States. The disappearance of the electronic companies suggests weaknesses of the highly diversified enterprise and of diversification into unrelated industries. GE, RCA, Ford with Philco, Xerox with SDS, by relying on profit centres and statistical cost controls, exited because they failed to put the resources into computer lines necessary to compete with the business machine companies and the few entrepreneurial firms which made first mover investments. On the other hand, Hewlett Packard, for 30 years a highly successful producer of electronic instruments, and even less diversified than the machinery firms, did make the investments necessary to become a major player in mini and microcomputers. In minicomputers, Digital has made a comeback through its VAX networking systems. The most important challenger, besides established foreign firms, is a venerable managerial enterprise from a related industry – AT&T with its UNIX operating system that permits portability of software across hardware of many different manufacturers.[22]

In 1987, American companies still enjoyed just under 60 per cent of the European market for mainframe and minicomputers, and just over 20 per cent of the Japanese. In Europe IBM's market share was 35 per cent, DEC's seven per cent, UNISYS' five per cent and Hewlett Packard's three per cent. In Japan IBM had 15 per cent, UNISYS three per cent, and NCR two per cent. In microcomputers Apple and IBM, together with NEC, accounted for 50 per cent of the world market. Except in some peripherals foreign competition in the United States remained limited.[23]

In semiconductors the story has been very different. This industry, which supplies critical components for telecommunications, factory automation, robotics, airspace, and production controls as well as for computers, was created in the United States. In the mid-1970s, the pioneering American firms held 60 per cent of the world market, 95 per cent of the domestic market, half the European market and a quarter of the Japanese. By 1987 their share of the world market share was reduced to 40 per cent, while the Japanese share had risen to 50 per cent. By then the United States had become a net importer, with the Japanese supplying 25 per cent of its market. The Japanese controlled over 80 per cent of the world's sales of dynamic random access memory (DRAMs) which had been invented by an American company, Intel. Intel, Motorola and Texas Instruments have moved into the most technically advanced sectors, producing particularly advanced microprocessors. Even here they are being challenged by the Japanese. IBM, now the only world class producer of semiconductors in the United

MANAGERIAL ENTERPRISE AND COMPETITION   **31**

States, is working with the Defense Department through SEMATECH, a consortium of American companies, to try to save the industry.[24]

What happened? Again the diversified electronics firms – RCA and GE – with the greatest capabilities for production and continuing research pulled out, while Ford's takeover of Philco destroyed the potential there. More serious, however, was the failure of the pioneering firms to make the investments in production, distribution and management essential to become first movers. If IBM is the prototype of the giant managerial enterprise as first mover, surely the semiconductor companies in California's Silicon Valley epitomise entrepreneurial enterprise. Instead of making the long-term investments, creating the necessary organisational capabilities and continuing to reinvest, these entrepreneurial enterprises remained small or sold out, often to the Japanese. Repeatedly groups of engineers left their companies to start new ones. Both old and new failed to make the necessary long-term commitments.

In Japan, on the other hand, large established firms did make the investments needed to become first movers in the new industry and did develop the organisational capabilities that permitted them so quickly to destroy American competitive advantages. As an MIT study on American productivity notes: 'The rapidity of the Japanese advance and the American retreat and the emphasis of the Japanese on those sectors with the greatest potential for the future suggests that without dramatic structural changes, the decline of the US industry will not only continue but will accelerate'.[25] But if the experience of the entrepreneurial chemical, electrical, and machinery firms in Britain in the 1880s and 1890s provides any indication, such restructuring is difficult and the opportunity to regain competitiveness is fleeting.

In light machinery, the response to intensified competition varied. The experience of sewing machines and agricultural machinery contrasted sharply from that of business machines. In both the leading firms have been destroyed. In sewing machines the American industry's capabilities deteriorated when Singer, the dominant firm, diversified into machine tools and several defence-related industries in which it had few strong organisational capabilities. Soon it dropped out of the sewing machine business altogether. As defence demands fell off so did Singer's profits. In 1987 a takeover specialist, Paul A. Bilzern, financed by Shearson and T. Boone Pickens, obtained the company. He had sold off eight of the remaining 12 divisions before he was convicted of fraud and sued by the Federal Government for over $30 million.[26]

In agricultural and construction equipment (International Harvester had moved into the latter in the 1920s) American firms did better. John

32 ORGANISATIONAL CAPABILITY & COMPETITIVE ADVANTAGE

Deere, Caterpillar, and other leading firms reinvested in improving product and process. International Harvester, however, was not dismembered by a corporate raider but by a highly touted business manager who came from Xerox with the largest salary yet offered a CEO in the United States. To increase shareholder value he concentrated on cutting costs, including a reduction of wages that led to a bitter strike. In the resulting sell-off in 1984 and 1985, American companies purchased the operating divisions of Harvester – Caterpillar acquired the Turbine Division, and Tenneco, a conglomerate, its agricultural equipment operations. As Tenneco already owned a long-established agricultural equipment enterprise, J.I. Case, it began to rationalise facilities and personnel in ways to regain competitive strength.[27]

In machine tools, on which American machinery, automobile, and other industries depend as much as does the computer industries on semiconductors, the story has relevant similarities to that of semiconductors. In both the pioneers failed to become first movers. The older industry had long been operated through small enterprises, many of which were in the 1960s still owned and managed by the founders' families. These firms had not made the investments necessary to exploit fully either the economies of scope, as had German machinery firms earlier in the century, nor to exploit the economies of scale, as the Japanese did after World War II. Conglomerates such as Textron and Houdaille moved in, consolidating many small firms. By 1982 85 per cent of American machine tool production was concentrated in 12 firms. But the conglomerates did not rationalise the consolidated facilities, as Tenneco has begun to do in farm machinery, or invest in new ones. Instead they used the firms as cash cows to generate income to be re-invested in other industries. When demand fell off in this cyclical business, they spun them off. As a result of this failure to restructure and re-invest, the United States share of world production dropped from 25 per cent in the mid-1960s to less than 10 per cent in 1986. More significant for an industry which, like semiconductors, remains critical to the productivity of the wide variety of other industries, was the fact that the United States imported 50 per cent of its machine tools in 1986, compared with four per cent in the mid-1960s.[28]

The post-1960s history of the motor vehicle industry remains one functional and strategic competition for market share. Diversification and mergers and acquisition have played only a small role. True, Ford's acquisition of Philco eliminated a potentially strong international electronics competitor. But the decline of the market share held by the American Big Three resulted largely from the ability of European and then Japanese firms to produce better products in terms of performance, price, and customer satisfaction, much as General Motors and Chrysler had done in competing with Ford and the smaller producers of middle-priced cars during the 1920s and the 1930s.

The new challengers in the United States and world markets were, of course, not small American entrepreneurial firms but established foreign managerial enterprises. Once their domestic markets had become large enough to assure a volume sufficient to reduce costs to a competitive level, these managerial firms began to move into the rich American market. American car makers, committed to high dividends and high wages, were slow to respond. By the 1980s, however, they were beginning to restructure their enterprises and their industries, improving product and process and their relationships with suppliers and dealers; and adjusting strategies and structures. So at present they are beginning to regain market share at home and abroad. According to the MIT's commission on productivity: 'The American-owned *firms* are now headed in the right direction, and the American based *industry* (including Japanese firms operating in the United States) is improving its international competitive position very rapidly'. Moreover the subsidiaries of General Motors and Ford were still strong competitors in Europe and Australia and all of the 'Big Three' had close links (strategic alliances) with Japanese firms.[29]

Until very recently, the venerable first movers in the electrical equipment industry, General Electric and Westinghouse, remained strong in their core products – systems generating and transforming electric power; electric motors, engines, components and other industrial products; and some long-established consumer appliances. While GE remains a world leader in the industry, in 1990 Westinghouse, which had disposed of its lighting division in 1986 to an American firm, sold off its electrical equipment and elevator divisions to Swiss companies. The proceeds of these sales were used to purchase businesses, largely in the service sector, where Westinghouse had not yet developed competitive capabilities. As its CEO, John C. Marous, explained to a reporter from the *Wall Street Journal*, his company was:

> boxed in by the rules of US capitalism. While European companies don't expect more than 12 per cent, he says, and the Japanese are even satisfied with 10 per cent or even as little as five per cent, if a product has a long lifecycle, American companies faced with a threat of takeover must do far better. 'Competition is tilted in favor of foreigners', declares Mr Marous, who has pushed Westinghouse to achieve a 22 per cent on equity last year.[30]

In this way pressure from the institutionalised market for corporate control pushed Westinghouse to abandon the long-term logic of industrial

34   ORGANISATIONAL CAPABILITY & COMPETITIVE ADVANTAGE

success – the logic which GE continued to follow by reinvesting heavily in those operating divisions in which it had the strongest competitive capabilities.

In consumer electronics – radio, television, and video equipment – the performance of the leaders and the smaller competitors has been uncommonly poor. Here over-diversification in the 1960s and 1970s appears to have been the culprit. GE and RCA became widely diversified and failed to concentrate resources on product development in consumer electronics; Philco and Admiral were acquired by firms (Ford and Rockwell, respectively) that had no experience in the industry. And Magnavox and Sylvania were purchased by the Dutch firm Philips. So by 1985 only 23 per cent of consumer electronic sales in the United States were for products made in American factories.[31]

Let me close this historical overview with a success story – that of the chemical industry, the industry that was hardest hit by the intensified competition of recent years. It remains one of the most significant generators of economic growth and transformation. In 1987 its US sales totalled $210 billion, as compared to auto sales of $125.6 billion. Its output of textiles far surpassed those produced by cotton, wool, and silk combined – products that had been the basis of powerful economies in the past. Its drug and pharmaceutical plants provided much of the world's medicine; its fertilizers had made possible the green revolution in many parts of the world; and its wide variety of other products had become essential in the production processes of its many and varied industries as those of the electrical and electronics industries. For a century the most research-intensive of all industries, its companies continued to expand by exploiting the economies of scope and entering markets related to their distinctive core production and research technologies. After World War II, American companies moved into Europe and European companies into the United States more than they had before 1939. Moreover, as the industry was dependent on oil for its basic raw materials, it suffered more than others from the sharp increase in oil prices in the 1970s.

As the leading managerial enterprises reshaped their own product lines and their organisational strategies, they restructured their industry. They narrowed their product lines, spinning off many of the commodity products, particularly petrochemicals, concentrated on expanding their output in existing higher value-added specialties and moving into new ones best fitted to their capabilities, including pharmaceuticals, biotechnical products and advanced materials. Thus, Dow's portion of commodities produced dropped from 63 per cent to 35 per cent in five years and Monsanto from 61 per cent to 35 per cent in four. As chemical companies reduced capacity much of petrochemical output was taken over by long-established oil companies. That is, the chemical companies moved into markets where they could utilise organisational capabilities developed to exploit economies of scope; and the oil companies into the petrochemicals where they could exploit capabilities based on understanding the economies of scale. Such restructuring based on long-term strategic plans involved heavy direct investment in new products and processes and the acquisition of pioneering firms in the growth areas as well as the divestiture of declining product lines. This restructuring was carried out almost wholly by the managerial enterprises that had long dominated their national industries – Bayer, BASF, and Hoechst in Germany; Ciba–Geigy in Switzerland; ICI in Britain; and in the United States Du Pont, Union Carbide, Dow, Monsanto (Allied Chemical, the most enthusiastic diversifier in the industry, is no longer a major player), and smaller, but still large, managerial enterprises such as Hercules, Rohm & Haas, and American Cyanamide. New start-up firms played almost no role; though a very few smaller firms were created to operate and occasionally consolidate the spun-off petrochemical activities. The United States remains an exporter of chemicals. Japanese firms have yet to become serious competitors in American or international markets.[32]

The Logic of Competitive Success and Failure

In the capital intensive industries, particularly those whose product and processes are technologically complex, the managerial enterprise has continued to dominate. (In this article I am speaking only of the capital-intensive industries that have been at the centre of growth and industrial competitiveness for the past century.) Such firms continued to grow by moving into new geographical and related product markets. Such growth continued to be based on the maintenance and improvement of product-specific facilities and skills whose activities were co-ordinated, monitored and planned by experienced full-time managers. And the test of such capabilities is their ability to compete functionally and strategically for market share.

The success and failure of American managers in competing for market share at home and abroad since the 1960s emphasises that those who ignore the logic of this dynamic do so, not necessarily at their own peril, but at the peril of the continuing long-term productivity and profitability of their enterprises, and of the industries and the national economies in which they operate. The failure of entrepreneurs to make the large long-term investments in manufacturing, marketing

36 ORGANISATIONAL CAPABILITY & COMPETITIVE ADVANTAGE

and management which are essential to create the capabilities needed to compete globally has meant that they and their enterprises lost out to those that did, both abroad and at home. This was as true of the entrepreneurs of Silicon Valley in semiconductors in the 1970s as it was of the entrepreneurs in Britain in chemicals, electrical equipment, machinery and metals in the 1880s and 1890s.

Similarly, the failure of managerial enterprises to improve their capabilities once created meant that they lost out in functional and strategic competition for market share to those that did. Just as General Motors and Chrysler took market share and profits from Ford by enhancing their organisational capabilities while Ford let its deteriorate, so too European and then Japanese automobile makers captured share and profit from the American 'Big Three' in the 1970s by improving their functional facilities and skills and by devising more effective long-term strategies for maintaining and gaining market share. And just as Ford regained its capabilities in the 1940s and 1950s, so too the Americans began to come back in the late 1980s.

The automobile story emphasizes that, while co-ordinated capabilities developed within the managerial enterprise are essential to competitive success, these managerial enterprises, like any human institution, can stagnate. Ford in the 1920s and the American 'Big Three' in the 1970s made wrong-headed decisions as to their markets, suppliers, dealers, and the activities of their competitors. In both cases, by improving process and product and restructuring their organizations, they were able to regain their capabilities and their competitive strength. The patterns of competition in automobiles have been much the same in nearly all capital-intensive and oligopolistic industries for the past century. Once established, a small number continued to dominate, with the market share and profitability changing constantly. Here the discipline of the market helped to enforce the logic of the dynamic of industrial growth.

More serious to the long-term health of enterprises and industries was the deliberate ignoring of that logic by managers who decided on a strategy of growth of acquiring companies in business in which they had little or no product-specific organizational capabilities that gave them a competitive edge. Such moves weakened the competitive strength of many American companies and industries. The American electrical and electronics companies had as great a potential for success in computers as did American machinery companies, and as great a potential for success in semiconductors and consumer electronics as did the large electrical and electronic companies in Europe and Japan. They failed in good part because these were only one of many product lines. So their

MANAGERIAL ENTERPRISE AND COMPETITION 37

top managers were unable to devote the time and resources necessary to compete effectively in computers, semiconductors, and consumer electronics. Nor did the top executives at Ford and Xerox have the capabilities to maintain the competitiveness of Philco and SDS. So, too, Singer's move away from its basic business was the beginning of its end. In comparable fashion, ITT, which had been since the 1920s a world-wide producer of telephone equipment was, after its diversification spree, out of that business. The conglomerates helped to bring down the machine tool industry. Finally, the diversification of automobile and machinery companies into unrelated industries made them much more vulnerable to the European and Japanese invasion of their market. By pulling back and concentrating on improving their functional capabilities, they are now beginning to regain competitive strength.

Ignoring the logic of industrial growth had even more far-reaching consequences than the destruction of the capabilities of a number of major American enterprises and industries. It led to changes in the capital markets that further encouraged inattention to the basic functions of managerial enterprises and to the maintenance of national competitive capabilities in global markets. The extraordinary number of acquisitions made in the late 1960s into unrelated and more distantly related industries, followed by a totally unprecedented number of divestitures in the early 1970s, suggest that many managers quickly realised the hazards of ignoring the logic. But it also made it clear that often more money was to be made in buying and selling companies than in operating them. Indeed, the new business turned many financial institutions, particularly investment banks, from carrying out what had been for almost a century their basic function, that of providing funds to supplement retained earnings in the reinvestment of facilities and skills essential to maintain competitive capabilities – a function that financial institutions in Japan and continental Europe continue to perform effectively. The new business, often personally as profitable to managers involved as to the financial institutions, was further encouraged by the new owners of American industry: the managers of portfolio and pension funds whose abilities were constantly tested by comparisons with their performance to the Standard & Poor indices. As time passed even the language of the financial community – such terms as 'bust-up takeovers', 'putting companies into play', and 'break-up value' – indicated that long-term investment was no longer the major concern of financial intermediaries. This trend away from the realities of global competition has been further stimulated by business schools and the business press. Just as in the 1960s the schools encouraged the hubris of American managers by teaching that those who learned the general principles of management need not

38   ORGANISATIONAL CAPABILITY & COMPETITIVE ADVANTAGE

be intimately concerned with its product-specific content; so the current discussion of shareholder value focuses on the obtaining of profit rather than on the product-specific capabilities necessary to achieve that profit – capabilities that differ considerably from industry to industry.

All this is not to say that the increased flexibility of the processes and products of the financial markets is not of significant value in restructuring American enterprises and industries so that they can regain or maintain their long-term competitive capabilities. The success of the chemical industry is a case in point. It is only to say that, as the experience of chemicals indicates, such flexibility is valuable only when capital is raised and businesses are bought and sold to enhance facilities and skills according to a carefully considered long-term strategy. Nor is this to say that conglomerates cannot play a significant role in maintaining and developing capabilities, as the case of Tenneco in agricultural implements suggests. Indeed, as long as the conglomerate operates a relatively small number of divisions and its full-time executives concentrate on maintaining those divisions' competitive capabilities, such executives can provide a more effective and more immediate discipline over managerial inertia than can the product markets. Nor is this to say that outside directors representing financial institutions or large stockholders do not have an important role in reviving stagnating companies whose capabilities have deteriorated, by bringing in outsiders, perhaps even from another industry, to turn the company around. The basic task of conglomerate managers, outside directors and a new CEO must, however, be to recruit managers who have the experience and skills essential to understand the enterprise's technologically complex products and processes, the intricacies of its many markets, and the activities of its competitors in these markets.

Individual financiers, managers and shareholders have often profited from ignoring the dynamics of managerial enterprises in capital-intensive industries, but the consequences of such actions have been serious to the long-term health of enterprises and industries involved. That logic has been ignored when managers and financiers view the assets of an enterprise as merely the value of existing facilities, and when they consider the employees and managers in terms of costs of wages and salaries instead of product-specific skills to be enhanced. The consequences can be particularly serious when deals involving the buying and selling of companies are based on such assumptions. It is ignored, too, when the goal of those involved in that buying and selling is the profit to be made from the transactions themselves rather than that made from the resulting improvements in the competitive capabilities of the enterprises involved in the transaction. The long-term consequences

MANAGERIAL ENTERPRISE AND COMPETITION   39

can be dangerous too when the transactions burden the enterprise involved with heavy debts whose interest reduces the funds essential for reinvestment in facilities and skills. They are serious too when the managers sacrifice funds needed to maintain and improve capabilities, to meet shareholder demands for higher dividends.

Why then should the weakening of organisational capabilities of managerial enterprises weaken the competitive strength of national industries and economies? The reason is that the development, production and distribution of goods for national and global markets must be a co-operative effort. It requires the carrying out of a wide variety of activities that in turn call for different facilities and skills. And only when these facilities and skills and the flow of goods through their processes of production and distribution are carefully co-ordinated can the activities be integrated in ways to reduce price, assure quality, and provide services essential to reach those markets. Such co-operative efforts are so profitable that if entrepreneurial enterprises fail to become managerial and managerial enterprises fail to maintain and nourish their competitive capabilities, they lose market share and profits to managerial enterprises from other nations and from related industries that do. At least that has been the experience in the industries that have done the most to transform the world since the coming of modern transportation and communication more than a century ago.

NOTES

This article was presented at the Business History Seminar at the Harvard Business School in September 1989. Very much reworked, it appeared as 'The Enduring Logic of Industrial Success', *Harvard Business Review*, Vol.90 (1990), pp.130–40. Because it was greatly shortened, because much of the basic data was deleted and because the data was not documented, it seemed worthwhile to have the original text published. Parts of this piece have been used in 'Learning and Technological Change: The Perspective from Business History', in R. Thomson (ed.) *Learning and Technological Change*, to be published by Macmillan, and in 'Competitive Performance of U.S. Industrial Enterprises: A Historical Perspective, 1880s–1990s' in M. Porter (ed.), *Time Horizons in American Industry*, to be published by the Harvard Business School Press. Both the title of the article and of the book are tentative.

1. S. Kuznets, *Economic Growth of Nations: Total Output and Productivity* (Cambridge, MA, 1971), pp.144–51, 160–1, 316–9; W.W. Rostow, *The World Economy: History and Prospects* (Austin, TX, 1978), pp.52–3.
2. The following paragraphs are based on A.D. Chandler, Jr., *Scale and Scope: The Dynamics of Industrial Capitalism* (Cambridge, MA, 1990), Ch.2.
3. For the British failure and German success in chemicals, pharmaceuticals, electrical equipment and other machinery and metals, see ibid., Ch.7 (particularly pp.274–86) and Ch.12 (particularly pp.463–86).
4. These two quotations are cited in ibid., p.476 from Carl Duisberg, 'Memorandum on the Construction and Organization of the Dye Works [Farben Fabriken], at Leverkusen', p.3 (Bayer Archives).

40 ORGANISATIONAL CAPABILITY & COMPETITIVE ADVANTAGE

5. L.F. Haber, *The Chemical Industry, 1900–1930: International Growth and Techno-logical Change* (Oxford, 1971), pp.121, 145, 179.
6. Chandler, *Scale and Scope*, Ch.6 for the dominance of US firms in light volume produced machinery.
7. M. Dertouzos *et al.*, *Made in America: Regaining the Competitive Edge* (Cambridge, MA, 1989), p.234.
8. Chandler, *Scale and Scope*, p.171. The collective history of the leaders of the US chemical industry in the inter-war years is told in ibid., pp.170–90.
9. Ibid., pp.205–8 for this paragraph and the next.
10. For information on computers, see K. Flamm, *Creating the Computer: Government, Industry and High Technology* (Washington, DC, 1987), Chs. 4–6 and for the history of individual companies, J. Cortada, *Historical Dictionary of Data Processing Organizations* (New York, 1987).
11. R. Sobel, *I.B.M.: Colossus in Transition* (New York, 1981), Ch.10.
12. *Datamation*, Vol.29 (1983), p.92.
13. Chandler, *Scale and Scope*, pp.611–12.
14. Flamm, *Creating the Computer*, pp.168, 201.
15. D.S. Ravenscrapt and F.M. Scherer, *Mergers, Sell-offs, and Economic Efficiency* (Washington, D.C., 1987), Ch.6.
16. For extent of diversification see A.D. Chandler and R.S. Tedlow, *The Coming of Managerial Capitalism: A Casebook on the History of American Economic Institutions* (Homewood, IL, 1985), pp.765–75.
17. T. Johnson and R. Kaplan, *Relevance Lost: The Rise and Fall of Managerial Accounting* (Boston, MA, 1987). As the book points out 'contemporary cost accounting and management control systems . . . are no longer providing accurate signals about the efficiency and profitability of internally managed transactions . . . Without receipt of appropriate cost and profitability information, the availability of the "visible hand" to effectively manage the myriad of transactions that occur in a complex hierarchy has been severely compromised'. Particularly useful are Ch.6, 'From Cost Management to Cost Accounting: Relevance Lost', and Ch.7, 'Cost Accounting and Decision Making: Academics Strive for Relevance'.
18. W.T. Grimm & Co., *Mergerstat Review, 1987* (Chicago, IL, 1988), pp.103–4.
19. New York Stock Exchange, *Share Ownership, 1980* (New York, 1981), p.1.
20. New York Stock Exchange, *New York Stock Exchange Fact Book, 1987* (New York, 1987) pp.70–1.
21. This information is taken from *Datamation*, Vol.34 (1988), p.30.
22. Flamm, *Creating the Computer*, pp.17, 102–127.
23. Ibid., pp.168, 201.
24. Dertouzos *et al.*, *Made in America*, pp.248–61. The US has remained strong in microprocessing chips but recently a Japanese firm, Kubota, purchased 20 per cent of MIPS Computer Systems, the first merchant vendor to commercialize an advanced microprocessor chip for reduced-instruction-set computing (RISC). In return, MIPS shares its technology with Kubota; while Matsushita manufactures the devices (pp.259–60).
25. Ibid., p.251.
26. *New York Times*, 3 May 1989, p.D19; 28 Sept. 1989, p.D1.
27. Marsh, *A Corporate Tragedy: The Agony of International Harvester Company* (Garden City, NY, 1987). Describes in detail the disintegration of this great American firm. Particularly useful are Chs.11–17. Valuable too is an article comparing Deere to Harvester in *Sales and Management*, Vol.32 (1985), pp.30–3. For Tenneco see, besides annual reports, *New York Times* (30 Dec. 1990), pp.D3–4.
28. Dertouzos *et al.*, *Made in America*, pp.232–3; M. Holland, *When the Machine Stoppes: A Cautionary Tale From Industrial America* (Boston, MA, 1989) provides a graphic account of the destruction of an innovating and well managed machine tool maker – Burgmaster Corporation.
29. Dertouzos *et al.*, *Made in America*, pp.171–87. The quotation is from p.187.

30. *Wall Street Journal*, 24 Jan. 1990, p.A4. For GE's continuing strength in the core lines see the company's annual report for 1989. This paragraph was revised after the completion of the original draft.

31. More detailed than Detouzos *et al.*, *Made in America*, pp.217–31 is 'The Decline of US Consumer Electronics Manufacturing: History, Hypothesis, and Realities', *The Working Papers of the MIT Commission on Industrial Productivity*, Vol.1, (Cambridge, MA, 1989), especially pp.15–21, 45.

32. As in the case of consumer electronics, the *Working Papers of the MIT, Commission*, Vol.1, 'The Transformation of the US Chemicals Industry' provides much more information on individual companies than does the summary volume *Made in America*. J.L. Bower, *When Markets Quake: The Management Challenge of Restructuring Industry* (Boston, MA, 1986), especially Chs.4–6 adds valuable information.

[7]

Scale and Scope: A Review Colloquium

> Scale and
> Scope The
> Dynamics of
> Industrial
> Capitalism
> Alfred D.
> Chandler, Jr.

Scale and Scope: The Dynamics of Industrial Capitalism. *By Alfred D. Chandler, Jr.*, with Takashi Hikino · Cambridge, Mass.: Harvard University Press, 1990. xix + 860 pp. Charts, figures, tables, appendixes, notes, and index. $35.00.

Editor's Introduction

In *Scale and Scope*, Alfred D. Chandler, Jr., sets out a complex and sustained interpretation of "the dynamics of industrial capitalism." His work, the culmination of decades of study, spanning three major economies (the United States, Great Britain, and Germany) from the 1880s to the 1940s, will undoubtedly be a central point of reference for all business historians for a very long time to come. More than that, it also makes contributions to, and has wide implications for, a great variety of fields of scholarship, research, and debate. It is hard to imagine any single book review that could do justice to the scale and the scope of Chandler's work.

Accordingly, this issue of the *Business History Review* devotes substantial space to a review colloquium to discuss the book. Under this format, several distinguished reviewers have been asked to discuss the implications of the book from their varying scholarly perspectives. Four historians examine the book from the perspective of the business history of their own national economies. Three of them are historians of the economies that Chandler has specifically discussed: the United States (Thomas Hughes), Germany (Jürgen Kocka), and Great Britain (Roy Church). The fourth reflects on the important implications of the book for the study of one country that Chandler has

Business History Review 64 (Winter 1990): 690–735. © 1990 by The President and Fellows of Harvard College.

Chandler's Scale and Scope / *691*

not addressed in this work—Japan (Hidemasa Morikawa). None of these reviews is, however, simply an evaluation of Chandler's national case studies by a specialist; rather, each contributor highlights international comparisons by using the leverage of his own national standpoint, and each focuses on key themes of the book.

Three other studies focus on the interdisciplinary contribution of the book from the points of view of an economist (Frederic Scherer) and a sociologist (Neil Fligstein) and from the perspective of broader changes in the global economy (Albert Fishlow). Again, the focus of each of these reviews is on the questions, insights, comparisons, and divergences that Chandler's work illuminates, and each demonstrates the resonance of Chandler's work far beyond the confines of business history.

Alfred Chandler kindly accepted an invitation to respond to these comments. In keeping with the spirit of the colloquium, his responses are not a "reply to critics." Rather, Chandler takes the opportunity to engage in broader debates and, as he says, "to clarify and to define more sharply the basic concepts, focus, and aims of the book."

As *Scale and Scope* becomes widely studied, more and more debates, discussions, and controversies will doubtless open up around Chandler's synthesis. This colloquium shows that *Scale and Scope* may be the conclusion to one chapter of business history, but it is also the first chapter of many future investigations.

— S. T.

Contributors

Alfred D. Chandler, Jr., Straus Professor of Business History emeritus, taught at MIT and the Johns Hopkins University before coming to the Harvard Business School in 1970. Besides his *Strategy and Structure* (1962) and *The Visible Hand* (1977), he edited, with Richard S. Tedlow, *The Coming of Managerial Capitalism* (1985). He is currently examining the experiences since the Second World War of many of the enterprises studied in *Scale and Scope*, particularly U.S. companies, focusing on the ways in which their organizational capabilities, as they were developed, expanded, maintained, damaged, and even destroyed, affected the competitive strength in global markets of the national industries in which these companies operated.

.   .   .

Review Colloquium / 692

Roy Church is professor of economic and social history at the University of East Anglia, Norwich. Until 1990 he was editor of the *Economic History Review*. His latest book is *The History of the British Coal Industry*, volume 3: *1830–1913, Victorian Pre-Eminence* (1986). Among his recent articles is "Family Firms and Managerial Capitalism: The Case of the International Motor Industry," *Business History* 28 (1986). His current research concerns industrial relations, specifically strikes in the British coal industry, and a short history of the British motor industry.

Albert Fishlow is dean of International and Area Studies at the University of California, Berkeley. In addition to his *American Railroads and the Transformation of the Ante-Bellum Economy* (1965) and many journal articles, he is the author of *The Mature Neighbor Policy: A New United States Economic Policy for Latin America* (1977), the coauthor of *Latin America's Emergence: Toward a U.S. Response* (1979), and a contributor to *Trade with Manufacturers in Developing Countries: Reinforcing the North-South Partnership* (1981).

Neil Fligstein is professor of sociology at the University of California, Berkeley. His most recent book, *The Transformation of Corporate Control* (1990), is a history of the large modern corporation that focuses on how the political-legal system and the attempts by managers to create stable worlds produced various forms of control over the past one hundred years. He is currently working on issues related to the 1992 Single Market Program of the European Community.

Thomas Hughes is Andrew W. Mellon Professor of the History and Sociology of Science at the University of Pennsylvania. His publications include two books about the nature of technological and social change: *Networks of Power: Electrification in Western Society, 1880–1930* (1983) and *Elmer Sperry: Inventor and Engineer* (1971). He recently published *American Genesis: A Century of Invention and Technological Enthusiasm, 1870–1970* (1990), and he edited, with Agatha Hughes, *Lewis Mumford: Public Intellectual* (1990).

Jürgen Kocka has held the Chair for the History of the Industrial World at the Free University of Berlin since 1988, and he is also a permanent fellow of the Wissenschaftskolleg zu Berlin (the Institute for Advanced Study). He has published widely in the field of modern social and economic history, including *White Collar Workers in America, 1890–1940* (1980), *Les employés in Allemagne, 1850–1980* (1989), and *Arbeitsverhältnisse und Arbeiterexistenzen: Grundlagen der Klassenbildung im 19. Jahrhundert* (1990). He is coeditor of the journal *Geschichte und Gesellschaft*.

Hidemasa Morikawa is professor of business history at the Graduate School of Business Administration at Keio University. He formerly was

Chandler's Scale and Scope / *693*

on the faculty of Hosei University and Yokohama National University. He specializes in the history of the *zaibatsu*, and his *Business History of the Zaibatsu* will shortly be published (in English). He is currently president of the Business History Society of Japan.

Frederic M. Scherer is professor of business and government at the John F. Kennedy School of Government, Harvard University. His research has emphasized industrial economics and technological change, leading to books on *The Weapons Acquisition Process* (1964), *Industrial Market Structure and Economic Performance* (1980), *Innovation and Growth* (1984), and *Mergers, Sell-offs, and Economic Efficiency* (1987). A new book on *International High-Technology Competition* will emerge from Harvard University Press in 1992.

·   ·   ·

Beyond the Three-Pronged Investment
Frederic M. Scherer

My view of *Scale and Scope* comes not only from the vantage point of an economist, but from that of an economist who once tried without notable success to find an explanation for industrial structure in detailed evidence on scale and scope economies.[1] Why does Alfred Chandler succeed where I failed?

One possible reason is a difference in time frames. He is concerned with a period from the late nineteenth century to 1945; I focused on the late 1960s. He found the minimum efficient scale (MES) for a petroleum refinery in 1885 to require a throughput of roughly 6,000 barrels a day. By 1965, my coauthors and I observed, the MES had increased to 200,000 barrels a day. Clearly, refiners could and did gain by repeatedly pushing out the scale frontier.

It is far from evident, however, why this striving for scale economies should explain how one or a very few firms came to dominate an industry. Efficient scales have been growing over time in many and perhaps most industries, but so have the markets into which their output is directed. For forty-six industries over the period 1904–47, Saul Sands found that demand grew on average slightly more rapidly than the physical output of the largest plants.[2] Studies covering the

---

[1] F. M. Scherer, et al., *The Economics of Multi-Plant Operation: An International Comparisons Study* (Cambridge, Mass., 1975).

[2] Saul S. Sands, "Changes in Scale of Production in United States Manufacturing Industry, 1904–1947," *Review of Economics and Statistics* 43 (Nov. 1961): 365–68.

period following the Second World War show consistently that in most manufacturing industries, efficient plant sizes were far too small to mandate highly concentrated structures. Other analyses reveal that rapid growth, which was typical in many of the industries that Chandler studies, erodes barriers to competitive entry. The conjunction of these findings implies that deeper explanations must be sought for persistently maintained positions of industrial dominance.

Chandler's petroleum refinery data exhibit a further problem. Chandler asserts (p. 25) that by expanding from a midpoint throughput of 1,750 barrels per day to 5,750 barrels, Standard Oil reduced its unit costs in Cleveland from 1.5 to 0.45 cents per gallon of kerosene—a decline of 70 percent. The percentage cost reduction is far too large to be consistent with the "two-thirds rule" used widely by engineers and economists to characterize scale economy relationships in chemical processing plants. Had the two-thirds rule held, unit costs would have fallen to 1.0 cents. Instead of the 0.67 exponent implied by the two-thirds rule, Chandler's data suggest a total cost function exponent close to zero. To see this, multiply the 1.5-cent unit cost by the 73,500-gallon daily throughput of the 1,750-barrel refinery, obtaining a daily processing cost of $1,103. Now multiply 0.45 cents times the 241,500-gallon throughput of the 5,750-barrel refinery. The result is $1,087. The increased output from a larger refinery comes as a free lunch! Free lunches are not impossible, but they must have stemmed from technological changes that shifted cost curves downward, not from riding down a scale economies curve of fixed position.[3] Thus, in the only fully articulated numerical example presented in the book, Chandler has confounded cost curve shifts with scale economy gains from moving down the cost curve.

Although it is more difficult to be certain, I suspect that similar confusion has crept into Chandler's analysis of economies of scope—that is, cost savings from producing a larger array of products. He asserts (pp. 26 and 475) that by increasing their product range from one dyestuff to "literally hundreds," the leading German chemical companies reduced their unit cost from 270 to 9 Marks per kilogram. My own analysis of scope economies in industries such as paint, textiles, shoes, and ball bearings (before the advent of flexible automation) revealed that the more products of a given volume a plant handled, the more overall unit costs were likely to be pushed up owing

---

[3] See Joel Mokyr, *The Lever of Power: Technical Creativity and Economic Progress* (New York, 1990), 1–2. For a graphical illustration, see my "Economies of Scale and Industrial Concentration" in *Industrial Concentration: The New Learning*, ed. Harvey J. Goldschmid, et al. (Boston, 1974), 21.

Chandler's Scale and Scope / 695

to greater managerial complexity, all else equal.[4] Assigning more products to a plant is commonly viewed as a second-best solution that will help firms realize greater *plant*-specific economies when the volumes of individual products are so small that a plant cannot be filled to optimal capacity with a narrow range of products, each realizing all *product*-specific economies of high-volume production. Canadian plants, for example, confronting a small domestic market, have traditionally handled broader product arrays than their U.S. counterparts.[5] In his German dyestuff cost figures, Chandler has probably confounded shifts in and movements along product-specific cost curves. And he does not distinguish with sufficient clarity between the advantages of producing individual products in larger volumes, those of packing more low-volume products into an otherwise underutilized plant, and the dynamic gains from tapping a pool of technical talent to develop new, profitable product variants.

I question also the quantitative support for Chandler's assertion (p. 23 and repeatedly thereafter) that scale economies are especially prevalent in capital-intensive industries. Using the list in table 18 (p. 225) augmented by qualitative references, I dichotomized the Federal Trade Commission's 1977 report on 234 "lines of business" into Chandler's "modern, capital-intensive" category and all others.[6] Assets averaged 70 percent of sales for 107 Chandlerian industries and 67 percent for all others—a difference that is not statistically significant. The two groups differed most significantly in the ratio of research and development outlays to sales: 1.64 percent on average for Chandler's industries and 1.38 percent for the others.

This leads to my most fundamental criticism of Chandler's argument: that only by making "three-pronged investments" in large-scale production, distribution channels, and management structures were firms able to gain first-mover advantages that allowed them to discourage competitive entry and to maintain positions of dominance in their industries. Chandler stresses repeatedly that technological inventiveness and being the market pioneer with a new product or process are insufficient to establish leadership. Rather, "The first movers were pioneers or other entrepreneurs who made the three interrelated sets of investment in production, distribution, and management

---

[4] Scherer, et al., *The Economics of Multi-Plant Operation*, 49–56 and 295–321.
[5] John R. Baldwin and Paul K. Gorecki, "The Relationship between Plant Scale and Product Diversity in Canadian Manufacturing Industries," *Journal of Industrial Economics* 34 (June 1986): 373–88.
[6] U.S. Federal Trade Commission, *Statistical Report: Annual Line of Business Report, 1977* (Washington, D.C., April 1985).

Review Colloquium / 696

required to achieve the competitive advantages of scale, scope, or both" (p. 35). His schema can be diagrammed as:

Investment   - - ->   Large Scale and/or Scope   - - ->   First-Mover Advantages   - - ->   Dominance

In this, I believe he paints with too broad a brush and blurs the subtle dynamics through which enterprises seize and retain dominance. Three illustrations must suffice to support my counterargument.

Consider Chandler's treatment of Henry Ford in *Scale and Scope*:

> Ford was the quintessential first mover. His investment in production facilities—the Highland Park works in Detroit—became the symbol of modern mass production and the exploitation of economies of scale. Ford's completion, in the spring of 1914, of the moving assembly line quickly reduced labor time in the production of the Model T from 12.5 hours to 1.5 hours. At the same time, Ford built an international distributing and marketing network which included the industry's first branch assembly plants (p. 205).

In his earlier *The Visible Hand*, Chandler put a different gloss on the initial dynamics:

> Henry Ford and his associates produced the low-priced model T in 1908 and then created a worldwide sales organization to distribute their sturdy, reliable, cheap car. The resulting almost insatiable demand created a constant pressure to increase output by accelerating throughput.[7]

In *The Visible Hand* it appears (correctly, I believe) that the first-mover advantages associated with the Model T were what made the Highland Park investment (with first operations in January 1910) profitable. *Before* the first moving assembly line was inaugurated at Highland Park, Ford's automobile market share had risen to 40 percent.

Similarly, in an extension of his analysis to the period following the Second World War, Chandler argues that "In 1965, a little more than a decade after the mainframe computer had first been commercialized, IBM had completed its System 360, which made it the first mover in the production and distribution of general-purpose main-

---

[7] Alfred D. Chandler, Jr., *The Visible Hand: The Managerial Revolution in American Business* (Cambridge, Mass., 1977), 280.

Chandler's Scale and Scope / *697*

frames for a wide variety of users" (p. 610). Granted, the System 360 entailed a massive investment—one that strained the financial capacity even of IBM, then a stock market favorite. But IBM's first-mover advantages were built up year by year during the mid- and late 1950s, when IBM correctly perceived that it could induce large numbers of business firms to lease computers if it helped them with applications software and exerted the hard sell it had honed to perfection while peddling punch-card machines. Market pioneer Remington Rand failed not because of deficient investment in production and marketing, but because it made the *wrong kinds* of investment, emphasizing scientific applications and doing too little hand-holding to win potential users among business firms. In 1964, before the System 360 appeared, IBM had built up a strong reputation and "software lock-in" advantages that gave it an 80 percent share of a billion-dollar market despite vigorous cloning and leapfrogging efforts by rivals. The System 360 was aimed not at providing first-mover advantages, but at consolidating those advantages by allowing the users of what had been two quite distinct operating systems to "upgrade" compatibly to a common family of machines. Had there been no loyal IBM user base, something quite different from the 360 would almost surely have been developed.

The Remington Rand story suggests still another weakness in Chandler's argument. Far too little attention is paid to firms that made substantial investments in production, distribution, and management, but failed because they backed the wrong technical or marketing approach or made decisions that for other reasons proved erroneous. To take another example, Harold Passer's careful analysis suggests that the American Electric and Illuminating Company made all the right kinds of arc lighting investments during the 1880s, but plunged into crisis in 1888 when it was found to have infringed a Thomson-Houston patent. Brush Electric likewise invested heavily and at first successfully in invention, production, marketing, and organization, according to Passer, but was forced by Thomson-Houston's patent to offer an inferior regulator design and eventually to sell out.[8]

From these and other examples, I would place much less emphasis than Chandler on investment in itself and much more on the complex feedback relationships among successful innovation, first-mover

[8] Harold C. Passer, *The Electrical Manufacturers, 1875–1900: A Study in Competition, Entrepreneurship, Technical Change, and Economic Growth* (Cambridge, Mass., 1953), 34–40, 14–21, 42, and 54.

advantages, investment for expansion, and further reinforcing advantages. Thus, my schema can be diagrammed as:

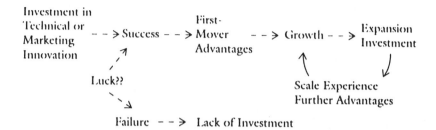

Chandler touches on all of these more complex phenomena in his book, but pride of place is given to the three-pronged investments. In his discussion of specific industry and company histories, the dynamic complexities fall by the wayside, perhaps because he attempted to cover too broad a canvas, surveying the leading two hundred industrial enterprises in each of three widely spaced time frames for three different nations. What is needed now is much more fine-grained research on the kinds of relationships Chandler identifies in *Scale and Scope*. In that further research, special attention must be paid to working out the detailed dynamics of firm growth and to disentangling quantitatively the contributions of capital intensity, movements down cost curves, and technological changes that shift cost curves. In sum, *Scale and Scope* is an erudite and stimulating first move, not the investment that defines and dominates this new field of inquiry for business historians.

·   ·   ·

Managerial Capitalism beyond the Firm
Thomas Hughes

Through his articles and books, Alfred D. Chandler, Jr., has earned international acclaim; European scholars acknowledge Americans' leadership in the field of business history largely because of his work. His influence, moreover, extends beyond business history into economic history and the history of technology. In fact, Chandler is not a business historian narrowly defined; he writes mainstream American history. In time, his interpretation will surely sift into general history, scholarly and popular. A century from now, when historians

Chandler's Scale and Scope / *699*

of America look back on the period extending from about 1870 to 1970, they may well agree that the most remarkable achievements of the nation occurred in the fields of technology and modern management. Earlier, in *The Visible Hand* (1977), and now in *Scale and Scope*, Chandler provides the prevailing interpretation of American modern management in this remarkably creative era.

In *Scale and Scope* Chandler boldly extends his intellectual horizons to take on the challenge of writing comparative history. He uses concepts such as economies of scale and scope to organize the history of what he calls competitive managerial capitalism in the United States, personal capitalism in Britain, and cooperative managerial capitalism in Germany. His time span covers roughly the period of the Second Industrial Revolution, from about 1870 to the present. As in his earlier books, Chandler conceives of managers in multidivisional manufacturing firms evaluating performance, planning long-term corporate strategy, and allocating funds, facilities, and personnel. As before, he delineates layers of management rationally monitoring and coordinating production, distribution, and marketing to achieve an efficient flow from raw materials processing to final consumption. Effective management, he believes, optimizes the organizational capabilities of a firm; it coordinates the autonomous, self-contained operating units that make up multidivisional firms.

Chandler's ideal type of industrial enterprise and its management might be labeled "modern," in contrast to "postmodern." He is writing about a management style that he argues prevailed throughout the era of the Second Industrial Revolution. He assumes a positive feedback interaction of modern production technology and modern management, each of which stresses order, control, and system. He analyzes a style of management that this reviewer finds analogous, in its emphasis on the rational and the functional, to the Modern style of architecture. Both were shaped by the modern technology of mass production. Chandler, like Henry Ford, Frederick W. Taylor, Walter Gropius, Le Corbusier, and Mies van der Rohe, assumes that the modern style, whether in management, technology, or architecture, has a timeless quality that will project it into the future. Just as none of these other men foresaw a postmodern technology or architecture, Chandler also does not foresee a postmodern management, one formulated in reaction against his ideal type of modern management. In the conclusion of this magisterial study, he lists the changes that he anticipates in management, but these are incremental, not radical, challenges to the past. He asks whether a new era of managerial capitalism approaches, but he foresees only evolution-

Review Colloquium / 700

ary changes (p. 621), and he clearly anticipates that the industrial firm engaged in production will remain the prime locus of managerial functions essentially like those he defines so well in his book.

Paradoxically, although Chandler formally designates the manufacturing firm—specifically the two hundred largest American, British, and German manufacturing firms—as his unit of analysis, a substantial part of his narrative concerns the management of firm-transcending enterprises. But, because he is focused on the firm, he does not analyze the spread of the firm-transcending enterprises that his narrative describes, and he does not consider the likelihood of their increasing importance in the future that his narrative implies.

In the extremely informative German section of the book, for instance, Chandler describes such firm-transcending enterprises as joint ventures, cartels, *Interessengemeinschaften*, and *Konzerne*. Earlier, he uses as a prime example of the modern economies of scale and scope the Standard Oil Trust in America, which was not a firm but a loose federation of forty companies tied to the Standard Oil Company through interchange of stock and other financial devices. Even though he devotes many pages to describing such firm-transcending industrial enterprises and implies that they make possible the fulfillment of managerial goals beyond those achievable by the firm, Chandler continues to insist that the firm is the proper unit of analysis for understanding management in an era of industrial capitalism.

Because of Chandler's concentration on the firm, *Scale and Scope* does not take into account, for instance, the rise of production systems that consist of many firms, systems formed and structured by government contracts. Management of the Manhattan Engineering District for production of explosives in the United States, for example, is not caught in Chandler's methodological net. The government-funded Manhattan Project involved and affected the management style then and subsequently of a host of major manufacturing firms, so the project seems a likely candidate for analysis in a study of modern industrial management.

Mixed government-industry enterprises that have been of central importance in Germany are also left out of his analysis, nor does he explore the management of the innovative superfirm relationships of electrical manufacturers and utilities in Germany and the United States. Chandler does provide a lengthy description and analysis of the management of Allgemeine Elektricitäts-Gesellschaft (AEG) and Siemens, the two leading German electrical enterprises during the period he surveys, but he ignores their complex interaction with electrical utilities. Through the investment banks with which they were closely allied, the managements of the two companies often provided the financing for the construction of utility power plants. AEG took part in the designing and building of utility facilities through its construction department, and from the late 1880s until the First World War, the company managed the Berliner Elektrizitäts-Werke, one of the country's largest urban utilities. Hugo Stinnes, whom Chandler associates only with his steel and iron holdings, also headed Germany's leading regional electrical utility, the Rheinisch-Westfälisches Elektrizitätswerk, and he coordinated the steel-, coal-, and energy-production enterprises under his control. In the United States, General Electric founded Electric Bond and Share Company (EBASCO) to finance, design, and construct utilities. Stone & Webster (which Chandler mistakenly identifies as a research company) also owned controlling shares in and financed, designed, and constructed utilities. The heads of these superfirm enterprises, such as Emil and Walther Rathenau of AEG, Stinnes, Charles Stone and Edwin Webster, and S. Z. Mitchell of EBASCO, had to evaluate performance, plan long-term strategy, and allocate funds, facilities, and personnel for superfirm enterprises. For them the problem of coordination transcended the self-contained operating units of the multidivisional firm; they had to coordinate nominally autonomous firms.

Chandler not only fails to acknowledge sufficiently the rise of firm-transcending enterprises and to analyze their management systematically; he also neglects to consider how the rise of modern transportation, communication, and energy utilities has shaped modern management. This is paradoxical, because in both *Scale and Scope* and *The Visible Hand* he maintains that mid-nineteenth century railways and communications networks made possible late nineteenth century and twentieth-century managerial capitalism. The rails and wires of these networks made possible the coordination, scheduling, and physical links that combined production and distribution into a single enterprise capable of supplying first a national and then an international market. If this were true of railroads and the telegraph, then by analogy we would expect transportation, communication, and energy networks to have continued to shape industrial management during the period since 1880.

In the case of electrical power networks, there is abundant evidence that modern managers devoted substantial organizational capability to interconnecting widespread production facilities with high-voltage power lines in order to exploit economies made possible by centralized management of diverse and widespread loads. Stinnes and his associates were particularly adept in fulfilling this goal in Rhineland

Review Colloquium / 702

Westphalia. Chandler, however, does not discuss the tactics and strategies of modern managers who used the electric power resources of
the modern era. He does not, for instance, explore the way in which
high-voltage interconnections have been used by management to tie
together superfirm enterprises. In his conclusion he refers to electricity as transforming the processes of production and distribution before
the turn of the century, but he does not develop the thesis in the
body of the book. He predicts that the electronic revolution will transform the processes of production, but he does not explore the possibility that information networks will facilitate the interconnection of
firms into superfirm enterprises on a global scale, just as rails, conveyors, and pipes had earlier facilitated the rise of the multidivisional
firm. Because Chandler has impressively shown in *The Visible Hand*
how managers used networks to knit together the multidivisional firm
during the late nineteenth century, one would expect him to see the
possibility that twentieth-century networks will be used to structure
firm-transcending enterprises capable of fulfilling the imperatives of
scale and scope.

Chandler has not only taken insufficient account of the way in
which twentieth-century communication and energy utility networks
have brought superfirm interconnections; he has also not considered
the ways in which the management of such organizations has
influenced industrial management style in general. In a masterly analysis
in *The Visible Hand*, he showed how railway management, especially
that of the Pennsylvania Railroad, provided a paradigm for modern
industrial management. He might have been expected in *Scale and
Scope*, then, to continue to monitor the influence of utility management during the Second Industrial Revolution. The managers of electrical utilities, with their emphasis on scale and scope as expressed
in the drive for high load factors and a cost-reducing economic mix
of power plants, have set a pace for Chandler's two hundred manufacturing firms. Even today a leading electrical utility provides seminars
in management for a leading manufacturer. Because electrical utilities do not usually store electricity, Chandler could not have found
a better example of managerial emphasis on flow, a characteristic of
modern management that he has rightly stressed throughout his works.

In the introductory sections of *Scale and Scope*, he states several
of his objectives. The most general is to provide a history of "the
modern industrial enterprise" and to explain the "dynamics of industrial capitalism." The most specific is to provide "collective histories
of the two hundred largest manufacturing companies—the prototypes
of the modern industrial enterprise . . . " (p. 11). The questions I

Chandler's Scale and Scope */ 703*

have raised about the scope of Chandler's latest contribution suggest that he has not fulfilled his broadly stated goal of describing and analyzing modern industrial enterprise. Instead, he has written a masterful description and a partial analysis of the management of the modern multidivisional manufacturing firm, *a* central institution in managerial capitalism, but not necessarily *the* central institution, as he presumes. If Chandler had dealt with the multidivisional firm as a "protoytpe" rather than as *the* modern form of business enterprise, *Scale and Scope* would have addressed the questions posed in this review.

Even in his concentration on manufacturing firms, Chandler has not encompassed the scope of the challenge for the managers of these firms, especially for those engaged in firm-transcending enterprises, such as trusts, holding companies, and contract-structured production systems. He has not seen the emergence of new forms of industrial enterprise, or at least has not chosen to introduce a further complexity into this major study by including such new forms. Future scholarship in these directions, however, will be founded on Chandler's seminal, prodigious, and profoundly sagacious works.

•   •   •

The Limitations of the Personal Capitalism Paradigm
Roy Church

Three characteristic features have contributed much to Alfred D. Chandler, Jr.'s reputation as the leading business historian of his generation. Combining a strong hypothesis, systematic and detailed empirical analysis, and a lucid exposition, he has enormously enriched and transformed the field of business history. He has created a model of the development of corporate capitalism that is neither totally abstract, based on economic theory, nor vulgarly empiricist, building one fact on another. *Scale and Scope* carries forward the model developed in *The Visible Hand* by comparing the dynamics of America's corporate history between the 1880s and the Second World War with those of Britain and Germany, elucidating similarities and differences in the pattern of industrial capitalism that he identifies in each of the three countries. With *Scale and Scope* Chandler has undoubtedly advanced the teaching of comparative business history; research will also be stimulated by Chandler's willingness to generalize on a heroic scale in a book of such scope that inevitably not all its generalizations will elicit universal concurrence.

Review Colloquium / 704

Chandler's thesis is that beginning in the late nineteenth century large industrial (manufacturing) firms developed by exploiting economies of scale and scope, and that a necessary condition for successful corporate development was "three-pronged investment" in large-scale production, international marketing and distribution networks, and a management organization adapted to administer very large business units. The three-pronged investment prerequisite for success is employed by Chandler both as a test of and an explanation for the performance of individual firms and for international industrial comparisons.

The section concerning Britain dwells on that nation's failure as measured by the inability to adapt corporate structures to compete effectively in the core industries of the Second Industrial Revolution: metals, machinery, industrial chemicals, and oil. Because of the technical and production complexity of these industries, optimal efficiency required large-scale enterprises administered by an extensive hierarchy of salaried managers, rather than firms characteristically either owned and managed by families or exhibiting some other form of "personal enterprise." Yet in Britain the transition from personal enterprise, characteristic of the First Industrial Revolution, to managerial capitalism was delayed. Laws that (unlike in the United States and Germany) allowed collusion without encouraging either cartelization or full-scale mergers enabled large British firms to become part of "global oligopolies," thereby inhibiting corporate expansion. The limited size of the British internal market and a lack of university graduates among those managing British companies are also cited as factors in Great Britain's failure to embrace managerial capitalism. Chandler argues that personal enterprise continued to dominate manufacturing in Britain. Britain's Victorian industrialists made their mark in branded, packaged products—food and drink, tobacco and consumer chemicals—which made fewer managerial demands in terms of the complexity of production and offered less opportunity for securing scale economies. These industries continued to compete successfully at least until the Second World War.

In such industries, personal enterprises—owner-controlled, frequently managed by founders or their families, and lacking extensive management hierarchies—proved adequate to the task, but in the core industries of the Second Industrial Revolution they did not. Just as new products and processes that were to typify consumption and production in the early twentieth century began to be developed, according to Chandler, British entrepreneurs "hesitated" (p. 294).

Chandler's Scale and Scope / 705

Even where investment was undertaken in complex, product-specific production and distribution facilities and where appropriate technical and managerial skills were created, personal management constrained the growth of enterprise in ways that ensured Britain's lag behind its international competitors in Germany and the United States. British enterprises moved overseas more hesitantly and less successfully than their foreign rivals. Between the wars U.S. and German firms, larger and uncommitted to the British form of personal capitalism, successfully created and developed organizational capabilities that were exploited by managers highly trained in science and technology, and who in the United States also possessed graduate professional management skills. Chandler concludes from his review of the collective histories of British enterprises that they demonstrate the necessity of creating and maintaining organizational capabilities, that the failure to do so weakened British industry and with it the British economy, and that more than any other single factor a commitment by British entrepreneurs to the personal enterprise was the cause of Britain's industrial failure.

Perhaps it is inevitable that a strong hypothesis of this kind, developed with the support of historical evidence of firms, entrepreneurs, and managers, should leave the reader with an uneasy feeling that the general competitive environment has been inadequately specified and explained. Factors other than organizational type, such as the law, tariffs, resources, factor costs, capital markets, labor and trade unions, and the specific market environment industry by industry receive little more than passing reference.

Chandler distinguishes two types of companies, which although rare in the United States and Germany dominated the British manufacturing industry by the Second World War: either "firms managed by individuals or by a small number of associates, often members, of founders' families, assisted by only a few salaried managers, or they were federations of such firms" (p. 235). These federations were holding companies, each legally controlling its small, personally managed operating subdivisions, but lacking a large central corporate office for coordination, monitoring, or resource allocation. Compared to the number in the United States, few enterprises in Britain were administered through extensive managerial hierarchies, and substantially fewer than in Germany.

Personal enterprises not only lacked extensive managerial hierarchies but also typically were controlled by founding entrepreneurs or families who continued to participate in management. The problems

Review Colloquium / 706

of British business, in Chandler's analysis, stem in part from the consequences of ownership control for motivation and the setting of objectives and in part from the quality of management that owner participation produces. Thus, "owner-managers might have been more hesitant to deprive themselves of short-term income in order to invest in long-term growth" (pp. 236–37). In contrast to American managerial firms, where the basic goals appear to have been long-term profit and growth, "in Britain the goal for family firms appears to have been to provide a steady flow of cash to owners—owners who were also managers" (p. 390). Chandler finds evidence for this analysis in companies' payment of high dividends and issuance of nonvoting preferred stock and debentures, rather than investment of retained earnings to finance expansion or research and development.

Several points need to be made. The contrast between the relative importance of family firms in Britain and in the United States and Germany may be overdone. Philip Burch's analysis of family control in America's large corporations suggested that in the late 1930s between 40 and 50 percent of the largest manufacturing and mining firms could be classified as being under family control, falling to around 36 percent by 1965. In those family-controlled firms in 1965, Burch identified family participation in various major executive capacities in 91 percent of the top two hundred industrial firms.[1]

The motivation of owner-managers compared with that of nonfamily managerial organizations has been a matter of considerable debate, as have the effects on performance and profitability of the behavioral characteristics identified with the two types of firms. It is not obvious that owner-managers should prefer short-term income to long-term growth in assets, since the latter strategy would be more likely to enable an enterprise to survive the vicissitudes of competition and economic fluctuations than high dividends and low investment. By the very nature of personal enterprises after the first generation, owners tended to possess wealth, rendering income a welcome but less crucial objective. The evidence that Chandler presents for marked differentials in dividend levels between U.S. and British firms consists of observations for a handful of firms that, with one exception covering ten years, deal with only two to five years before the First World War (p. 390n161).

Chandler adduces further evidence from Wayne Lewchuk's study of the financing of the British motor industry before 1939 to support the hypothesis that British personal enterprises pursued policies

---

[1] Philip Burch, *The Managerial Revolution Reassessed* (Lexington, Mass., 1972).

Chandler's Scale and Scope / 707

of high dividends and low profit retention.[2] However, this evidence is insufficient to bear the weight placed on it in Chandler's model. The pattern of finance in one industry cannot be assumed to hold good for others, and in addition Lewchuk accepted balance sheet data as believable, making no attempt at a flow-of-funds analysis. More important, Lewchuk's analysis is less than conclusive even for the motor industry. He acknowledged that direct comparisons between the financing of British and American firms before 1919 are not possible, because British companies enjoyed access to a capital market attuned to and enthusiastic about public issues, whereas American firms had to rely on private sources and retained earnings to finance the public market for funds. Averaging a sample of British motor companies from 1919 to 1932 results in a relatively low proportion of retained profits. Yet Morris Motors, excluded from Lewchuk's sample before 1926 because it was entirely privately owned, was retaining some 90 percent of pretax profits for development during this period. As Morris produced over 50 percent of all motor vehicles made by the Big Six motor manufacturers in Britain in 1929, and Austin (which declared virtually no dividends on ordinary shares throughout the 1920s) produced 37 percent (together 58 percent of total production in 1935), the dividend history of these firms tends to invalidate the significance for the industry's course of development of the *average* picture implied by Lewchuk's sample. Since the basis for the Anglo-American comparison is the period before 1926, the terminal date for L. H. Seltzer's American study, the conclusions drawn by Chandler are of dubious validity.[3] There is evidence that during the 1930s lower levels of retained profits were characteristic of Morris and Austin (though comparisons with the United States are not available); however, the existence of changing patterns over time tends to negate the notion of a British bias toward short-termism explained by the structural features of personal capitalism.

Even if enterprises in the United States did tend to rely on internal financing more than their British counterparts, it does not necessarily follow that American managerial firms were more growth oriented, reflecting differences in "the basic goals of British and American enterprises, or, more properly, between enterprises managed per-

[2] Wayne Lewchuk, "Motor Vehicles" in *Decline of the British Economy*, ed. W. Bernard Elbaum and William Lazonick (New York, 1986), 135–61, and in greater detail Wayne Lewchuk, "The Return to Capital in the British Motor Vehicle Industry, 1896–1939" *Business History* 27 (1985): 3–25.

[3] L. M. Seltzer, *A Financial History of the American Automobile Industry* (Cambridge, Mass., 1928): 36–63.

sonally or by families and those administered by salaried managers"
(p. 390). Chandler asserts that in personally managed firms, "growth
was not a primary objective" (p. 292). To the extent that personally
and family-managed enterprises were more prevalent in the United
States than *Scale and Scope* suggests, the explanatory significance for
Anglo-American performance and international competition merits
less emphasis. Moreover, there are further justifications for doubting
the explanatory value of the attribution of contrasting behavioral
characteristics to different kinds of corporate structures. The work of
Oliver Williamson, K. J. Monsen and A. Downs, Robin Marris, and
others has stressed characteristics common to large enterprises in the
setting of goals, irrespective of ownership, control, and management
participation (crucial characteristics of personal enterprises).[4] The
bureaucratic structures set up to administer large organizations cannot be controlled by those at the apex of the decision-making hierarchy; their goals are frustrated by diverging interests and objectives
shared by lower and middle management. The systematic deviations
from whatever goals the organization may be pursuing occur because
top managers in larger managerial firms must delegate responsibility
to subordinates. The outcome is the pursuit of steady and probably
slower growth instead of the maximum profits typically associated with
owner-managed firms.

Irrespective of the type of enterprise, in Chandler's terminology
the quality of decision making—by entrepreneurs or by managers—is
crucial to ensure that the three-pronged investment strategy is adopted.
Chandler is critical not only of the slowness with which enterprises
in Britain recruited external managers, but he also condemns the failure
of British institutions of higher learning for their slow response to
the needs of the new industrial enterprise for science, technology, and
management graduates. Quoting Eric Ashby,Chandler endorses the
view that the aim of universities during the early twentieth century
was"to be 'a nursery for gentlemen, statesmen and administrators'"
(p. 293) and that the link between education and industry remained
tenuous, at least until the Second World War. J.M.Sanderson has
exposed this interpretation, widespread in the literature on Britain's
industrial decline, as false, particularly with respect to the civic universities, for even in 1914 Oxford and Cambridge graduates were a

---

    [4] Oliver Williamson, "The Modern Corporation: Origins, Evolution, Attributes," *Journal
of Economic Literature* 19 (1981): 1537–68; K. J. Monsen and A. Downs, "The Behavior
of the Large Managerial Firm," *Journal of Political Economy* 3 (1965): 221–36; Robin Marris
and D. Mueller, "The Corporation, Competition, and the Visible Hand," *Journal of Economic Literature* 18 (1980): 36–63.

Chandler's Scale and Scope / 709

minority.[5] Chandler quotes Robert Locke in condemning the contribution of British higher education to Britain's decline. However, Locke's verdict was that, although the contributions of German institutions to higher technological education were superior to those in Britain and the United States, "since they were industrialized countries with systems of higher technical and scientific education, the insufficiencies were marginal at worst."[6] Sanderson's study showed that at least at the civic universities and at Imperial College, London, the ethos was not anti-industrial, and the overall percentage of university-age cohorts attending university in 1913 was 4 percent in the United States compared with 1.47 percent in Britain; the figure for Germany, with which Britain is also adversely compared, was 1.65 percent.

Chandler is justified in underlining the British failure, in comparison with the United States and Germany, to introduce management education, which reflects the lack of interest by business in the recruitment of graduates in commerce or business subjects. However, the prejudice against the employment of graduates (other than those within the family), except in narrowly defined scientific or technical roles (or for lower level responsibilities) was deeply ingrained within the business sector until after 1945; Imperial Chemical Industries (ICI) was an exception. This prejudice existed in British firms regardless of ownership, control, and management hierarchies and was to be found in both managerial and personal enterprises.

As an explanatory concept, therefore, the "personal enterprise" possesses serious weaknesses; some of the evidence presented in elucidation of its nature and operation is partial, and occasionally the evidence that can be drawn from business histories cautions further against uncritical acceptance of Chandler's classifications. An extreme example is his account of the Birmingham Small Arms Company (BSA), which he ranks alongside the Anglo-Persian Oil Company, Dunlop in rubber, and Stewarts & Lloyds in steel tubes as firms that created organizational capabilities to a degree that brought success and dominance in their respective markets. Chandler's discussion implies that the reconversion of BSA's plant from wartime production after 1918 to produce cycles, motorcycles, and machine tools was a major achievement: the company "had the facilities and skills—the organizational capabilities—to remain the dominant producer of motorcycles at home and Britain's major representative in that line abroad" (p.

[5] J. M. Sanderson, *The Universities and British Industry, 1850–1950* (London, 1972).
[6] Robert Locke, *The End of Practical Man* (Greenwich, Conn., 1984), 78.

345). In terms of the volume of sales, BSA was successful, but the company was unprofitable, recording a financial loss even in its peak year of sales in 1935. Between 1918 and 1940 BSA experienced a series of irrelevant structural reorganizations, reshuffling of top managers, and abortive efforts to develop new products[7]. Mediocrity characterized the board of directors despite the rapid turnover of personnel, with the resulting failure to coordinate the productive and marketing elements of BSA.

Production series or other unidimensional proxy indicators employed as evidence can be unreliable bases from which to deduce the character, functioning, and achievements of organizational structures. Lack of sufficient substantive evidence,except for various measures of sector and enterprise size, notably for output and market shares compels Chandler to rely heavily on a handful of individual company histories for detailed elaboration and validation of his principal arguments (Courtaulds, ICI, Pilkingtons, and Cadbury in particular). By adducing evidence from other studies, however, it is possible to offer serious reservations to Chandler's thesis. Until further detailed research is carried out to test the various elements contained in his argument, the availability of evidence that points to a lack of congruence between forms of corporate structure and behavioral characteristics and corporate "style" counsels caution. It would be unwarranted to infer either strengths or weaknesses in strategy and achievement only from the fact that personal capitalism may (or may not) have been the phenomenon that most distinguished British manufacturing industry from that of the United States and Germany. Both the extent of personal capitalism in these countries and its behavioral significance have yet to be examined in adequate depth.

Such a task could not be expected of a work encompassing so enormous a range of issues on an international comparative basis. Chandler's forceful presentation of his argument should ensure that these questions will soon figure high on the research agenda of business historians. For this reason, notwithstanding all reservations, the appearance of *Scale and Scope* is a milestone for all interested in the history of the structure, organization, conduct, and performance of business institutions, not only for the lucidity with which the hypotheses are presented, but also for the insights that Chandler has to offer and for the debates that this study will inevitably provoke.

---

[7] R. P. T. Davenport-Hines, *Dudley Docker: The Life and Times of a Trade Warrior* (Cambridge, England, 1985).

Chandler's Scale and Scope / 711

·   ·   ·

Germany: Cooperation and Competition
Jürgen Kocka

Alfred D. Chandler Jr.'s *Scale and Scope* is comparative economic history at its best. It begins with a set of related assumptions, concepts, questions, and hypotheses developed from previous in-depth research on the American case and explicitly stated in the first part of the book. Chandler's basic interests are in the rise and the changing character of the modern industrial enterprise and its fundamental role in the growth and the transformation of Western economies in the period of advanced industrialization.

Changing markets as well as new transportation and communication systems on the one hand and improved processes of production on the other created the possibility of increased regularity, volume, and speed in the flows of goods and materials. Consequently, in some industries substantial economies of scale and scope became possible. In order to benefit from them, entrepreneurs had to invest heavily in production facilities, marketing networks, and management. The resulting modern industrial enterprise was large-scale and capital- and management-intensive; it tended to expand at home and abroad, to diversify into a multiproduct enterprise, to be led by salaried managers and coordinated by managerial hierarchies, and to integrate forward (into sales) and sometimes backward (into supply). The first entrepreneurs to create such enterprises acquired powerful competitive advantages and good prospects for long-term success. The economies in which these changes toward the modern managerial enterprise were made early and broadly did better than economies in which these changes were delayed. Chandler uses this analysis to explain the much better performance of the American and the German economies compared with the British between the 1880s and the 1930s and again after 1945.

In order to be manageable, a historical comparison must restrict itself to a limited number of questions. Consequently, Chandler excludes several topics of social and cultural history—for example, changing labor relations, the broader cultural environment, and business-government relationships (though he does try to consider the impact of different legal and educational systems). Chandler chooses to compare the United States, Great Britain, and Germany, which together accounted for about two-thirds of the world's indus-

Review Colloquium / 712

trial output between the 1870s and the 1930s. For each of these countries he constructs comparable tables of the two hundred largest industrial enterprises, ranked by assets and listed by industrial groups, at three points between 1913 and 1953—a major achievement in itself.[1] Chandler mobilizes information on the history of a substantial minority of these largest industrial enterprises in the three countries by exploiting an impressive wealth of printed and unprinted materials, company histories, and research literature. By careful country-to-country and industry-to-industry comparisons, he describes and explains the different timing and varying patterns of the rise of the modern industrial enterprise. By applying the same concepts and hypotheses to structure the materials in each case, Chandler succeeds in pointing out what was common and what was specific to the three national cases, and why. In this way he checks and supports his main causal hypotheses.

Chandler's analyses are dependent on the quality of the available literature and the state of research on each country. Consequently, the section on the revolution of distribution is weaker in the part on Germany than in the two other parts because of the imperfect state of research. Of course such synthetic overviews must be selective, reflecting the author's analytical aims. As a result, for example, the chapters on textiles are short and sketchy, and other labor-intensive industries are hardly touched on. Chandler's approach seems to illuminate more about the American and the German cases than about the British one, but developments in each of the three nations become more understandable and appear in a new light as a result of Chandler's comparative method.

The field of business and entrepreneurial history abounds with individual studies of single companies, single aspects, sometimes single industries; systematic analysis is rare. Chandler's chapter on Germany is a splendid exception, a welcome synthesis, an innovative piece of research. Because of his comparative approach, Chandler succeeds in bringing in branches of industry and specific companies that are usually neglected or at least not integrated into the picture one has of German business history: rayon and alkali producers, the chocolate maker Stollwerck, and the tire manufacturer Continental. The

---

[1] However, Hannes Siegrist has produced more detailed and more complete lists on the *hundred* largest enterprises in German manufacturing and mining in 1887, 1907, and 1927 (on the basis of nominal capital, including the large personal enterprises). Cf. the tables in Norbert Horn and Jürgen Kocka, eds., *Law and the Formation of the Big Enterprises in the Nineteenth and Early Twentieth Centuries* (Göttingen, 1979), 98–112, and Hannes Siegrist, "Deutsche Grossunternehmen vom späten 19. Jahrhundert bis zur Weimarer Republik," in *Geschichte und Gesellschaft* 6 (1980): 60–102, esp. 93–102.

Chandler's Scale and Scope / 713

information is tremendously rich, accurate as far as I can judge, and—most important—it is part of a well-structured, well-integrated argument. Chandler's comparative research produces new insights—for example, his analysis of IG Farben's limited ability to develop new and promising lines of production in the 1920s and 1930s (pp. 580–81). Chandler also succeeds in establishing and detailing what we had assumed in a more general, less well supported, and sometimes inaccurate way: the striking similarities in the early rise of German and American managerial capitalism, in sharp contrast to Britain, where the commitment to personal capitalism and to market instead of to hierarchies continued much longer; the pioneering role of the leading German electrical manufacturer Siemens in the development of the multidivisional structure before the First World War; the particular modernity of German producer-goods industries and the relative backwardness—or fragmentation—of some of the German "lesser industries," especially producers of food, tobacco, and consumer chemicals. Chandler convincingly shows that the larger (though declining) role of the banks and the legality and abundance of cartels (with or without common selling agencies) and other forms of intensive interfirm cooperation distinguished the German brand of "cooperative managerial capitalism" from American-style "competitive managerial capitalism."[2]

As a consequence of this full-fledged comparison, which is based on an admirable amount of painstaking research in the literature and archives of three countries, Chandler has slightly modified his approach. First, he no longer simply contrasts American with European developments.[3] Indeed, differences within Europe (between Germany and Great Britain, for example) are more pronounced than differences between single European countries (especially Germany) and the United States. Second, functional integration backward and forward is now less clearly interpreted as an indicator of a firm's modernity than it was in Chandler's earlier writings. Indeed, in established industries vertical integration sometimes decreased as a consequence of better developed and more stable markets, particularly after 1945 (p. 613). Finally, in his earlier writings, Chandler tended to assume that international differences in the rise of the large-scale, diversified,

---

[2] As Chandler knows, this reconfirms the notion of "organized capitalism" developed in a more sweeping way in a controversial debate that started in the early 1970s. Cf. H. A. Winkler, ed., *Organisierter Kapitalismus* (Göttingen, 1974).

[3] This was done, for example, in Alfred D. Chandler, Jr., and Herman Daems, "Administrative Coordination, Allocation and Monitoring: Concepts and Comparisons," in Horn and Kocka, eds., *Law and the Formation of the Big Enterprises*, 28–54.

Review Colloquium / 714

integrated, managerial enterprise resulted from different market sizes and growth rates. In *Scale and Scope* the causal analysis has become much more differentiated and complex. Besides markets and other strictly economic factors, Chandler now stresses the different organizational capabilities of entrepreneurs and the skills and motivations of managers as explanatory factors, and he tries to account for them in a variety of ways—by considering, among other issues, the different educational, cultural, and legal traditions within the three countries. In the case of Germany, for example, he convincingly stresses the importance of the long tradition of bureaucratic management (p. 500).

The causal analysis of the observed national differences could be further enriched. First, the concrete links between education, recruitment, skill, and motivation of managers on the one hand, their strategic decisions and the performance of their enterprises on the other, need further clarification. In Chandler's book managerial capabilities and resources are described in only a general way; the real working of the managerial structures remains something of a "black box" (with some exceptions, for example, p. 595). Second, for the late nineteenth and early twentieth centuries at least, the relationship between the relative backwardness of an economy at large and the relative modernity of some of its largest firms should be explored. West European entrepreneurs may have had fewer incentives to build large and sophisticated managerial hierarchies because they could rely on well-developed market structures and a high degree of overall economic specialization, whereas in the less developed economies of Central and Eastern Europe entrepreneurs were forced to internalize more functions and to use formal organization to compensate for deficient markets. Under different market conditions English and German entrepreneurs behaved differently, but both of them made choices that were rational relative to the constellation in which they found themselves. However, the more backward situation led to entrepreneurial solutions that, in the long run, turned out to be favorable to modernization and growth, whereas the more developed constellation in the West permitted strategic decisions and firm structures that later became a liability.[4]

Compared with that of the United States, German managerial capitalism can certainly be qualified as "cooperative." Chandler has ample evidence supporting this view. But it seems to me that he sometimes tends to underestimate the severity of competition and the seri-

---

[4] The Gerschenkronian idea is not incompatible with Chandler's analysis. Cf. J. Kocka and H. Siegrist, "Die hundert grössten deutschen Industrieunternehmen im späten 19. und frühen 20. Jahrhundert: Expansion, Diversifikation und Integration im internationalen Vergleich," in ibid., 91–95.

ousness of rivalries between the large firms in spite of their common cartels, joint ventures, and shared bank connections. Compared with the situation in Japan, German managerial capitalism would probably appear to be highly competitive.

There is much continuity in the German system of large-scale industry, in spite of the deep ruptures of social and political history between the 1880s and the 1960s. Firms that moved first had a good chance to endure. Those at the top around 1900 were likely to be in the top group a quarter of a century later, and perhaps even in the 1950s and 1960s. Chandler describes and explains the long-term success of many "first movers" and the difficulties of the "new challengers," particularly if they came from the large field of small and middle-sized firms. Still, as Chandler knows, there was much turnover. Fifty-four of the one hundred largest German manufacturing and mining firms of the year 1887 no longer belonged to the top one hundred in 1907, and only twenty-four of them could still be found in the top group in 1927.[5] Perhaps one should offer more explanation of why early success stories so frequently turned into stories of decline and failure.

Chandler is certainly not unaware that large-scale economic institutions *may* be unfavorable to economic growth. He remarks that real innovations frequently came from outside the large firms (p. 604). One should push this line of thought a bit farther and consider the masses of small and medium-sized firms that hardly appear in Chandler's account. Now and then Chandler admits that expansion, integration, and diversification can go too far and become obstacles to a firm's or an economy's success (for example, pp. 510, 626–27). Greater emphasis could be placed on the fact that attempts to build large-scale empires and organizations can be economically irrational. Small personal firms are not necessarily less effective than large-scale managerial firms; it depends on the circumstances.

But basically Chandler is right in stressing the dynamic role of managerial capabilities and large-scale structures and their important "independent" contributions to economic growth. They not only respond to market incentives, but they shape and influence them as well. They are not just tools of business leaders' decisions, but they develop a momentum of their own. It is Chandler's outstanding achievement to have rediscovered the firm between markets and entrepreneurs and to have reintroduced it into American economic history. It does not appear that Chandler's thought has been deci-

---

[5] Ibid., 84. Also see appendix C.4 in *Scale and Scope*, 722–32.

sively influenced by Max Weber, but in some respects his approach is Weberian. He has produced a masterful and unparalleled synthesis that will soon become a classic.

.   .   .

The View from Japan
Hidemasa Morikawa

Scale and Scope is a testament to Alfred D. Chandler, Jr.'s enduring intellectual vigor. The two most important elements of the book, I believe, are a new theoretical framework erected on an examination of the collective histories of large-scale industrial enterprises covering more than a century and the comparative study of the development and transformation of modern industrial enterprises in the United States, Great Britain, and Germany. Although Japan, as a later industrializing nation, is not included in Chandler's discussion, much of what he says has important implications for the study of Japanese business history.

Although the "scale" and "scope" of the title are important key words in this book, the core concept of Chandler's new framework is "organizational capabilities," which he employs for the first time here. He argues that economists and sociologists have not developed a dynamic theory to explain the evolution of modern industrial enterprises and modern industrial capitalism. Chandler's historical analysis of modern industrial enterprise leads him to the conclusion that "[a]t the core of this dynamic were the organizational capabilities of the enterprise as a unified whole" (p. 594).

Organizational capabilities refer to the physical facilities and human skills that are organized within an enterprise. They can be generated and maintained by a three-pronged investment in production, distribution, and management; according to Chandler, "Functional and strategic competition for market share between the major players of the new oligopolies was a major force in sharpening these organizational capabilities. Such competition provided a spur to counter inevitable bureaucratic inertia, and the enhanced capabilities provided profits to finance continued growth" (p. 230). Significantly, financial capital is excluded from the category of organizational capabilities; it is considered as the means for making the necessary investments and as the result of a successful enterprise.

Chandler's Scale and Scope / 717

Because it sets organizational capabilities at the core of its theoretical framework, *Scale and Scope* makes considerable progress from Chandler's previous books, which tended to emphasize surrounding changes in technology and in the market without focusing on the nucleus of the enterprise. Although Chandler does not discuss the "organizational capabilities" paradigm in general terms, but rather specifically in connection with the exploitation of economies of scale and scope to acquire powerful competitive advantages, the term nevertheless expresses the key subjective factor of entrepreneurial activity. It shows Chandler's recognition that a business enterprise does not consist of only the functioning of objective forces such as technology and the market.

I believe that Chandler's use of "organizational capabilities" also results from his need to evaluate properly the human skills in the development of modern industrial enterprises. Human skills are the decisive element in a firm's organizational capabilities, because physical facilities are chosen, built, and operated by the managers and the work force. When oligopolistic competition hones capabilities, it is working not on the buildings, but on the skills of people. In addition, the coordination and integration of facilities and expertise are made possible by the skills of management. According to Chandler, "The combined capabilities of top and middle management can be considered the skills of the organization itself. These skills were the most valuable of all those that made up the *organizational capabilities* of the new modern industrial enterprise" (p. 36).

Many Japanese business historians have studied the competitive strength of Japanese industries and the management system that supported it from the viewpoint of the accumulation of technological and managerial skills within those industries. Indeed, Japan's later industrial development made this subject a matter of more than academic interest, and it is hence more developed there than in the United States. A few colleagues still attempt to explain the success of Japanese businesses in terms of a mysterious Japanese "culture" or the existence of a brutal system of worker exploitation, but these interpretations are losing esteem. Historians cannot verify human skill levels empirically in any direct way, because the evolution of knowledge and the influence of external factors such as culture and social norms cannot be easily measured. At best, we can research the environment in which skills grow and accumulate within business enterprises. For Japanese business historians, therefore, the "organizational capabilities" concept advanced in *Scale and Scope* is a delightful gift.

Review Colloquium / 718

Many conventional studies of Japanese business history have limited their discussion of managerial resources to financial functions, because available source materials often provide more financial and other quantitative data than interpretative or qualitative information. Following the flow of financial resources alone, however, cannot produce a comprehensive picture. The growth of healthy enterprises does not automatically result from the accumulation of financial resources, which can be used simply to speculate in corporate shares and real estate. Investing those financial resources in physical facilities for production and distribution alone also does not guarantee the competitiveness of a firm, because the essential ingredient is the formation and development of human skills to operate the facilities. The arrangement of a huge bureaucratic hierarchy is much less effective if it lacks networks of managerial skills that actually coordinate the organization.

Thus the concept of organizational capabilities centered around human skills will be a key idea for understanding the growth potential and competitiveness of firms as we try to analyze both the reasons for Japanese success and why American large firms, at least at the present moment, cannot compete against their Japanese counterparts.

Despite Chandler's excellent theoretical work, I did find some points of disagreement. The first of these is the discussion of vertical integration, which I believe is less compelling than that presented in *The Visible Hand*. In *The Visible Hand* vertical integration, together with product diversification, was presented as one pattern of aggressive strategy for the growth of the business enterprise. Vertical integration included both backward and forward integration, though Chandler especially emphasized the relationship of production and distribution—that is, forward integration. But *Scale and Scope* considers only backward integration, so that vertical integration becomes nothing more than a method "to withhold supplies from competitors and so create barriers to entry in the industry" (p. 37) and "to assure a steady supply of materials into the enterprise's production processes" (p. 38). Increased productivity and cost reduction therefore do not result from vertical integration.

I do not understand the shift in Chandler's interpretation of vertical integration from *The Visible Hand* to *Scale and Scope*. If vertical integration is taken to include forward integration, it requires the three-pronged investment, intensifies organizational capabilities, and helps to assure the cost advantages of scale and scope. All of this certainly suggests aggressive strategy. Furthermore, even if vertical integration

Chandler's Scale and Scope / 719

is limited to backward integration, it cannot be characterized as only defensive except in the case where the motive for assuring supplies is speculative.

Second, I find a decrease in the conceptual clarity of "the managerial enterprise" in this book. In his earlier work, Chandler clearly defined managerial enterprises as "firms in which representatives of the founding families or of financial interests no longer make top-level management decisions—where such decisions are made by salaried managers who own little of companies' stock."[1] This definition points to a significant historical trend: that the governors of business enterprises have changed from venture capitalists, founding families, financiers, and their representatives to salaried managers.

In *Scale and Scope*, Chandler's definition of "managerial enterprise" has become more vague. Although he continues to look at the relationship between owners and salaried managers, he now attaches importance to the relationship between "inside" and "outside" directors, which he defines as follows: "The inside directors, who were full-time managers, included senior members of the salaried hierarchy and members of the founder's family who were also full-time top managers. The outside directors, who were part-time directors with other business and social interests, represented major stockholders, including family members who were not full-time managers" (p. 85). The focus on "inside" and "outside" directors leads to confusion. For example, in the cases of oil, rubber, industrial materials, and primary metals, Chandler concludes that "by the 1920s . . . there were enterprises whose managers owned less than 1% of the stock of the company they administered. These salaried managers, unencumbered by the wishes of large stockholders (whether members of founding families, venture capitalists, or outside investors) selected their own boards of directors and nominated their own successors" (p. 145). In some cases, founding family members and venture capitalists who were full-time inside directors could take part in decision making at the highest level with top salaried managers; in others, inside directors might be removed from the top management position by the salaried managers. Which of these two scenarios becomes the dominant trend?

Chandler writes, "It must be stressed, however, that management control cannot be measured in terms of the amount of stock held.

---

[1] Alfred D. Chandler, Jr., "The United States: Seedbed of Managerial Capitalism," in *Managerial Hierarchies: Comparative Perspectives on the Rise of the Modern Industrial Enterprise*, ed. Chandler and Herman Daems (Cambridge, Mass., 1980), 14.

Review Colloquium / 720

The managers of these companies gained control because they, not the outside directors, had the knowledge, experience, and information required to make and implement the strategies essential to keep such enterprises profitable. Only those family members who worked as full-time managers were in a position to influence such decisions" (p. 192). Where are the salaried managers? Such a description is utterly inconsistent with Chandler's previous argument on the development of the managerial enterprise. Indeed, we can find Chandler making two inconsistent statements in the same paragraph: He writes,

> In the machinery industries, as in the chemical and chemically oriented food industries, the complex and technical nature of decisions critical to current and future health of their enterprises meant that they were made by trained and experienced, full-time salaried managers. Here, as in chemicals, the information, knowledge, and experience of the inside directors gave them the authority to plan and implement long-term strategy, as well as to make short-term operating decisions (p. 222).

But the inside directors are not necessarily the same people as the salaried managers.

In Chandler's original definition, the "managerial" of managerial enterprise meant the dominant role of salaried managers, not of full-time directors. Under Chandler's earlier definition, one would expect that even full-time owner-directors would hand over their control of the company to salaried managers in the course of development toward managerial enterprises. In *Scale and Scope* Chandler intertwines the owner-salaried manager relationship with the inside (full-time)-outside (part-time) director relationship, creating, it seems to me, a much less clear distinction.

In his international comparison among the United States, Great Britain, and Germany, Chandler summarizes the basic factors that encouraged the expansion of modern industrial enterprise and competitive managerial capitalism in the United States as follows: "(1) the large, rapidly growing, geographically extensive, affluent domestic market; (2) the continuing development of capital-intensive technologies of production; and (3) the legal environment that prevented the enforcement of the contractual price-and-output arrangements that were attempted through horizontal federations of small firms" (p. 89). The reasons why personal or family capitalism in Britain and cooperative or organized capitalism in Germany, both in contrast to American managerial capitalism, developed before the First World War are analyzed in light of these three factors.

The conclusions of Chandler's comparative analysis among the three countries are somewhat contradictory. He seems to answer the critical question of why British entrepreneurs failed to make the three-pronged investment in production, distribution, and organization and to exploit the opportunities of the new technologies of the Second Industrial Revolution by pointing to the scale of the market and the continued personal management of family enterprises. Of these two, he considers the size of the market as the controlling factor, as when he writes, referring to the British steel industry, "Their relatively small initial investment in new production technologies, their reliance on commercial intermediaries, and their personal management—all these reflected the presence of a market still too small to exploit fully the economies of scale" (p. 285).

The argument for the importance of market scale is not entirely convincing. First, Chandler mentions the small geographical size of Britain, but it is in fact not so different from that of Germany or Japan. Second, he points out that Britain was more geographically separated from foreign markets than was Germany. But one must wonder if the distances of Britain and Germany from many European markets were significantly different. Moreover, Chandler seems to call the whole issue into question when he writes of the extraordinarily rich consumer market in Britain in the early twentieth century.

Even if the scale of Britain's domestic and foreign markets is admitted to be limited in the ways Chandler describes, it is a mistake to view market inelasticity as the sole cause of the lack of substantial three-pronged investment among British entrepreneurs. Some firms operating within that market situation did make the necessary investments, both before and after the First World War.

More important than the market situation, I believe, is the persistence of personal management in British family enterprises. Chandler himself considers this topic in some detail. "Throughout the late nineteenth century," he writes, "British entrepreneurs continued to view their businesses in personal rather than organizational terms, as family estates to be nurtured and passed on to heirs" (p. 286). Even after the First World War, "there is a good deal of evidence to support the view that in Britain a large and stable income for the family was more of an incentive than the long-term growth of the firm. . . . These and other family firms were reluctant to recruit nonfamily managers and even slower to bring such salaried executives into top management" (p. 390).

This distinctive persistence of personal management surely hampered the growth of technological and managerial skills—that is, of organizational capabilities within British business enterprises. However, more concrete research needs to be done on the decline of organiza-

Review Colloquium / 722

tional capabilities within British businesses. Although family enterprise does tend to continue personal management based on ongoing family control, this is not always the case. For example, prewar Japan's large family-owned enterprise groups, the *zaibatsu*, notwithstanding their ostensible family control, built up managerial hierarchies with powerful salaried managers in senior positions. Thus the personal management style unique to British companies cannot be explained solely on the basis of family structure. Family-run businesses in Britain produced personal management that obstructed the development of organizational capabilities, whereas in Japan the leadership of salaried managers checked family control and personal management, encouraging the growth of organizational capabilities.

Chandler also argues that the growth of British organizational capabilities was arrested by "less vigorous competition between firms." British firms did tend to avoid competition and to negotiate with each other for market share in the domestic market and with foreign companies in the world market. However, this tendency toward cooperation was seen not only in Britain, but also in Germany, and German firms successfully developed powerful organizational capabilities.

Chandler's description of German managerial capitalism as cooperative naturally raises the question of the nature of "cooperation" in Japanese capitalism. Such well-known elements as prewar *zaibatsu*, postwar *keiretsu*, and the active role of the government inevitably give a strong impression of cooperation in Japanese business affairs, but the situation is more ambiguous than it first appears. Japanese capitalism preserves the fundamental nature of competitive capitalism while utilizing cooperative instruments when they serve a purpose.

The *zaibatsu* and most of the *keiretsu* are certainly cooperative. In both cases, their headquarters, where collective managerial resources are cumulated and overall policies formulated, coordinated cooperation among affiliated and integrated enterprises. The cooperation in this context is more extensive than that of German cartels, combinations, and trusts. Moreover, the scope of cooperation in Japan has been much wider than that which Chandler describes for Germany. In Japan enterprises cooperated in multi-industry and multi-business areas, whereas in Germany the cooperation remained within each industry.

However, the behavior of enterprises within the same industry in Japan is fiercely competitive. For firms affiliated with the *zaibatsu* or an enterprise group, this took the form of intergroup competition. In this sense Japanese capitalism since the nineteenth century up to the present has been a competitive capitalism. Cartels were once legal in Japan, and between the wars cartels were organized in the cotton spinning, coal, copper, iron and steel, cement, and electrical machinery industries. But they were not effective in their original functions of controlling the prices and quantities of their products. Sometimes their basic purposes were different, as in cotton textiles, where cartels were formed to organize the financial activities of wholesalers. Coal cartels were organized to lobby the government to limit imports. Most enterprises emphasized the development of organizational capabilities rather than extensively employing cartels, which played only a minor role in management policies. Cartels often simply served as "gentleman's clubs" to facilitate the exchange of information among companies, and that is the role played today by most of Japan's informal cartels.

The Japanese government, which without doubt played a significant role in shaping the industry structure, did not regulate the competitive behavior of enterprises, except on two occasions: in the transition to the wartime economy of the 1930s and in the acceptance of depression cartels in the 1970s. Even in its industrial development policies, the government was careful to target more than two companies in an industry to preserve and encourage competition among enterprises. Thus, in the prewar years two groups, Mitsubishi and Kawasaki, competed in building battleships; Mitsubishi and Nakajima were fierce rivals in developing military airplanes.

The Japanese story may also have something to contribute to a consideration of the explanatory power of Chandler's distinction between "personal" and "managerial" capitalism. Chandler sees the development of managerial enterprises in Germany as comparable to that in the United States and much greater than their development in Britain: "in Germany, as in the United States, salaried managers with little or no equity in the enterprises for which they worked participated in making decisions concerning current production and distribution, as well as in planning and allocating resources for future production and distribution" (p. 393). Nevertheless, when reading *Scale and Scope*, we can find everywhere substantial evidence that family enterprises continued to be as firmly rooted in Germany as in Britain, so that Chandler's focus on managerial capitalism in Germany may be excessive. However, even if we argue that many German enterprises persisted in family control and personal management after the Second World War, we must admit that they were able to develop considerably more powerful organizational capabilities than their British counterparts. Why? Chandler lists various factors that encouraged the growth of German organizational capabilities, such as dependence on

Review Colloquium / 724

teams of salaried managers stemming from the long tradition of bureaucratic management and German industry's close relationship with "universities that served both as training grounds for managers and as sources of technological information and innovation" (p. 500).

A deeper analysis of these circumstances would be useful in explaining the dynamic development of Japanese organizational capabilities. Numerous family enterprises played a significant role in prewar Japan. Certain wealthy families, in particular, developed diversified enterprises in widely scattered industries and exclusively owned those firms. Many family enterprises, including some *zaibatsu*, did emphasize the preservation of family business assets; those with that outlook simply declined in the process of industrial growth. Most *zaibatsu*, as well as many other family businesses—probably a higher proportion than in Germany and considerably higher than in Britain—developed Chandler's organizational capabilities and stressed the significance of long-term corporate growth. In the process, the *zaibatsu* became a significant force in Japan's industrialization.

Many *zaibatsu*, from their early phases of growth, aggressively recruited highly educated salaried managers and promoted them to middle and top positions in the managerial hierarchy. The top management of Mitsui and Sumitomo thus became almost exclusively controlled by salaried managers. At Mitsubishi, family members and salaried managers shared the duties of top management; some conservative groups, such as Yasuda and Asano, limited the role of salaried managers to middle management. Although the families still owned the companies, salaried managers were responsible for strategic and operational decision making, which resulted in diversified, often risky, investment. Families generally trusted the salaried managers and usually accepted their decisions even when they did not agree with the strategies adopted by the managers. In prewar Japan, therefore, the managerial enterprise was firmly established despite the persistence of widespread family ownership.

In the last eight pages of the concluding chapter, Chandler's unhappiness with current conditions, in which he sees a decline in managerial capitalism, is evident. Since the 1960s, in the United States, Europe, and Japan, large-scale managerial enterprises grew and diversified broadly. As a result, there occurred an unprecedented degree of competition for market share among large enterprises equipped with effective organizational capabilities. Facing contracting market share, increasing excess capacity, and a decreasing return on investment, these big industrial enterprises believed that "the opportunities for profit from investment in their own or closely related industries had become

Chandler's Scale and Scope / 725

limited" (p. 622). Since the 1960s, therefore, they converted to strategies of investing extensively in businesses in which they had no experience and no product-specific organizational capabilities. Furthermore, they engaged enthusiastically in mergers and acquisitions, and they are now suffering from the organizational overload of administering a wide variety of businesses. Moreover, the fever of merger and acquisition fueled the businesses of buying and selling companies and their securities. Enormous sums are being directed not into the improvement of the organizational capabilities of industrial enterprises, but into the speculative money game.

Chandler sees this scenario as more pervasive in the United States than in Europe, although, he writes, "As competition increased, . . . Europe's large industrial enterprises also began to move into distantly related and unrelated markets, and overdiversification into other industries and overexpansion into foreign markets certainly occurred" (p. 626). According to Chandler, only Japan appears to be avoiding this disastrous formula.

Chandler's argument is cogent, but it is only a brief sketch, leaving a more in-depth study of this problem for another time. It is unreasonable, I think, to trace the deterioration of large industrial enterprises in the United States and elsewhere to the unprecedented competition since the 1960s. In Chandler's own framework, strategic and functional competition for market share sharpen organizational capabilities, forcing industrial enterprises in each country to develop new markets, new technologies, and new resources in the future. The recent phenomenon of suffering American industrial enterprises is the result of their failure to gain a victory in the competition with Japan and other countries, and this failure itself stems from the weakened organizational capabilities in American industry. But the competition is not over. The Japanese firms, winners today, may be defeated one day by American firms because of their arrogance as leaders and their own failure to continue to improve organizational capabilities. Entrepreneurs in the United States, who have a long and brilliant history of creating powerful organizational capabilities, cannot be the ultimate losers. They will learn to understand and to avoid unsuitable activities within enterprises and to devise more effective organizational capabilities. In that process, they will continue to learn a great deal from the experiences of their European and Japanese counterparts.

.   .   .

Developing Countries and the Modern Firm
Albert Fishlow

Alfred Chandler's *Scale and Scope* is a persuasive and rich account of the dynamics of industrial capitalism between 1880 and 1940 in the three leading industrial nations—the United States, Great Britain, and Germany—that is destined to become a definitive work on the subject. Chandler's argument, familiar to many from his earlier *The Visible Hand*, is briefly put. Industrial development, and thereby economic growth, was dependent on the emergence of the modern enterprise. Large, integrated, and hierarchically managed firms came to dominate their competitors because they could best exploit: 1) the economies of scale and scope—that is, product diversification—inherent in the new capital-intensive technologies characteristic of the Second Industrial Revolution; 2) the economies of marketing, distribution, and purchasing that were essential to achieving competitive advantage and staving off potential challengers; and 3) the economies of strategic management over a host of decisions, ranging from rationalization of production to investment in research and development to expansion into new markets.

The heart of the book is not theoretical elaboration of this thesis, but rather presentation of historical evidence in its support. The experiences of the two hundred largest firms in the United States, Britain, and Germany over a sixty-year period form the information set. So effective is the weaving of detail within this framework, whether relating to firms, industries, or countries and whether stressing similarities or differences, that the fundamental propositions sometimes appear to be self-evident. That skillful and graceful exposition understates the novelty and the importance of Chandler's contribution.

Implicit in Chandler's affirmations is rejection of other plausible hypotheses regarding the process of economic growth. First, in his attention to dynamic industry as the motor of capitalist expansion through its positive externalities, he minimizes the utility of static comparative advantage and specialization in primary production as guides to investment. Second, in emphasizing the positive contribution of the large firm, despite the market concentration it fosters, Chandler rejects the view that atomistic competition is a preferable form for encouraging growth; indeed, at one point, in a concluding comparison drawing on post–Second World War developments, he speaks of "a new era—one characterized by more competition than growth" (p. 628), thereby placing the two in direct opposition. Third, in Chan-

Chandler's Scale and Scope / 727

dler's elevation of the importance of managerial competence, he minimizes the adverse effects of the separation of ownership and management, a theme raised by Adolf Berle and Gardiner Means in the 1930s, reiterated in the defense of market takeovers in the 1980s, and salient again in the privatization debate now taking place in Eastern Europe and elsewhere. Fourth, in lauding product and functional diversity within the single enterprise, he rejects the gains deriving from specialization of the firm as well as the diseconomies inherent in managerial complexity and instead affirms the ubiquity of the advantage of reducing transaction costs through integration.

Scale and Scope does not pursue a rigorous confrontation of these competing hypotheses by applying statistical methods to the array of enterprise data from different time periods and different countries. Chandler relies instead on the conformity of the general pattern of these three experiences with his organizing principles. His conclusions are not based wholly on similarities; contrasts also work to underscore the points he makes. His is the subtle art of the business historian weaving a consistent tale rather than the bluntness of the cliometrician systematically testing hypotheses.

My assigned task is not to reconsider the validity of Chandler's central propositions by reexamining the historical evidence or by elaborating other theoretical models of industrial organization. Rather, it is to ponder the relevance of the argument for the dynamics of contemporary developing countries. In a number of respects, there is clear compatibility. The very choice of an industrialization strategy by the vast majority of such countries after the Second World War affirms a parallel. But there is more. In her enlightening study of Korea, *Asia's Next Giant*, Alice Amsden concludes that not only there, but "in all late-industrializing countries, the agent of expansion is [Chandler's] modern industrial enterprise."[1] What is fundamentally different, however, as she also stresses, is the ubiquitous role of the state in shaping the character of enterprise in these countries. There are more citations to Henry Ford in the index of *Scale and Scope* than to the role of government.

There is good reason. Chandler's concern is with the three nineteenth-century leaders in industrialization. Despite their differences, they did not confront the combination of severe constraints and the need for creative response characteristic of Alexander Gerschenkron's successful latecomers. Institutional adaptation, although

---

[1] Alice H. Amsden, *Asia's Next Giant: South Korea and Late Industrialization* (New York, 1989), 8, 9.

central to the evolution of capitalism in the leaders, took on a more exaggerated form in the followers. Subject to limitations of capital, entrepreneurship, skilled labor, and foreign exchange, developing countries after 1945 were the late latecomers, in need of means not only to overcome these constraints but also to accelerate economic growth.

Chandler's central tasks of restructuring production, improving distribution of inputs and final product, and reorganizing management of these processes consequently fell less to the firm and more to the state. In many instances, the large, modern industrial enterprises were wholly or partially owned by the state. Even when ownership remained private, the critical element in determining the level of investment and the choice of technology remained public policy through the state's macroeconomic signals, its complementary investment in infrastructure, and its sectoral direction. The role of the firm in most developing countries was to absorb foreign technology and not to create it; to invest public savings and to rely on internal earnings or capital markets; and to manage with agility the interface between private profits and social benefits and to achieve both.

The domestic managers of state enterprises and even those of private firms did not achieve their positions as a result of victories won in the marketplace. In some countries they were likely to emerge from the military; in virtually all, they would have had extensive public experience. In several, particularly early on, a strong foreign presence was to be found. The theory of rent-seeking posits that the managers who would be most successful in this climate of state activism would be those who were especially privileged by public intervention. Import quotas and licenses would assure special gains to recipients; credit subsidies would lower costs; regulations would grant monopoly powers and bolster profits. So lucrative were the potential gains that recipients would spend significant resources to lobby state bureaucrats. The consequence was a double loss: that emanating from distortion and that emerging from resources spent to influence public decisions.

It takes special care for a state to shape its incentives in ways that do not simply spill over into wasteful expenditure and inefficient production. Japan and Korea stand out as positive examples where vigorous developmental states tempered private monopoly power and harnessed the advantages of scale and scope to social advantage. But the successful *keiretsu* (Japan) and *chaebol* (Korea) have their counterparts in economic groups that dominated activity more to the benefit of a select few than for society as a whole. Their impact is not on growth alone. Income distribution can also be adversely affected. Within large firms, excessively hierarchical structures emerged with

Chandler's Scale and Scope / *729*

disproportionate rewards to managers insulated from market forces. Such positions tend to become entrenched. Expanded supply of a more educated labor force does not erode large differential returns.

Given more limited market size, monopoly power is more ubiquitous in developing countries over a wider gamut of activity than it was in the leading industrial countries at the end of the nineteenth century. Firms did not achieve their preeminence through repeated cycles of Schumpeterian creativity. There is more tension between absence of competition and sustained economic growth in these developing countries than Chandler posits in the industrial leaders. State managerial capacity then becomes central to the result.

One dimension is of special significance: the management of integration into the international economy. Developing countries that were closed to trade may have been especially penalized in their continuing industrial ascent. The state has to take its cues about performance not exclusively from the regulated domestic market but also from the more informative global economy. Excessive and continuing import protection can stifle initiative; inability to compete in exports signals inefficiency and poor use of technology. Not all countries can replicate the enormous export stimulus to growth experienced by the Four Tigers, but all can use international market signals to make resource allocation in the domestic economy more effective.

One's faith in large firms is further challenged by the dichotomy between the modern and traditional sectors found in so many developing countries. A frequent outcome has been disarticulated growth: a stagnant agricultural sector and impoverished cities beside a modern capital-intensive industry. Critics of state intervention attribute this result to public measures that provided excessive incentive to large-scale firms and to regulation that dampened private entrepreneurship. Critics of free enterprise find fault with income inequality and private monopoly power. Both add up to a denial that big is beautiful.

I have emphasized several ways in which developing-country experience amends Chandler's historical tale of the creative contribution of the modern firm. Similar form can belie important functional difference. That the larger institutional setting is an important determinant of outcomes is a conclusion that Chandler himself should find quite amenable. *Scale and Scope* was conceived to shed light on "questions on how growth and performance were affected by legal requirements, government rulings, educational systems, and cultural values" (p. 11). Its powerful thesis is enriched, if modified, by extension to new terrain.

.   .   .

The *Organizational Sociology of* Scale and Scope
Neil Fligstein

My purpose in this essay is to discuss the organizational sociology that I believe underlies Alfred Chandler's *Scale and Scope* and then to consider what theories of organizations this perspective undermines. Most of the reviews of *Scale and Scope* published elsewhere have concentrated on the theory of managerial success that is presented in the first few chapters, but I think that the book as a whole contains a much more interesting organizational sociology, one that is partially complementary but also contradictory to that presented in the early chapters. This organizational sociology seems to me not only theoretically richer, but also empirically more able to explain the trajectories of American, British, and German firms.

The central tension of the text, I think, occurs between the organizational sociology, which explains how the differences between countries were decisive for the organizational patterns observed, and the claims of the first few chapters, which stress how a few simple factors had to exist in all successful firms and thereby imply the organizational convergence of these firms. I would like to reconstruct Chandler's theory from the micro (technology, organization, managerial strategic action), to the meso (social and political embeddedness), to the macro (societal entry into modernity) in order to demonstrate how it provides an account of the differences in organizational forms across countries.

In Chandler's theory at the micro level, technology determines the possibility of achieving economies of scale and scope and provides the opportunity for managers and entrepreneurs to find new markets for their products. The ability to make a product is not enough; one must be able to produce it in sufficient quantity and quality to establish a market for it. Thus, although the existence of a technology is a necessary condition for the emergence of large firms, it is not sufficient to explain them.

The existence of an organization and managerial skills are required to take advantage of the possibilities opened up by technologies. The creation of technologies in the first place is subsumed by firms and is directed by managers and entrepreneurs. The essence of organization for Chandler is the creation of standard operating procedures, or routines, to utilize technologies to produce things. The creation of routines requires managerial trial and error, some failure, and considerable managerial time and energy. These routines will tend to be unique, because the set of conditions that gives rise to them is unique to each firm, industry, and historical context. They will be stable, because once they are discovered, managers will act to preserve and perfect them. Indeed, those who learn these operating procedures first will have advantages that others will find difficult to duplicate, because trying to catch up will be very costly. In its strongest form, Chandler's argument is that the ability to develop and exploit these organizational routines is the decisive characteristic of large, successful firms. Conversely, enterprises that fail to generate and maintain these advantages will be overtaken by competitors.

Managerial strategic actions focus on two spheres: the organization of production (that is, creating routines that include inputs, distribution, marketing, and finance) and finding niches to create markets. The central problem of managers (and entrepreneurs) is to create a long-term strategy: to discover what market opportunities exist and then to organize to take advantage of them. Managers will be oriented toward gaining first-mover advantages and, where such advantages exist, toward preserving them. To achieve these rewards, they must be able to deliver their goods cheaply and reliably. Once those advantages accrue, "smart" managers will figure out how to improve on existing products and operating routines. This will entail investment in research and development, new plant, the expansion of marketing and distribution, or the making of new products.

First movers in a new technology have two sorts of organizational advantages. They gain market share by virtue of being first: they can lock suppliers and customers into their products and make it more difficult for others to follow. Once a firm gains this kind of advantage, a massive infrastructure arises to service it and without a revolution in technology, displacing such a firm will be very difficult. Second, first movers will develop organizational routines difficult for others to reproduce. These routines enable firms to turn out their products reliably; moreover, the organization will discover even better ways of producing their goods. In this way, first-mover advantages will be cemented by organizational learning.

But the establishment of organizational routines, the use of technology, and the strategic actions of managers say nothing about the form and substance of organization. For the substance of these organizational routines, one must consider how the meso- and macro-embeddedness of organizations creates the opportunities and constraints that make the possibility of large organizations feasible. In this regard at the meso level, Chandler emphasizes a small number of factors: political and legal relations, particularly laws governing incorporation and competition, the nature of existing competitors, and a country's stage of industrial development. The kinds of organizational routines that emerge are the results of current circumstances and of the possibilities for managers and entrepreneurs.

Chandler's organizational sociology includes an emphasis on political and legal systems, particularly on issues regarding incorporation and regulation of competitive relations. Without the limited liability joint stock company, for example, it is difficult to see how the large modern corporation could exist. Although he does not believe that these relations have a decisive effect on which organizations will produce efficiently, Chandler does acknowledge that such institutions can shape market behavior. He recognizes, for instance, that the American antitrust laws encouraged firms to merge at the turn of the century, whereas the German cartel laws encouraged firms to cooperate rather than to compete; these circumstances had important effects on firm size, strategies, and integration. Chandler argues, however, that managers who relied solely on these factors did not survive long in the world marketplace. He asserts that internal organization had to be rationalized to create routines that could exploit technology and first-mover advantages. To paraphrase Karl Marx, though political and legal issues mattered, in the last instance the organizational response to the market was determinative for survival.

The actions of competitors are important as well. A firm that obtains first-mover advantages will be difficult to challenge, and similar firms will be better off entering other lines of business. On the other hand, competitors can serve as role models for appropriate behavior in a given industry. By copying the example of firms that have achieved first-mover advantages, a company can potentially compete, particularly if it develops advanced technology and deploys management appropriately.

At the broadest macro level, Chandler's theory of organizations is focused on the long-run emergence of new national economies in the world economy. The problem of founding new organizational forms is quite different depending on the timing and the character of capitalist development. For the British economy at the turn of the century, Chandler makes the case that the high income and geographical concentration of the market made it profitable for British firms to cling to what they knew. Since they routinely made money by concentrating in the industries that they dominated, such as textiles, British entrepreneurs had little incentive to enter the new industries of the

Chandler's Scale and Scope / 733

Second Industrial Revolution. This behavior demonstrates two features of Chandler's earlier model. First, once British firms learned certain routines that reliably delivered profits, British managers would not risk the firm by changing the routines. Second, this lock-in meant not only that the costs of entering fields dominated by British firms were high, but also that these firms had little incentive to enter fields where no such domination occurred.

The Germans and the Americans faced quite different problems. The geographical spread of the American economy meant that firms had to overcome the fragmentation of local markets to create a national market. American firms were larger than European firms, even before the turn-of-the-century merger movement, because the distances and the size of the market were so large. Germany was a relatively late entrant into the international economy, and it had a small local market. The only path to successful development was to produce goods in the newly emerging industries where firms possessing routines to dominate markets did not yet exist, and to develop export-oriented markets. A similar argument is made today regarding Japan's advantages in international markets. The late arrival of industrialization in Japan meant that the decision to invest in the most modern industries was undertaken with no previous set of social or economic institutions in the way, allowing Japanese firms in the postwar era to build into their organizations the most up-to-date plants and methods.

The decisive difference between the strategies and structures of British, American, and German firms thus hinged on their local political and legal systems and on their moment of entry into the modern capitalist world. The types of routines that they created were quite different precisely because of the different conditions faced by their respective managers and entrepreneurs. But, once each chose to produce a given set of organizational routines, those organizations persisted for long periods.

This theory of organizational behavior may be used to criticize three other theories: the theory that Chandler himself presents in the first few chapters of *Scale and Scope*, modern finance economics, and the "small is beautiful," or manufacturing flexibility, school of thought that dominates current opinion about appropriate organizational forms. Chandler's theory provides real challenges to all three by illuminating the forces that have produced significant organizational advances in the past one hundred years.

The theory in the early chapters of *Scale and Scope* is quite simple: managers who build hierarchies that include functional specialization into distribution and marketing will be able to take advantage of scale and scope economies and thereby be successful. This creates a convergence in organizational forms around the large industrial enterprise in spite of differences in the macro- and meso-level factors just discussed. The organizational theory that I have drawn out from the rest of the book undermines this view on a number of fronts. First, the larger view is richer, makes more sense of the data, and helps account for the unique features of capitalist development. Second, it points out that the organizational routines that have been developed do not hinge solely on extensions into marketing or distribution, but depend on opportunistic actions to take advantage of new technologies, local political systems, and the timing of entry of a country into world development. Indeed, from this point of view, one would not expect convergence, but the continual emergence of new and unique organizational forms.

Chandler's view also undermines the finance economics conception of the corporation that dominates economic discourse on the large firm. From the finance perspective, firms are really their capital structures, and the goal of managers is to balance equity and debt in order to maximize short-run returns. Chandler's rich historical analysis shows quite clearly that if firms had always taken this approach, they would have been unable to produce anything. The establishment of dominance requires that managers perceive market opportunities, use first-mover advantages to exploit those opportunities, and create organizational routines to produce goods reliably. Firms cannot make these kinds of investments if the goals of the capital markets must be their first concern. Indeed, the short-termism of the capital markets plagues American managers and, from Chandler's perspective, keeps them from doing their real job: making investments for the long run to produce things that generate wealth.

I think Chandler's theory also undermines the current claims that American firms are too large and bureaucratized and that smaller firms engaging in flexible specialization or network relations with one another are the wave of the future. From a Chandlerian perspective, small firms are handicapped by their inability to achieve economies of scale or scope and so are unable to compete in markets that require the investment of large amounts of capital over a long period. Further, large firms can make the investment in research and development and can create organizational routines to make a product efficiently. Network organizations lack the ability to make these kinds of investments collectively.

Chandler's answer to the industrial problems of the United States is simple. Managers should be less concerned with short-run gain and

Chandler's Scale and Scope / 735

more concerned with what made American business great: investment in scale and scope and organizational routines to produce goods reliably. The large firm is the best vehicle to do this because it possesses the deep pockets, expertise, and forward-looking management that the capital markets and network firms cannot have at their disposal.

However, Chandler's organizational sociology might lead to another prediction as well. Given that large firms have enormous sunk costs in business as usual and given that many of the organizational routines reflect a highly developed system of interfirm and state-firm relations, one could argue that the current inclination of most managers in large firms will be to continue business as usual unless their enterprises become very unprofitable. If this is the case, then we should look for managerial leadership in newly emerging technologies, which are likely to be generated by new firms from a great many countries. Indeed, the view of organizational change deeply embedded in *Scale and Scope* may be a pessimistic one for the future of large American firms precisely because their previous success has locked them into organizational forms that will not readily change.

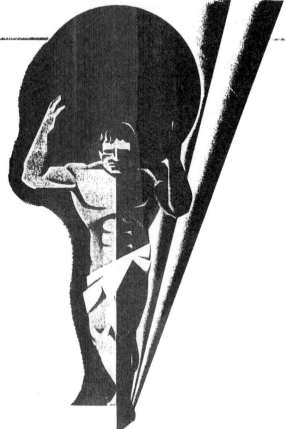

The Competitive Advantage of Nations

by Michael E. Porter

National prosperity is created, not inherited. It does not grow out of a country's natural endowments, its labor pool, its interest rates, or its currency's value, as classical economics insists.

A nation's competitiveness depends on the capacity of its industry to innovate and upgrade. Companies gain advantage against the world's best competitors because of pressure and challenge. They benefit from having strong domestic rivals, aggressive home-based suppliers, and demanding local customers.

In a world of increasingly global competition, nations have become more, not less, important. As the basis of competition has shifted more and more to the creation and assimilation of knowledge, the role of the nation has grown. Competitive advantage is

Harvard Business School professor Michael E. Porter is the author of Competitive Strategy *(Free Press, 1980) and* Competitive Advantage *(Free Press, 1985) and will publish* The Competitive Advantage of Nations *(Free Press) in May 1990.*

created and sustained through a highly localized process. Differences in national values, culture, economic structures, institutions, and histories all contribute to competitive success. There are striking differences in the patterns of competitiveness in every country; no nation can or will be competitive in every or even most industries. Ultimately, nations succeed in particular industries because their home environment is the most forward-looking, dynamic, and challenging.

These conclusions, the product of a four-year study of the patterns of competitive success in ten leading trading nations, contradict the conventional wisdom that guides the thinking of many companies and national governments—and that is pervasive today in the United States. (For more about the study, see the insert "Patterns of National Competitive Success.") According to prevailing thinking, labor costs, interest rates, exchange rates, and economies of scale are the most potent determinants of competitiveness. In companies, the words of the day are merger, alliance, strategic partnerships, collaboration, and supranational globalization. Managers are pressing for more government support for particular industries. Among governments, there is a growing tendency to experiment with various policies intended to promote national competitiveness—from efforts to manage exchange rates to new measures to manage trade to policies to relax antitrust—which usually end up only undermining it. (See the insert "What is National Competitiveness?")

These approaches, now much in favor in both companies and governments, are flawed. They fundamentally misperceive the true sources of competitive advantage. Pursuing them, with all their short-term appeal, will virtually guarantee that the United States—or any other advanced nation—never achieves real and sustainable competitive advantage.

We need a new perspective and new tools—an approach to competitiveness that grows directly out of an analysis of internationally successful industries, without regard for traditional ideology or current intellectual fashion. We need to know, very simply, what works and why. Then we need to apply it.

How Companies Succeed in International Markets

Around the world, companies that have achieved international leadership employ strategies that differ from each other in every respect. But while every successful company will employ its own particular strategy, the underlying mode of operation—the char-

acter and trajectory of all successful companies—is fundamentally the same.

Companies achieve competitive advantage through acts of innovation. They approach innovation in its broadest sense, including both new technologies and new ways of doing things. They perceive a new basis for competing or find better means for competing in old ways. Innovation can be manifested in a new product design, a new production process, a new marketing approach, or a new way of conducting training. Much innovation is mundane and incremental, depending more on a cumulation of small insights and advances than on a single, major technological breakthrough. It often involves

> **The lure of the huge U.S. defense market has diverted the attention of U.S. companies from global commercial markets.**

ideas that are not even "new"—ideas that have been around, but never vigorously pursued. It always involves investments in skill and knowledge, as well as in physical assets and brand reputations.

Some innovations create competitive advantage by perceiving an entirely new market opportunity or by serving a market segment that others have ignored. When competitors are slow to respond, such innovation yields competitive advantage. For instance, in industries such as autos and home electronics, Japanese companies gained their initial advantage by emphasizing smaller, more compact, lower capacity models that foreign competitors disdained as less profitable, less important, and less attractive.

In international markets, innovations that yield competitive advantage anticipate both domestic and foreign needs. For example, as international concern for product safety has grown, Swedish companies like Volvo, Atlas Copco, and AGA have succeeded by anticipating the market opportunity in this area. On the other hand, innovations that respond to concerns or circumstances that are peculiar to the home market can actually retard international competitive success. The lure of the huge U.S. defense market, for instance, has diverted the attention of U.S. materials and machine-tool companies from attractive, global commercial markets.

Information plays a large role in the process of innovation and improvement—information that either is not available to competitors or that they do not seek. Sometimes it comes from simple investment in research and development or market research; more often, it comes from effort and from openness and from looking in the right place unencumbered by blinding assumptions or conventional wisdom.

This is why innovators are often outsiders from a different industry or a different country. Innovation may come from a new company, whose founder has a nontraditional background or was simply not appreciated in an older, established company. Or the capacity for innovation may come into an existing company through senior managers who are new to the particular industry and thus more able to perceive opportunities and more likely to pursue them. Or innovation may occur as a company diversifies, bringing new resources, skills, or perspectives to another industry. Or innovations may come from another nation with different circumstances or different ways of competing.

With few exceptions, innovation is the result of unusual effort. The company that successfully implements a new or better way of competing pursues its approach with dogged determination, often in the face of harsh criticism and tough obstacles. In fact, to succeed, innovation usually requires pressure, necessity, and even adversity: the fear of loss often proves more powerful than the hope of gain.

Once a company achieves competitive advantage through an innovation, it can sustain it only through relentless improvement. Almost any advantage can be imitated. Korean companies have already matched the ability of their Japanese rivals to mass-produce standard color televisions and VCRs; Brazil-

---

> Change is an unnatural act, particularly in successful companies; powerful forces are at work to avoid it at all costs.

---

ian companies have assembled technology and designs comparable to Italian competitors in casual leather footwear.

Competitors will eventually and inevitably overtake any company that stops improving and innovating. Sometimes early-mover advantages such as customer relationships, scale economies in existing technologies, or the loyalty of distribution channels are enough to permit a stagnant company to retain its entrenched position for years or even decades. But sooner or later, more dynamic rivals will find a way to innovate around these advantages or create a better or cheaper way of doing things. Italian appliance producers, which competed successfully on the basis of cost in selling midsize and compact appliances through large retail chains, rested too long on this initial advantage. By developing more differentiated products and creating strong brand franchises, German competitors have begun to gain ground.

Ultimately, the only way to sustain a competitive advantage is to *upgrade it* – to move to more sophisticated types. This is precisely what Japanese automakers have done. They initially penetrated foreign markets with small, inexpensive compact cars of adequate quality and competed on the basis of lower labor costs. Even while their labor-cost advantage persisted, however, the Japanese companies were upgrading. They invested aggressively to build large modern plants to reap economies of scale. Then they became innovators in process technology, pioneering just-in-time production and a host of other quality and productivity practices. These process improvements led to better product quality, better repair records, and better customer-satisfaction ratings than foreign competitors had. Most recently, Japanese automakers have advanced to the vanguard of product technology and are introducing new, premium brand names to compete with the world's most prestigious passenger cars.

The example of the Japanese automakers also illustrates two additional prerequisites for sustaining competitive advantage. First, a company must adopt a global approach to strategy. It must sell its product worldwide, under its own brand name, through international marketing channels that it controls. A truly global approach may even require the company to locate production or R&D facilities in other nations to take advantage of lower wage rates, to gain or improve market access, or to take advantage of foreign technology. Second, creating more sustainable advantages often means that a company must make its existing advantage obsolete – even while it is still an advantage. Japanese auto companies recognized this; either they would make their advantage obsolete, or a competitor would do it for them.

As this example suggests, innovation and change are inextricably tied together. But change is an unnatural act, particularly in successful companies; powerful forces are at work to avoid and defeat it. Past approaches become institutionalized in standard operating procedures and management controls. Training emphasizes the one correct way to do anything; the construction of specialized, dedicated facilities solidifies past practice into expensive brick and mortar; the existing strategy takes on an aura of invincibility and becomes rooted in the company culture.

Patterns of National Competitive Success

To investigate why nations gain competitive advantage in particular industries and the implications for company strategy and national economies, I conducted a four-year study of ten important trading nations: Denmark, Germany, Italy, Japan, Korea, Singapore, Sweden, Switzerland, the United Kingdom, and the United States. I was assisted by a team of more than 30 researchers, most of whom were natives of and based in the nation they studied. The researchers all used the same methodology.

Three nations – the United States, Japan, and Germany – are the world's leading industrial powers. The other nations represent a variety of population sizes, government policies toward industry, social philosophies, geographical sizes, and locations. Together, the ten nations accounted for fully 50% of total world exports in 1985, the base year for statistical analysis.

Most previous analyses of national competitiveness have focused on single nation or bilateral comparisons. By studying nations with widely varying characteristics and circumstances, this study sought to separate the fundamental forces underlying national competitive advantage from the idiosyncratic ones.

In each nation, the study consisted of two parts. The first identified all industries in which the nation's companies were internationally successful, using available statistical data, supplementary published sources, and field interviews. We defined a nation's industry as internationally successful if it *possessed competitive advantage relative to the best worldwide competitors.* Many measures of competitive advantage, such as reported profitability, can be misleading. We chose as the best indicators the presence of substantial and sustained exports to a wide array of other nations and/or significant outbound foreign investment based on skills and assets created in the home country. A nation was considered the home base for a company if it was either a locally owned, indigenous enterprise or managed autonomously although owned by a foreign company or investors. We then created a profile of all the industries in which each nation was internationally successful at three points in time: 1971, 1978, and 1985. The pattern of competitive industries in each economy was far from random: the task was to explain it and how it had changed over time. Of particular interest were the connections or relationships among the nation's competitive industries.

In the second part of the study, we examined the history of competition in particular industries to understand how competitive advantage was created. On the basis of national profiles, we selected over 100 industries or industry groups for detailed study; we examined many more in less detail. We went back as far as necessary to understand how and why the industry began in the nation, how it grew, when and why companies from the nation developed international competitive advantage, and the process by which competitive advantage had been either sustained or lost. The resulting case histories fall short of the work of a good historian in their level of detail, but they do provide insight into the development of both the industry and the nation's economy.

We chose a sample of industries for each nation that represented the most important groups of competitive industries in the economy. The industries studied accounted for a large share of total exports in each nation: more than 20% of total exports in Japan, Germany, and Switzerland, for example, and more than 40% in South Korea. We studied some of the most famous and important international success stories – German high-performance autos and chemicals, Japanese semiconductors and VCRs, Swiss banking and pharmaceuticals, Italian footwear and textiles, U.S. commercial aircraft and motion pictures – and some relatively obscure but highly competitive industries – South Korean pianos, Italian ski boots, and British biscuits. We also added a few industries because they appeared to be paradoxes: Japanese home demand for Western-character typewriters is nearly nonexistent, for example, but Japan holds a strong export and foreign investment position in the industry. We avoided industries that were highly dependent on natural resources: such industries do not form the backbone of advanced economies, and the capacity to compete in them is more explicable using classical theory. We did, however, include a number of more technologically intensive, natural-resource-related industries such as newsprint and agricultural chemicals.

The sample of nations and industries offers a rich empirical foundation for developing and testing the new theory of how countries gain competitive advantage. The accompanying article concentrates on the determinants of competitive advantage in individual industries and also sketches out some of the study's overall implications for government policy and company strategy. A fuller treatment in my book, *The Competitive Advantage of Nations*, develops the theory and its implications in greater depth and provides many additional examples. It also contains detailed descriptions of the nations we studied and the future prospects for their economies.

– Michael E. Porter

Successful companies tend to develop a bias for predictability and stability; they work on defending what they have. Change is tempered by the fear that there is much to lose. The organization at all levels filters out information that would suggest new approaches, modifications, or departures from the norm. The internal environment operates like an immune system to isolate or expel "hostile" individuals who challenge current directions or established thinking. Innovation ceases; the company becomes stagnant; it is only a matter of time before aggressive competitors overtake it.

The Diamond of National Advantage

Why are certain companies based in certain nations capable of consistent innovation? Why do they ruthlessly pursue improvements, seeking an ever-more sophisticated source of competitive advantage? Why are they able to overcome the substantial barriers to change and innovation that so often accompany success?

The answer lies in four broad attributes of a nation, attributes that individually and as a system constitute the diamond of national advantage, the playing field that each nation establishes and operates for its industries. These attributes are:

1. *Factor Conditions.* The nation's position in factors of production, such as skilled labor or infrastructure, necessary to compete in a given industry.

2. *Demand Conditions.* The nature of home-market demand for the industry's product or service.

3. *Related and Supporting Industries.* The presence or absence in the nation of supplier industries and other related industries that are internationally competitive.

4. *Firm Strategy, Structure, and Rivalry.* The conditions in the nation governing how companies are created, organized, and managed, as well as the nature of domestic rivalry.

These determinants create the national environment in which companies are born and learn how to compete. (See the diagram "Determinants of Na-

tional Competitive Advantage.") Each point on the diamond – and the diamond as a system – affects essential ingredients for achieving international competitive success: the availability of resources and skills necessary for competitive advantage in an industry; the information that shapes the opportunities that companies perceive and the directions in which they deploy their resources and skills; the goals of the owners, managers, and individuals in companies; and most important, the pressures on companies to invest and innovate. (See the insert "How the Diamond Works: The Italian Ceramic Tile Industry.")

When a national environment permits and supports the most rapid accumulation of specialized assets and skills – sometimes simply because of greater effort and commitment – companies gain a competitive advantage. When a national environment affords better ongoing information and insight into product and process needs, companies gain a competitive advantage. Finally, when the national environment pressures companies to innovate and invest, companies both gain a competitive advantage and upgrade those advantages over time.

Factor Conditions. According to standard economic theory, factors of production – labor, land, natural resources, capital, infrastructure – will determine the flow of trade. A nation will export those goods that make most use of the factors with which

Determinants of National Competitive Advantage

it is relatively well endowed. This doctrine, whose origins date back to Adam Smith and David Ricardo and that is embedded in classical economics, is at best incomplete and at worst incorrect.

In the sophisticated industries that form the backbone of any advanced economy, a nation does not inherit but instead creates the most important factors of production—such as skilled human resources or a scientific base. Moreover, the stock of factors that a nation enjoys at a particular time is less important than the rate and efficiency with which it creates, upgrades, and deploys them in particular industries.

The most important factors of production are those that involve sustained and heavy investment and are specialized. Basic factors, such as a pool of labor or a local raw-material source, do not constitute an advantage in knowledge-intensive industries. Companies can access them easily through a global strategy or circumvent them through technology. Contrary to conventional wisdom, simply having a general work force that is high school or even college educated represents no competitive advantage in modern international competition. To support competitive advantage, a factor must be highly specialized to an industry's particular needs—a scientific institute specialized in optics, a pool of venture capital to fund software companies. These factors are more scarce, more difficult for foreign competitors to imitate—and they require sustained investment to create.

Nations succeed in industries where they are particularly good at factor creation. Competitive advantage results from the presence of world-class institutions that first create specialized factors and then continually work to upgrade them. Denmark has two hospitals that concentrate in studying and treating diabetes—and a world-leading export position in insulin. Holland has premier research institutes in the cultivation, packaging, and shipping of flowers, where it is the world's export leader.

What is not so obvious, however, is that selective disadvantages in the more basic factors can prod a company to innovate and upgrade—a disadvantage in a static model of competition can become an advantage in a dynamic one. When there is an ample supply of cheap raw materials or abundant labor, companies can simply rest on these advantages and often deploy them inefficiently. But when companies face a selective disadvantage, like high land costs, labor shortages, or the lack of local raw materials, they *must* innovate and upgrade to compete.

Implicit in the oft-repeated Japanese statement, "We are an island nation with no natural resources," is the understanding that these deficiencies have only served to spur Japan's competitive innovation. Just-in-time production, for example, economized on prohibitively expensive space. Italian steel producers in the Brescia area faced a similar set of disadvantages: high capital costs, high energy costs, and no local raw materials. Located in Northern Lombardy, these privately

COMPETITIVE ADVANTAGE

owned companies faced staggering logistics costs due to their distance from southern ports and the inefficiencies of the state-owned Italian transportation system. The result: they pioneered technologically advanced minimills that require only modest capital investment, use less energy, employ scrap metal as the feedstock, are efficient at small scale, and permit producers to locate close to sources of scrap and end-use customers. In other words, they converted factor disadvantages into competitive advantage.

Disadvantages can become advantages only under certain conditions. First, they must send companies proper signals about circumstances that will spread to other nations, thereby equipping them to innovate in advance of foreign rivals. Switzerland, the nation that experienced the first labor shortages after World War II, is a case in point. Swiss companies responded to the disadvantage by upgrading labor productivity and seeking higher value, more sustainable market segments. Companies in most other parts of the world, where there were still ample workers, focused their attention on other issues, which resulted in slower upgrading.

The second condition for transforming disadvantages into advantages is favorable circumstances elsewhere in the diamond—a consideration that ap-

---

> ## Demanding buyers in the domestic market can pressure companies to innovate faster.

---

plies to almost all determinants. To innovate, companies must have access to people with appropriate skills and have home-demand conditions that send the right signals. They must also have active domestic rivals who create pressure to innovate. Another precondition is company goals that lead to sustained commitment to the industry. Without such a commitment and the presence of active rivalry, a company may take an easy way around a disadvantage rather than using it as a spur to innovation.

For example, U.S. consumer-electronics companies, faced with high relative labor costs, chose to leave the product and production process largely unchanged and move labor-intensive activities to Taiwan and other Asian countries. Instead of upgrading their sources of advantage, they settled for labor-cost parity. On the other hand, Japanese rivals, confronted with intense domestic competition and a mature home market, chose to eliminate labor through automation. This led to lower assembly costs, to products with fewer components and to improved quality and reliability. Soon Japanese companies were build-

ing assembly plants in the United States—the place U.S. companies had fled.

Demand Conditions. It might seem that the globalization of competition would diminish the importance of home demand. In practice, however, this is simply not the case. In fact, the composition and character of the home market usually has a disproportionate effect on how companies perceive, interpret, and respond to buyer needs. Nations gain competitive advantage in industries where the home demand gives their companies a clearer or earlier picture of emerging buyer needs, and where demanding buyers pressure companies to innovate faster and achieve more sophisticated competitive advantages than their foreign rivals. The size of home demand proves far less significant than the character of home demand.

Home-demand conditions help build competitive advantage when a particular industry segment is larger or more visible in the domestic market than in foreign markets. The larger market segments in a nation receive the most attention from the nation's companies; companies accord smaller or less desirable segments a lower priority. A good example is hydraulic excavators, which represent the most widely used type of construction equipment in the Japanese domestic market—but which comprise a far smaller proportion of the market in other advanced nations. This segment is one of the few where there are vigorous Japanese international competitors and where Caterpillar does not hold a substantial share of the world market.

More important than the mix of segments per se is the nature of domestic buyers. A nation's companies gain competitive advantage if domestic buyers are the world's most sophisticated and demanding buyers for the product or service. Sophisticated, demanding buyers provide a window into advanced customer needs; they pressure companies to meet high standards; they prod them to improve, to innovate, and to upgrade into more advanced segments. As with factor conditions, demand conditions provide advantages by forcing companies to respond to tough challenges.

Especially stringent needs arise because of local values and circumstances. For example, Japanese consumers, who live in small, tightly packed homes, must contend with hot, humid summers and high-cost electrical energy—a daunting combination of circumstances. In response, Japanese companies have pioneered compact, quiet air-conditioning units powered by energy-saving rotary compressors. In industry after industry, the tightly constrained requirements of the Japanese market have forced companies to innovate, yielding products that are *kei-haku-tan-*

sho—light, thin, short, small—and that are internationally accepted.

Local buyers can help a nation's companies gain advantage if their needs anticipate or even shape those of other nations—if their needs provide ongoing "early-warning indicators" of global market trends. Sometimes anticipatory needs emerge because a nation's political values foreshadow needs that will grow elsewhere. Sweden's long-standing concern for handicapped people has spawned an increasingly competitive industry focused on special needs. Denmark's environmentalism has led to success for companies in water-pollution control equipment and windmills.

More generally, a nation's companies can anticipate global trends if the nation's values are spreading—that is, if the country is exporting its values and tastes as well as its products. The international success of U.S. companies in fast food and credit cards, for example, reflects not only the American desire for convenience but also the spread of these tastes to the rest of the world. Nations export their values and tastes through media, through training foreigners, through political influence, and through the foreign activities of their citizens and companies.

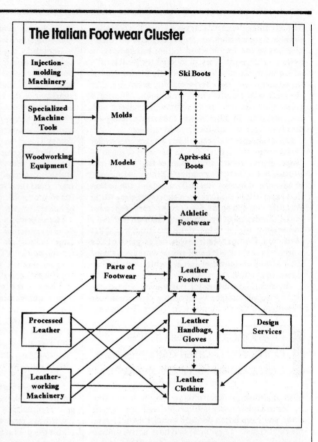

The Italian Footwear Cluster

Related and Supporting Industries. The third broad determinant of national advantage is the presence in the nation of related and supporting industries that are internationally competitive. Internationally competitive home-based suppliers create advantages in downstream industries in several ways. First, they deliver the most cost-effective inputs in an efficient, early, rapid, and sometimes preferential way. Italian gold and silver jewelry companies lead the world in that industry in part because other Italian companies supply two-thirds of the world's jewelry-making and precious-metal recycling machinery.

Far more significant than mere access to components and machinery, however, is the advantage that home-based related and supporting industries provide in innovation and upgrading—an advantage based on close working relationships. Suppliers and end-users located near each other can take advantage of short lines of communication, quick and constant flow of information, and an ongoing exchange of ideas and innovations. Companies have the opportunity to influence their suppliers' technical efforts and can serve as test sites for R&D work, accelerating the pace of innovation.

The illustration of "The Italian Footwear Cluster" offers a graphic example of how a group of close-by, supporting industries creates competitive advantage in a range of interconnected industries that are all internationally competitive. Shoe producers, for instance, interact regularly with leather manufacturers on new styles and manufacturing techniques and learn about new textures and colors of leather when they are still on the drawing boards. Leather manufacturers gain early insights into fashion trends, help-

COMPETITIVE ADVANTAGE

ing them to plan new products. The interaction is mutually advantageous and self-reinforcing, but it does not happen automatically: it is helped by proximity, but occurs only because companies and suppliers work at it.

The nation's companies benefit most when the suppliers are, themselves, global competitors. It is ultimately self-defeating for a company or country to create "captive" suppliers who are totally dependent on the domestic industry and prevented from serving foreign competitors. By the same token, a nation need not be competitive in all supplier industries for its companies to gain competitive advantage. Companies can readily source from abroad materials, components, or technologies without a major effect on innovation or performance of the industry's products. The same is true of other generalized technologies – like electronics or software – where the industry represents a narrow application area.

Home-based competitiveness in related industries provides similar benefits: information flow and technical interchange speed the rate of innovation and upgrading. A home-based related industry also increases the likelihood that companies will embrace new skills, and it also provides a source of entrants who will bring a novel approach to competing. The Swiss success in pharmaceuticals emerged out of previous international success in the dye industry, for example; Japanese dominance in electronic musical keyboards grows out of success in acoustic instruments combined with a strong position in consumer electronics.

Firm Strategy, Structure, and Rivalry. National circumstances and context create strong tendencies in how companies are created, organized, and managed, as well as what the nature of domestic rivalry will be. In Italy, for example, successful international competitors are often small or medium-sized companies that are privately owned and operated like extended families; in Germany, in contrast, companies tend to be strictly hierarchical in organization and management practices, and top managers usually have technical backgrounds.

No one managerial system is universally appropriate – notwithstanding the current fascination with Japanese management. Competitiveness in a specific industry results from convergence of the management practices and organizational modes favored in the country and the sources of competitive advantage in the industry. In industries where Italian companies are world leaders – such as lighting, furniture, footwear, woolen fabrics, and packaging machines – a company strategy that emphasizes focus, customized products, niche marketing, rapid change, and breathtaking flexibility fits both the dy-

namics of the industry and the character of the Italian management system. The German management system, in contrast, works well in technical or engineering-oriented industries – optics, chemicals, complicated machinery – where complex products demand precision manufacturing, a careful development process, after-sale service, and thus a highly disciplined management structure. German success is much rarer in consumer goods and services where image marketing and rapid new-feature and model turnover are important to competition.

Countries also differ markedly in the goals that companies and individuals seek to achieve. Company goals reflect the characteristics of national capital markets and the compensation practices for managers. For example, in Germany and Switzerland, where banks comprise a substantial part of the nation's shareholders, most shares are held for long-

> No one managerial system is universally appropriate – notwithstanding the current fascination with Japanese management.

term appreciation and are rarely traded. Companies do well in mature industries, where ongoing investment in R&D and new facilities is essential but returns may be only moderate. The United States is at the opposite extreme, with a large pool of risk capital but widespread trading of public companies and a strong emphasis by investors on quarterly and annual share-price appreciation. Management compensation is heavily based on annual bonuses tied to individual results. America does well in relatively new industries, like software and biotechnology, or ones where equity funding of new companies feeds active domestic rivalry, like specialty electronics and services. Strong pressures leading to underinvestment, however, plague more mature industries.

Individual motivation to work and expand skills is also important to competitive advantage. Outstanding talent is a scarce resource in any nation. A nation's success largely depends on the types of education its talented people choose, where they choose to work, and their commitment and effort. The goals a nation's institutions and values set for individuals and companies, and the prestige it attaches to certain industries, guide the flow of capital and human resources – which, in turn, directly affects the competitive performance of certain industries. Nations tend to be competitive in activities that people admire or depend on—the activities from which the nation's heroes emerge. In Switzerland, it is banking and pharmaceuticals. In Israel, the highest callings have been agriculture and defense-related fields. Sometimes it is hard to distinguish between cause and effect. Attaining international success can make an industry prestigious, reinforcing its advantage.

The presence of strong local rivals is a final, and powerful, stimulus to the creation and persistence of competitive advantage. This is true of small countries, like Switzerland, where the rivalry among its pharmaceutical companies, Hoffmann-La Roche, Ciba-Geigy, and Sandoz, contributes to a leading worldwide position. It is true in the United States in the computer and software industries. Nowhere is the role of fierce rivalry more apparent than in Japan, where there are 112 companies competing in machine tools, 34 in semiconductors, 25 in audio equipment, 15 in cameras—in fact, there are usually double figures in the industries in which Japan boasts global dominance. (See the table "Estimated Number of Japanese Rivals in Selected Industries.") Among all the points on the diamond, domestic rivalry is argu-

> Local rivalries go beyond economic competition—they become intensely personal feuds for "bragging rights."

ably the most important because of the powerfully stimulating effect it has on all the others.

Conventional wisdom argues that domestic competition is wasteful: it leads to duplication of effort and prevents companies from achieving economies of scale. The "right solution" is to embrace one or two national champions, companies with the scale and strength to tackle foreign competitors, and to guarantee them the necessary resources, with the government's blessing. In fact, however, most national champions are uncompetitive, although heavily subsidized and protected by their government. In many of the prominent industries in which there is only one national rival, such as aerospace and telecommunications, government has played a large role in distorting competition.

Static efficiency is much less important than dynamic improvement, which domestic rivalry uniquely spurs. Domestic rivalry, like any rivalry, creates pressure on companies to innovate and improve. Local rivals push each other to lower costs, improve quality and service, and create new products and processes. But unlike rivalries with foreign competitors, which tend to be analytical and distant,

Estimated Number of Japanese Rivals in Selected Industries

Air conditioners	13
Audio Equipment	25
Automobiles	9
Cameras	15
Car Audio	12
Carbon Fibers	7
Construction Equipment*	15
Copiers	14
Facsimile Machines	10
Large-scale Computers	6
Lift Trucks	8
Machine Tools	112
Microwave Equipment	5
Motorcycles	4
Musical Instruments	4
Personal Computers	16
Semiconductors	34
Sewing Machines	20
Shipbuilding†	33
Steel‡	5
Synthetic Fibers	8
Television Sets	15
Truck and Bus Tires	5
Trucks	11
Typewriters	14
Videocassette Recorders	10

Sources: Field interviews; *Nippon Kogyo Shinbun, Nippon Kogyo Nenkan,* 1987; Yano Research, *Market Share Jitan,* 1987; researchers' estimates.

*The number of companies varied by product area. The smallest number, 10, produced bulldozers. Fifteen companies produced shovel trucks, truck cranes, and asphalt-paving equipment. There were 20 companies in hydraulic excavators, a product area where Japan was particularly strong.

†Six companies had annual production exports in excess of 10,000 tons.

‡Integrated companies.

local rivalries often go beyond pure economic or business competition and become intensely personal. Domestic rivals engage in active feuds; they compete not only for market share but also for people, for technical excellence, and perhaps most important, for "bragging rights." One domestic rival's success proves to others that advancement is possible and often attracts new rivals to the industry. Companies often attribute the success of foreign rivals to "unfair" advantages. With domestic rivals, there are no excuses.

Geographic concentration magnifies the power of domestic rivalry. This pattern is strikingly common around the world: Italian jewelry companies are located around two towns, Arezzo and Valenza Po; cutlery companies in Solingen, West Germany and Seki, Japan; pharmaceutical companies in Basel, Switzerland; motorcycles and musical instruments in Hamamatsu, Japan. The more localized the rivalry, the more intense. And the more intense, the better.

Another benefit of domestic rivalry is the pressure it creates for constant upgrading of the sources of competitive advantage. The presence of domestic competitors automatically cancels the types of advantage that come from simply being in a particular nation – factor costs, access to or preference in the home market, or costs to foreign competitors who import into the market. Companies are forced to move beyond them, and as a result, gain more sustainable advantages. Moreover, competing domestic rivals will keep each other honest in obtaining government support. Companies are less likely to get hooked on the narcotic of government contracts or creeping industry protectionism. Instead, the industry will seek – and benefit from – more constructive forms of government support, such as assistance in opening foreign markets, as well as investments in focused educational institutions or other specialized factors.

Ironically, it is also vigorous domestic competition that ultimately pressures domestic companies to look at global markets and toughens them to succeed in them. Particularly when there are economies of scale, local competitors force each other to look outward to foreign markets to capture greater efficiency and higher profitability. And having been tested by fierce domestic competition, the stronger companies are well equipped to win abroad. If Digital Equipment can hold its own against IBM, Data General, Prime, and Hewlett-Packard, going up against Siemens or Machines Bull does not seem so daunting a prospect.

The Diamond as a System

Each of these four attributes defines a point on the diamond of national advantage; the effect of one point often depends on the state of others. Sophisticated buyers will not translate into advanced products, for example, unless the quality of human resources permits companies to meet buyer needs. Selective disadvantages in factors of production will not motivate innovation unless rivalry is vigorous and company goals support sustained investment. At the broadest level, weaknesses in any one determinant will constrain an industry's potential for advancement and upgrading.

But the points of the diamond are also self-reinforcing: they constitute a system. Two elements, domestic rivalry and geographic concentration, have especially great power to transform the diamond into a system – domestic rivalry because it

promotes improvement in all the other determinants and geographic concentration because it elevates and magnifies the interaction of the four separate influences.

The role of domestic rivalry illustrates how the diamond operates as a self-reinforcing system. Vigorous domestic rivalry stimulates the development of unique pools of specialized factors, particularly if the

> **Nations are rarely home to just one competitive industry; the diamond promotes industry *clusters*.**

rivals are all located in one city or region: the University of California at Davis has become the world's leading center of wine-making research, working closely with the California wine industry. Active local rivals also upgrade domestic demand in an industry. In furniture and shoes, for example, Italian consumers have learned to expect more and better products because of the rapid pace of new product development that is driven by intense domestic rivalry among hundreds of Italian companies. Domestic rivalry also promotes the formation of related and supporting industries. Japan's world-leading group of semiconductor producers, for instance, has spawned world-leading Japanese semiconductor-equipment manufacturers.

The effects can work in all directions: sometimes world-class suppliers become new entrants in the industry they have been supplying. Or highly sophisticated buyers may themselves enter a supplier industry, particularly when they have relevant skills and view the new industry as strategic. In the case of the Japanese robotics industry, for example, Matsushita and Kawasaki originally designed robots for internal use before beginning to sell robots to others. Today they are strong competitors in the robotics industry. In Sweden, Sandvik moved from specialty steel into rock drills, and SKF moved from specialty steel into ball bearings.

Another effect of the diamond's systemic nature is that nations are rarely home to just one competitive industry; rather, the diamond creates an environment that promotes *clusters* of competitive industries. Competitive industries are not scattered helter-skelter throughout the economy but are usually linked together through vertical (buyer-seller) or horizontal (common customers, technology, channels) relationships. Nor are clusters usually scattered physically; they tend to be concentrated geographically. One competitive industry helps to create an-

What Is National Competitiveness?

National competitiveness has become one of the central preoccupations of government and industry in every nation. Yet for all the discussion, debate, and writing on the topic, there is still no persuasive theory to explain national competitiveness. What is more, there is not even an accepted definition of the term "competitiveness" as applied to a nation. While the notion of a competitive company is clear, the notion of a competitive nation is not.

Some see national competitiveness as a macroeconomic phenomenon, driven by variables such as exchange rates, interest rates, and government deficits. But Japan, Italy, and South Korea have all enjoyed rapidly rising living standards despite budget deficits; Germany and Switzerland despite appreciating currencies; and Italy and Korea despite high interest rates.

Others argue that competitiveness is a function of cheap and abundant labor. But Germany, Switzerland, and Sweden have all prospered even with high wages and labor shortages. Besides, shouldn't a nation seek higher wages for its workers as a goal of competitiveness?

Another view connects competitiveness with bountiful natural resources. But how, then, can one explain the success of Germany, Japan, Switzerland, Italy, and South Korea – countries with limited natural resources?

More recently, the argument has gained favor that competitiveness is driven by government policy: targeting, protection, import promotion, and subsidies have propelled Japanese and South Korean auto, steel, shipbuilding, and semiconductor industries into global preeminence. But a closer look reveals a spotty record. In Italy, government intervention has been ineffectual – but Italy has experienced a boom in world export share second only to Japan. In Germany, direct government intervention in exporting industries is rare. And even in Japan and South Korea, government's role in such important industries as facsimile machines, copiers, robotics, and advanced materials has been modest; some of the most frequently cited examples, such as sewing machines, steel, and shipbuilding, are now quite dated.

A final popular explanation for national competitiveness is differences in management practices, including management-labor relations. The problem here, however, is that different industries require different approaches to management. The successful management practices governing small, private, and loosely organized Italian family companies in footwear, textiles, and jewelry, for example, would produce a management disaster if applied to German chemical or auto companies, Swiss pharmaceutical makers, or

American aircraft producers. Nor is it possible to generalize about management-labor relations. Despite the commonly held view that powerful unions undermine competitive advantage, unions are strong in Germany and Sweden – and both countries boast internationally preeminent companies.

Clearly, none of these explanations is fully satisfactory; none is sufficient by itself to rationalize the competitive position of industries within a national border. Each contains some truth; but a broader, more complex set of forces seems to be at work.

The lack of a clear explanation signals an even more fundamental question. What is a "competitive" nation in the first place? Is a "competitive" nation one where every company or industry is competitive? No nation meets this test. Even Japan has large sectors of its economy that fall far behind the world's best competitors.

Is a "competitive" nation one whose exchange rate makes its goods price competitive in international markets? Both Germany and Japan have enjoyed remarkable gains in their standards of living – and experienced sustained periods of strong currency and rising prices. Is a "competitive" nation one with a large positive balance of trade? Switzerland has roughly balanced trade; Italy has a chronic trade deficit – both nations enjoy strongly rising national income. Is a "competitive" nation one with low labor costs? India and Mexico both have low wages and low labor costs – but neither seems an attractive industrial model.

The only meaningful concept of competitiveness at the national level is *productivity*. The principal goal of a nation is to produce a high and rising standard of living for its citizens. The ability to do so depends on the productivity with which a nation's labor and capital are employed. Productivity is the value of the output produced by a unit of labor or capital. Productivity depends on both the quality and features of products (which determine the prices that they can command) and the efficiency with which they are produced. Productivity is the prime determinant of a nation's long-run standard of living; it is the root cause of national per capita income. The productivity of human resources determines employee wages; the productivity with which capital is employed determines the return it earns for its holders.

A nation's standard of living depends on the capacity of its companies to achieve high levels of productivity – and to increase productivity over time. Sustained productivity growth requires that an economy continually *upgrade itself*. A nation's companies must relentlessly improve productivity in existing industries by raising product quality, adding desirable features, improving product technology, or boosting production efficiency. They must develop the necessary

COMPETITIVE ADVANTAGE

capabilities to compete in more and more sophisticated industry segments, where productivity is generally high. They must finally develop the capability to compete in entirely new, sophisticated industries.

International trade and foreign investment can both improve a nation's productivity as well as threaten it. They support rising national productivity by allowing a nation to specialize in those industries and segments of industries where its companies are more productive and to import where its companies are less productive. No nation can be competitive in everything. The ideal is to deploy the nation's limited pool of human and other resources into the most productive uses. Even those nations with the highest standards of living have many industries in which local companies are uncompetitive.

Yet international trade and foreign investment also can threaten productivity growth. They expose a nation's industries to the test of international standards of productivity. An industry will lose out if its productivity is not sufficiently higher than foreign rivals' to offset any advantages in local wage rates. If a nation loses the ability to compete in a range of high-productivity/high-wage industries, its standard of living is threatened.

Defining national competitiveness as achieving a trade surplus or balanced trade per se is inappropriate. The expansion of exports because of low wages and a weak currency, at the same time that the nation imports sophisticated goods that its companies cannot produce competitively, may bring trade into balance or surplus but lowers the nation's standard of living. Competitiveness also does not mean jobs. It's the *type* of jobs, not just the ability to employ citizens at low wages, that is decisive for economic prosperity.

Seeking to explain "competitiveness" at the national level, then, is to answer the wrong question. What we must understand instead is the determinants of productivity and the rate of productivity growth. To find answers, we must focus not on the economy as a whole but on *specific industries and industry segments*. We must understand how and why commercially viable skills and technology are created, which can only be fully understood at the level of particular industries. It is the outcome of the thousands of struggles for competitive advantage against foreign rivals in particular segments and industries, in which products and processes are created and improved, that underpins the process of upgrading national productivity.

When one looks closely at any national economy, there are striking differences among a nation's industries in competitive success. International advantage is often concentrated in particular industry segments. German exports of cars are heavily skewed toward high-performance cars, while Korean exports are all compacts and subcompacts. In many industries and segments of industries, the competitors with true international competitive advantage are *based in only a few nations*.

Our search, then, is for the decisive characteristic of a nation that allows its companies to create and sustain competitive advantage in particular fields – the search is for the competitive advantage of nations. We are particularly concerned with the determinants of international success in technology- and skill-intensive segments and industries, which underpin high and rising productivity.

Classical theory explains the success of nations in particular industries based on so-called factors of production such as land, labor, and natural resources. Nations gain factor-based comparative advantage in industries that make intensive use of the factors they possess in abundance. Classical theory, however, has been overshadowed in advanced industries and economies by the globalization of competition and the power of technology.

A new theory must recognize that in modern international competition, companies compete with global strategies involving not only trade but also foreign investment. What a new theory must explain is why a nation provides a favorable *home base* for companies that compete internationally. The home base is the nation in which the essential competitive advantages of the enterprise are created and sustained. It is where a company's strategy is set, where the core product and process technology is created and maintained, and where the most productive jobs and most advanced skills are located. The presence of the home base in a nation has the greatest positive influence on other linked domestic industries and leads to other benefits in the nation's economy. While the ownership of the company is often concentrated at the home base, the nationality of shareholders is secondary.

A new theory must move beyond comparative advantage to the competitive advantage of a nation. It must reflect a rich conception of competition that includes segmented markets, differentiated products, technology differences, and economies of scale. A new theory must go beyond cost and explain why companies from some nations are better than others at creating advantages based on quality, features, and new product innovation. A new theory must begin from the premise that competition is dynamic and evolving; it must answer the questions: Why do some companies based in some nations innovate more than others? Why do some nations provide an environment that enables companies to improve and innovate faster than foreign rivals?
— Michael E. Porter

other in a mutually reinforcing process. Japan's strength in consumer electronics, for example, drove its success in semiconductors toward the memory chips and integrated circuits these products use. Japanese strength in laptop computers, which contrasts to limited success in other segments, reflects the base of strength in other compact, portable products and leading expertise in liquid-crystal display gained in the calculator and watch industries.

Once a cluster forms, the whole group of industries becomes mutually supporting. Benefits flow forward, backward, and horizontally. Aggressive rivalry in one industry spreads to others in the cluster, through spin-offs, through the exercise of bargaining power, and through diversification by established companies. Entry from other industries within the cluster spurs upgrading by stimulating diversity in R&D approaches and facilitating the introduction of new strategies and skills. Through the conduits of suppliers or customers who have contact with multiple competitors, information flows freely and innovations diffuse rapidly. Interconnections within the cluster, often unanticipated, lead to perceptions of new ways of competing and new opportunities. The cluster becomes a vehicle for maintaining diversity and overcoming the inward focus, inertia, inflexibility, and accommodation among rivals that slows or blocks competitive upgrading and new entry.

The Role of Government

In the continuing debate over the competitiveness of nations, no topic engenders more argument or creates less understanding than the role of the government. Many see government as an essential helper or supporter of industry, employing a host of policies to contribute directly to the competitive performance of strategic or target industries. Others accept the "free market" view that the operation of the economy should be left to the workings of the invisible hand.

Both views are incorrect. Either, followed to its logical outcome, would lead to the permanent erosion of a country's competitive capabilities. On one hand, advocates of government help for industry frequently propose policies that would actually hurt companies in the long run and only create the demand for more helping. On the other hand, advocates of a diminished government presence ignore the legitimate role that government plays in shaping the context and institutional structure surrounding companies and in creating an environment that stimulates companies to gain competitive advantage.

Government's proper role is as a catalyst and challenger; it is to encourage – or even push – companies to raise their aspirations and move to higher levels of competitive performance, even though this process may be inherently unpleasant and difficult. Government cannot create competitive industries; only companies can do that. Government plays a role that is inherently partial, that succeeds only when working in tandem with favorable underlying conditions in the diamond. Still, government's role of transmitting and amplifying the forces of the diamond is a powerful one. Government policies that succeed are those that create an environment in which compa-

> ## Competitive time for companies and political time for governments are fundamentally at odds.

nies can gain competitive advantage rather than those that involve government directly in the process, except in nations early in the development process. It is an indirect, rather than a direct, role.

Japan's government, at its best, understands this role better than anyone – including the point that nations pass through stages of competitive development and that government's appropriate role shifts as the economy progresses. By stimulating early demand for advanced products, confronting industries with the need to pioneer frontier technology through symbolic cooperative projects, establishing prizes that reward quality, and pursuing other policies that magnify the forces of the diamond, the Japanese government accelerates the pace of innovation. But like government officials anywhere, at their worst Japanese bureaucrats can make the same mistakes: attempting to manage industry structure, protecting the market too long, and yielding to political pressure to insulate inefficient retailers, farmers, distributors, and industrial companies from competition.

It is not hard to understand why so many governments make the same mistakes so often in pursuit of national competitiveness: competitive time for companies and political time for governments are fundamentally at odds. It often takes more than a decade for an industry to create competitive advantage; the process entails the long upgrading of human skills, investing in products and processes, building clusters, and penetrating foreign markets. In the case of the Japanese auto industry, for instance, companies made their first faltering steps toward exporting in the 1950s – yet did not achieve strong international positions until the 1970s.

COMPETITIVE ADVANTAGE

But in politics, a decade is an eternity. Consequently, most governments favor policies that offer easily perceived short-term benefits, such as subsidies, protection, and arranged mergers – the very policies that retard innovation. Most of the policies that would make a real difference either are too slow and require too much patience for politicians or, even worse, carry with them the sting of short-term pain. Deregulating a protected industry, for example, will lead to bankruptcies sooner and to stronger, more competitive companies only later.

Policies that convey static, short-term cost advantages but that unconsciously undermine innovation and dynamism represent the most common and most profound error in government industrial policy. In a desire to help, it is all too easy for governments to adopt policies such as joint projects to avoid "wasteful" R&D that undermine dynamism and competition. Yet even a 10% cost saving through economies of scale is easily nullified through rapid product and process improvement and the pursuit of volume in global markets – something that such policies undermine.

There are some simple, basic principles that governments should embrace to play the proper supportive role for national competitiveness: encourage change, promote domestic rivalry, stimulate innovation. Some of the specific policy approaches to guide nations seeking to gain competitive advantage include the following:

Focus on specialized factor creation. Government has critical responsibilities for fundamentals like the primary and secondary education systems, basic national infrastructure, and research in areas of broad national concern such as health care. Yet these kinds of generalized efforts at factor creation rarely produce competitive advantage. Rather, the factors that translate into competitive advantage are advanced, specialized, and tied to specific industries or industry groups. Mechanisms such as specialized apprenticeship programs, research efforts in universities connected with an industry, trade association activities, and, most important, the private investments of companies ultimately create the factors that will yield competitive advantage.

Avoid intervening in factor and currency markets. By intervening in factor and currency markets, governments hope to create lower factor costs or a favorable exchange rate that will help companies compete more effectively in international markets. Evidence from around the world indicates that these policies – such as the Reagan administration's dollar devaluation – are often counterproductive. They work against the upgrading of industry and the search for more sustainable competitive advantage.

The contrasting case of Japan is particularly instructive, although both Germany and Switzerland have had similar experiences. Over the past 20 years, the Japanese have been rocked by the sudden Nixon currency devaluation shock, two oil shocks, and, most recently, the yen shock – all of which forced Japanese companies to upgrade their competitive advantages. The point is not that government should pursue policies that intentionally drive up factor costs or the exchange rate. Rather, when market forces create rising factor costs or a higher exchange rate, government should resist the temptation to push them back down.

Enforce strict product, safety, and environmental standards. Strict government regulations can promote competitive advantage by stimulating and upgrading domestic demand. Stringent standards for product performance, product safety, and environmental impact pressure companies to improve quality, upgrade technology, and provide features that respond to consumer and social demands. Easing standards, however tempting, is counterproductive.

When tough regulations anticipate standards that will spread internationally, they give a nation's companies a head start in developing products and services that will be valuable elsewhere. Sweden's strict standards for environmental protection have promoted competitive advantage in many industries. Atlas Copco, for example, produces quiet compressors that can be used in dense urban areas with minimal disruption to residents. Strict standards, however, must be combined with a rapid and streamlined regulatory process that does not absorb resources and cause delays.

Sharply limit direct cooperation among industry rivals. The most pervasive global policy fad in the competitiveness arena today is the call for more cooperative research and industry consortia. Operating on the belief that independent research by rivals is wasteful and duplicative, that collaborative efforts achieve economies of scale, and that individual com-

 Most Japanese companies participate in MITI research projects for defensive reasons.

panies are likely to underinvest in R&D because they cannot reap all the benefits, governments have embraced the idea of more direct cooperation. In the United States, antitrust laws have been modified to allow more cooperative R&D; in Europe, megaprojects such as ESPRIT, an information-technology project, bring together companies from several countries. Lurking behind much of this thinking is the fascination of Western governments with – and fundamental misunderstanding of – the countless cooperative research projects sponsored by the Ministry of International Trade and Industry (MITI), projects that appear to have contributed to Japan's competitive rise.

But a closer look at Japanese cooperative projects suggests a different story. Japanese companies participate in MITI projects to maintain good relations with MITI, to preserve their corporate images, and to hedge the risk that competitors will gain from the project – largely defensive reasons. Companies rarely contribute their best scientists and engineers to cooperative projects and usually spend much more on their own private research in the same field. Typically, the government makes only a modest financial contribution to the project.

The real value of Japanese cooperative research is to signal the importance of emerging technical areas and to stimulate proprietary company research. Cooperative projects prompt companies to explore new

---

Tax incentives for long-term capital gains encourage long-term investment.

---

fields and boost internal R&D spending because companies know that their domestic rivals are investigating them.

Under certain limited conditions, cooperative research can prove beneficial. Projects should be in areas of basic product and process research, not in subjects closely connected to a company's proprietary sources of advantage. They should constitute only a modest portion of a company's overall research program in any given field. Cooperative research should be only indirect, channeled through independent organizations to which most industry participants have access. Organizational structures, like university labs and centers of excellence, reduce management problems and minimize the risk to rivalry. Finally, the most useful cooperative projects often involve fields that touch a number of industries and that require substantial R&D investments.

Promote goals that lead to sustained investment. Government has a vital role in shaping the goals of investors, managers, and employees through policies in various areas. The manner in which capital markets are regulated, for example, shapes the incentives of investors and, in turn, the behavior of companies. Government should aim to encourage sustained investment in human skills, in innovation, and in

physical assets. Perhaps the single most powerful tool for raising the rate of sustained investment in industry is a tax incentive for long-term (five years or more) capital gains restricted to new investment in corporate equity. Long-term capital gains incentives should also be applied to pension funds and other currently untaxed investors, who now have few reasons not to engage in rapid trading.

Deregulate competition. Regulation of competition through such policies as maintaining a state monopoly, controlling entry into an industry, or fixing prices has two strong negative consequences: it stifles rivalry and innovation as companies become preoccupied with dealing with regulators and protecting what they already have; and it makes the industry a less dynamic and less desirable buyer or supplier. Deregulation and privatization on their own, however, will not succeed without vigorous domestic rivalry – and that requires, as a corollary, a strong and consistent antitrust policy.

Enforce strong domestic antitrust policies. A strong antitrust policy – especially for horizontal mergers, alliances, and collusive behavior – is fundamental to innovation. While it is fashionable today to call for mergers and alliances in the name of globalization and the creation of national champions, these often undermine the creation of competitive advantage. Real national competitiveness requires governments to disallow mergers, acquisitions, and alliances that involve industry leaders. Furthermore, the same standards for mergers and alliances should apply to both domestic and foreign companies. Finally, government policy should favor internal entry, both domestic and international, over acquisition. Companies should, however, be allowed to acquire small companies in related industries when the move promotes the transfer of skills that could ultimately create competitive advantage.

Reject managed trade. Managed trade represents a growing and dangerous tendency for dealing with the

---

Better than managed trade: pressure Japan to buy more manufactured imports.

---

fallout of national competitiveness. Orderly marketing agreements, voluntary restraint agreements, or other devices that set quantitative targets to divide up markets are dangerous, ineffective, and often enormously costly to consumers. Rather than promoting innovation in a nation's industries, managed trade guarantees a market for inefficient companies.

COMPETITIVE ADVANTAGE

Government trade policy should pursue open market access in every foreign nation. To be effective, trade policy should not be a passive instrument; it cannot respond only to complaints or work only for those industries that can muster enough political clout; it should not require a long history of injury or serve only distressed industries. Trade policy should seek to open markets wherever a nation has competitive advantage and should actively address emerging industries and incipient problems.

Where government finds a trade barrier in another nation, it should concentrate its remedies on dismantling barriers, not on regulating imports or exports. In the case of Japan, for example, pressure to accelerate the already rapid growth of manufactured imports is a more effective approach than a shift to managed trade. Compensatory tariffs that punish companies for unfair trade practices are better than market quotas. Other increasingly important tools to open markets are restrictions that prevent companies in offending nations from investing in acquisitions or production facilities in the host country—thereby blocking the unfair country's companies from using their advantage to establish a new beachhead that is immune from sanctions.

Any of these remedies, however, can backfire. It is virtually impossible to craft remedies to unfair trade practices that avoid both reducing incentives for domestic companies to innovate and export and harming domestic buyers. The aim of remedies should be adjustments that allow the remedy to disappear.

The Company Agenda

Ultimately, only companies themselves can achieve and sustain competitive advantage. To do so, they must act on the fundamentals described above. In particular, they must recognize the central role of innovation—and the uncomfortable truth that innovation grows out of pressure and challenge. It takes leadership to create a dynamic, challenging environment. And it takes leadership to recognize the all-too-easy escape routes that appear to offer a path to competitive advantage, but are actually short-cuts to failure. For example, it is tempting to rely on cooperative research and development projects to lower the cost and risk of research. But they can divert company attention and resources from proprietary research efforts and will all but eliminate the prospects for real innovation.

Competitive advantage arises from leadership that harnesses and amplifies the forces in the diamond to promote innovation and upgrading. Here are just a few of the kinds of company policies that will support that effort:

Create pressures for innovation. A company should seek out pressure and challenge, not avoid them. Part of strategy is to take advantage of the home nation to create the impetus for innovation. To do that, companies can sell to the most sophisticated and demanding buyers and channels; seek out those buyers with the most difficult needs; establish norms that exceed the toughest regulatory hurdles or product standards; source from the most advanced suppliers; treat employees as permanent in order to stimulate upgrading of skills and productivity.

Seek out the most capable competitors as motivators. To motivate organizational change, capable competitors and respected rivals can be a common enemy. The best managers always run a little scared; they respect and study competitors. To stay dynamic, companies must make meeting challenge a part of the organization's norms. For example, lobbying against strict product standards signals the organization that company leadership has diminished aspirations. Companies that value stability, obedient customers, dependent suppliers, and sleepy competitors are inviting inertia and, ultimately, failure.

Establish early-warning systems. Early-warning signals translate into early-mover advantages. Companies can take actions that help them see the signals of change and act on them, thereby getting a jump on the competition. For example, they can find and serve those buyers with the most anticipatory needs; investigate all emerging new buyers or channels; find places whose regulations foreshadow emerging regulations elsewhere; bring some outsiders into the management team; maintain ongoing relationships with research centers and sources of talented people.

Improve the national diamond. Companies have a vital stake in making their home environment a better platform for international success. Part of a company's responsibility is to play an active role in forming clusters and to work with its home-nation buyers, suppliers, and channels to help them upgrade and extend their own competitive advantages. To upgrade home demand, for example, Japanese musical instrument manufacturers, led by Yamaha, Kawai, and Suzuki, have established music schools. Similarly, companies can stimulate and support local suppliers of important specialized inputs—including encouraging them to compete globally. The health and strength of the national cluster will only enhance the company's own rate of innovation and upgrading.

In nearly every successful competitive industry, leading companies also take explicit steps to create

How the Diamond Works:
The Italian Ceramic Tile Industry

In 1987, Italian companies were world leaders in the production and export of ceramic tiles, a $10 billion industry. Italian producers, concentrated in and around the small town of Sassuolo in the Emilia-Romagna region, accounted for about 30% of world production and almost 60% of world exports. The Italian trade surplus that year in ceramic tiles was about $1.4 billion.

The development of the Italian ceramic tile industry's competitive advantage illustrates how the diamond of national advantage works. Sassuolo's sustainable competitive advantage in ceramic tiles grew not from any static or historical advantage but from dynamism and change. Sophisticated and demanding local buyers, strong and unique distribution channels, and intense rivalry among local companies created constant pressure for innovation. Knowledge grew quickly from continuous experimentation and cumulative production experience. Private ownership of the companies and loyalty to the community spawned intense commitment to invest in the industry.

Tile producers benefited as well from a highly developed set of local machinery suppliers and other supporting industries, producing materials, services, and infrastructure. The presence of world-class, Italian-related industries also reinforced Italian strength in tiles. Finally, the geographic concentration of the entire cluster supercharged the whole process. Today foreign companies compete against an entire subculture. The organic nature of this system represents the most sustainable advantage of Sassuolo's ceramic tile companies.

The Origins of the Italian Industry

Tile production in Sassuolo grew out of the earthenware and crockery industry, whose history traces back to the thirteenth century. Immediately after World War II, there were only a handful of ceramic tile manufacturers in and around Sassuolo, all serving the local market exclusively.

Demand for ceramic tiles within Italy began to grow dramatically in the immediate postwar years, as the reconstruction of Italy triggered a boom in building materials of all kinds. Italian demand for ceramic tiles was particularly great due to the climate, local tastes, and building techniques.

Because Sassuolo was in a relatively prosperous part of Italy, there were many who could combine the modest amount of capital and necessary organizational skills to start a tile company. In 1955, there were 14 Sassuolo area tile companies; by 1962, there were 102.

The new tile companies benefited from a local pool of mechanically trained workers. The region around Sassuolo was home to Ferrari, Maserati, Lamborghini, and other technically sophisticated companies. As the tile industry began to grow and prosper, many engineers and skilled workers gravitated to the successful companies.

The Emerging Italian Tile Cluster

Initially, Italian tile producers were dependent on foreign sources of raw materials and production technology. In the 1950s, the principal raw materials used to make tiles were kaolin (white) clays. Since there were red- but no white-clay deposits near Sassuolo, Italian producers had to import the clays from the United Kingdom. Tile-making equipment was also imported in the 1950s and 1960s: kilns from Germany, America, and France; presses for forming tiles from Germany. Sassuolo tile makers had to import even simple glazing machines.

Over time, the Italian tile producers learned how to modify imported equipment to fit local circumstances: red versus white clays, natural gas versus heavy oil. As process technicians from tile companies left to start their own equipment companies, a local machinery industry arose in Sassuolo. By 1970, Italian companies had emerged as world-class producers of kilns and presses; the earlier situation had exactly reversed: they were exporting their red-clay equipment for foreigners to use with white clays.

The relationship between Italian tile and equipment manufacturers was a mutually supporting one, made even more so by close proximity. In the mid-1980s, there were some 200 Italian equipment manufacturers; more than 60% were located in the Sassuolo area. The equipment manufacturers competed fiercely for local business, and tile manufacturers benefited from better prices and more advanced equipment than their foreign rivals.

As the emerging tile cluster grew and concentrated in the Sassuolo region, a pool of skilled workers and technicians developed, including engineers, production specialists, maintenance workers, service technicians, and design personnel. The industry's geographic concentration encouraged other supporting companies to form, offering molds, packaging materials, glazes, and transportation services. An array of small, specialized consulting companies emerged to give advice to tile producers on plant design, logistics, and commercial, advertising, and fiscal matters.

With its membership concentrated in the Sassuolo area, Assopiastrelle, the ceramic tile industry association, began offering services in areas of common interest: bulk purchasing, foreign-market research, and consulting on fiscal and legal matters. The growing tile cluster stimulated the formation of a new, specialized

COMPETITIVE ADVANTAGE

factor-creating institution: in 1976, a consortium of the University of Bologna, regional agencies, and the ceramic industry association founded the Centro Ceramico di Bologna, which conducted process research and product analysis.

Sophisticated Home Demand

By the mid-1960s, per-capita tile consumption in Italy was considerably higher than in the rest of the world. The Italian market was also the world's most sophisticated. Italian customers, who were generally the first to adopt new designs and features, and Italian producers, who constantly innovated to improve manufacturing methods and create new designs, progressed in a mutually reinforcing process.

The uniquely sophisticated character of domestic demand also extended to retail outlets. In the 1960s, specialized tile showrooms began opening in Italy. By 1985, there were roughly 7,600 specialized showrooms handling approximately 80% of domestic sales, far more than in other nations. In 1976, the Italian company Piemme introduced tiles by famous designers to gain distribution outlets and to build brand name awareness among consumers. This innovation drew on another related industry, design services, in which Italy was world leader, with over $10 billion in exports.

Sassuolo Rivalry

The sheer number of tile companies in the Sassuolo area created intense rivalry. News of product and process innovations spread rapidly, and companies seeking technological, design, and distribution leadership had to improve constantly.

Proximity added a personal note to the intense rivalry. All of the producers were privately held, most were family run. The owners all lived in the same area, knew each other, and were the leading citizens of the same towns.

Pressures to Upgrade

In the early 1970s, faced with intense domestic rivalry, pressure from retail customers, and the shock of the 1973 energy crisis, Italian tile companies struggled to reduce gas and labor costs. These efforts led to a technological breakthrough, the rapid single-firing process, in which the hardening process, material transformation, and glaze-fixing all occurred in one pass through the kiln. A process that took 225 employees using the double-firing method needed only 90 employees using single-firing roller kilns. Cycle time dropped from 16 to 20 hours to only 50 to 55 minutes.

The new, smaller, and lighter equipment was also easier to export. By the early 1980s, exports from Ital-

ian equipment manufacturers exceeded domestic sales; in 1988, exports represented almost 80% of total sales.

Working together, tile manufacturers and equipment manufacturers made the next important breakthrough during the mid- and late 1970s: the development of materials-handling equipment that transformed tile manufacture from a batch process to a continuous process. The innovation reduced high labor costs—which had been a substantial selective factor disadvantage facing Italian tile manufacturers.

The common perception is that Italian labor costs were lower during this period than those in the United States and Germany. In those two countries, however, different jobs had widely different wages. In Italy, wages for different skill categories were compressed, and work rules constrained manufacturers from using overtime or multiple shifts. The restriction proved costly: once cool, kilns are expensive to reheat and are best run continuously. Because of this factor disadvantage, the Italian companies were the first to develop continuous, automated production.

Internationalization

By 1970, Italian domestic demand had matured. The stagnant Italian market led companies to step up their efforts to pursue foreign markets. The presence of related and supporting Italian industries helped in the export drive. Individual tile manufacturers began advertising in Italian and foreign home-design and architectural magazines, publications with wide global circulation among architects, designers, and consumers. This heightened awareness reinforced the quality image of Italian tiles. Tile makers were also able to capitalize on Italy's leading world export positions in related industries like marble, building stone, sinks, washbasins, furniture, lamps, and home appliances.

Assopiastrelle, the industry association, established trade-promotion offices in the United States in 1980, in Germany in 1984, and in France in 1987. It organized elaborate trade shows in cities ranging from Bologna to Miami and ran sophisticated advertising. Between 1980 and 1987, the association spent roughly $8 million to promote Italian tiles in the United States.

—Michael J. Enright and Paolo Tenti

Michael J. Enright, a doctoral student in business economics at the Harvard Business School, performed numerous research and supervisory tasks for The Competitive Advantage of Nations. *Paolo Tenti was responsible for the Italian part of research undertaken for the book. He is a consultant in strategy and finance for Monitor Company and Analysis F.A. – Milan.*

specialized factors like human resources, scientific knowledge, or infrastructure. In industries like wool cloth, ceramic tiles, and lighting equipment, Italian industry associations invest in market information, process technology, and common infrastructure. Companies can also speed innovation by putting their headquarters and other key operations where there are concentrations of sophisticated buyers, important suppliers, or specialized factor-creating mechanisms, such as universities or laboratories.

Welcome domestic rivalry. To compete globally, a company needs capable domestic rivals and vigorous domestic rivalry. Especially in the United States and Europe today, managers are wont to complain about excessive competition and to argue for mergers and acquisitions that will produce hoped-for economies of scale and critical mass. The complaint is only natural—but the argument is plain wrong. Vigorous domestic rivalry creates sustainable competitive advantage. Moreover, it is better to grow internationally than to dominate the domestic market. If a company wants an acquisition, a foreign one that can speed globalization and supplement home-based advantages or offset home-based disadvantages is usually far better than merging with leading domestic competitors.

> Innovating to overcome local disadvantages is better than outsourcing; developing domestic supplies is better than relying on foreign ones.

Globalize to tap selective advantages in other nations. In search of "global" strategies, many companies today abandon their home diamond. To be sure, adopting a global perspective is important to creating competitive advantage. But relying on foreign activities that supplant domestic capabilities is always a second-best solution. Innovating to offset local factor disadvantages is better than outsourcing; developing domestic suppliers and buyers is better than relying solely on foreign ones. Unless the critical underpinnings of competitiveness are present at home, companies will not sustain competitive advantage in the long run. The aim should be to upgrade home-base capabilities so that foreign activities are selective and supplemental only to over-all competitive advantage.

The correct approach to globalization is to tap selectively into sources of advantage in other nations' diamonds.. For example, identifying sophisticated buyers in other countries helps companies understand different needs and creates pressures that will stimulate a faster rate of innovation. No matter how favorable the home diamond, moreover, important research is going on in other nations. To take advantage of foreign research, companies must station high-quality people in overseas bases and mount a credible level of scientific effort. To get anything back from foreign research ventures, companies must also allow access to their own ideas—recognizing that competitive advantage comes from continuous improvement, not from protecting today's secrets.

Use alliances only selectively. Alliances with foreign companies have become another managerial fad and cure-all: they represent a tempting solution to the problem of a company wanting the advantages of foreign enterprises or hedging against risk, without giving up independence. In reality, however, while alliances can achieve selective benefits, they always exact significant costs: they involve coordinating two separate operations, reconciling goals with an independent entity, creating a competitor, and giving up profits. These costs ultimately make most alliances short-term transitional devices, rather than stable, long-term relationships.

Author's note: Michael J. Enright, who served as project coordinator for this study, has contributed valuable suggestions.

COMPETITIVE ADVANTAGE

Most important, alliances as a broad-based strategy will only ensure a company's mediocrity, not its international leadership. No company can rely on another outside, independent company for skills and assets that are central to its competitive advantage. Alliances are best used as a selective tool, employed on a temporary basis or involving noncore activities.

Locate the home base to support competitive advantage. Among the most important decisions for multinational companies is the nation in which to locate the home base for each distinct business. A company can have different home bases for distinct businesses or segments. Ultimately, competitive advantage is created at home: it is where strategy is set, the core product and process technology is created, and a critical mass of production takes place. The circumstances in the home nation must support innovation; otherwise the company has no choice but to move its home base to a country that stimulates innovation and that provides the best environment for global competitiveness. There are no half-measures: the management team must move as well.

The Role of Leadership

Too many companies and top managers misperceive the nature of competition and the task before them by focusing on improving financial performance, soliciting government assistance, seeking stability, and reducing risk through alliances and mergers.

> Using alliances as a strategy will only ensure a company's mediocrity, not its international leadership.

Today's competitive realities demand leadership. Leaders believe in change; they energize their organizations to innovate continuously; they recognize the importance of their home country as integral to their competitive success and work to upgrade it. Most important, leaders recognize the need for pressure and challenge. Because they are willing to encourage appropriate – and painful – government policies and regulations, they often earn the title "statesmen," although few see themselves that way. They are prepared to sacrifice the easy life for difficulty and, ultimately, sustained competitive advantage. That must be the goal, for both nations and companies: not just surviving, but achieving international competitiveness.

And not just once, but continuously.   ⊟

Reprint 90211

[9]

Strategic Management Journal, Vol. 12, 61–74 (1991)

WHY DO FIRMS DIFFER, AND HOW DOES IT MATTER?

RICHARD R. NELSON
School of International and Public Affairs, Columbia University, New York, U.S.A.

In virtually all economic analyses, differences among firms in the same line of business are repressed, or assumed to reflect differences in the market environments that they face. In contrast, for students of business management and strategy, firm differences are at the heart of their inquiry. This paper explores the reasons behind this stark difference in viewpoint. It argues that economists really ought to recognize firm differences explicitly.

INTRODUCTION

This paper is concerned with the sources and significance of interfirm differences, from the viewpoint of an economist. How might an economist's perspective on this differ, say, from that of a student of business management? I would argue that the most important difference is that economists tend to see firms as players in a multi actor economic game, and their interest is in the game and its outcomes, rather than in the particular play or performance of individual firms. That is, economists are interested in how the automobile industry works, and its performance in various dimensions, and not in General Motors or Toyota *per se*, but only insofar as the particularities of these firms influence the industry more broadly. This perspective is quite different, it seems to me, than that of a student of management who is concerned with the behavior and performance of individual firms in their own right.

My objective in this essay is to make a strong case for the economic significance, in the sense above, of discretionary firm differences. My

position certainly has been influenced by the work of scholars of firm management who have persuasively documented significant differences among firms in an industry in behavior and performance, and proposed that these differences largely reflect different choices made by firms. However, because the interests of those authors have differed from the interests of economists, almost no attention has been paid to the industry or economy wide implications of such different choices. Thus while the management literature provides a start for my argument, there is much that I need to build myself, in cooperation with like thinking friends.

It should be recognized that, in trying to make a case for the economic significance of discretionary firm differences, I and my co-arguers are fighting against a strong tide in economics, particularly in theoretical economics, that downplays or even denies the importance of such differences. The argument in economics is not that firms are all alike; economists recognize that computer firms differ from textile firms, and in both industries, German firms almost certainly differ from Taiwanese firms. Rather, the position is that the differences aren't discretionary, but rather reflect differences in the contexts in which firms operate: computer design and production

Key words: Firms, innovation, evolution, competition

0143–2095/91/100061–14$07.00

technology and the computer market differ from the situation in textiles. Factor prices and availabilities and product markets in Germany differ from those in Taiwan. Thus, firms are forced to be different.

The tendency to ignore discretionary firm differences in part reflects that economists are not interested in behavior and performance at the level of firms, but rather in broader aggregates—industry or economy wide performance. It reflects, as well, some strong theoretical views held by most main line economists about what economic activity is all about, and about the role and nature of firms in economic activity. My argument that discretionary firm differences within an industry exist and do matter significantly is part and parcel of my broader argument that neoclassical economic theory is badly limited.

Let me flag here, for future elaboration, what I do and don't mean by the term 'discretionary'. I do mean to imply a certain looseness of constraints, both in the short and long run, that gives room so that firms that differ in certain important respects can be viable in the same economic environment. I do mean that to some extent these differences are the result of different strategies that are used to guide decision making at various levels in firms. On the other hand, I do not mean that what a firm is and does is under the tight control of high level decision makers. And I certainly do not mean that what makes a firm strong or weak at any time is well understood, even within the firms themselves, although there well may be an articulated point of view on this. More on these matters later.

The remainder of this essay is structured as follows. In the following section I shall flesh out my above remarks about the very significant differences in perspective between scholars trained or inclined to see discretionary firm level variables as important, and economists who see firm differences as determined largely by more aggregative economic forces. Then I focus on the basic theoretical preconceptions of neoclassical economic theory that lead to this position, and which make it very difficult to move any distance from it. I follow with an exploration of evolutionary economic theory which provides a very different view of what economic activity is all about and within which firm differences are central, and go on to consider the role of firm differences in the evolution of technology and

modes of organizing economic activity. Finally, a reprise.

THE DIVERGENT LITERATURES ON 'COMPETITIVENESS'

The differences in perspective can be seen clearly in the divergent literatures concerned with what now popularly is called the 'competitiveness' issue—the recent weakness of American firms, particularly *vis-à-vis* Japanese ones, in industries where not so long ago U.S. firms were doing very well. There is a sharp split between studies that focus on the differences between American and Japanese firms, and studies by economists that are focused on more aggregated variables.

Made in America, a publication put out in the summer of 1989 by the MIT Commission on Industrial Productivity, is a good example, and summary, of the former line of research. While the staff of the Commission undertook considerable research on its own, the multifaceted diagnosis it presents is quite consistent with that presented in a number of prior studies concerned with why American firms have been losing out.

American firms are hooked on old style mass production methods, in an era where flexible manufacturing has become a more effective mode of operation. Similarly, our hierarchical mode of organization and custom of specifying job assignments narrowly, while perhaps appropriate in an earlier era, now are sources of weakness. Research and product design and development stand too distant from manufacturing and production engineering; thus it takes American companies much longer than the Japanese to go from conception to production, and our production costs and quality often are inferior. American firms are myopic, both in the sense of their failure to look at world rather than national markets, and in the sense that time horizons are short. The latter partly has to do with the high cost of capital in the United States, but also with the way our managers think and the tools of analysis they are taught in business schools. Compared with the Japanese and Germans, our blue collar work force comes to the work place poorly trained by the public education system. This is compounded by a weakness of in-company training and retraining programs. Together, this puts American firms at a significant disadvantage regarding labor skills. American firms are less willing to cooperate with each other on matters where cooperation would yield pay-off, partly because of the attitudes of managers, but also partly because government looks on cooperation with suspicion or hostility. More generally, business and government seldom work together and often are at odds.

Others might summarize the central arguments somewhat differently, but I believe the above does represent fairly the kinds of propositions about firm differences made in the report. The arguments are plausible and provocative, and may provide important guidance to American management, and for public policy.

However, there are two important issues one can raise about the conclusions of the study. First, one can question the confidence one should place in the causal connections asserted in studies like *Made in America*. Second, one also can question whether the variables treated there as basic really are so, as contrasted with themselves being determined by broader forces.

At this stage I want only to flag the former issue. However, there really is a big question about just what Japanese firms in the automobile industry, or the semiconductor industry, are doing that lies behind their evident stronger performance, in various dimensions, than American or European firms. Later in this essay I shall focus on this uncertainty, and some of its implications.

For the present I want to focus on the latter question, because it gets sharply into view the contrast between analyses like *Made in America*, and the standard views of economists about the determinants of 'competitiveness'. There is some discussion in *Made in America* of macro or national level variables, like the exchange rate, the cost of capital, or more generally the system of corporate finance, the effectiveness of the public education system, government policies, etc. However, this is not where the focus is. It is firm level variables that receive the top billing, and it is presumed that these are discretionary to a considerable degree. In contrast, the inclination of economists is to focus on macro, or environmental level variables, and to play down or ignore the role of firm discretion.

The same year that *Made in America* was published, three economists, Baumol, Blackman, and Wolff, published their interpretation and diagnosis of lagging American productivity growth rates, and the convergence of productivity and living standards among the major industrial nations. The focus of *Productivity and American Leadership: The Long View* (1989) is usually at the level of the national economy, and sometimes at the level of the sector or industry. The variables considered are national savings and investment rates, investments in education, processes through which technology flows from creators to followers, and the like. There is scarcely a word about discretionary behavior at the level of firms.

It is strongly tempting, and I think right headed, to propose that each of the studies has described part of the elephant. The argument in the MIT study, that many of the difficulties American firms are having are self inflicted, is quite persuasive. At the same time the economist's proposition, that to a considerable extent firms are molded by the broader economic conditions surrounding them, is compelling. What seems sorely needed is an analysis that sees both of these matters, in a coherent way.

While the authors of *Made in America* never quite got into serious analyses of environmental variables, it does not seem difficult to augment an analysis that starts at the firm level to consider the environments that firms are in. Two new books are exemplary in that they do just this. Both recognize explicitly that national or environmental variables strongly influence firm strategy and structure, and that firms have considerable range of choice about these variables. Chandler's *Scale and Scope* (1990) describes in considerable depth how the different economic conditions, institutions, and cultures of the U.S., Great Britain, and Germany, molded the nature of the modern manufacturing firms that grew up in these different countries in the first decade of the twentieth century, and influenced the industries in which the nations developed special strength. However, there is nothing deterministic about Chandler's description of how the environment shapes firms and influences their performance.

Porter's *The Competitive Advantage of Nations* (1990) presents a similar perspective in which environmental influences matter greatly, but the firms have a considerable range of freedom regarding whether, or just how, they will take advantage of the opportunities the environment affords. Indeed both authors see the firms as to some extent molding their own environment as, for example, in calling forth significant public investments in education in the U.S. and Germany.

Chandler is an historian by training. Porter's formal training is in economics, but his career has been at a Business School and his research focus has been on management. It should be recognized that the orientation of these authors to 'firms' is quite different than that in most of economics. Indeed it is apparent that for both authors the center of attention is the firms, and the central questions are 'how are they doing' and 'what makes them strong or weak'. They are drawn to wider economic mechanisms and institutions in the search for answers to these questions. Now firm performance clearly is related to broader economic performance, but I have argued above they are not the same thing. Since neither Chandler nor Porter presents a coherent statement of the economy wide problem, their analyses stop considerably short of providing an answer that would satisfy economists to the question of 'why do firms differ and how does it matter?'

FIRMS IN NEOCLASSICAL ECONOMIC THEORY

To get at that question from an economist's perspective, one needs to start with a broad understanding of what economic activity is all about, and what constitutes good economic performance or poor. Neoclassical theory, which provides the current conventional wisdom on these matters for economists, militates against paying attention to firm differences as an important variable affecting economic performance for several reasons.

The first is the perception of what economic activity is all about. Since the formulation of general equilibrium theory almost a century ago, the focus has largely been on how well an economy allocates resources, given preferences and technologies. This position is far from universal. Empirically oriented economists have been interested in things like technical change and, recently, there has been a rash of work on economic institutions and how and why these change over time. Schumpeter some time ago

put forth a strong general theoretical challenge to the effect that innovation ought to be the center of economic analysis. But it is hard to overestimate the degree to which economists continue to see the central economic problem as that of meeting preferences as well as possible, given resources, and prevailing technologies and institutions. This perspective implies a rather limited view of what firms are about.

Second, partly reflecting this general orientation, but not the only possible formulation of firms' decision processes consistent with it, economists became wedded to a theory of firm behavior that posited that firms face given and known choice sets (constrained for example by available technologies) and have no difficulty in choosing the action within those sets that is the best for them, given their objectives (generally assumed to be as much profit as possible). Thus the 'economic problem' is basically about getting private incentives right, not about identifying the best things to be doing, which is assumed to be no problem.

The perspective on the economic problem and the theory of firm behavior described above do not invite a careful inquiry into what goes on in firms. However, the tradition in economics of treating firms as 'black boxes,' was not inevitable either. The fact that until recently at least, this has been the norm deserves recognition in its own right.

The overall result is a view that what firms do is determined by the conditions they face, and (possibly) by certain unique attributes (say a choice location, or a proprietary technology) they possess. Firms facing different markets will behave and perform differently, but if the market conditions were reversed so would be firm behaviors. Where the theory admits product differentiation, different firms will produce different products but, in the theoretical literature, any firm can choose any niche. Thus there are firm differences but there is no essential autonomous quality to them.

The theoretical orientation in economics thus leans strongly against the proposition that discretionary firm differences matter. Of course economists studying empirical or policy questions have a proclivity to wander away from the tethers of theory when the facts of the matter compel them to do so. Thus in doing industry studies, economists often have been forced to recognize, even highlight, firm differences, and differences that matter. One cannot study the computer industry sensitively without paying attention to the peculiarities of IBM. The recent history of the automobile industry cannot be understood without understanding Toyota and G.M. But as the Baumol, Blackman, and Wolff book testifies, the theoretical preconceptions shared by most economists lead them to ignore firm differences, unless compelled to attend to them.

Several recent developments in theoretical economics would appear to be changing this somewhat. Thus the same summer that *Made in America*, and *Productivity and American Leadership* were published, the long awaited *Handbook of Industrial Organization* (1989) was also. Included in the chapters were several that survey theoretical work that does recognize firm differences.

There are, first of all, the essays by Ordover and Saloner, and by Gilbert, which are expressly concerned with theoretical work that aims to explain firm differences, or at least some consequences of firm differences. In the models reported, there usually is an incumbent in the industry, or in the production of a particular product, who has certain advantages over firms who might think of joining the action. The presence of these advantages, or threats of action should a newcomer try to encroach, is enough to make the advantages durable. Gilbert deals more generally with models where there are costs to firms of changing their market positions. However, with few exceptions the models surveyed in these chapters do not consider in much depth or detail original sources of firm differences.

Reinganum's chapter, which surveys modern neoclassical models of technological innovation, is focused on what certainly is an important source of such differences—industrial R&D and the innovation R&D makes possible. In the models she surveys, a firm's technology may differ from a rival's because of the luck of an R&D draw, with the advantages made durable by patent protection or subsequent learning curve advantages. Given an initial difference, firms may face different incentives and thus find different courses of action most profitable. However, while these models may rationalize the observation that firms possess different technologies, the answers as to why certainly aren't very deep. And one comes away from

them, or at least I do, with very little theoretical insight into why IBM is different, or Toyota, and so what.

There has been a certain amount of recent theoretical work by economists that looks inside of firms, at their structure, and thus seems to give promise of a theoretical window for a deeper look into why firms differ. The chapters by Holmstrom and Tirole, and by Williamson, report on such work. The questions explored in the surveyed work include what determines, through make or buy decisions, the boundaries of a firm, how it is organized, the relative bargaining power of owners, managers, and workers, etc. But, again, the ultimate reason for why firms differ is rather superficial. Implicitly they differ because some chance event, or some initial condition, made different choices profitable.

In my view, recent theoretical developments in neoclassical theory have loosened two of the theoretical constraints making it difficult if not impossible to see firm differences as important. Economists are getting away from the theoretical tethers of static general equilibrium theory and are treating technology as a variable not a given. And they are trying to look inside the black box of the firm. However, for the most part there has been failure to get away from the third tether—taking a firm's choice sets as obvious to it and the best choice similarly clear and obvious. And because of that, the reasons for firm differences, in technology or organization, are ultimately driven back to differences in initial conditions, or to the luck of a draw, which may make choice sets different. Given the same conditions, all firms will do the same thing.

As I indicated above, I certainly do not want to play down the role of environment in constraining and molding what firms do. And I do not want to play down the role of chance in causing large and durable subsequent differences among firms. But in my view the models most economists keep playing with do not effectively come to grips with what lies behind the firm differences highlighted in *Made in America*, or the implications of those differences.

The reason, I want to argue, is that while the surveyed work purports to be concerned with 'innovation', with the introduction of something new to the economy in the form of new technology or a new way of organizing a firm, the models in question completely miss what is involved in innovation. Thus nowhere in the models Reinganum describes is the fundamental uncertainty, the differences of opinion, the differences in perceptions about the feasible paths, that tend to stand out in any detailed study of technical advance, even recognized, much less analyzed in any detail. Williamson's own work on the determinants of firm organization has been much influenced by Chandler, and he dedicates a certain space in his chapter to a transactions cost interpretation of Chandler's account of the rise of the modern corporation. But nowhere does he recognize explicitly the halting, trial and feedback, often reactive rather than thought-through, process that led to the new ways of organizing that Chandler describes.

Put compactly, the treatment of technological and organizational 'innovation' described in these chapters simply takes the given 'choice set' and 'maximizing over it' presumptions of standard neoclassical theory and applies them to 'innovation.' That is, innovation is treated as basically like any other choice. Investment costs may need to be incurred before the new product or organizational design is ready to be employed, but in neoclassical theory this is true of other capital goods like a bridge or a machine. There may be high risks involved in doing something new, in a formal sense of that term, but this is treated as statistical uncertainty with the correct probability distribution known to all as is standard in micro economic theory. The innovation may yield a new latent or manifest public good, and this raises theoretical problems of 'market failure', but this is no different than investment in, say, public health.

But what if effective treatment of innovation (and perhaps other activities) requires breaking away from the assumptions of clear and obvious choice sets and correct understanding of the consequences of making various choices? Does it really make sense to work with a model that presumes that the transistor, or the M form of organization, were always possible choices out there and known to all relevant parties, and that they simply were chosen and thus came into existence and use when conditions made profitable the relevant investments? Does the assumption that 'actors maximize' help one to analyze situations where some actors are not even aware of a possibility being considered by others?

If one reflects on these issues, one may be moved to adapt a very different view of the economic problem. Within this view, which I will call evolutionary, firm differences play an essential role.

INNOVATION AND FIRMS IN EVOLUTIONARY THEORY

The models of technological innovation surveyed by Reinganum show economists interested in the theory of the firm struggling to break away from the orientation of general equilibrium theory, which sees the economic problem as allocating resources efficiently, given technologies. So too the new literature on organizational innovation. Here economists seem to be basically interested in how new ways of doing things—technologies, and ways of organizing and governing work—are introduced, winnowed, and where proven useful, spread, as contrasted with how familiar technologies and organizational modes are employed. Many years ago Schumpeter insisted that the focus of general equilibrium theory was on questions that, over the long run, were of minor importance compared with the question of how Capitalist economies develop, screen, and selectively adopt new and better ways of doing things. Many of the writers surveyed by Reinganum call themselves 'neo Schumpeterians'.

However, the dynamic processes Schumpeter described are not captured by the new neoclassical models. As he put it 'in dealing with Capitalism, you are dealing with an evolutionary process'. He clearly had in mind a context in which people, and organizations, had quite different views about what kinds of innovations would be possible, and desirable, and would lay their bets differently. There are winners and losers in Schumpeter's 'process of creative destruction', and these are not determined mainly in ex-ante calculation, but largely in ex-post actual contest.

In his 1911 *Theory of Economic Development*, Schumpeter saw the key innovative actors as 'entrepreneurs'. His 'firms' were basically the vessels used by entrepreneurs, and other decision makers forced to adapt to the changes wrought by entrepreneurial innovators or to go under. By the time (1942) he wrote *Capitalism, Socialism, and Democracy*, Schumpeter's view of the sources of innovation had changed, or rather it might be better to say that there had been a transformation of the principal sources of innovation from an earlier era, and Schumpeter's views reflected this transformation. Modern firms, equipped with research and development laboratories, became the central innovative actors in Schumpeter's theory. The chapter by Cohen and Levin in the *Handbook* admirably surveys the wide range of empirical research that has been inspired by Schumpeter, particularly the research concerned with the relationships among innovation, firm size and other characteristics, and market structure.

In our book, *An Evolutionary Theory of Economic Change* (1982), Winter and I spent quite a bit of space presenting a 'theory of the firm' which is consistent with, and motivates, a Schumpeterian or evolutionary theoretic view of economic process and economic change. Our formulation drew significantly on Simon (1957), on Cyert and March (1963), and on Penrose (1959), as well as on Schumpeter. With the vision of hindsight, it is clear that our writing then was handicapped by insufficient study of the writings of Chandler, particularly his *Scale and Scope* (1966).

Since the time we wrote, there have been a number of theoretical papers on firm capabilities and behavior that draw both on Chandler and on our early formulation, and which add significantly to the picture. Papers by Teece (1980, 1982), Rumelt (1984), Cohen and Levinthal (1989), Dosi, Teece and Winter (1989), Prahalad and Hamel (1990), Pavitt (1987, 1990), Cantwell (1989, 1990), Kogut (1987), Henderson (1990), Burgelman and Rosenbloom (1989), Langlois (1991), and Lazonick (1990), all present a similar or at least a conformable theoretical view, although with differences in stress. The recent paper by Teece, Pisano, and Shuen (1990) provides an overview of many of these works, and I believe correctly states that the common element is a focus on firm specific dynamic capabilities.

This emerging theory of dynamic firm capabilities can be presented in different ways. Here it is convenient to focus on three different if strongly related features of a firm that must be recognized if one is to describe it adequately: its strategy, its structure, and its core capabilities. While each has a certain malleability, major changes in at least the latter two involve considerable cost. Thus they define a relatively stable firm character.

The concept of strategy in this theory of the firm is basically what business historians and scholars of management mean, as contrasted with game theorists. It connotes a set of broad commitments made by a firm that define and rationalize its objectives and how it intends to pursue them. Some of this may be written down, some may not be but is in the management culture of the firm. Many economists would be wont to propose that the strategy represents a firms solution of its profit maximization problem, but this seems misconceived to me. In the first place, the commitments contained in a strategy often are as much a matter of faith of top management, and company tradition, as they are of calculation. Second, firm strategies seldom determine the details of firm actions, but usually at most the broad contours. Third, and of vital importance, there is no reason to argue *a priori* that these commitments are in fact optimal or even not self destructive. If it is proposed that competition and selection force surviving strategies to be relatively profitable, this should be a theorem not an assumption.

The concept of firm structure in this literature also is in the spirit of Chandler, as is the presumption that strategy tends to define a desired firm structure in a general way, but not the details. Structure involves how a firm is organized and governed, and how decisions actually are made and carried out, and thus largely determines what it actually does, given the broad strategy. A firm whose strategy calls for being a technological leader that does not have a sizeable R&D operation, or whose R&D director has little input into firm decision making, clearly has a structure out of tune with its strategy. However, the high level strategy may be mute about links between its R&D lab and universities, whether to have a special biotech group, etc.

Change in strategy may require a change in management as well as a change in articulation; indeed for the latter to be serious may require the former. However, within this theory of the firm structure is far more difficult to change effectively than is strategy. While changing formal organization, or at least the organization chart, is easy, and selloffs and buyups are possible, significantly changing the way a firm actually goes about making operating level decisions and carries them out is time consuming and costly to do. Or rather, while it may not be too difficult to destroy an old structure or its effectiveness, it is a major task to get a new structure in shape and operating smoothly. Thus to the extent that a major change in strategy calls for a major change in structure, effecting the needed changes may take a long time.

The reason for changing structure, of course, is to change, possibly to augment, the things a firm is capable of doing well. Which brings the discussion to the concept of core capabilities. Strategy and structure call forth and mold organizational capabilities, but what an organization can do well has something of a life of its own.

Winter and I have proposed that well working firms can be understood in terms of a hierarchy of practiced organizational routines, which define lower order organizational skills, and how these are coordinated, and higher order decision procedures for choosing what is to be done at lower levels. The notion of a hierarchy of organizational routines is the key building block under our concept of core organizational capabilities. At any time the practiced routines that are built into an organization define a set of things the organization is capable of doing confidently. If the lower order routines are not there for doing various tasks, or if they are but there is no practiced higher order routine for invoking them in the particular combination needed to accomplish a particular job, then the capability to do that job lies outside the organization's extant core capabilities.

The developing theory of dynamic firm capabilities I am discussing here starts from the premise that, in the industries of interest to the authors, firms are in a Schumpeterean or evolutionary context. Simply producing a given set of products with a given set of processes well will not enable a firm to survive for long. To be successful for any length of time a firm must innovate. The capabilities on which this group of scholars focus are capabilities for innovation and to take economic advantage of innovation.

In industries where technological innovation is important, a firm needs a set of core capabilities in R&D. These capabilities will be defined and constrained by the skills, experience, and knowledge of the personnel in the R&D department, the nature of the extant teams and procedures for forming new ones, the character

of the decision making processes, the links between R&D and production and marketing, etc. This means that at any time there will be certain kinds of R&D projects that a firm can carry out with some confidence and success, and a wide range of other projects that, while other firms might to able to do them, this particular firm can not, with any real confidence.

R&D capabilities may be the lead ones in defining the dynamic capabilities of a firm. However, in a well tuned firm, its production, procurement, marketing and legal organizations must have built into them the capabilities to support and complement the new product and process technologies emanating from R&D. In Teece's terms, the firm's capabilities must include control over or access to the complementary assets and activities needed to enable it to profit from innovation. And in an environment of Schumpeterian competition, this means the capability to innovate, and to make that innovation profitable, again and again.

The concept of organizational capabilities, and the theory that Winter and I proposed as to what determines and limits them, does not directly imply any coherency to the set of things a firm can do. However, Dosi *et al.* (1989) argue that, in effective firms, there is a certain coherency. There would appear to be several reasons. The ones stressed by Dosi *et al.* basically are associated with localized learning in a dynamic context, and follow on the arguments that Winter and I made some time ago that, to be under control, a routine needs to be practiced. Firms need to learn to get good at certain kinds of innovation, and at the things needed to take advantage of these, and this requires concentration or at least coherency, rather than random spreading of efforts. Further, in many technologies one innovation points more or less directly to a set of following ones, and the learning and complementary strengths developed in the former effort provide a base for the next round.

But I think it also is the case that to be effective a firm needs a reasonably coherent strategy, that defines and legitimizes, at least loosely, the way the firm is organized and governed, enables it to see organizational gaps or anomalies given the strategy, and sets the ground for bargaining about the resource needs for the core capabilities a firm must have to take its next step forward. Absent a reasonably coherent and accepted strategy, decision making about rival claims on resources has no legitimate basis. Decisions from above have no supportive rationale, and there is no way to hold back log rolling bargaining among claimants other than arbitrary high level decisions. There is no real guidance regarding the capabilities a firm needs to protect, enhance, or add in order to be effective in the next round of innovative competition.

But I think I simply am restating what Chandler, Lazonick, Williamson, and other scholars of the modern corporation, have been saying for some time. To be successful in a world that requires that firms innovate and change, a firm must have a coherent strategy that enables it to decide what new ventures to go into and what to stay out of. And it needs a structure, in the sense of mode of organization and governance, that guides and supports the building and sustaining of the core capabilities needed to carry out that strategy effectively.

If one thinks within the frame of evolutionary theory, it is nonsense to presume that a firm can calculate an actual 'best' strategy. A basic premise of evolutionary theory is that the world is too complicated for a firm to comprehend, in the sense that a firm understands its world in neoclassical theory. There are certain characteristics of a firm's strategy, and of its associated structure, that management can have confidence will enhance the chances that it will develop the capabilities it needs to succeed. There are other characteristics that seem a prescription for failure. However, there is a lot of room in between, where a firm (or its management) simply has to lay its bets knowing that it does not know how they will turn out.

Thus diversity of firms is just what one would expect under evolutionary theory. It is virtually inevitable that firms will choose somewhat different strategies. These, in turn, will lead to firms having different structures and different core capabilities, including their R&D capabilities. Inevitably firms will pursue somewhat different paths. Some will prove profitable, given what other firms are doing and the way markets evolve, others not. Firms that systematically lose money will have to change their strategy and structure and develop new core capabilities, or operate the ones they have more effectively, or drop out of the contest.

THE EVOLUTION OF TECHNOLOGY

In real capitalist economies, in contrast with the neoclassical models, technical advance proceeds through an evolutionary process, with new products and processes competing with each other and with prevailing technology in real time, rather than solely in ex-ante calculation. Some of the innovations will be winners, other losers. With the vision of hindsight the whole process looks messy and wasteful, and a more coherent planning approach to technological advance appears attractive.

However, it is striking how inefficient and misguided efforts to plan and control significant technical advance have been. Where, for one reason or another, society has been denied the advantages of multiple independent approaches to advance technology, which flows naturally from a basis of independent rivalrous firms, almost always the approach chosen has turned out, after the fact, to have major limitations. And since alternatives had not been developed to a point where they could be tried in comparison, there has been lock in. A number of U.S. military R&D efforts since 1960 are striking examples. Nuclear power programs are another. The fact is that in virtually every field where we have had rapid technical advance that has met a market test or its equivalent, we have had multiple rivalrous sources of new technology.

While Winter and I formally modelled company R&D programs as generating results through a random draw, in fact in the industries that I know well there has tended to be a certain consistency in the R&D efforts of particular companies. This consistency reflects a basically stable company 'strategy', and the core R&D and other dynamic capabilities it has put in place to carry it out. Where company strategies and associated capabilities differ significantly, their patterns of innovation are likely to differ significantly as well.

This has an important consequence often overlooked in the literature on technological imitation. When one firm comes up with a successful innovation, its competitors may differ significantly among themselves in their ability effectively to imitate or develop something comparable. Contrary to many economic models, effective technological imitation very often requires the imitating firm to go through many of the same design and development activities as did the innovator, and to implement similar production and other supporting activities. Thus firms with similar strategies and core capabilities are in a much better position to imitate or learn and build from each others work than firms with different strategies and capabilities.

Thus to an extent the market is selecting on strategies and companies, as well as new technologies. This suggests that in some circumstances strategic diversity may get extinguished.

There is something to this argument. A number of analysts, some working in the tradition of economic research, some in a business school research tradition, have suggested that there is a natural industry life cycle. When an industry or a broad technology is new, a wide variety of approaches to technological innovation—strategies—is taken by different firms. As experience grows, certain of the approaches begin to look significantly better than others. Firms who have made the right bets do well. Those who have not, need to switch over, or drop out. A number of studies have shown that, as an industry or technology matures, there is a significant reduction in the number of firms, and in some cases the emergence of a 'dominant design' with all surviving firms producing some variety of that tuned to the niche they have found.

One fascinating question is what happens in a relatively mature industry when a new and potentially superior technology comes into existence. The evidence suggests that it matters whether the new technology is conformable with the core capabilities of extant firms, or requires very different kinds of capabilities. Tushman and Anderson (1986) call these two kinds of developments 'competence enhancing' and 'competence destroying'. Under the latter circumstances, new firms are likely to be the innovators, and old firms often are unable to respond effectively. Tushman and Anderson note that a change in management, and presumably a major change in strategy, often is necessary if the old firm is to survive in the new environment. But it may not be sufficient. Structure and core capabilities are far more difficult to change than management and articulated strategies.

For a student of business management the question of what enables a firm to change directions effectively, and be a viable competitor in the new regime, is of central interest in its own right. For an economist what matters is that pharmaceutical R&D take advantage of the new possibilities opened by new biotechnology, and not whether the old pharmaceutical firms do it, or whether they fail, so long as new ones take up the torch.

However, the fact that the leading edge companies in a field often change is a fascinating matter. It is consistent with the theory of focused and constrained core capabilities presented above. And it is a central reason why, for an economist interested in technological advance, firm differences matter importantly.

THE EVOLUTION OF FIRM ORGANIZATION

There has been far more study of the way technology advances than there has been of the way firm organization changes. By organization I mean what I think Chandler (1966) means by strategy and structure, those aspects of a firm that are wider and more durable than the particular technologies and other routines it employs at any moment, or even its extent core capabilities, and which in effect guide the internal evolution of these. It is apparent that change in organization in this broad sense, as well as advance in technology, has been an essential feature of the enormous economic progress that has been experienced over the last century and a half.

Some writers clearly would like to give organizational change separate and equal billing with technical advance as a source of economic progress. I would like to argue here, however, that one needs to understand organizational change as usually a handmaiden to technological advance, and not a separate force behind economic progress.

If I understand him correctly, this would be Chandler's position. The new technology of the railroads required, for its effective implementation, the development of organizational capabilities far beyond that possessed by traditional owner managed firms. Line and staff organizational form, along with the development of the position of hired manager, enabled the railroads to be effectively 'governed', to use Williamson's term. Later, new technologies which promised economies of scale and scope in manufacturing called for large firms operating in several different product fields, or market areas. The M form of managerial structure evolved to govern effectively this kind of business operation.

Over the long run what has mattered most has been organizational changes needed to enhance dynamic innovative capabilities. Reich (1985), Hounshell and Smith (1988), and other writers have described how the organizational device of the industrial research and development laboratory came into existence, to permit firms to shield a portion of their scientific and technical personnel from the pressures of day by day problem solving so that they could work on the development of new products and processes. This development was preconditioned by the rise of a new 'technology' for product and process development, one employing the understandings and techniques of the sciences and engineering disciplines in a systematic way. One can read Chandler's and Lazonick's account of the rise of other aspects of the modern corporation in terms of Teece's arguments about needed complementary assets or capabilities.

As I read the case study evidence, devising and learning to use effectively a significantly new organizational form involves much the same kind of uncertainty, experimental groping, and learning by making mistakes and correcting them, that marks technological invention and innovation. New modes of organization aren't simply 'chosen' when circumstances make them appropriate. They, like technologies, evolve in a manner that is foreseen only dimly. And even when a firm makes a conscious decision to change organization, it may take a long time before it is comfortable and effective in its new suit of clothes.

I want to return here to a point I made at the start of this paper. I suspect that the uncertainties about new organization are even greater than those surrounding technological innovations. This is especially so regarding organization which molds effective dynamic innovative capabilities and the abilities to profit from innovation. At the present time there is little in the way of tested and proved theory (let me use the less pretentious word—knowledge) that enables confident prediction of the best way of organizing a particular activity, or what will be the consequences of adopting a different mode of organiz-

ation. If the 'rationally choosing' view of technological advance is misguided, the 'rationally choosing' view of organizational change is even more so.

Just as important, it is common, not infrequent, for a particular mode of organization put in place for one reason to turn out to have advantages, or disadvantages, in arenas that were not considered at the time the original move was contemplated and made. It also is common, not infrequent, that there be considerable dispute about just what features of a firm's organization are responsible for certain successes or failures.

Thus, as I understand it, large Japanese firms adapted 'life time employment' for their skilled workers in the early post war era to try to deal with a problem of skill shortages and labor unrest. It is quite unclear how many Japanese managers foresaw advantages associated with worker loyalty, and ability of a firm to do in-house training without fear of losing the investment through worker defection. Just in time was, I understand, largely a response to scarce space, high inventory costs, and input shortages. It is not clear how many saw that it would facilitate quality control.

American companies looking at their Japanese competitors often have been uncertain about just why the Japanese are better in some respects, and just what they can effectively transplant. They only will be able to learn by trying some things, seeing what happens, and having the good luck to see it right.

The evidence is very limited, but there is reason to believe that firms have greater ability to replicate themselves in another setting in a way that preserves their strength, than to comprehend and adopt what gives their rivals strength. Thus as Womack, Jones, and Roos (1991) and Clark and Fujimoto (1991) document convincingly, American automobile manufacturers still are struggling to catch up with the Japanese in terms of productivity and quality of production. Where they are coming close it seems to be in cases where the Japanese are serving as partners. This does not look accidental. Florida and Kenney (1991) report that Japanese owned automobile assembly plants in the United States have rather quickly been able to establish practices—strategies and structures—similar to their home operations, and with comparable outcomes.

72   *R. R. Nelson*

I want to put forth the argument that it is organizational differences, especially differences in abilities to generate and gain from innovation, rather than differences in command over particular technologies, that are the source of durable, not easily imitable, differences among firms. Particular technologies are much easier to understand, and imitate, than broader firm dynamic capabilities.

From one point of view it is technological advance that has been the key force that has driven economic growth over the past two centuries, with organizational change a handmaiden. But from another perspective, we would not have got that technological advance without development of new ways of organization that can guide and support R&D and enable firms to profit from these investments.

I have been concentrating on firm organization. However, it is clear that the organizational changes that have enabled nations to support the modern R&D system and the technological advance it generates go far beyond those of firm organization. Universities had to change. New scientific disciplines and societies had to come into being. In many cases new bodies of law were needed. Some technologies required major new public infrastructure for their effective development.

The coevolution of technology and institutions is a fascinating subject. Chandler, and a few other scholars such as Hughes (1983) and Freeman (1989), have begun to address it. There clearly have been major national differences in how the institutions needed to support particular evolving technologies themselves evolved. Perhaps in the study of the coevolution of technology and institutions we will begin to develop a serious theory of how national comparative advantage comes into being, or is lost. But I now am far beyond the scope of this paper.

REPRISE

Students of firm management, in particular those working in the strategy field, treat discretionary firm differences as their bread and butter. Economists have tended to play down these differences, or to argue that they are the result not the cause of general economic differences. In good part the difference in viewpoints is due to differences in basic interests—the student of firm management concerned with the fate of individual firms, and the economist interested in general economic performance of an industry or nation. But I have argued that the lack of interest by economists in discretionary firm differences stems as well from a particular theoretical view of economic activity and the role and behavior of firms.

If one takes an evolutionary rather than a neoclassical view of what economic activity is about, then firm differences matter importantly regarding issues that traditionally have been the central concern of economists. Competition can be seen as not merely about incentives and pressures to keep prices in line with minimal feasible costs, and to keep firms operating at low costs, but, much more important, about exploring new potentially better ways of doing things. Long ago Schumpeter remarked that the former function was trivial compared with the latter, if the measure was contribution to the economic well-being of humankind.

From the perspective of evolutionary theory, firm diversity is an essential aspect of the processes that create economic progress. Monopoly, or tight oligopoly with strong barriers to entry, can be seen as a serious economic problem, not so much because such structures permit a large gap between price and cost, but because they are unlikely to generate the variety of new routines, and the attendant shifts in resource allocation on which economic progress depends. One is suspicious of arguments to 'rationalize' production and innovation for the same reasons, particularly when the winds of change are blowing from uncertain angles.

Thus, the 'dynamic capabilities' view of firms being developed by scholars in the strategy field can be seen to be important not only as a guide to management, but also as the basis for a serious theory of the firm in economics. It, when embedded in an evolutionary theory of economic change, instructs us regarding 'Why do Firms Differ, and How Does it Matter?'

ACKNOWLEDGEMENTS

The author is indebted to the Sloan Foundation, through its funding of the Consortium on Competitiveness and Cooperation, and to the

Conference on Fundamental Issues and Strategy for whom this essay was written, for support in its undertaking. Many people have commented helpfully on an earlier draft. I especially want to thank Alfred Chandler, Wesley Cohen, Rebecca Henderson, Richard Langlois, William Lazonick, Richard Rosenbloom, Donald Sexton, David Teece, and Michael Tushman.

REFERENCES

Baumol, W., S. Blackman and E. Wolff. *Productivity and American Leadership: The Long View*, MIT Press, Cambridge, MA, 1989.

Burgelman R. and R. Rosenbloom. 'Technology strategy: An evolutionary process perspective'. In R. Burgelman and R. Rosenbloom (eds.), *Research on Technological Innovation, Management, and Policy*, Vol. 4, JAI Press, Greenwich, CT, 1989, pp. 1–23.

Cantwell, J. *Technological Innovation and Multinational Corporations*, Basil Blackwell, London, 1989.

Cantwell, J. 'The technological competence theory of international production and its implications', University of Reading Discussion Paper #149, 1990.

Chandler, A. D., Jr. *Strategy and Structure*, Doubleday & Co., Anchor Books Edition, New York, 1966.

Chandler, A. D., Jr. *Scale and Scope: The Dynamics of Industrial Capitalism*, Harvard University Press, Cambridge, MA, 1990.

Clark, K. and T. Fujimoto. *Product Development Performance: Strategy Management and Organization in the World Auto Industry*, Harvard Business School Press, Cambridge, MA, 1991.

Cohen W. and R. Levin. 'Empirical Studies of Innovation and Market Structure'. In R. Schmalensee and R. Willig (eds.), *Handbook of Industrial Organization*, North Holland, New York, 1989, pp. 1059–1107.

Cohen W. and D. Levinthal. 'Innovation and learning: The two faces of R & D,' *Economic Journal*, Sept. 1989, pp. 569–596.

Cyert R. and J. March. *A Behavioral Theory of the Firm*, Prentice Hall, Englewood Cliff, NJ, 1963.

Dertouzos, M., R. Lester and R. Sulow. *Made in America*, MIT Press, Cambridge, MA, 1989.

Dosi, G., D. J. Teece and S. Winter. 'Toward a theory of corporate coherence: Preliminary remarks', unpublished paper, Center for Research in Management, University of California at Berkeley, 1989.

Florida R. and M. Kenney. 'Transplanted organizations: The transfer of Japanese industrial organization to the United States', *American Sociological Review*, June, 1991, pp. 381–398.

Freeman, C. 'The nature of innovation and the evolution of the production system', OECD Paris, Xerox, 1989.

Gilbert R. 'Mobility barriers and the value of

incumbency'. In R. Schmalensee and R. Willig (eds.), *Handbook of Industrial Organization*, North Holland, New York, 1989, pp. 475–535.

Henderson, R. 'Underinvestment and incompetence as responses to radical innovation: Evidence from the photolithographic alignment equipment industry', MIT Sloan School Discussion paper, 1990.

Hounshell, D. and J. Smith. *Science and Corporate Strategy: Du Pont R&D 1902–1980*, Cambridge University Press, New York, 1988.

Hughes, T. *Networks of Power: Electrical Supply Systems in the U.S., England, and Germany*, Johns Hopkins Press, Baltimore. MD, 1983.

Holmstrom B. and J. Tirole. 'The theory of the firm'. In R. Schmalensee and R. Willig (eds.), *Handbook of Industrial Organization*, North Holland, New York, 1989, pp. 61–133.

Kogut, B. 'Country patterns in international competition: Appropriability and oligopolistic agreement'. In N. Hood and J. Vahlne (eds.), *Strategies in Global Competition*, Croom-Helm, London, 1987, pp. 315–340.

Langlois, R. 'Transaction cost economics in real time' *Industrial Corporate Change*, June 1991, pp. 99–127.

Lazonick, W. *Competitive Advantage on the Shop Floor*, Harvard University Press, Cambridge, MA, 1990.

Nelson, R. and S. Winter. *An Evolutionary Theory of Economic Change*, Harvard University Press, Cambridge, MA, 1982.

Ordover, J. and G. Saloner. 'Predation, monopolization, and antitrust'. In R. Schmalensee and R. Willig (eds.), *Handbook of Industrial Organization*, North Holland, New York, 1989, pp. 537–596.

Pavitt, K. 'On the nature of technology' Inaugural lecture given at the University of Sussex, 23 June 1987.

Pavitt, K. 'The nature and determinants of innovation: A major factor in firms' (and countries') competitiveness.' Paper prepared for the conference on 'Fundamental Issues in Strategy: A Research Agenda for the 1990s', 1990.

Penrose, E. *The Theory of the Growth of the Firm*, Basil Blackwell, London, 1959.

Porter, M. E. *The Competitive Advantage of Nations*, Free Press, New York, 1990.

Prahalad, C. K. and G. Hamel. 'The core competence of the corporation', *Harvard Business Review*, 68(3), 1990, pp. 79–91.

Reich, L. *The Making of American Industrial Research: Science and Business at G.E. and Bell*, Cambridge University Press, New York, 1985.

Reinganum, J. 'The timing of innovation: Research, development and diffusion'. In R. Schmalensee and R. Willig (eds.), *Handbook of Industrial Organization*, North Holland, New York, 1989, pp. 849–908.

Rumelt, R. P. 'Towards a strategic theory of the firm'. In R. B. Lamb (ed.), *Competitive Strategic Management*, Prentice-Hall, Englewood Cliffs, NJ, 1984, pp. 556–570.

74   *R. R. Nelson*

Schmalensee, R. and R. Willig (eds.), *Handbook of Industrial Organization*, North Holland, New York, 1989.

Schumpeter, J. *The Theory of Economic Development*, Harvard University Press, Cambridge, MA, 1934 (first published 1911).

Schumpeter, J. *Capitalism, Socialism, and Democracy*, Harper, New York, 1950 (first published 1942).

Simon, H. *Administrative Behavior*, The Free Press, New York, 1957.

Teece, D. 'Economics of scope and the scope of an enterprise', *Journal of Economic Behavior and Organization*, Sept. 1980, pp. 223–247.

Teece, D. 'Towards an economic theory of the multiproduct firm', *Journal of Economic Behavior and Organization*, March 1982, pp. 39–63.

Teece, D. 'Profiting from Technological Innovation', *Research Policy*, December, 1986, pp. 285–305.

Teece, D., G. Pisano and A. Shuen. 'Firm capabilities, resources, and the concept of strategy', CCC Working Paper 90-8, Center for Research on Management, University of California, Berkeley, 1990.

Tushman, M. and P. Anderson. 'Technological discontinuities and organizational environments', *Administrative Science Quarterly*, Sept. 1986, pp. 439–465.

Williamson, O. 'Transaction Cost Economies'. In R. Schmalensee and R. Willig (eds.), *Handbook of Industrial Organization*, North Holland, New York, 1989, pp. 135–182.

Womack, J., D. Jones and D. Roos. *The Machine that Changed the World*, MIT Press, Cambridge, MA, 1991.

[10]

Strategic Management Journal, Vol. 13, 111–125 (1992)

CORE CAPABILITIES AND CORE RIGIDITIES: A PARADOX IN MANAGING NEW PRODUCT DEVELOPMENT

DOROTHY LEONARD-BARTON

Graduate School of Business Administration, Harvard University, Boston, Massachusetts, U.S.A.

This paper examines the nature of the core capabilities of a firm, focusing in particular on their interaction with new product and process development projects. Two new concepts about core capabilities are explored here. First, while core capabilities are traditionally treated as clusters of distinct technical systems, skills, and managerial systems, these dimensions of capabilities are deeply rooted in values, which constitute an often overlooked but critical fourth dimension. Second, traditional core capabilities have a down side that inhibits innovation, here called core rigidities. Managers of new product and process development projects thus face a paradox: how to take advantage of core capabilities without being hampered by their dysfunctional flip side. Such projects play an important role in emerging strategies by highlighting the need for change and leading the way. Twenty case studies of new product and process development projects in five firms provide illustrative data.

INTRODUCTION

Debate about the nature and strategic importance of firms' distinctive capabilities has been heightened by the recent assertion that Japanese firms understand, nurture and exploit their core competencies better than their U.S.-based competitors (Prahalad and Hamel, 1990). This paper explores the interaction of such capabilities with a critical strategic activity: the development of new products and processes. In responding to environmental and market changes, development projects become the focal point for tension between innovation and the *status quo*—microcosms of the paradoxical organizational struggle to maintain, yet renew or replace core capabilities.

In this paper, I first examine the history of core capabilities, briefly review relevant literature, and describe a field-based study providing illustrative data. The paper then turns to a deeper description of the nature of core capabilities and detailed evidence about their symbiotic relationship with development projects. However, evidence from the field suggests the need to enhance emerging theory by examining the way that capabilities inhibit as well as enable development, and these arguments are next presented. The paper concludes with a discussion of the project/capabilities interaction as a paradox faced by project managers, observed management tactics, and the potential of product/process development projects to stimulate change.

THE HISTORY OF CORE CAPABILITIES

Capabilities are considered *core* if they differentiate a company strategically. The concept is not new. Various authors have called them distinctive

Key words: Core capabilities, innovation, new product development

0143-2095/92/060125-15$12.50

112   *D. Leonard-Barton*

competences (Snow and Hrebiniak, 1980; Hitt and Ireland, 1985), core or organizational competencies (Prahalad and Hamel, 1990; Hayes, Wheelwright and Clark, 1988), firm-specific competence (Pavitt, 1991), resource deployments (Hofer and Schendel, 1978), and invisible assets (Itami, with Roehl, 1987). Their strategic significance has been discussed for decades, stimulated by such research as Rumelt's (1974) discovery that of nine diversification strategies, the two that were built on an existing skill or resource base in the firm were associated with the highest performance. Mitchell's (1989) observation that industry-specific capabilities increased the likelihood a firm could exploit a new technology within that industry, has confirmed the early work. Therefore some authors suggest that effective competition is based less on strategic leaps than on incremental innovation that exploits carefully developed capabilities (Hayes, 1985; Quinn, 1980).

On the other hand, institutionalized capabilities may lead to 'incumbent inertia' (Lieberman and Montgomery, 1988) in the face of environmental changes. Technological discontinuities can enhance or destroy existing competencies within an industry (Tushman and Anderson, 1986). Such shifts in the external environment resonate within the organization, so that even 'seemingly minor' innovations can undermine the usefulness of deeply embedded knowledge (Henderson and Clark, 1990). In fact, all innovation necessarily requires some degree of 'creative destruction' (Schumpeter, 1942).

Thus at any given point in a corporation's history, core capabilities are evolving, and corporate survival depends upon successfully managing that evolution. New product and process development projects are obvious, visible arenas for conflict between the need for innovation and retention of important capabilities. Managers of such projects face a paradox: core capabilities *simultaneously* enhance and inhibit development.[1] Development projects reveal friction between technology strategy and current corporate practices; they also spearhead potential new strategic directions (Burgelman, 1991). However, most studies of industrial innovation focus on the new

product project as a self-contained unit of analysis, and address such issues as project staffing or structure (Souder, 1987; Leonard-Barton, 1988a; Clark and Fujimoto, 1991. Chapter 9).[2] Therefore there is little research-based knowledge on managing the interface between the project and the organization, and the interaction between development and capabilities in particular. Observing core capabilities through the lens of the project places under a magnifying glass one aspect of the 'part-whole' problem of innovation management, which Van de Ven singles out as '[p]erhaps the most significant structural problem in managing complex organizations today. . . ' (1986:598).

Recent field research on 20 new product and process development projects provided an opportunity to explore and conceptually model the relationship between development practices and a firm's core capabilities. As described in the Appendix, four extensive case studies in each of five companies (Ford, Chaparral Steel, Hewlett Packard, and two anonymous companies, Electronics and Chemicals) were conducted by joint teams of academics and practitioners.[3] (Table 1). Before describing the interactions observed in the field, I first define core capabilities.

Dimensions of core capabilities

Writers often assume that descriptors of core capabilities such as 'unique,' 'distinctive,' 'difficult to imitate,' or 'superior to competition' render the term self-explanatory, especially if reference is also made to 'resource deployment' or 'skills.' A few authors include activities such as 'collective learning' and explain how competence is and is not cultivated (Prahalad and Hamel, 1990). Teece, Pisano and Shuen provide one of the clearest definitions: 'a set of differentiated skills, complementary assets, and routines that provide the basis for a firm's competitive capacities and sustainable advantage in a particular business' (1990: 28).

---

[1] According to Quinn and Cameron, '(t)he key characteristic in paradox is the simultaneous presence of contradictory, even mutually exclusive elements' (1988:2.)

[2] Exceptions are historical cases about a developing technical innovation in an industry (see for example, Rosenbloom and Cusumano, 1987.)

[3] Other members of the data-collection team on which I served are: Kent Bowen, Douglas Braithwaite, William Hanson, Gil Preuss and Michael Titelbaum. They contributed to the development of the ideas presented herein through discussion and reactions to early drafts of this paper.

Table 1.   Description of projects studied

Company	Product/process description
Ford Motor Company	**FX15** Compressor for automobile air conditioning systems **EN53** New full-sized car built on carryover platform **MN12** All new car platform including a novel supercharged engine **FN9** Luxury automobile built on carryover platform with major suspension system modifications
Chaparral Steel	**Horizontal Caster** New caster used to produce higher grades steel **Pulpit Controls** Furnace control mechanism upgrade from analog to digital **Microtuff 10** New special bar quality alloy steel **Arc Saw** Electric arc saw for squaring ends of steel beams
Hewlett-Packard Company	**Deskjet** Low cost personal computer and office printer using new technology **Hornet** Low cost spectrum analyzer **HP 150** Terminal/PC linked to high-end computer **Logic Analyzer** Digital logic analyzer
Chemicals	Special use camera Large format printer for converting digital input to continuous images New polymer used in film 21st century 'factory of the future'
Electronics	New RISC/UNIX workstation Local area network linking multiple computer networks Software architecture for desktop publishing High-density storage disk drive

In this article, I adopt a knowledge-based view of the firm and define a core capability as the knowledge set that distinguishes and provides a competitive advantage. There are four dimensions to this knowledge set. Its content is embodied in (1) employee *knowledge and skills* and embedded in (2) *technical systems*. The processes of knowledge creation and control are guided by (3) *managerial systems*. The fourth dimension is (4) the *values and norms* associated with the various types of embodied and embedded knowledge and with the processes of knowledge creation and control. In managerial literature, this fourth dimension is usually separated from the others or ignored.[4] However, understanding it is crucial to managing both new product/process development and core capabilities.

The first dimension, knowledge and skills embodied in people, is the one most often associated with core capabilities (Teece *et al.*, 1990) and the one most obviously relevant to new product development. This knowledge/skills dimension encompasses both firm-specific techniques and scientific understanding. The second, knowledge embedded in technical systems, results from years of accumulating, codifying and structuring the tacit knowledge in peoples' heads. Such physical production or information systems represent compilations of knowledge, usually derived from multiple individual sources; therefore the whole technical system is greater than the sum of its parts. This knowledge constitutes both information (e.g. a data base of product tests conducted over decades) and procedures (e.g. proprietary design rules.) The third dimension, managerial systems, represents formal and informal ways of creating knowledge (e.g. through

---

[4] Barney (1986) is a partial exception in that it poses organizational culture as a competitive advantage.

114   *D. Leonard-Barton*

sabbaticals, apprenticeship programs or networks with partners) and of controlling knowledge (e.g. incentive systems and reporting structures).

Infused through these three dimensions is the fourth: the value assigned within the company to the content and structure of knowledge (e.g. chemical engineering vs. marketing expertise; 'open-systems' software vs. proprietary systems), means of collecting knowledge (e.g. formal degrees v. experience) and controlling knowledge (e.g. individual empowerment vs. management hierarchies). Even physical systems embody values. For instance, organizations that have a strong tradition of individual vs. centralized control over information prefer an architecture (software and hardware) that allows much autonomy at each network node. Such 'debatable, overt, espoused values' (Schein, 1984: 4) are one 'manifestation' of the corporate culture (Schein, 1986: 7).[5]

Core capabilities are 'institutionalized' (Zucker, 1977). That is, they are part of the organization's taken-for-granted reality, which is an accretion of decisions made over time and events in corporate history (Kimberly, 1987; Tucker, Singh and Meinhard, 1990; Pettigrew, 1979). The technology embodied in technical systems and skills usually traces its roots back to the firm's first products. Managerial systems evolve over time in response to employees' evolving interpretation of their organizational roles (Giddens, 1984) and to the need to reward particular actions. Values bear the 'imprint' of company founders and early leaders (Kimberly, 1987). All four dimensions of core capabilities reflect accumulated behaviors and beliefs based on early corporate successes. One advantage of core capabilities lies in this unique heritage, which is not easily imitated by would-be competitors.

Thus a core capability is an interrelated, interdependent knowledge system. See Figure 1. The four dimensions may be represented in very different proportions in various capabilities. For instance, the information and procedures embedded in technical systems such as computer programs are relatively more important to credit card companies than to engineering consulting firms, since these latter firms likely rely more on

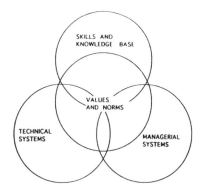

Figure 1. The four dimensions of a core capability.

the knowledge base embodied in individual employees (the skills dimension).[6]

Interaction of development projects and core capabilities: Managing the paradox

The interaction between development projects and capabilities lasts over a period of months or years and differs according to how completely aligned are the values, skills, managerial and technical systems required by the project with those currently prevalent in the firm. (See Figure 2). Companies in the study described above identified a selected, highly traditional and strongly held capability and then one project at each extreme of alignment: highly congruent vs. not at all (Table 2). Degree of congruence does not necessarily reflect project size, or technical or market novelty. Chaparral's horizontal caster and Ford's new luxury car, for instance, were neither incremental enhancements nor small undertakings. Nor did incongruent projects necessarily involve 'radical' innovations, by market or technological measures. Electronic's new workstation used readily available, 'state-of-the-shelf' components. Rather, unaligned projects

---

[5] Schein distinguishes between these surface values and 'preconscious' and 'invisible' 'basic assumptions' about the nature of reality (1984: 4).

[6] Each core capability draws upon only *some* of a company's skill and knowledge base, systems and values. Not only do some skills, systems and norms lie outside the domain of a particular core capability, but some may lie outside *all* core capabilities, as neither unique nor distinctly advantageous. For instance, although every company has personnel and pay systems, they may not constitute an important dimension of any core capability.

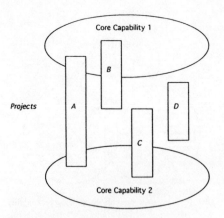

Figure 2.   Possible alignments of new product and process development projects with current core capabilities at a point in time.

were nontraditional for the organization along several dimensions of the selected core capability.

For instance, Chemicals' project developing a new polymer used in film drew heavily on traditional values, skills and systems. In this company, film designers represent the top five

percent of all engineers. All projects associated with film are high status, and highly proprietary technical systems have evolved to produce it. In contrast, the printer project was nontraditional. The key technical systems, for instance, were hardware rather than chemical or polymer and required mechanical engineering and software skills. Similarly, whereas the spectrum analyzer project at Hewlett Packard built on traditional capabilities in designing measurement equipment, the 150 terminal as a personal computer departed from conventional strengths. The 150 was originally conceived as a terminal for the HP3000, an industrial computer already on the market and as a terminal, was closely aligned with traditional capabilities. The attempt to transform the 150 into a personal computer was not very successful because different technical and marketing capabilities were required. Moreover, the greater system complexity represented by a stand-alone computer (e.g. the need for disk drives) required very untraditional cross-divisional cooperation.

Similar observations could be made about the other projects featured in Table 2. Chaparral's horizontal caster pushed the traditional science of molds to new heights, whereas the arc saw required capabilities that turned out to be

Table 2.   Relationship of selected projects with a very traditional core capability in each company studied

		Degree of alignment	
Company name	Traditional core capability	Very high	Very low
Ford Motor Co.	Total Vehicle Architecture	luxury car built on carryover platform (FN9)	compressor for air conditioner system (FX15)
Chaparral Steel	Science of Casting Molds	horizontal caster	electric arc saw
Hewlett Packard	Measurement Technology	low cost spectrum analyzer	150 terminal/ personal computer
Chemicals	Silver Halide Technology	new polymer for film	factory of the future
Electronics	Networking	local area network link	stand-alone workstation

unavailable. The local area networks project at Electronics grew directly out of networking expertise, whereas the new RISC/UNIX workstation challenged dominant and proprietary software/hardware architecture. At Ford, the three car projects derived to varying degrees from traditional strengths—especially the new luxury car. However, the air-conditioner compressor had never been built in-house before. Since all new product development departs somewhat from current capabilities, project misalignment is a matter of degree. However, as discussed later, it is also a matter of kind. That is, the type as well as the number of capability dimensions challenged by a new project determines the intensity of the interaction and the project's potential to stimulate change.

THE UP SIDE: CAPABILITIES ENHANCE DEVELOPMENT

In all projects studied, deep stores of knowledge embodied in people and embedded in technical systems were accessed; all projects were aided by managerial systems that created and controlled knowledge flows, and by prevalent values and norms. That is, whether the projects were aligned or not with the prominent core capability identified by the company, *some* dimensions of that capability favored the project. However, the closer the alignment of project and core knowledge set, the stronger the enabling influence.

In order to understand the dynamic interaction of project with capabilities, it is helpful to tease apart the dimensions of capabilities and put each dimension separately under the microscope. However, we must remember that these dimensions are interrelated; each is supported by the other three. Values in particular permeate the other dimensions of a core capability.

Skills/knowledge dimension

Excellence in the dominant discipline

One of the most necessary elements in a core capability is excellence in the technical and professional skills and knowledge base underlying major products. The professional elite in these companies earn their status by demonstrating remarkable skills. They expect to 'achieve the

impossible'—and it is often asked of them. Thus managers of development projects that draw upon core capabilities have rich resources. In numerous cases, seemingly intractable technical problems were solved through engineering excellence. For instance, although engineers working on the thin film media project at Electronics had little or no prior experience with this particular form of storage technology, (because the company had always used ferrite-based media) they were able to *invent* their way out of difficulties. Before this project was over, the geographically dispersed team had invented new media, new heads to read the data off the thin film media, as well as the software and hardware to run a customized assembly and test line for the new storage device.

Pervasive technical literacy

Besides attracting a cadre of superbly qualified people to work in the dominant discipline, time-honored core capabilities create a reservoir of complementary skills and interests outside the projects, composed of technically skilled people who help shape new products with skilled criticism. In the Electronics Software Applications project, the developers enlisted employees through computer networks to field test emerging products. After trying out the software sent them electronically, employees submitted all reactions to a computerized 'Notes' file. This internal field testing thus took advantage of both willing, technically able employees and also a computer system set up for easy world-wide networking. Similarly, Electronics Workstation developers recruited an internal 'wrecking crew' to evaluate their new product. Employees who found the most 'bugs' in the prototype workstations were rewarded by getting to keep them. At Chemicals, developers tested the special purpose camera by loading down an engineer going on a weekend trip with film, so that he could try out various features for them. In these companies, internal testing is so commonplace that it is taken for granted as a logical step in new product/process creation. However, it represents a significant advantage over competitors trying to enter the same market without access to such technically sophisticated personnel. Internal 'field testers' not only typify users but can translate their reactions into technical enhancements; such swift feedback helps development teams hit market windows.

The technical systems dimension

Just as pervasive technical literacy among employees can constitute a corporate resource, so do the systems, procedures and tools that are artifacts left behind by talented individuals, embodying many of their skills in a readily accessible form. Project members tap into this embedded knowledge, which can provide an advantage over competitors in timing, accuracy or amount of available detail. At Ford Motor Company, the capability to model reliability testing derives in part from proprietary software tools that simulate extremely complex interactions. In the full-sized car project, models simulating noise in the car body allowed engineers to identify nonobvious root causes, some originating from interaction among physically separated components. For instance, a noise apparently located in the floor panel could be traced instead to the acoustical interaction of sound waves reverberating between roof and floor. Such simulations cut development time as well as costs. They both build on and enhance the engineers' skills.

The management systems dimension

Managerial systems constitute part of a core capability when they incorporate unusual blends of skills, and/or foster beneficial behaviors not observed in competitive firms. Incentive systems encouraging innovative activities are critical components of some core capabilities, as are unusual educational systems. In Chaparral Steel, all employees are shareholders. This rewards system interacts with development projects in that employees feel that every project is an effort to improve a process they own. 'I feel like this company partly belongs to me,' explains a millwright. Consequently, even operators and maintenance personnel are tenacious innovation champions. The furnace controls upgrade (incorporating a switch from analog to digital) was initiated by a maintenance person, who persevered against opposition from his nominal superiors. Chaparral Steel also has a unique apprenticeship program for the entire production staff, involving both classroom education and on-the-job training. Classes are taught by mill foremen on a rotating basis. The combination of mill-specific information and general education (including such unusual offerings as interpersonal

skills for furnace operators) would be difficult to imitate, if only because of the diversity of abilities required of these foremen. They know what to teach from having experienced problems on the floor, and they must live on the factory floor with what they have taught. This managerial system, tightly integrating technical theory and practice, is reflected in every development project undertaken in the company (Leonard-Barton, 1991).

Values dimension

The values assigned to knowledge creation and content, constantly reinforced by corporate leaders and embedded in management practices, affect all the development projects in a line of business. Two subdimensions of values are especially critical: the degree to which project members are empowered and the status assigned various disciplines on the project team.

Empowerment of project members

Empowerment is the belief in the potential of every individual to contribute meaningfully to the task at hand and the relinquishment by organizational authority figures to that individual of responsibility for that contribution. In HP, 'Electronics,' and Chaparral, the assumption is that empowered employees will create multiple potential futures for the corporation and these options will be selected and exercised as needed. The future of the corporation thus rests on the ability of such individuals to create new businesses by championing new products and processes. Since strategy in these companies is 'pattern in action' or 'emergent' rather than 'deliberate' (Mintzberg, 1990), empowerment is an especially important element of their core capabilities, and project members initiating new capabilities were exhilarated by the challenges they had created. The Hewlett Packard printer and the Electronics storage teams actually felt that they had turned the course of their mammoth corporate ship a critical degree or two.

High status for the dominant discipline

A business generally recognized for certain core capabilities attracts, holds, and motivates talented people who value the knowledge base underlying that capability and join up for the challenges, the camaraderie with competent peers, the status associated with the skills of the dominant discipline or function. Each company displays a cultural bias towards the technical base in which the corporation has its historical roots. For Chemicals, that base is chemistry and chemical engineering; for Hewlett Packard and Electronics, it is electronics/computer engineering and operating systems software. A history of high status for the dominant discipline enables the corporation and the projects to attract the very top talent. Top chemical engineers can aspire to become the professional elites constituting the five percent of engineers who design premier film products at Chemicals. At Hewlett Packard and Electronics, design engineers are the professional elite.

A natural outgrowth of the prominence of a particular knowledge base is its influence over the development process. In many firms, a reinforcing cycle of values and managerial systems lends power and authority to the design engineer. That is, design engineers have high status because the new products that are directly evaluated by the market originate in design engineering; in contrast, the expertise of manufacturing engineers is expended on projects less directly tied to the bottom line and more difficult to evaluate. The established, well-paid career path for product designers attracts top engineering talent, who tend to perform well. The success (or failure) of new products is attributed almost entirely to these strong performers, whose high visibility and status constantly reinforce the dominance of their discipline.

As the above discussion suggests, projects derive enormous support from core capabilities. In fact, such capabilities continually spawn new products and processes because so much creative power is focused on identifying new opportunities to apply the accumulated knowledge base. However, these same capabilities can also prove dysfunctional for product and process development.

THE DOWN SIDE: CORE RIGIDITIES INHIBIT DEVELOPMENT

Even in projects that eventually succeed, problems often surface as product launch approaches. In response to gaps between product specifi-

cations and market information, or problems in manufacture, project managers face unpalatable choices. They can cycle back to prior phases in the design process (Leonard-Barton, 1988a), revisiting previous decisions higher up the design hierarchy (Clark, 1985), but almost certainly at the cost of schedule slippage. Or they may ship an inadequate product. Some such problems are idiosyncratic to the particular project, unlikely to occur again in the same form and hence not easily predicted. Others, however, occur repeatedly in multiple projects. These recurring shortfalls in the process are often traceable to the gap between current environmental requirements and a corporation's core capabilities. Values, skills, managerial systems, and technical systems that served the company well in the past and may still be wholly appropriate for some projects or parts of projects, are experienced by others as core rigidities—inappropriate sets of knowledge. Core rigidities are the flip side of core capabilities. They are not neutral; these deeply embedded knowledge sets actively create problems. While core rigidities are more problematic for projects that are deliberately designed to create new, nontraditional capabilities, rigidities can affect all projects—even those that are reasonably congruent with current core capabilities.

Skills and knowledge dimension

Less strength in nondominant disciplines

Any corporation's resources are limited. Emphasizing one discipline heavily naturally makes the company somewhat less attractive for top people in a nondominant one. A skilled marketing person knows that she will represent a minority discipline in an engineering-driven firm. Similarly, engineers graduating from top U.S. schools generally regard manufacturing in fabrication industries less attractive than engineering design, (see Hayes *et al.*, 1988) not only because of noncompetitive salaries, but because of a lower level of expertise among potential colleagues.

In each of the nonaligned and hence more difficult projects (Table 2), specific nontraditional types of knowledge were missing. Chaparral Steel's electric arc saw project required understanding electromagnetic fields for a variety of alloys—a very different knowledge set than the usual metallurgical expertise required in casting.

The Hewlett Packard 150 project suffered from a lack of knowledge about personal computer design and manufacture. The company has a long history of successful instrument development based on 'next-bench' design, meaning the engineering designers based their decisions on the needs and skills of their colleagues on the bench next to them. However, such engineers are not representative of personal computer users. Therefore traditional sources of information and design feedback were not applicable for the 150 project. Similarly, the new workstation project of Electronics met with less than optimal market acceptance because the traditional focus on producing a 'hot box,' i.e. excellent hardware, resulted in correspondingly less attention to developing software applications. The knowledge relevant to traditional hardware development flows through well-worn channels, but much less knowledge exists about creating application software. Therefore, the first few working prototypes of the UNIX/RISC workstation were shipped to customers rather than to third-party software developers. While this practice had worked well to stimulate interest in the company's well-established lines of hardware, for which much software is available, it was less appropriate for the new hardware, which could not be used and evaluated without software.

Technical systems dimension

Physical systems can embody rigidities also, since the skills and processes captured in software or hardware become easily outdated. New product designers do not always know how many such systems they are affecting. For example, in the RISC/UNIX workstation project at Electronics, the new software base posed an extreme challenge to manufacturing because hundreds of diagnostic and test systems in the factory were based on the corporate proprietary software. The impact of this incompatibility had been underestimated, given the very tight 8 month product delivery targets.

Management systems dimension

Management systems can grow just as intractable as physical ones—perhaps more so, because one cannot just plug in a new career path when a new project requires strong leadership in a hithertofore underutilized role. Highly skilled people are understandably reluctant to apply their abilities to project tasks that are undervalued, lest that negative assessment of the importance of the task contaminate perceptions of their personal abilities. In several companies, the project manager's role is not a strong one—partly because there is no associated career path. The road to the top lies through individual technical contribution. Thus a hardware engineer in one project considered his contribution as an engineering manager to be much more important than his simultaneous role as project manager, which he said was 'not my real job.' His perception of the relative unimportance of project leadership not only weakened the power of the role in that specific project but reinforced the view held by some that problem-solving in project management requires less intelligence than technical problem-solving.

Values dimension

Core rigidities hampered innovation in the development projects especially along the values dimension. Of course, certain generic types of corporate cultures encourage innovation more than others (Burns and Stalker, 1961; Chakravarthy, 1982). While not disagreeing with that observation, the point here is a different one: the very same values, norms and attitudes that support a core capability and thus enable development can also constrain it.

Empowerment as entitlement

A potential down side to empowerment observed is that individuals construe their empowerment as a psychological contract with the corporation, and yet the boundaries of their responsibility and freedom are not always clear. Because they undertake heroic tasks for the corporation, they expect rewards, recognition and freedom to act. When the contract goes sour, either because they exceed the boundaries of personal freedom that the corporation can tolerate, or their project is technically successful but fails in other ways, or their ideas are rejected, or their self-sacrifice results in too little recognition, they experience the contract as abrogated and often leave the company—sometimes with a deep sense of betrayal.

Engineers in projects that fall towards the 'incongruity' end of the spectrum speak of 'betting their [corporate identification] badges,' on the outcome, and of having 'their backs to the cliff' as ways of expressing their sense of personal risk. One engineering project manager describes 'going into the tunnel,' meaning the development period, from which the team emerges only when the job is done. 'You either do it or you don't. . . You don't have any other life.' Such intrapreneurs seem to enjoy the stress—as long as their psychological contract with the company remains intact. In this case the manager believed her contract included enormous freedom from corporate interference with her management style. When corporate management imposed certain restrictions, she perceived her contract as abrogated, and left the company just 2 months before product launch, depriving the project of continuity in the vision she had articulated for an entire stream of products.

Empowerment as a value and practice greatly aids in projects, therefore, until it conflicts with the greater corporate good. Because development requires enormous initiative and yet great discipline in fulfilling corporate missions, the management challenge is to channel empowered individual energy towards corporate aims—without destroying creativity or losing good people.

Lower status for non-dominant disciplines

When new product development requires developing or drawing upon technical skills traditionally less well respected in the company, history can have an inhibiting effect. Even if multiple subcultures exist, with differing levels of maturity, the older and historically more important ones, as noted above, tend to be more prestigious. For instance, at Chemicals, the culture values the chemical engineers and related scientists as somehow 'more advanced' than mechanical engineers and manufacturing engineers. Therefore, projects involving polymers or film are perceived as more prestigious than equipment projects. The other companies displayed similar, very clear perceptions about what disciplines and what kinds of projects are high status. The lower status of nondominant disciplines was manifested in pervasive but subtle negatively reinforcing cycles that constrained their potential for contributions to new product development and therefore limited the cross-functional integration so necessary to innovation

(Pavitt, 1991). Four of these unacknowledged but critical manifestations are: who travels to whom, self-fulfilling expectations, unequal credibility and wrong language.[7]

One seemingly minor yet important indication of status affecting product/process development is that lower status individuals usually travel to the physical location of the higher. Manufacturing engineers were far more likely to go to the engineering design sites than vice versa, whether for one-day visits, or temporary or permanent postings. Not only does such one-way travel reinforce manufacturing's lower status, but it slows critical learning by design engineers, reinforcing their isolation from the factory floor. The exception to the rule, when design engineers traveled to the manufacturing site, aided cross-functional coordination by fostering more effective personal relationships. Such trips also educated the design engineers about some of the rationale behind design for manufacture (Whitney, 1988). A design engineer in one project returned to alter designs after seeing 'what [manufacturing] is up against' when he visited the factory floor.

Expectations about the status of people and roles can be dangerously self-fulfilling. As dozens of controlled experiments manipulating unconscious interpersonal expectations have demonstrated, biases can have a 'pygmalion effect': person A's expectations about the behavior of person B affect B's actual performance—for better or worse (Rosenthal and Rubin, 1978). In the engineering-driven companies studied, the expectation that marketing could not aid product definition was ensured fulfillment by expectations of low quality input, which undermined marketers' confidence. In the Electronics Local Area Network project, the marketing people discovered early on that users would want certain very important features in the LAN. However, they lacked the experience to evaluate that information and self-confidence to push for inclusion of the features. Not until that same information was gathered directly from customers by two experienced consulting engineers who presented it strongly was it acted upon. Precious time was lost as the schedule was slipped

---

[7] Such cycles, or 'vicious circles' as psychiatry has labeled them, resemble the examples of self-fulfilling prophecies cited by Weick (1979: 159–164).

four months to incorporate the 'new' customer information. Similarly, in the Hewlett Packard printer project, marketing personnel conducted studies in shopping malls to discover potential customers' reactions to prototypes. When marketing reported need for 21 important changes, the product designers enacted only five. In the next mall studies, the design engineers went along. Hearing from the future customers' own lips the same information rejected before, the product developers returned to the bench and made the other 16 changes. The point is certainly not that marketing always has better information than engineering. Rather history has conferred higher expectations and greater credibility upon the dominant function, whereas other disciplines start at a disadvantage in the development process.

Even if nondominant disciplines are granted a hearing in team meetings, their input may be discounted if not presented in the language favored by the dominant function. Customer service representatives in the Electronics LAN project were unable to convince engineering to design the computer boards for field repair as opposed to replacing the whole system in the field with a new box and conducting repairs back at the service center, because they were unable to present their argument in cost-based figures. Engineering assumed that an argument not presented as compelling financial data was useless.

Thus, nondominant roles and disciplines on the development team are kept in their place through a self-reinforcing cycle of norms, attitudes and skill sets. In an engineering-dominated company, the cycle for marketing and manufacturing is: low status on the development team, reinforced by the appointment of either young, less experienced members or else one experienced person, whose time is splintered across far too many teams. Since little money is invested in these roles, little contribution is expected from the people holding them. Such individuals act without confidence, and so do not influence product design much—thus reinforcing their low status on the team.

THE INTERACTION OF PRODUCT/PROCESS DEVELOPMENT PROJECTS WITH CORE RIGIDITIES

The severity of the paradox faced by project managers because of the dual nature of core capabilities depends upon both (1) the number and (2) the types of dimensions comprising a core rigidity. The more dimensions represented, the greater the misalignment potentially experienced between project and capability. For example, the Arc Saw project at Chaparral Steel was misaligned with the core metallurgical capability mostly along two dimensions: technical systems (not originally designed to accommodate an arc saw), and more importantly, the skills and knowledge-base dimension. In contrast, the Factory-of-the-Future project at Chemicals challenged all four dimensions of the traditional core capability. Not only were current proprietary technical systems inadequate, but existing managerial systems did not provide any way to develop the cross-functional skills needed. Moreover, the values placed on potential knowledge creation and control varied wildly among the several sponsoring groups, rendering a common vision unattainable.

The four dimensions vary in ease of change. From technical to managerial systems, skills and then values, the dimensions are increasingly less tangible, less visible and less explicitly codified. The technical systems dimension is relatively easy to alter for many reasons, among them the probability that such systems are local to particular departments. Managerial systems usually have greater organizational scope (Leonard-Barton, 1988b), i.e. reach across more subunits than technical systems, requiring acceptance by more people. The skills and knowledge content dimension is even less amenable to change because skills are built over time and many remain tacit, i.e. uncodified and in employees' heads (see von Hippel, 1990). However, the value embodied in a core capability is the dimension least susceptible to change; values are most closely bound to culture, and culture is hard to alter in the short term (Zucker, 1977), if it can be changed at all (Barney, 1986).

Effects of the paradox on projects

Over time, some core capabilities are replaced because their dysfunctional side has begun to inhibit too many projects. However, that substitution or renewal will not occur within the lifetime of a single project. Therefore, project managers cannot wait for time to resolve the paradox they face (Quinn and Cameron, 1988).

In the projects observed in this study, managers handled the paradox in one of four ways: (1) abandonment; (2) recidivism, i.e. return to core capabilities; (3) reorientation; and (4) isolation. The arc saw and factory-of-the-future projects were abandoned, as the managers found no way to resolve the problems. The HP150 personal computer exemplifies recidivism. The end product was strongly derivative of traditional HP capabilities in that it resembled a terminal and was more successful as one than as a personal computer. The special-use camera project was reoriented. Started in the film division, the stronghold of the firm's most traditional core capability, the project languished. Relocated to the equipment division, where the traditional corporate capability was less strongly ensconced, and other capabilities were valued, the project was well accepted. The tactic of isolation, employed in several projects to varying degrees, has often been invoked in the case of new ventures (Burgelman, 1983). Both the workstation project at Electronics and the HP Deskjet project were separated physically and psychologically from the rest of the corporation, the former without upper management's blessing. These project managers encouraged their teams by promoting the group as hardy pioneers fighting corporate rigidities.

Effects of the paradox on core capabilities

Although capabilities are not usually dramatically altered by a single project, projects do pave the way for organizational change by highlighting core rigidities and introducing new capabilities. Of the companies studied, Chaparral Steel made the most consistent use of development projects as agents of renewal and organization-wide learning. Through activities such as benchmarking against best-in-the-world capabilities, Chaparral managers use projects as occasions for challenging current knowledge and for modeling alternative new capabilities. For instance, personnel from vice presidents to operators spent months in Japan learning about horizontal casting and in the case of the new specialty alloy, the company convened its own academic conference in order to push the bounds of current capabilities.

In other companies, negative cycles reinforcing the lower status of manufacturing or marketing were broken—to the benefit of both project and corporation. In the workstation project at Electronics, the manufacturing engineers on the project team eventually demonstrated so much knowledge that design engineers who had barely listened to 20 percent of their comments at the start of the project, gave a fair hearing to 80 percent, thereby allowing manufacturing to influence design. In the deskjet printer project at Hewlett Packard, managers recognized that inequality between design and manufacturing always created unnecessary delays. The Vancouver division thus sought to raise the status of manufacturing engineering skills by creating a manufacturing engineering group within R&D and then, once it was well established, moving it to manufacturing. A rotation plan between manufacturing and R&D was developed to help neutralize the traditional status differences; engineers who left research to work in manufacturing or vice versa were guaranteed a 'return ticket.' These changes interrupted the negative reinforcing cycle, signalling a change in status for manufacturing and attracting better talent to the position. This same project introduced HP to wholly unfamiliar market research techniques such as getting customer reactions to prototypes in shopping malls.

As these examples indicate, even within their 1–8-year lifetime, the projects studied served as small departures from tradition in organizations providing a 'foundation in experience' to inspire eventual large changes (Kanter, 1983). Such changes can be *precipitated* by the introduction of new capabilities along any of the four dimensions. However, for a capability to become *core*, all four dimensions must be addressed. A core capability is an interconnected set of knowledge collections—a tightly coupled system. This concept is akin to Pfeffer's definition of a paradigm, which he cautions is not just a view of the world but 'embodies procedures for inquiring about the world and categories into which these observations are collected. Thus', he warns, 'paradigms have within them an internal consistency that makes evolutionary change or adaptation nearly impossible' (1982: 228). While he is thinking of the whole organization, the caution might apply as well to core capabilities. Thus, new technical systems provide no inimitable advantage if not accompanied by new skills. New skills atrophy or flee the corporation if the technical systems are inadequate, and/or if the managerial systems such as training are incompatible. New values will not take root if associated behaviors are not rewarded. Therefore, when the development process encounters rigidities, projects can be managed consciously as the 'generative' actions characteristic of learning organizations (Senge, 1990) only if the multidimensional nature of core capabilities is fully appreciated.

CONCLUSION

This paper proposes a new focus of inquiry about technological innovation, enlarging the boundaries of 'middle range' project management theory to include interactions with development of capabilities, and hence with strategy. Because core capabilities are a collection of knowledge sets, they are distributed and are being constantly enhanced from multiple sources. However, at the same time that they enable innovation, they hinder it. Therefore in their interaction with the development process, they cannot be managed as a single good (or bad) entity.[8] They are not easy to change because they include a pervasive dimension of values, and as Weick (1979: 151) points out, 'managers unwittingly collude' to avoid actions that challenge accepted modes of behavior.

Yet technology-based organizations have no choice but to challenge their current paradigms. The swift-moving environment in which they function makes it critical that the 'old fit be consciously disturbed. . . ' (Chakravarthy, 1982: 42). Itami points out that 'The time to search out and develop a new core resource is when the current core is working well,' (1987: 54)—a point that is echoed by Foster (1982). Development projects provide opportunities for creating the 'requisite variety' for innovation (Van de Ven, 1986: 600; Kanter, 1986). As micro-level social systems, they create conflict with the macro system and hence a managerial paradox. Quinn and Cameron argue that recognizing and managing paradox is a powerful lever for change: 'Having multiple frameworks available. . . is probably the single most powerful attribute of self-renewing. . . organizations' (1988: 302).

---

[8] This observation is akin to Gidden's argument that structure is 'always both constraining and enabling' (1984: 25).

Thus project managers who constructively 'discredit' (Weick, 1979) the systems, skills or values traditionally revered by companies may cause a complete redefinition of core capabilities or initiate new ones. They can consciously manage projects for continuous organizational renewal. As numerous authors have noted, (Clark and Fujimoto, 1991; Hayes *et al.*, 1988; Pavitt, 1991) the need for this kind of emphasis on organizational learning over immediate output alone is a critical element of competition.

ACKNOWLEDGEMENTS

The author is grateful to colleagues Kim Clark, Richard Hackman and Steven Wheelwright as well as members of the research team and two anonymous reviewers for comments on earlier drafts of this paper, to the Division of Research at Harvard Business School for financial support, and to the companies that served as research sites.

A full report on the research on which this paper is based will be available in Kent Bowen, Kim Clark, Chuck Holloway and Steven Wheelwright, *Vision and Capability: High Performance Product Development in the 1990s*, Oxford University Press, New York.

REFERENCES

Barney, J. B. 'Organizational culture: Can it be a source of sustained competitive advantage?, *Academy of Management Review*, 11(3), 1986, pp. 656–665.

Burgelman, R. 'A process model of internal corporate venturing in the diversified major firms', *Administrative Science Quarterly*, 28, 1983, pp. 223–244.

Burgelman, R. 'Intraorganizational ecology of strategy making and organizational adaptation: Theory and field research', *Organization Science* 2(3), 1991, pp. 239–262.

Burns, T. and G. M. Stalker. *The Management of Innovation*, Tavistock, London, 1961.

Chakravarthy, B. S. 'Adaptation: A promising metaphor for strategic management', *Academy of Management Review*, 7(1), 1982, pp. 35–44.

Clark, K. 'The interaction of design hierarchies and market concepts in technological evolution' *Research Policy*, 14, 1985, pp. 235–251.

Clark, K. and T. Fujimoto. *Product Development Performance*, Harvard Business School Press, Boston, MA, 1991.

Foster, R. 'A call for vision in managing technology,' *Business Week*, May 24, 1982, pp. 24–33.

Giddens, A. *The Constitution of Society: Outline of the Theory of Structuration*. Polity Press, Cambridge, UK, 1984.

Hayes, R. H. 'Strategic planning—forward in reverse?', *Harvard Business Review*, November–December 1985, pp. 111–119 (Reprint # 85607).

Hayes, R. H., S. C. Wheelwright and K. B. Clark. *Dynamic Manufacturing: Creating the Learning Organization*, Free Press, New York, 1988.

Henderson, R. and K. B. Clark. 'Architectural innovation: The reconfiguration of existing product technologies and the failure of established firms', *Administrative Science Quarterly*, 35, 1990, pp. 9–30.

Hitt, M. and R. D. Ireland. 'Corporate distinctive competence, strategy, industry and performance', *Strategic Management Journal*, 6, 1985, pp. 273–293.

Hofer, C. W. and D. Schendel. *Strategy Formulation: Analytical Concepts*. West Publishing, St. Paul, MN, 1978.

Huber, G. and D. J. Power. 'Retrospective reports of strategic-level managers: Guidelines for increasing their accuracy', *Strategic Management Journal*, 6(2), 1985, pp. 171–180.

Itami, H. with T. Roehl. *Mobilizing Invisible Assets*, Harvard University Press, Cambridge, MA, 1987.

Kanter, R. M. *The Change Masters*. Simon and Schuster, New York, 1983.

Kanter, R. M. 'When a thousand flowers bloom: Structural, collective and social conditions for innovation in organizations', Harvard Business School Working Paper #87–018, 1986.

Kimberly, J. R. 'The study of organization: Toward a biographical perspective'. In J. W. Lorsch (ed.), *Handbook of Organizational Behavior*, Prentice-Hall, Englewood Cliffs, NJ, 1987, pp. 223–237.

Leonard-Barton, D. 'Implementation as mutual adaptation of technology and organization', *Research Policy*, 17, 1988a, pp. 251–267.

Leonard-Barton, D. 'Implementation characteristics in organizational innovations', *Communication Research*, 15(5), October 1988b, pp. 603–631.

Leonard-Barton, D. 'The factory as a learning laboratory', Harvard Business School Working Paper # 92–023, 1991.

Lieberman, M. and D. B. Montgomery. 'First-mover advantages', *Strategic Management Journal*, 9, Summer 1988, pp. 41–58.

Mintzberg, H. 'Strategy formation: Schools of thought'. In J. W. Fredrickson (ed.), *Perspectives on Strategic Management*, Harper & Row, New York, 1990.

Mitchell, W. 'Whether and when? Probability and timing of incumbents' entry into emerging industrial subfields', *Administrative Science Quarterly*, 34, 1989, pp. 208–230.

Pavitt, K. 'Key characteristics of the large innovating firm', *British Journal of Management*, 2, 1991, pp. 41–50.

Pettigrew, A. 'On studying organizational cultures', *Administrative Science Quarterly*, 24, 1979,

pp. 570–581.

Pfeffer, J. *Organizations and Organization Theory*, Ballinger Publishing, Cambridge, MA, 1982.

Prahalad, C. K. and G. Hamel. 'The core competence of the corporation', *Harvard Business Review*, 68(3), 1990, pp. 79–91, (Reprint # 90311).

Quinn, J. B. *Strategies for Change: Logical Incrementalism*, Richard D. Irwin, Homewood, IL, 1980.

Quinn, R. and K. Cameron. 'Organizational paradox and transformation'. In R. Quinn and K. Cameron (eds), *Paradox and Transformation*, Cambridge, MA, Ballinger Publishing, 1988.

Rosenbloom, R. and M. Cusumano. 'Technological pioneering and competitive advantage: The birth of the VCR industry', *California Management Review*, 29(4), 1987, pp. 51–76.

Rosenthal, R. and D. Rubin. 'Interpersonal expectancy effects: The first 345 studies', *The Behavioral and Brain Sciences*, 3, 1978, pp. 377–415.

Rumelt, R. P. *Strategy, Structure and Economic Performance*, Harvard Business School Classics, Harvard Business School Press, Boston, MA, 1974 and 1986.

Schein, E. 'Coming to a new awareness of organizational culture', *Sloan Management Review*, Winter, 1984, pp. 3–16.

Schein, E. *Organizational Culture and Leadership*, Jossey-Bass, San Francisco, CA, 1986.

Schumpeter, J. *Capitalism, Socialism, and Democracy*, Harper, New York, 1942.

Senge, P. 'The leader's new work: Building a learning organization', *Sloan Management Review*, 32(1), 1990, pp. 7–23, (Reprint # 3211).

Snow, C. C. and L. G. Hrebiniak. 'Strategy, distinctive competence, and organizational performance', *Administrative Science Quarterly*, 25, 1980, pp. 317–335.

Souder, W. E. *Managing New Product Innovations*, Lexington Books, Lexington, MA, 1987.

Teece, D. J., G. Pisano and A. Shuen. 'Firm capabilities, resources and the concept of strategy', Consortium on Competitiveness and Cooperation Working Paper # 90–9, University of California at Berkeley, Center for Research in Management, Berkeley, CA, 1990.

Tucker, D., J. Singh and A. Meinhard. 'Founding characteristics, imprinting and organizational change'. In J.V. Singh (ed.), *Organizational Evolution: New Directions*, Sage Publications, Newbury Park, CA, 1990.

Tushman, M. L. and P. Anderson. 'Technological discontinuities and organizational environments', *Administrative Science Quarterly*, 31, 1986, pp. 439–465.

Van de Ven, A. 'Central problems in management of innovations', *Management Science*, 32(5), 1986, pp. 590–607.

von Hippel, E. 'The impact of 'Sticky Data' on innovation and problem-solving', Sloan Management School, Working Paper # 3147-90-BPS, 1990.

Weick, K. E. 'Theory construction as disciplined imagination', *Academy of Management Review*,

14(4), 1989, pp. 516–531.
Weick, K. E. *The Social Psychology of Organizing*,
    Random House, New York, 1979.
Whitney, D. 'Manufacturing by design', *Harvard*

Business Review, 66(4), 1988, pp. 83–91.
Zucker, L. G. 'The role of institutionalization in
    cultural persistence', *American Sociological Review*,
    42, 1977, pp. 726–743.

APPENDIX: METHODOLOGY

Structure of research teams

Four universities (Harvard, M.I.T., Standford and Purdue) participated in the 'Manufacturing Visions' project. Each research team was composed of at least one engineering and one management professor plus one or two designated company employees. The research was organized into a matrix, with each research team having primary responsibility for one company and also one or more specific research 'themes' across sites and companies. Some themes were identified in the research protocol; others (such as the capabilities/project interaction) emerged from initial data analysis. In data collection and analysis, the internal company and outside researchers served as important checks on each other—the company insiders on the generalizability of company observations from four cases and the academics on the generalizability of findings across companies.

Data-gathering

Using a common research protocol, the teams developed case histories by interviewing development team members, including representatives from all functional groups who had taken active part and project staff members. These in-person interviews, conducted at multiple sites across the U.S., each lasted 1–3 hours. Interviewers toured the manufacturing plants and design laboratories and conducted follow-up interview sessions as necessary to ensure comparable information across all cases. The data-gathering procedures thus adhered to those advocated by Huber and Power (1985) to increase reliability of retrospective accounts (e.g. interviews conducted

in tandem, motivated informants selected from different organizational levels, all responses probed extensively). In addition, the interviewers' disparate backgrounds guarded against the dominance of one research bias, and much archival evidence was collected. I personally interviewed in 3 of the 5 companies.

Data analysis

Notes compiled by each team were exchanged across a computer network and joint sessions were held every several months to discuss and analyze data. Company-specific and theme-specific reports were circulated, first among team members and then among all research teams to check on accuracy. Team members 'tested' the data against their own notes and observations and reacted by refuting, confirming or refining it. There were four within-team iterations and an additional three iterations with the larger research group. Thus observations were subjected to numerous sets of 'thought trials' (Weick, 1989).

Each team also presented interim reports to the host companies. These presentations offered the opportunity to check data for accuracy, obtain reactions to preliminary conclusions, fill in missing data and determine that observations drawn from a limited number of projects were in fact representative of common practice in the company. The examples of traditional core capabilities presented in Table 2 were provided by the companies as consensus judgments, usually involving others besides the company team members. While the 20 projects vary in the degree of success attributed to them by the companies, only two were clear failures. The others all succeeded in some ways (e.g. met a demanding schedule) but fell short in others (e.g. held market leadership for only a brief period).

[11]

Cambridge Journal of Economics 1982, **6**, 167–184

The Emilian model: productive decentralisation and social integration

Sebastiano Brusco*

Introduction

The following essay presents a dynamic analysis of the interaction between the productive structure, the labour market, and the principal political institutions in Emilia-Romagna.

There are at least three reasons why, in recent times, many economists have focused their attention on the economy of the region (Bagnasco and Messori, 1975; Bagnasco, 1977; Filuppucci, 1978; Capecchi *et al.*, 1979).

The first is that over the last fifteen years Emilia-Romagna has had an economic performance distinctly better than many other regions in Italy, and has shown itself more resilient to crisis.

Secondly, the industrial structure which developed in Emilia-Romagna, and which is the basis for its economic performance, may also be found in other parts of Italy, so that the study of Emilia is of general interest and its results may help to understand the working of industrial districts elsewhere in Italy.

Finally, in Emilia-Romagna almost all local authorities, including the regional government, are controlled by the communist party, often in alliance with the socialist party. The region, therefore, represents a kind of test for a coalition of left wing parties in Italy which is of broader European interest.

The superior economic performance of Emilia-Romagna

Table 1 compares both the participation rate and the unemployment rate in Emilia-Romagna and in Italy as a whole over the last twelve years.

According to ISTAT (the Central Statistical Office), which generally underestimates these figures, the rate of participation in the labour force reached almost 46% in 1980, 6% higher than the national average. The contrast is even more striking if Emilia is compared with Southern Italy where less than one third of the population participates in the labour force.

On the other hand, the rate of unemployment is in general lower in Emilia-Romagna than in Italy. More detailed figures would also show that recessions reach Emilia later than other regions, and their effects are more temporary.

Two other indicators also show the superiority of economic performance of Emilia-Romagna when compared with the rest of Italy.

* Università degli studi di Modena. This article originally appeared in *Problemi della transizione*, 1980, no. 5, pp. 86–105, and has been translated and abridged by Jonathan Zeitlin and Diego Gambetta.

0309–166X/82/020167 + 18 $03.00/0

168   S. Brusco

Table 1. *Participation rate and unemployment rate in Emilia-Romagna and in Italy, 1971 to 1980 (percentages)*

	Participation rate				Unemployment rate			
	Emilia		Italy		Emilia		Italy	
	Old series	New series	Old series	New series	Old series	New series	Old series	New series
1971	42·7	n.a.	36·2	38·4	2·7	n.a.	3·2	5·4
1972	41·2	n.a.	35·5	37·9	3·0	n.a.	3·7	6·4
1973	42·2	n.a.	35·5	38·0	2·9	n.a.	3·5	6·4
1974	42·4	n.a.	35·7	38·0	2·3	n.a.	2·9	5·4
1975	42·5	n.a.	35·7	38·1	2·9	n.a.	3·3	5·9
1976	42·3	n.a.	35·9	38·5	2·8	n.a.	3·7	6·7
1977		44·8		38·9		5·2		7·1
1978		44·8		38·9		5·7		7·2
1979		45·0		39·4		5·9		7·6
1980		45·9		39·9		5·7		7·6

Source: From 1970 to 1976 see ISTAT, *Rilevazione trimestrale delle forze di lavoro;* from 1977 to 1980 see ISTAT, *Rilevazione trimestrale delle forze di lavoro—nuova serie.*

From 1970 to 1979, the rate of growth of money income per head in Italy was 17·15% per year: in Emilia-Romagna over the same period income grew at an annual rate of about 18·5% (Unioncamere, 1981). Consequently, Emilian income rose from an already favourable position in 1970 to 5·6 million lire per head in 1979 compared with the average Italian income of 4·4 million per head. Moreover, the provinces of Modena and Reggio had in 1979 an income per head of 6·2 and 6·0 million lire respectively, and were the second and the fourth richest provinces in Italy (whereas in 1970, in the classification of the richest provinces, they occupied the 17th and the 12th position respectively).

Another interesting indicator is the amount of exports which originate in the region. Table 2 shows that the share of Emilian exports in total Italian exports continued to increase, almost without interruption, from 1963 to 1980.

Table 2. *Exports from Emilia-Romagna, as a percentage of total Italian exports*

1963	1964	1965	1966	1967	1968	1969	1970	1971
6·0	6·3	6·3	7·0	7·0	6·5	7·1	7·7	7·9

1972	1973	1974	1975	1976	1977	1978	1979	1980
8·1	7·9	7·5	8·6	8·4	8·8	8·8	8·9	9·4

Source: Unioncamere, *Statistiche provinciali dei movimenti valutari inerenti alle importazioni e alle esportazioni.*

The characteristics of Emilia

There are no great differences between Emilia-Romagna and Italy in the distribution of the labour force among sectors and among industries (see Tables 3 and 4). More significant are the differences in other aspects of the region's industrial structure, in particular the size distribution of firms. Table 5 shows that the proportion of the labour force employed in small productive units is always greater in Emilia than in Italy as a whole.

But the most significant point is that these small firms, often with less than 10 employees (see Table 5), are frequently grouped in relatively small zones according to their product, and give rise to monocultural areas in which all firms have a very low degree of vertical integration and the production process is carried on through the collaboration of a number of firms. In these areas only a proportion of the small enterprises market finished goods; the others work as subcontractors, executing operations commissioned by the first group of firms. Production has become widely decentralised as more and more firms which previously manufactured their own components increasingly resorted to outside suppliers. Despite union opposition, 'putting out' is now a common phenomenon.

There are many possible examples of these industrial districts: knitwear in Modena; clothes and ceramic tiles in Modena and Reggio; cycles, motorcycles and shoes in Bologna; buttons in Piacenza; tomato canning and ham in Parma; pig breeding in Reggio Emilia. But it would be a mistake to think that this phenomenon is confined to the production of

Table 3. *Employees by sector, 1980 (percentages)*

	Emilia	Italy
Agriculture	15·8	14·1
Industry	38·6	37·6
Services	45·6	48·3
Total	100·0	100·0

Source: ISTAT, *Rilevazione trimestrale delle forze di lavoro—nuova serie.*

Table 4. *Employees by industry, 1971 (percentages)*

	Emilia	Italy
Food and tobacco	11·3	7·6
Textiles	7·4	10·3
Clothing and shoes	11·4	12·2
Wood and furniture	7·8	7·5
Engineering	38·7	40·6
Non-metal minerals	11·5	6·1
Chemical	4·9	7·5
Paper and printing	3·5	4·4
Others	3·5	3·8
Total	100·0	100·0

Source: ISTAT, *5° Censimento generale dell'industria e del commercio, 1971.*

Table 5. *Employees in manufacturing industries, by size of the establishment, 1971 (percentages)*

	Emilia	Italy
Up to five employees	20·5	17·6
6–9	7·3	5·8
10–19	10·4	8·4
20–49	14·7	12·5
50–99	12·7	10·2
100–249	15·3	13·2
250–499	8·4	9·0
500 and more	10·7	23·3
Total	100·0	100·0

Source: ISTAT, *5° Censimento generale dell'industria e del commercio, 1971.*

consumer goods. Industrial districts are also common in engineering: the production of automatic machinery and packaging machinery in Bologna; of agricultural machinery and oleodynamic apparatus in Modena and Reggio; of woodworking machine tools in Carpi; of food processing machinery in Parma. In these cases, the industrial districts are less clearly defined, since they form specialised parts of the engineering sector where component producers supply the manufacturers of a wide range of finished products. This concentration of small firms also extends to the service sector and is found widely on the Adriatic riviera to which four million foreign tourists come every year.

It is also notable that there is a clear connection between the proliferation of small enterprises and the use of 'black' labour. This concept has been given many definitions (Frey, 1975). It has been applied to situations where social welfare contributions are evaded and again to cases where labour is paid lower wages than the minimum set by national agreement, works in substandard conditions, or does not receive agreed levels of supplementary bonuses and holiday pay. However defined, black labour is extremely common in Emilia-Romagna, and underpayment, tax evasion and the extraordinary flexibility of labour are all important features of the productive system.

The economy of the region is also characterised by a high income per head of the labour force engaged in agriculture (in 1971 Emilian agriculture gave work to 8·6% of all Italian agricultural workers, and produced 11·5% of the total Italian agricultural product); by active and increasingly strong cooperatives, which although concentrated in food and construction exert a powerful influence on the social and productive structure as a whole; and by a limited presence of wholly or partially state-owned enterprises.

The following sections of this paper consider various aspects of the region's industrial system—the industrial structure and industrial relations. Particular attention is paid to dynamic interactions between these, the market and the government in order to study their impact on the region's economy.

Inter-firm relations

Recent research in the Faculty of Economics at the University of Modena sheds significant light on the relations between different types of firms in this industrial structure (Brusco and Malagoli, 1981). This study focuses on the garment industry in Modena, Reggio

Emilia and the adjacent provinces, as a sector marked by an extremely low level of vertical integration. It shows that in Modena and Reggio the artisanate considered as a legal category can be divided economically into three groups: half are homeworkers inscribed under the category of artisans purely for the purpose of evading taxes and social welfare payments; one-quarter produce on their own account, having direct relations with the market for finished goods; and a final quarter are subcontractors. It is important to note that many of the independent artisans put out a good deal of the components of the finished product both to the other artisans and to the numerous female homeworkers of the region. In order to understand this structure, one must also consider the larger industrial firms of the region. Half of these enterprises undertake internally only the preparation of samples and the packing and distribution of the garments, while the bulk of the work is decentralised. The other half perform directly at least some of the work, though even these also decentralise an often substantial part.

In the neighbouring provinces, the picture is totally different. There the artisans producing on their own account constitute only 8% of the total, while the larger firms are in most cases owned by entrepreneurs from Modena and Reggio. To interpret these findings, it is necessary to consider together Modena and Reggio on the one hand and the neighbouring provinces on the other. Those artisans with direct access to the market need the dependent artisans of the neighbouring or secondary provinces as a bulwark for their own productive structure. The relationship between Modena and Reggio on the one hand and the neighbouring provinces on the other thus appears to be that of metropolis to colony, and the two together constitute a single system.

It would be tempting to interpret the relationship between the purchasers of components and their subcontractors in monopsonistic terms, as if, in other words, the enterprises producing on their own account were price makers able to compel the subcontractors to accept extremely low profits. But this is untrue, as we will see more fully below. Here it suffices to stress that the market between the two parties is almost invariably competitive. The great majority of subcontractors in fact have the ability to switch customers, if the prices offered are too low, and there is no collusion among the latter strong enough to enforce artificially low prices.

The sources of decentralisation

The principal sources of the movement towards decentralisation of the productive structure in Emilia, and in Italy more generally, are twofold. The first cause can be found in the rise of trade union power since the 1960s. Since the victories of the late 1960s, the union has acquired enough strength in the large firms to make redundancies almost impossible; to protect their shop-floor representatives and to force the employers into plant-level bargaining; to exercise a certain degree of control over working conditions; and sometimes even to impose changes in the organisation of work. Since these developments did not take place to the same extent in the smaller firms, it is only natural that the large employers sought to offset the effect of unionism by shifting production towards the small firm sector. Thus it is no coincidence that the process of vertical disintegration gathered force in Italian industry towards the end of the 1960s.

The second cause can be found in the emergence since the mid-1960s of a significant demand for more varied and customised goods, produced in short series, alongside that for standardised goods. Among the examples of this trend one can point to the much greater number of versions of each model of car than existed fifteen years ago; a multiplying of styles

172   S. Brusco

in clothing and shoes; a growth in the publication of new books and magazines; and an increase in the varieties of furniture, refrigerators and sewing machines. Before the market experienced this evolution, these goods were most often produced according to the techniques originally developed by Taylor and Ford. Many of the components used in these products were made with specialised machinery, the so-called transfer machines, which were designed for the production of a single part, and which were therefore both very productive and very costly. These products were put together on elaborate assembly lines, designed in such a way that each operation was often to be completed in less than thirty seconds. Assembly lines, too, were highly costly, since they were both expensive to build, and required large amounts of planning, work study and running-in time. Both types of technology were restricted to large industry: transfer machinery because of its cost and rigidity, and assembly lines because of their dimensions alone.

The advantages of mass-production technology were reduced by the diversification of the product market and the competition in terms of quality and variety which this implies. The new demand requires more flexible, even if less productive, machinery than the transfer machines, as well as methods of assembly in which tasks are less fragmented so that slightly more diverse products can be assembled. This flexible technology is much less expensive than its predecessor and, more importantly, it is quite compatible with the needs of small firms.

This trend in turn affects investment goods. Without going into much detail, one should note that the construction of sophisticated machine tools was synonymous with that of transfer machines, which were custom-built in small series or single examples. For this reason they were particularly suitable for production with a fragmented structure, insofar as the small firms possessed the relevant know-how. During the past few years, however, the shift in consumer demand has cut down the demand for these machines. What will happen in the future will depend both on the extension of the current standardisation of components and on the diffusion of numerically-controlled machine tools which may be produced in long series. It seems probable in either case, however, that even in the investment goods sector there will remain space for short runs and therefore for small firms.

Alongside the increase in unionisation and changes in demand which have provoked the fragmentation of the industrial structure, there is another element which without acting directly constitutes a necessary condition allowing the process to occur without reduction in productivity. The sectors in which decentralisation is particularly marked are those in which it is possible to fragment the productive process without having recourse to an inferior technology. For example, the Morini motorcycle plant in Bologna has 100 employees and produces an average of 20 motorcycles per day. Most of the workers in the plant are engaged in assembly, on lines on which the tasks are not very subdivided. Except for the camshaft and the engine mounting, all of the components are put out: the frame, the tank, the shock absorbers, the handlebars, the brakes, the gears and the wheels; almost the whole machine is produced by subcontractors. And the key point is that they are produced with precisely the same techniques which would have been used had the firm decided to make them directly.

In other words one should bear in mind that, despite the increase in the scale of production in the 1950s and 1960s, with certain technologies there is no advantage in producing all the components of a product under a single roof: whether they produce similar or different pieces, twenty lathes have substantially the same productivity if they are gathered together or dispersed in separate buildings. This is what economists mean when they assert that economies of scale should be calculated in the first instance for phases of production, and that the economies which result from the juxtaposition of similar operations are often negligible

(Brusco, 1975; Muller, 1976). It should be noted, therefore, that generally the sectors in which this type of industrial structure prevails are those characterised by limited economies of vertical integration. Where these conditions do not hold, as in the ceramic tiles sector, decentralisation is nearly non-existent or assumes purely legal forms.

Even if it is accepted that for many industries the importance of technical economies of scale has often been overstated in the past, it might still be objected that there exist nonetheless both indivisibilities in the administrative work of firms and significant pecuniary economies of scale. Thus small firms might experience difficulties in book keeping, in obtaining raw materials, and in obtaining credit at the same price paid by larger firms with greater bargaining power. But in this context it is extraordinary to observe how the artisans and small entrepreneurs of Emilia-Romagna have overcome these difficulties by creating associations to provide these administrative services and to coordinate purchasing and credit negotiations, thus establishing on a co-operative basis the conditions for achieving minimum economic scales of operation. These associations, which cover the whole region, prepare the pay slips, keep the books, and pay the taxes of the small firms, giving to the latter the expertise of a large office in administration and accountancy at a minimal price. Furthermore, these associations also establish technical consultancy offices, consortia for marketing and the purchase of raw and semi-fabricated materials and, most importantly, co-operatives which provide guarantees for bank loans which can thus be obtained at the lowest possible rate of interest.

Industrial relations

Turning to the field of industrial relations, the first premise of the analysis is that the industrial structure, as we have already suggested, is divided into two segments by the size of the firms. In the 'primary' sector, the trade union has two main characteristics. First of all, it is extremely strong: there labour legislation is almost always respected; trade union representatives are recognised on the shop floor; plant bargaining yields wages above those negotiated at national level, and seeks—with intermittent success—to influence the organisation of work and to establish job ladders within the firm; finally, there is a tradition of popular mobilisation which in practice enables the unions to block any factory closure. The strength of the unions both depends on and is illustrated by the fact that in Emilia, by contrast to Piedmont and Lombardy, the 'primary' sector extends downwards to include all enterprises with more than 30 employees, so that roughly half of the labour force is unionised. Secondly, the union is generally 'reasonable'; it does not bid up wages too strongly in plant bargaining and is prepared to be flexible, even if within fairly strict limits, in enforcing contractual provisions concerning layoffs, overtime, and health and safety regulation; finally, it does not put forward over-bold projects of work reorganisation within the factory.

These characteristics of trade unionism in Emilia ensure a prompt, and generally non-violent, resolution of industrial disputes. The point at which agreement will be reached is usually recognised by both parties in advance, since it can be easily derived from the going rate for plant settlement in the country. It is precisely the strength of the union and its flexibility which guarantee at the same time that the negotiations will produce a satisfactory result without concessions and that the terms of the agreement will be enforced without subsequent flare-ups of localised conflict or idleness among the workers. Thus even though the union exercises a real control over working conditions in the plant, the employer enjoys a secure climate which makes possible a greater degree of planning of the volume of production and investment.

174   **S. Brusco**

In the 'secondary' sector, in contrast, everything works differently. But before going on to examine the 'rules of the game' in this segment of the labour market, it is necessary to draw attention to the heterogeneity of those to be found within it. Besides the artisans working on their own account and the subcontractors we have already discussed, there can be found four main groups. First, highly skilled workers, often specialised in maintenance work, who have registered as artisans in order to free their wages from the limits established in the national agreements, but who continue to perform exactly the same job during the same hours as before. Second, the various types of homeworkers: those already mentioned who are forced by their bosses to register as artisans in order to evade social security payments; those whose position has been regularised according to recent labour legislation; and those whose position remains 'irregular', some highly qualified and others without any particular skill, whether elderly or from the South. Third, moonlighters and pensioners who have returned to work, who often agree with the employer to evade all social security payments and divide the proceeds. And finally, women and students who, in evasion of all controls, accept seasonal, temporary, and precarious work of every kind.

In this world the dispersion of wages is extremely high, extending from the maintenance workers registered as artisans who can earn twice as much as their factory fellows, to the elderly or immigrant homeworkers who get less than one-third of what they would receive in the factory. Here there is little evidence of the struggle for egalitarianism which has formed so noteworthy a part of the history of the Italian unions. The Emilian unions attempt to regulate wages, unlike their counterparts elsewhere, by making collective agreements with the artisanal associations, which in turn press their members to regularise the working conditions of their employees and to respect the contracts; certain recent legislation has a similar intention (Malagoli and Mengoli, 1979). But the level of wages is fundamentally determined by three factors: the level of demand for the product; the intensity of labour; and finally the level of skill.

In this sector, moreover, redundancies are possible. Here firms are able to hire and fire as the volume of orders changes, both because legislation against unfair dismissals does not apply to firms with less than 15 employees and because of their scanty unionisation. In this sector all variations in the level of output are translated into variations in employment. By contrast, as a recent study shows, the large firms fear that a subsequent recession will leave them unable to dispose of surplus manpower and they therefore refrain from hiring unless they install new machinery (Brusco, Giovannetti and Malagoli, 1979).

The segmentation of the labour market

The two labour markets which correspond to these two types of firms are, in general, linked and movement from one to the other is possible. There are, to be sure, significant numbers of workers who are unable to gain access to the 'primary' sector: elderly or immigrant women; middle-aged peasants; and at least for a time recent agricultural immigrants working in small firms with particularly unhealthy working conditions. But when demand is expanding, anyone accustomed to factory life and able to work intensively, even if not very skilled, can find work where he or she pleases. And each worker is ultimately able to choose in which segment to work. Under such conditions of increasing demand, wage differentials between the sectors narrow markedly and choices between them are not determined by earnings. For women, their family situation is the most important consideration, while the central influences for men are such factors as preferences concerning the atmosphere in large and small factories, possibilities of acquiring skills, and networks of personal or family contacts.

Many young people, in these conditions, are able consciously to choose a temporary or part-time job, or to decide to work at whatever job, however disagreeable. This choice is possible in some cases because of the level of family income which ultimately guarantees subsistence; in other cases, it is based on a light-hearted trade-off of lower earnings against shorter hours of work. Often, this latter attitude springs from a sharp critique of the capitalist use of labour-power; always, it depends on the expectation that it will be possible to find a job when necessary.

For highly skilled workers, it is possible not only to choose the plant, but also to decide to go into business for themselves. The latter choice, while it brings a higher income, also requires longer and more intensive hours of work. Thus the question for the worker is whether or not to opt for more work and higher earnings. What is striking is not how many become artisans, but how many of those who are able do not. This is ultimately a further sign of the health of this regional economy.

If instead the labour market should become depressed, the situation would change significantly. The less skilled workers would experience much more difficulty in changing segments; then the absence of collective bargaining and of union guarantees would make themselves sharply felt. The very flexibility which currently constitutes an advantage for this sector would become an insurmountable obstacle to the organised defence of employment. The effects of a crisis would be much less for the highly skilled workers whose bargaining power gives them greater means of self-defence.

No major recession has struck Emilia-Romagna since the 1960s, and the system has easily absorbed the effects of the central bank's credit restrictions. However, some indication of what might happen in recession can be seen from what happened during the downturn in the garment industry in 1974, when many homeworkers were left without work, while those who were employed suffered cuts in real and even money wages. The black economy of the South indirectly suggests what might happen in recessionary conditions. There the overall level of unemployment is so high that even when the product market is booming individual bargaining gives rise to wages well below those agreed nationally, to frequent evasions of social security payments, and to very poor working conditions (David and Pattarin, 1975; Botta *et al.*, 1976).

In conclusion, the possibility of mobility from one segment of the labour market to the other depends on the same factors which determine wages: skill, the intensity of work, and the state of the product and labour market.

Mechanisms of labour market adjustment

Certain channels exist whereby the power to shed labour is transmitted between the small and the large firm sectors so that the system as a whole retains its flexibility. There are two main mechanisms, which are complementary rather than alternatives. The garment sector provides the most clearcut example of the first of these. There the impact of a fall in demand for the products of a particular firm depends on its level of vertical integration: where this is high, such a fall in demand will produce unemployment; where it is low, the workers employed in subcontracting firms will simply receive their orders from more successful competitors. To follow the process in more detail: when the level of integration is highest, each firm circulates its collection of samples through its own agents; collects and executes the orders; finishes, packs and sends the final product. When the level of integration is lowest, the firm which had prepared the samples and received the order will execute it through subcontractors from whom it will collect the final product for despatch.

Now suppose that (1) in both cases firms are sufficiently numerous to guarantee competition; (2) that the total demand for garments is constant, so that orders lost by one firm are taken up by another; (3) that all commissioning firms belong to the primary segment, and all subcontractors to the secondary; (4) finally, that subcontractors are able to shift easily from the production of one model to that of another.

We can now see what would happen in both cases when the styles offered by a firm are rejected by the market. In the first case (high vertical integration) the crisis in the firm will hit all the workers involved in the various phases of production. If orders fall to zero, they will have to be made redundant, even if they will be hired soon afterwards by the more successful firms. In this case the system has reached a new equilibrium by redistributing workers among firms, requiring a certain number of redundancies, which by hypothesis are tense and difficult for the firm concerned.

Under similar assumptions, we can now consider what would happen in the second type of structure, i.e. one which is characterised by a minimal degree of vertical integration. This time the firm struck by the crisis does not employ weavers, cutters, stitchers, pressers and finishers; it employs only people working on prototypes, and workers in packing and despatching goods. Only these workers directly employed by the firm will be made redundant. The vast majority of the workers actually producing the garment would continue to work as before for the subcontracting firm which employs them directly. The work which is no longer coming to the subcontractor from the firm whose styles have been rejected by the market will simply be replaced by that commissioned by its more successful competitors. In this case, too, the system imposes some redundancies in order to find its equilibrium, but these are fewer than in the preceding one, and are made by firms which have fewer employees for the same gross turnover. The equilibrium has been restored not so much through a shift in manpower as through a shift in orders. The response to a downturn has been rendered that much easier.

In presenting the second mechanism to which we initially referred, our simplifying assumptions will be to some extent opposed to those employed in describing the first. Here the global movement of demand and the type of price-formation mechanism operating in this sector will be unimportant; it is rather assumed that the subcontractors are *unable* to shift their production. The only assumption which remains as before is that the commissioning firms belong to the primary segment and the subcontracting firms to the secondary one.

We can now illustrate the second mechanism with an example. Imagine a firm with 1000 employees in which a decrease in production of 10% would provoke 100 redundancies. This level of redundancies would be highly problematic in the primary segment. Imagine instead a firm which decentralises 80% of the same volume of production, which would therefore be left with 200 workers. This firm would still belong to the primary sector, while the other 800 workers would be scattered among the small enterprises of the secondary sector. This time a fall in production of 10% would require 20 redundancies in the primary sector and 80 in the secondary. The first poses no great problems, both because 20 workers are few in absolute terms and because the union is weaker in a firm with 200 employees than in one with 1000. The other 80 redundancies would pose no problems at all since they belong to the secondary sector. In this case, too, it is ultimately the secondary sector which absorbs the tensions coming from the large firms. The difference is that in this case the small firms perform this role by assuming responsibility for the major portion of the redundancies, while in the first case they coordinate the flow of subcontracted labour from the less to the more successful firms.

We can add four observations in order to clarify what has been said so far. First, the link between the two segments of the labour market has an important implication: all attempts to impose rigidities on the secondary sector would immediately reverberate on the system as a whole. Any successful initiative, whether by the unions or by public policy, which aimed to limit the small firms' power to hire and fire would automatically rigidify the manpower management of the large enterprises. It seems as if there is, therefore, a clear alternative between two objectives, both desirable: that of maintaining the system's flexibility, and that of limiting the small enterprises' power to make workers redundant when they want.

There is only one way to avoid the dilemma of ensuring primary conditions of employment in all Emilian firms and yet preserving the flexibility of the system as a whole in a situation where demand is uncertain. To achieve such a result it would be necessary to construct a new secondary sector of firms and workers outside the region. Beyond the need to find manpower which has become ever more scarce in Emilia, this is to some extent the significance of the extension of decentralisation to the Veneto, the Marche, and even Puglia. The internal contradictions of Emilia gradually become in this way external ones, which other regions have to face and resolve.

Secondly, it often happens in some productive activities that the great majority of firms cluster in the secondary sector, irrespective of the role played by the enterprise. This is, for example, the case of knitwear in which 50% of the 'parent' firms (i.e. those with direct access to the market for finished goods) have less than 30 employees. This state of affairs reaches its limits in Prato, a Tuscan town with an analogous industrial structure, where the commissioning firm very often has no employees other than the proprietor, the so-called *impannatore* who designs the fabric and commissions the spinning, weaving, and finishing from other other enterprises.

Thirdly, it will be useful to dwell for a moment on the difference between the mechanisms discussed above and another interpretation of decentralisation as a sort of 'productive lung' for the commissioning enterprises (Paci, 1975). There it is assumed that short period variations in the demand for the product of the commissioning firm may lead from time to time to the expulsion of certain operations from the factory and their subsequent recall. In this case, variations in the level of vertical integration of the firm are understood as conjunctural manoeuvres. In our view, this practice is difficult to realise, and it has no place in the mechanisms of the 'Emilian model'.

Finally, it is necessary to ask how frequently each of our hypothetical mechanisms of labour market adjustment might actually occur. As will be apparent from the assumptions on which they are based, the answer depends on two main considerations. The first is the demand for the product: the longer and more frequent the recessions, the more often the second mechanism will operate. The other consideration points instead towards the technology used by the subcontracting firms and the ease with which they are able to shift their production.

How plausible is this hypothesis that Emilian firms are easily able to shift from one product to another? In this context we should note there are variations between the production of components and assembly and in the experience of individual sectors. In the knitwear industry, for example, there are virtually no difficulties in switching models, neither in the production of components nor in assembly; in that of women's clothes, the production of components is highly flexible, whereas the adaptation of assembly lines poses some problems, though these are easily resolved; in the food industry, the flexibility is also very high. More careful attention should be paid to the engineering sector. Generally, components are more flexible than assembly and this is the reason why decentralisation is more prominent in the former. It should be noted that in this case a subcontracting firm can easily shift not only models but also subsectors: a firm producing stamped metal has no problem in switching from the production of, say, gas stoves to that of chair frames. Single-purpose machine tools, as remarked earlier, have next to no flexibility, whereas that of numerically controlled machine tools is extremely high. Finally, the flexibility of assembly lines is itself very variable: it is least where tasks are very fragmented and greatest where each position is assigned longer operations. Given the diversification of demand, this capacity to adapt easily to different products becomes synonymous in practice with the capacity to produce in short series at competitive costs.

In conclusion, the hypothesis that it is possible to shift quickly and easily from one product to another is certainly true for many firms and in many industries. And this fact is closely related to the capacity of Emilian firms to produce in short series.

The solidity of the industrial structure

The capacity of the 'Emilian model' to resist foreign competition, in particular that of Third World countries, is rooted in three main factors. First of all, flexibility in the use of manpower. We can add to what has been observed earlier that this feature of the industrial structure becomes all the more important when compared to the rigidity of industrial structures, such as, say, that of Milan, which are dominated by large firms. Second, there is the rather high technical level of the machinery employed. The flexible use of labour facilitates the introduction of innovations, even when they are labour-saving. As we observed earlier, when demand is expanding wages in the primary and secondary segments of the labour market are more or less the same; there is, therefore, no possibility for firms to recoup with low wages the low productivity of their machinery. It will be remembered that most markets, including those for semi-finished products, are highly competitive and this too speeds up the adoption of more sophisticated machinery. There is evidence, moreover, that in the most industrialised regions small firms experience no disadvantage relative to large ones in raising credit (Guglielmi, 1978; Filippi, 1979).

Finally, the solidity of the 'Emilian model' derives from the fact that this type of industrial structure more than any other fosters the skills and initiatives of its entrepreneurs in a variety of ways. In the first place, it spurs their emergence. The number of artisans or even major entrepreneurs previously employed as workers is very high, particularly as foremen, maintenance workers, and coordinators of putting-out networks. For each of these groups, their knowledge of some part of the productive process facilitates their passage to independent work. Even easier in some sectors, particularly that of garments, is the transition from subcontracting to direct contact with the market. Many subcontractors through their relations with their customers learn how to prepare samples, come into contact with the network of distribution, and eventually reach the point where they can circulate samples on their own. If these are well received they will produce a few copies within the firm and will put out the rest. At the same time, they will continue to work as subcontractors, thus avoiding undue risks. The system therefore operates as a 'forcing' ground for entrepreneurship.

Second, by using the foresight and imagination of so many artisans and entrepreneurs, this productive structure is able to offer an extraordinary variety of products, many of them novel, which cleverly interpret the needs of consumers and the shifts in their tastes. The garment sector is an obvious example. It is sufficient to realise that it would be impossible for a few large firms to produce the enormous range of styles which are created by the hundreds of small firms. An idea, seen at a Parisian or Florentine fashion show, can be reworked in a multitude of workshops. And in this way thousands of options are offered to domestic and foreign buyers. But more important examples can be cited from the investment goods sector, such as machines which dispense railway tickets, pack cigarettes and medicine capsules, or clean the streets; the extraordinary variety of agricultural machinery, from light tractors to fruit-harvesting platforms; or the many sophisticated hydraulic devices used in servo-mechanisms. These are all cases in which new needs are satisfied by a multitude of competing small firms which emulate and imitate each other and which as a result can give shape to new ideas with a speed that would be unthinkable in larger enterprises.

Finally, the small firms' capacity to develop new products and to devise new machines is enhanced both by the proximity of so many entrepreneurs engaged in similar activities and by the extensive collaboration between skilled workers and technicians within each firm (Brusco and Sabel, 1981). This phenomenon, which is particularly characteristic of monocultural areas, should be emphasised since it undercuts the conventional idea that research is only what scientists and technicians do in the laboratories of the big firms and not the on-the-job creativity of ordinary people who know their own needs. For instance, in the ceramic tile industry, the machines which move the tiles uninterruptedly along the glazing lines, or which detect breakages through the use of sonic waves, were not the product of formal research, but were rather developed through the collaboration of the tile firms with a number of small engineering firms.

Emilia: an 'interstitial' case?

The idea of 'interstices' is connected with a view of the world in which goods can be divided into two groups. The first group consists of goods produced in long series by large firms with highly subdivided labour; strong economies of scale mark such production processes. The second group reverses these characteristics, and is accordingly neglected by the large firms. As a result, their production, concentrated in small firms, is considered 'interstitial'. In such a classificatory system, the first type of goods are usually but often implicitly considered technologically advanced and the second backward. To this view is often added the assumption that goods produced in long series in large factories can only be reproduced with great difficulty in the Third World, in contrast to those of the second type, and are therefore less exposed to competition from developing countries. This has led some observers to conclude that the second type of production is ultimately destined to disappear from the advanced countries.

As we have seen, however, many goods produced in short series are nonetheless the fruit of enterprises which employ advanced technology and have some real market power. The simplest example is that of investment goods, which are often produced in short series or even on a one-off basis. The limit case, among these goods, is that of transfer machines, the robots used at Fiat, or the special pieces used in chemical plants; but, among Emilian products, this is true also of many automatic machines, machine tools, agricultural machines, and those used in ceramic tile production and food processing.

It is also true, to be sure, that some goods produced in short series are vulnerable to competition from Third World countries: for instance, the garment and knitwear industries, which on occasion suffer from the influx of Rumanian jackets and Indian T-shirts, or the producers of toys and stoves who face competition from Hong Kong and Poland. But on the whole it can be noted in most cases that the products of the underdeveloped countries are aimed at the bottom of the market. In other words, it seems possible to counteract the competition from these countries by shifting production up-market. These types of goods can only be produced with difficulty by such countries because of their distance from the consumers, their consequent difficulty in predicting shifts in tastes, and the low skill-level of their workforces.

180   S. Brusco

The history of the Italian monocultural area is precisely the history of this specialisation and movement up-market. This is the case of ceramics in Sassuolo, or to choose a case from outside Emilia, of textiles in Prato. This process can, of course, lead to a progressive narrowing of the market, and an attendant contraction of the industry and its labour force. So far, though, the process seems to go slower than is commonly expected, either because, as in Prato, sidelines have been found to make up the lost ground or because, as we have already seen, consumer demand for quality and variety is becoming increasingly pronounced. This slow expansion in the market for sophisticated products goes alongside the need to produce in shorter series and therefore to find a means of controlling the labour force different from that developed by Fordism. All this naturally increases the space in which the small firm can operate efficiently. In conclusion, therefore, the notion of interstices seems to be weak and of limited value.

Agriculture

We can now turn our attention to the relation between industry and agriculture. There is a basic distinction to be made in this regard. Agriculture has not been able to survive in the Appenine mountains which mark the southern boundary of the region. To varying degrees, therefore, the mountains have lost their population and, to schematise a bit, only those areas which can attract tourists have managed to maintain their per capita income relative to that of the region as a whole. By contrast, the Po valley, which includes the most fertile soil in Italy, has been able to dispute with industry the labour force it requires. As a consequence, the incomes of many agricultural workers, including the day labourers, are often comparable to those of their industrial counterparts. This prosperity constitutes the principal feature of Emilian agriculture even though there remains a stratum of poor peasants which some estimate at one-third of the total agricultural labour force (Brusco, 1979).

The general prosperity of agriculture in the region can be ascribed to three main causes. First, there is the extraordinary fertility of the soil. Yet this is not a sufficient cause, since there are areas in Campania and Puglia which are even more fertile but less prosperous. The second reason is the presence of co-operatives which heavily influence the market for a wide variety of agricultural products. The diffusion and strength of co-operatives which sell Emilian agricultural products directly to consumers throughout Italy has eliminated the parasitic middlemen who still flourish in other regions. The co-operatives even manage to obtain for their members a share in the profits of the food processing industry. It is for this reason that the regional government has quite correctly chosen them as its main channel for influencing the agricultural sector, to such an extent that since its creation at the beginning of the 1970s the region has directed more than 20% of its total agricultural expenditure towards co-operatives.

It should be noted in passing that this practice of co-operative work has had its impact on industry as well. While there are no co-operative firms as such outside construction, it is plausible to suppose that these traditions of co-operation have influenced those associations of artisans and small entrepreneurs of which we have already spoken.

Finally, and most importantly, the superiority of Emilian agriculture can be explained by the transformation of agrarian property relations since the war. Of all Italian regions, Emilia-Romagna was one of those in which sharecropping was most widely practiced in 1947. In the province of Modena, this type of contract covered 70% of the soil. Its decay, due more to the growth of industry than to legislation, has had deep repercussions. Many of the old landlords, whose estates often included ten to twenty sharecroppers' plots, once freed from this system have unified them into a single capitalist farm. Some of the minor landlords, almost always belonging to the urban bourgeoisie, have preferred to keep their farms as a second activity run by a salaried manager. All the remaining proprietors, large and small, have sold their land to the peasants. These sales, which were in some cases preceded by a period of rental, have selected out a wide stratum of highly skilled peasants.

The situation, therefore, has evolved along radically different lines to those of the southern regions. There, apart from the effects of the agrarian reforms, the importance of large and medium landed property has remained unchanged; the only modifications of agricultural techniques have been those linked to irrigation; the small properties freed by migration have in practice remained blocked and often uncultivated. In Emilia, where as we have seen, the land market has been extremely active, a major part of the capital accumulated through the sale of large estates was invested in the growing industrial sector. The initial capital of many engineering, ceramic, textile, and food processing firms was drawn from this source. A final example of the integration of agriculture and industry in Emilian development can be seen in the growing tendency for workers and artisans who are employed in the towns to go to live in the countryside, where they engage in a certain amount of part-time farming.

The state and local government

The central state administration appears to play a lesser role in this region than in others. First of all, tax collection is less effective here than elsewhere, both as regards firms and private households. One might expect that in such a fragmented productive structure the longstanding deficiencies of Italian public administration might be even more striking than elsewhere. One might expect, in other words, that something similar to what happens to the trade unions (or by that token to the central statistical agencies) might happen to the state: the smaller the unit in question, the less such institutions will be able to control it. If this were true it would follow that Emilia-Romagna contributes less to the state than the other rich regions of the country. In this sense, then, it would be as if there were a transfer of income from these regions to Emilia. On the other hand, it is necessary to recall that the state also contributes less to Emilia since there are fewer public and semi-public enterprises there than in other regions.

In the case of public works, too, the absence of sound data makes any conclusions speculative. It seems certain, however, that the 'red belt' is discriminated against in terms of the distribution of public funds and credit concessions. Today perhaps this bias has eased off and is less pressing than in the past: there is no doubt, however, that such discrimination has never troubled the public conscience of the Christian Democratic Party. Another phenomenon, however, acts in the opposite direction: the extraordinary efficiency of Emilian municipal government in organising public interventions, no matter how complex; in providing financial resources; and in mobilising local forces, including Christian Democrats, in support of demands directed to the state.

A specific case may serve to exemplify this political efficiency, peculiar in Italian terms. The river Panaro, which separates the province of Modena from that of Bologna, had flooded thousands of acres of Modenese land several times between 1966 and 1973. These disasters were due to the absence of adequate flood-gates. The intervention which should have been planned by the Ministry of Public Works was instead prepared by the provincial administrations of Modena and Reggio Emilia, and was ready by 1972. The Ministry had accepted it but by 1976 nothing had happened. When the river flooded in this year for the fifth time, the municipal government of Modena convoked an assembly in the city square of its citizens and those of the other affected towns; with the collaboration of *all* the MPs of the province so much pressure was brought to bear on the Ministry of Public Works that the funds for the long-planned flood-gates were released within fifteen days.

There is no doubt in fact that the efficiency of local government has markedly raised the real wages of Emilian workers, and has improved the quality of life. Using the minimal, even non-existent, spaces provided by a hazy legislative framework, the local governments have managed to implement policies unheard of in the rest of Italy. Two areas of intervention stand out in this respect. The first is that of social services: for example, in Reggio Emilia and Modena, nursery schools can absorb the entire demand for their services, in sharp contrast to the situation elsewhere, particularly in the South. Thus it is striking that in Bologna there are enough places in creches and nursery schools for 25% and 65% of the respective age groups; in Naples, by contrast, the corresponding figures are only 1·5% and 4% (Capecchi and Pugliese, 1978).

The second is that of urban planning and control of speculative building development. After some initial mistakes, the local governments have opted for a policy of controlled development. All possible legal instruments from expropriation and agreements to threats and inducements have been used to control the price of commercial property. As a consequence the Emilian cities have a higher proportion of publicly and co-operatively funded accommodation and lower house prices than elsewhere in Italy. The new neighbour-hoods are often architecturally undistinguished but the proportion of green space per inhabitant is certainly quite high. The low price of property not only benefits private households but also promotes the prosperity of local firms. By planning for artisanal districts this policy allows small firms to buy lofts at relatively reasonable prices, and thus promotes their growth.

In other areas, too, the municipal administrations are active. Despite a certain delay they are attempting to control pollution as much as possible. They are creating a network of psychiatric consultation centres and family counselling centres. A wide range of cultural initiatives have been launched, ranging from opera to theatre to rock concerts. Finally, particularly in the past few years, attempts have been made to revive the old urban centres from which traffic has long been excluded.

Summary and conclusions

In conclusion, let us re-examine the principal component parts of the 'Emilian model' and their relation to the operation of the system as a whole. First, agriculture in this region has emerged strengthened from the reorganisation of the past two decades. Some poor peasants remain who have not been able to establish an independent farm from the collapse of share-cropping. But these groups are destined to disappear. The regional labour market is too tight to permit a rigid compartmentalisation, and the next generation is more prone to acquire industrial skills. In any case, the presence of agricultural co-operatives makes this sector rather cohesive, and certainly more resistant to recessions than elsewhere.

Second, there is a 'primary' industrial sector with advanced technology, innovative ability, high wages, and considerable union presence. Its only limitation comes from restraints on redundancies. The industrial relations system, however great its powers of mediation, imposes serious rigidities on the employers, and it is in this context that the third component of the 'Emilian model' finds its place. The 'secondary' industrial sector, consisting of small firms, shares with the 'primary' sector its advanced technology, its innovative capacity and its ability to compete on the world market, and at least when business is good pays similar wages to most of its workforce. The true role of this sector, therefore, at least in periods of expansion, is to return flexibility in the use of labour to the entire productive structure, rather than to exploit cheap labour and so make possible the use of backward machinery. There is, however, another mechanism by which the system as a whole escapes the rigidity imposed by the unions in the larger firms: the putting-out of work to other regions, in which the classic secondary labour market characteristics of low pay and backward machinery can to some extent be found.

Finally, all this takes place under the watchful eye of a local government which helps to raise real wages and to improve the quality of life. The state on the other hand, for better and for worse, plays a lesser role than in other regions.

This complex productive apparatus gives the worker a wide range of choices and opportunities: to the more skilled the opportunity to go into business for themselves; to others the ability to choose in which firm to work; and to young people the possibility of alternating periods of work with periods of 'life'. The work force can be set along a continuum with two opposite poles: artisans working to the limit of their capacity to earn a high income, and youth prepared to trade off low wages for short hours of work. More generally, therefore, it can be stated that each worker is able to decide how to divide life between work and leisure in a context which measures precisely the amount of labour expended and converts it into income.

From this above all comes the widespread certitude that this system is rich in opportunities for all, and that everyone is ultimately the master of his own fate. Such certitude is amongst the basic elements of the political consensus enjoyed by those who have attempted to guide and control this development process. For the same reason, however, there is little sympathy for those who do not share the basic values of the system and hostility and even contempt for those who criticise it from outside.

Cohesion and closure have been reinforced by the virtuous circle fuelled by the continuous prosperity of the past two decades. Flexibility and entrepreneurship produce high rates of growth, which push up family incomes; high incomes permit increased education and the accumulation of skills; and local government keeps the environmental consequences of development within tolerable limits. This circle depends on one basic condition: 'when you work you work, without cheating yourself or anyone else'.

Thus cultural as well as economic factors lead us to emphasise the freer role played by market forces in Emilia and the more authentically capitalist character of its development as compared to other Italian regions. This can be seen in the extensive role played by individual initiative; in the system's capacity to regain the flexibility lost to the unions in the large factory by segmenting the productive structure and exporting its contradictions; and in the relative absence of the national state, both in terms of public spending and tax collection. To a certain extent, however, this absence of the state has been compensated for by the initiatives of those few efficient public institutions more closely linked to the civil society of the region. Thus there has been realised in Emilia a harmonious mixture of discordant elements, but one whose complexity makes it difficult to take it as a model: efficient institutions despite the absence of the state, and active trade unions which control only half of the labour force.

So long as demand continues to expand, this social and productive structure will face only the problem of integrating into itself those who declare themselves to be outside it. But some doubt remains that this system might react badly to a deep and prolonged recession. Consider for example what happened to Turin in response to the Fiat redundancies in October 1980, and what would happen in Emilia if the success of a new Mary Quant were to

184   S. Brusco

create as many redundancies among knitwear workers. In Turin the clash between employer and resistant workers was clear cut and was moderated by special state unemployment funds and so the situation was controlled.

In Emilia, unless the local entrepreneurs could quickly copy and improve on the new styles (which could well happen), the dynamic interaction of the parts of the industrial district which guarantee a flexible response to the product market could quickly deteriorate in a competitive scramble for orders. This, in the condition where trade unions only partially control the labour market, could put downward pressure on wages, and cause a reduction of prosperity and a dismantling of the productive structure upon which that prosperity is based.

Bibliography

Bagnasco, A. 1977. *Tre Italie: la problematica territoriale dello sviluppo*, Bologna, Il Mulino

Bagnasco, A. and Messori, M. 1975. *Tendenze dell'economia periferica*, Torino, Valentino

Botta, P., Fonte, M., Improta, L., Pugliese, E. and Ruggero, F. 1976. La struttura del settore calzaturiero a Napoli, *Inchiesta*, no. 23

Brusco, S. 1975. Organizzazione del lavoro e decentramento produttivo nel settore metalmeccanico, *Sindacato e piccola impresa* (a cura della FLM di Bergamo), Bari, De Donato

Brusco, S. 1979. *Agricoltura ricca e classi sociali*, Milano, Feltrinelli

Brusco, S., Giovannetti, E. and Malagoli, W. 1979. *La relazione tra dimensione e saggio di sviluppo nelle imprese industriali: una ricerca empirica*, Modena

Brusco, S. and Malagoli, W. 1981. Disintegrated firms and industrial districts: the case of the knitwear industry in Italy, paper presented at the Third Conference of the International Working Party on Labour Market Segmentation, mimeo, Modena

Brusco, S. and Sabel, C. 1981. Artisan production and economic growth, in Wilkinson, F. (ed.), *The Dynamics of Labour Market Segmentation*, London, Academic Press

Capecchi, V. *et al*. 1979. *La piccola impresa in Italia*, Bari, De Donato

Capecchi, V. and Pugliese, E. 1978. Bologna Napoli: due città a confronto, *Inchiesta*, no. 34–36

David, P. and Pattarin, E. 1975. Retroterra rurale e condizione operaia femminile: il settore della maglieria, *Inchiesta*, no. 20

Fillippi, E. 1979. La struttura finanziaria delle medie imprese italiane, *Thema*, no. 4

Filippucci, C. 1978. L'occupazione ed il valore aggiunto in Emilia-Romagna: un'analisi disaggregata per settore di attività economica, *Statistica*, no. 3

Frey, L. (ed.) 1975. *Lavoro a domicilio e decentramento dell'attività produttiva nei settori tessile e dell'abbigliamento in Italia*, Milano, Angeli

Guglielmi, M. 1978. I problemi finanziari dello sviluppo della piccola e media impresa—un confronto regionale, *Orientamenti nuovi per la piccola e media industria*, no. 9

ISTAT, *5° Censimento generale dell'industria e del commercio—1971*, Roma

ISTAT, *Rilevazione trimestrale della forze di lavoro*, Roma

ISTAT, *Rilevazione trimestrale delle forze di lavoro—nuova serie*, Roma

Malagoli, W. and Mengoli, P. 1979. Lavoro a domicilio e artigianato nel comparto della maglieria, *Città e regione*, no. 5

Muller, J. 1976. La dimensione dell'impresa e l'integrazione verticale, *Rivista di Economia e Politica Industriale*, no. 2

Paci, M. 1975. Crisi, ristrutturazione e piccola impresa, *Inchiesta*, no. 20

Unioncamere 1981. *Il reddito prodotto nelle provincie italiane nel 1979*, Roma

Unioncamere, *Statistiche provinciali dei movimenti valutari inerenti alle importazioni e alle esportazioni*, Roma

[12]

Ronald Dore

Goodwill and the spirit of market capitalism

HOBHOUSE MEMORIAL LECTURE

Why have large factories given way to the co-ordinated production of specialized family units in segments of the Japanese textile industry? One reason is the predominance of 'obligated relational contracting' in Japanese business. Consumer goods markets are highly competitive in Japan, but trade in intermediates, by contrast, is for the most part conducted within long-term trading relations in which goodwill 'give-and-take' is expected to temper the pursuit of self-interest.

Cultural preferences explain the *unusual* predominance of these relations in Japan, but they are in fact more common in Western economies than textbooks usually recognize. The recent growth of relational contracting (in labour markets especially) is, indeed, at the root of the 'rigidities' supposedly responsible for contemporary stagflation. Japan shows that to sweep away these rigidities and give markets back their pristine vigour is not the only prescription for a cure of stagflation. The Japanese economy more than adequately compensates for the loss of allocative efficiency by achieving high levels of other kinds of efficiency — in many respects thanks to, rather than in spite of, relational contracting. We would do well to be more concerned about those kinds of efficiency too.

One of economists' favourite Adam Smith quotations is the passage in the *Wealth of Nations* in which he sets out one of his basic premises.

It is not from the benevolence of the butcher, the brewer and the baker, that we expect our dinner, but from their regard to their own interest. We address ourselves, not to their humanity, but to their self-love, and never talk to them of our necessities but of their advantages.[1]

The British Journal of Sociology Volume XXXIV Number 4
© R.K.P. 1983 0007-1315/83/3404-459 $1.50

I wish to question that sharp opposition between benevolence and self-interest. Perhaps, so that he should be alert for signs of possible bias, the reader should be warned that a prolonged soaking in the writings of Japanese eighteenth- and nineteenth-century Confucianists at an early age has left me with a soft spot for the virtue of benevolence, even a tendency to bristle when anyone too much disparages it. At any rate I wish to argue, apropos of benevolence, or goodwill, that there is rather more of it about than we sometimes allow, further that to recognize the fact might help in the impossible task of trying to run an efficient economy and a decent society — an endeavour which animated Hobhouse's life, and about which, as Ginsburg makes clear in his 1950s preface to *Morals in Evolution*, even the pains of old age and the rise of fascism in the 1920s did not destroy his eventual optimism.

My title refers to goodwill rather than benevolence because benevolence, in my Confucian book, though not I think in Adam Smith's, is something shown in relations between unequals, by superior to inferior, the reciprocal of which is usually called loyalty. Goodwill is more status-neutral, more an expression of Hobhouse's 'principle of mutuality'. And it is that broader meaning which I intend. A formal definition of my subject might be: the sentiments of friendship and the sense of diffuse personal obligation which accrue between individuals engaged in recurring contractual economic exchange. (By 'economic', I mean only that the goods and services exchanged should be commonly subject to market valuation.)

Goodwill, of course, is a term of art in the commercial world. In the world of petty proprietorships, familiar to most of us, if you are selling a corner store you set a price on the premises, a price on the stock and a price on the goodwill. Back in the old Marshallian days when economists took their concepts from everyday life rather than trying to take everyday life from their concepts, goodwill meant the same thing to economists too. Palgrave's 1923 dictionary of economics defines goodwill as:

> The expectancy of a continuance, to the advantage of a successor in an established business, of the personal confidence, or of the habit of recurring to the place or premises or to the known business house or firm, on the part of a circle or connection of clients or customers.[2]

The next economics dictionary I find, McGraw-Hill's exactly half a century later, has a very different definition of goodwill:

> An accounting term used to explain the difference between what a company pays when it buys another company and what it gets in the form of tangible assets.[3]

Samuelson, to his credit one of the very few textbook writers in whose index one will find the word goodwill, illustrates the concept with J. P. Morgan taking over Carnegie's steel interests, making it clear that Morgan paid a premium well over the market value of the fixed assets primarily because he thereby advanced significantly towards a monopoly position.[4] In other words the goodwill concept is extended to cover not just the benefits accruing to the purchaser of a business from the affectionate or inertial habits of its customers, but also those accruing out of his consequent shift from the position of price-taker to that of price-maker — his enhanced ability to hold those customers up to ransom. To be fair to the economists who have adopted this use of the term, and partially to retract my earlier gibe, one could say that the standard definition of the term has changed because everyday life has changed. A world in which the terms appropriate to the small owner-managed business formed the dominant norm, has given way to a world dominated by the large corporations and their accountants' terms. Certainly, if anyone wanted to write an Old Testament Prophet-style denunciation of modern capitalism *à la* Marx, he could hardly ask for a better illustration than the corruption of the concept of 'goodwill', that primordial embodiment of basic social bonds, into a term for some of the more ugly anti-social forms of profit-seeking.

THE DISAGGREGATION OF FACTORY PRODUCTION

I have been caused to ponder the role of goodwill in economic life by the recent experience of studying the organization of the textile industry, or to be more precise, the weaving segment of it, in Britain and Japan. One place I visited in the course of that research was the small town of Nishiwaki in western Japan whose industry is almost wholly devoted to the weaving of ginghams chiefly for export to Hong Kong to be made up into garments for Americans to wear when square-dancing in the Middle West. This is an area where hand-loom weaving goes back some centuries. Power-looms came in in the late nineteenth century and they brought with them the factory system as they did everywhere else. And 25 years ago, although many small weaving establishments had survived, the bulk of the output was accounted for by larger mills, many of which were part of vertically integrated enterprises with their own cotton-importing, spinning and finishing establishments.

By 1980, however, the picture had changed. The larger mills had closed. The integrated firms had retreated, as far as direct production was concerned, to their original base in spinning. Most of them were still, either alone or in collaboration with a trading company, producing their own brand cloth, dyed and finished. But they were doing so through the co-ordination of the activities of a large number of family enterprises. The key family business was that of the merchant-converter who contracted with the spinning company to turn its yarn into a certain type of cloth at a given contract price. The converter would send the yarn to another small family concern specializing in yarn dyeing, then it would go on to a specialist beamer who would wind it on to the warp beams in the desired pattern and also put the warp through the sizing process. Then it would be delivered to the weaver who might do his own weft preparation and the drawing-in (putting the harness on the beams ready for the looms) or might use other family businesses — contract winders or drawers in — for the process. And so on to the finishers who did the bleaching or texturizing or over-printing.

What is the reason for this fragmentation? What changes in Japanese society and the Japanese economy account for what most orthodox notions of the direction of the evolution of modern economies would count as a regression — the replacement of a system of production co-ordination within a vertically integrated firm by a system of production co-ordination between a large number of fragmented small firms; the replacement, to use Williamson's terms, of co-ordination through hierarchy by co-ordination through the market?[5]

I can think of four possible long-term secular trends which might help to explain the change.

1. The first is the rise in wages and the shorter working week of employees in union-organized firms. Wages are commonly lower in small firms — especially in Japan where the privileged position of the large enterprise elite has become firmly conventionalized, and inter-scale wage differentials are very great. But that is not all. Family enterprisers themselves are often willing to work much longer than 40 hours a week for what may or may not be a larger *total* income than wage workers get, but for an *average* return per hour of labour — hence wage cost per metre of cloth — which is below the employee's wage. If you like, family enterprisers are now willing to exploit themselves more than the unions or the law permit employees to be exploited — a condition which did not hold when *employees* were already working close to the human maximum — a 70 hour week for a subsistence level wage. The clear superiority of the factory system at that time may have been lost since.

2. Second, the secular trend to high taxation and higher levels of taxation-allergy make the family enterpriser's advantage in both tax avoidance and tax evasion more attractive — *vide* the growth of the secondary 'black' and quasi-black economy in many other countries.

3. Third, there is a technical factor: the capital lumpiness of some of the new technology. For example expensive, large and fast sizing machines can hardly get the through-put necessary to make them profitable within a single firm. Inter-firm specialization becomes the best way of realizing economies of scale.
4. Fourth, much higher levels of numeracy and literacy mean a much wider diffusion of the accounting and managerial skills necessary to run a small business, the prudent ability to calculate the rentability of investments, etc.

These are all features common to societies other than Japan and may well be part of the explanation why the woollen industry of Prato has also moved to a fragmented structure in recent years. But there is another factor which applies especially in Japan. The reason why the dominant trend in the west seems to be in the reverse direction — away from co-ordination through the market towards co-ordination through the hierarchy of a vertically integrated firm — is, as Oliver Williamson is never tired of telling us, because of the transaction costs entailed, the costs arising from the imperfections of markets with small numbers of buyers and sellers in which the bargaining transactions are made difficult by what the jargon calls 'impacted information'. These features so enhance the bargaining power of each party that, when there are no significant economies of scale to be gained by their mutual independence one party (usually the stronger one) buys out the other to put a stop to his 'opportunism' (rapid response not only to price signals — which of course is always admirable — but also to information about vulnerable weaknesses of the other party.)

RELATIONAL CONTRACTING

Here is another of those timeless generalizations about 'capitalist economies' about which Japan gives pause. Transaction costs for large Japanese firms may well be lower than elsewhere. 'Opportunism' may be a lesser danger in Japan because of the explicit encouragement, and actual prevalence, in the Japanese economy of what one might call moralized trading relationships of mutual goodwill.

The stability of the relationship is the key. Both sides recognize an obligation to try to maintain it. If a finisher re-equips with a new and more efficient dyeing process which gives him a cost advantage and the opportunity of offering discounts on the going contract price he does not immediately get all the business. He may win business from one or two converters if they had some *other* reason for being dissatisfied with their own finisher. But the more common consequence is that the other merchant-converters go to their finishers and say: 'Look how X has got his price down. We hope you can do the same because we really would have to reconsider our position if the price difference goes on for months. If you need bank finance to get the new type of vat we can probably help by guaranteeing the loan.'

It is a system, to use a distinction common in the Williamson school, of relational contracting rather than spot-contracting[6] – or to use Williamson's more recent phrase[7] 'obligational contracting'. More like a marriage than a one-night stand as Robert Solow has said about the modern employment relation.[8] The rules of chastity vary. As is commonly the case, for those at the lower end of the scale, monogamy is the rule. A weaver with a couple of dozen automatic looms in a back garden shed will usually weave for only one converter, so that there should be no dispute about prior rights to the fruits of his looms – no clash of loyalties. Specialists with faster, larger volume, through-puts, like beamers – scarcer, more attractive, more in demand, therefore – may have a relation *à trois* or *à quatre*. For the converters themselves, at the top of the local hierarchy, there have grown up curious conventions rather like polyandrous concubinage. The Japan Spinners Association is dominated by the so-called Big Nine firms. None of the Big Nine will tolerate one of its converters taking cotton yarn from *another* of the Big Nine. However, one rank below the Big Nine are the so called New Spinners, and below them the post-war upstarts, the New New Spinners. A Big Nine spinner will tolerate its converters having relations with them, though, of course a New Spinner will not tolerate a relation with another New Spinner. So the converter can end up with one of each – a first husband and a number two and a number three husband as it were.

As in nearly all systems of marriage, divorce also happens. That is why I said that a finisher with a cost advantage could attract other converters who happen for other reasons to be dissatisfied with their finisher. When I use the analogy of divorce, I mean traditional divorce in obligation-conscious societies, rather than the 'sorry I like someone else better: let's be friends' divorce of modern California. That is to say, the break usually involves recrimination and some bitterness, because it usually has to be justified by accusing the partner of some failure of goodwill, some lack of benevolence – or, as the Japanese phrase is more often translated, 'lack of sincerity'. It is not enough that some external circumstances keep his prices high.

I have made these relations sound like the kinship system of a Himalayan village, but of course the specific patterns of who may trade with whom are of very recent origin. What are entirely traditional, however, are, first, the basic pattern of treating trading relations as particularistic personal relations; second, the values and sentiments which sustain the obligations involved, and third such things as the pattern of mid-summer and year-end gift exchange which symbolizes recognition of those obligations.

But how on earth, the economist will want to know, do the prices and ordered quantities get fixed? The answer seems to be that, once established, prices can be re-negotiated at the initiative of either party on the grounds either of cost changes affecting either party, or else of changes in the competitive conditions in the final market in which the brand cloth is sold. There are also fringe spot-markets for cotton yarn and grey cloth, and the prices ruling in these markets and reported in the daily textile press provide guides. To further complicate the issue there is some collective bargaining. Both the weavers and the converters in Nishiwaki have their own co-operative union and guide prices may be agreed between them; alternatively, in some other textile areas, the weavers co-op sets a minimum contract price which its members are not supposed to undercut, though there is general scepticism about the effectiveness of such an agreement.

RELATIONAL CONTRACTING BETWEEN UNEQUALS

The basic principles on which these price and quantity negotiations rest appear to be three-fold. First that the losses of the bad times and the gains of the good times should be shared. Second, that in recognition of the hierarchical nature of the relationship — of the fact that weavers are more dependent on converters than converters are on weavers — a fair sharing of a fall in the market may well involve the weaker weaver suffering more than the converter — having his profits squeezed harder. But, third, the stronger converter should not use his bargaining superiority in recession times, and the competition between his weavers to have their orders cut as little as possible, to drive them over, or even to, the edge of bankruptcy.

It is in the interpretation of these principles, of course, that ambiguity enters. Benevolence all too easily shades into exploitation when the divorce option — the option of breaking off the relationship — is more costlessly available to one party than to the other. There is, even, an officially-sponsored Association for the Promotion of the Modernization of Trading Relations in the Textile Industry in Japan which urges the use of written rather than verbal contracts in these relationships and is devoted to strengthening moral constraints on what it calls the abuse — but our economic textbooks would presumably call the legitimate full use — of market power. As for the nature of such abuse, surveys conducted by the Association show that suppliers with verbal contracts are more likely to have goods returned for quality deficiencies than those with proper written contracts.[9] Weavers will wryly remark that returns become strangely more common when the price is falling (and a rejected lot contracted at a higher price can be replaced by a newly contracted cheaper lot).

The work of the Association is an interesting illustration of the formal institutionalization of the ethics of relational contracting — doing, perhaps, for contracting what the post-war labour reform did to transform the employment system of large firms from manipulative paternalism into something less exploitative and better described as welfare corporatism.[10] All one can say about the contemporary trading reality is that those ethics appear to be sufficiently institutionalized, to be sufficiently constraining on a sufficient number of the firms and families in Nishiwaki textiles, for the pattern of trading I have described to be a stable and viable one.

That pattern is repeated in many other areas of the Japanese economy — between, for example, an automobile firm like Toyota and its sub-contractors. Here again, the obligations of the relationship are unequal; the sub-contractor has to show more earnest goodwill, more 'sincerity', to keep its orders than the parent company to keep its supplies. But equally the obligatedness is not entirely one-sided, and it does limit the extent to which the parent company can, for example, end its contracts with a sub-contractor in a recession in order to bring the work into its own factory and keep its own workforce employed.

I have been taken to task by Okumura, the Japanese economist who has written most interestingly about these relationships, for speaking of the 'obligatedness' of a firm like Toyota as if a corporation was, or behaved like, a natural person.[11] But I still think the term is apt. The mechanisms are easy to intuit, if ponderous to spell out. First of all, there are *real* personal relations between the purchasing manager of Toyota and the manager or owner-manager of a sub-contracting firm. But, of course, managers change frequently, particularly in firms with a bureaucratic career-promotion structure like Toyota. It is part of the commitment of such managers, however, that they identify with their firm and their department. If it were said, therefore, in the world outside, that Toyota, or its purchasing department in particular, had behaved badly by playing fast and loose with its sub-contractors, the manager responsible would feel that he had let his firm down. If the accountants in the costing department urge a tough line with sub-contractors, he may well tell them that they are short-sighted and even disloyal to the firm in under-estimating the importance of its reputation. These seem to me readily understandable mechanisms by which the patterns of obligation between individual owner-managing converters and weavers in Nishiwaki can be duplicated between corporations.

I have discussed two cases of obligated trading relationships which are explicitly hierarchical. If there is any doubt as to who pecks whom in the pecking order look at the mid-summer and year-end gifts. Although it may vary depending on the precise nature of the concessions sought or granted in the previous six months or anticipated in the next, the weaver's gift to the converter will usually cost more than vice versa — unless, that is, either of them miscalculates the gift inflation rate, the point of transition, say, from Black Label against Suntory Old to Napoleon brandy against Dimple Haig.

RELATIONAL CONTRACTING BETWEEN EQUALS

But these relations are not confined to the hierarchical case. Even between firms of relatively equal strength the same forms of obligated relational contracting exist. Competition between Japanese firms is intense, but only in markets which are (a) consumer markets and (b) expanding. In consumer markets which are not expanding cartelization sets in rather rapidly, but that is a rather different story which does not concern us here. What does concern us here are markets in producers' goods, in intermediates. And for many such commodities markets can hardly be said to exist. Take steel, for instance, and one of its major uses for automobiles. The seven car firms buy their steel through trading companies, each from two or three of the major steel companies, in proportions which vary little from year to year. Prices, in this market, are set by the annual contract between the champions — Toyota on the one side, New Japan Steel on the other.

It is the concentration of such relationships which is the dominant characteristic of the famous large enterprise groups, known to Japanese as *grūpu*, and to foreigners, usually, as *zaibatsu* or *keiretsu*. There are six main ones of which the two best known are Mitsui and Mitsubishi. These groups are quite distinct from the hierarchical groupings of affiliates and subsidiaries around some of the giant individual firms like Hitachi or Matsushita or MHI. The Mitsubishi group, for example, has no clear hierarchical structure. In its core membership of 28 firms, there is a certain amount of intra-group share ownership — on average about 26 per cent of total equity widely dispersed throughout the group in three or four per cent shares. There is a tiny amount of interlocking directorships — about three per cent of all directors' seats. And most of the firms have the group bank as their lead bank, and bank of last pleading resort, but that bank provides on average less than 20 per cent of all loan finance to group firms. The only thing which formally defines the identity of the group is the lunch on the last Friday of the month when the Presidents of every company in the group get together, often to listen to a lecture on, say, the oil market in the 1990s, to discuss matters like political party contributions, sometimes to hear news of, or give blessings to, some new joint venture started up by two or more member firms, or a rescue operation for a member firm in trouble.[12]

But the main *raison d'etre* of these groups is as networks of preferential, stable, obligated *bilateral* trading relationships, networks of relational contracting. They are not conglomerates because they have no central board or holding company. They are not cartels because they are all in diverse lines of business. Each group has a bank and a trading company, a steel firm, an automobile firm, a major chemical firm, a shipbuilding and plant engineering firm and so on — and, except by awkward accident, not more than one of each. (The 'one set' principle, as the Japanese say.) Hence, trade in producer goods within the group can be brisk. To extend earlier analogies; it is a bit like an extended family grouping, where business is kept as much as possible within the family, and a certain degree of give and take is expected to modify the adversarial pursuit of market advantage — a willingness, say, to pay above the market price for a while to help one's trading partner out of deep trouble.

THE PREFERENCE FOR RELATIONAL CONTRACTING: CULTURAL SOURCES?

The starting point of this discussion of relational contracting was the search for reasons to explain why it made sense for the spinning firms producing brand cloth to co-ordinate production neither through hierarchy in the usual Williamson sense of full vertical integration, nor through the market in the normal sense of continuously pursuing the best buy, but through 'relational contracting'. It was, I said, because such arrangements could be *relied on* in Japan more than in most other economies. There is one striking statistic which illustrates the extent to which it is in fact relied on. The volume of wholesale transactions in Japan is no less than four times as great as the volume of retail transactions. For France the multiple is not four but 1.2; for Britain, West Germany and the USA the figure is between 1.6 and 1.9.[13]

How does one explain the difference between Japan and other capitalist economies? Williamson has 'theorized' these 'obligational relationships' and explained the circumstances in which they will occur — when the extent to which the commodities traded are idiosyncratically specific (such that the economies of scale can be as easily appropriated by buyer or by seller), and the extent to which either party has invested in equipment or specialized knowledge for the trading relationship, are not quite such that vertical integration

makes sense, but almost so. He also asserts that in such relationships quantity adjustments will be preferred to price adjustments
and price adjustments will be pegged to objective exogenous indicators (though he allows, in passing, for the not very 'relevant' or
'interesting' possibility that 'ad hoc price relief' might be given as
an act of kindness by one party to the other.)[14]

Perhaps Williamson has evidence that that is the way it is in
America and the fact that his argument is couched in the terms of
a timeless generalization merely reflects the tendency of American
economists to write as if all the world were America. (Just as British
economists write micro-economics as if all the world were America,
and macro-economics as if all the world were Britain.) Or perhaps
he does not have much evidence about America either, and just
assumes that 'Man' is a hard-nosed short-run profit-maximizer
suspicious of everyone he deals with, and allows everything else to
follow from that. At any rate Williamson's account does not provide
the tools for explaining the difference between the Japanese and
the British or American economies. There is nothing particularly
idiosyncratic about the steel or cloth traded in many of the obligated
relationships, little specialized assets involved (though there are in
automobile sub-contracting). Nor is there clear avoidance of price
adjustments — weaving contract prices, in fact, look like graphs of
nineteenth century business cycles.

Clearly we have to look elsewhere for an explanation. Try as one
might to avoid terms like 'national character' which came naturally
to Hobhouse, in favour of the scientific pretensions of, say, 'modal
behavioural dispositions', it is clearly national differences in value
preferences, or dispositions to action, with which we are concerned.
And, as Macfarlane showed when he looked into the origins of
English individualism,[15] to attempt to explain *those* takes one on a
long speculative journey — at least into distant ill-recorded history,
even if, for ideological reasons, one wishes to rule out genes. But it
is legitimate and useful to ask: what are the concomitants of these
dispositions? What do they correlate with? Are they an expression
of more general traits?

One candidate explanation is that the Japanese are generally very
long-term-future-oriented. At this moment, for example, the Japanese
Industry Ministry's Industrial Structure Council is already com-
posing what it calls a 'vision' of the shape of the world economy in
the mid-1990s. The economist is likely to seize on this explanation
with relief, because it will allow him to ignore all dangerous thoughts
about benevolence, and accommodate the relational contracting
phenomenon in the conventional micro-economics of risk aversion
and low time-discounts. Any sacrifice of short-run market advantage
is just an insurance premium for more long-term gains.

And he would find some good evidence. Nakatani has recently

done an interesting calculation comparing 42 large firms inside one of the large kinship groupings like Mitsui and Mitsubishi which I have just described and a matched sample of 42 loners. The loners had higher average profit levels and higher growth rates in the 1970s. *But* they also had a considerably higher dispersal around the means. The group firms were much more homogeneous in growth and profit levels. What went on in the groups, he concluded, was an overall sacrifice of efficiency in the interests of risk-sharing and greater equality.[16]

Relational contracts, in this interpretation, are just a way of trading off the short term loss involved in sacrificing a price advantage, against the insurance that one day you can 'call off' the same type of help from your trading partner if you are in trouble yourself. It is a calculation, perhaps, which comes naturally to a population which until recently was predominantly living in tightly nucleated hamlet communities in a land ravished by earthquake and typhoon. Traditionally, you set to, to help your neighbour rebuild his house after a fire, even though it might be two or three generations before yours was burnt down and your grandson needed the help returned.

But you could be *sure* that the help *would* be returned. And this is where we come back to Adam Smith. The Japanese, in spite of what their political leaders say at summit conferences about the glories of free enterprise in the Free World, and in spite of the fact that a British publisher with a new book about Adam Smith can expect to sell half the edition in Japan, have never really caught up with Adam Smith. They have never managed actually to bring themselves to *believe* in the invisible hand. They have always insisted — and teach in their schools and their 'how to get on' books of popular morality — that the butcher and the baker and the brewer *need* to be benevolent as well as self-interested. They need to be able to take some personal pleasure in the satisfaction of the diners quite over and above any expectation of future orders. It is not just that benevolence is the best policy — much as we say, rather more minimally, that honesty is the best policy. They do not doubt that it is — that it is not a matter of being played for a sucker, but actually the best way to material success. But that is not what they most commonly say. They most commonly say: benevolence is a duty. Full stop. It is that sense of duty — a duty over and above the terms of written contract — which gives the assurance of the pay-off which makes relational contracting viable.

Note that this is a little different from what Durkheim had in mind when he was talking about the non-contractual elements in contract and refuting Spencer's claim that modern societies were held together solely by an organic web of individualistic contracts.[17] Durkheim was talking about the intervention of *society* both in enforcing the basic principles of honesty and the keeping of promises, and in regulating the content of contracts, deciding what was admissible and what offended social decency or basic human rights. And in Durkheim's book it is the consciousness of an obligation imposed by society as a whole — or, on its members, by an occupational group of professional practitioners — which enforces those rules. Hobhouse, likewise, in his brisker and more historically rooted discussion of the way freedom of contract and the rights of private property come to be curtailed by, for example, redistributive welfare measures, stressed the benefits the individual receives from society and the corresponding obligations to society.[18] In Japanese relational contracting, by contrast, it is a particular sense of diffuse obligation to the individual trading partner, not to society, which is at issue. To put the matter in Parson's terms, relational contracting is to be understood in the universalism/particularism dimension, whereas the Durkheim point relates to the fifth dichotomy that Parsons later lost from sight: collective-orientation versus individual-orientation. To put it another way, the Japanese share with Durkheim the perception that contract, far from being fundamentally integrative, is basically a marker for conflict. Every harmonization of interest in a contract simply conceals a conflict either latent or adjourned, as Durkheim said.[19] The Durkheim solution is to have universalistic social institutions contain the conflict — an engine-cooling system to take away the heat. The Japanese prefer particularistically to reduce the friction in all the moving parts with the emollient lubrication of mutual consideration.

Perhaps one should not overdraw the contrast, however, in view of the empirical fact that the Japanese, who stand out among other capitalist societies for their addiction to relational contracts, also stand out as the nation whose businessmen and trade unionists seem to have a more lively sense of their obligated membership in the national community than those of other nations. Japan has fewer free-rider problems in the management of the national economy; patriotism seems to supplement profit-seeking more substantially in, say, the search for export markets, and so on. Perhaps the common syndrome is a generalized dutifulness, or to put it in negative form, a relatively low level of individualistic self-assertion. I am reminded of the Japanese scholar and publicist, Nitobe. In his lectures in the USA in the 1930s he used to tell the national character story about the international prize competition for an essay about the elephant. In his version the Japanese entry was entitled 'The duties and domestication of the elephant'.

But there is, it seems to me, a third element in the Japanese preference for relational contracting besides risk sharing and long-term advantage on the one hand and dutifulness on the other. That is the element, to go back to Parsons' variables again, best analysed in his affectivity/affective-neutrality dimension. People born and brought up in Japanese society do not much *like* openly adversarial bargaining relationships — which are inevitably low-trust relationships because information is hoarded for bargaining advantage and each tries to manipulate the responses of the other in his own interest. Poker is not a favourite Japanese game. Most Japanese feel more comfortable in high-trust relations of friendly give-and-take in which each side recognizes that he also has some stake in the satisfaction of the other.

All of which, of course, is not necessarily to say that the affect is geniune. Pecksniffs can do rather well in exploiting these relationships when they are in a stronger bargaining position — the point made earlier about the ambiguities of these relationships.

EMPLOYMENT PRACTICES AND RELATIONAL CONTRACTS

The discussion so far has centred on markets in intermediates and capital goods, and about relational contracting between enterprises. I have not so far mentioned labour markets, though the predominance of relational contracting in Japanese labour markets is, of course, much more widely known than its predominance in inter-firm trading. By now every television viewer has heard of the life-time commitment pattern — the transformation of the employment contract from a short-term spot contract agreement to provide specific services for a specific wage (termination by one week or one month's notice on either side), into a long-term commitment to serve as needs may from time-to-time dictate, with wages negotiated according to criteria of fairness which have precious little to do with any notion of a market rate-for-the-job. The contract is seen, in fact, less as any kind of bilateral bargain, than as an act of admission to an enterprise community wherein benevolence, goodwill and sincerity are explicitly expected to temper the pursuit of self-interest. The parallel between relational contracting in the intermediates market and in the labour market is obvious. There can be little doubt that the same cultural values explain the preferred patterns in both fields.

RELATIONAL CONTRACTING AND EFFICIENCY

But anyone looking at the competitive strength of the Japanese economy today must also wonder whether this institutionalization of relational contracting, as well as serving the values of risk-sharing security, dutifulness and friendliness *also* conduces to a fourth valued end — namely economic efficiency. Any economist, at least any economist worth his neo-classical salt, would be likely to scoff

Goodwill and the spirit of market capitalism   473

at the idea. Just think, he would say, of the market imperfections, of the misallocation and loss of efficiency involved. Think how many inefficient producers are kept out of the bankruptcy courts by all this give-and-take at the expense of the consuming public. Think of the additional barriers to entry against new, more efficient, producers. Gary Becker, in a lecture at the LSE a couple of years ago, claimed that give-and-take trading was even an inefficient way of being altruistic. In the end, he said, through greater survival power, you get more dollars-worth of altruism by playing the market game and then using the profits to endow a charitable foundation like Rockefeller — which I suppose is true and would even be significant. if 'altruism' were a homogeneous commodity indifferently produced either by being friendly to your suppliers or by posthumously endowing scholarship.[20]

But that apart, the main point about sub-optimality is well-taken. The Japanese economy is riddled with misallocation. A lot of the international dispute about non-tariff barriers, for example, has its origin in relational contracting. Take the market for steel which I mentioned earlier. Brazil and Korea can now land some kinds of steel in Japan more cheaply than Japanese producers can supply it. But very little of it is sold. Japan can remain as pure as the driven snow in GATT terms — no trigger prices, minimal tariffs, no quotas — and still have a kind of natural immunity to steel imports which Mr. MacGregor would envy. None of the major trading companies would touch Brazilian or Korean steel, especially now that things are going so badly for their customers, the Japanese steel companies. Small importers are willing to handle modest lots. But they will insist on their being landed at backwater warehouses away from where any domestic steel is going out, so that the incoming steel is not seen by a steel company employee. If that happens, the lorries taking the steel out might be followed to their destination. And the purchaser, if he turned out to be a disloyal customer, would be marked down for less than friendly treatment next time a boom brings a seller's market. What distortions, an economist would say. What a conspiracy against the consumer! What a welfare loss involved in sacrificing the benefits of comparative advantage! If the Japanese economy has a good growth record, that can only be *in spite of* relational contracting and the consequent loss of efficiency.

And yet there are some good reasons for thinking that it might be *because of*, and not *in spite of* relational contracting that Japan has a better growth performance than the rest of us. There is undoubtedly a loss of allocative efficiency. But the countervailing forces which more than outweigh that loss can *also* be traced to relational contracting. Those countervailing forces are those which conduce to, not allocative efficiency, but what Harvey Leibenstein calls X-efficiency — those abilities to plan and programme, to cooperate without bitchiness in production, to avoid waste of time or of materials, capacities which Leibenstein tries systematically to resolve into the constituent elements of selective degrees of rationality and of effort.[21] We have recently been told by a solemn defender of the neo-classical paradigm that we need not bother about Leibenstein and X-efficiency because he is only reformulating the utility-maximizing paradigm of the generalized equilibrium theory as developed by the Williamson school (i.e. that which incorporates transaction costs, property-right constraints, etc.)[22] To argue thus is not only to destroy the usefulness of 'utility-maximization' for any precise calculations, it is also to ignore the achievement of Leibenstein in actually noticing (a) that individuals, firms and nations differ greatly in degrees of generalized *sloppiness*, and (b) that other kinds of sloppiness are far more important for output growth and welfare than that involved in failing to fine-tune economic behaviour in response to changes in price signals — or *even* in failing to calculate the relative transaction costs of internal and external procurement.

In his book Leibenstein tries a rough comparison between the estimated welfare loss from tariffs and price distortions in a number of empirical cases, and that implied by the 'inefficiency' of business firms inferrable from the range in outputs with similar inputs as between 'best practice' and 'worst practice' firms. His evidence that for most economies for most of the time the latter vastly exceeds the former is of crucial policy importance, and any theory which succeeds in assimilating both phenomena within the same umbrella framework is, like unisex fashions, less an achievement than a distraction. The distinction between allocative efficiency which has to do with rational responses to price signals and all those other kinds of efficiency which raise the productivity of inputs in a business organization is an extremely useful one, and X-efficiency is as good a catch-all term for the second bundle of qualities as any other.

It is in the second dimension, in its effect in making 'best practice' better and more widely diffused, that the Japanese system of relational contracting has merits which, I suggest, more than compensate for its price-distorting consequences. To take the case of employment and the life-time commitment first, the compensatory advantages which go with the disadvantage of inflexible wage costs, are reasonably well known. In a career employment system people accept that they have continually to be learning new jobs; there can be great flexibility, it makes more sense for firms to invest in training, the organization generally is more likely to be a learning environment open to new ideas. If a firm's market is declining, it is less likely to respond simply by cutting costs to keep profits up, more likely to search desperately for new product lines to keep busy the workers it is committed to employing anyway. Hence a strong growth dynamism. And so on.

Goodwill and the spirit of market capitalism   475

As for relational contracting between enterprises, there are three things to be said. First, the relative security of such relations encourages investment in supplying firms. The spread of robots has been especially rapid in Japan's engineering sub-contracting firms in recent years, for example. Second, the relationships of trust and mutual dependency make for a more rapid flow of information. In the textile industry, for example, news of impending changes in final consumer markets is passed more rapidly upstream to weavers and yarn dyers; technical information about the appropriate sizing or finishing for new chemical fibres is passed down more systematically from the fibre firms to the beamers and dyers. Third, a by-product of the system is a general emphasis on quality. What holds the relation together is the sense of mutual obligation. The butcher shows his benevolence by never taking advantage of the fact that the customer doesn't know rump from sirloin. If one side fails to live up to his obligations, the other side is released from his. According to the relational contract ethic, it may be difficult to ditch a supplier because, for circumstances for the moment beyond his control, he is not giving you the best buy. It is perfectly proper to ditch him if he is not giving the best buy and not *even trying* to match the best buy. The single most obvious indicator of effort is product quality. A supplier who consistently fails to meet quality requirements is in danger of losing even an established relational contract. I know that even sociologists should beware of anecodotal evidence, but single incidents can often illustrate national norms and I make no apology for offering two.

1. The manager of an automobile parts supplier said that it was not uncommon for him to be rung up at home in the middle of the night by the night-shift supervisor of the car factory 60 miles away. He might be told that they had already found two defective parts in the latest batch, and unless he could get someone over by dawn they were sorry, but they'd have to send the whole lot back. And he would then have to find a foreman whom he could knock up and send off into the night.

2. The manager of a pump firm walking me round his factory explains that it is difficult to diagnose defects in the pump-castings before machining though the founders are often aware when things might have gone wrong. 'I suspect', he said cheerfully, 'our supplier keeps a little pile of defective castings in the corner of his workshop, and when he's got a good batch that he thinks could stand a bit of rubbish he throws one or two in'.

I leave the reader to guess which is the Japanese and which the British story.

HOW *UNIQUELY* JAPANESE?

So if it is the case that relational contracting has some X-efficiency advantages which compensate for allocative inefficiencies, what lessons should we draw from all this about how to run an efficient economy and build a decent society? The first thing to do is to look around at our economies and take stock of the ways in which benevolence/goodwill actually modify the workings of the profit motive in daily practice. So far I have referred to relational contracting as something the Japanese have an *unusual* preference for. But that is far from saying that they are *uniquely* susceptible to it. If we look around us we will find far more evidence of relational contracting than we think. This is so even in America where capitalism seems generally to be more hard-nosed than in Europe. In an interesting article written 20 years ago, Stewart Macaulay examined the relative importance of personal trust and enforceable legal obligation in business contracts in the USA. He found many businessmen talking of the need for give-and-take, for keeping accountants and lawyers, with their determination to press every advantage, out of direct dealings with other firms.[23] Among those with experience of large projects in the civil construction industry it is a truism that successful work requires a bond of trust between client and contractor. Engineers, as fellow-professionals, sharing a commitment to the project's success, can create that trust. Their firms' lawyers can endanger it by the confrontational stance with which they approach all potential conflicts of interest. Recently I got a simple questionnaire answered by seven managers or owner-managers of weaving mills in Blackburn asking them about their trading practices, and found a strong preference for stable long-term relationships with give-and-take on the price, and a claim that, on average, two-thirds of their business already was that way. In the British textile trade, of course, Marks and Spencers is well known for its relational contracting, squeezing suppliers a bit in times of trouble but not ditching them as long as they are maintaining quality standards, and accepting some responsibility for helping them technically. In the supermarket world, Sainsbury's have the same reputation, supposedly very different from that of Tesco's which believes that frequent switching of suppliers encourages the others to keep the price down.

QUALITY, AFFLUENCE AND RELATIONAL CONTRACTING

There may be something very significant in the nature of these examples. Try adding together the following thoughts.

1. Marks and Spencers is well known for one thing besides

>   relational contracting, namely that it bases its appeal on product quality more than on price.
> 2. There is also an apparent relation between a quality emphasis and relational contracting in Japan.
> 3. Sainsburys is up-market compared with Tesco which is for keen pricers.
> 4. Japan's consumer markets are *generally* reckoned to be more middle-class, more quality sensitive and less price sensitive than Britain's. (Textile people, for instance, have given me rough estimates that if one divides the clothing market crudely into the AB groups, fastidious about quality and not too conscious of price, and the rest who look at price and super-ficial smartness rather than the neatness of the stitching, in Britain the proportions are: 25:75; in Japan 60:40.)
> 5. Japan of the 1920s, and again in the post-war period, was much more of a cut-throat jungle than it is today. Not the ethics of relational contracting nor the emphasis on product quality nor the life-time employment system, seem to have been at all characteristic of earlier periods of Japanese in-dustrialization.

Add all these fragments together and an obvious hypothesis emerges that relational contracting is a phenomenon of affluence, a product, Hobhouse would say, of moral evolution. It is when people become better off and the market-stall haggle gives way to the world of *Which*, where best buys are defined more by quality than by price criteria, that relational contracting comes into its own.

It does so for two reasons: first because quality assurance has to depend more on trust. You always *know* whether the butcher is charging you sixpence or sevenpence. But if you don't know the difference between sirloin and rump, and you think your guests might, then you *have* to trust your butcher: you have to depend on his benevolence. Also, I suspect, when affluence reduces price pressures, any tendencies to prefer a relationship of friendly stability to the poker-game pleasures of adversarial bargaining — tendencies which might have been formerly suppressed by the anxious concern not to lose a precious penny — are able to assert themselves. Japan's difference from Britain, then, is explained both by the fact that the cultural preferences, the suppressed tendencies, are stronger *and* by the fact that the price pressures have been more reduced by a much more rapid arrival at affluence, and consequently a greater subjective sense of affluence.

The fragmentary evidence about relational contracting in inter-firm trading relations in Britain, is much more easily complemented by evidence of its growth in the labour market. Not only Britain, but Europe in general — even the USA to a lesser extent — are no longer countries where employers hire and fire without compunction. Statutory periods of notice gradually lengthen. National redundancy payment schemes recognize the expectation of continuance of an employment contract as a property right. In industries like steel, job tenures are valued at well over a year's wages. More generally, labour mobility has been falling for 15 years. Factory flexibility agreements take the employment contract further away from the original rate-for-the-specific-job basis. More attention to career-promotion systems within the firm, managerial doctrines about 'worker involvement' in the affairs of the enterprise and, inter-mittently, talk of, and even occasional moves towards, enterprise-based industrial democracy all exemplify the transformation of the employment contract into a more long-term, more diffuse commitment.

RELATIONAL CONTRACTING, RIGIDITIES AND ECONOMIC POLICY

Economists have occasionally noted these trends, but have generally treated them as market imperfections, basically lag problems of the long and the short run — for in the end, habit always succumbs to the pursuit of profit. And among imperfection problems they have found them less interesting to analyse than other kinds like monopoly. And those bold souls among them who *have* taken aboard the new phenomenon of stagflation, and tried to explain the tendency for contraction in demand to lead to a contraction in output not a fall in price, to increased unemployment but only slow, delayed and hesitant deceleration in the rate of wage increase, have rarely recognized the importance of a general growth in relational con-tracting — of the effects on the effectiveness of fiscal and monetary regulators of the fact that more and more deals are being set by criteria of fairness not by market power. More commonly, they speak of the growth of oligopoly on the one hand and on the other of trade union monopoly consequent on statutory job protection and higher welfare benefits. They have explained stagflation, in other words, not as the result of creeping benevolence — the diffusion of goodwill and mutual consideration through the economy — but as the result of creeping malevolence, increasing abuse of monopoly power. And the cure which our modern believers in the supreme virtues of the market have for these 'rigidities', is a deflation stiff enough to restore the discipline of market forces, to make firms competitive again and force the inefficient out of business, to weaken trade union monopolies and get firms hiring and firing according to their real needs.

A few people have given relational contracting and its growth the importance it is due. Albert Hirschman, first in this as in so many things, described the general syndrome of voice and loyalty taking over from exit and entry as the characteristic disciplining force of advanced capitalism.[24] More recently Arthur Okun developed before his untimely death a similarly comprehensive view of relational contracting and, moreover, explained in his *Prices and Quantities* its connection to worsening stagflation.[25] He wrote of the tendency in capital goods and intermediate markets, and to some extent in consumer markets, for what he called 'customer markets', to grow at the expense of 'auction markets', and of the corresponding growth of 'career labour markets' — employment characterized by an implicit contract of quasi-permanence — the invisible handshake is one of his phrases — all adding up to what he called a 'price-tag economy' as opposed to the 'auction economy' of orthodox text books. What I do not think he fully took aboard is the way in which social relations in customer markets and career-labour markets take on a moral quality and become regulated by criteria of fairness. Consequently, his remedies, apart from being far more imaginatively interventionist, are not so very different in kind from the more common marketist prescriptions for dealing with the rigidities of stagflation. That is to say, he also concentrates on devices to change (a) incentives and (b) expectations under the unchanged assumption that economic behaviour will continue to be guided solely by short-run income-maximizing considerations.

There is no mention of Japan in his index, and none that I have discovered in his book. But if we do think of Japan, a society which has far more developed forms of relational contracting than ours and glories in it, *and* achieves high growth and technical progress, we might think of a different prescription.

It would run something like this. First, recognize that the growth of relational contracting can provide a very real enhancement of the quality of life. Not many of us who work in a tenured job in the academic career market, for example, would relish a switch to freelance status. I hear few academics offering to surrender their basic salary for the freedom to negotiate their own price for every lecture, or even demanding personally negotiated annual salaries in exchange for tenure and incremental scales. And if you overhear a weaving mill manager on the telephone, in a relaxed friendly joking negotiation with one of his long-standing customers, you may well wonder how much more than the modest profits he expects would be required to tempt him into the more impersonal cut-and-thrust of keen auction-market-type competition.

But the second point is this. Having recognized that relational contracting is something that we cannot expect to go away, and that inevitably a lot of allocative efficiency is going to be lost, try to achieve the advantages of X-efficiency which can compensate for the loss.

This prescription has a macro-part and a micro-part. The macro-part includes, first of all, maintaining the conditions for free competition in the one set of markets which remain impersonally competitive — the markets for final consumer goods. This is necessary to provide the external stimulus for the competing chains or pyramids of relational-contract-bound producers to improve their own internal efficiency. It means on the one hand an active competition policy, and on the other, where monopoly is inevitable, the organization of countervailing consumer watchdog groups. Also included in the macro-part are first, an incomes policy, since if it *is* now criteria of fairness rather than the forces of supply and demand which determine wages in career labour markets, those fairness criteria had better be institutionalized. Second it means an attempt, if you like, to tip the ideology towards benevolence; in Fred Hirsch's terms, to try to revive an 'ethos of social obligation' to replenish the 'depleting moral legacy' which capitalism inherited from an earlier more solidary age[26], not least by stressing the importance of quality and honest thoughtful service, the personal satisfactions of doing a good job well as a source of pride and self-respect — letting profits be their own reward, not treated as if they were a proxy measure of social worth. The Department of Industry's recent announcement of an £8 million programme of subsidies for improvement in quality assurance systems in British factories is at least a recognition of the enhanced importance of quality in the modern world, even if there are no signs of a recognition that this might entail new attitudes and values (or a new affirmation of old ones now lost), a move away from the spirit of *caveat emptor*.

The micro-part of the prescription involves a better specification of the ethics of relational contracting; perhaps, as the French have been contemplating, criteria for deciding what constitutes unfair dismissal of a sub-contractor, parallel to those for employees, with protection depending on performance, including quality criteria and conscientious timing of deliveries. Second, at the enterprise level, it means taking the growth of job tenure rights not just as an unfortunate rigidity, but as an opportunity for developing a sense of community in business enterprises. It means, that is to say, reaping the production advantages which can come from a shared interest in the firm's success, from co-operation and free flow of information and a flexible willingness not to insist on narrow occupational roles. What those advantages can be we can see in Japan, but in Britain, where attitudes to authority are very different from those of Japan, the prescription probably means not manipulative policies of worker 'involvement' in existing hierarchies, but some real moves towards constitutional management, industrial democracy or what you will — anything *except* the extension of traditional forms of collective bargaining made for, and growing out of, the era of auction markets for labour.

Goodwill and the spirit of market capitalism 481

I think Hobhouse would not have objected to a lecture in his honour being used as an occasion for preaching, though I am not sure that he would have approved of the contents. I am enough of an old-fashioned liberal, however, to hope that he might.

Ronald Dore

NOTES

1. A. Smith, *The Wealth of Nations*, London, J. M. Dent, 1910, p. 13.

2. R. H. I. Palgrave, *Dictionary of Political Economy*, ed. H. Higgs, London, Macmillan, 1923-6.

3. D. Greenwald, *McGraw-Hill Dictionary of Modern Economics*, New York, McGraw-Hill, 1973.

4. P. A. Samuelson, *Economics*, Eleventh Edition, New York, London, McGraw-Hill, 1980, pp. 121-2.

5. O. E. Williamson, 'The modern corporation: Origins, evolution, attributes', *Journal of Economic Literature*, vol. 19, no. iv, December 1981.

6. V. P. Goldberg, 'A relational exchange perspective on the employment relationship', Paper for SSRC Conference, York, 1981.

7. O. E. Williamson, 'Transaction-cost economics: the governance of contractual relations', *Journal of Law and Economics*, vol. 22, no. ii, 1979, pp. 233-61.

8. R. M. Solow, 'On theories of unemployment', *American Economic Review*, vol. 70, i, 1980.

9. Seni Torihiki Kindaika Suishin Kyogikai (Association for the Promotion of the Modernization of Trading Relations in the Textile Industry), *Nenji Hōkoku* (Annual Report), 1980.

10. R. Dore, *British factory: Japanese Factory: The Origins of National Diversity in Industrial Relations*, Berkeley, University of California Press, 1973, pp. 269 ff.

11. H. Okumura, 'Masatsu o umu Nihonteki keiei no heisa-sei' (The closed nature of Japanese corporate management as a source of international friction), *Ekonomisuto*, 6 July

1982. H. Okumura, 'The closed nature of Japanese intercorporate relations', *Japan Echo*, vol. 9, no. iii, 1982.

12. H. Okumura, 'Interfirm relations in an enterprise group: The case of Mitsubishi', *Japanese Economic Studies*, Summer 1982. H. Okumura, *Shin Nihon no Rokudai-kigyō-shūdan. (A new view of Japan's six great enterprise groups)*, Tokyo, Diamond, 1983.

13. Okumura in *Japan Echo*, 1982.

14. O. E. Williamson, 'Transaction-cost economics: the governance of contractual relations', *Journal of Law and Economics*, vol. 22, no. ii, 1979, pp. 233-261.

15. A. Macfarlane, *The Origins of English Individualism*, Oxford, Basil Blackwell, 1978.

16. I. Nakatani, *The Role of Intermarket keiretsu Business Groups in Japan*, Australia-Japan Research Centre, Research Paper, no. 97, Canberra, ANU. I. Nakatani, Risuku-shearingu kara mita Nihon Keizai, ('Risk-sharing in the Japanese economy'), 'Osaka-daigaku Keizaigaku', col. 32, nos. ii-iii, December 1982.

17. E. Durkheim, *De la Division du travail social*, Paris, Felix Alcan, 1893, tr. G. Simpson, *The Division of Labour in Society*, 1960.

18. L. T. Hobhouse, *Morals in Evolution*, London, Chapman & Hall, 1908, 7th ed., 1951.

19. Durkheim, op. cit., p. 222.

20. G. Becker, *Altruism in the Family and Selfishness in the Market Place*, Centre for Labour Economics, LSE, Discussion Paper No. 73, 1980.

21. H. Leibenstein, *Beyond Economic Man: A New Foundation for Micro Economics*, Cambridge, Mass., Harvard University Press, 1976.

22. L. De Alessi, 'Property rights transaction costs and X-efficiency: An essay in economic theory', *American Economic Review*, vol. 73, no. i, March, 1983.

23. S. Macaulay, 'Non-contractual relations in business: a preliminary study', *American Sociological Review*, vol. 28, no. i, February, 1963.

24. A. O. Hirschman, *Exit, Voice and Loyalty: Responses to Decline in Firms, Organizations and States*, Cambridge, Mass., Harvard University Press, 1970.

25. A. Okun, *Prices and Quantities*, Oxford, Basil Blackwell, 1981.

26. F. Hirsch, *Social Limits to Growth*, London, Routledge & Kegan Paul, 1977.

[13]

KEYNOTE ADDRESS

Organizational Capabilities in American Industry: The Rise and Decline of Managerial Capitalism

William Lazonick[1]
Barnard College, Columbia University
and
Institute for Advanced Study, Princeton

Organizational Capabilities

Organizational capabilities represent the power of planned and coordinated specialized divisions of labor to achieve organizational goals. Through planned coordination, the specialized productive activities of masses of individuals can coalesce into a coherent collective force. Through planned coordination, organizations can integrate the various types of knowledge needed to develop new products and processes. Through planned coordination, organizations can speed the flow of work from purchased inputs to sold outputs, thereby enabling the enterprise to achieve lower unit costs.

Over the past century the growing technical and social complexity of the specialized divisions of labor that must be planned and coordinated to achieve economic success have made organizational capabilities ever more critical for attaining and sustaining competitive advantage. Increasingly and across a widening range of industries, the benefits of planned coordination in developing and utilizing productive resources have justified the high fixed costs of building the organizations that can plan and coordinate.

Organization building is a social phenomenon that can be supported or hindered by the particular political, cultural, and economic environments in which any given business enterprise purchases its inputs, produces its goods, and markets its products. It is therefore possible to characterize not only particular enterprises but also the national economies in which those enterprises operate by the existence of more or less powerful organizational capabilities. From the late nineteenth century, when international industrial

---

[1]A version of this paper will appear in Howard Gospel, ed., *Industrial Training and Technological Innovations* (London, 1990).

BUSINESS AND ECONOMIC HISTORY, Second Series, Volume Nineteen, 1990.
Copyright (c) 1990 by the Business History Conference. ISSN 0849-6825.

36

leadership passed from Britain to the United States and Germany, superior organizational capabilities were critical. So too with the rise to dominance of Japan over Britain in cotton textiles in the 1920s and 1930s--a shift in international competitive advantage that rehearsed the more recent and more broad-based successes of Japanese industry against American and European competitors [6, 16, 17].

My purpose here is to provide an outline of the development and erosion of organizational capabilities in American industry during the twentieth century--a century that has witnessed the rise and relative decline of U.S. "managerial capitalism." The general historical perspective that I shall sketch out is by no means definitive. Only in recent years has scholarly research begun to discover and comprehend the internal evolution of business organizations. There is much more detailed research to be done. My hope is that a synthesis of existing knowledge on the development and erosion of organizational capabilities in the United States will be helpful for undertaking that research, as well as for stimulating debate over the institutional dynamics of capitalist development in the late twentieth century.

The Rise of Managerial Capitalism

Since the early nineteenth century, the geographic, occupational, and social mobility of labor in the United States has placed a premium on the building of managerial structures for successful industrial enterprise. The U.S. experience contrasted with that of Britain where geographic concentrations of skilled labor, reproduced on the job and in local communities from generation to generation, made it possible to conduct a successful business enterprise with little in the way of managerial planning and coordination. In Britain, capital could move to existing supplies of labor. In the United States, capital had to entice labor to move to it or alternatively develop and utilize technologies that made the enterprise less dependent on skilled manual labor that was in scarce supply. To solve the labor problem, U.S. industrialists had to build managerial structures that could ensure the sustained availability of the requisite labor services and that could plan and coordinate the development and utilization of labor-displacing technologies [4, 15, 16].

In the nineteenth century, as today, building a managerial structure meant training personnel in relevant industrial knowledge and motivating them to use that knowledge to further the goals of the enterprise. Higher education was as yet unimportant in the training of managers. They acquired relevant knowledge on the job--typically on the shop floor--and often moved from firm to firm to expand their knowledge base, bringing with them the skills as well as business connections that they already had acquired.

The interfirm, and interindustry, mobility of such technically trained personnel was a major factor in the diffusion of new technology in the nineteenth-century United States [10, 24]. With enough acquired experience, and some financial backing, some technologists would start their own firms. But if an entrepreneur wished to take advantage of expanding market opportunities in the nineteenth century, he had to create incentives for technical specialists to remain in his employ rather than go to work for the competition. To retain these specialists, and to ensure that they used their positions of responsibility and authority for the benefit of the firm, the entrepreneur often gave key personnel stakes in the enterprise in the forms of equity shares and promises of promotion to positions of greater power and pay. Gaining the commitment of managerial personnel to the firm was a cumulative dynamic process: the more successful the firm, the greater its ability to retain and reward key managerial personnel and the more the personnel would seek to further the interests of the firm [5, 6, 14].

The building of managerial structures was, therefore, both an effect and cause of the growth of American enterprises. Extensive managerial structures evolved in industries in which high fixed costs of technology and organization could, through planned coordination and the resultant achievement of large market shares, be transformed into low unit costs. The Lowell textile firms that launched the industrial revolution in the United States had managerial structures that were more extensive and costly than those that existed in the dominant British cotton industry. But it was the growth of the railroads from the 1840s that launched the managerial revolution in the United States. Particularly as the railroads evolved into regional and national systems, it became necessary to build managerial structures to plan and coordinate the flow of people and goods [5].

The railroads not only provided a school for industrial managers-- Andrew Carnegie was the most famous "graduate"--but also gave industrial enterprises the ready access to national supply and product markets that could make high fixed-cost investments in productive technology and managerial organization potentially worthwhile. Through planned coordination, enterprises that undertook these high fixed-cost investments in organization and technology could surge ahead of their rivals in the development and utilization of productive resources. For example, with railroads providing access to national markets for materials and finished products, the leading steel and oil refining companies--Carnegie Steel and Standard Oil in particular--made huge investments in plant and equipment as well as raw materials, and then, through the planned coordination of productive activities, captured the large market shares that enabled the transformation of these high fixed costs into low unit costs. As a result, these enterprises were able to underprice their competitors and emerge as dominant in their respective industries [5, 6].

Dominant firms also emerged in machinery manufacture, such as sewing machines (Singer) and agricultural equipment (McCormick). To compete in these industries required large investments not only in production facilities but also in marketing capabilities. To be competitive, companies had to invest in the training and motivation of knowledgeable and reliable salesmen who could provide after-sales service to the equipment users and who could also supply information from the field to manufacturing personnel concerning the need and potential for product development. As product innovation became central to successful industrial enterprise, the building of an effective marketing organization became as important, if not more important, to commercial success as the building of an effective

38

production organization. In a growing number of industries, the planned coordination of production and distribution activities within an organization provided the basis for attaining and sustaining competitive advantage. To accomplish the necessary planned coordination required the building of managerial structures--firm-specific investments in, and long-term commitments to, highly trained personnel [14].

The building of organizational capabilities became even more important in the next wave of managerial enterprises that emerged from the last decades of the nineteenth century in the science-based electrical and chemical industries. As these industries developed it became apparent that the integration of production and distribution facilities would not be sufficient for a firm to sustain whatever initial competitive advantage it may have had. The further growth of the enterprise required continuous innovation, which in turn required investments in research and development facilities. Firms such as General Electric, American Telephone and Telegraph, and Du Pont led the way in establishing R & D capabilities and integrating scientific personnel into the managerial structure [11, 23].

With the rise of the science-based industries came the growing need for personnel who had attained a conceptual comprehension of science and technology prior to taking up positions in industry. Following the successful German example of wedding higher education and industrial development, American businesspeople began to look to the educational system to provide their firms with the requisite personnel. Prior to the 1890s the U.S. system of higher education, like the British Oxbridge system on which it originally was modeled, was not integrated into the industrial sphere. Even the land-grant college system that had come into being in the 1860s and that would play a key role in the integration of higher education into the economy had been created primarily to enhance the social stature of America's farmers and artisans rather than to improve their productive capabilities. As individuals trying to make a living off the land or in their workshops, however, farmers and artisans had little use for the land-grant colleges [14].

These institutions only became integrated into economic activity from the late 1880s as the United States Department of Agriculture, with the subsequent support of rural bankers, agricultural machinery makers, and mail-order houses (all interested in rural prosperity), began using the land-grant colleges to develop new agricultural technologies and train agricultural "salesmen" who, through university extension courses, could help diffuse the new technologies to the farmers. At about the same time, some land-grant colleges--most notably M.I.T.--began training mechanical, electrical, and chemical engineers and scientists ready and willing to take up employment in managerial enterprises. Many of these engineers and scientists went on to climb the managerial hierarchy to positions of industrial leadership [14, 21].

Increasingly, after the turn of the century, major firms adopted the practice of regularly recruiting most new managerial personnel--and not just scientists and engineers--from the system of higher education. At the same time, dominant business interests--Carnegie and Rockefeller to name just two of the most important--pumped financial resources back into the system of higher education to ensure that, among other things, it would be able to fulfill its new-found function of peopling the burgeoning managerial structures. The competition for business funding ultimately forced the elite institutions such as Harvard and Yale to direct some of their educational attention toward servicing the personnel needs of managerial capitalism [14].

By the 1920s the U.S. system of higher education had taken its present form and had become deeply integrated into the economic system. Higher education provided future managerial personnel not only with the basic cognitive equipment needed to comprehend the nature of increasingly complex technology but also with the behavioral socialization needed to function within the new managerial organizations. As a result, higher education became a standard credential for embarking on a managerial career. It provided the pre-employment foundations for the development of managerial personnel within the firm. Educated recruits could be expected to have the cognitive capabilities for acquiring industry-specific technical knowledge as well as the behavioral characteristics required to interact within the organizational context and respond positively to organizational incentives.

American industry now had available the semi-processed human resources on which the organizational capabilities of U.S. corporate enterprises would be built. The graduates of higher education entered the firm as lower-level technical specialists, and over the next several years were rotated from one department and function to another to enable them to gain the experience necessary to move up the corporate ladder into positions requiring general managerial capabilities. In the process the corporation determined who would move up the hierarchy furthest and fastest. But even for the most promising of managers, the climb to the top was a career-long process, during which the employee had to demonstrate continuously his (until recent years rarely her) commitment to the organization. Compared to many of the fast tracks of today, rewards for devoted performance would come slowly, but steadily and surely. With the widespread separation of ownership from control that had occurred in American industry by the first decades of this century, moreover, an ambitious managerial employee ostensibly could envision ending his career at the pinnacle of the company's hierarchy of status and power [14].

In return for the employee's long-term commitment to the organization, the enterprise made a long-term commitment to the "organization man" to provide him with employment security and social status. The firm also had a strong incentive to invest in the productive potential of the career manager. A precondition for the firm to make this commitment was an entrenched position in its relevant product markets. The firm could only offer the employee long-term security, and would only make long-term investments in human resources, if the firm itself had sound prospects for long-term survival as a productive entity.

Enterprises that experienced sustained growth, moreover, could continually create new opportunities for the exercise of authority and responsibility that could be offered to loyal managerial employees. Hence the importance for personnel management of a diversification strategy that would continually take the firm into new product and geographic markets in which it could make use of the organizational capabilities it already had

40

developed in capturing existing markets. By generating not only employment stability but also new opportunities and rewards, the continuous growth of the firm was critical to creating incentives for career managers to contribute their skills and efforts to the pursuit of organizational goals. Success bred success.

The successful implementation of a diversification strategy required the building of an appropriate organization structure. The ability to integrate technical specialists into the organization and transform some of them into general managers was the key to the success of the multidivisional structures, which, as Alfred Chandler has shown, emerged in the 1920s and diffused rapidly in the 1930s and 1940s across dominant firms in American industry [4]. The multidivisional structure enabled the firm to augment its organizational capabilities for the purpose of expanding the scope of its activities to a wider range of product lines and more geographically extensive markets.

By separating strategic from operating decision-making, top management could focus all of its attention on planning long-term investment strategies. But in focusing on strategic decision-making top management had to ensure that the operating divisions would respond to the overall goals of the firm--top management had to delegate authority to middle managers without losing control over the pursuit of the strategic objectives that had been set at the top. Essential to the superior performance of the enterprise that adopted the multidivisional structure was the organizational integration of the managerial structure through the training and motivation of salaried personnel.

Centralized control facilitated the planning and coordination of management development programs that fostered organizational integration. Management development built on the pre-employment technical and social training that managerial personnel had acquired in the nation's education system. The training acquired through management development was not confined to particular functional activities, product divisions, or geographic regions of the firm. Enterprise-wide management development programs made it possible to adopt job-rotation schemes that were part of a continuous process of transforming specialists into generalists. Often the schemes involved the movement of people not only between divisions but also from divisions to centralized staff functions and back.

Besides providing training, management development also became integral to the incentive system within the managerial structure. Management development programs expanded the potential for advancement within the firm, while encouraging junior and middle managers to conform to enterprise goals rather than to the goals of particular workgroups, functions, divisions, or regions. Given the dependence of top management on salaried employees to whom it had delegated considerable authority and in whose training the firm had made significant investments, positive incentives of promotion up the hierarchy were much more powerful inducements to securing superior performance than were negative sanctions of demotion and dismissal.

Just as the delegation of authority extended decision-making responsibility down the firm's hierarchy, so did open lines of promotion help to ensure that the loyalty of managerial personnel would extend up the hierarchy. Moreover, the very possibility for moving up the hierarchy made middle managers willing to pass on information and delegate authority to subordinates who might one day take their places, thus extending appropriate training and effective incentives further down the organizational structure. At the same time, by separating control of key staff functions from the divisions, top management ensured that critical information would not become the property of self-serving entities within the firm [14].

The Managerial Structure and the Shop Floor

The long-term attachment of salaried employees to particular organizations in effect made managerial personnel members of the firm. Not so for shop-floor workers who, even to the present in the United States, generally have the status of hourly workers who are paid set rates for performing particular jobs. A blue-collar worker may spend a "lifetime" with the firm, especially when employment operates under seniority-based union rules. But American ideology has it that the shop-floor worker is a dispensable cog in the productive machine.

Indeed, since the late nineteenth century American management has sought to put this ideology into practice through the structuring of the hierarchical and technical divisions of labor [16]. The very formation of coherent managerial structures in U.S. firms created a clear-cut segmentation between salaried managers and wage workers that contrasted sharply with the integrated character of the managerial structures themselves. The process of segmentation between managers and workers began in the late nineteenth century, and its impetus was an obsession of American managers with taking skills off the shop floor. Up until the 1870s, American industrialists, and particularly those in metal and wood manufactures, relied extensively on craft workers to organize productive activities on the shop floor. These workers often were immigrants from Britain and Germany who had acquired their skills within the more traditional workplaces of Europe. But in the last decades of the nineteenth century, the combination of expanding national markets and rapid changes in process technology gave American managers both the incentive and ability to dispense with skilled craft workers [16].

Through the planned coordination of mechanized production processes, American managers could achieve the high rates of throughput that made it possible to gain competitive advantage or were essential just to remain competitive in capital-intensive industries. The attempts by craft workers to maintain their traditional shop-floor prerogatives, even in the face of deskilling technological change, threatened the achievement of what Alfred Chandler has called economies of speed [5]. Having invested in interconnected and expensive process technologies that were capable of high levels of throughput, management did not want to be bound by traditional craft norms concerning the allocation and pace of work as well as rates of pay.

It was the challenge to the position of craft control that prompted the workers to form the American Federation of Labor in the late 1880s.

42

The rise of craft unionism, however, only strengthened the resolve of U.S. mass producers to rid their workplaces of craft control. This they did not only by the violent suppression of strikes and the victimization of union labor but also by the cooptation of some of the more skilled craftsmen-- particularly those engaged in the set-up and maintenance of machinery--- into the managerial structure as engineers and supervisors. At the same time, American managers found ready at hand a massive influx of unskilled immigrant labor, primarily from southern and eastern Europe, eager to work in the mechanized factories.

A portion of these workers were assigned to unskilled heavy labor that had not yet been mechanized. But an increasing proportion found themselves assigned to "semi-skilled" operations. The cognitive requirements of semi-skilled jobs were minimal. Besides eliminating heavy labor, machines performed what for human minds and hands had previously been complex technical functions. Meanwhile a small group of elite, skilled personnel set up and maintained the machines. Left to semi-skilled workers were routine operative functions required to maintain the flow of work. What made these jobs demanding, both physically and mentally, was the pace of work, as managers tried to extract the maximum output from the high-throughput technologies in which their firms had invested. To avoid costly downtime on, and damage to, the expensive high-throughput machinery, it was essential that the semi-skilled operatives remain attentive and cooperative on the shop floor.

Not all machine operatives obliged. In the last two decades of the nineteenth century "scientific management" arose in enterprises that had invested in modern equipment. The goal of "scientific managers" was to get these workers to cooperate in the generation of high levels of throughput. The new technologies that were being put in place were not only skill-displacing but also *effort-saving*--the same amount of output could be produced with less effort on the part of the shop-floor worker, so that generating high levels of throughput no longer *necessarily* required that the operative actually work harder and longer. If only workers would trust "scientific managers" to set output norms consistent with the effort-saving capabilities of the new technologies and to fix piece rates that would give workers a fair share of the productivity gains, both capital and labor could, as Frederick Taylor put it, "together turn their attention toward increasing the size of the surplus until this surplus becomes so large that it is unnecessary to quarrel over how it shall be divided" [16, 19].

Taylor and his disciples had little success in gaining the cooperation of workers in the generation of high levels of throughput. Workers were disinclined to place their trust in the "scientific managers," because the industrial capitalists who really ran the factories were committed to extending and prolonging the "non-union era." The capitalists simply refused to bargain with the workers' representatives. Undermining even further the quest for high throughput was the rise after the turn of the century of a more militant labor movement, headed by the Industrial Workers of the World who advocated sabotage of the flow of work in order to pose a threat to the capitalists and thereby protect the interests of shop-floor labor.

With the struggle over "restriction of output" taking center stage in capital-labor relations, industrial managers became even more insistent that skill and initiative not be left on the shop floor, and that, by the same token, shop-floor workers not have control over the reproduction of relevant skills through craft-regulated apprenticeship training. Fearful that skilled shop-floor workers would use their scarce resources to reduce their effort and increase their pay, management deemed that knowledge of the shop-floor production process must reside within the managerial structure. In the short run, as already mentioned, management transformed skilled workers into managerial personnel. In the long run, management invested in new machine technologies that displaced shop-floor skills. In the process, the semi-skilled positions were increasingly filled by new immigrants who had arrived with few skills or by blacks who had left the South in search of a better living. Ethnically as well as organizationally and economically, a social gulf separated shop-floor workers from the managers who planned and coordinated their work [16, 19].

To get these increasingly alienated shop-floor workers to supply sufficient effort to maintain the flow of work, management turned in the early decades of this century to an extensive reliance on supervisory labor --a strategy that, however, often served to exacerbate the conflict on the shop floor, especially when labor markets were tight. In its reliance on the "drive system," moreover, management had not yet resolved the problem of how to ensure that supervisors, typically recruited from among the shop-floor workers and with meager prospects for rising further up the managerial hierarchy, would act in ways that furthered organizational goals [12, 16].

From the late 1910s, pressured by the exigencies of wartime labor shortage, the mass producers began to solve the problem of restriction of output on the shop floor. With the support of a repressive state, management attacked and eliminated the radical elements in the labor movement. In the aftermath of World War I, management also rebuffed large-scale efforts--in particular the Great Steel Strike of 1919--by the more conservative AFL to organize mass-production workers. By removing the possibility for workers to gain their ends through collective union voice, the demonstration of capitalist power set the stage for more progressive measures, particularly in firms that had attained dominant market shares, to gain a degree of cooperation from semi-skilled workers.

Personnel departments were put in place to rationalize labor policies, thereby eroding the autonomy of the foremen to whom management had been obliged to delegate substantial control. "Company unions" or "employee representation committees" were set up to provide an institutional context for workers to air their grievances to management. Attention was paid to the training of foremen to promote rather than undermine cooperative shop-floor relations, and lines of authority were put in place to ensure that foremen exercised control in accordance with company personnel policy [12].

Most important, during the boom of the 1920s, a significant number of dominant enterprises began to provide their shop-floor workers with "good jobs"--employment that offered higher pay and more job security than

44

could be found in the more competitive sectors of the economy. The managements of entrenched firms began, however modestly, to share with workers the huge surpluses that their firms were accumulating, and in an era during which the labor movement was in any case weakened, workers who landed the "good jobs" were inclined to cooperate in ensuring the rapid flow of work through the production process. With effective managerial coordination of high-throughput production processes now extending down to the shop floor, the 1920s saw phenomenal productivity growth in American manufacturing. Skills had been taken off the shop floor and production workers remained but "hourly," and ostensibly dispensable, labor. Nevertheless the planned coordination of the specialized division of labor was enabling dominant managerial enterprises to win a measure of cooperation from these workers. As a result, these firms were able to transform the high fixed costs of their investments in organization and technology into low unit costs, large market shares, and huge profits [16].

Managerial Capitalism in the Age of Mass-Production Unionism

With the depression of the 1930s, the "good jobs" of shop-floor workers vanished. At the beginning of the downturn, dominant enterprises sought to maintain employment for their shop-floor workers. But as the depression deepened in the early 1930s, massive layoffs of production workers became the rule. It appears, however, that dominant enterprises made greater efforts to keep their managerial structures intact. Top executives recognized that it would be difficult to recreate integrated managerial organizations that had taken decades to build if they were permitted to break apart. The economic success of the 1920s meant that most dominant firms had the financial power to take the long view in maintaining the integrity of their managerial organizations; they came into the 1930s with huge surpluses and little debt. It also appears that many dominant firms used the doldrums of the 1930s to create new products and search for new markets, and to implement multidivisional organizational structures to carry these strategies through. If, in the crisis of the 1930s, deskilled shop-floor workers were deemed dispensable, integrated managerial structures were not [15].

As good jobs vanished, shop-floor workers sought to remake their relations with their capitalist employers. Supported by a government that recognized the political and economic advantages of a viable union movement in the mass-production industries, workers successfully put an end to the "non-union era." The major objective of the mass-production unions that arose in the last half of the 1930s was "security"--the assurance that their members would enjoy both employment stability and substantial shares in their firms' prosperity.

The key to security was seniority. Unionized mass-production workers continued to be paid hourly rates attached to jobs, the form of payment suggesting that any individual worker was dispensable to the firm. But, barring another Great Depression, seniority provisions gave workers the prospects of steady employment as well as protection against discriminatory treatment for their involvement in unions. Indeed, over time, and typically through plant-level bargaining, seniority became the basis on which shop-floor workers moved up internal job ladders to positions that paid progressively higher hourly rates. Mass-production unionism gave workers substantially more collective power that could be used to challenge managerial prerogatives to control conditions of work and pay. But by giving workers employment security mass-production unionism also helped to overcome the legacy of workers' mistrust of corporate management created by the massive layoffs during the Great Depression. The accord between organized labor and corporate management created a basis for labor-management cooperation in creating value on the shop floor [3, 6].

U.S. industrial corporations also ensured that unionization did not extend too far up the organizational hierarchy. Specifically, in the mid-1940s attempts at unionization by foremen were stifled, helped by a legal ruling that declared that foremen were part of management, and hence could not demand union recognition under the National Labor Relations Act. With well-developed personnel departments in place--and extending a process of organizational integration that had already begun in the non-union era of the 1920s--corporate management was able to delegate supervisory authority to foremen without fear that these recruits from the shop floor would abuse their managerial power. By definitively according managerial status to foremen, moreover, corporations extended a powerful positive incentive to shop-floor workers by giving them the opportunity of rising to managerial positions, even if there was little chance of promotion beyond the level of first-line supervisor. In the 1940s the problem of "the man in the middle" was resolved in a way that established effective lines of authority and communication between the higher management levels and the shop floor. These organizational linkages enhanced managerial control [16, 18].

This modified structure of managerial capitalism enabled U.S. mass producers to take advantage of the propitious macroeconomic conditions of the 1940s and dominate the international economy into the 1960s. But it is important to note that the organizational structures available to U.S. mass producers were not creations of the post-World War II era. Rather they were extensions of a process of organization building that had begun in the late nineteenth century and that permitted most of the enterprises that had emerged as dominant in the rise of managerial capitalism to remain dominant into the second half of the twentieth century. Although unions now shared power with management in bargaining over shares of value gains, workers left investment decisions to management; unlike the earlier craft organizations, their unions were not inherently opposed to technological change and redivisions of labor on the shop floor. In the postwar era of economic growth and U.S. international dominance, mass-production unionism showed itself to be compatible with the transformation of high fixed costs into low unit costs in mass-production enterprises.

Ensuring the continued dominance of the U.S. economy in the 1940s and 1950s was the movement of many U.S. firms into new product and geographic markets. The growth of multinational operations would not have been possible if the U.S.-based enterprises that went multinational had not already developed the organizational capabilities needed to dominate the

46

vast U.S. domestic market. The continued growth of many of these firms, and their ability to share the gains of success with their managers and workers, would not have been possible without huge investments in research and development--activities that enabled enterprises to build on their existing technological capabilities to generate product innovations. In the United States during the 1940s and 1950s, these firm-level investments in R & D received substantial support from private and public funding that enabled a vast expansion of the system of higher education, as well as from direct government financial support, generally justified as military expenditures, but with apparently significant spillovers into commercial uses [20].

The Decline of Managerial Capitalism

Since the 1960s U.S. industry has entered into a period of long-term relative decline, not unlike the experience of British industry since the late nineteenth century. As both cause and effect of this decline has been the erosion of the organizational capabilities that U.S. industrial corporations had built up over the previous half century, if not longer. During the 1960s the erosion of the organizational capabilities of U.S. industrial enterprises began on the shop floor--the weakest link in the structure of organizational integration that had been achieved previously. Shop-floor workers had never been extended "membership" in the firms for which they labored; in their work they had been reduced to "appendages of the machines" (to use Karl Marx's apt phrase), and they belonged to powerful union organizations that could refuse to cooperate with management in the bargaining process if workers' interests were not being met. During the 1970s and 1980s, however, the erosion of the organizational capabilities of the major U.S. industrial corporations has gone much further than loss of control over the shop-floor labor force. As we shall see, the erosion of organizational capabilities has also occurred within the managerial structures themselves.

The result has been the waning of "managerial capitalism" as a dominant force in international industrial competition. The decline of managerial capitalism has not occurred in a competitive vacuum. The U.S. economy has been in *relative* decline. That is, the dominant managerial enterprises that form the core of the U.S. economy have continued to grow, and in many cases even innovate, but in their competitive capabilities, these enterprises have been surpassed by more powerful modes of business organization, particularly those emanating from the Japanese economy.

Elsewhere I have elaborated on the characteristics of the organizational capabilities of Japanese "collective capitalism" that have made the institutions of "managerial capitalism" obsolete [16, 17]. Suffice it to say here that the strength of Japanese enterprise derives from organizational integration that extends beyond the limits of the planned coordination of the specialized division of labor as practiced under U.S. managerial capitalism. First, organizational integration in Japan extends across horizontally and vertically related *firms* to a much greater extent than in the United States (where such integration is indeed often illegal) so that planned coordination spans units of financial control to encompass multifirm business organizations. Second, within dominant Japanese enterprises, organizational integration extends further down the organizational hierarchy, beyond the managerial structure itself, to include male blue-collar workers.

Both these extensions of organizational integration significantly enhance the organizational capability available to Japanese industry while significantly increasing the risks confronted by American firms that would attempt to make the huge investments in facilities and personnel necessary to remain competitive. Confronted by an international economy that they no longer dominate, many major U.S. enterprises have sought to adapt on the basis of the past successes, thereby reaping the returns on their prior investments without committing sufficient resources to ensure their future prosperity. Short-run adaptive responses inevitably lead to the erosion of organizational capabilities as the business enterprise can no longer maintain the incentives for key employees to remain committed to the organization --even if, as is increasingly less likely to be the case, these employees have the training and the physical facilities available that are necessary to enable the enterprise to remain at the forefront of innovation.

Deskilling on the Shop Floor

As already indicated, the vulnerability of American industrial enterprises to superior organizational capabilities from abroad was greatest on the shop floor. With a few exceptions such as IBM and Kodak, U.S. industrial enterprises had never made long-term employment *commitments* (as distinct from implicit promises) to their shop-floor workers. Inherent in insistence by American managers of their "right to manage" the shop floor was the ideology that, at any time and for any job, any individual shop-floor worker was dispensable--paid by the "hour" for the job at hand and no more.

In terms of workers' *skills*, managerial ideology could claim some relevance. Intent on taking skills off the shop floor where workers might use them to control the pace of work, U.S. managerial enterprises had not made significant investments in the skills of shop-floor workers. Management tended not to count the deskilled shop-floor worker among the firm's valued assets. But in terms of workers' *efforts*, this managerial ideology was much less well-founded. In practice, to gain the cooperation of shop-floor workers in maintaining the rapid and steady flow of work so essential to achieving low unit costs, management had to offer them a measure of employment security and a share (however indirect) in the prosperity of the enterprise [16].

Prior to the Great Depression, some of the more farsighted industrial managers had systematized their personnel policies to provide hardworking shop-floor workers with realistic promises of economic security. As we have seen, when the promises were not kept during the Great Depression, workers took the matter of economic security into their own hands. Once the major industrial corporations had recognized the new mass-production unions, it was not managerial personnel policy but rather the workers' own collective organizations with their emphasis on seniority rights that would provide workers with the employment security and economic gains critical for gaining their cooperation in the workplace. In effect managers of most

48

of the great U.S. industrial corporations came to rely on independent union organizations to ensure the stability of the long-term relation between shop-floor workers and the firms for which they worked.

This institutional arrangement remained viable as long as the U.S. industrial corporations continued to dominate their markets. But when, in the 1960s and 1970s, the corporations stumbled in the face of international competition and sought to roll back the bargaining gains that workers had made over the previous decades, the adversarial character of U.S. labor-management relations broke through the cooperative veneer. In industries such as steel and automobiles that were dominated by adaptive (as distinct from innovative) oligopolists, the costs of the accord with labor that had been struck in the 1940s began to outstrip productivity gains. As long as there was no serious foreign competition and the U.S. national firms in an industry did not engage in significant price competition among themselves, U.S. corporations were able to pass off higher labor costs to consumers in the form of higher prices. By the late 1960s, however, the limits of the adaptive strategy had been reached. With powerful international competitors on the scene, domestic inflation only served to erode U.S. international competitive advantage [16].

The U.S. competitiveness problem was not only higher wages but also lagging productivity growth. High wages, tight labor markets, and the availability of unemployment benefits--not to mention the restiveness of younger blue-collar workers, both black and white, in the wake of the civil rights and antiwar movements--had weakened managerial control over shop-floor workers. Alienated in any case by the routine nature of their work and without any formal power to influence the nature of the work environment, blue-collar workers sought to control their expenditure of effort by unauthorized work stoppages, work to rule, and absenteeism, all of which had adverse consequences for productivity.

In the 1970s many observers of American industry pointed to the alienated shop-floor worker, confined to routine and repetitive tasks requiring little skill development, as an explanation of the slowdown in the growth of labor productivity in American manufacturing that had begun in the mid-1960s. In many plants around the country, experiments in job enlargement and job enrichment were undertaken to try to enhance "the quality of worklife" (as it was called) in order to elicit more effort from workers. Although the initial impacts of these programs were generally positive, many of the experiments in the early 1970s were cut short when the workers whose jobs had been enriched and enlarged began questioning traditional managerial prerogatives. In the long run, attempts such as these at piecemeal transformation of the organizational structure may well have reduced rather than enhanced organizational capability by creating expectations for more meaningful work which in the end were not fulfilled [13, 16, 25].

In the 1980s Japanese success in taking market share away from once-dominant U.S. mass producers made it clear that the prime source of Japanese competitive advantage was not low wages (as many Americans had chosen to believe in the 1970s) but superior organizational capabilities. Many American industrial managers also came to recognize that the major difference between the internal organization of U.S. and Japanese enterprises was the extent to which Japanese managers *developed* skills on the shop floor and delegated authority to blue-collar workers to use those skills to ensure a rapid flow of high-quality work. As a result of the Japanese challenge, American industrial managers began to realize that enhancing "the quality of worklife" was not just a means of eliciting effort from workers (as had been the case in the failed experiments of the 1970s).

Rather industrial managers came to recognize that upgrading the skills of the shop-floor labor force was an end in itself because it augmented the firm's human-resource "assets." To maintain the rapid flow of high-quality work using new, automated manufacturing technologies requires shop-floor workers with the cognitive capabilities to ensure that the machines work properly with a minimum of downtime. U.S. mass-production industries can no longer compete using workers whose own mechanical motions merely complement those of the machine, as previously has been the case. The effective use of the new technologies requires shop-floor workers who can ensure the quality, as well as the quantity, of work [16, 22].

As a precondition for technology-specific training for workers under the auspices of the employing enterprise itself, the large-scale adoption of new "flexible" technologies requires a supply of more highly educated shop-floor workers than U.S. industry has used or has had available in the past. To generate a large supply of workers capable of acquiring the requisite training both within and outside the manufacturing enterprise, institutional rigidities in the U.S. educational system must be confronted. When, in the early twentieth century, vocational schooling entered U.S. secondary education to track youths away from college and into the blue-collar labor force, the resultant segmentation of the labor force was consistent with the social division of labor between managers and workers in the world of work [2]. But in recent decades the same educational system has lost touch with the changing human-resource needs of an industrial era in which the potential for automation has created a new role for shop-floor workers in monitoring the quality, as well as ensuring the quantity, of work [22].

Mass Education and Deskilled Labor

What is now needed is an educational system that rejects the conception of the worker as a mere appendage of the machine and prepares future workers for active involvement in speeding the flow of work while maintaining its quality in the "flexible" factory. There is no point, however, in building new organizational structures and educational systems if those who run the largest industrial corporations eschew innovative investment strategies that can make use of skilled workers who are encouraged to exercise initiative on the shop floor. Yet prevailing organizational structures within U.S. manufacturing enterprises may be inhibiting the adoption of innovative investment strategies because they reflect a century-long managerial obsession with taking skills, and initiative, off the shop floor. It would appear that even entering the 1990s many, if not most, American

50

managers are reluctant to develop skills on the shop floor for fear of losing control of the flow of work [16].

Despite conservative investment strategies in the mass-production industries, the 1980s witnessed, somewhat belatedly, the widespread recognition of the need to improve the quality of mass education in the United States.   At the same time, however, blue-collar workers have experienced massive, and typically permanent, layoffs in the face of international competition.   Good blue-collar jobs have vanished in the United States, not because of a lack of effective demand as in the 1930s but because of the supply-side effectiveness of international competitors. Youths in working-class schools and communities see that the good jobs are no longer there. Yet they are confronted with an educational system that is geared toward generating blue-collar workers who will be able and willing to spend their lives doing routine work. The system no longer has a hold on them. Particularly in black communities, class discipline, a modicum of which was previously secured by the prospects of steady and well-paying blue-collar jobs, has broken down.

The Decline of Innovation

Although mass education for blue-collar workers has been deteriorating, the United States still possesses a powerful system of higher education, capable of generating technical specialists required for innovation in the late twentieth century. But the system of higher education is less integrated into the U.S. industrial economy than it used to be. For one thing, international competitors, with their powerful organizational capabilities in place, are able to make ample use of the open U.S. system of higher education.   One reason why U.S. industrial corporations are having increasing difficulty in maintaining control over intellectual property is that they have become too reliant on the publicly funded educational institutions to foot the bills for R & D, rather than, as they did in the past, use the higher educational system as the foundation for investments in in-house R & D. In addition, over the post-World War II decades, the spillover of military R & D expenditures to civilian uses appears to have diminished [20].

At the same time, the evolution of U.S. financial institutions has generated strong disincentives for highly educated Americans to become technical specialists and pursue the types of managerial careers with particular enterprises that, as outlined above, were critical to the building of organizational capabilities in the era of U.S. industrial dominance. The deregulation movement of the 1970s and the related financial revolution of the 1980s opened up new opportunities for the graduates of higher education to make large sums of money quickly with little experience in either technology or the organizations for which they worked. The new opportunities made the slow climb up the managerial hierarchy of an industrial corporation distinctly less attractive for these educated personnel. When combined with the rise of formidable international competition, moreover, the financial revolution has placed the long-term existence of many once-stable industrial corporations in jeopardy, so that the firm-specific career that a college graduate could once take for granted is now by no means assured [15].

More generally, the domination of financial interests over industrial interests has been eroding U.S. organizational capabilities even at the managerial level where historically organizational integration in the United States had been most complete. To be innovative in the late twentieth century requires not only appropriate human-resource development and far-reaching organizational integration but also massive financial commitments in the face of returns that are more uncertain than ever. In general, financial commitment means that those who, as employees, creditors, or owners, can lay claim to the revenues of the firm will not enforce those claims in ways that undermine the development and utilization of the firm's organizational capabilities [15]. In the private-sector enterprise, financial commitment generally means the retention of earnings for the sake of developing the resources of the firm. High degrees of financial commitment characterize those industrial enterprises in Japan and Germany that are the major international competitors in the late twentieth century. In international competition, financial commitment has become ever more critical to the development and utilization of organizational capabilities. Yet since the 1950s a number of forces in the U.S. economy have been eroding financial commitment.

The erosion began within the industrial enterprise itself. During the first half of the century when the major U.S. industrial corporations rose to international dominance, ownership was increasingly separated from control. Stockholding was widely dispersed among portfolio investors who, by virtue of the fragmentation of ownership, ceded to professional managers the right to determine the allocation of the firm's financial resources. The interests of these top managers were bound up with the interests of their managerial organizations. They had typically pursued their careers with the firms that they now ran. As salaried managers, moreover, their only claims to higher levels of remuneration derived from the long-run competitive performance of the enterprise.

During the 1950s, however, top managers ceased to be merely salaried employees. Through stock-based compensation systems, they became substantial owners, and hence the beneficiaries of the prolonged run up in stock prices that ended only at the close of the 1960s. During the 1950s and 1960s, the incentives increased for top managers of the major corporations to identify with the short-run market performance of their companies' stocks. The methods for improving short-run performance often conflicted with the long-term financial requirements for building organizational capability for the sake of sustained innovation.

By the same token, top managers now had vastly more scope than previously to use their positions of strategic management as the basis for their own individual aggrandizement rather than as the basis for the development of the organizational capabilities of their enterprises as a whole. Hence as an alternative to engaging in innovative investment strategies in their current or technologically related lines of business, many top managers of the 1960s became conglomerateurs, each one with financial control over a multitude of industrial enterprises in which he had neither

52

organizational roots nor technological expertise. These conglomerate managers controlled the financial resources required to undertake innovative investment strategies. But the planning and coordination of these strategies was the task of the new "middle" managers--often (initially at least) the former top managers of the acquired companies who now headed the conglomerate divisions and who had the requisite understanding of the division's organizational capabilities to manage the innovation process.

Besides knowledge of products, processes, and people, however, the management of innovation requires financial commitment--and more specifically control over the allocation of enterprise earnings--which is precisely what the new "middle" managers whose role it was to manage innovation within the conglomerate structure no longer had the power to provide. Moreover, evaluated by the head office on the basis of their short-term performance, the divisional heads who indeed pursued innovative investment strategies quickly learned (if they were still around to make use of their knowledge) that adaptive behavior--managerial behavior that did not make large and sustained demands on enterprise earnings--got a better reception from the conglomerate bosses.

Although the conglomerate movement abated and indeed reversed itself somewhat in the 1970s as many ill-managed divisions were sold off, considerable damage to the organizational capability of many U.S. industrial corporations had been done. At the same time, increasingly powerful international competitive challenges made the top managers of U.S. industrial enterprises think twice about committing their firms' resources to long-run innovative strategies. Instead the tendency was for these firms to try to adapt on the basis of their successful investments of the past. In this adaptive mode, the rewards of promotion to top management positions went to those who displayed the most talent for improving the "bottom line." We can conjecture that it was this type of top manager, driven by financial goals, who was most likely to cooperate with the raiders in the hostile takeover movement of the 1980s. The popularity of "golden parachutes" and other compensation schemes designed to bribe top management to make way for corporate raiders revealed that America's industrial leaders could pursue their own individual ends not only through the medium of the securities markets but also by selling their very offices of financial control.

The use of securities markets to buy and sell industrial enterprises for the sake of individual gain has often torn apart U.S. organizational capabilities without creating the conditions for putting more powerful organizational capabilities in their place. The problem is not mergers and acquisitions per se, but the purposes for which, and the conditions under which, they are undertaken. It may make strategic sense for an innovative firm to acquire or merge with other existing enterprises which have already developed unique capabilities rather than adopt the much slower and more uncertain strategy of developing these operations from the ground up. The success of such mergers and acquisitions in permitting the production of higher quality goods at lower unit costs depends on the willingness and the ability of the previously distinct and separate enterprises to integrate their capabilities so as to join forces in pursuit of a common organizational goal.

As demonstrated by the history of British economic decline, however, the simple vertical or horizontal amalgamation of firms or operations without organizational integration does not result in sustained competitive advantage--a lesson that was repeated in the United States with the rise and fall of the conglomerate movement in the 1960s and 1970s [6]. Financial integration does not imply organizational integration. And as demonstrated by the organizational advantages of the Japanese system of enterprise groups, organizational integration can occur across units of distinct financial control [1].

As financial commitment and organizational capability have eroded, the United States has lost competitive advantage not only in the "mature" industries of the Second Industrial Revolution but also in the high-technology industries of the Third Industrial Revolution [7, 8]. The formation of Sematech as a consortium of the major U.S. electronic firms to combine resources in the research and development of semiconductors was a step in the direction of a more collective capitalism that might have been able to respond to the new competition. Yet even IBM--the U.S. industrial organization par excellence--is so consumed with its struggles for restructuring its own product lines that it has been unable to provide effective leadership in restructuring the supply of its industry's vital capital inputs. The example of Japan suggests that the generation of innovation and the attainment of competitive advantage in such technologically complex and high fixed-cost industries require thoroughgoing vertical integration of the industry's productive capabilities as well as a degree of horizontal cooperation among major competitors in ensuring the supply of high-quality capital goods.

In the high fixed-cost, high-technology industries, it is only such collectivized organizations that can effectively nurture and sustain innovative new ventures into dynamic going concerns. The experience of the 1980s showed that the mode of venture capital that provided the financial commitment to innovative new ventures in the past is no longer adequate to meet the exigencies of the new international competition. Although the venture capital funds grew enormously during the 1980s, a plethora of venture capital firms competing for scarce high-technology personnel and eager for short-term returns have undermined the building of the organizational capabilities that the success of innovative investment strategies requires [15].

The comparative history of capitalist development--and in particular the successful Japanese challenge to the once-dominant United States, not to mention the previously dominant Britain--shows that now more than ever industrial leadership requires the long-term commitment of resources to organizations that can plan and coordinate the development and utilization of productive capabilities. In developed capitalist economies, however, those who control wealth can choose to live off the past rather than invest in the future. A necessary condition for continued investment in innovation, marked by the building of organizational capabilities, is that such adaptive behavior be constrained. A sufficient condition is that the economic uncertainty inherent in innovative investments be reduced by means of

54

policies that educate the labor force, mobilize committed financial resources, and coordinate interdependent innovative efforts [17].

References

1. Michael Best, The New Competition (Cambridge, MA, 1990).
2. Samuel Bowles and Herbert Gintis, *Schooling in Capitalist America* (New York, 1976).
3. David Brody, *Workers in Industrial America* (New York, 1980).
4. Alfred D. Chandler Jr., *Strategy and Structure* (Cambridge, MA, 1962).
5. _____, *The Visible Hand* (Cambridge, MA, 1977).
6. _____, *Scale and Scope: The Dynamics of Industrial Capitalism* (Cambridge, MA, 1990).
7. Stephen S. Cohen and John Zysman, *Manufacturing Matters* (New York, 1987).
8. Michael L. Dertouzos, Richard K. Lester, and Robert M. Solow, *Made in America: Regaining the Productive Edge* (Cambridge MA, 1989).
9. Robert Hayes and William Abernathy, "Managing Our Way to Economic Decline," *Harvard Business Review*, 58 (July-August 1980).
10. David Hounshell, *From the American System to Mass Production 1800-1932* (Baltimore, 1984).
11. _____, and John K. Smith Jr., *Science and Corporate Strategy: Du Pont R & D, 1902-1980* (Cambridge, ENG, 1988).
12. Sanford Jacoby, *Employing Bureaucracy: Managers, Unions, and the Transformation of Work in American Industry, 1900-1945* (New York, 1985).
13. Thomas A. Kochan, Harry C. Katz, and Robert B. McKersie, *The Transformation of American Industrial Relations* (New York, 1986).
14. William Lazonick, "Strategy, Structure, and Management Development in the United States and Britain," in Kesaji Kobayashi and Hidemasa Morikawa, eds., *Development of Managerial Enterprise* (Tokyo, 1986).
15. _____, "Controlling the Market for Corporate Control: The Historical Significance of Managerial Capitalism." Paper presented to the Third International Joseph A. Schumpeter Society Meetings, Airlie, Virginia, June 3-5, 1990.
16. _____, *Competitive Advantage on the Shop Floor* (Cambridge, MA, 1990).
17. _____, *Business Organization and the Myth of the Market Economy* (Cambridge, ENG, 1991).
18. Nelson Lichtenstein and Stephen Meyer, eds., *On the Line: Essays in the History of Auto Work* (Urbana IL, 1989).
19. David Montgomery, *The Fall of the House of Labor* (Cambridge, ENG, 1987).
20. Richard R. Nelson, "U.S. Technology Leadership: Where Did It Come From and Where Did It Go?" Paper presented to the Third International Joseph A. Schumpeter Society Meetings, Airlie, Virginia, June 3-5, 1990.
21. David Noble, *America by Design* (New York, 1977).
22. Michael Piore and Charles Sabel, *The Second Industrial Divide* (New York, 1984).
23. Leonard Reich, *The Making of American Industrial Research* (Cambridge, ENG, 1985).
24. Ross Thomson, *The Path to Mechanized Shoe Production in the United States* (Chapel Hill, NC, 1989).
25. Richard E. Walton, "From Control to Commitment: Transforming Work Force Management in the United States," in Kim B. Clark, Robert H. Hayes, and Christopher Lorenz, eds., *The Uneasy Alliance: Managing the Productivity-Technology Dilemma* (Boston, 1985).

Part III
The Dynamics of Success

[14]

William Mass

Mechanical and Organizational Innovation: The Drapers and the Automatic Loom

The Draper Company's commitment to research and development was unparalleled among other nineteenth-century American manufacturers in older industries. This innovative drive, coupled with a strategy of patent defense and control, carried the firm to the top of the cotton textile machine industry by the end of the century. The company's 1907 decision to follow a less innovative path seemed sensible in light of its secure position in a volatile market, but the costs in long-term competitive strength were high.

From the 1870s until the mid-twentieth century, the Draper Company was the single most important innovative force in the cotton textile machine industry (see Table 1). In the 1870s and 1880s, it was the leading actor in the development and continued improvement of high-speed ring spinning, the most important spinning innovations of the late nineteenth century textile industry. In weaving technology, the Draper automatic loom, introduced in 1895, was a breakthrough invention whose fundamental design remained the industry standard, unrivaled by any twentieth-century textile innovation until the development of shuttleless looms after the Second World War.

Behind this record of success in mechanical invention lies a history of innovation in business organization as well. By the early twentieth century, the Drapers had achieved a dominant market position, protected by barriers to competition. They faced the strategic choice

WILLIAM MASS is associate professor in the Policy and Planning Department of the College of Management Science at the University of Lowell.

I would like to thank William Lazonick in particular for helpful comments on earlier drafts of this paper, as well as the editors and two anonymous referees of this journal, Dane Morrison, and the participants in the University of California Intercampus Group in Economic History, 1988. Parts of this research were supported by grants-in-aid from the Museum of American Textile History and the University of Connecticut Research Foundation.

Business History Review 63 (Winter 1989): 876–929. © 1989 by The President and Fellows of Harvard College.

Draper and the Automatic Loom / 877

Table 1
A Chronology of Draper-Associated Firms, 1816–1967

1816–1830	Ira Draper
1825–1830	Ira Draper (with son James)
1830–1838	James Draper
1838–1852	E. D. Draper
1852–1868	E. D. & G. Draper
1856–1897	Dutcher Temple Company (1856–1867 W. W. Dutcher Temple Co.)
1856–1897	Hopedale Machine Company (1880—merged with Hopedale Furnace Co., est. 1856) (1896—bought Hopedale Elastic Goods Co., est. 1887)
1868–1877	George Draper & Son (E. D. Draper's share bought out by his nephew William F. Draper in 1868)
1873–1912	Sawyer Spindle Company
1877–1897	George Draper & Sons (George's sons George A. and Eben S. Draper admitted as partners in 1877 and 1880; William F. Draper's sons, William F., Jr., and George Otis Draper, made partners in 1887 and 1889)
1888–1897	Hopedale Machine Screw Company
1892–1897	Northrop Loom Company
1897–1916	Draper Company (1897 absorbed George Draper & Sons, Hopedale Machine Co., Dutcher Temple Co., Hopedale Machine Screw Co.; assumed exclusive agency for the Sawyer Spindle Co. and the U.S. rights of the Northrop Loom Co.)
1916–1967	Draper Corporation[a]

[a]In 1967 the Draper Corporation, by then including several subsidiary firms, merged with the North American Rockwell Corporation.

Sources: George Otis Draper, *Facts and Figures for Textile Manufacturers* (Hopedale, Mass., 1896), v–viii; *Cotton Chats*, no. 73 (June 1908); G. O. Draper, *Textile Texts*, 3d ed. (Hopedale, Mass., 1907), v–vii; Thomas R. Navin, *The Whitin Machine Works* (Cambridge, Mass., 1950), 202; "Notice of Special Meeting of Stockholders," Draper Corporation, 26 May 1967, photocopy in possession of author.

that confronts any entrenched innovative firm when it considers what to do with its legacy of previous technological success: whether to continue the commitment to the development of significant new technologies or to mine existing resources through more adaptive technical change. In 1907 a struggle among Draper family factions resulted in a change in top management and a reorientation of the company's development policy toward a more adaptive path. This article describes the history of the Draper Company's rise to technological leadership and the critical 1907 shift in strategic policy, and it briefly examines the consequences of that decision.

William Mass / 878

Little is known about the extent of industrial research during the mid-nineteenth century in industries associated with the First Industrial Revolution, but the Draper Company's early and extensive commitment of resources to industrial research seems distinctive. Recent studies of early industrial research have emphasized its origins in changes in the business environment that do not apply to the Draper experience—in the growth of science-based chemical and electrical firms identified as the core of the Second Industrial Revolution and in the establishment of industrial laboratories as part of the central office rationalization and planning that often followed extensive mergers.[1] In contrast to these models, the Draper Company successfully developed new technologies in the oldest of mechanical industries rather than in the newly emerging sectors characterized by high concentrations of scientific and engineering personnel. The Drapers employed few formally trained engineers or scientists, and well into the twentieth century most of their inventors were trained through industry experience as operators, draughtsmen, or mechanics. Moreover, increased administrative coordination of research efforts more often led than followed the company's success as a manufacturer.

Within the textile industry, most of the conventional picture of technical progress is based on the more extensively studied early British textile industry. Technical change there, including the origins of mechanized spinning and power loom weaving, occurred through incremental, fragmented improvements in firms across the industry, and innovation was not characterized by concentrated research and development expenditures. After mechanized factory production was established, the next major British technological breakthrough was the development of the self-acting mule. The engineering firm of Sharp, Roberts & Company committed sufficient resources to invent a self-acting mule only after spinning manufacturers, responding to striking mule spinners in 1825, collectively asked Richard Roberts to develop a self-actor.[2]

In the United States, the Waltham system was noted for its relatively high capital costs, but early American technology was "bor-

[1] Leonard Reich, *The Making of American Industrial Research* (New York, 1985); David Mowery, "The Emergence and Growth of Industrial Research in American Manufacturing, 1899–1945" (Ph.D. diss., Stanford University, 1981); David Mowery and Nathan Rosenberg, *Technology and the Pursuit of Economic Growth* (New York, 1989), chaps. 3 and 4; Alfred D. Chandler, Jr., "From Industrial Laboratories to Departments of Research and Development," in *The Uneasy Alliance: Managing the Productivity-Technology Dilemma*, ed. Kim Clark, Robert H. Hayes, and Christopher Lorenz (Boston, Mass., 1985).
[2] H. Catling, *The Spinning Mule* (Newton Abbot, 1970), 37.

Draper and the Automatic Loom / 879

rowed" from abroad (although subsequent technical improvements and adaptations were of dramatic cumulative importance).[3] The pattern of industrial research and the trajectory of textile machine design in the United States diverged from the pattern of the British machine industry after the mid-nineteenth century.[4] The Drapers' contribution to high-speed ring spinning and automatic weaving made them worldwide leaders in the development of textile technology, and the scale of inventive activities within the Draper Company by the beginning of the twentieth century was comparable to that within the new, large, science-based firms. Yet the degree to which this one U.S. firm was central to the innovation process in the textile industry has received little attention.

Origins of the Draper Business and Early Inventions: Temples

The origins of the American textile machinery industry from the 1790s to the 1820s are well known. In both the extensive, capital-intensive Waltham system and the smaller, more specialized Slater operations, the "bootstrap" tasks of equipping the early cloth factories took place within the textile machine shops and gave mechanical form to the Industrial Revolution in America. From the late 1820s to the end of the 1840s, many new and independent machine shops were formed, selling a large variety of machinery over a widening geographical area. By the mid-nineteenth century, the industry consisted of firms with broad product lines as machine builders increasingly diversified their production. Nineteen firms were responsible for most of the sales of textile machinery: seven fully diversified machine shops, five firms increasingly diversified yet without a complete machinery line, and six specialized producers making only looms or one or two types of carding or spinning frames.[5]

---

[3] David J. Jeremy, *Transatlantic Industrial Revolution: The Diffusion of Textile Technologies between Britain and America, 1790–1830's* (Cambridge, Mass., 1981).

[4] For a review of the technologies and institutional factors permitting continued expansion of the British cotton industry, see William Lazonick and William Mass, "The Performance of the British Cotton Industry, 1870–1913," *Research in Economic History*, ed. Paul Uselding, vol. 9 (Spring 1984); William Lazonick, "Industrial Organization and Technological Change: The Decline of the British Cotton Industry," *Business History Review* 57 (Summer 1983): 195–236; and William Mass and William Lazonick, "The British Cotton Industry and Competitive Advantage: The State of the Debates," *Business History* 32 (Oct. 1990): 9–65, also reprinted in *International Competition and Strategic Response in the Textile Industry since 1870*, ed. Mary B. Rose (London, 1991).

[5] George Gibb, *The Saco-Lowell Shops* (Cambridge, Mass., 1950), 169–70, 208–9; Thomas R. Navin, *The Whitin Machine Works Since 1831* (Cambridge, Mass., 1950), 485–86.

William Mass / 880

Although most fundamental textile machine designs had been smuggled in from Britain, American firms were noted for contributing significant technical improvements during the formative years. By the middle of the century, few significant innovations were originating in the larger machine shops.[6] The relative contribution of the large shops as a group to technological advance continued to decline, an important factor in their ultimate demise. The most important improvements came from independent inventors, most often mill overseers or mechanics. Such inventors often did not open their own shops, but instead sold the use of their patent rights. They either accepted a lump sum payment or licensed one or more machine manufacturers to serve as intermediaries, collecting royalties from mill customers.[7]

Ira Draper, a resident of Weston, Massachusetts, came out of this milieu. He was a prolific inventor of farm equipment and was sufficiently prominent in his patent activity to be mentioned by John Quincy Adams among those considered (but not appointed) as Commissioner of Patents.[8] But Draper's primary business was based on two textile-related patents—one for a revolving loom temple dating from 1816 and another for an improved version in 1829. In New England, the necessity of manually readjusting the temples on the edges of the cloth as it was woven limited each weaver to the operation of a single power loom. Ira Draper's invention enabled a New England weaver to run two looms at a time.

Ira sold his textile patent rights and the temple business to his eldest son, James. As the sole patentee from 1830 to 1837, James Draper primarily, if not exclusively, licensed other companies as manufacturers and suppliers of the loom temples. Whatever the specific terms of these licensing arrangements with independent suppliers, he retained sufficient control and incentive to advertise temples personally, both to cloth mills and to loom manufacturers. The temples sold for $2 a pair including royalty rights.[9] James Draper brought in his stepbrother E[benezer]. D. Draper as managing partner in 1837 and retired to farming.

[6] Gibb, *Saco-Lowell Shops*, 192, 214.
[7] Navin, *Whitin Machine Works*, 112–13.
[8] William F. Draper, *Recollections of a Varied Career* (Boston, Mass., 1908), 3–4; George O. Draper, *Textile Texts*, 2d ed. (Hopedale, Mass., 1903), 261; *Cotton Chats*, no. 1 (July 1901). *Cotton Chats* was the Draper Company house organ.
[9] *Cotton Chats*, no. 2 (Aug. 1901): The *Boston Daily Evening Transcript* ran the following advertisement on 24 July 1830:

NOTICE TO MANUFACTURERS
Draper's Patent Self-Moving Temples, are now in operation on all looms at Waltham and Lowell, also at various other factories. . . . Any person wishing to obtain said

Draper and the Automatic Loom / 881

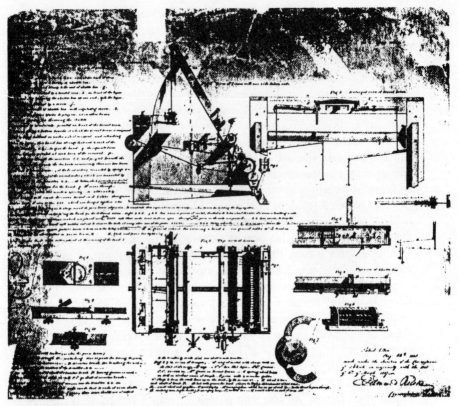

Ira Draper's Revolving Loom Temple Patent · A pair of temples holds the cloth at the proper width during the weaving process in order to prevent the drag of the filling yarns from condensing the cloth to a narrower width than desired. Figs. 8–10 (lower left) show the temple. (U.S. patent drawing 2608; photograph courtesy National Archives, Washington, D.C.)

In 1842 E. D. Draper moved his business and family to Hopedale, Massachusetts, to join the Christian Socialist community led by Adin Ballou.[10] Although the transitional stages toward increased

---

Temples can examine them at either of the above named Factories, or at the Counting Room of Mr. J.A. Lowell. . . .

Price of the Temples, including patent right, is $2 a pair. Any person desirous of purchasing may be supplied by the Boston Manufacturing Co. at Waltham. For the right to make them, apply to the subscriber at East Sudbury.

James Draper, Patentee

[10] For more on the early history of the Draper Company, its roots in Hopedale, and its origins in a Christian Socialist utopian community, see Adin Ballou, *History of the Hopedale Community* (Lowell, Mass., 1897); Barbara Louise Faulkner, "Adin Ballou and the Hopedale Community" (Ph. D. diss., Boston University, 1965); John S. Garner, *The Model Company Town* (Amherst, Mass., 1984).

William Mass / 882

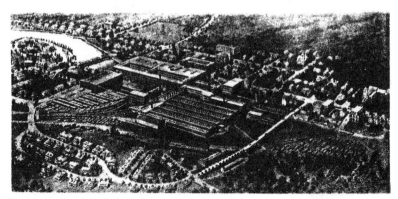

Draper Corporation Works and Surroundings, 1918 · This view of the corporation's facilities shows them considerably enlarged from the company's original existence as the Hopedale
Machine Works. After the demise of Adin Ballou's utopian community, Hopedale became
a Draper company town. The company sponsored beautification projects and each year
gave awards to the best-maintained homes and yards. (Reproduced from *Cotton Chats*, no.
184 [Feb. 1918].)

Draper manufacturing are not known, the Hopedale Company soon
became the principal supplier of Draper temples and began manufacturing other textile machinery parts as well. As the Hopedale community encountered financial difficulties, E. D. Draper led the efforts
to increase the surplus generated by his textile machinery business in
order to finance the rest of the community's activities. In 1852
E. D. brought in his younger brother George as managing copartner.
George was clearly attracted by the business prospects and at best tolerated the governing community ideals. He purchased the copartner-
ship for $5,000 and took the position of manager of operations. Like
his brother, George had developed his machinery experience as a weaving overseer prior to joining in the family business. He had worked
in several positions as a mill manager and as a mill superintendent
prior to 1852, and he had already patented several loom-related inventions. George and E. D. Draper's Hopedale partnership employed
seventeen workmen in the manufacture of loom attachments by 1855.
Their enterprise was a pioneering effort in specialized manufacturing
within the textile equipment industry.

In 1856 the religious settlement was declared insolvent, and the
community sold its assets to E. D. and George Draper "for their sole

Draper and the Automatic Loom / 883

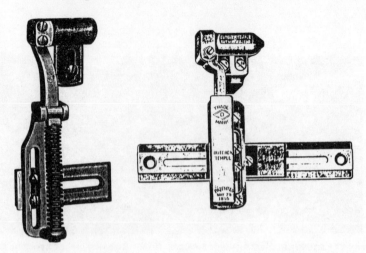

Early and Improved Dutcher Temples · From the mid-nineteenth century (left) to the early twentieth century (right), Dutcher's fundamental temple design remained remarkably stable. By 1900, the Draper Company supplied temples for every new loom produced in the United States. (Reproduced from *Cotton Chats*, no. 5 [Nov. 1901].)

use, behoof, and disposal forever."[11] At that time the Drapers reorganized the settlement solely for the purpose of manufacturing textile equipment. George Draper directed the expansion and reorganization of the E. D. and G. Draper Company's business activities. Facing competition from an improved loom temple patented and manufactured by Warren W. Dutcher and his brother in 1851, the Drapers purchased Elihu Dutcher's 50 percent interest in the patent in 1854. The Drapers convinced Warren Dutcher to move his operations to Hopedale in 1856, and Dutcher became the manager of the W. W. Dutcher Temple Company there. Warren Dutcher subsequently took out twenty patents on temples and on machines for manufacturing them. Some of his ideas were never patented, however; instead, the Drapers kept them under lock and key in an effort to prolong their monopoly beyond the seventeen years that a patent would cover. Dutcher's patents and his carefully guarded manufacturing methods for making temples enabled the W. W. Dutcher Company to gain control of the temple market.[12]

[11] Adin Ballou, *History of the Hopedale Community*, 307, as cited by Garner, *Model Company Town*, 119.
[12] Garner, *Model Company Town*, 130, 132; *Cotton Chats*, no. 5 (Nov. 1901); *Cotton Chats*, no. 24 (1904); George O. Draper, *Textile Texts*, 2d ed. (1903), 6, 261.

William Mass / 884

The Drapers formed two other copartnerships in 1856 with Joseph Bancroft, George Draper's brother-in-law. Bancroft was named manager of what became the other major Draper manufacturing facility, the Hopedale Machine Company, which manufactured and tested all non-temple inventions produced at Hopedale. The second, the Hopedale Furnace Company, was established as a partnership of the Drapers, Bancroft, and Dutcher. Principally a foundry managed by Dutcher, it made the castings required by the other two manufacturing facilities. In an arrangement continued until the end of the century, the Drapers maintained control of all three companies by acquiring the principal shareholding interest and by making the E. D. and G. Draper Company the exclusive selling agent for the affiliated manufacturers. It served as George Draper's main vehicle for controlling patent rights in addition to being the marketing agency for all Hopedale-manufactured machines, machine parts, and attachments.[13]

The Drapers were part of an active, but changing, business environment. From 1850 to the mid-1870s, the number of textile machine builders increased to its peak level. At least twenty-seven American textile machine manufacturers were in operation in 1874, and five British companies exported to the U.S. market. Eight of the American firms and one of the British offered a more or less complete line of mill equipment, but fifteen American machinery builders specialized in the production of two or fewer machines. The entry of new firms with narrower product lines contrasted with the earlier trend toward diversification.[14] Almost all of the American textile machine companies that had begun as mill machine shops were formally independent entities by the 1870s. As the textile industry expanded from 1840 to 1880, it came to be based on fewer but larger firms. Cultivating loyalty among these rapidly expanding customers was therefore an important sales strategy for the increasing number of specialized machine producers.[15]

Even before it assumed a dominant role, the Draper organization was set apart from other makers of textile machinery by several structural and strategic characteristics. First, using minimal manufacturing capacity, the company specialized in the development of widely marketed machine parts and attachments. Product development was a major focus within the company, but internal research was complemented by aggressive acquisition of patents having commercial

---

[13] Garner, *Model Company Town*, 132; *Cotton Chats*, no. 73 (June 1908).
[14] Navin, *Whitin Machine Works*, 108, 239–40, 485–87; Gibb, *Saco-Lowell Shops*, 761–62.
[15] Navin, *Whitin Machine Works*, 91–93; Gibb, *Saco- Lowell Shops*, 203, 230.

Draper and the Automatic Loom / 885

Main Drafting Room, Draper Company · From its beginnings the Draper Company placed greater emphasis on research and innovation than many other companies, early on employing a sizable research and design staff. It developed not only major inventions in textile machinery, but also hundreds of incremental changes in the parts that it furnished the trade. (Reproduced from *Cotton Chats*, no. 39 [May 1905].)

potential and by the direct employment of the most promising inventors. Even when they pooled patents, as with Dutcher, the Drapers maintained overall patent control. The Draper agency not only marketed both parts and licensing rights to other manufacturers of new machines, but they also sold replacement parts directly to mills in all regions and for nearly all loom models. Their success in this market was unique in an era when mill repair shops usually made their own spare parts.[16]

The Spindle Patent Pool and Patent Defense

When the key Dutcher patent expired in 1868, E. D. Draper was bought out by his nephew William F. Draper, and the company was reorganized as George Draper & Son, father and son holding equal interests.[17] George Draper's experience with patented inventions,

[16] Navin, *Whitin Machine Works*, 41.
[17] W. F. Draper, *Recollections*, 179–80; *Cotton Chats*, no. 36 (1905).

William Mass / 886

including the patents pooled with Dutcher, placed George Draper & Son at center stage in the key innovations in the textile machine industry over the next two decades. The company first seized the initiative in the development of high-speed spinning, and then pioneered a patent pool around the principle of the high-speed spindle, one of the earliest such pools in America.[18]

As early as 1870, the Drapers operated a separate department for research and testing, and they continued to diversify their control of patented textile parts. Although no figures are available, the scale of inventive activity attests that the Draper Company's expenditures on applied research not only set the pace for the textile industry, but also established the company as a leader among all U.S. industries.[19] Sufficient evidence to assess the full extent of the Draper Company's diversification in 1870 does not exist, but one large diversified machine manufacturer, the Whitin Machine Works, held eight out of its ten use-licensing arrangements from the Drapers. The Drapers received 25 percent of their royalties from Whitin for patents related to cotton-processing prior to spinning, 30 percent for those related to spinning, and 45 percent for weaving-related patents.[20]

As their royalty revenues grew, the Drapers extended their product line to include complete machinery. In the early 1870s their Hopedale plants began to manufacture spoolers, warpers, and, by the second half of the decade, twisters. All three machines processed and repackaged yarns to be used as warp yarns, the vertical yarns that create a pattern of "sheds" through which the shuttles pass carrying filling yarns on bobbins during weaving. The Draper warper soon controlled the bulk of the trade. Still, the Draper products were confined to the fringes of the industry, since all of these machines together made up 4 percent at most of the total machinery cost of a textile mill.[21]

By 1870 the Drapers had made a conscious decision to redirect their efforts in securing patentable inventions from primarily loom-related mechanisms to the field of spinning. Textile industry interest in the potential of a lighter and faster spindle was sparked in April 1871, when Jacob H. Sawyer, the mill agent of the Appleton Mills

---

[18] Navin, *Whitin Machine Works*; see chaps. 10 and 12 for the history of the relations between the Whitin and the Draper companies. The earliest American patent pool, controlling sewing machine patents, was established in 1856; see David Hounshell, *From the American System to Mass Production, 1800–1932* (Baltimore, Md., 1984), chap. 2 and p. 71.
[19] George Draper, "Let-Off Motions for Looms," *New England Cotton Manufacturers' Association*, no. 8 (Boston, Mass., 1870).
[20] Navin, *Whitin Machine Works*, 112.
[21] G. O. Draper, *Textile Texts*, 2d ed. (1903), 6–7, 179–80; Gibb, *Saco-Lowell Shops*, 632; Navin, *Whitin Machine Works*, 535.

Draper and the Automatic Loom / 887

in Lowell, presented the successful results of his spindle experiments to the New England Cotton Manufacturers' Association. George Draper had already gotten the jump on the rest of the industry by securing a large, although not controlling, interest in Sawyer's patent at least a month prior to Sawyer's public presentation. Thomas R. Navin highlights this episode as foreshadowing Draper's sustained risk-taking and "heroic" daring.[22] But it was actually one among several examples, and not the first occasion, of periodic radical change in which Draper's organizational capabilities were systematically utilized to take pioneering steps in product development.

Just as George Draper had done with Warren Dutcher earlier, the Drapers brought Jacob Sawyer to Hopedale to manage the Sawyer Spindle Company. George Draper's ownership interest rose from 29 percent in 1873 to 56 percent by 1875. Other Draper family members also held shares, making the total Draper interest in the Sawyer Spindle Company 30 percent in 1873 and 80 percent by 1875.[23]

The Hopedale Machine Company had sufficient production capacity to meet the demand for Sawyer spindles as replacements in spinning frames already in place, and the Drapers controlled the sales of high-speed spindles for use in retrofitting old frames of various types from the start. As manufacturers, the Drapers were aware of direct competition from the primary market and therefore designed and sold replacement spindles that could be transferred easily into new spinning frames at a later date. But the Drapers did not manufacture spinning frames, and their ability to supply the primary market for high-speed spindles in new frames was problematical. Limited in production capacity and dependent on selling to several competing frame manufacturers, the Drapers' early priority was to secure the higher-margin replacement sales rather than the higher-volume primary market. However, this strategy created difficulties that were reflected in the company's shifting licensing relations with suppliers and customers. The company first tried to meet orders for Sawyer spindles in new frames by subcontracting with several small specialty manufacturers. For a time they tolerated deliveries of Sawyer spindles that were periodically late and inferior in quality, rather than risk licensing the large machinery manufacturers. They accurately feared the larger companies' capabilities for developing competing spindle patents.

As their capacity increased, the Drapers tried to sell Sawyer spindles manufactured at Hopedale directly to the spinning frame manufac-

[22] Navin, *Whitin Machine Works*, 184, 591n9.
[23] Ibid., 186.

William Mass / 888

turers, but this strategy encountered other sorts of difficulties. The Whitin Machine Works, which from the early 1870s sold more spinning frames than its three largest competitors combined, was the Drapers' largest direct customer. Draper initially refused to allow Whitin to manufacture Sawyer spindles, so any mill encountering operating problems had to navigate through the mutual recriminations passing between Draper and Whitin as to whether the fault lay in the spindle or in the frame.

Customer confidence could hardly be enhanced in this manner. Whitin did make the investment necessary for the redesign of its frame, but not with a whole-hearted commitment to the Sawyer spindle: Whitin's new frame design permitted use of either the common or the Sawyer spindle. The Draper Company was concerned about the lack of confidence shown in its high-speed spindle, and finally, by the start of 1874, they consented to license Whitin for the manufacture of Sawyer spindles for Whitin's own frames. Draper also licensed six other sizable textile machine shops for the manufacture of spindles applied to their new frames. The terms for sharing patent control included the conditions for licensing the manufacture of patented spindles, the division of the primary and replacement parts markets, the responsibility for sales promotion, and even mechanisms for arbitration to set adjustments to royalty fees.

The technological barrier to increased spindle speed lay in the accompanying increases in vibration, which required greater consumption of power and created more frequent yarn breakage. Sawyer's patented invention entailed a change in the support of the spindles that enabled a reduction in their weight and in the diameter of bearings. The Sawyer spindle design was deficient in sustaining its promised high speeds, however, and it required extensive complementary modification of basic components for improved operation across the full range of yarns by fineness and type. The Sawyer spindle's greatest advantage lay in permitting significant decreases in power consumption.

Numerous patentable alterations in spindle design were undertaken that led both to incremental, cumulative improvements and to many alternative models with varying tradeoffs between speed and power consumption. The Drapers faced competition from inventors and investors pursuing the goal of high-speed spinning with a variety of often closely related designs. Despite the competitive stimulus to rapid technical advance, a mass of separate patent claims could impede commercial development of spinning innovations in three ways: by blocking the integration of complementary patented design modifi-

Draper and the Automatic Loom / 889

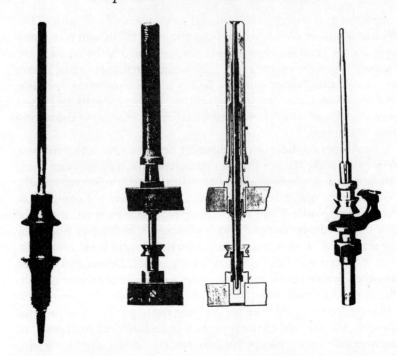

The Evolution of Spindles • A spindle is a revolving upright shaft with the simple function of carrying a rotating bobbin; it has relatively few basic components and moving parts, about five and fifteen, respectively. The above illustration shows an early spindle from a Slater mill, the Sawyer spindle design, and a Rabbeth "centrifugal clutch" spindle produced by Draper in 1915. (Sawyer spindle drawings reproduced courtesy of the Museum of American Textile History, North Andover, Mass.; Slater and Rabbeth spindles from *Cotton Chats*, no. 150 [April 1915].)

cations through the mutual obstruction of suit and countersuit; by deterring the exchange of unpatentable technological expertise essential for the easy use of a patent or for complementary invention; and by fragmenting the market, thereby significantly lowering profits. Patent pooling sought to overcome these impediments by regulating patent competition; it also reflected the increasingly cooperative nature of research and product development. Like other pooling arrangements, patent pooling was a transitional stop on the way to increasingly centralized and administratively coordinated activities.[24]

[24] Edith Penrose, *The Economics of the International Patent System* (Baltimore, Md., 1951), 104–5, 191; Alfred E. Kahn, "Fundamental Deficiencies of American Patent Law," *American Economic Review* 30 (1940): 482–87.

William Mass / 890

The stability of patent pooling agreements required the regulation of all other important forms of competitive behavior, including product prices and market spheres. The two most serious threats to the market control of the Sawyer Spindle Company came from large-scale frame manufacturers. One, a new patent controlled by Fales & Jenks Machine Company for the Rabbeth spindle, was "founded on a completely new principle," whereas the second, developed at the Whitin Machine Works, only "contained elements of independent value." In both cases, the Drapers exchanged a small number of Sawyer Spindle Company shares for patent rights to maintain control over the patent pool.[25]

The strategy of the Draper Company (now George Draper and Sons, as William's brothers, George A. and Eben S. Draper were admitted as partners in 1877 and 1880) was three-pronged. First, they committed company resources to further invention and patent activity. Second, they sought to purchase the rights to competitors' inventions and to consolidate them into their pool, even if on occasion the purchase price included sharing some degree of control over the patent pool. Finally, if patent competition could not be prevented by the first two strategies, patent litigation was the inevitable third step. The three prongs of their strategy complemented each other; a strong position in each enhanced the potential effectiveness of the other two.

By raising the costs of patent competition through unrelenting and effective litigation, the Drapers created a wide berth for their internally developed patents and enhanced their bargaining leverage when acquiring patent rights from others. Describing the last of five major cases of patent litigation, Thomas Navin comments, "Only the foolhardy or the ill-advised would have had the daring to back the litigious Drapers into a corner. . . . Court actions were part of the Draper stock-in-trade. The very foundation of their firm was cemented with lawsuits and reinforced with injunctions. George Draper & Sons were famed for invincibility before the bar."[26] The human and financial resources spent by the firm in support of litigation were impressive. From 1874 to 1880, George Draper and his son William were in court frequently enough to generate over ten thousand printed pages of testimony. The younger Draper reported that during these six years he spent more than half of his days appearing in court, consulting with

[25] Navin, *Whitin Machine Works*, 190–96.
[26] Ibid., 198, 189–203.

Draper and the Automatic Loom / 891

lawyers, or conducting experiments required to demonstrate the scientific basis to the company's cases.[27]

Much of the Draper patent activity was defensive, using a credible threat of legal action to raise patent barriers to competition even when the patents were not utilized. For example, the Drapers successfully brought suit against the Eureka Spindle Company for infringement of a patent that was not in use in any form.[28] This instance of defensive patent protection was not exceptional. The Drapers explained and justified their general strategy:

> It is possible that were the several hundred spindle inventions built for the trade, in approved form, a fair per cent of them might find converts, and give good satisfaction in use. Such a multiplicity, however, would cause confusion to our customers, and consternation to ourselves; so that we prefer to continue the responsibility of decision as to type, for as long as conditions warrant.[29]

The Drapers' unwavering commitment to universal patent defense was demonstrated by their suit against the Wauregan Mill. This case revolved around the priority of invention of a lot of 500 custom bobbins with a total value of $5.00. The Drapers had their lawyers interview all the mill employees who could be found for the years 1868 to 1871, incurring legal costs for this case in excess of $25,000.[30]

The relative importance of intrafirm development of spindle patents and external patent acquisition to the Drapers' control can also be assessed. In 1903 the Drapers reviewed the performance of the spindle market and listed all the inventors of important spindle innovations since 1870 and the number of spindle patents issued to each (see Table 2). As the Drapers reported, "The great mass of patents taken out by the [listed] men are, or have been, owned by the Sawyer Spindle Co., the control of this single element, in a wide field of mechanisms, necessitating the ownership of hundreds of patents within the dates mentioned."[31]

The eight Draper in-house inventor-patentees included four employees who were granted thirty spindle patents over this period. The remaining four in-house inventors were Draper family members. Their eighty-eight patents were the result not only of their capabilities for prolific invention, but also of their command of resources as

[27] W. F. Draper, *Recollections*, 183.
[28] Gibb, *Saco-Lowell Shops*, 263.
[29] G. O. Draper, *Textile Texts*, 2d ed. (1903), 144.
[30] W. F. Draper, *Recollections*, 184.
[31] G. O. Draper, *Textile Texts*, 2d ed. (1903), 142–43.

William Mass / 892

Table 2
Spindle Patentees, 1870–1 January 1903

All Spindle Inventors	54
Total patents granted patentees	463
Spindle Inventors "employed" by Draper	8
Total patents granted Draper patentees	118

Sources: G. O. Draper, *Textile Texts*, 2d ed. (Hopedale, Mass., 1903), 142–43, 308–9. Since all coinventors are listed separately as patentees, the total number of patents granted patentees will overstate the actual number of distinct patents represented.

owner-supervisors of the research and engineering department. Roughly one-quarter of the spindle patents under Draper control were developed in-house.

The acquisition of three-quarters of the patents in the pool from external sources indicates how the Drapers consolidated their control. Navin, who wrote that "At the height of their power, the Drapers owned or controlled every important spindle patent in America and Europe—some two hundred in number," in fact significantly underestimated the extent of the Drapers' patent holdings.[32] The peak number of *unexpired* patents controlled by the patent pool exceeded 250 in the 1880s, the years of peak spindle patent activity. But the company's ability to sustain control over spindle technology is better reflected by the total number of different spindle patents it controlled between 1871 and 1903, which was 463.[33]

Draper control of the spindle patent pool was built, first, on the early recognition of key patents, such as the Sawyer spindle, which they rapidly acquired whenever possible. They continued the aggressive acquisition of spindle patent rights in three ways: by direct purchase, in exchange for participation in the spindle patent pool, and through the in-house development of patentable inventions. The Drapers not only maintained their technological leadership in improved spindles, but, by increasing their stock of patents, they also gained bargaining leverage in negotiating patent acquisitions and enhanced their capability for legal defense of the patents they controlled. As the history of their patent litigation attests, the Drapers sought direct patent protection and raised barriers to technical developments that might circumvent their key patents.

[32] Navin, *Whitin Machine Works*, 181.
[33] Digest of Assignment of Property Rights in Patents, D. no. 12, 21 March 1895 to 7 Aug. 1897, 240–41, RG 241, National Archives, Washington, D.C.

Draper and the Automatic Loom / 893

In the spindle business, although they were the first and strongest among a few partners, they contended with formidable rivals both inside and outside the pooling arrangements. In contrast, in the business they went on to build around their loom patents, there would be no surviving competitors and no need of partners. The Drapers developed unassailable control over the returns to their loom innovations through an unprecedented buildup in the scale of in-house inventive activity. As a result, the Drapers relied much less on actual litigation to protect their loom innovations, and the financial resources committed to legal purposes declined compared to those applied to research and development.[34]

The Northrop Loom and Draper Company Invention

After power loom weaving was established in the early nineteenth century, the only major time-consuming manual task left to be mechanized was replenishing the filling. The magnitude of this task can be better understood when it is broken down into its several steps. When the filling in the shuttle of a common loom was exhausted or broken, the loom automatically stopped. Weaving ceased until the weaver released the shipper-brake, pushed the lay back, withdrew the shuttle from the box or shed, put in the reserve shuttle, and operated the shipper handle to start the loom. The weaver then rubbed the cloth below the front breast beam to prevent the occurrence of a thin place. In preparation for the next cycle, the weaver took up the empty shuttle, pulled the shuttle-spindle out at an angle, removed the exhausted bobbin (or cop tube containing mule-spun yarns), put in a new supply of filling, pulled off a sufficient length of filling from the carrier, snapped the shuttle-spindle back into place, held the filling over the eye entrance with a finger, sucked the filling through the hole, and inserted the shuttle in its receptacle, where it remained until needed. Each weaver tended eight looms (increasingly the norm in New England by the mid-1890s) and was required to repeat these tasks once or twice every minute.[35]

---

[34] In 1903 the Draper Company reported that the average per-patent costs associated with the 679 patents developed in-house since Ira Draper's first were: $100 for "fees and legal expenses," $200 for "incidental expenses and litigation," and at least $1,000 for "experiments." G. O. Draper, *Textile Texts*, 2d ed. (1903), 308.

[35] Draper Corporation pamphlet, "The Advance of the Northrop Loom" (1900), 10 (Hopedale Public Library).

William Mass / 894

Between 1840 and 1890 thirty-one patents were issued for inventions related to mechanized filling replenishment, eight in the United States and twenty-three in England, but none proved successful.[36] In the late 1880s, George Draper and Sons faced both the impending expiration of several key Sawyer spindle patents and renewed patent competition from the Whitin Machine Works. Patent royalties had provided the Drapers with a singularly large and liquid capital fund among textile machinery manufacturers.[37] In 1889 the company decided on a radical departure in new product development and committed "their large force of inventors and skilled mechanics" to experimentation in redesigning the common power loom.[38]

An important impetus to Draper inventive efforts came from a July 1888 visit by William F. Draper to Providence, Rhode Island, where he witnessed the operation of an automatic shuttle-changing loom. He later deemed that invention impractical, but he was prompted to begin an exhaustive investigation of existing patents. Draper Company inventors developed their own shuttle-changing looms and tested them at the Seaconnet Mills in Fall River in 1889. During these experiments, it occurred to James H. Northrop, a Draper employee, to change the bobbin in the shuttle while the loom continued weaving. Before the end of the year he had designed a self-threading shuttle, a bobbin with rings or corrugations on the base, spring jaws of grooved metal plate within the shuttle to grasp the bobbin rings, and a thread cutter to sever the thread trailing the bobbin after the first pick was laid.[39] By the end of 1891 Northrop had added a rotating battery (also known as the hopper or magazine) for holding the bobbins and a filling motion, a device to regulate the transfer of the bobbin from the battery to the shuttle when the filling was

---

[36] George O. Draper, *History of the Northrop Loom Evolution*, vol. 1, *1886–1892* (Milford, Mass., 1897), 156–57. Of the other twenty-three English patents, nine were issued between 1864 and 1866. George Otis Draper kept a daily record of machine developments and experimentation, including the results of investigations of related patent claims. Three volumes are referred to but I have found only volume 1. Together they would provide an abundance of information about the evolution of loom design.

[37] Thomas R. Navin, "Innovation and Management Policies—The Textile Machine Industry: Influence of the Market on Management," *Bulletin of the Business Historical Society* 25 (Spring 1951): 18n3.

[38] William Chase, *Five Generations of Loom Builders* (Hopedale, Mass., 1950), 13.

[39] The bobbin rings and "peculiar" spring inside the shuttle were the key inventions among the many embodied in the redesigned automatic loom. These patents prevented the successful development of any alternative patentable bobbin-changing devices. See *Transactions of the New England Cotton Manufacturers Association* (hereafter *NECMA*) 113 (Oct. 1922): 117.

Draper and the Automatic Loom / 895

James H. Northrop in the Draper Experiment Room · This photograph shows Northrop (in the center foreground) standing beside looms equipped with his battery and filling motion in Draper's experimental weave room at Hopedale. (Photograph reproduced courtesy of the Museum of American Textile History, North Andover, Mass.)

broken or exhausted.[40] These key patented inventions led the Drapers to organize the Northrop Loom Company in 1892, just as they had earlier established companies based on the patents and continued participation of Dutcher and Sawyer. In the case of Northrop's inventions, however, the entire endeavor was internally directed from the start. Thus, the new automatic loom, often referred to as the Draper loom, was originally known as the Northrop loom.

Marketing of the bobbin-changing loom was delayed several years, however, as George Draper and Sons found it necessary to develop a practical warp stop motion as well. As it turned out, "designing a suitable stop motion took longer and cost more than designing the battery."[41] The Drapers identified "every patent for a warp stop motion ever granted in this country or abroad"; they contacted the original patentees wherever possible, hiring the most promising or buying the

[40] This stage of development is reported in Chase, *Five Generations of Loom Builders*, 13–15, and George O. Draper, *Labor Saving Looms*, 1st ed. (Hopedale, Mass., 1904), 22–24; G. O. Draper, *History of the Northrop Loom Evolution*, vol. 1.
[41] G. O. Draper, *Labor Saving Looms*, 1st ed. (1904), 25.

William Mass / 896

patent rights.[42] An early explicit recognition of the importance of the warp stop motion to the progress of weaving experiments was stated by George Otis Draper (William's son) on 2 April 1892:

> The way the matter lies: Our weavers average to tend six [automatic] looms apiece, and there is only one who I would dare to give more than his present allowance.
>
> This looks bad when we used to count on a poor weaver running eight looms, and a good weaver, twelve.
>
> The evident trouble is the watching. An ordinary loom stops so often a pickout does not have time to become so serious as ours, and I believe ours require more careful oversight per loom on that account alone. With the same number of looms this watching is more of a necessity, and to increase the number multiplies it. I am not at all sure after seeing the looms run that a perfect warp stop motion would not enable a weaver to get off more cloth than a filling changer, give him all the looms he wanted.[43]

Later company publications describe how the relief from the manual task of changing the filling made the weavers "uneasy," anticipating more broken warp yarns while tending more looms. The Drapers "saw it would be absolutely necessary to furnish protection in the way of an accurate warp stop motion, so that there would be no mental anxiety or necessity for alert observation."[44] The Drapers believed that a successful automatic loom would double the number of looms tended by each weaver, but only if a mechanism that would replace the monitoring as well as the manual tasks formerly done by the weaver could be developed.

The filling changer thus gave impetus to efforts to redesign the warp stop motions, which had been little changed since the 1860s, when forty to fifty patents for such mechanisms had been granted. They were made of round wire, suitable for use in weaving only the coarsest cloth. The 1890s Draper experiments introduced warp stop motions of extremely thin wire, and the company began developing applications for weaving with finer warp yarns and closer weaves.[45] The newly designed stop motion was attractive because it did not complicate or increase the cost of drawing-in, but it was limited to simple (two-harness) weaves. Drop wire devices were soon developed to apply to individual warp yarns or to serve two or more at the same time.

[42] Chase, *Five Generations of Loom Builders*, 15.
[43] G. O. Draper, *History of the Northrop Loom Evolution*, 1: 423.
[44] G. O. Draper, *Textile Texts*, 1st ed. (1901), 11.
[45] Henry I. Harriman, *Transactions of NECMA* 68 (April 1900): 318–19.

Draper and the Automatic Loom / 897

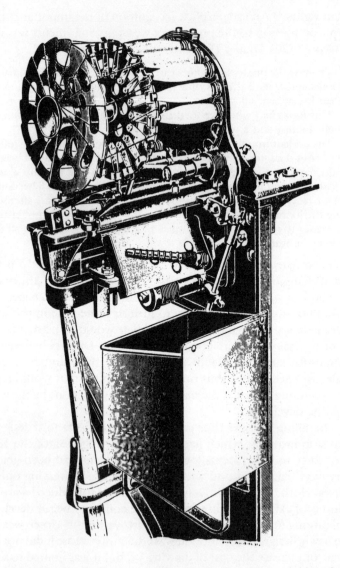

Detail of Rotating Bobbin Battery · Northrop's hopper, or magazine, held new bobbins ready for transfer to the shuttle when the old bobbin was exhausted. Here, the transferrer mechanism is just placing a new bobbin in the shuttle as the empty bobbin falls into the bin below. Originally designed to hold fourteen bobbins, by 1904 the hopper held twenty-four. (Reproduced from George Otis Draper, *Labor Saving Looms*, 3d ed. [Hopedale, Mass., 1907], 41.)

William Mass / 898

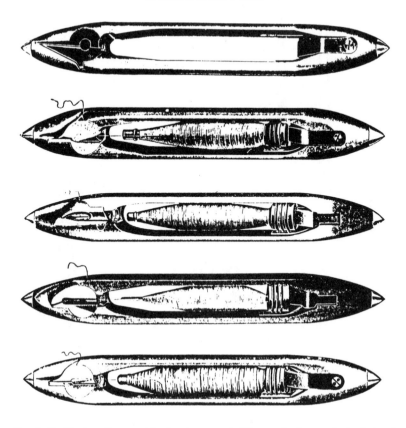

Shuttles for Northrop Looms · Northrop's automatic filling mechanism required redesigned bobbins and shuttles, and these illustrations show both the basic shuttle components of spring, gripper, and self-threading eye and a variety of Draper bobbin styles, all having the characteristic rings. (Reproduced from George Otis Draper, *Labor Saving Looms*, 1st ed. [Hopedale, Mass., 1904], 58–59.)

By early 1895 the Drapers felt ready to market the Northrop loom devices on a large scale.

Early Loom Marketing and Integrated Production

The history of the production of automatic looms is fundamentally a story of how establishing a mass market accelerated integration backward into mass production. When it organized the Northrop Loom Company in 1892, the Draper Company had very limited manufac-

Draper and the Automatic Loom / 899

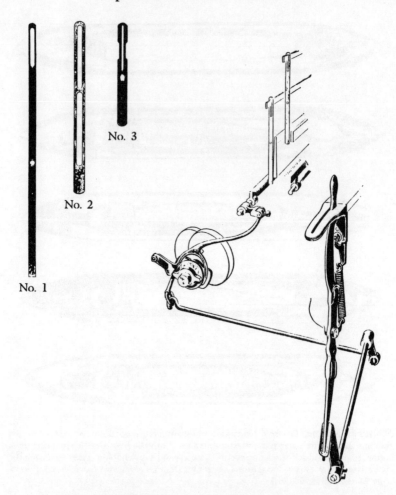

No. 3

No. 2

No. 1

Warp Stop Motion and Drop Wires · By 1904, Draper was marketing four distinct types of warp stop motion for use in multiple-harness weaving. In the steel harness stop motion shown, the heddles (see no. 1) themselves acted as warp stop devices, dropping when a thread broke to interfere with a vibrator that in turn operated the shipper brake. Drop wires no. 2 and 3 were used, respectively, with the Roper warp stop for a cotton harness and with single-thread looms. (Reproduced from Draper, *Labor Saving Looms*, 1st ed. [1904], 64, 67.)

turing capacity at Hopedale. The Drapers therefore hoped to reproduce arrangements similar to those of the spindle patent pool, and they secured licensing agreements with six major loom manufacturers, under which Draper would receive royalties for the use of its patents on auto-

William Mass / 900

matic loom attachments.[46] In particular, the Draper Company expected to manufacture filling-changers and warp stop motions for use on looms manufactured by the other companies.

The Draper Company had an extensive history of marketing replacement temples and spindles directly to mills, but the novelty of the Northrop loom's automatic features and its higher price—triple that of the common loom—required a dramatic introduction to break down sales resistance. As the company history described the situation, "They had to buy mills of their own to prove to other textile manufacturers that their new loom could be successfully operated under regular mill conditions."[47]

On the announcement of the availability of the new automatic loom, the Drapers received orders for several thousand before the looms ever ran in outside mills. Despite this interest, however, they encountered unanticipated difficulties in marketing the filling and warp stop motions. The early period of experimentation and product development had brought frustrations both in relations with mill management and weavers and with design and materials. At Seaconnet, there were accounts of recurring loom stoppage due to broken parts, especially shuttles, during the experiments, and there were two episodes of direct union opposition.[48] In the spring of 1891, the Draper Company was concentrating on the development of the bobbin-changer, and they transferred the testing of their new mechanisms from Fall River to the Pacific Mills in Lawrence.[49] Later, from November 1892 until 1894, the focus of testing was a weave room of eighty looms in Draper's own machine company at Hopedale.[50] Success in an experimental environment, however, was not sufficient to overcome industry skepticism in the face of possible equipment failure, union opposition, and the higher price of the Northrop loom.

The Drapers had already incurred high fixed costs during the stages of invention and development, but they decided to assume even greater

[46] The agreements were with Whitin Machine Works, Mason Machine Works, Lowell Machine Shop, the Lewiston Machine Works, Kilburn, Lincoln and Company, and Knowles Loom Company. Jonathan T. Lincoln, "Cotton Textile Machinery—American Loom Builders," *Harvard Business Review* 12 (Oct. 1933): 101–2; Navin, *Whitin Machine Works*, 274; see also Lincoln, "The Cotton Textile Machine Industry," *Harvard Business Review* 11 (Oct. 1932).

[47] Chase, *Five Generations of Loom Builders*, 15. As the Drapers sought to break down resistance to later loom models in various industry submarkets, they assumed the role of mill organizers on four later occasions.

[48] G. O. Draper, *History of the Northrop Loom Evolution*, 1: 147, 220.

[49] G. O. Draper, "The Present Development of the Northrop Loom," *Transactions of NECMA* 59 (1895): 90; G. O. Draper, *Labor Saving Looms*, 1st ed. (1904), 25.

[50] G. O. Draper, "Present Development," 90.

Draper and the Automatic Loom / 901

Table 3
The Northrop Loom: The Costs of Invention

1) Direct costs of inventions and experiments	$185,000
2) Other general expenses and time not charged to the above account (conservatively estimated)	150,000
Initial Production and Marketing Costs	
3) Inventory costs: loom parts & extra stock	300,000
4) Patterns, legal expenses, and "stock taken in new mills that use the loom"[a]	215,000
5) Plant enlargement and new machinery	150,000
Total Investment	$1,000,000[a]

[a]The Queen City Cotton Mill investment is included in item 4.

[b]The specific cost estimates may have been influenced by a desire to advertise a "million-dollar loom," but the investment in bringing the Northrop loom to market was probably the largest for a single machine in the nineteenth century.

Source: George O. Draper, *Facts and Figures for Textile Manufacturers* (Hopedale, Mass., 1896), 175.

capital risks in order to market the loom (see Table 3). The Drapers subscribed to $50,000 worth of shares in the first mill fully equipped with Draper looms, the Queen City Cotton Mill, in Burlington, Vermont. The site was chosen in part because, as the Drapers expressed it to Burlington city officials, "there are no labor organizations in Vermont to lead them and others into trouble."[51] The Queen City Cotton Company began full operation on 1 May 1895, and, though there were three strikes in five years despite the lack of unions, management had a much freer hand to adjust piece rates to capture productivity gains in the nonunion environment than they would have had in the unionized textile centers of southern Massachusetts.[52]

By establishing a mill under their direct control, the Drapers simultaneously presented a demonstration of the loom's reliability to the

[51] *Burlington Free Press*, 5 May 1894; the Drapers also expected lower coal costs and freight rates than in Massachusetts, and that the cost of construction of the mill would be 10 percent less; *Burlington Free Press*, 16 May 1894. A British observer, reporting to the *Manchester Guardian* about the U.S. textile industry in 1903–4, wrote, "The reason given me was that in Vermont they could get cheap labour, and there was no factory laws and no unions to give trouble over the trial of a new machine." T. W. Uttley, *Cotton Spinning and Manufacturing in the United States of America* (Manchester, 1905), 21.
[52] T. D. Seymour Bassett and David Blow, "The Lakeside Story, 1894–1948," *Chittendon County Historical Society Bulletin* 7 (May 1972); *Burlington Free Press*, 11, 13, 22, 24 Jan. 1898; 4–5, 10–11, 16–17, 19 April, 14 May 1900.

William Mass / 902

Model A Northrop Loom, 1894 · An early version of the automatic loom, the Model A was the type installed in the Queen City Cotton Mill in Burlington, Vermont. (Reproduced from Draper, *Labor Saving Looms*, 1st ed. [1904], 76.)

rest of the industry and gained a closely controlled proving ground for further development of both the machine and labor practices. They were able to demonstrate that the Northrop loom would lower production costs, by dramatically increasing the number of looms a single weaver could tend, to a degree that would more than compensate for the initial high investment

The Queen City Cotton Mill demonstrated the commercial viability of weaving with the new looms. However, the strategy of licensing the use of Draper motions to other loom builders was not successful. Most of the early orders were directed to the Draper Company itself for Northrop looms manufactured at its own facility, and sales of components to other loom manufacturers under licensing arrangements were never considerable.

The Whitin Machine Works and the Lowell Machine Shop objected to the high royalty fee, equivalent to the full price of a plain loom, and to a contract clause requiring them to sign over to Draper all improvements added to the Northrop looms they manufactured, although such an arrangement was not unusual at that time or later.[53]

[53] Navin, *Whitin Machine Works*, 274; Gibb, *Saco- Lowell Shops*, 769n29.

Draper and the Automatic Loom / 903

Table 4
Whitin Looms and Draper Motions

Year	Total U.S. Whitin Loom Orders	Percentage Fitted for Draper Motion
1895	8,563	45
1896	5,159	96
1897	2,499	82
1898	1,348	25
1899	4,943	21
1900	2,038	76
1901	4,646	8

Sources: Whitin Loom Order Books, Museum of American Textile History, North Andover, Mass.

The other four loom manufacturers agreed to cooperate, but in a February 1897 letter to the Whitin front office, selling agent Stuart Cramer assessed the situation: "The Drapers are pushing the loom for all it is worth and it seems to be doing well, yet it is not being bought in the North. Again several of the Northern shops have been licensed to build the loom, but they don't build it and they don't try to sell it."[54]

The Whitin Machine Works did manufacture a significant proportion of all their looms sold from 1895 to 1900 according to customer specification that the loom be fitted for a "shuttle box for Draper Motion." Few of the Whitin looms, however, were ever actually fitted with Draper attachments, and after 1901 they built no more looms fitted for Draper motions (see Table 4). Why did the market coordination of Whitin looms and Draper attachments break down in this way? Although the innovations were dramatic, the Queen City Cotton Mill had demonstrated their practicality.

A likely explanation of the resistance from rival loom manufacturers lies in their recognition that the Drapers had the basis to appropriate the present and future lion's share of the profits from innovation. Unlike the case of the high-speed spindle, when Whitin reserved the right to manufacture its own spindles for new frames, loom manufacturers were not going to get the opportunity to produce the Northrop mechanisms. Whitin could thus never develop the

---

[54] William F. Draper, comment, *Transactions of NECMA* 60 (April 1896): 133; Navin, *Whitin Machine Works*, 275.

William Mass / 904

Table 5
Draper Loom Models

Model	Description	Year
A	First model	1895
B	Standard to 1898	1896
D	First heavy loom	1898
E	Standard (1898–1930)	1898
Mod. D	Heavy deep loom (24-harness)	1899
F	First wide sheeting loom	1899
G	Special model (not put out)	1899
H	Side cam—corduroy	1899
I	Improved E model	1900
J	2-harness anti-bang loom	1901
K	Standard dobby loom (24-harness)	1901
L	Wide sheeting (replaces F)	1905
Nar. E	Same as E, but 3″ less depth	1909
M	New departure loom (cut gears)	1911
O	Heavy wide loom for jacquard or dobby	1912
P	Heavy duck loom	1912
R	Extra heavy duck loom	1922
S-4	Silk loom	1928
HC	Worsted loom	1928
X	Standard high-speed cotton loom	1930

Source: Hopedale Public Library, undated.

resources necessary for independent patent development and the leverage to assure a return on any substantial investment in modifying the Whitin loom to take the Draper motion.

By 1899 the Draper Company had concluded that other manufacturers would not push the automatic loom, and it decided to build a plant capable of meeting the entire national market for single-shuttle looms.[55] As a consequence, the period of most rapid change in the Northrop loom, after its initial development, was during the early years of manufacturing in Hopedale, from 1899 to 1906.

On developing their manufacturing capacity, the Drapers found that the quality of performance of the Northrop attachments was superior to the operation of the rest of the loom. Between 1899 and 1903 they redesigned several of the basic loom motions, making their loom, even without Northrop attachments, superior to those of competitors (see Table 5). Furthermore, in about 1903 the Draper loom

[55] Navin, *Whitin Machine Works*, 275–76.

Draper and the Automatic Loom / 905

Model E Northrop Loom · This was the standard Draper automatic loom between 1898 and 1930, accounting for the majority of Northrop looms sold. The company registered this cut of the loom as a trademark and used it on stationery and notes as a form of advertising. (Reproduced from *Cotton Chats*, no. 117 [July 1912].)

models also incorporated several improvements in other loom mechanisms, dramatically improving cost competitiveness through technical changes. To select only the most important example, the Draper Company thought that the development of a new take-up mechanism, considerably enlarging the capacity of the cloth roll and thereby reducing the frequency and labor cost of cloth doffing (removing full rolls of cloth), would alone give its loom an edge over the competition.[56]

The Drapers' expansion program did more than increase their manufacturing capacity in order to satisfy national demand. They simultaneously consolidated their organization as an integrated

[56] William F. Draper, *Transactions of NECMA* 74 (1903): 170. The increase in the capacity of the cloth roll of course added to its weight, thus increasing the strength requirement for removing the cloth from the loom. This was possibly an important factor in the increase in male weavers that accompanied the introduction of the automatic loom, particularly in the South, but it is unlikely to have been the sole cause of the changing gender division of labor in the weave room.

William Mass / 906

producer of all parts required for loom manufacturing and improved the quality of the loom by incorporating the best-known manufacturing practices from the United States and abroad.[57]

When they began manufacturing looms, the Draper Company, like other loom builders, had been organized more like a job shop than as a mass producer. The typical method of manufacture of looms began with the construction of a loom sample to order. The parts were made from rough castings and "unfinished" joints. To run properly, the machine parts required further "fixing." The rest of the loom order was then built according to sample specifications. The 1904–5 foundry facilities of the Draper Company included new molding machines that allowed superior milling of loom frames. The cost of these machines required an investment that the Draper Company was confident no other loom manufacturer could afford. With the use of these and other modern machine tools, Draper produced increasingly standardized parts and cut gears, and they were able to end the practice of sample loom construction. The greater "harmony" and "uniformity" in the operation of the various loom parts not only resulted in lower repair costs, but probably also reduced yarn breakages by decreasing strain and friction.[58] By 1905 the Draper Company's major improvements in loom design and construction were complete.

Draper Patent Control

In 1897 the Drapers had absorbed all of their Hopedale enterprises except the Sawyer Spindle Company into the newly incorporated Draper Company and established a centralized experimental staff. By 1900, the closely held Draper Company owned thirty-one patents for bobbin filling-changers, of which twenty-seven had been developed within the firm, and sixty-seven warp stop motion patents, involving forty-seven intrafirm patentees (eight separate inventors) and twenty-four extrafirm patentees (twelve inventors).[59] However, the

---

[57] Navin, *Whitin Machine Works*, 275–76.

[58] *Cotton Chats*, no. 31 (Sept. 1904), which explained that the price of the Northrop loom was originally based on looms per weaver increasing from eight to sixteen. The price had been unchanged (and would remain a fixed list price until 1916), though the loom's "efficiency" had been increased. The Drapers claimed that new attachments and other improvements increased their manufacturing costs by $15 per loom. *Cotton Chats*, no. 38 (April 1905); no. 137 (March 1914); no. 249 (Feb. 1924); April 1952 (available as a mimeograph in the "Little Red Shop," Hopedale, Mass.).

[59] Draper Company, "Advance of the Northrop Loom," 58–59.

Draper and the Automatic Loom / 907

total scale of loom-related inventive activity controlled by the Drapers went far beyond these two essential mechanisms.

On three occasions, in 1896, 1900, and 1904, the Draper Company published information indicating the breadth and depth of its control of loom-related patents, listing the names of the inventors and the number of patents issued to each.[60] By identifying the inventors "directly employed" by the Draper-controlled companies and the patents they were issued (and then assigned to their employer), the number of patents acquired internally can be compared to the purchase of patent rights from independent inventors. Most of the rapidly accumulating extrafirm patent rights acquired by the Drapers were from new sources. Between 1900 and mid-1904, seventy-seven newly listed extrafirm inventors were responsible for 173 of a total of 195 loom-related patent rights sold to the Drapers during this period.

The top five in-house inventors continued to generate the bulk of the patentable inventions developed internally throughout the period. The key inventors were William F. Draper and his son, George O. Draper, along with employees C. F. Roper, E. S. Stimpson, and most important, the principal inventor and developer, James H. Northrop. The total number of patents granted these five inventors made them responsible for 90, 79, and 63 percent of all in-house loom-related patentees cited in 1896, 1900, and 1904, respectively. These inventors were responsible for 48 percent of the total of 178 new Draper in-house loom patentees from 1900 to mid-1904.

In their efforts to increase their market and to protect it from competitors, the Drapers committed themselves to further substantial growth in the scale of in-house industrial research around the turn of the century, and they also continued to increase their acquisition of patent rights from extrafirm inventors. From 1901 to 1907, the Draper Company gained control of an additional 718 patents, 45 percent from in-house inventors. By 1907 the cumulative total of patents acquired by the Draper Company rose to 2,070, of which 1,330 were still active and enforceable.[61]

Although the Drapers' major commitment in product development after 1890 was clearly the automatic loom, they also continued

---

[60] G. O. Draper, *Facts and Figures for Textile Manufacturers* (Hopedale, Mass., 1896), 176–77; Draper Company, "Advance of the Northrop Loom," 58–59; G. O. Draper, *Labor Saving Looms*, 1st ed. (1904), 208–11.

[61] G. O. Draper, *Textile Texts*, 1st ed. (1901), 295–97; 2d ed. (1903), 308–9; 3d ed. (1907), 321–23.

William Mass / 908

to channel resources to patent acquisition in other areas. Presumably spindle and temple product development, especially for technical changes complementary to automatic weaving, received much of the remaining resources. The Draper Company's patent acquisition peaked in 1903 and 1904, and the firm's patent activity relative to the rest of American industry was at its zenith. The 1904 annual report of the Commisioner of Patents listed 55 inventors who assigned patents to the Draper Company, a number greater only at General Electric (134), with Westinghouse and affiliates a close third (46) and the rest of American businesses relatively far behind. The rate of invention controlled by the Draper Company in the first decade of the twentieth century was all the more remarkable because its scale of manufacture did not approach that of the other leading research companies.[62]

The patent data suggest that the proportion of loom-related patents acquired from extrafirm inventors was increasing during this period, so that in the early 1900s the Draper company acquired roughly equal numbers of patent rights from its own and outside inventors. However, these proportions understate the extent of direct control that the Drapers exerted over inventive and patent activity, because the Draper Company coordinated the invention and patent process to a significant degree even when it acquired patent rights from extrafirm inventors. According to the company's policy and descriptions, the patent sale was far from an arm's-length transaction:

> We always prefer to acquire an invention before it has been patented, as we are unwilling to trust to the ordinary methods by which patents are obtained. It is impossible for the average patent attorney to grasp all the possibilities in any single line like this, for the majority have never been in a cotton mill, and few of course are educated as to the state of the art, or the detail of the necessities of operation.
>
> . . . the value of the patent, however, independent of whether the device works well, depends largely upon the nature of the description or specification in the patent, and the claims that are allowed. Unless the claims are carefully drawn to cover just what is new and patentable, it may be possible to evade the patent by a slightly different construction. There is absolutely no remedy for an improperly prepared patent. . . . [63]

Table 6 summarizes the scale of ongoing inventive activity taking place within the Draper Company for loom-related R&D (for 1900 through mid-1904) and for total R&D (for 1901 through 1906).

---

[62] *Cotton Chats*, no. 36 (Feb. 1905), and no. 41 (July 1905).

[63] G. O. Draper, *Textile Texts*, 1st ed. (1901), 295, and 3d ed. (1907), 320; *Cotton Chats*, no. 96 (Oct. 1910).

Draper and the Automatic Loom / 909

Table 6

Distribution of Draper In-House Inventors,
by Number and Type of Patents Granted, 1900–1906

Type of Patent:	*Loom-Related Only*	*All Patents*
Number of Patents Issued Individual Inventors	Number of Inventors 1900–June 1904	Number of Inventors 1901–1906
1	14	25
2–3	9	17
4–6	3	4
7 or more	8	14
	34	60

Sources: George Otis Draper, *Facts and Figures for Textile Manufacturers* (Hopedale, Mass., 1896), 176–77; Draper Company, "The Advance of the Northrop Loom" (Hopedale, Mass., 1900), 58–59; G. O. Draper, *Labor Saving Looms*, 1st ed. (Hopedale, Mass., 1904), 208–11; G. O. Draper, *Textile Texts* (Hopedale, Mass.), 1st ed. (1901), 295–97; 2d ed. (1903), 308–9; 3d ed. (1907), 321–23.

Although the periods summarized are unequal in duration and incompletely overlapping, the data conservatively indicate the number of inventors involved in R&D at the Draper Company, their relative scale of patent activity, and the proportion that was directly committed to developing the Northrop loom. Clearly, the Draper Company was built around the development of patentable inventions. As in other mechanical sectors, a significant number of the in-house patentees were no doubt sales, service, and production personnel, but on the basis of the evidence in Table 6, we can conclude that the Draper Company maintained a research, engineering, and product development staff of at least twenty people by the early twentieth century. Even this conservative estimate places the Draper Company in the forefront of companies that committed personnel resources to research and development.

Loom Competition and Patent Litigation

No other textile machinery company was able to mount a significant challenge to the Northrop loom. There were only twelve loom manufacturers in the United States, including the Drapers, in the 1890s.[64] By the early 1900s, five new companies had attempted to

[64] Lincoln, "Cotton Textile Machinery—American Loom Builders," 99.

William Mass / 910

market automatic filling-changing looms. Only one ongoing loom manufacturer, the Crompton Loom Works, attempted to market an "automatic" loom, and they soon withdrew their loom from the market. One of the five new firms was bought out by the Draper Company and three others failed. The sole survivor was the American Loom Company, soon to be reorganized as the Stafford Loom Company, which manufactured an automatic shuttle-changing loom.[65]

Although its control of Northrop loom patents was overwhelming and the competition was weak, the Draper Company was as aggressive as ever in repeatedly and forcefully stating its intention to litigate against patent infringement. The early cash reserves secured by spindle patent royalties increased the company's ability to bear the costs of litigation and made the threat of legal action all the more effective. Indeed, by 1906 the company could boast of a record of continuous patent litigation against infringers for the previous thirty-five years that was "aggressive, persistent and almost uniformly successful."[66] Draper soon added to its record of legal victories, as it sued the Stafford Loom Company, a shuttle manufacturer, and others.[67] The lawsuits against the Stafford Company merit brief review to document the persistent use of patent litigation against this sole survivor among contemporary loom competitors.

Sales figures are not available, but all accounts indicate that the Stafford Company never gained a significant share of the loom market. As the Draper experimental staff discovered, the mechanical problems of automatically changing the shuttle were greater than those of changing the bobbin in the shuttle. In addition, the Stafford shuttle-changer was a slower loom; it came to a full stop when the shuttles were changed, and refilling shuttles required more time than refilling batteries. Still, shuttle-changing looms were developed in England, and in Japan a shuttle-changing loom made by Toyoda (the forerunner of Toyota Motor Corporation) was a more widely used automatic loom than the bobbin-changing type.[68] Hence the Drapers monitored developments at Stafford carefully.

[65] G. O Draper, *Labor Saving Looms*, 3d ed. (1907), 37.

[66] *Cotton Chats*, no. 52 (July 1906). The company also threatened, "It will be understood that it is just as much an infringement to *use* a patented invention as to make or sell the same." Ibid., no.146 (Dec. 1914).

[67] See footnote 69 for the references concerning the Stafford company. The suit against the U.S. Bobbin and Shuttle Company is reviewed in *Cotton Chats*, no. 175 (May 1917).

[68] *Cotton Chats*, no. 51 (June 1906); *Textile World*, May 1905, 167; see Toru Yanagihara, "Development of Cotton Textile Industry and Textile Machinery Industry in Prewar Japan", Institute of Developing Economies, unpub. paper, 1979, 40–45, and Mass and Lazonick, "The British Cotton Industry and Competitive Advantage."

Draper and the Automatic Loom / 911

The importance of this litigation is shown by the fact that it has been twice before the District Court and twice before the United States Court of Appeals for the First Circuit. Moreover, after the Court of Appeals, on May 1, 1914, had affirmed the validity of claim 23 of this patent, The Stafford Company applied for a rehearing, which the court refused, and then petitioned the Supreme Court of the United States to revise the decision of the Court of Appeals, which petition was refused on October 26, 1914.

This Finally Establishes
The Validity of the Patent.

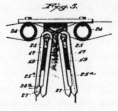

We annex a portion of a drawing of the patent, showing the patented arrangement of the drop-bars (drop-wires) hung on the lower shade of the warp-threads, so as to minimize chafing of the threads by the drop-bars. The original opinion of the District Court rightly said:

"The very extensive use of these devices, and especially their use on fine and delicate fabrics, shows that the refinement was of practical value and a substantial advance in the art."

WE AGAIN WARN THE TRADE

that the rights granted by this patent, and now finally established, will be enforced against all persons who unlawfully appropriate the patented invention.

The Stafford Company has been under injunction, forbidding it to make, use or sell this invention, since the decree of the District Court on August 7, 1913, but we have reason to believe that the patented arrangement is still employed in many Stafford Looms; and, as we have repeatedly notified the trade of our rights since the beginning of this long-contested litigation, we shall feel obliged to enforce these rights without further notice and prevent the further unlicensed use of this valuable invention.

It will be understood that it is just as much an infringement to use a patented invention as to make or sell the same.

Draper Advertises a Victory Over Stafford · Nearly every issue of *Cotton Chats* contained news of the Draper Company's legal victories or ongoing suits, accompanied by stern warnings. This example refers to the successful litigation against the Stafford Loom Company for infringement of a Draper warp stop wire patent. (Reproduced from *Cotton Chats*, no. 146 [Dec. 1914].)

The patents controlled by Draper were the basis for three separate suits against the Stafford Company that extended, respectively, from 1901 to 1911, from 1909 to 1918, and from 1912 to 1919.[69] The constraints of staying clear of Draper Company patents and, where that was not possible, bearing the costs, uncertainty, and consequences of patent litigation contributed to the Stafford Loom Company's limited growth. A small niche competitor specializing in fine yarn weaving, Stafford was ultimately absorbed by Draper (reincorporated as the Draper Corporation in 1916) amid the Depression in 1932.

Furthermore, the likelihood of similar difficulties effectively deterred the entry of powerful potential competitors. The Whitin Machine Works, the largest producer of cotton textile machinery in the United States, was also the producer of the highest-priced nonau-

[69] The three successful suits against the Stafford Loom Company involved a shuttle-changing mechanism—*Cotton Chats*, no. 2 (Aug. 1901); no. 51 (June 1906); no. 71 (March-April 1908); no. 99 (Jan. 1911); a feeler mechanism— *Cotton Chats*, no. 83 (Sept. 1909); no. 183 (Jan. 1918); no. 193 (Nov. 1918); and a warp stop motion—*Cotton Chats*, no. 117 (July 1912), no. 129 (July 1913), no. 146 (Dec. 1914); no. 204 (Oct. 1919).

William Mass / 912

tomatic loom on the market. Of all American loom manufacturers, it was likely to lose the most in competition with the Draper automatic loom. In 1898 Whitin executives were telling customers that they were slowly perfecting an automatic loom, but the company in fact never directed its experimental staff's attention in that direction. When independent inventors approached Whitin with various devices to make plain-goods looms automatic, the company decided that the inventions either would not operate adequately under mill conditions or would not stand clear of Draper Company patents, particularly Northrop's broadly drawn patent claims.[70]

Market Penetration and Market Control

By 1907 a majority of Draper's top management were confident that they had developed the Northrop loom sufficiently to ensure its conquest of the market for single-shuttle looms for both new mills and loom replacements. The rapid growth in production capacity at Hopedale certainly reflected the Drapers' confidence in future growth in loom sales. The pattern of diffusion and adoption of the Draper loom can be briefly summarized.[71]

In 1899 there were more than 113,000 looms in place in the southern United States. The greatest absolute increase in the South's cotton textile capacity (measured by looms in place) occurred in the next ten years, and the growth in production was based on the Draper loom. In the first five years of the century, the sales of Northrop looms to the South were equivalent to 54 percent of the region's growth in capacity. Between 1904 and 1909, the sales of Northrop looms in every major textile-producing southern state exceeded the net growth in capacity. Not only had the Draper Company captured the fastest-growing segment of the national market, but it was also securing a large share of the replacement market in the newer region.

Most historians agree on the overriding importance of southern labor cost advantages, but there is no similar agreement on the other factors that impeded or accelerated the pace and progress of the industry's relocation, notably the relative labor, managerial, financial, and technical advantages of the two regions for producing various types

---

[70] Navin, *Whitin Machine Works*, 275–76, 278.

[71] William Mass, "Technological Change and Industrial Relations: The Diffusion of Automatic Weaving in the United States and Britain" (Ph.D. diss., Boston College, 1984). What follows is a synopsis of relevant aspects of chaps. 3 and 4 presented in "desperate brevity."

Draper and the Automatic Loom / 913

Weave Room with Northrop Looms, 1916 · Taken at the Naumkeag Steam Cotton Company in Salem, Mass., this photograph presents a typical scene in the mills being constructed in the early twentieth century. The weave room was said to contain seven acres of Northrop looms. (Reproduced from *Cotton Chats*, no. 161 [March 1916].)

of cloth.[72] Central controversies relate to the suitability of the Northrop loom for weaving a wider range of cloth types and its cost advantages over common looms already in place. In 1900 three-quarters of existing U.S. loom capacity remained outside the South, and the number of looms in New England cotton textile mills would increase an additional 27 percent before the region's loom capacity peaked in 1914. The outlook for the Northrop loom's penetration of the New England market therefore continued to be an important part of the Draper Company's calculations.

Early in the twentieth century, there were greater technical difficulties in adapting the Draper automatic mechanisms for fancy weaves (which the Drapers were in the process of accomplishing) and multi-shuttle weaves (which Crompton-Knowles made automatic). By 1907, Draper looms were powerfully placed in the replacement market for plain single-shuttle looms in every New England state and in all the

[72] For a small sampling of this large body of research, see recent surveys of the literature (on the North) in Mass, "Technological Change and Industrial Relations," and Martha Schary, "Exit, Investment and Technological Diffusion in a Declining Industry: An Empirical Study" (Ph.D. diss., MIT, 1987); and on the South, see Gavin Wright, *Old South, New South* (New York, 1986), and Nancy Kane, *Textiles in Transition: Technology, Wages, and Industry Relocation in the U.S. Textile Industry, 1880–1930* (Westport, Conn., 1988).

William Mass / 914

larger textile centers except for the two largest concentrations of cotton textile production—Fall River and New Bedford in southern Massachusetts. The share of national weaving capacity in these two cities remained constant at 21 percent of all looms in the nation from 1899 to 1919. Yet, by 1909, the proportion of all looms accounted for by Northrops was only 4 percent in Fall River and 6 percent in New Bedford, and their rates of adoption of Northrops would continue to lag far behind rates in the rest of New England.

Why did these southern Massachusetts mills persist in their use of common looms? What were the prospects for foreseeable technical improvements that would open up the two largest loom markets to Draper on a scale comparable to its success in the rest of the country? What shifts in automatic loom design and construction would be necessary to meet or beat the costs that firms incurred by adapting common looms to various uses?

The pattern of labor relations, wages, and productivity permitted continued adaptation by most of the Fall River mills in their efforts to lower costs on the common loom.[73] However, this ability to lower unit labor costs was limited and sustained competitiveness only where the Fall River mills already had a competitive advantage: in the custom-order cloth market. The importance of this market for Fall River and New Bedford had resulted in a distinctive organization of marketing compared to the rest of the industry. From the start, most southern Massachusetts mills sold their own goods and were not represented by the commission houses.[74] Originally producing staple print cloth of unvarying construction, the mills sold directly to merchant-converters, who subcontracted with printers to finish the cloth and then distributed to wholesale and retail units, or to printers "converting" the goods on their own account. Southern New England towns had a transportation cost advantage that promoted their development as textile centers and structured their marketing orientation. The mills were close to the finishing establishments centered in Rhode Island, and steamboat lines could deliver goods in less than a day to New York jobbers.[75]

---

[73] The industrial relations conflicts in Fall River centered around the determination of the weaver's piece rate. See Mass, "Technological Change and Industrial Relations," chap. 4.

[74] The importance of individual commission houses and their influence over mill production in directing the diffusion of Draper looms in the South is emphasized by Martha Schary, "Financial Structure and Competition: Entry, Investment and Exit in the Cotton Textile Industry" (unpub. paper).

[75] T. R. Smith, *The Cotton Textile Industry of Fall River, Massachusetts* (New York, 1944), 63.

Draper and the Automatic Loom / 915

The fundamental change in the industry's marketing organization from 1880 until the 1920s was the growing importance of the merchant converter. The converter's basic function was to develop new styles and fabrics accompanying the growth of new markets, primarily the growth of garment manufacturing.[76] The number of converters in New York increased from 108 to 181 between 1907 to 1911, and there were 385 converters based in New York by 1927.[77]

The industry trade journal, *Textile World*, commented on the changing market organization in 1907:

> It is interesting to note that in the rapid growth of the converting business we are following closely the long established English methods of transacting the cotton goods business. . . . These converting houses work at their own styles, plan the construction of the fabrics, place their orders for the goods in the grey through brokers by specifications, and send the goods to be bleached, dyed, printed or finished, and finally sell them under their trade-mark names.[78]

The extensive product diversification that came with the increased role of the converter developed along several dimensions: cloth width, fineness of yarn, and fancy patterns. Product diversification was a response to changes in general market conditions and to growing southern competition in coarse and medium standard cloths. The expansion in fine and fancy mills largely took place through construction of new mills and enlargement of existing fine and fancy mills, not through scrapping and replacement in mills making coarser products. In Fall River, the greater absolute expansion in diversified production until 1910 came in new mills and print cloth mills producing more varied products with medium rather than fine-count yarn.[79]

In Fall River, in particular, an increasing proportion of products classified as print cloth were known as "odd goods." Odd goods varied from standard print cloth in width, number of threads per inch, or

[76] See Louis Bader, *World Developments in the Cotton Industry* (New York, 1925), 146–49. See the literature on the developing converter-commission houses, in Melvin Copeland and Edmund Learned, *Merchandising of Cotton Textiles*, Harvard University Graduate School of Business Administration, Business Research Studies, no. 1 (1933) and also *25 Years, The Association of Cotton Textile Merchants of New York, 1918–1943* (New York, 1944).

[77] *Textile World* 32 (March 1907); Herbert Burgy, *The New England Cotton Textile Industry: A Study in Industrial Geography* (Baltimore, Md., 1932), 207.

[78] *Textile World* 32 (March 1907).

[79] Smith, *Cotton Textile Industry*, 109. These measures of capacity represent the percentage of Fall River spindleage. The total Fall River spindleage was 1.27, 2.6, 3.6, and 3.95 million for 1875, 1895, 1910, and 1925, respectively. Since finer cloth requires a higher spindle-to-loom ratio, this measure is biased toward overstating weaving capacity in fine goods mills.

William Mass / 916

yarn count. Although generally made from yarns in the medium-count print cloth range, odd goods also included cloth made with finer yarns. They were not specialty products, but frequent variation in thread count and cloth construction required more attention in operating and managing the mills that produced them. Also, since selling odd goods required greater sensitivity to changes in demand, it also required close contact with the market.[80]

The mills in Fall River that had originally been built to make only print cloth easily adapted their facilities to make odd goods like gauze (made with print cloth yarns but with fewer yarns per square inch), fancy shirtings, and even fine goods. Though the costs of making the necessary physical adjustments in equipment are not available, they were not so great that conversion back to print cloth production in a favorable market would be uneconomical. In fact, Seth Hammond, attempting to chronicle the shift in the type of cloth produced by the Fall River mills, noted that the mills frequently produced print cloth even after having turned to other products.[81]

Variety in cloth production did, however, cause greater increase in costs on Northrop looms relative to ordinary looms. The initial investment in labor and material to adapt equipment may not have been prohibitive, but the increased downtime due to changeovers was more costly on the more expensive loom. On one occasion of a favorable shift in the price of staple print cloth compared to cloth of "non-standard [yarn] counts," it was estimated that it would take over three weeks to complete a changeover and turn off regular cloth on Northrop looms.[82] The costs of downtime and lost production were also greater on Northrops because for some applications the adjusted looms could not produce the different cloth style as successfully as the one they were constructed to turn out.[83]

The nature of the odd goods production gaining importance in the Fall River and New Bedford area meant that the Draper Company was unlikely to develop a technology that would make the North-

---

[80] *Dry Goods Economist*, Jubilee Issue (1896), 73, cited in Smith, *Cotton Textile Industry*, 111.

[81] Seth Hammond, "The Cotton Industry of this Century" (Ph. D. diss., Harvard University, 1941), 788–90.

[82] *Fall River Daily Globe*, 7 Oct. 1905.

[83] By 1923, the Draper Company acknowledged that "Experience has taught that an automatic loom may make one kind of weave successfully and need much in the way of experiment and changes before it will produce another kind equally well." They explained that the operation of the automatic appliances had to be worked out for each weave, though by this time a print cloth loom could be "fitted to run silk filling or make denim, light duck," or other cloth of a similar weight. *Cotton Chats*, no. 247 (Nov. 1923).

Draper and the Automatic Loom / 917

Old Looms for New · In a photograph similar to many others displayed in *Cotton Chats*, the Draper Company depicted part of its foundry yard, showing thousands of common looms scrapped and presumably being replaced by Northrop looms. (Reproduced from *Cotton Chats*, no. 164 [June 1916].)

rop loom sufficiently adaptable and cost-effective to penetrate this market, at least not without a sizable and appropriately targeted R&D effort.

Internal Conflicts and Shifts in Strategic Policy

Against this background, a growing conflict over basic business strategy came to a head within the company in 1907. The Draper Company had completely integrated production and had capacity adequate to meet industry demand. The firm had gained sufficient control of loom-related inventive activity within and outside the firm to attain two goals. The technical development of the automatic loom had progressed to make it applicable to almost all single-shuttle weaves and, except in southern New England mills, there were clear indications that the company had successfully opened the market for replacing common looms with Northrops. In the case of the one-fifth of the industry located in Fall River and New Bedford, there was little prospect for significant near-term inroads through further technical innovation. Moreover, once Draper had successfully penetrated all

William Mass / 918

Joseph B. Bancroft, 1821–1909 · An early partner of E. D. and George Draper, Bancroft became president of the reconstituted Draper Company in 1907 when William Draper and his sons left. (Reproduced from *Cotton Chats*, no. 84 [Oct. 1909].)

other markets for new looms, the company's market share and profit rate would increasingly depend on the growth in sales for replacement parts and supplies.

In addition, their three-pronged strategy of in-house research, market acquisition of competing and complementary patents, and aggressive patent litigation limited the potential for competitors to survive, much less to capture any of the returns to the Drapers' technical innovations. All competitors except Stafford had been vanquished, and its threat appeared inconsequential.

Alternative strategies were advocated by two management groups. The first included William F. Draper, who had initiated the company's commitment to the development of the Northrop loom, and his two sons. George Otis Draper had supervised most of the early development of the Northrop loom, and his younger brother Clare Draper was most active in furthering its technical development. The heart of their organizational priorities was centered in the Draper Experiment Committee, which pursued new product development. The opposition was led by the other senior Drapers, William's two brothers—Eben S. Draper, the top marketing executive, and George A. Draper, the treasurer and the corporate officer with "full respon-

Draper and the Automatic Loom / 919

Eben S. Draper · For many years the chief agent of the Draper Company, in charge of all its sales, Eben S. Draper sided with the management group that wished to concentrate on consolidation in 1907. (Reproduced from *Cotton Chats*, no. 138 [April 1914].)

sibility for the financial affairs of the company." They wished to expand the profitability of sales to both primary and secondary markets by increasingly standardizing production. The older Drapers secured majority support from the nine-member board of directors when they gained the votes of three minority shareholders and directors: Joseph Bancroft, his son Eben D. Bancroft, and Frank Dutcher.

The early steps taken to redirect business strategy included the disbanding of the Experiment Committee and the ouster of William Draper as president of the company in July 1907.[84] A general exodus of the company officials and inventors responsible for the development of the Draper looms up to that time soon followed. George Otis and Clare Draper left the company, and they took with them four employee-inventors, including two of the company's top three inventors—Charles Roper, who had been instrumental in the design of warp stop motions, and Jonas Northrop, who had assumed the position of chief loom inventor after his brother James left the company in 1898. The seven officials and employees who left the Draper Company had been issued 328 patents by 1907, and they constituted

[84] *Cotton Chats*, no. 138 (April 1914); no. 238 (20 Feb. 1923); no. 63 (July 1907).

William Mass / 920

William F. Draper · President of the Draper Company and chairman of the "Committee on Experiments and Improvements," William Draper was forced to resign in 1907; he died in 1910. (Reproduced from *Cotton Chats*, no. 63 [July 1907].)

nearly one-third of all intrafirm patentees who ever assigned patent rights to the company. Clearly, the remaining Draper management viewed a great deal of talent for innovation as expendable in their desire to pursue an alternative course of business.[85]

Those left in control decided "to continue certain standard machinery unchanged" and to pursue sales in the secondary market for supplies, replacement parts, and repairs.[86] Joseph Bancroft was elected president, clearly an interim measure, for at eighty-six he served less than two years before his death. The key managers and inventors assuming control over the direction of research and engineering development were Frank Dutcher, E. S. Stimpson, his son Wallace I. Stimpson, and Alonzo E. Rhoades. Bancroft was succeeded by Frank Dutcher, who had started as an apprentice to his father at the W. W. Dutcher Temple Company, then served as treasurer of that company

---

[85] *Cotton Chats*, no. 71 (March and April 1908); George Otis Draper, "Nordray Loom Catalogue" (Milford, Mass., c. 1921), 8, in the possession of William F. Northrop (grandson of Jonas Northrop), photocopy in author's possession; G. O. Draper, *Facts and Figures for Textile Manufacturers*, 176–77; Draper Company, "Advance of the Northrop Loom," 58–59; G. O. Draper, *Labor Saving Looms*, 1st ed. (1904), 208–11. For one participant's observations on the disagreements, see W. F. Draper, *Recollections*, 326, 375–77.

[86] G. O. Draper, "Nordray Loom Catalogue," 14.

Draper and the Automatic Loom / 921

George Otis Draper · Son of William F. Draper, George O. Draper joined the company in 1889 and served as secretary, giving special attention to patent matters. He wrote much of the material in the company's trade catalogues and in its house monthly, *Cotton Chats*. (Reproduced from *Cotton Chats*, no. 71 [March and April 1908].)

for twenty years until becoming assistant agent to Eben S. Draper in 1896. Dutcher served as president of the company for twenty years and then as chairman for two more years, until his death in 1930. For all of his last twenty-two years Frank Dutcher also served as the supervisor of the Department of Patents.

The most accomplished inventor-employee retained by the Draper Company was E. S. Stimpson, who had been foreman in charge of manufacturing at the W. W. Dutcher Temple Company for thirty years. Stimpson had been issued seventy patents assigned to the Draper Company before 1907, most involving improved weaving mechanisms. As the senior member of the experimental staff, he assumed a central role in directing the continuing development of the Northrop loom, and he went on to patent an additional ninety-one inventions before his death in 1924. Wallace I. Stimpson also began his employment at W. W. Dutcher, and he was one of the company's most successful salesmen for twenty-five years. He succeeded Eben S. Draper as agent of the Draper Company in 1914, and he later assumed charge of the further improvement of the Draper looms.[87]

[87] *Cotton Chats*, no. 84 (Oct. 1909); no. 254 (Aug. 1924); no. 302 (May 1930); no. 333 (Dec. 1939).

William Mass / 922

Alonzo E. Rhoades was the most prolific inventor in the history of the Draper Corporation. The first inventor assigned to develop an automatic loom for Draper, he had concentrated on the more traditional shuttle-changing approach; he was reassigned to nonweaving mechanisms after James H. Northrop succeeded with his bobbin-changing designs. Prior to 1907 Rhoades had secured fifty-three patents (almost all nonweaving) assigned to the Draper Company, after which his inventions were overwhelmingly loom-related. He obtained an additional 258 patents between 1907 and 1927.[88]

The top executives asserting control over corporate strategy had witnessed at least seventeen years of continuous investment in new product development. To the investment in R&D were added the costs of marketing the new looms (including the financing of new mills) and the costs of rapid expansion of capacity sufficient to produce 25,000 looms annually. A second stage of expansion, with a net addition of 40 percent of the final foundry capacity, was made in response to high sales in 1900 and 1902. The subsequent slowdown in sales, linked as always to a volatile textile trade cycle and an uneven rate of mill expansion, must have given these company officers reason to reconsider their commitment to continual large-scale innovation (see Figure 1).

The Draper Company had also taken steps to develop sales to the secondary market. In 1902, they purchased 30,000 acres of New Hampshire timberland and built nearby facilities for seasoning wood and manufacturing bobbin blanks.[89] In 1906 the Draper Company opened a southern office and supply warehouse in Atlanta, Georgia, as "more or less of an experiment." Their initial concern was to discourage mill customers from getting crude, local castings for repair parts, which diminished loom performance and consequently tarnished the Draper Company's reputation. Using the original Draper patterns avoided the problem of otherwise inevitable metal shrinkage in molds patterned from machine parts. The southern office's immediate success led to its enlargement within the year to provide a full line of loom parts locally.[90]

[88] G. O. Draper, *Textile Texts*, 1st ed. (1901), 295–97; 2d ed. (1903), 308–9; 3d ed. (1907), 321–23; *Annual Report of the Commissioner of Patents*, 1907–25 (Washington, D.C.); *Index of Patents Issued from the United States Patent Office*, 1926–27 (Washington, D.C.); Patent Assignments Index Card File, Patents and Trademarks Agency, Washington, D.C.

[89] *Cotton Chats*, no. 141 (July 1914). The Draper Company later acquired 75,000 acres of New York timberland for manufacturing shuttle blanks, but the date of that acquisition is unknown. Garner, *Model Company Town*, 126 and 255n35.

[90] *Cotton Chats*, no. 61 (May 1907).

Draper and the Automatic Loom / 923

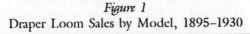

Figure 1
Draper Loom Sales by Model, 1895–1930

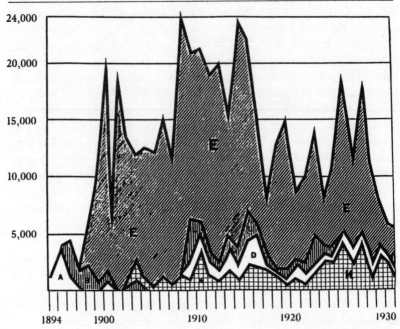

Source: Hopedale Public Library, undated chart.

With the ability to define an industry standard without a challenger on the horizon, the Draper Company could maximize profits by controlling its costs and by increasing the combined sales of the new loom and replacement parts. Standardization assured greater manufacturing economies of throughput by increasing the utilization of already existing specialized assets. The firm could turn from a strategy dominated by innovation to a more adaptive strategy of farming the assets accumulated in the era of rapid innovation. The human and capital resources remaining within the firm could still aim at new product development, but now within the constraint of complementarity with the standard loom designs. The patent strategy was likely to be even more defensive to guard against encroachment by inventors focusing on the secondary markets for supplies and replacement parts.

The direction of product development was placed in the hands of managers who had risen to executive positions largely through the temple division. These key personnel provided continuity and extensive

William Mass / 924

experience in manufacturing and sales, and they had learned how to maintain monopoly control even as patent control subsided in relative importance. After 1907 the number of new patents related to the Northrop loom assigned to the company dwindled, providing clear evidence of their decision to decrease the firm's efforts at technical innovation (see Table 7). Ironically, the most severe test of their organizational performance came from the officers and inventors ousted from the Draper Company.

William F. Draper died in January 1910, less than three years after his forced retirement from the Draper Company. Clare Draper inherited "a lot of loom patents and devices prepared by [William Draper] with assistance of Jonas Northrop."[91] Clare reluctantly sold these patent rights back to the Draper Company for one-third his asking price. The company next initiated negotiations with both Clare Draper and Jonas Northrop to convince them to forgo inventive efforts and other activities related to their past business in return for financial compensation. The negotiations quickly broke down, however, and the two remained fully independent actors.

In 1912, the year the original Northrop loom patents expired, Clare Draper and Jonas Northrop established the Hopedale Manufacturing Company under their own direction. They made their presence felt immediately. Their success in gaining warp stop motion orders prompted sharp price competition, and the prevailing prices on comparable motions dropped 50 percent. Their initial strategy was to sell automatic filling-changers to attach to looms "with twenty years' life left." The company explained that many cast iron looms could operate for fifty years. Although worn-out looms would be better replaced by automatic looms, Hopedale Manufacturing sold a set of "Nordray" attachments at one-third the price of a new loom that could "economically" convert looms with twenty years' life remaining for automatic weaving.[92] It also sold a smaller number of Nordray attachments on new Mason Machine Works looms until the company began selling its own complete Nordray looms in 1919.[93]

---

[91] Ibid., no. 87 (Jan. 1910); G. O. Draper, "Nordray Loom Catalogue," 14–15.

[92] G. O. Draper, "Nordray Loom Catalogue," 15. Most of the information about the Hopedale Manufacturing Company comes from several issues of its house organ, *Textrin Themes*: no. 15 (Aug. 1920); no. 16 (Sept. 1920); no. 19 (Dec. 1920); no. 20 (Feb. 1921); no. 22 (April 1921). In 1921, the Nordray attachments sold for $123; they included filling changer and battery, warp stop motions, shuttle, and feeler motions; *Textrin Themes*, no. 22. The claim of one-third the cost of new automatic looms is made in no. 15. The Dan River mills bought 1,271 Model E Drapers in 1921 at an average cost of $346.18, so the Hopedale claim seems accurate. Robert S. Smith, *Mill on the Dan* (Durham, N.C., 1960), 121.

[93] *Textrin Themes*, nos. 19–20. In 1918 the Draper Company gained control of Whitin

Draper and the Automatic Loom / 925

Table 7
Northrop Loom-Related Patents
Assigned to the Draper Company, 1899–1915

Year	*Number of Patents*
1899	13
1900	16
1901	11
1902	5
1903	18
1904	14
1905	7
1906	11
1907	10
1908	10
1909	9
1910	8
1911	2
1912	6
1913	2
1914	5
1915 (to 7/15)	3

Source: *Cotton Chats*, no. 162 (April 1916). The list of patents was presented as a "notice in regard to patents prepared under counsel and used on our Northrop Looms."

During this time the Draper Company continued to make good on its threats of aggressive legal action against patent infringement. First, in 1916, it gave notice by publishing the application dates of every Northrop loom patent still in effect (see Table 7). Patent protection was utilized in the secondary market as well. Each shipment of shuttles was packed with a notice announcing, "These shuttles are sold and licensed to be used only in looms made by Draper Company and its licensees."[94] The next year, the message was sent directly and forcefully to their challenging "offspring" as the Draper Company sued for infringement of a patent for a misthreading device, which

---

patents that Mason had previously leased; see Navin, *Whitin Machine Works*, 278. The importance of selling complete looms grew as the stock of nonautomatic looms aged and shrank.

[94] *Cotton Chats*, no. 170 (Dec. 1916). The text accompanying the reproduced notice explicitly threatened suit for patent infringement in these cases. There is no doubt the threat was aimed at the Hopedale Manufacturing Company, since it was the only other manufacturer of looms equipped to use Northrop shuttles.

William Mass / 926

ensured high cloth quality, that had originally been issued and assigned to its past managers and new competitors at the Hopedale Manufacturing Company. Hopedale had felt clear of Draper legal action because of mistakes in the original patent application, for which Jonas Northrop was the inventor of record. However, the Draper Company won a court victory that required Northrop to sign the reapplication forms. In another round of lawsuits, the Draper Company forced the mills that had purchased the invention from Hopedale Manufacturing to remove the misthreading devices from their looms.[95]

By 1920, at least 260 of the Draper Company's Northrop loom patents had expired, and the Hopedale Manufacturing Company was increasingly free to copy and improve on the Northrop loom design. In that year, Hopedale's first full year of deliveries, they shipped three thousand complete Nordray looms and had sufficient capacity to produce five thousand. Interestingly, the Hopedale Manufacturing Company made less than 2 percent of the looms in Fall River and New Bedford automatic by 1920, a rate that corroborates the view that a stronger commitment to technical innovation in automatic weaving mechanisms was insufficient to elicit their widespread adoption in southeastern Massachusetts.[96] Having only one-fifth the capacity of the Draper Corporation plant, the Hopedale Manufacturing Company continued more like a job order shop than a mass producer. They specialized in the production of custom-fit attachments for other manufacturers' looms, which they referred to as their "own peculiar field." But as they established their capability for integrated loom manufacture, they did increase their production of relatively small runs of custom-order looms.[97]

As passing time depleted the Draper Company arsenal of key patents, they increasingly relied on the advantages of scale economies. Reducing prices was particularly important for maintaining their share of the secondary market, where a small firm could grab for a toehold in the marketplace as the Hopedale Manufacturing Company was

---

[95] *Cotton Chats,* no. 165 (July 1916); no. 171 (Jan. 1917); no. 179 (Sept. 1917).

[96] *Textrin Themes,* nos. 15 and 19; Irwin I. Feller, "The Diffusion and Location of Technological Change in the American Cotton-Textile Industry, 1890–1970," *Technology and Culture* 15 (Oct. 1974).

[97] *Textrin Themes,* no. 19; *Cotton Chats,* no. 306; G. O. Draper, "Nordray Loom Catalogue," 28. By the end of 1920 the Hopedale Manufacturing Company had sold 23,882 sets of Nordray attachments and 4,851 complete automatic looms. After introducing the Nordray loom, Hopedale's sales of complete looms were about equal to the number of looms made automatic through the sale of attachments. For the years 1917–20, the total sales of automatic looms by the Draper Company was two and a half times the number of looms made automatic by the Hopedale Manufaturing Company.

beginning to do. For example, in 1923 Draper identified three frequently ordered shuttles as "standard shuttles." They established a policy of maintaining stocks in these models rather than producing for order and of giving price discounts on these and on any future shuttle ordered in sufficient volume to warrant designation as a "standard shuttle."[98]

The inventor-managers remaining at the Draper Company were highly talented inventors, but their inventive functions were constrained by both their own broader managerial responsibilities and the priorities of their colleagues. Whether these managers were more conservative by experience, socialization, or inclination, or just more accurate in anticipating the future, their strategy brought continued success in a more slowly expanding market.

The top managers at the Hopedale Manufacturing Company were by nature innovators, and certainly their previous roles in the shop culture of the Draper Company Experiment Committee reinforced these inclinations. On their own, they lacked the counteracting ballast of more conservative managers who might better prepare for rougher times ahead by first securing more predictable markets and steadier sales. The Hopedale Manufacturing Company continued operation until 1927, when the family division was bridged by Hopedale's absorption into the Draper Corporation, where Clare Draper was made a director.[99]

Conclusions and Implications

By the early 1930s, the Draper Corporation was the sole producer of single-shuttle looms, but it confronted renewed domestic and international technological competition with the development of shuttleless looms in the 1950s. Draper looms continued to dominate American markets, although they increasingly lagged technologically. Nevertheless, the company was still the largest loom producer in the world in the late 1960s. In 1967 Draper, the five hundredth largest U.S. corporation, was acquired by the antecedent of Rockwell International, the twenty-seventh largest, and a very research-intensive company. Despite promises to infuse new technology into the Draper Division, however, by 1975 Rockwell had withdrawn significant financial

[98] *Cotton Chats*, no. 238 (1923). Until then, the Draper Company had shipped 2,100 different shuttles. Mills could choose combinations among 242 shuttle blanks, 115 springs, 34 spring covers, 151 shuttle eyes, and several other devices.

[99] Ruth Lawrence, supervisor, *Draper, Preston and Allied Families* (New York, 1954), 58.

William Mass / 928

support for R&D, choosing to concentrate on other areas for growth.[100]

How did a leader in industrial research, a firm that at an early date acted like a modern research-oriented firm, lose its capabilities for further related product development and diversification? Why did the Draper Corporation fail to sustain its early leadership in industrial research? In its later years, Draper's ultimate failure was due to its inability to succeed in export competition and to diversify into other mechanical sectors, failings that are often seen as symptomatic of the competitive failures afflicting many large mechanically based U.S. industries in the late twentieth century.

The problem of exporting Draper technology, which was so successful in textile mills in the United States, really begins with ring spinning. Although Draper led in the development of this innovation, British firms early on adapted ring spinning to their domestic conditions and soon dominated world exports of ring spindles and spinning frames. Draper did take a major share in the British Northrop Loom Company, a firm licensed to manufacture and sell automatic looms on overseas markets. But British Northrop never penetrated the British market significantly, and it was a major competitor in the principle markets in continental Europe only for a relatively brief period after the Second World War. Draper's experience was typical in the textile machinery industry, since at its peak in 1922 the U.S. share of total world textile machinery exports was only 4 percent.[101]

The barriers to export market penetration were considerable. The poor performance of Draper in world markets despite its technological lead resulted from variations in the role of mechanization in international competition in different markets. The U.S. textile firms developed on the basis of high-wage, high-throughput technology, which required a high quality of cotton. The British developed a technology on the basis of lower-grade cotton inputs that was cost-competitive by offsetting low throughput with cheaper cotton and

---

[100] For a more complete history see William Mass, "Decline of a Technological Leader: Capabilities, Strategy, and Shuttleless Weaving, 1945–1974," *Business and Economic History*, 2d ser. 19 (1990): 234–44.

[101] D. A. Farnie, "The Textile Machine-Making Industry and the World Market, 1870–1815," *Business History* 32 (Oct. 1990): 150–70; Gary Saxonhouse and Gavin Wright, "Rings and Mules Around the World: A Comparative Study in Technological Choice," in *Technique, Spirit and Form in the Making of Modern Economies*, ed. Saxonhouse and Wright (Greenwich, Conn., 1984); Colin Simmons, "Hollins, Denis Machell: Textile Machinery Manufacturer," in *Dictionary of Business Biography: A Biographical Dictionary of Business Leaders Active in Britain in the Period 1860–1980*, vol. 3, ed. David Jeremy (London, 1985); Mass, "Technological Change and Industrial Relations," chap. 5.

Draper and the Automatic Loom / 929

low wages. Japan's later success was based on adapting and developing relatively high-throughput mechanical technologies that could also utilize cheaper, low-grade cotton and low-wage labor.[102] Draper technology was not suitable for most foreign markets, and with a large home market, the company never developed the distinctive organizational and technical capabilities required to adapt its technology for foreign customers.

Relative insulation from foreign markets offered little stimulus to product development for export. But why were opportunities for domestic diversification into related sectors not pursued? The Toyoda Automatic Loom Company, the dominant Japanese textile machine manufacturer, became the foundation for Japan's largest automobile manufacturer. A cursory contrast of the Draper company and the Toyoda Automatic Loom works suggests that the limits to diversification probably do not lie in inherent limits to integrating technical and organizational capabilities developed in loom manufacture (or in advanced mechanical technology more broadly). In fact, Taiichi Ohno, the originator of the famed Toyota production system, credits experience with warp stop motions on automatic looms as central to organizational learning about the importance of designing self-regulating machinery. Yet the origins of this principle lay in the development of various stop motions at the Draper Company.[103]

When the senior Drapers reacted to the current market for their machinery and the state of the textile industry generally by concentrating on volume production of Northrop loom technology, they consolidated the success created by their years of innovation, but perhaps at the price of long-term competitive advantage. As George O. Draper, the dominant personality at the Hopedale Manufacturing Company, wrote in the early 1920s, "The [Draper Corporation] earnings made public in the intervening years certainly justify such policy for periodic application, but it leaves the path open for others to enter and for others to design the improvements which might have been made."[104]

---

[102] See Mass and Lazonick, "The British Cotton Industry and Competitive Advantage."
[103] Taiichi Ohno, "How the Toyota Production System Was Created," in *The Anatomy of Japanese Business*, ed. K. Sato and Y. Hoshino (Armonk, N.Y., 1984); see also Michael Cusumano, *The Japanese Automobile Industry* (New York, 1985), esp. 27–32, 58–65.
[104] G. O. Draper, "Nordray Loom Catalogue," 14.

[15]

Continuity and Change in the Management of Industrial Research: The Du Pont Company, 1902–1980

David A. Hounshell

INTRODUCTION

The often used expression, 'the more things change, the more they stay the same', perfectly fits the history of the Du Pont Company's research and development programmes from their formal beginning in 1902 until 1980. Managing research during this period was always problematical. Despite changes in the size of the company and the nature of its business, despite new developments in the worlds of science and technology, despite changes in the scale and sophistication of the company's research efforts, Du Pont's executives have from the very outset faced a certain set of perennial issues in the management of research: what role should research play in the company's strategy? Should the company conduct research in a centralized organization or along decentralized, departmental lines? How much money should the company spend on research, and in what areas? What kind of time horizons should the company's research programmes have—short or long range? Should researchers be closely managed or pretty much left alone? This chapter is an attempt to highlight briefly the major areas of change and continuity in Du Pont's twentieth-century research programmes while summarizing very briefly the rich history of the company's research experience.

If I were forced to identify a single, dominant element of continuity in Du Pont's R. & D. history during the first eight decades of this century, I would say that it was faith in and commitment to R. & D. Despite changes in overall corporate

This chapter draws from Hounshell and Smith (1989), to which we refer for a detailed bibliography.

232   *David A. Hounshell*

strategy, the company's leaders have maintained a steadfast faith in the value of research and have consistently outspent—both in absolute figures and as a percentage of sales—its major competitors.

For the sake of analysis, I have divided the history of Du Pont's R. & D. programmes into six periods: founding (1902–10), centralization and diversification (1911–21), decentralization, acquisition, and rationalization (1921–35), nylon and the 'new nylons' mentality (1936–60), maturation and response (1960–70), and rethinking and restructuring (1970–80). I present also some charts (see Appendix) to provide a quick guide to the major events of the period, the internal and external forces that affected the company's R. & D. programmes, and the major fruits of those programmes in terms of products and processes.

FOUNDING, 1902–1911

In 1902 two signal events occurred in the Du Pont Company. First, the hundred-year-old firm passed into the hands of three younger du Pont cousins, T. Coleman, Pierre S., and Alfred I. The older generation of du Ponts was tired, leaderless, and without any real idea of the assets of their company. In the new generation, Coleman and Pierre du Pont in particular saw their acquisition as a major opportunity to consolidate the entire explosives industry of the United States. By 1905 they had succeeded, bringing three-quarters of the industry under the control of a central management, the Executive Committee of E. I. du Pont de Nemours Powder Company. The consolidated Du Pont Company manufactured three types of explosives: black powder (an old, fragmented, and declining business), dynamite (a newer, concentrated, growing, and highly profitable product), and smokeless powder (a product aimed mainly at the military market and one that was just becoming profitable).

The second major event of 1902 occurred when the Eastern Dynamite Company, a subsidiary of Du Pont soon to be consolidated into the larger company, established the Eastern Laboratory, a facility divorced from any immediate manufacturing responsibilities and with a specific mission to improve the company's high explosives products and processes through scientific research and development. From the time Du Pont interests had first entered the high explosives

The Du Pont Company, 1902–1980 233

business, its managers had been aware of the economic benefits that accrued from technical improvements. A small increase in chemical yields meant important savings in materials that could easily be measured in dollars and cents. But not until 1902 did the managers of the dynamite business decide to build a laboratory removed from the day-to-day operations of the plant. The wisdom of this decision was quickly demonstrated. Under the direction of the German-educated Dr Charles L. Reese, Eastern Laboratory made a big showing in only a few years. In 1911, for example, Reese calculated the annual profits stemming from only four among many of Eastern Laboratory's developments at a million dollars; the total cost of research at Eastern was but a third of these profits.

Eastern Laboratory's success contrasted sharply with the experience of the Experimental Station, the second Du Pont R. & D. laboratory, established in 1903 north of Wilmington, Delaware, on the Brandywine River immediately downstream from the company's original hundred-year-old black-powder works. Shortly after Coleman du Pont had organized the executive committee to run the newly acquired company, Francis I. du Pont (another cousin) and Alfred—both members of the Executive Committee— decided not to establish laboratories similar to Eastern for their respective businesses, smokeless powder and black powder. Rather, they agreed with A. J. Moxham, the executive Coleman had appointed to watch over the newly organized development department, that the company should organize a 'general experimental laboratory' whose mission would be to support all three of the company's existing businesses and to do pioneering research for the company along broad lines such as the synthesis of natural raw materials used in explosives manufacture. Hence the Experimental Station, which today must be one of the largest corporate research complexes in the world.

When Charles Reese's counterpart at the Experimental Station was compelled in 1911 to prepare a statement of the Station's contributions to profits, he was unable to demonstrate any such profits. In fact, he was hard pressed to show that the laboratory operated on a break-even basis. He argued that several of the Station's projects were of enormous proportions and, though of great cost and risk, might ultimately pay handsome dividends. Executives in 1911—at least most of them—accepted this argument because it was consistent with the policy established in 1907 by Pierre S. du Pont while he was briefly in charge of supervising the director of the Experimental Station. Pierre had maintained that:

In our Experimental [Station] Laboratory we should at all time endeavor to have some investigations in which the reward of success would be very great, but which may have a correspondingly great cost of development, calling for an extended research of possibly several years, and the employment of a considerable force. (Pierre S. du Pont, 1908)

Pierre du Pont's statement captures the very essence of the Du Pont Company's philosophy of research for much of this century—pursue big, high-risk, high-reward projects that demand extensive commitment of research personnel and financial resources over a long period of time.

The director of the Experimental Station stressed that his laboratory's performance had to be measured by means other than its immediate contribution to profits. Specifically, he alluded to the qualitative success of the Station in that the United States army and navy ordnance officials continued to view Du Pont as a scientifically advanced manufacturer of smokeless powder in spite of the growing public criticism by Progressives of Du Pont as an evil 'trust'. The army and the navy continued to purchase smokeless powder from Du Pont even though some members of Congress wanted to prohibit these purchases. Congress actually passed the 1908 Naval Appropriations Bill with a specific clause banning the Navy from buying powder from a 'trust'.

Du Pont's success in being viewed by military officials as a progressive manufacturer of smokeless powder was not accidental. In 1903, Francis I. du Pont had written what essentially became the charter of the Experimental Station and had stressed the necessity of Du Pont's remaining well out in front of the government in the development of military propellants. Both the army and the 'new' navy had established their own R. & D. laboratories for smokeless powder and had also built or planned to build small-scale experimental manufacturing plants. The full weight of Du Pont's success in staying ahead of the army and navy in the development of military propellants was not felt until after Du Pont lost its first big anti-trust case. In 1912 the company was convicted of violating the Sherman Act and was forced to divest a big chunk of its business. But the army and navy interceded on Du

The Du Pont Company, 1902–1980   235

Pont's behalf and convinced the court to keep intact all of the company's smokeless powder operations, largely because of Du Pont's R. & D. prowess in this area. The consent decree went into effect in 1913, so Du Pont was perfectly positioned to reap several hundred million dollars in profits from sales of smokeless powder that mushroomed when World War I broke out in Europe in 1914.

CENTRALIZATION AND DIVERSIFICATION, 1911–1921

In 1911, however, this vast fortune from smokeless powder manufacture was not evident. A minority of members of the executive committee were not convinced that the pursuit of research in a general or central laboratory like the Station was the best allocation of resources. That year, for reasons that had nothing to do with R. & D., T. Coleman and Pierre du Pont reorganized the managerial structure of the company. As Alfred Chandler has written in his classic *Strategy and Structure* (Chandler, 1962:63), the net effect of this reorganization was the centralization of the company under one general manager, Hamilton Barksdale. The selection of Barksdale had an important impact on the company's R. & D. He had been the cofounder of the highly successful Eastern Laboratory and the staunchest opponent of the Experimental Station as a general laboratory. Seeking increased funding for the expansion of Eastern Laboratory in 1904, Barksdale had led a campaign to convince the Executive Committee to choose once and for all how it would manage its R. & D. (in decentralized departmental laboratories like Eastern or in a centralized general laboratory like the Experimental Station). Barksdale believed that the Station's fuzzy mission, its duplication of Eastern's high explosives research, and its location away from manufacturing plants resulted in inefficient and ineffective research. He strongly advocated the establishment of separate R. & D. laboratories for black powder and smokeless powder, to be located at appropriate plant sites and managed by the respective industrial divisions.

Barksdale's efforts led to extensive debates within the full executive committee about how best to manage industrial R. & D. As was its custom, the committee formed a subcommittee to study the issue, which issued two majority reports accompanied by two

236   *David A. Hounshell*

minority reports. When the full committee took up the issue, it too was unable to resolve the issue in 1904 and decided instead that there was no 'one best way' to manage research. Because of the company's adequate resources, the committee decided to continue to pursue both centralized and decentralized approaches to research.

When Barksdale assumed the position of general manager in 1911—only a month after the directors of Eastern Laboratory and the Experimental Station had issued their reports about their respective laboratories' contributions to profits—he quickly seized the opportunity he had been waiting for since 1904. He determined to put the unwieldy Experimental Station under the control of Charles L. Reese, the founding director of the Eastern Laboratory, who by this time was known as the Chemical Director of the High Explosives Operating Department. In that position, Reese was in charge of not only the Eastern Laboratory but also the chemical control of all of the department's plants. That is, he was responsible for monitoring the actual plant yields as compared to the theoretical yields derived by the Eastern Laboratory. Barksdale created a corporate-wide position of chemical director and elevated Reese to this position. Barksdale obviously hoped that Reese would do for the Experimental Station what he had done for the Eastern Laboratory—that is, to align research closely with production problems and product opportunities.

Paradoxically, Barksdale's move resulted in the greatest centralization of research in the company's history. In the short run, Reese did exert considerable pressure on the Station to look more closely at the company's businesses, but for reasons discussed below, the Station took increasing responsibility for the diversification of the company. This meant that the bulk of its research moved away from immediate commercial needs in smokeless powder and black powder. Moreover, Reese liked power, and over the next five or six years, he built a large, centrally controlled organization that for some in the company seemed to exist for itself.

This increasing centralization in the management of research and development occurred at precisely the time that the company's top managers had determined to diversify the company. Talk of diversification began when Progressive agitation against the 'powder trust' threatened Du Pont's sales to the armed services. In 1908, when Congress prohibited the navy from buying any powder from 'trusts', Du Pont's executives were forced to close down

The Du Pont Company, 1902–1980 237

much of the company's smokeless powder manufacturing plant and to begin searching for products to make with this idle plant. Smokeless powder is nitrocellulose, so Du Pont concentrated on diversifying into other nitrocellulose products, such as celluloid plastics and nitrocellulose-coated fabrics. Even at this early date, Du Pont had developed a noticeable hubris about its R. & D. capabilities, and managers initially thought they could easily develop products and processes in these areas. But after doing enough work to learn the true complexity of these businesses, Du Pont bought its way into both the 'artificial leather' (nitrocellulose-coated fabrics) business and the celluloid industry.

Although the Congressional attack on Du Pont abated and thus took immediate pressure off the company to find ways to utilize its excess smokeless powder plant capacity, World War I suddenly amplified this concern to unprecedented proportions. With the company building more and more capacity, its executives worried more and more about overcapacity in the post-war era. In 1916, after two years of anxiety, Du Pont's executives realized that their strategy of finding uses for the company's smokeless powder plants did not utilize Du Pont's greatest resources, which were people, know-how, and plenty of cash.

In place of the old plan, Du Pont's Development Department fashioned a new diversification strategy that was so bold that it was expected to take a generation to execute fully. The goal was to move Du Pont away from its core business in explosives and turn the firm into a well-diversified chemical giant. Formulated largely by Fin Sparre, the director of the Experimental Station who was on loan to the Development Department and who would play a key role in Du Pont's diversification until his retirement in 1944, the new strategy including entry into vegetable oils, paints, pigments, and organic chemicals, including dyestuffs, pharmaceuticals, and photographic chemicals.

Du Pont bought its way into paints and pigments but stayed out of vegetable oils. With organic chemicals, however, the company ventured into dyestuffs on its own largely because there was no American dye firm to buy; the Germans totally dominated the industry, and after 1914 the United States was cut off from German supplies. Reese quickly brought all of the company's technical resources to bear on the dyestuffs venture, and he began an intensive campaign to hire organic chemists who knew something

238   *David A. Hounshell*

about the dye industry—an impossible mission. Du Pont quickly learned that there was far more to the synthetic dye industry than its chemists knew and that it would be difficult and expensive to do in a few years what it had taken the Germans fifty years to achieve. The company soon worked out an agreement with the British dye house of Levenstein, which, excepting synthetic indigo, knew little more about the business than Du Pont did. Reese had had organic chemists at both the Station and the Eastern Laboratory working on dyestuffs, but in 1917, he consolidated these efforts in the new Jackson Laboratory, located at the site of the company's new dye works. Soon well over half of the company's thousand-strong R. & D. staff were working at Jackson Laboratory and its sister institution, the Technical Laboratory, the end-use research laboratory also located at the dye works.

DECENTRALIZATION, ACQUISITION, AND RATIONALIZATION, 1921–1935

By 1920, Du Pont was rapidly losing money on its dyestuffs business and all of its other non-explosives businesses. This trend continued into mid-1921 and reached such proportions that after extended and hotly debated discussions, the executive committee took a dramatic step and decentralized the company's organization into separate industrial departments, each with its own manufacturing and sales divisions. The committee believed that if each business had better control over its functions it would perform better than in the centrally managed firm.

This decentralization radically affected Du Pont's R. & D. programme because the men whom the executive committee put in charge of the various businesses—general managers, as they were called—had been generally unsatisfied with the chemical department's performance. They believed that the department served its own ends rather than theirs. Soon after assuming their new duties, the general managers banded together and demanded that R. & D. functions also be decentralized—that the chemical department be split up. Although the president of the company, Irenee du Pont, did not like the idea, he was unwilling to vote against the general managers. The chemical department was 'disembodied', as one research manager observed, but not totally eliminated. Eastern Laboratory became the responsibility of the explosives department; the new dyestuffs department took charge of the Jackson Laboratory; and so on. (By this time, the chemical department was managing five geographically separated laboratories.) A mere vestige of the once glorious chemical department survived; eighteen researchers remained at the Experimental Station under the nominal direction of Charles Reese, who retired a few years later.

Looking back on the decade from 1911 to 1921, the most important development—at least as far as the future of Du Pont was concerned—was the decision to diversify the company. That decision led eventually to the decentralization of the company's organization, which in turn facilitated future diversification activities. The decentralization of the company in 1921 forced the company's executives to debate again the merits of centralized versus decentralized management of R. & D. The resulting decision to split up the once powerful central chemical department reaffirmed the executive committee's decision of 1904 to support both approaches to R. & D. Since 1921 Du Pont has not materially departed from this basic structure for managing R. & D.

Du Pont's experience with diversification in the half decade after 1916 led not only to the decentralization of the corporation but also to some important conclusions by executives about how future diversification would be undertaken. In 1921 executives knew that they were in well over their heads in dyestuffs. The dye works had proven to be essentially a sink-hole for Du Pont's cash. Du Pont had invested perhaps $20 million in the business and faced investments of another $20 million before profits would become apparent. No doubt with some regrets, executives had accepted the fact that Du Pont did not have all of the necessary know-how in dye chemistry and dye manufacturing, so they had approved and helped carry out a somewhat clandestine operation to recruit a number of German dye chemists to provide this critical know-how. The lesson these executives drew from the dye experience was that diversification by acquisition was easier than diversification through the internal generation of science and technology. Over the next decade and a half, du Pont built a chemicals empire through acquisitions, not through internal means.

Between 1921 and 1933, Du Pont's executives pursued a growth strategy predicated on diversification through acquisition of companies or technologies. The decentralized structure of the corporation suited this strategy well because when Du Pont brought a company or a major technology, the acquisition often became a new industrial department. In terms of R. & D., Du Pont typically built a research organization around the acquisition and then began the very important process of rationalizing the acquired technology, pushing it to its limits, finding new markets for its products, and developing new products as well. In this way Du Pont moved into the production of rayon fibres (French technology purchase), cellophane films (French technology purchase), synthetic ammonia and other high-pressure reaction products (French technology purchase), tetraethyllead (TEL) gasoline antiknock (Du Pont manufacturing process of compound discovered by GM), and Freon refrigerants (Du Pont manufacturing process of compound discovered by GM), titanium-dioxide pigments (initial process purchased and the chloride process developed later), and electrochemistry (purchase of Roessler and Hasslacher Chemical Company). The last major acquisition Du Pont made during this period was the Remington Arms Company in 1933, which was well outside its chemical industry realm and therefore did not really fit the diversification strategy developed by Fin Sparre in 1916. Indeed, not until very recently did Du Pont purchase the balance of Remington's stock and fully merge the company into the larger corporation.

The growth of the Du Pont Company during the period from 1921 to 1935 was clearly world class. After their formation, two other firms were in the same league, I. G. Farben and Imperial Chemical Industries. Du Pont had had international market-sharing agreements with predecessors of both firms and clearly wanted those agreements, which were restricted to certain explosive products, to be put in force again and to be greatly expanded to cover other products. Wanting to capture part of the large American market, I. G. Farben was not anxious to divide world markets. ICI and Du Pont, however, reached an agreement in 1929 called the Patents and Processes Agreement, which was clearly designed to divide world markets between the two firms. Du Pont's Sparre believed that by licensing one another's patents and processes, Du Pont and ICI could divide world markets without violating the Sherman Act.

Although clearly a market-sharing agreement, this device affected Du Pont's R. & D. programmes because the presidents of the two chemical companies also reached a gentlemen's agreement that their R. & D. laboratories would exchange not only information on existing products and processes but also on all research being done in the two companies (that is, on research from its inception). Until anti-trust action ended this arrangement in the late 1940s, the ICI agreement significantly broadened Du Pont's research base. For example, in the mid to late 1940s when Du Pont was trying to develop dyes for its new, hydrophobic Orlon acrylic and Dacron polyester fibres, research managers relied heavily upon the dye research unit at ICI for fundamental work. When the agreement was cancelled, Du Pont's research managers estimated that Du Pont would have to hire thirty first-class researchers to make up for the loss of ICI information. Moreover, since ICI did many things differently from Du Pont, considerable cross-fertilization of ideas occurred when the hundreds of research delegations from the two companies visited each other's laboratories and plants and when researchers from both companies read the tens of thousands of research reports that were exchanged during the lifetime of the agreement.

During this period from 1921 well into the 1930s Du Pont had access to much of the world's chemical research. The company's strategy called for R. & D. to play a supporting role of assimilating, improving, and extending acquired technology and knowledge. Du Pont did not see its R. & D. as the principal means of generating new technology and new business. But within a very short period, owing to both internal and external factors, the company completely changed its strategy. Du Pont moved into an explosive new era.

NYLON AND THE 'NEW NYLONS' MENTALITY, 1936–1960

In the 1920s, while the industrial departments were laying the foundations of the Du Pont chemical empire, the remnant of the central chemical department struggled to find a role in the company. Under the leadership of Reese's successors, Charles M. A. Stine in the 1920s and Elmer K. Bolton in the 1930s, the chemical department rose to prominence primarily because of the discoveries of neoprene synthetic rubber and nylon by Wallace H. Carothers's fundamental research group. Until this time, the chemical department had survived by doing research for the industrial departments essentially

242   *David A. Hounshell*

on a contract basis. But Stine sought a more central and independent role for his department. In 1926 he asked the executive committee for more money for general investigations and proposed what he called a 'radical departure', the establishment of a 'pure research' programme. The executive committee was uneasy about the concept of pure research and asked Stine to reformulate his proposal.

When Stine came back to the committee, his ideas had developed significantly. Now he proposed a 'fundamental research' programme, not 'pure research'. He convinced the executive committee that Du Pont's seemingly disparate businesses really possessed common scientific bases. If these common scientific bases were better understood, Du Pont's businesses would inevitably benefit. But because of the shorter-range focus of each of the industrial department research divisions, such fundamental work was not apt to get done; only the central chemical department could engage in such important work on a long-term basis and thus it could now fulfil its logical role as a central laboratory in the now well-diversified Du Pont Company.

Stine identified several areas in which his department could contribute to the welfare of the company. One item on his list was polymers. He argued that there was virtually no fundamental understanding of polymer chemistry, yet many of Du Pont's businesses were polymeric in nature. These included paints, plastics, rayon, and cellophane film. Du Pont could not rely on universities to generate knowledge of polymer chemistry because universities simply were not doing such chemistry. The same was true, argued Stine, in such areas as catalysis, high-pressure reactions, physico-chemical phenomena, and chemical engineering. Stine stressed that his plan would not only lead inevitably to improvements in Du Pont's products and processes but more importantly would serve as a major piece of public relations, thereby allowing Du Pont to recruit higher-calibre researchers and improve the company's relationship with colleges and universities. Thoroughly convinced by Stine, who incidentally was a great, almost evangelical salesman of research, the executive committee granted Stine a much larger budget for 'general research' and generous funds for his fundamental research programme.

Soon the chemical department was building a new laboratory at the Experimental Station to hold the researchers Stine envisioned recruiting for his programme. Other researchers at the Station promptly and somewhat facetiously dubbed this laboratory 'Purity Hall'. But even with a new laboratory, very high salaries, generous research support, and a supposedly 'unlimited' publication policy, Stine found it impossible to recruit the top-tier chemists away from the universities. These men—and they were all men in those days—were very suspicious of industrial research and reckoned it industrial slavery. Rebuffed by established university professors, Stine had to turn to young academics who could be more easily lured by the money and promising opportunities.

One of these more vulnerable chemists was Wallace H. Carothers, an instructor at Harvard, who agreed to join Du Pont only after repeated assurances that he could pursue 'pure science'. Carothers and Stine agreed that he would investigate polymers and would have a group of several scientists with fresh Ph.D.s helping him. Within three years, Carothers had conducted his classic research on the nature and formation of polymers that propelled him to the forefront of the new discipline, thereby accomplishing Stine's original goal of building Du Pont's image as a high-calibre scientific organization. But this academic era would not last much longer.

In April 1930, two of Carothers's assistants made unexpected discoveries, neoprene and the first truly synthetic fibre. Carothers was pleased by these discoveries but quickly moved on to other areas of polymer chemistry that interested him more, leaving the organic-chemicals department to develop neoprene and dropping the synthetic fibre work altogether after publishing several papers on the subject. A few months after the initial discoveries, Stine was promoted to the executive committee and was replaced by Elmer Bolton, who had directed Du Pont's dyestuff research since the early 1920s and who had voiced objections to Stine's fundamental research programme when he first heard about it. Whereas Stine had symbolized the expansive visions of the 1920s, Bolton represented the practical, tough-minded Depression decade. He believed that Du Pont could not afford to allow its élite group of scientists in Purity Hall to pursue only scientific goals, and he accordingly started to bring fundamental research down from its ethereal realm. After constant badgering by Bolton and his assistant Ernest Benger, who had come from the Rayon Department's research division, Carothers agreed in 1934 to renew work on fibres, which had languished for about three years after the initial exciting results. He soon discovered nylon.

244   *David A. Hounshell*

This discovery resulted in the chemical department being turned inside out to develop nylon into a commercial product. While nylon was being developed, Carothers essentially went into a tailspin; his bouts of depression, which had plagued him since early manhood, grew worse and worse until he committed suicide in 1937. By this time Bolton had essentially done away with Stine's original fundamental research programme (that is, a group of élite researchers pursuing their own agenda as long as it seemed to be related to Du Pont's businesses). Most of those that had been in the fundamental research programme found themselves working in one way or another on the development of nylon. Bolton made fundamental research something that all of the chemical department's groups did some of when it was appropriate.

The virtually instantaneous success of nylon came at roughly the same time as the more radically oriented members of President Roosevelt's 'brain trust' had gained the upper hand in diagnosing the United States' economic problems. They laid the Depression at the feet of big business in America and launched the late New Deal's attack on large corporations. Under Thurman Arnold, a sharp critic of Du Pont, the Anti-trust Division of the Justice Department expanded rapidly between 1938 and 1942 and instituted some 180 cases—50 per cent of all those that had been pursued since the Division was created in 1903! Arnold and his successors vigorously went after Du Pont, bringing some eight anti-trust cases against the firm by the end of the 1940s. To Du Pont executives in the late 1930s and early 1940s, this new wave of attacks on the firm yielded one very solid conclusion: Du Pont's future growth would have to stem from some means other than acquisition.

Nylon provided the way. It became the new archetype for Du Pont's strategy: nylon (and neoprene) had emerged from fundamental research. If Du Pont were to expand its fundamental research efforts, not only in the central chemical department but also by carrying it out in the industrial research divisions, then its laboratories would become cornucopias of 'new nylons'. Executives derived this new formula for success between 1941 and 1945 as the United States was engaged in World War II. Du Pont's highly successful experience in turning a piece of exotic physics into the massive Hanford Plutonium Works, a critical part of the Manhattan Project, reinforced the power of this formula.

The Du Pont Company, 1902–1980   245

Between 1946 and 1954, Du Pont dramatically expanded the firm's R. & D. facilities, personnel, and expenditures. In particular, executives convinced the general managers of most of the industrial departments (who were very independent in those days) to build new laboratories on the grounds of the Experimental Station and to devote these facilities to basic and pioneering research. The Station rapidly took on the appearance of a university campus, and a similar atmosphere, with all of its polar attributes of interchange and insularity, also followed. The model of fundamental science inducing corporate growth became the foundation of Du Pont's corporate culture. Science was now firmly at the centre of Du Pont's corporate strategy.

During this period, the industrial departments became more autonomous than before. Many of them carried out their own fundamental research programmes on polymers, the area of chemistry that now formed Du Pont's core technology. Ironically, the chemical department—soon to be renamed the central research department—was instructed to leave polymer research to the industrial departments, a move contrary to the central research philosophy that Stine had articulated in 1927 when he won approval to establish the company's first fundamental research programme. In developing a mentality of 'new nylons', executives and research managers alike had forgotten why the company had so easily and swiftly developed nylon. The chemical department's pioneering work had fitted neatly into the company's existing businesses, technologies, and levels of expertise. With central research's programmes being pushed away from the company's commercial interests, the nylon model became skewed.

The role of central research in the company therefore became highly problematic. The department was urged simply to explore new areas rather than to provide the fundamental knowledge base for Du Pont's technologies. Executives still believed, however, that central research would discover new nylons. As the department moved into physics and biology, it began to lose contact with many of the industrial departments and consequently took on the trappings of a high-powered scientific research establishment divorced from any commercial objectives. Eventually, many in the company began to criticize central research for pursuing science that was out of step with corporate strategy.

These sentiments began to grow when it became apparent that

246   *David A. Hounshell*

Du Pont had not come up with another nylon. This is not to say that research had not produced anything, but rather that no new products were developed during this period that approached nylon's impact on the company's growth and earnings. During the 1950s Du Pont developed important insecticides and herbicides and new plastics with outstanding properties. The textile fibers department (successor to the rayon department) had produced the most significant products with its Orlon acrylic and Dacron polyester fibres. Moreover, intensive R. & D. on nylon itself had yielded new products and processes that continued to make nylon a major money-maker. Commanding the lion's share of total company R. & D. expenditures, textile fibers provided almost half of Du Pont's earnings on one-third of the company's sales in 1960.

Du Pont and its R. & D. programmes were affected by other trends external to the company during the 1940s and 1950s. The most important was the growth of competition in the chemical industry. World War II had rapidly accelerated the development of Du Pont's competitors. The wartime emergency had led many of them to engage in R. & D. projects and manufacturing operations that were extraordinary for them at the time but that would become commonplace after the war. In this sense, the war was a great leveller in terms of scientific and technical talent in the chemical industry. Du Pont's executives perhaps underrated the abilities of their competitors; certainly most of Du Pont's R. & D. personnel believed they were head and shoulders above their competition. This hubris sometimes had dire consequences for Du Pont's products.

MATURATION AND RESPONSE, 1960–1970

By the late 1950s, Du Pont's rate of growth and earnings began to decline, a sign that the chemical industry had begun to mature. Although the company's research programmes had been expanded significantly, the number of important new products introduced annually had not. The increasing size of the company required R. & D. to turn out a larger number of new products each year if Du Pont were to achieve its performance goals. After assessing the situation, the executive committee concluded that Du Pont research was more productive than ever but that the results were not getting beyond the laboratory, particularly those discoveries that

The Du Pont Company, 1902–1980   247

would lead Du Pont into new businesses. Therefore, in 1960 the committee called for a corporate-wide push to develop products from Du Pont's accumulated riches of research. Executives likened their new venture programme to Du Pont's first diversification efforts when the company successfully moved away from being purely an explosives manufacturer. Rather than acquisition of new technologies and small companies, however, the new venture programme would be based on Du Pont's own R. & D.

Du Pont had learned in the 1910s how difficult it was to diversify through R. & D. alone. The anti-trust climate of the post-war era, however, and the company's self-definition as a chemical company (a definition stemming from the post-war planning conducted by the executive committee during World War II) limited Du Pont's alternatives. Two brief examples illustrate these factors. Had Du Pont had the legal go-ahead and the intention to purchase a large pharmaceuticals company, the company's life sciences programme would probably be far ahead of where it is today. Second, Du Pont pioneered the production of pure silicon, but not wishing to compete with its primary customer, Texas Instruments, and seeing itself as a chemical firm, Du Pont did not integrate forwards into doping and eventually lost out when TI integrated backwards to produce its own silicon.

Not discouraged by the setbacks of the late 1950s, all of Du Pont's technical organizations responded enthusiastically to the executive committee's call for new products. The company had money to spend on new ventures—about $300 million, the executive committee estimated. In the ensuing decade of the 1960s, Du Pont doubled its rate of new product introduction from 2.5 to 5 per year but at an extraordinary cost—$2 billion.

The new venture programme led to the revitalization of the once-powerful development department, which had atrophied following Fin Sparre's retirement in 1944. The Executive Committee gave the department responsibility for developments that did not fall logically into the province of any industrial department or that the industrial departments did not want to pursue. This marked something of a departure from the company's post-war decentralized research strategy, which placed complete responsibility for diversification on the industrial departments. The Development Department launched seven major new ventures and invested in a like number of embryonic companies (i.e. became minority

248   *David A. Hounshell*

shareholder in what the development department hoped would become emerging technology-driven growth companies). Five of the new ventures, which included the successful Automatic Clinical Analyzer, were commercialized, but Du Pont eventually divested itself of its holdings in the small companies.

Although the development department was beefed up, the Executive Committee's actions fell well short of what the manager of the new venture programme, Edwin Gee, wanted. Gee advocated the establishment of a diversification department, but the committee did not see the need and reasserted that the industrial departments were still expected to be the principal seat of innovation within the firm. Instead of moving the company in new directions, the new venture programme of the 1960s resulted in a deepening of commitment to Du Pont's existing lines of business—to more of the same, in other words. Many of the largest and most expensive ventures were, in fact, in the textile fibers department. There is irony in this because much of the rationale for launching the entire new venture programme was to lessen the company's dependence on textile fiber earnings, which had dominated the company and which could not last forever.

Without a programme for reallocating corporate resources, textile fibers continued to dominate the company. When that department's earnings suffered a significant drop in 1966, just six years after the beginning of the new venture programme, doubts began to arise about the entire programme. The new ventures that had been launched were not yet capable of contributing much to the company's profits. In fact, most were still losing money. Moreover, textile fibers' profits dived just when Du Pont needed unprecedented amounts of cash to finance its new venture programme. Sizing up the situation in 1967, the executive committee concluded that a major cause of the deterioration of the company's position was poor investment decisions in new ventures, and estimated that about one-third of them would have to be written off as losses.

In the late 1960s, Du Pont attempted to deal with this situation by terminating some ventures and scrutinizing more carefully departmental requests for additional new venture funds. Mostly, though, the company rode out the storm initiated by the burst of innovation that had marked the first part of the decade. By the end of the 1960s, the executive committee declared the entire new venture programme a failure; the company had spent $2 billion to develop over forty new products. But many of these were facing extended periods of operating losses, and some appeared to be beyond hope.

Du Pont's predicament called into question the company's entire post-war strategy. Large-scale projects had become so expensive and risky that the company could afford only a limited number of them—a far different situation from that which had previously prevailed, when the company funded any project that had sound technical merits. Nevertheless, the executive committee remained reluctant to play a stronger role in the direction of research and development activities until capital shortages in the mid-1970s forced it to select particular projects for development and commercialization. Only gradually did the committee assume a larger role in the management of Du Pont research.

RETHINKING AND RESTRUCTURING, 1970–1980

When the executive committee declared the entire new venture programme a failure, thereby also condemning the policy of long-term, high-risk, high-investment, high-projected-earnings innovation first enunciated by Pierre S. du Pont in 1907, it was truly at a loss about what to do. Therefore, during much of the 1970s, a decade marked by extreme economic turmoil, the company used its research organizations to keep its existing businesses healthy and to try to salvage the more promising of the new ventures of the 1960s. In the early part of the decade, the committee was unwilling or unable to revise or restructure the way in which the company managed its R. & D. function. Simple cutting back on expenditures was the easiest course to follow, and that is what the company did. But the Arab oil embargo of 1974 hit the company very hard in all of its polymer areas; textile fibers was particularly vulnerable. Du Pont faced unprecedented cash shortages. The situation called for radical action.

The election of Edwin A. Gee to the executive committee in 1970 provided the critical catalyst for change. As noted earlier, Gee had been the one selected by president Crawford Greenewalt to head the development department's new venture efforts of the 1960s. He had called for the creation of a diversification department charged with the responsibility of moving the company into new businesses and had lost that battle. Both as the development department's new ventures manager and later as head of the development department Gee had also lost all of his attempts to wrest primary responsibility for diversification away from the industrial departments. He had consistently argued that the industrial departments were too busy protecting their businesses to think radically about the future and that until Du Pont had some means to reallocate its research resources, it would be business as usual. Later, as general manager of the fledgling photo-products department, Gee well knew how much he could have done in developing new businesses for the company if he had only had some of textile fibers' huge R. & D. funds to work with. Nevertheless, by taking over the development department's Automatic Clinical Analyzer venture and purchasing Berg Electronics, Gee's photo products became a star performer. The department demonstrated that Du Pont could build high-return businesses in entirely new areas without vast outlays of R. & D. expenses and capital.

Gee brought to the executive committee an agenda for the restructuring of Du Pont R. & D. When Irving Shapiro, an attorney without any intellectual or emotional commitments to R. & D., became the chief executive officer, Gee was able to achieve most of his goals before he left the company to head International Paper. Gee's agenda contained several items. First, he proposed to cut fundamental research and concentrate on areas in which Du Pont had an existing competitive advantage. He argued that central research's areas of excellence should follow, not precede, the company's areas of business and corporate commitment. Gee also maintained that Du Pont should be more wary of launching high-risk and high-investment ventures. After a major venture was initiated, the executive committee had to pay more attention to it than in the past, because the venture could become a significant drain on the company's earnings. Gee also advocated cutting R. & D. expenditures on products that had fallen to commodity status, and he called for more emphasis on the purchase and sale of technology. Much of Du Pont's research, Gee believed, should be aimed at lowering production costs as a means of gaining competitive advantage. Gee urged his colleagues on the executive committee to find a means by which the committee could assume a greater role in the allocation of the company's research resources; that is, Gee wanted to establish a mechanism for the reallocation of

The Du Pont Company, 1902–1980   251

research resources in the company. Finally—and this was a bitter pill for those in the research ranks to swallow—Gee advocated cutting R. & D. spending by 10 to 15 per cent in the early 1970s in addition to reductions caused by inflation.

Except for the final recommendation, the Executive Committee did not act immediately on Gee's recommendation. But by the end of the decade, the committee had seized control of the research process along the lines advocated by Gee. Short-range research on existing businesses was emphasized under both Gee's leadership as research liaison on the committee and that of his successor in that role, Richard Heckert, the current chief executive officer at Du Pont. Central research was forced to take a more careful look at how it could aid the industrial departments. The vehicle Heckert arrived at to achieve this was to establish a goal for CRD's funding; within a few years Heckert wanted 50 per cent of CRD's budget to come from industrial department research contracts. (As late as 1950, CRD had derived half of its expenditures from the departments, but by the 1970, this figure was less than 10 per cent.)

In 1975, the executive committee split up the development department. A small piece of the department was grafted on to central research, and that department became known as central research and development. The new department was given primary responsibility for diversification, and the industrial departments were encouraged to stick close to the businesses that they were already in.

The other segment of the old development department was renamed the corporate plans department and given the important charter of evaluating overall corporate strategy, helping chart the company's future strategy, and recommending to the executive committee how it should allocate its resources to implement that strategy.

To provide tighter control over the company's extensive R. & D. activities the executive committee decided in 1978 to have Central Research and Development report directly to one of its members. The committee also charged this research executive with the responsibility for overseeing the work of the research directors of the industrial departments, although these research directors continued to report formally to their respective industrial department heads. In Du Pont parlance, the research executive had 'dotted line' responsibility over all departmentally controlled R. & D.

Thus, these 1978 changes signalled yet another step back towards the centralization of research that had prevailed at Du Pont in the 1910s.

At the same time that the strategic functions of research management were being centralized, there was also a countercurrent to this development: the proliferation of profit centres throughout the company. Profit centres were created to make particular segments of Du Pont's businesses more responsive to the market. The thinking was along much the same lines as the original decentralization of 1921: industrial departments had become too large and unwieldy to be responsive to the market. By decentralizing the departments through the creation of profit centres, whose managers were given responsibility for research, manufacturing, and marketing functions, these businesses would be more competitive.

While achieving their goals, profit centres have created definite problems in the management of research at Du Pont. Foremost among these problems is the process of promotion. With relatively small research groups associated with these profit centres, little opportunity exists for advancement except by leaving research and going into general management. Reassignment of research personnel has also proved problematical. Because of these problems, Du Pont has not reached a set formula for the creation or management of profit centres, and it has been done case by case, with each centre tailoring its research to its own particular needs.

When the executive committee determined to have central research and development report directly to one of its members, Edward G. Jefferson was chosen to assume that expanded role. Working with both the head of the corporate plans department and the director of central research and development, Jefferson determined to move the company into an expanded research and development programme in the life sciences. The rapid development of recombinant DNA technology and related developments in the life sciences in the later 1970s appeared to be opening major growth opportunities for Du Pont if it correctly positioned its R. & D. Jefferson saw particular possibilities for the new technology in crop protection, pharmaceuticals, and medical diagnostics, areas in which Du Pont had been trying to become leader. Largely through Jefferson's persuasion, Du Pont announced in 1980 that it would be dramatically expanding its life science research and would build a major new laboratory at the Experimental Station to house this research. This facility, dedicated in 1984 as the Greenewalt Laboratory, is located at the Experimental Station not far from a greatly expanded agricultural chemical research laboratory. The company has also invested in other laboratory space at other locations devoted to life sciences research in a number of areas. The life sciences venture represents the most dramatic expansion of Du Pont R. & D. since the late 1940s and perhaps the most significant departure from its once strictly tailored self-image as a chemical company.

Jefferson's subsequent purchase of Conoco in 1981 definitely ended that self-image. But more importantly, for reasons that are beyond the scope of this chapter, it has allowed the top management at Du Pont to centralize more fully control over Du Pont's industrial departments, thereby reinforcing the slightly earlier centralization of the company's overall research and development programme.

CONCLUSION

It is difficult to summarize in a few words eight decades of research and development at Du Pont. What impresses me, however, is the continuity in the company's faith in R. & D. throughout this century. Except in the turbulent decade of the 1970s, Du Pont did not question its faith in R. & D. In that decade, some executives recognized that the company's zealousness about R. & D. had led to sloppy management of R. & D. and excessive allocation of resources. Therefore they determined not to destroy R. & D. but rather to cut back on it a little and, more importantly, to give it sharper focus—a development that was probably long overdue. While being fully faithful to the value of R. & D. to the company, executives at Du Pont, from members of the first executive committee to those on the committee in the 1980s, have not really found a permanent solution to the problem of finding the best way to manage R. & D. Du Pont's management of R. & D. has varied significantly over the last eight decades, moving back and forth between decentralized and centralized structures. This is but one of the perennial problems of managing research in a large modern corporation.

254　　　　　　　　*David A. Hounshell*

APPENDIX
DEVELOPMENT OF
DU PONT R. & D.

1. *Founding, 1902–11*

Company focus: explosives manufacture; consolidation and rationalization of the industry.

Major institutional development:
- consolidation of two-thirds to three-fourths of explosives industry;
- establishment of Eastern Laboratory for high explosives research, 1902;
- estabishment of Experimental Station for general research, 1903;
- decision to pursue both centralized and decentralized research simultaneously, 1904;
- beginning of anti-trust action against Du Pont, 1907;
- initial thoughts on need for diversification.

Major R. & D. projects:
- Eastern Laboratory:
  non-freezing dynamite;
  safety explosives;
  improved manufacturing processes.
- Experimental Station:
  Stabillite military powder (failure);
  continuous black powder manufacturing process (failure);
  pulp powder keg (failure);
  glycerine synthesis (failure);
  stabilization of smokeless powder with diphenylamine.

Company sales and earnings ($ millions)

	1904	1906	1907	1911
Gross receipts	26.1	30.8	31.7	33.4
Net earnings	4.4	5.3	3.9	6.5
Total assets	57.2	66.6	70.9	83.2

R. & D. expenditures

	1904	1906	1907	1911
Total expenditure ($ 000)	n.a.	150	219	309
% of sale	n.a.	0.5	0.7	0.9
% of earnings	n.a.	2.8	5.6	4.7
R. & D. staff (no.)	n.a.	n.a.	n.a.	111

Note: n.a. = not available

The Du Pont Company, 1902–1980   255

2. Centralization and Diversification, 1911–21

Company focus: movement away from being purely an explosives
manufacturer, diversification into chemicals, paints, plastics, nitrocellulose-
coated sheet structures.

Major institutional developments:
- centralization of company under one general manager, 1911;
- centralization of research, 1911;
- tighter centralization from reorganizations in 1914;
- anti-trust conviction, 1912;
- forced divestment of part of black powder and high
  explosives businesses (formation of Hercules and Atlas), 1913;
- initial diversification efforts and approval by Executive Committee
  of Development Department's master plan for diversification:
  purchase of Fabrikoid Company, 1910,
  purchase of Arlington Company, 1915,
  purchase of Harrison Brothers Paint Company, 1917,
  other minor acquisitions, 1917–20;
- establishment of Jackson Laboratory (dyestuffs), 1917;
- establishment of Delta Laboratory (Celluloid), 1917;
- establishment of Redpath Laboratory (photographic film), 1920;
- World War I (vast expansion of smokeless powder capacity, vast
  profits, vast problems of utilizing capacity after war).

Major R. & D. projects:
- TNT;
- TNX;
- tetryl;
- synthesis of amyl acetate;
- synthesis of glycerine (failure);
- synthesis of diphenylamine;
- synthesis and manufacture of dyestuffs.

Company sales and earnings ($ millions)

	1911	1914	1916	1918	1919	1921
Gross receipts	33.4	25.2	318.8	329.1	105.4	55.3
Net earnings	6.5	5.6	82.1	43.1	17.7	7.6
Total assets	83.2	83.4	217.9	303.3	241.0	252.2

R. & D. expenditures

	1911	1914	1916	1918	1919	1921
Total ($ 000)	309	250	639	2,748	3,447	1,734
% of sales	0.9	1.0	0.2	0.8	3.3	3.1
% of earnings	4.7	4.5	0.8	6.4	19.5	22.8
R. & D. staff (no.)	111	95	200	475	652	135

256   *David A. Hounshell*

3. Decentralization, Acquisition and Rationalization, 1921–35

Company focus: diversified chemical company, achieved through acquisition and rationalization of technologies and companies.

Major institutional developments:
- decentralization of management (including R. & D.), 1921;
- acquisition of French rayon technology, 1920–1;
- acquisition of French cellophane technology, 1923;
- acquisition of French (Claude) high-pressure ammonia process, 1924;
- joint venture with French in photographic film, 1924;
- acquisition of French cellulose acetate technology, 1928;
- other acquisitions: Viscoloid (1925), National Ammonia (1926), Grasselli (1928), Krebs Pigment (1929), Roessler and Hasslacher Chemical (1930), Commercial Pigments (1931), Newport Chemical (1931), Remington (1933);
- establishment of élite fundamental research programme in central Chemical Department, 1927;
- Patents and Processes Agreement with ICI, 1929.

Major R. & D. projects:
- TEL process;
- Freon process;
- straightening out Claude process;
- Duco fast-drying lacquer;
- discovery and development of neoprene, 1930 onwards;
- discovery of first truly synthetic fibre, 1930;
- discovery and development of nylon, 1934–40;
- major fundamental research work in polymer chemistry under Wallace H. Carothers.

Company sales and earnings ($ millions)

	1921	1926	1931	1936
Sales	55.3	90.4	163.5	250.1
Operating income	7.3	90.4	19.0	44.3
Ave. operating investment	84.7	140.8	365.4	449.5
Ave. no. employees	n.a.	15,228	31,041	45,938

Note: n. a. = not available.

R. & D. expenditures

	1921	1926	1931	1936
Total exp. ($ 000)	1,734	2,224	5,400	7,652
% of sales	3.1	2.5	3.3	3.0
% of earnings	23.8	23.9	28.4	17.3
R. & D. staff (no.)	135	241	755	912

The Du Pont Company, 1902–1980   257

4. Nylon and the 'New Nylons' Mentality, 1936–60

Company focus: 'chemical' company growing through internal generation of technology based on fundamental research.

Major institutional developments:
- nylon a smash hit, grows like Topsy;
- late New Deal attacks on Big Business, resulting in eight anti-trust cases against Du Pont, 1944–52;
- Nye Committee hearings, 1934–46; Du Pont labelled 'Merchant of Death';
- World War II (Du Pont not anxious to be involved in armament);
- Manhattan Project (Du Pont designs, builds, and operates Hanford plutonium works; designs and builds semiworks pile and separation facilities at Oak Ridge, Tenn.);
- total 'new nylons' strategy worked out by 1944–6;
- dramatic expansion of Du Pont R. & D., particularly at Experimental Station;
- rapid growth of world-wide competition in post-war period.

Company sales and earnings ($ millions)

	1936	1941	1946	1951	1956	1961
Sales	258.1	480.1	648.7	1,531.1	1,888.4	2,191
Operating income	44.3	57.5	84.0	139.4	254.8	258
Ave. operating investment	449.5	628.4	891.8	1,553.2	2,251.7	3,121
Ave. no. employees	45,938	60,029	72,002	86,878	89,449	87,057

R. & D. expenditures

	1936	1941	1946	1951	1956	1961
Total ($ millions)	7.65	12.4	26.0	71.9	140.3	160.8
% of sales	3.0	2.6	4.0	4.7	7.5	7.3
% of earnings[a]	17.3	21.6	31.0	51.6	55.1	62.3
R. & D. staff (no.)	912	1,341	1,800	3,376	4,582	3,787

[a]These figures are 30–40% lower if calculated as exp./exp. + income.

258   *David A. Hounshell*

5. *Maturation and Response, 1960–70*

Company focus: diversification through new ventures based on storehouse of Du Pont knowledge.

Major institutional developments:
- court-ordered General Motors stock divestiture;
- reactivation of the Development Department;
- establishment of formal new venture programme, 1960;
- capital shortages begin to be experienced for first time in almost sixty years.

Major R. & D. projects:
- during this decade Du Pont commercialized forty-one new products. See Table 22.1 in Hounshell and Smith, 1988: 528.

Company sales and earnings ($ millions)

	1961	1965	1970
Sales	2,191.0	2,999.3	3,618.4
Earnings	258.0	384.9	328.7
Ave. operating investment	3,120.6	4,267.0	6,505.0
Ave. no. employees	87,057	106,013	115,126

R. & D. expenditures

	1961	1965	1970
Total expenditures ($ millions)	160.8	238.0	270.0
% of sales	7.3	8.0	7.5
% of earnings[a]	62.3	61.9	82.2
R. & D. staff (no.)	3,787	4,295	4,362

[a] Expenditures/income.

The Du Pont Company, 1902–1980 259

6. Rethinking and Restructuring, 1970–80

Company focus: fuzzy—prop up existing businesses, minimize launching of high-cost new products, contend with wide, energy-related swings in the economy, cash flow out of existing businesses, coping with apparent collapse of synthetic fibres business.

Major institutional developments:
- tightening reins on industrial department heads;
- increasing centralization of research units of company under one Executive Committee member;
- break-up of Development Department:
  addition of one piece to form the Central Research and Development Department,
  other piece becomes the Corporate Plans Department;
- increasing willingness of Executive Committee to reallocate research resources along consciously developed strategic lines;
- purchase of Continental Oil Company (Conoco), 1981.

Major R. & D. projects:
- Kevlar development;
- process improvement in a number of key intermediates;
- life sciences research launched.

Company sales and earnings ($ million)

	1970	1975	1980
Sales	3,618.4	7,221.5	13,652.0
Net operating income	328.7	271.8	716.0
Ave. operating investment	6,585.0	11,418.0	17,448.0
Ave. no. employees	115,126	132,235	135,900

R. & D. expenditures

	1970	1975	1980
Total expenditures ($ millions)	270.0	336.0	484.0
% of sales	7.5	4.7	3.6
% of earnings[a]	82.2	123.6	67.6
R. & D. staff (no.)	4,362	4,593	4,050

[a]Expenditures/income.

260   *David A. Hounshell*
REFERENCES

CHANDLER, ALFRED D., Jr. (1962), *Strategy and Structure* (Cambridge, Mass.: MIT Press).

DU PONT, PIERRE S. (1908), Letter to C. M. Barton of 17 Aug., Papers of E. I. Du Pont de Nemours & Co. (ser. II, pt 2, box 167, Hagley Museum and Library, Wilmington, Del.).

E.I. Du Pont de Nemours & Co. (n.d.), *The Story of the Eastern Laboratory, 1902–52* (Pamphlet Collection, Hagley Museum and Library, Wilmington, Del.).

HOUNSHELL, D. A., and SMITH, J. K. (1988), *Science and Corporate Strategy: Du Pont R & D, 1902–80* (New York: Cambridge University Press).

[16]

The Growth of the Firm

A Case Study: The Hercules Powder Company

❡ *Growth is governed by a creative and dynamic interaction between a firm's productive resources and its market opportunities. Available resources limit expansion; unused resources (including technological and entrepreneurial) stimulate and largely determine the direction of expansion. While product demand may exert a predominant short-term influence, over the long term any distinction between "supply" and "demand" determinants of growth becomes arbitrary.*

by Edith T. Penrose

LECTURER AND RESEARCH ASSOCIATE
AT THE JOHNS HOPKINS UNIVERSITY

The following analysis of the growth of the Hercules Powder Company was originally intended for inclusion in my *Theory of the Growth of the Firm*,[1] but was omitted in order to keep down the size of the book. The Hercules case was designed to illustrate the argument of that study; the interpretation of im-

[1] Edith T. Penrose, *The Theory of the Growth of the Firm* (New York and Oxford, 1959).

portant factors in the growth of Hercules is shaped by the case histories of other firms studied. Consequently I shall begin with a brief summary of some of the relevant conclusions presented in my larger work. In doing this I necessarily risk appearing either dogmatic, since oversimplification and absence of supporting argument are unavoidable, or trite, since demonstration of the theoretical and empirical significance of the conclusions is impracticable here.[2]

A firm is both an administrative organization and a pool of productive resources. In planning expansion it considers two groups of resources; its own previously acquired or "inherited" resources, and those it must obtain from the market in order to carry out its program. All expansion must draw on some services of the firm's existing management and consequently the services available from such management set a fundamental limit to the amount of expansion that can be either planned or executed even if all other resources are obtainable in the market. This is as true for expansion through acquisition as it is for internal expansion, although acquisition permits a faster rate of growth and often facilitates diversification. A firm is not confined to "given" products, but the kind of activity it moves into is usually related in some way to its existing resources, for there is a close relationship between the various kinds of resources with which a firm works and the development of the ideas, experience, and knowledge of its managers and entrepreneurs. Furthermore, changing experience and knowledge of management affect not only the productive services available from resources, but also the "demand" which the firm considers relevant for its activities.

At all times there exist, within every firm, pools of unused productive services and these, together with the changing knowledge of management, create a productive opportunity which is unique for each firm. Unused productive services are, for the enterprising firm, at the same time a challenge to innovate, an incentive to expand, and a source of competitive advantage. It is largely because such unused services are related to existing resources and partly

[2] NOTE ON SOURCES: This study of the Hercules Powder Company was made possible by a Fellowship granted me by the Foundation for Economic Education in cooperation with the company, which enabled me to spend six weeks studying the company from within in the summer of 1954 with the full cooperation of all of its personnel. The paper was completed in 1956; when I decided to publish it now I inquired of the company about subsequent developments, receiving the following reply: "More recent events, while of great interest within Hercules (and we believe in the industry), are largely a continuation of the types of growth you have shown to be typical and more or less to be expected, except at possibly a somewhat faster rate. Actually, the manuscript can never be quite up to date in an expanding company, nor for your purpose does this seem to be necessary." I agree with the last statement and for this reason have made no attempt to bring it to the present.

because of the pressures of competition that firms tend to specialize in broad technological or marketing areas, which I have called technological or market "bases." In a sense, the final products being produced by a firm at any given time merely represent one of several ways in which the firm could be using its resources, an incident in the development of its basic potentialities. Over the years the products change, and there are numerous firms today that produce few or none of the products on which their early reputation and success were based. Their basic strength has been developed above or below the end-product level as it were — in technology of specialized kinds and in market positions. Within the limits set by the rate at which the administrative structure of the firm can be adapted and adjusted to larger and larger scales of operation, there is nothing inherent in the nature of the firm or of its economic function to prevent the indefinite expansion of its activities as time passes.

Entrepreneurial services are as much productive services as are the services of management, labor, or even machines. Entrepreneurial incompetence, or general cautiousness, including a conservative attitude toward financing, should be looked on not as a failure to "maximize" profits, whatever that may mean, but as a limitation on the supply of productive services to the firm.

In the explanation of the course of expansion of a particular firm and of the limits on its rate of expansion, it is illuminating to put the chief emphasis on the firm's "inherited" resources and productive services, including its accumulated experience and knowledge, for a firm's productive opportunity is shaped and limited by its ability to use what it already has. Not only is the actual expansion of a firm related to its resources, experience, and knowledge, but also, and most important, the kinds of opportunity it investigates when it considers expansion. Moreover, once a firm has made its choice and has embarked on an expansion program, its expectations may not be confirmed by events. The reactions of the firm to disappointment — the alteration it makes in its plans and activities and the way in which it adapts (or fails to adapt) — are again to be explained with reference to its resources.

These relationships are portrayed in the chronology of the changing productive opportunity of the Hercules Powder Company. The history of this company illustrates the nature and significance of the areas of specialization of a firm — its technological and market bases — as well as some of the difficulties encountered when an attempt is made to move to new bases markedly different from the old. The outlines of the company's diversification are presented in Chart I. The following story elaborates, explains, and discusses the significance of the movements implied therein.

In 1912 a large United States firm, E. I. Dupont de Nemours, then looked upon as dangerously close to monopoly in the explosives business, was broken into three parts by action of the federal courts as a result of an antitrust suit initiated by the federal government in 1907. One of the two "new" firms thus created was the Hercules Powder Company. At the time of its formal organization in 1913 Hercules had a thousand employees and nine plants; it produced explosives only: black powder and dynamites.

During the next forty-odd years this amputated piece of DuPont, like a cutting from a plant, continued to grow.[3] It, like DuPont, has over the years branched out in numerous directions in response to external opportunities and internal developments. The parent and its involuntary offspring have not grown in the same directions, and in only a few fields are they in direct competition with each other. Hercules is not only completely independent of DuPont, but has acquired its own personality and its own position in the industrial world quite unrelated to DuPont's position. By 1956 it had 11,365 employees, 22 domestic plants, and total assets of nearly $170 million, making it the 165th largest industrial company in the United States measured by total assets.[4]

The company's rate of growth has been modest (something over 5 per cent per year in terms of fixed assets) but fairly steady. Its financing has been conservative, virtually all of its growth having been financed with internally generated funds. It has engaged in little acquisition, only eight small companies with total assets at the time of acquisition of less than 10 per cent of the company's present net worth having been acquired in its entire lifetime. Its "entrepreneurship" has been what I have called "product-minded," reasonably venturesome and imaginative, but concentrating on "workmanship" and product development rather than on expansion for its own sake or for quick profits.

---

[3] The story of Hercules also illustrates the point that the splitting up of large companies will often not have an adverse effect on efficiency if the advantages they have in expansion are economies of growth and not economies of size. For a discussion of these two types of economies and their significance see Penrose, *The Theory of the Growth of the Firm*, Chap. VI.

[4] This rank is the one given in the *Fortune Directory* of the 500 largest United States industrial corporations. Supplement to *Fortune* (July, 1957). In addition to the above, Hercules had three plants in wholly owned subsidiaries abroad and employed some 6,000 workers in government owned Hercules-operated ordnance facilities.

CHART I

DIRECTION OF EXPANSION

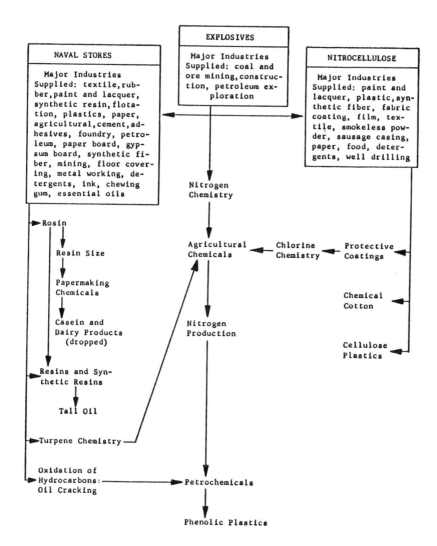

DEVELOPMENT OF THE TECHNOLOGICAL AREAS OF SPECIALIZATION

The original technological base of the Hercules firm was explosives and for the first few years of its existence it was kept busy with the expansion of this field. Two new plants were acquired and improvements were made in existing plants and in the processes of production of dynamite, smokeless powder, and cordite. One of the innovations — the production of acetone (a solvent used in the manufacture of cordite) and other products from the giant kelp found on the Pacific Coast — involved an extension of the firm's knowledge and experience in a type of organic chemistry which was to become significant in its subsequent diversification.

The manufacture of explosives is still of considerable importance for Hercules (accounting for 18 per cent of sales in 1951) and at times has been its most profitable operation, providing funds for the extension of activities in other directions. Substantial innovations have been made in the field of semigelatin explosives, smokeless powder, packaging of explosives, and explosive supplies. Some diversification into the production of chemicals used in explosives production, notably nitric acid, anhydrous ammonia, and other nitrogenous compounds, has been made, and this development has contributed in recent years to Hercules' position in the agricultural chemicals industry.

In spite of the innovations and enlarged activity, however, the explosives business was not one to permit extensive growth and development of the firm. In particular, it provided little opportunity for the use of the experience in the field of organic chemistry that had been developed by Hercules men in the course of the firm's operations. Furthermore, at the end of the First World War the plant, organization, and accumulated funds of the firm were much greater than could be used in explosives in view of the drastic decline in demand after the war. In the immediate postwar period numerous opportunities for profitable investment were open on all sides in the expanding, changing economy. But which of them would furnish opportunities for the growth of a still relatively small and specialized explosives company?

Nitrocellulose and New Areas of Specialization

Nitrocellulose is one of the most important basic raw materials in the production of explosives. In 1915 Hercules had bought the Union Powder Company, which had a plant for the nitration of cotton linters (the "fuzz" on cotton seeds and a by-product of cotton production) into nitrocellulose, then used primarily for smoke-less powder, but also for celluloid and collodion ("new skin"). Already by 1917 the company was experimenting with the production of nitrocellulose for industries other than explosives, for if it could produce a suitable soluble nitrocellulose it felt sure of a large market supplying the needs of the lacquer, film, and protective coatings industries generally. It succeeded in developing an appropriate product, and by 1923 was firmly established in the field. Between 1918 and 1944 Hercules' production of soluble nitrocellulose increased from 100,000 pounds annually to 28,000,000 pounds and the price was lowered from 75 to 33 cents a pound.

So efficient was Hercules' production and quality control and so well-developed its control of explosive hazards in the manufacture of the basic product and also in its use by customers, that a number of companies withdrew from the field. Some of these were integrated companies, producing for their own use, who found it more economical to buy their requirements from Hercules; others simply withdrew in the face of Hercules' competition. The automobile industry turned out to be the biggest consumer, using nitrocellulose in its lacquers. In consequence, Hercules was in a position to profit from the rapid growth of this then relatively new industry. Nevertheless, here, as in other fields, continual attention to the development of new products and new methods to meet or surpass competitive developments has been required. For example, the advent of baked enamel for automobile finishes, which reduced the labor time required for finishing, was a serious threat to lacquer; and Hercules developed new lacquers which could be sprayed on hot and meet the new competition in cost.

Successful development of nitrocellulose for nonexplosive uses provided for Hercules an extensive technological base as well as an important market area of specialization. The development of the technological base led to expansion in still other markets; the development of the market base furthered expansion into still other branches of chemistry. Broadly speaking, the technological base was that of cellulose chemistry; the market base, supplier to the protective coatings industry.

Cellulose Chemistry

Hercules' base in cellulose chemistry enabled it to take advantage of the growing markets in the artificial fiber and plastics industries. Cellulose acetate, an important raw material in the rayon industry and used for the production of some grades of plastics, soon became, for the firm's Cellulose Products Department, an important product in quantity, though disappointing in profitability.

The cellulose acetate market is highly competitive, and, in this as well as in most of its other products, one of the firm's biggest competitive problems arises from the ever-present possibility that its customers will integrate vertically and start producing their own requirements. In the long run Hercules can prevent this only by producing a high-quality product and selling it at a price that makes integration unprofitable for customers. Hence a relatively low sales margin is earned and continual research and experimentation are carried on. (Hercules has even experimented with the spinning of fibers in order to acquire knowledge which might be of use to its customers. As we shall see, "technical service" is one of the "utilities" Hercules sells with all of its products in order to maintain its market position.)

With the development of synthetic rubber during the Second World War came a new petrochemical base for cheap plastics (polystyrene) which soon began to displace cellulose acetate in molding powders, the basic material from which molded plastics can be made. Petrochemicals, however, involved a branch of chemistry in which Hercules had only limited experience at the time. Many of the companies producing the new plastic material had developed extensive experience during the war which gave them a new "base" in petrochemicals. Hercules' wartime activities were in very different areas. The firm's lack of an adequate technological base was sufficient to prevent it from taking up the production of polystyrene and similar petrochemical products. Consequently the company attempted to reach new markets with its own cellulose acetate by taking up the production of molding powders.

The extensive knowledge of cellulose chemistry possessed by Hercules has provided a continuous inducement to the firm to search for new ways of using it. For example, during the war Hercules, in an attempt to replace a lubricant no longer available, took up the production of an extraordinary versatile cellulose gum — sodium carboxymethy-cellulose (CMC). The firm was much impressed with the properties of this chemical composition, but was not sure to what use American industry could put it. Perhaps CMC could be used in the sizing of textiles (Hercules already produced some types of fabric coating). No one knew; nevertheless, advertisements were placed in trade papers describing the qualities of the product and inquiring "What do you see in CMC?"

The product caught on. Here, surely, is an almost perfect example of the creation of consumer demand as a consequence of entrepreneurial desire to find a use for available productive resources. The biggest uses for CMC, initially, turned out to be as a stabilizer in foods, ice cream, lotions, drugs, and cosmetics. CMC also proved to have an industrial application in oil-well drilling mud — an outlet the firm had not anticipated. It is now also used in textile sizes, finishes, and printing pastes; in ointment bases, in thickening rubber latex; in can-sealing compounds and grease-proof paper coatings; in tooth paste; in emulsion paints and lacquers; in leather pasting; in ceramic glazes; and as a binder for crayons and lead pencils. Innovations in use and in the product continue. In 1955 a new type of CMC was introduced which was expected still further to expand the market and the variety of uses.

There are other cellulose products and specialties that have been developed by Hercules which we shall not take the time to discuss here, but our account cannot leave out the firm's early diversification into the production of its own requirements for chemical cotton, the raw material for cellulose products of all kinds. In 1926 Hercules purchased the Virginia Cellulose Company at Hopewell, Virginia, in order to produce one of its own basic raw materials and, in particular, to control its quality. The purchasing of cotton linters — of which the second cut is used for chemical cotton — is a highly specialized business. Hercules buys around 40 per cent of that part of the nation's production of cotton linters destined for chemical uses, and supplies not only all of its own requirements but sells outside as well, for production must be on a large scale to be efficient. When Hercules went into production of chemical cotton its chief use was in paper making and in nitrocellulose products. The expanding rayon industry provided a new and growing outlet, and later another important use was found in the manufacture of high tenacity viscose rayon for tire cord.

Developing a New Base — Naval Stores

Broadly speaking, as can be seen in Chart I, the operations of the Hercules Powder Company, apart from explosives, can be divided into two large chemical branches, with a third becoming clearly evident in recent years. They all overlap in the markets they serve, and each leads in its later stages into new areas of chemistry which may well provide new technological bases for further diversification. The movement into new aspects of cellulose chemistry, just described, was an obvious entrepreneurial response to the postwar decline of nitrocellulose markets in the explosives field.

The subsequent branching out of the company was the logical (though not inevitable) effect of its continually increasing knowledge of cellulose chemistry as well as of its developing position in its various market areas. Later we shall discuss the interaction between the technological and market bases of the firm; for the present we are concerned primarily with the technological aspects of its diversification, although clearly technological developments are of use only if profitable markets can be found.

Important as the opportunities were in the field of cellulose chemistry, however, they did not appear to the firm to promise sufficient scope for the entrepreneurial, managerial, labor, and technical services available to it at the end of the First World War. In 1919 the company had created an industrial research department for the express purpose of investigating products Hercules could profitably produce. This department decided that the firm could go into the production of wood naval stores (rosin, turpentine, and pine oil) obtained from the stumps of the long-leaf southern pine — like linters, a waste product of another industry.

Naval stores production was not as obvious an opportunity for Hercules as was cellulose chemistry, but, again it was expected to provide openings for the use of the existing resources of the firm. Hercules believed that it could use its knowledge of organic chemistry to produce a purified wood rosin good enough to compete with the gum rosin when gum prices were high; incidentally, the naval stores operation would also provide a use for dynamite in the blasting out of the stumps. Extensive lumbering operations during the First World War had resulted in a large-scale cutting of suitable trees, and it was widely believed that the consequent reduction in the supply of gum rosin would lead to an extended period of high prices which would make profitable the production of wood rosin.

Consequently, in 1920 Hercules built a plant in Mississippi for the steam distillation of rosin from pine stumps; it also bought another company owning a deteriorated plant but with a large supply of stumps. The mining of the pine stumps produced three joint products: rosin, turpentine, and pine oil, the main product for Hercules being rosin. Hercules did succeed in developing a purified wood rosin suitable as a substitute for gum in many uses, and it improved the productivity of the old plant it had bought, increasing rosin output by one third in three years and liquids production by 100 per cent. But the firm's original expectations of demand for wood naval stores turned out to have been too optimistic. Although wartime lumbering did sharply deplete the supply of standing pine available for the production of gum naval stores, the second growth of trees came in, output rose, and gum prices fell drastically. Wood rosin could not compete with gum when gum prices were low, and the naval stores business of Hercules went into the red for many years. Notwithstanding its heavy investment in rosin chemistry research, Hercules came close to withdrawing from the business.

Rosin and Terpene Chemistry

But research paid off; unable to sell rosin in its existing forms in competition with gum, Hercules learned how to modify the product by hydrogenation, disproportionation, and polymerization and thus to convert it into various kinds of rosins for which many new uses could be found. Rosin is essentially abietic acid; when esterified with various polyols it makes hard resins valuable in the manufacture of paints and varnishes, and Hercules already had a position in the protective coatings field. Customers could be found for hard resins and rosin esters, and these, together with a variety of specialty resins as well as straight esters, were developed into an important outlet for rosin production. The naval stores operation became the equal of cellulose chemistry as a central technological base of the firm and in 1928 was organized as a separate department. In 1936 still another department was created, charged with the task of developing new uses and new outlets for resin-based products. As we shall see, the knowledge generated in this department, together with its market opportunities, soon led it outside the field of rosin chemistry and into new areas.

Further description of the range of products produced by Hercules and based in rosin chemistry would involve us in too much detail (and, incidentally, in too much chemistry), although we shall return to some of the more interesting developments in our discussion of the interaction between the technological and market bases of the firm. It is fairly easy for small firms and "in-and-out" producers to take up the production of resins; profit margins are consequently low, and the profitability of the industry for Hercules depends on large volume. To sustain its position, the firm has to rely on technological knowledge, low production costs, service facilities to customers, and continual improvements in production, in quality, and in variety of its products. Hardly a year passes without the introduction of several new products or improved varieties of old products, developed under the stimulus of actual or potential competition, the pressures of technical men with ideas to

GROWTH OF A FIRM   11

put across, and the hope of profit from innovations in which the firm has special advantages because of its accumulated experience.

But rosin is only one of the three joint products of the pine stump, and markets had to be found both for turpentine and for pine oil, a relatively new industrial product in the 1920's, derived only from the wood operation. Fractional distillation methods were perfected which permitted the production of higher grades of turpentine and pine oil. In 1929 pine oil outlets were not developing fast enough to keep pace with production, and Hercules intensified its research into pine oil chemistry looking for derivative products. Thanite was developed, a terpene thiocyanoacetate providing a toxicant for insecticides, and later toxaphene, a chlorinated camphene. These products put Hercules firmly in the field of agricultural insecticides which in turn stimulated research into agricultural chemicals generally. At times the demand for pinene has exceeded the company's output and it has had to buy crude products from pulp mills for refining. As was the case in cellulose chemistry, a large variety of chemical products and processes has been developed in the field of terpene chemistry. One of the latest processes bids fair to give Hercules a more established base in petrochemicals, a field which, as was noted above, had up to recently been outside Hercules' major fields of specialization, thereby handicapping the firm in its ability to meet competitive developments.

Petrochemicals – A New Base

In several of its manufacturing processes Hercules has always been involved in petrochemical operations. Although the manufacture of explosives is not in itself a chemical process, the production of the essential ammonia is. Nitric acid used for making explosives is obtained from ammonia, and the process used by Hercules to produce ammonia involves the cracking of natural gas. Furthermore, some of the processes in the rosin and terpene operations of its naval stores activities are similar in nature to the cracking of oil. Indeed, some of them can be and are used in oil cracking. Finally, in experimenting with the chemistry of terpenes and with the oxidation of the hydrocarbon by-products of naval stores, Hercules developed a reaction that utilized benzol and propylene and that resulted in a new process for making phenol. These developments opened up two new branches of chemistry for the firm: air oxidation processes and petrochemicals; new plants have been built for operation in both areas. The phenol plant, established near an oil refinery, uses a by-product of the refinery. Among the important uses of phenol is the manufacture of synthetic resins for phenolic plastics; it is also used in the manufacture of varnishes, enamels, herbicides, and pharmaceuticals. Lack of any raw material "base" in petrochemicals had prevented Hercules from participating fully in the rising markets for rubber-base paints and for phenolic plastics. One of the primary hopes of management in establishing the phenol plant was to open the way for the acquisition of further knowledge in order to provide a base for expansion in this wide field of chemistry, as well as to put the company in a position to keep up with competitive developments arising in petrochemistry and affecting the market for some of its major products.

Finally, Hercules in 1955 took up the production of polyethylene for plastics. The technology was based on the work of German scientists who had discovered in experimenting with new types of catalysts that ethylene could be polymerized at low pressures to give a new type of high molecular weight polyethylene. This not only further extends Hercules' activities in plastics, but also takes it further into catalytic chemistry, which may, in time, lead into still further technological areas.

INTERACTION BETWEEN TECHNOLOGICAL AND MARKET BASES

Hercules is a producer of chemical products for other industries; it does not manufacture final products for the nonindustrial consumer. To obtain knowledge of the "demand" for its products, one of its principal tasks is to watch industrial developments in all relevant sectors of the economy in order to discover where its products might be made to supply the requirements of industrial consumers as well as or better than existing products. It is a conscious policy of the firm systematically to review its resources with an eye on external developments, asking the question, "What have we got to offer?"

Because of the nature of its market, Hercules stresses "technical service" to customers; salesmen are for the most part technically trained men. In selling their products the salesmen are expected to take an active interest in the production and market problems of their customers. This permits them to acquire an intimate knowledge of the customers' businesses and not only to demonstrate the uses of their own products and to suggest to customers new ways of doing things, but also to adapt their products to customers' requirements and learn what kinds of new products can be used. It is standard practice in the development of new products to get

GROWTH OF A FIRM   13

customers to try them out on a "pilot plant" basis and thus to assist Hercules in the necessary research and experimentation.

Obviously, it is in those areas where Hercules' personnel have the greatest experience and the most extensive relationships with customers that the opportunities for the sale of existing products and for the promotion of new products will be widest. Hence, in spite of the enormous variety of possible end uses of Hercules' chemical products, the firm nevertheless remains in a relatively few broad "areas of specialization." Approximately 40 per cent of the total value of sales are accounted for by three industry groups: protective coatings, paper, and mining and quarrying, and an additional 40 per cent by six others: synthetic fibers, plastics, agricultural chemicals, petroleum, rubber, and identifiable military uses (the last including fees obtained from the operation of government owned ordnance plants).

The interaction between the market opportunities of the firm and the productive services available from its own resources can be seen in the development of almost any field we examine. A few examples will illustrate.

Paper-making Chemicals

The biggest customer of rosin is the paper-making industry which uses rosin largely in the form of rosin size, a sodium soap of rosin. As a result of the close association with the paper industry consequent upon its entry into naval stores production, Hercules in 1931 acquired the Paper Makers Chemical Corporation, a diversified, loosely organized company producing a variety of industrial chemicals. On acquiring the corporation, Hercules reorganized its productive activities, consolidating production in the more efficient plants and getting rid of others; it eliminated alum production and the jobbing activities of the old company. Eventually a separate department, called the Paper Makers Chemical Department, was created to take over the remaining collection of activities.

Although the basic reason for the acquisition of the old PMC was the outlet it provided for rosin and the possibilities for growth that Hercules saw in the rosin-size business, the activities of the new department in Hercules rapidly extended not only to many other chemicals useful in the paper-making industry but also to other industries using the same or similar chemicals. Thus, with the advent of synthetic rubber production, Hercules looked into the possibilities of using rosin soap as an emulsifier in the production of synthetic rubber, and now sells a very large proportion of its rosin soap to the synthetic rubber industry.

This in turn stimulated interest in the general field of synthetic rubber production, now one of the more important areas of Hercules' research. Hercules' interest in the paper industry, arising from rosin sizes, has in recent years been substantially reinforced by the growing uses of chemical cotton in paper making. Much research has gone into the characteristics imparted to paper when chemical cotton is substituted for other raw materials. As a result, Hercules has been able to establish its raw material for many uses in paper making.

Among the activities of the old Paper Makers Chemical Corporation when it was acquired by Hercules was the production and sale of casein, a milk product used in the paper industry. Hercules retained this business for some twenty years and attempted to develop the field. For a while the operation was profitable, but owing to rising support prices of dairy products, imported casein became so much cheaper than the domestic product that it was no longer profitable to produce it. On the other hand, since the firm had an organization and a sales staff that it wanted to use, attempts were made to develop a chemical to displace casein in paper manufacturing. These attempts continue, but the casein operation itself was finally discontinued in 1953, after many years of unsatisfactory performance.

Protective Coatings

Protective coatings is a broad term including paints, lacquers, and other forms of providing a "coating" to protect wood, metal, cement, textiles, and other materials. Hercules' market position in this field goes back to its early production of soluble nitrocellulose for the lacquer industry; it was subsequently extended as the firm developed rosin products, also valuable in the paint and lacquer industry. The interest in the general market area of protective coatings imparted by these important uses of its basic raw materials led to developments within the firm which took it into the production of other products from other raw materials, but products that served the same types of customers and involved similar types of technological processes.

One of the early successful innovations in the field was the development of Parlon, a chlorinated rubber, valuable as an ingredient in paints for chemical plants and in other places where resistance to alkalies and acids is important. This product is pro-

GROWTH OF A FIRM   15

duced in the large cellulose products plant of Hercules but is not related to cellulose through either raw materials or production processes. It was introduced to broaden the firm's base in the market for protective coatings. During the Second World War, rubber was in short supply and the firm, in order to use its plants, produced Clorafin, a chlorinated paraffin used as a plasticizer in synthetic rosins and as an ingredient in compounds for imparting flame, water, and mildew resistance to textile materials. After the war, the production of this product was continued and the production of Parlon resumed.

Development of the general field of protective coatings and of plasticizers also led the Synthetics Department beyond its original specialty of finding outlets for rosin in various forms, into research with chemical materials, unrelated to rosin, for the manufacture of new ingredients for protective coatings, new types of plasticizers, polyols used in rosins, and raw materials for synthetic fibers. By 1951, substantially more than 50 per cent of the sales of this department were of nonrosin-based products.

Agricultural Chemicals

All three of the major technological fields of Hercules have combined to give it an interest in the field of agricultural chemicals. The fact that nitrogen chemistry, in particular ammonia, is important in the manufacture of explosives and also one of the major bases of commercial fertilizers early gave Hercules a connection with agriculture. With the progressive development of chlorine and terpene chemistry and the introduction of the new insecticides, Thanite and toxaphene, mentioned above, this interest broadened. Although the original stimulus to the entry of Hercules into agricultural chemicals stemmed directly from the types of resources it possessed, once the firm had entered the field in a major way and created a technical and sales force to serve this market, the market possibilities became the primary stimulus. Extensive research activities were undertaken to develop further the firm's position in the field. A new laboratory for research into agricultural chemicals was opened in 1952, and in 1954 Hercules, together with the Alabama By-Products Corporation, set up the Ketona Chemical Corporation to produce anhydrous ammonia using by-product coke-oven gas as a raw material, the first ammonia plant to use this process in the United States. The plant produces for both agricultural and industrial nitrogen users in southeast United States.

Plastics

Celluloid, which is virtually nothing but nitrocellulose and camphor, was the forerunner of modern plastic materials (and, incidentally, is still important in many uses). This product was produced by Hercules from the very beginning; the development of cellulose acetate further committed the firm to the plastics industry. The various kinds of chemical plastics, which in a broad sense can often be regarded as the same "product," are made by substantially different chemical processes. Hence, the widening of Hercules' position in the plastics field stems from different types of chemical technology, the development of which has itself been stimulated by the firm's attempt to maintain and improve its position as a supplier to manufacturers of plastic products. Thus much research effort has been directed specifically toward the development of plastics, not only based on the firm's primary raw materials and on chemical processes used in its several other operations, but also going far afield into new processes and new raw materials. Hercules' research is broad and many different areas of activity are being explored, but which of the possible products are finally selected for "basic" expansion depends on the firm's estimate not only of the new markets they may create for the firm but also of how they fit in and can be developed along with existing resources and market areas. Many of the technological developments discussed above, such as the development of phenolic chemistry, were to a large extent stimulated by a desire to take full advantage of the growing opportunities in plastics.

Oil Additives

The story of Abalyn, tall oil, and Metalyn, is a minor one in the history of Hercules but is interesting from our point of view as an illustration not only of an interaction between technological and market bases, but also of the way in which new raw material sources can be developed in order to maintain an existing market position.

We have noted that rosin is one of the primary raw material bases of the firm. Under the pressure of the 1947 recession, Hercules was eagerly looking for new outlets for rosin. As we have seen, one of the primary measures adopted by the firm lay in the conversion of rosin to other products for which markets could be found. Among these products was Abalyn, a methyl ester of rosin, useful as an oil additive in high pressure greases because of its ability to hold grit and other foreign matter in suspension. The important competitive substitutes were lard and sperm oil, which were expensive compared to rosin when Abalyn was introduced. These, however, fell in price and Abalyn became relatively expensive. To keep its markets, Hercules decided to buy tall oil, a by-product of paper mills, from which rosin could be obtained more cheaply than from the naval stores operations. This by-product, esterified, yielded a substance which used the same equipment as Abalyn for its production, did the same or better job as an oil additive, and was substantially cheaper. The product, called Metalyn, became an important product of the Synthetics Department, but at the same time lost for the firm an outlet for its own rosin. On the other hand, tall oil became a new and significant raw material for Hercules, and in 1954 the firm announced plans to build a plant for the processing of crude tall oil and the manufacture of rosin and fatty acids from it, thus establishing itself in another new field also based on a by-product of another industry. This development may be of especial importance in the future in view of the fact that the naval stores production is essentially a mining operation (the supply of existing stumps is being steadily depleted and no new stumps are being "produced"). Hence this source of wood rosin will eventually run out and substitutes will be required.

Food Industries

Finally, the latest venture of Hercules again illustrates the constantly changing and cumulative process involved in the interaction between the resources and markets of a firm. In 1956 Hercules acquired the Huron Milling Company, a small firm processing wheat flour to produce amino acids, food supplements, and wheat-based food flavoring, including monosodium glutamate. At first sight this acquisition looked rather far afield, although Hercules did have earlier connections with the food business through its CMC, discussed above, as well as chewing gum (a rosin derivative) and antioxidants for food products. Hence, although food chemistry and food markets had not been of primary concern to the firm, they were not completely alien to its experience. Nevertheless, the primary incentive for this particular acquisition and for the choice of this specific direction of expansion was somewhat different.

It will be recalled that Hercules produces its own chemical cotton from cotton linters. Production is carried on in the Virginia cellulose plant and the scale of activity depends not only on the demand for the product but on the supply of linters, which is a function of the size of the cotton crop. The supply of linters has not been sufficient in recent years to employ fully the services of the personnel connected with the Virginia cellulose operation, and the firm has been looking for some suitable activity to absorb these "unused services." The Huron Milling Company was on the market. It was a family firm whose owners wanted to get out and retire from business and also to put their assets in a different form. (Estate tax considerations may well have had something to do with their desire to sell.) At the same time, the firm's activities were of such a nature that Hercules saw an opportunity to extend its knowledge in the food field, especially in the chemistry of amino acids, and to use the personnel of the Virginia cellulose plant. The Huron Milling Company was accordingly purchased with an exchange of shares and is now operated as the Huron Milling Division of the Virginia Cellulose Department. Whether a new base will develop for Hercules remains to be seen, but a start has been made which, if it fits in well with the general nature of Hercules' activities, may not only mean new markets for the firm, but new technology as well.

The Changing Productive Opportunity of the Firm

The diversification of the Hercules Powder Company, while unique in its details, is by no means unique in its general pattern and will be found repeated in greater or less degree in the story of any number of long-established successful firms. The company's history illustrates the impossibility of separating "demand" and "supply" as independent factors explaining the growth and diversification of a firm. The Hercules story illustrates the crucial role of changing knowledge about its own resources in the determination of a firm's course of expansion; at the same time it illustrates the restraining influence of a firm's existing areas of specialization, in particular its technological bases. Whether or not the appearance of new industries, of new "demand," in the economy as a whole will provide profitable opportunities for the expansion of a particular firm depends largely on whether that firm has, or can obtain, an adequate "base" in the relevant field.

Although no single group of industries served by Hercules accounts for more than around 16 per cent of Hercules' sales, two of its primary technological bases, cellulose chemistry and rosin and terpene chemistry, have until recently accounted for over three quarters of its business, with nitrogen chemistry a third important base. Within these bases new products and new markets are continually being created; at the same time petrochemicals have become a leading activity and the emergence of new bases for future operations can already be discerned. By 1926, a bare thirteen years after the firm's creation, new product lines accounted for 35 per cent of total sales; by 1952, 40 per cent of its sales consisted of products that had originated from the firm's research activities after 1930.

The market-creating activities of Hercules are of two kinds; we have discussed one, its extensive reliance on "technical service" to its customers. The other lies in extensive promotion activities related to its customers' products and only indirectly to its own products. For example, Hercules does not manufacture hot lacquers, but it devotes considerable effort to developing the market for these lacquers; only if the end product is extensively used will the demand for the components made by Hercules be high. The firm even goes as far as to promote the sale of aerosol lacquers (lacquers packaged in aerosol cans under pressure), although it produces neither the lacquers nor the cans.

Because of the nature of its market, Hercules is peculiarly sensitive to business fluctuations. When the demand for final products falls off in the economy, the decline in sales affects the intermediate products and raw materials produced by Hercules in magnified form. The question of the desirability of vertical integration therefore arises, for a producer of intermediate products can usually reduce the sensitivity of its total activities to fluctuations in demand by itself undertaking to produce products destined for the final consumer. This has been a solution adopted by many firms, but it is a solution largely denied Hercules by the nature of its market connections. Forward integration would immediately adversely affect one of the pillars of the sales and market policy of Hercules, for customers would no longer be willing to open their plants, disclose their processes, and discuss their problems with the technical servicemen of Hercules. The technical relationship with customers so carefully cultivated and so important for the creation of new opportunities would be impaired if customers had any reason to fear that Hercules would itself become a competitor.

The Rate of Growth of the Firm

The discussion so far has been concerned exclusively with the direction of expansion. What about the rate of growth of the firm? Hercules has not grown so fast as some other firms in related fields of activity, but it has grown faster than industry as a whole. Can one identify a basic factor limiting the firm's rate of growth? Here, of course, we can only speculate, draw inferences from the course of events, and attempt to interpret statements made by the officials of the firm.

Practically all of the growth of Hercules has been financed with internally generated funds. There has been some criticism within the firm of its conservative financing, and the allegation is made by many, particularly by junior executives who feel that their opportunities have been unnecessarily limited on this account, that the firm's growth has been restricted by its preference for internal financing and its insistence on a strong "cash position." On the other hand, one of the older executives, long a senior official in the firm, asserted categorically that it was not finance but rather the availability of profitable opportunities for expansion which controlled the firm's rate of expansion. He said that if Hercules found new opportunities for profitable investment exceeding its own financial resources it would borrow the money (or preferably raise it from existing stockholders) to take advantage of them.

The same executive stated that neither was expansion held back by the ability of the firm's personnel. He felt that the war record of the firm showed that if the opportunities were there it could do a great deal more than it was doing. In contrast, another senior executive took a different view: "Give us the men," he said, "and we will do the job."

These appear to be conflicting explanations of the limits on the rate of expansion of the firm. Although it is obvious that an insistence on financing all expansion from retained earnings would limit the firm's growth, it is unsafe to assume that this has provided the effective limit on expansion merely because little outside capital has in fact been raised. On the other hand, it is undoubtedly true that from a purely managerial point of view the administrative organization of Hercules could have been expanded much more rapidly than it was. In other words, it is probable that the managerial services available from the administrative and technical staff of the firm have rarely been fully used. Under these circumstances we must examine the nature of the firm's "entrepreneurship."

Hercules has clearly been imaginative, versatile, and venturesome in the introduction of new products, even at times going into production on a small scale before any market for a particular product was clearly evident; at the same time it has been cautious and conservative in entering new and alien fields of technology. It has been willing to venture extensive funds in speculative research in new fields; it has been unwilling to move into production and invest in plant and equipment in new fields before it had established a research base of its own. And it has been conservative in the methods chosen for entering new fields. For example, it was long after petrochemicals had become an important and growing aspect of the field of industrial chemistry that Hercules decided to enter in a significant way, and then it moved cautiously, relying largely on production processes the firm itself had developed. Another firm, technologically less conservative, might have entered much earlier and through extensive acquisition; Hercules has tended to emphasize the importance of establishing a technological position based on some specialty arising from its own experience. On the other hand, once the firm has become "basic" in a field, as some of the officials of the firm like to put it, this conservatism largely disappears and the variety and quantity of product is expanded as rapidly as developing technology and markets will permit.

This means, in effect, that the growth of the firm is fundamentally constrained by the knowledge and experience of its existing personnel. Hercules has apparently been loath to go into new fields of activity except through the relatively slow process of building up its internal technical resources. New people are continually being brought into the firm and trained in the processes and methods of the firm; new ideas are eagerly sought from the outside, particularly from abroad, and incorporated into the firm's research program. But new *bases* are not acquired "ready-made," so to speak, through extensive and rapid absorption of new people in new fields that are not easily integrated with some existing and internally developed unit in the firm.

The profitability of opportunities for expansion is examined not only in the light of the expected market for certain products or types of products, but largely in the light of how Hercules, with its existing resources and types of operation, could take advantage of and develop them. If the growth of the firm has been restrained by a "lack" of profitable opportunities for expansion, this merely reflects the lack of entrepreneurial confidence in the profitability *for Hercules* of areas of activity with which the officials of the firm are insufficiently familiar. Since a "technological base" consists not of buildings, kettles, and tubes, but of the experience and know-how of personnel, the basic restriction comes down to the services available from existing personnel; the problem of entrepreneurial confidence is fundamentally a problem of building up an experienced managerial and technical team in new fields of activity. Here, again, we can see the nature of the market as a restraining influence on expansion. To the extent that limited opportunities in existing fields force firms to go into new ones, the rate of growth is retarded by the need for developing new bases and by the difficulties of expanding as a coordinated unit. The speed with which firms *try* to move, however, is to a large extent a question of the nature of their "entrepreneurship."

The above interpretation of the growth of Hercules is based on a study of past history and of recent attitudes. It is clear that entrepreneurial attitudes, the "firm's conception of itself," have had a pervasive influence not only on its direction of growth but also on the method of growth and on the rate of growth. Whether these attitudes will persist depends on the way in which the entrepreneurial resources of the firm change as time goes on. Hercules takes pride in the long service of its people and in the fact that its board of directors is not only a "working board" but is also drawn from men who have spent a great part of their working life within the firm. The first president of the firm served in that capacity for 26 years, was chairman of the finance committee until 1952, and only retired from the board in 1956; of the 15 members of the board in 1950 all but 2 had been with the firm at least 25 years. As the men who built up the firm and carried it through its first few decades retire, it remains to be seen whether the growth of Hercules will be shaped in the future by the same considerations as it has in the past, for in spite of the importance of technological and market considerations, the entrepreneurship of a firm will largely determine how imaginatively and how rapidly it exploits its potentialities.

[17]

The Managerial Revolution and the Developmental State: The Case of U.S. Agriculture

Louis Ferleger
Department of Economics
University of Massachusetts, Boston

William Lazonick
University of
Massachussetts, Lowell
and
Harvard Institute for International Development

A Public-Sector Managerial Revolution[1]

The dominant view among Americans is that government intervention into the operation of the economy can only result in inferior economic performance. It is a view, however, that is currently being questioned by a growing awareness of the successes of the developmental state in places such as Japan, Korea, and Taiwan [see Johnson, 1982; Amsden, 1989; Wade, 1990]. Yet many American academics and policymakers who recognize the accomplishments of the developmental state abroad still retain strong doubts about the applicability of such governmental intervention to the United States. However appropriate the developmental state may be for the late-developing nations, the skeptics argue, it is not suited to a nation such as the United States, which became highly industrialized a century ago on the basis of individualism and *laissez-faire*.

Such mistrust of the possibilities for an American developmental state reflects a misunderstanding of American economic history. No-

1 Versions of this paper were presented at the Economic History Workshop, Harvard University, May 1, 1992; the Cliometrics Conference, Miami, Ohio, May 16, 1992; the Business History Seminar, Harvard Business School, December 7, 1992; and the Business History Conference, Boston, March 19-21, 1993. We are grateful to Michael Best, Fred Carstensen, Richard DuBoff, Stanley Engerman, Alan Kauffman, Stephen Marglin, and William Mass for comments and criticisms.

where is the neglect of the historical record of the role of the government more evident than in the case of U.S. agriculture. Here was a sector of the economy that in 1890 represented 43 percent of the American labor force working on over four-and-a-half million farms [U.S. Bureau of the Census, 1961, pp. 72, 278]. In the aggregate, labor productivity in agriculture was somewhat higher than labor productivity in manufacturing in the 1890s. But low prices for agricultural commodities meant that the income generated from the products (including nonmarketed output) of these farms accounted for only 17.1 percent of national income [U.S. Bureau of the Census, 1961, p. 140]. The importance of agriculture to the national economy derived not only from the large numbers of people who were supported (even if barely) by it but also from the preponderance of agricultural products among U.S. exports. In 1890, agricultural products accounted for almost 75 percent of total U.S. exports, with cotton and grain products making up close to 50 percent of the agricultural export total [U.S. Department of Agriculture, 1891]. Especially in the context of a shrinking frontier of unutilized land, the discovery of new sources of productivity growth became critical to agriculture's ability to contribute to the economic development of the nation.

Acting as an individual enterprise, the family farmer had neither the financial resources nor the scientific knowledge to develop new technologies that could dramatically improve productivity. The agricultural machinery and implements sector--which included such giants as McCormick (soon to form the core of International Harvester) and John Deere--developed labor-saving mechanical technologies that increased the amount of land that could be tilled, planted, and harvested by a given number of labor hours. But, in addition, continued productivity growth in agriculture required scientific advances that could be embodied in the land and the products of the land to increase yields per acre.

To secure productivity gains from machines and scientific advances, farmers had to learn how properly to utilize these new technologies. In the transfer of knowledge to the farm, government, through the United States Department of Agriculture [USDA] and the state experiment stations, played the central role. The transfer of relevant knowledge also flowed from the farmer to the government agencies. Improvements in seeds, fertilizers, disease control, as well

L. Ferleger & W. Lazonick / 69

as new product development, required that the scientific community, largely based in the USDA, land-grant colleges, and state experiment stations, receive information back from farmers concerning their experiences under widely varying climatic and geological conditions.

Finally, farmers had to have the financial resources to purchase these inputs. Yet, prior to the 1930s, volatile agricultural prices -- the consequence of unregulated competition in the sale of undifferentiated commodities -- meant that farmers rarely could rely on their own financial resources to invest in new technologies. Even when loans were available, many farmers were reluctant to borrow for fear of losing their land. Indeed, some farmers who did borrow to make significant capital investments ended up in bankruptcy and had their land foreclosed [Clarke, 1992].

The development of new agricultural products and processes, the diffusion of these technologies to the farmers, and the provision of financial incentives that could induce farmers to invest in the productivity-enhancing inputs had to be undertaken by some entities other than the farmers themselves. To some extent, private-sector businesses assumed these roles, especially in the development and diffusion of farm implements and machinery. The fact is, however, that in the economic development of U.S. agriculture, governments at the federal, state, and county levels became deeply involved in developing productive resources for agriculture and ensuring their effective utilization. Over the long run, moreover, the activities of the private and public sectors became inextricably linked in the development of U.S. agriculture.

An understanding of the roles of the government in the development of U.S. agriculture makes it difficult to argue that a successful developmental state is foreign to the experience of the United States. But the case of U.S. agriculture has even more profound implications for understanding the sources of successful economic development in the United States. The contribution of federal, state, and local governments in the United States to agricultural productivity represents one of the most successful examples in modern economic history of the beneficial impact of the developmental state on a single economic sector. In our view, an accurate understanding of the role of the government in the development of U.S. agriculture substantially undermines the "myth of the market economy" [Lazonick, 1991]. The

The Managerial Revolution / 70

rediscovery of the history of the role of the government in American economic development during the twentieth century should compel a rethinking of how, as the "American century" nears its close, the United States should, and can, respond to ever-intensifying global competition.

The key to rethinking the role of the government in American economic history is, we shall argue, an understanding of the "managerial revolution" that occurred in the United States in roughly the half century from the 1880s to the 1930s. Our argument is that the managerial revolution occurred not only in manufacturing, as Alfred Chandler [1977, 1990] and others have amply documented, but also in agriculture. In manufacturing, the managerial revolution occurred primarily (although not entirely) within private-sector enterprises that came to dominate their industries. In agriculture, the managerial revolution occurred primarily (although not entirely) within public-sector organizations that defined the strategies and structures of the developmental state. We shall argue that the developmental state was central to technological change and productivity growth in U.S. agriculture from the late nineteenth century, and that the managerial revolution within the public sector was the essence of the developmental state.

The Managerial Revolution and the Family Farm

To begin to comprehend the role of the developmental state in U.S. agriculture, one must understand what made the managerial revolution such a powerful engine of economic development. As Joseph Schumpeter [1942] argued, economic development requires innovation -- the generation of higher-quality products at lower-unit costs than those goods and services that had previously been available. Innovation that is economically successful requires the development of new technology and its diffusion to producers who can generate high-quality products at low unit costs. The development of new technology requires that a specialized division of labor be coordinated to generate new knowledge that can be embodied in new productive inputs. The diffusion of new technology requires that the users of these productive inputs have both the incentive to invest in the new technology and the ability -- namely, knowledge that is complementary to the utilization of machines and scientific advances -- to

L. Ferleger & W. Lazonick / 71

generate high-quality products at low-unit costs.

The managerial revolution occurred to plan and coordinate the development and diffusion of those technologies that required large-scale investments in plant and equipment and sustained access to personnel with highly specialized complementary knowledge. In many manufacturing industries such as automobiles, consumer electronics, electrical machinery, and chemicals (among others), the technological possibilities for product differentiation and high throughput permitted individual business organizations that pursued innovative investment strategies to gain distinct competitive advantages in their industries. Those innovative enterprises that used the returns from innovation (in the form of retained earnings) to pursue a strategy of continuous innovation were often able to gain sustained competitive advantage and dominate their industries. This innovative investment strategy typically entailed not only technological innovation in products and processes but also organizational innovation in planning and coordinating complex specialized divisions of labor. Within major enterprises, these divisions of labor could include tens of thousands of highly trained individuals whose specialist activities often extended from the production of capital inputs to the sale of the final products. The managerial revolution enabled these manufacturing enterprises to develop their own technologies and diffuse them to their own production facilities around the nation and eventually around the world.

In agriculture, the technological limitations on product differentiation and throughput meant that it was very difficult for any individual business enterprise to gain a sustained competitive advantage. These limitations, along with the federal government policies of land distribution during the nineteenth century, resulted in the widespread persistence of the family farm in the twentieth century. As Table 1 shows, the number of farms in the United States reached 6.4 million in 1920.

Table 1 also shows that even as the number of farms in the United States dropped by two-thirds between 1920 and 1990, there was little growth in the number of acres in farms. Yet over this period, agricultural productivity per unit of input increased over two-and-a-half times [U.S. Bureau of the Census, 1976, pp. 498-99; U.S. Bureau of the Census, 1992, p. 657], while from 1920 to 1986 agricultural productivity per labor hour increased over fifteen times (see Table 2). How did this

The Managerial Revolution / 72

Table 1
Total Farms and Acreage, United States, 1890-1990

	Number of Farms (1000s)	Land in Farms (1000 acres)
1880	4,009	536,082
1890	4,565	623,219
1900	5,740	841,202
1910	6,366	881,431
1920	6,454	958,677
1930	6,295	990,112
1940	6,102	1,065,114
1950	5,388	1,161,420
1960	3,962	1,176,946
1970	2,954	1,102,769
1980	2,440	1,039,000
1990	2,143	988,000

Sources: U.S. Bureau of the Census, 1976, p. 457; U.S. Bureau of the Census, 1991, p. 644.

Table 2
Farm Output per Labor-Hour, 1910-1986

Year	Output per labor-hour
1910	14
1920	16
1930	17
1940	21
1950	35
1960	67
1970	113
1980	191
1986	254

Sources: U.S. Department of Agriculture, 1954:458; U.S. Department of Agriculture, 1972, p. 540; U.S. Bureau of the Census, 1974, p. 614; U.S. Bureau of the Census, 1981, p. 709; U.S. Bureau of the Census 1989, p. 642.

L. Ferleger & W. Lazonick / 73

remarkable productivity growth occur?   Even when private-sector enterprises manufactured and marketed the productive inputs, the
government did much of the research required to improve the productivity of the inputs and the training required to enable farmers to use
these inputs more effectively.   To develop and diffuse these yield-in-
creasing technologies required the building up of extensive links
between, on the one hand, state experiment stations and land-grant colleges and, on the other hand, millions of farmers.

The key actor in linking the research process with the production
process was the county agent, a government employee who was an integral member of local farm communities.   In 1924, ten years after
the passage of the Smith-Lever Act, which established a nationwide
cooperative extenstion service, there were 2,251 county agents in the
United States, spread out over about three-quarters of the agricultural
counties in the nation [McConnell, 1969, p. 46; see also Smith, 1926,
pp. 4-5].   The cooperative extension service made the results of research at the USDA, experiment stations, and land-grant colleges and
universities available and accessible to farmers. Supported by federal,
state, and local funds (see Table 3), the main task of the county agents
was to inform farmers about new agricultural practices [Rasmussen
1989].

Through cooperative extension services, the county agent took
new methods of farming from the agricultural experiment stations and
the USDA to groups of farmers in particular localities.   The county
agent also took back to the experiment stations information on the
varying performance of new technologies under differing geological
and climatic conditions as well as in combination with various other
farming practices. This information then permitted the experiment stations to improve the technologies for use under different conditions.

The role of the county agents was, however, not only technological. They played central roles in organizing farmers on the local level
for purposes of educating them collectively and sharing information
among themselves.

The county agents were typically the key figures in organizing local farm bureaus -- organizations that when amalgamated into
the American Farm Bureau Federation quickly became the most potent

The Managerial Revolution / 74

advocates of the interests of commercial farmers on the national level [Kile, 1948, Pt. I; McConnell, 1969, ch. 5; Howard, 1983, ch. 10].

Table 3

Cooperative Extension Funds, by Source, 1915-1988

	Total (000 $)	Federal (%)	State (%)	County (%)	Private (%)
1915	3,597	41	29	22	8
1920	14,685	40	36	20	4
1925	19,250	36	37	20	7
1930	23,804	37	29	30	4
1935	20,042	45	25	26	4
1940	32,764	57	20	20	3
1945	37,836	50	24	23	3
1950	73,394	44	32	21	3
1955	100,617	39	36	22	3
1960	140,071	38	38	23	1
1965	188,884	38	39	21	2
1970	290,688	39	41	18	2
1975	448,334	40	41	18	2
1980	682,698	34	45	19	2
1985	996,629	33	46	18	3
1988	1,144,996	30	48	18	4

Source: Rasmussen, 1989, p. 252.

From the U.S. Secretary of Agriculture down through the state experiment stations to the army of county agents, an elaborate managerial organization evolved in the American agricultural sector between the late 1880s and the 1920s. Not by coincidence, it was during this very same period that the managerial revolution in manufacturing occurred. These decades witnessed a science-based industrial revolution in which the building of complex organizations was critical to the development and utilization of scientific knowledge. These decades also saw a transformation in the American system of higher education that developed highly educated personnel who were ready and willing to pursue careers in the complex science-based or-

L. Ferleger & W. Lazonick / 75

ganizations. The potential for innovation and productivity growth through the application of science to industrial pursuits was enormous in agriculture as well as manufacturing. In both agriculture and manufacturing, a managerial revolution occurred.

Our purpose in the remainder of this paper is to describe the managerial revolution that occurred in U.S. agriculture from the Hatch Act of 1887 to World War II. In the conclusion, we shall indicate some of the implications of this managerial revolution for the growth of productivity in American agriculture subsequent to the legislation of the New Deal as well as for some major social problems that American society faces as we near the end of the twentieth century.

The Commitment of Finance to Agricultural Development

Economic development requires committed finance that enables those who make direct investments in productive assets to develop the productive capabilities of these assets until such time as they yield returns. Committed finance generally takes the form of retained earnings. For many farmers who did not make significant investments in farm equipment, such ongoing "financial" commitment was literally the seed corn that they planted. But in a business world of purchased inputs and sold outputs, the basic source of financial commitment for small family farms as well as giant corporations was (and remains) those revenues that are left over after workers, suppliers, landlords, owners, creditors, and governments have taken their shares. With the prospects of a steady stream of this "seed corn," the business enterprise can, if it so desires, secure additional finance through borrowing.

In the manufacturing enterprises that Chandler [1977] describes, retained earnings formed the basis for investments in not only plant and equipment but also research and development [see Brooks 1992]. In the agricultural sector, funding for research and development came from federal and state governments. In 1887, the Hatch Act allocated $15,000 per year to every state for the purposes of setting up and operating an agricultural experiment station. After the passage of the Hatch Act, the individual states took over more of the funding of the experiment stations, with the states' proportionate contributions rising steadily from 24 percent in 1896 to 36 percent in 1905 [True, 1937].

The Managerial Revolution / 76

The passage of the Adams Act in 1906 bolstered the national movement to advance agricultural science within the state experiment station system. This act established a separate fund (initially $5,000 per year per state) of federal subsidies to support science-based research projects at experiment stations. The USDA and the Office of Experiment Stations [OES] also encouraged state governments to appropriate more funds to supplement federal aid to agriculture for station activities. Some states had previously made substantial contributions to stations, while others had provided no funds or had parsimonious records of funding station work. After the Adams Act, state appropriations expanded, with more states increasing their contributions to station work [True, 1937, pp. 138, 212]. In 1906, when the act was passed, nonfederal funding of experiment stations represented 41 percent of total station revenues. From 1912 until 1955, nonfederal funds amounted to anywhere from 60 to 80 percent of the total budgets of state stations [Huffman and Evenson, 1991, pp. 4-43].

The Smith-Lever Act increased the financial commitment of the federal government to agricultural research. The act authorized specific federal appropriations, with dollar-for-dollar state matching funds over an initial $10,000 per year per state, for cooperative agriculture and extension work. The act significantly enhanced the capacity of the experiment stations to diffuse knowledge to farmers.

The passage of the Purnell Act in 1925 further rewarded the USDA's efforts to increase federal appropriations for scientific research. The act authorized additional funds -- $20,000 per station in 1926, $60,000 by 1930 -- for research purposes (including some economic and sociological studies).

The Bankhead-Jones Act of 1936, similar to the Adams Act and Purnell Act, provided for project oversight by the OES [ESR 78, February 1938, p. 146]. The act also stipulated that states had to provide matching funds, similar to the Smith-Lever Act. The USDA only distributed 60 percent of the appropriation. It allocated the rest to regional laboratories that were often located near land-grant colleges and stations. The Bankhead-Jones Act was amended in 1946 with the passage of the Agricultural Research and Marketing Act which increased funding for basic research as well as marketing and distribution of agricultural products.

L. Ferleger & W. Lazonick / 77

Not all land-grant colleges benefited equally from the public funding of agricultural experimentation. The "colleges of 1890" -- the separate black colleges set up under the Morrill Land-Grant College Act of 1890 -- got virtually none of the research funds. For example, in 1971, the "colleges of 1890" received just one-tenth of one percent of all the funds distributed to the land-grant colleges by the Cooperative State Research Service [Hightower, 1978, p. 12].

As the potential user of the new technologies, the family farm also needed finance to enable it to invest in new technologies. Volatile prices and mortgages of short duration, however, made it difficult, and often imprudent, for the farmer to invest in the new technologies. Clarke [1992] shows convincingly that New Deal legislation that remained in force after the 1930s vastly improved the prospects for financing high fixed-cost farm investments without setting the stage for high levels of farm foreclosures because of insufficient returns to these investments.

The pre-Depression cumulation of organizational capabilities that were the essence of the managerial revolution in agriculture were critical for securing the passage and implementation of the New Deal legislation. Central to these organizational capabilities were the United States Department of Agriculture and its Office of Experiment Stations, the land-grant colleges, the state experiment stations, and the cooperative extension service.

The Development of Agricultural Science

The Morrill Land-Grant College Act of 1862, which created a nationwide system of publicly funded state colleges for agriculture and mechanical arts, was not meant to provide critical institutional foundations for the managerial revolution. Rather, when it was passed, the act was aimed at upgrading the social standing of the farmer and artisan by providing these "industrial classes" with institutions of higher education that were on a par with existing elite universities like Harvard and Yale. Unfortunately for this Jeffersonian vision, farmers and artisans found little use for the land-grant colleges during the first quarter century of their existence, in part because of the underdevelopment of the secondary education system that was supposed to supply the colleges with students, and in part because of the irrelevance of a four-year college degree for Americans who intended to earn their livelihoods as farmers and artisans [Lazonick, 1977]. It was only in the 1880s, with agricultural exports accounting for some three-quarters of all U.S. exports and with the limits to the American frontier rapidly being reached, that the federal government sought to make the land-grant colleges centers of agricultural research.

As already indicated, the critical legislation was the Hatch Act of 1887, for it marked the beginning of governmental actions to contribute to agricultural productivity. The USDA supported the establishment of an experiment station system to aid farmers nationwide, develop links with agricultural scientists across states, and raise funding for agricultural research. Each state in the Union, as a recipient of Hatch Act funds, had at least one central experiment station. In 1888 the Secretary of Agriculture established the Office of Experiment Stations as the administrative division of the USDA responsible for coordinating and monitoring the use and allocation of funds under the Hatch Act (see Figure 1).

Advocates of an experiment station system noted the advances that German agriculture had achieved because of sustained government support for agricultural research. Americans admired three characteristics of the German system: highly trained teachers and scientists, a commitment to high-caliber scientific investigations, and sufficient time and freedom to carry out research projects [Ferleger, 1990, pp. 12-13; Kerr, 1987, pp. 2-3].

One section of the Hatch Act specified that American experiment stations should make an effort "to conduct original researches or verify experiments . . . bearing directly on the agricultural industry of the United States" [Marcus, 1985]. USDA and experiment station proponents of original research rejected the idea that stations should function mainly as bureaus of information. Instead, they thought that the future of American agriculture depended on successful experimentation in the lab or field leading to scientific discoveries that were beneficial to the development of the industry. These innovations could then be disseminated to farmers through farmers' institutes and agricultural schools at the land-grant colleges.

L. Ferleger & W. Lazonick / 79

Figure 1
Federal Agricultural Research Organizations, 1862-1953

Chemical and Biological   **USDA (1862)**   Statistics and Economics
_____Research_____   _____
Divisions: **Bureaus/Offices:**
Chemistry (1862)
Entomology (1863)   Statistics (1863,1903)
Botany (1868)

Veterinary (1883)
Veterinary and
  Animal Industry (1884)
                          OES (1888)

Vegetable, Physiology, and
  Pathology (1890,1895)
Agricultural Soils (1894)
Agroscopy (1895)

Bureaus:
Soils (1901)
Plant Industry (1901)
Entomology (1904)   Crop Estimates (1914)
                                             Markets (1917)
                                             Farm Management and Farm
                                               Economics (1919)
Home Economics (1923)   Markets and Crop Estimates (1921)
Dairy Industry (1924)   Agricultural Economics (1922)
Chemistry and Soils (1927)

Entomology and Plant
  Quarantine (1934)
Plant Industry and Soils (1938)   Foreign Agricultural Service
Agricultural Chemistry and   (1938)
  Engineering (1938)
Human Nutrition and
  Home Economics (1943)
Agricultural and Industrial
  Chemistry (1943)
Plant Industry, Soil, and   Production and Marketing
  Agricultural Engineering (1943)   Administration (1945)

                          ARS (1953)

                                             Agricultural Marketing
                                               Service (1953)

Sources: Huffman and Evenson, 1991, ch.2,47-48; Baker et al., 1963; Rasmussen and Baker, 1972.

The Managerial Revolution / 80

For example, in 1890 basic research by the USDA's Bureau of Animal Industry revealed that cattle ticks transmitted from one animal to another a fatal disease that became known as tick fever. Subsequent public research on disease-producing organisms, particularly those borne by insects, built on the USDA's original investigations [Baker, et al., 1963, pp. 32-33; Moore, 1967, pp. 8-9].

The early directors of the OES attempted to define the objectives of research work at the stations. Because the OES had oversight responsibilities for the federal grants provided to states, it acted as a central clearinghouse for keeping track of the kinds of research projects that stations initiated as well as avoiding excessive duplication of experiments. OES staff, particularly the director, presented OES policy recommendations regarding agricultural research practices in, among other places, two critical forums: editorial exhortations and articles in the *Experiment Station Record* (*ESR*), and professional meetings of USDA/OES staff with scientists from land-grant colleges and experiment stations [Ferleger, 1990].

Meanwhile, some station directors faced tremendous pressure from various statewide groups to spend Hatch funds on nonresearch work. Some land-grant college administrators wanted station scientists to do more teaching rather than research. Some farmers who were skeptical about the merits of agricultural science wanted the stations to provide quick answers to isolated problems. Some political leaders who failed to appreciate the long-term benefits to their constituents of advances in agricultural science demanded that stations orient their work to solving immediate farm crises. Despite these conflicting pressures on the allocation of experiment station time and effort, by the end of the first decade of the twentieth century many stations had begun to focus their activities on original agricultural investigations that required fundamental research [Ferleger, 1990; Fletcher, 1937].

As stated by a Montana experiment station scientist in 1905, these investigations were defined as pure science or fundamental research when "scientific research is carried on for the acquisition of truth only and the mere sake of extending the boundaries of knowledge" [quoted in Eddy, 1957, p. 124; see also *ESR*, 18, January 1907, p. 413]. Under the joint leadership of James Wilson, Secretary of Agriculture from 1897 to 1913, and Alfred True, director of the OES from 1893 to

L. Ferleger & W. Lazonick / 81

1915, the value of using public funds to extend basic scientific knowledge became firmly imbedded as the prime mission of the government.

Project review procedures contained in the Adams Act allowed the OES to exercise more control over expenditures and projects than was possible under the Hatch Act. The OES maintained that its review process enabled it to exercise effective influence over station work. The review process was critical, the OES argued, because expenditures under the Hatch Act were too often used for nonresearch work, such as enforcement of agricultural regulations, correspondence, and administrative tasks. The OES had repeatedly suggested that non-Hatch funds (that is, state appropriations) be used to cover nonresearch expenditures [Knoblauch et al., 1962, p. 112]. To avoid the confusion that had emerged under the Hatch Act regarding the uses of federal funds, Secretary Wilson, a vociferous proponent of agricultural science, sent instructions to the experiment stations on March 20, 1906, that explained that the Adams Act prohibited the use of federal funds for nonresearch work. He specifically indicated that "expenses for administration, care of buildings and grounds, insurance, office furniture and fittings, general maintenance of the station and animals, verification and demonstration experiments, compilations, farmers' institute work, traveling, except as is immediately connected with original researches in progress . . . and other general expenses for the maintenance of the experiment stations, are not to be charged to this fund" [Kerr, 1987, p. 44; Office of Experiment Stations, 1906, pp. 67-68]. This exercise of firm control over the use of federal funds forced the states to secure other funding to support the nonresearch expenditures of their experiment stations.

The evolution of USDA-OES control over this far-flung system of research says much about the public-sector managerial revolution that was taking place in the decades spanning the turn of the century. In 1895 the Secretary of Agriculture threatened to terminate appropriations for the experiment stations unless the stations agreed to a federal fiscal review of their expenditures. The stations, represented by the American Association of Agricultural Colleges and Experiment Stations (AAACES), agreed to submit their expenditures to the OES. In the same year Alfred True, director of the OES, visited 35 stations to review their work. True was concerned about the progress of not only particular projects but also "entire research programs." In 1899, upon

The Managerial Revolution / 82

request of the OES, the attorney general of the United States ruled that Hatch funds could not be used for academic instruction. Similarly, in that year, James Wilson, the Secretary of Agriculture, told USDA scientists to stop making informal agreements with selected station scientists for joint cooperative research. Instead the secretary wanted all approved proposals for cooperative work to be monitored and implemented by the OES [Kerr, 1987, pp. 41-44]. These directives illustrate the USDA's resolve to manage the station's work by implementing the policies adopted by the OES -- policies that were formulated in consultation with the secretary of the USDA.

The Adams Act stipulated advance reviews of station work, thus allowing the OES to make recommendations about the scope and nature of project outlines before investigations began. The OES also had legislative power to recommend curtailment of Adams funding for a station that did not abide by the OES's standards for scientific investigations; and during the first three decades of this century several stations did have their funding cut off temporarily [Kerr, 1987, pp. 58-61, 66-68]. As a result, the review process, known as the "project system," gave the OES a powerful managerial mechanism to oversee scientific work under the Adams Act. In subsequent years *all* reviews occurred under this system irrespective of source of funding. In sum, according to Edward Eddy, with the Adams Act "for the first time in Land-Grant College history a Federal Department had been given direct authority over state units" [Eddy, 1957, p. 125].

The OES, in its advisory capacity, recognized that station autonomy over research projects remained a politically explosive issue, one in which station directors had to contend with various constituencies while also conforming to scientific standards set by the OES for funding under the Adams Act. The act enabled the USDA, through an administrative unit, the OES, to formally monitor federal subsidies for research work. As a result, the USDA had a mechanism to strengthen scientists' commitment to basic research within an organizational structure that would, they believed, enhance future opportunities for fundamental discoveries leading to innovations.

Alfred True sent a memorandum to station directors on April 30, 1906, describing in minute detail how a project outline should be submitted to his office. He included a sample project outline that explicitly specified the scope and character of the study to be carried

L. Ferleger & W. Lazonick / 83

out, and a budget that broke down estimated expenses by, among other items, employee function (for example, salary of expert in charge, salary of analyst) [*Annual Report*, 1906, pp. 68-70]. To handle the burgeoning number of projects that had to be examined, True's staff at OES grew rapidly from 38 in 1897 to over 200 in 1912 [Kerr, 1987, p. 45].

In the OES's annual report to Congress of Adams work completed in 1907, True remarked that "the system . . . of having projects outlined by the stations and passed upon by the Office in advance of beginning work . . . has worked very satisfactorily" [quoted in Knoblauch et al., 1962, p. 164]. In practice, under this project approach, experimentation on a project could not begin without meeting what came be to be known as the "True Standard." How original did a project have to be to conform to this standard? Although True was not a scientist, he understood the complexities that pure agricultural science research projects entailed. In his evaluations of projects, he did not require complete originality. Instead he wanted some aspect of the work to involve science-based principles. Knoblauch et al. state that True was "more intent on measuring station projects for their scientific caliber than for their academic uniqueness, [and he] relied on the certainty that a scientific investigation, planned and conducted in conformity with the project system, would achieve prior to its termination a significant penetration in depth." True believed that 'originality' in accomplishment, gained by an assault against the unknown, would unfailingly emerge" [Knoblauch et al., 1962, pp. 164-65].

An AAACES commission report in 1908 emphasized a mission-directed approach to promote agricultural research in the United States. The five-person commission (which included, in addition to two prominent agricultural researchers and a representative of the USDA, Carroll D. Wright and David Starr Jordan) had been set up in 1906 to evaluate how successfully federally funded agricultural research had been carried out. They also made recommendations on the nature and types of research on which experiment stations and the USDA should concentrate their efforts. The report spelled out the functional relationship between the USDA and experiment stations, thus reinforcing the already evident central role that the USDA played as manager of the nation's agricultural research agenda. In particular the report noted:

The Managerial Revolution / 84

There should be a clearer definition of the relative fields of work of the United States Department of Agriculture and the experiment stations. The dominance of the stations within their respective fields should be preserved and their growth fostered, as agencies for the investigation of local questions and of the more individual scientific problems. The Federal agency, on the other hand, should cultivate the almost limitless field offered by questions having national or interstate relations, and by those broad scientific problems requiring heavy expenditures, elaborate equipment, long continued study, and the correlation of the results of many investigators, which efforts are usually beyond the means of an individual station. On many questions the harmonious cooperation of the two agencies is essential to the highest efficiency of effort . . . . Research work, both national and state, should be provided for by separate, lump-sum appropriations, to be distributed according to the discretion of the responsible executive head of each agency . . . . An advisory board is suggested consisting of members appointed by the Secretary of Agriculture and by the Association of American Agricultural Colleges and Experiment Stations, respectively, which shall confer with the Secretary of Agriculture regarding the mutual interests of the Department and the Stations and shall consider the promotion of agricultural investigation in general. [Knoblauch et al., 1962, p. 125]

Prior to the passage of the Adams Act, the AAACES recognized that it needed a new committee to coordinate "operational harmony" with other administrative units [Knoblauch et al., 1962, p. 107]. The Experiment Station Committee on Organization and Policy (ESCOP) included representatives from other administrative units engaged in agricultural research, in particular the USDA. Within the USDA's organizational hierarchy, the ESCOP played a critical role in resolving administrative disputes among different units while preserving organizational harmony and cohesion.

L. Ferleger & W. Lazonick / 85

By the first decade of the twentieth century the USDA had in place a managerial organization to enhance the nation's capability to promote agricultural science. Greater appropriations to the USDA during the sixteen years (1897-1913) in which Secretary Wilson headed the department meant that the USDA could expand its research programs. Moore provides a succinct summary of Wilson's vital role: "His sixteen years in the Cabinet . . . established a record for unbroken service that has never been equaled. His interest in scientific work made him a frequent visitor in the Department laboratories. He knew all the scientists and what they were doing" [1967, p. 16]. Secretary Wilson's emphasis on strengthening the department resulted in larger USDA appropriations, jumping from about 3 million dollars in 1897 to close to 25 million dollars in 1913. During Wilson's term, the USDA hired hundreds of scientists, developed new lines of inquiry, especially in the fields of entomology and animal and dairy husbandry, purchased equipment, and modernized facilities. It also expanded research and regulatory work on plants, soils, and nutrition [Kerr, 1987, pp. 44-45; Baker et al., 1963, pp. 42-51; Moore, 1967, p. 16].

In the years after the Adams Act, federal-state relations regarding agricultural research proceeded relatively smoothly. ESCOP played a mediating role in resolving those jurisdictional or administrative disputes that did arise. Federal-state relations were characterized by collusion, compromise, and cooperation, with the USDA encouraging agreements among competing research units so as to maintain public support for agriculture [Baker and Rasmussen, 1971]. Over the years many joint committees were set up to coordinate policies among AAACES, the OES, and the USDA.

An important force for the organizational integration of the nationwide system of agricultural research was the movement of agricultural scientists over the course of their careers between the public and private sectors and between state and federal public institutions. In earlier years some station scientists (so-called "research entrepreneurs") cultivated relationships with various client groups in order to ensure political support for their work [Rosenberg, 1971; Danbom, 1988, pp. 21-22]. These clients included private agricultural firms and commercial farmers who needed research done in a specific area related to monoculture agriculture.

The Managerial Revolution / 86

Scientists at the USDA also cultivated similar relationships. In Ruttan's words: "The major research bureaus of the USDA were initially established in a manner to take full advantage of the link between the bureau's mission and its clientele interests both within and outside of the Congress" [Ruttan, 1980, p. 530]. Station scientists did change their affiliations, with many department heads departing for positions with the USDA, land-grant colleges, or private firms. One glimpse of the problem is captured in a study of the 1914-1919 period that found that stations experienced an 80 percent turnover rate, with some leading scientists leaving the station system. In particular, the OES reported that "370 department heads and leaders of special lines [departed] . . . . Of this expert class, upward of 150 went into industrial or commercial lines, . . . 50 into extension work, [and] an equal number to the National and State departments of agriculture . . ." [True, 1937, p. 237; Kerr, 1987, pp. 62-63].

High turnover rates could delay or slow ongoing station projects. But they also provided the USDA and private agricultural firms with a readily available pool of trained scientists [see Huffman and Evenson, 1991, ch.3]. Those scientists who moved back and forth between government and industry established key public-private links that contributed to the improvement of technologies.

As the main coordinating force, the USDA maintained its mission of directing the various centers of basic agricultural research. Between the Smith-Lever Act of 1914 and the Purnell Acts of 1925, the USDA reorganized its departments to streamline operations (see Figure 1). New departments were established to respond to changing economic conditions, particularly falling prices caused by overproduction. One new department, the Bureau of Agricultural Economics, carried out studies to help farmers market and distribute farm products.

The OES maintained its historical position as a separate unit within the USDA. Its chief of operations also assumed the title of assistant director of the Office of Scientific Work, reporting directly to the USDA's director of Scientific Work [Baker et al., 1963, pp. 64-67]. OES's project system was firmly in place in the 1920s, so that few proposals were turned down, though many were substantially revised. The review process involved an examination of the project by an OES scientist in a particular specialization (for example, field

L. Ferleger & W. Lazonick / 87

crops) and consultation with scientists within the USDA. The OES project system was not a pro forma process, although, as in the case of USDA reviews of proposals, the OES deliberately attempted to reformulate the objectives of a project rather than reject it outright [Key, 1937, pp. 43-44]. Kerr [1987, p. 67] states that in 1928 "only twenty-three of the nearly 400 proposals were turned down. Yet in the same year, Washington reviewers insisted upon substantial modifications in another 105 of those proposed projects in an attempt to promote scientific productivity in the state agricultural experiment stations."

Thus, the OES continued its role of coordinating the expenditures and projects of the state experiment stations while promoting cooperative research efforts between the USDA and the stations. Cooperative research projects grew over the 1920s, as was noted at the 1930 AAACES meeting, where the Joint Committee on Projects and Correlation of Research reported that almost 1,100 USDA-experiment station projects were currently under way, about 200 more than the previous year. Finally, state agricultural departments absorbed some regulatory functions previously carried out by stations while appropriating more state funds for experiment work [*ESR* 60, 1930, pp. 103-04].

Experiment station scientists published the results of their research in many places, including popular publications and scientific journals. Scientific discoveries irrespective of field were published in the *Journal of Agricultural Research*, edited by USDA and AAACES scientists. The journal, published from 1913 to 1949, reported important scientific findings of agricultural scientists for the public and private scientific communities.

In 1931 an ESCOP special commission survey of the experiment stations noted that the "role of the Department [of Agriculture] in a national system for agricultural research should be that of advisor, contributor, and coordinator, rather than administrator . . . . The Department, . . . because of its detachment from local influences, could be expected to bring into cooperation broad and unbiased views of the purposes and relations of research projects. It is in the position to coordinate the net results of all local research and translate them into the broadest and most fundamental meaning." The commission also suggested that "the United States Department of Agriculture [should] establish and operate field stations or laboratories in any state only in

The Managerial Revolution / 88

definite cooperation with the state experiment stations" [Knoblauch et al., 1962, p. 127]. In addition, various AAACES committees examined the nature of cooperative research projects. In 1931, for example, a special committee report on federal-state relations remarked that the "fundamental finding of the committee [is] that in general mutually cordial and helpful relations exist between the Federal and State agencies, and there is constant improvement in the administration of the details of cooperative research" [*ESR* 66, February 1932, p. 107 and *ESR* 68, February 1933, p. 139].

The 1931 ESCOP special commission survey contributed to the passage five years later of the Bankhead-Jones Act which appropriated additional funds for state stations and the establishment of regional research laboratories to support cooperative research. Each laboratory worked on a specific problem: for example, poultry in Michigan or swine breeding in Iowa [Kerr, 1987, pp. 74-75].

These laboratories represented another significant step in the USDA's efforts to contribute, through research, to the alleviation of the problems of American agriculture. During the 1920s and 1930s, one of the most pressing and persistent problems was overproduction. With large agricultural surpluses flooding depressed markets during the 1930s, President Roosevelt signed the Agricultural Adjustment Act of 1938. This act committed federal funds to establish and operate four regional laboratories that would investigate new uses of farm products [Moore, 1967, p. 22].

These laboratories centered their work on chemical and engineering research in order to improve the range of uses of agricultural products, especially by-products. Each research center focused on regional crops; for example, the Southern laboratory concentrated on cotton, peanuts, and sweet potatoes, while the Northern laboratory carried out research projects on corn, wheat, and soybeans. Especially during World War II, these research laboratories contributed to the development of many new industrial and agricultural products, including rubber substitutes from dairy products (Northern), drugs from tobacco and buckwheat plants (Eastern), tire cord from cotton (South), and dried food products from fruits and vegetables (West) [Harding, 1947, pp. 53-57].

L. Ferleger & W. Lazonick / 89

In 1947 the Secretary of Agriculture reorganized the research departments of the USDA (including the OES) and put them under the authority of the Agricultural Research Administration (renamed the Agricultural Research Service [ARS] in 1953). The USDA streamlined its operations again in the 1950s after all funding for research purposes was consolidated in the Act of 1955 Consolidating the Hatch Act and Laws Supplementary Thereto. As had been the case in earlier reorganizations dating back to the days of James Wilson and Alfred True, the 1955 reorganization of the USDA was a basis for realigning its administrative structure to manage more effectively its new and varied activities [Ruttan, 1980].

During the first half of the twentieth century, research by agricultural scientists at experiment stations and the USDA contributed enormously to the productivity of American agriculture. Robert Evenson, Paul Waggoner, and Vernon Ruttan [1979, p. 1103] have documented the enormous returns to investments in agricultural research (often on the order of 30-40 percent per year, and in some cases much higher) in the United States and abroad throughout the twentieth century. Specifically, they estimated an annual rate of return on U.S. agricultural research expenditures of 65 percent for the period 1868-1926 and of between 95 and 110 percent for the period 1927-1950. According to the estimates of Evenson et al. [1979, p. 1102], federally sponsored research accounted for productivity growth rates of 1 percent per year from 1870 to 1900, and over 1 percent per year since 1925.

Underlying these remarkable productivity results were sustained scientific advances over a wide range of crops and applications. The USDA and station scientists recorded notable successes in fending off damaging insects, particularly two formidable pests: the Hessian fly that infested wheat and the boll weevil that infested cotton [Harding, 1947]. Coordinated work between the USDA and stations successfully eradicated or reduced the impact of particular plant diseases--for example, black rot that damaged sweet potatoes and wilt diseases that harmed cotton and other crop plants. Besides plant disease work, USDA and station scientists carried out plant-science research directed toward developing geographically specific soybean, wheat, cotton, orchards, and tobacco varieties. In later years other research projects expanded the market for cotton by developing new uses for the raw material, such as wash and wear cottons, stretch cottons, and flame-proof cottons. Soybean projects that focused on improved methods of processing the crop resulted in soybean oil and high protein meal from soya [Moore, 1967, p. 24].

The Developmental State: Past and Present

The story that we have told about the managerial revolution in the developmental state has focused on the role of the USDA and OES in planning and coordinating the production of knowledge in the land-grant colleges and experiment stations in the United States. This managerial organization in the public sector is analogous to that which exists in the private sector, where the corporate headquarters of indus-trial enterprises plan and coordinate the activities of their divisions [on the historical evolution of the multidivisional organizational structure, see Chandler, 1962]. From the late 1880s, the federal government had a strategy to develop American agriculture, and over the next half cen-tury or so put in place an organizational structure to generate the productive resources that economic development required. To be sure, numerous interested parties on the state and local levels influenced the evolution of the strategy and structure of the developmental state in American agriculture. But, as in the cases of the public-sector Ameri-can Association of Agricultural Colleges and Experiment Stations or the private-sector American Farm Bureau Federation, state and local interests quickly built national organizations that could interact with the federal government in shaping the nation's agricultural strategy.

Some economists have stressed the role of decentralized decision making in the successful development of American agriculture. For example, Zvi Griliches [1957] emphasizes the role of investment deci-sions at the farm level in response to market incentives in the diffusion of hybrid corn, although, in a subsequent article [Griliches, 1958], he also calculates enormously high returns to the public-sector research that generated the technology.

Farmers did respond to market incentives in adopting the new technologies. But as Clarke [1991, 1992] has argued persuasively, it was the political process, and in particular the New Deal legislation of the 1930s that stayed in place in the following decades, that structured market forces to induce farm investment. New Deal legislation that supported farm prices and that provided low-cost and secure farm credit made it possible for farmers to adopt high-fixed cost technologies like tractors that yielded substantial productivity gains and sharp declines in farm foreclosures [Clarke, 1992]. Although Clarke analyzes the case of tractors, an agricultural input produced in the private sector, she also recognizes that scientific advances coming mainly from the public sector increased yields per acre, which in turn increased the potential productivity gains that could be derived from mechanization that could decrease the number of labor-hours per acre. The perspective that we have presented suggests that it was the managerial revolution within the developmental state prior to the 1930s that made it possible for the government to restructure markets effectively during the crisis of the Great Depression.

Evenson, Waggoner, and Ruttan [1979], whose productivity figures on the returns to agricultural research we have already cited, have focused on the role of the public sector in the development of technology but have emphasized the decentralized character of the system of land-grant colleges and experiment stations as the key to the success of what we have called the developmental state. Specifically, Evenson et al. [1979, p. 1105] argue that the distribution of agricultural researchers across many different regions of the nation "exposes scientists to the problems of farmers, gives farmers and extension workers easy access to specialists and their libraries, spins off talent and ideas to a locality and gives a region the technological capacity essential to development."

We recognize the importance of this decentralized structure for diffusing and improving agricultural technology but view its evolution as the outcome of a national strategy to increase agricultural productivity. The very existence of scientific advances to be diffused and improved as well as the very existence of the land-grant colleges, experiment stations, and cooperative extension services to do the diffusing and improving can only be understood in terms of the historical evolution of a national system of agricultural innovation [on national systems of innovation more generally, see Nelson, 1993].

The events leading up to the federal funding of cooperative extension services is a case in point. In 1913 the Joint Committee on Projects and Correlation, composed of representatives selected by the AAACES and the Secretary of Agriculture, analyzed federally funded

The Managerial Revolution / 92

work of the USDA, agricultural colleges, and experiment stations. Their report noted the need for an expansion of extension services. The committee's report contributed to the passage in 1914 of the Smith-Lever Act, which funded the diffusion of knowledge to farmers through extension services provided by the land-grant colleges and the experiment stations. Commenting on the Act in 1914, David F. Houston, the Secretary of Agriculture noted: "We are in reality one family, working in different jurisdictions to serve the same people" [Knoblauch et al., 1962, p. 113].

The extension service would now be responsible for all rural farmer educational activities, including demonstration farms, adult education programs, and farmers' institutes. Many local substations were set up to bring experiment station scientists in closer contact with farmers. The service's task, carried out by a multitude of county agents, was to inform farmers of the latest agricultural improvements generated by publicly supported research [Rasmussen, 1989; Huffman and Evenson, 1991, ch.2, pp. 52-53].

By the 1920s, on a nationwide basis in agriculture, a highly integrated, committed, and productive public-sector organization for developing knowledge was complemented by a highly integrated, committed, and productive public-sector organization for diffusing knowledge. In The *Wallaces of Iowa*, Russell Lord [1947, pp. 380-81], a prominent farm journalist and associate of Henry A. Wallace, summed up the organizational revolution that had occurred in middle and lower management of the developmental state:

> When we lament, as we often do in this republic, the lack of a college-trained group of civil servants specifically trained in tasks of administration and statesmanship, we overlook the fact that in one important particular we are well supplied. The Land Grant Agricultural Colleges, established in the states in the time of Lincoln, have been turning out year by year not only thousands of trained technicians in the special branches of agriculture, but economists, sociologists, and administrators whose approach to events is trained and generally realistic. And the in-service training which many such men and women acquire after graduation in the Agricultural Extension Service, as county

L. Ferleger & W. Lazonick / 93

agents, state supervisors, and state or regional administrators, for instance, inclines to instill a considerable
degree of skill and competence in public affairs.
These men and women customarily work facing real
people, out on the ground. One reason that Triple-A
was able to forward its programs, it may well be argued, where NRA so largely failed, lies in the fact that
Triple-A could be and was staffed from the very first
with specifically trained and, on the whole, educated
people [Lord, 1947, pp. 380-81].

Particularly at the lower management level of agricultural extension, the contribution of the public-sector organization to the success
of the New Deal legislation was organizational as well as technological. From the 1910s, county agents had become key figures in
organizing private-sector farm bureaus that brought together local
farmers for educational and political purposes. In 1919 these local
farm bureaus quickly amalgamated to form the American Farm Bureau
Federation, a private-sector organization that became the most powerful advocate of the interests of commercial farmers over the following
decades [Kile, 1948; McConnell, 1969; Howard, 1983]. Those interests, they understood, were served by the federal government through
a national system of innovation designed to develop and diffuse technology to farmers. During the crisis years of the 1930s, the county
agents, in conjunction with the farm bureaus, were called upon not
only to diffuse technical knowledge to farmers but also to implement
New Deal programs such as crop reduction [see, for example, Kirkendall, 1966].

With the passing of the Great Depression, however, there was a
growing concern that public-sector employees in agriculture were becoming the servants of only the wealthier segment of the farm
population rather than of the farm population as a whole. Early in the
New Deal, in an address to the American Economic Association, M. L.
Wilson, a major agricultural economist in the Roosevelt administration, had recognized the dangers of an "engineered agriculture" as
opposed to a "living agriculture" for a large segment of the agricultural
population.

An engineered agriculture is going to require much
fewer workers than a mode of living agriculture. It has

been estimated that we could easily release two million
of the six million farm families now on the land for
other productive industry and thereby improve both the
status of the four million families remaining on the
land and increase the productivity of society as a
whole. The question arises, where will the two million
families go, especially as we have now between eight
and ten million unemployed? How can they be fitted
into new walks of life without great human sacrifice?
This comes very near to the crux of the agricultural
problem [Quoted in Lord, 1947, p. 370; see also
Kirkendall, 1966].

Subsequent history would show that the reduction of two million
farms of which Wilson spoke in 1933 would take about two decades,
with another reduction of two million farms taking about two decades
more [U.S. Bureau of the Census, 1976, p. 457]. As an "engineered
agriculture" took hold, the farm sector became much more productive
and much less populous.

By the second half of the twentieth century, there was reason to
argue that private-sector interest groups -- the Farm Bureau in Grant
McConnell's *The Decline of Agrarian Democracy* [1969; originally
published in 1953] and agribusiness in James Hightower's *Hard Tomatoes, Hard Times* [1978; originally published in 1972] -- dominated
the agricultural sector, including the land-grant colleges and the experiment stations, in pursuit of their own ends. In the aftermath of the
New Deal, poor (or what the USDA called "non-commercial") farmers
had little future in agriculture, while the richer ("commercial") farmers
as well as the private-sector suppliers of agricultural equipment, implements, fertilizers, and seeds had privileged access to highly
effective public-sector organizations for developing and diffusing
technology.

In the process, the developmental state in American agriculture
was a success in introducing new technology and raising productivity
in American agriculture. The developmental state has also been important in opening up and expanding global markets for U.S.
agricultural exports [Vogel, 1985, ch.8]. In the late twentieth century,
the agricultural sector remains of prime importance to American economic prosperity. In 1989, primary agricultural products were 11.6

L. Ferleger & W. Lazonick / 95

percent of all U.S. exports, with grain products, soya products, and cotton making up over half of the value of the agricultural exports. In these products and many others, the United States outstrips the productivity levels of every other nation in the world.

But the American-style developmental state also was exclusive in the sense that, with the passing of the New Deal and its coterie of social reformers close to President Roosevelt, little attention was paid to the fate of the millions of farm families who could not continue to make a living in agriculture. No comparable developmental state existed in industry where the vast majority of the displaced farmers had to find work in blue-collar jobs that demanded little in the way of skills [see Lazonick, 1990, ch.7-9].

This legacy of unskilled shop-floor work, as well as a more recent decline of concerted commitments to scientific research, are now pressing problems facing American industry in its attempts to be internationally competitive. The case of American agriculture shows that the developmental state is not alien to the nation. For developing and utilizing productive resources, moreover, the organizational principles of an effective developmental state are analogous to the organizational principles of an effective business organization in the private sector. The lessons of the past in agriculture suggest that the United States can build a developmental state in its efforts to be a world industrial leader. The demands of the present for a highly skilled work force suggest that the developmental state that is put in place will have to be more inclusive in its distribution of productive capabilities than the developmental state that gave the nation the world's most productive agricultural sector.

References

Amsden, Alice, *Asia's Next Giant: South Korea and Late Industrialization* (New York, 1989).

Baker, Gladys L., and Wayne D. Rasmussen, *The Department of Agriculture* (New York, 1972).

Baker, Gladys L., Wayne D. Rasmussen, Vivian Wiser, and Jane Porter, *Century of Service: The First Hundred Years of the USDA* (Washington, 1963).

The Managerial Revolution / 96

Brooks, Jennifer J. S., "Debt and Equity in the American Corporate Financial Structure, 1900-1991," photocopy (1992).

Chandler, Jr., Alfred D., *Scale and Scope: the Dynamics of Industrial Capitalism* (Boston, MA, 1990).

Chandler, Jr., Alfred D., *Strategy and Structure: Chapters in the History of the Industrial Enterprise* (Boston, MA, 1962).

Chandler, Jr., Alfred D., *The Visible Hand: The Managerial Revolution in American Business* (Boston, MA, 1977).

Clarke, Sally, "'Innovation' in U.S. Agriculture: A Role for New Deal Regulation," *Business and Economic History*, 21 (1992), 46-55.

Clarke, Sally, "New Deal Regulation and the Revolution in American Farm Productivity: A Case Study of the Diffusion of the Tractor in the Corn Belt, 1920-1940," *Journal of Economic History*, 51 (March 1991), 101-123.

Danbom, David, B., *'Our Purpose Is to Serve': The First Century of the North Dakota Agricultural Experiment Station,* (North Dakota Institute for Regional Studies, 1990).

Eddy, Edward D., *Colleges for Our Land and Time* (New York, 1957).

Evenson, Robert E., Paul E. Waggoner, and Vernon W. Ruttan, "Economic Benefits from Research: An Example from Agriculture," *Science*, 205 (September 14, 1979).

Experiment Station Record [ESR], Washington, various years.

Ferleger, Lou, "Uplifting American Agriculture: Experiment Station Scientists and the Office of Experiment Stations in the Early Years After the Hatch Act," *Agricultural History*, 64 (Spring 1990).

Fletcher, S.W., "The Major Research Achievements Made Possible Through Grants Under the Hatch Act," *Proceedings, Associated Land Grant Colleges & Universities*, 51 (1937).

Griliches, Zvi, "Hybrid Corn; An Exploration in the Economics of Technological Change," *Econometrica*, 25 (October 1957), 501-522.

Griliches, Zvi, "Research Costs and Social Returns: Hybrid Corn and Related Innovations," *Journal of Political Economy*, 66 (1958), 419-431.

Harding, T. Swann, *Two Blades of Grass: A History of Scientific Development in the U.S. Department of Agriculture*, reprint, (New York, 1947).

Hightower, James, *Hard Tomatoes, Hard Times* (Cambridge, ENG, 1978).

L. Ferleger & W. Lazonick / 97

Howard, Robert P., *James R. Howard and the Farm Bureau,*(Ames, IA, 1983).

Huffman, Wallace E., and Robert E. Evenson, *Science for Agriculture*, photocopy (Ames, IA, 1991).

Johnson, Chalmers, *MITI and the Japanese Miracle: The Growth of Industrial Policy, 1925-1975* (Palo Alto, 1982).

Kerr, Norwood A., *The Legacy: A Centennial History of the State Agricultural Experiment Stations* (Missouri Agricultural Experiment Station, 1987).

Key, V.O., *The Administration of Federal Grants to States* (Public Administration Service, Chicago, 1937).

Kile, Orville Mertin, *The Farm Bureau Through Three Decades* (1948).

Kirkendall, Richard S., *Social Scientists and Farm Politics in the Age of Roosevelt* (Columbia, 1966).

Knoblauch, H.C., et al., *State Agricultural Experiment Stations: A History of Research Policy and Procedure* (Washington, 1962).

Lazonick, William, *Business Organization and the Myth of the Market Economy* (New York, 1991).

Lazonick, William, *Competitive Advantage on the Shop Floor* (Boston, MA, 1990).

Lazonick, William, "The Integration of Higher Education into Agricultural Production," photocopy, 1977.

Lord, Russell, *The Wallaces of Iowa* (Boston, MA, 1947).

McConnell, Grant, *The Decline of Agrarian Democracy* (New York, 1969).

Marcus, Alan I., *Agricultural Science and the Quest for Legitimacy* (Ames, 1985).

Moore, Ernest G., *The Agriculture Research Service* (New York, 1967).

Nelson, Richard R., ed., *National Innovation Systems* (New York, 1993).

Office of Experiment Stations, *Annual Report* (Washington, 1906).

Rasmussen, Wayne D., *Taking the University to the People: Seventy-Five Years of Cooperative Extension* (Ames, 1989).

Rosenberg, Charles, "Science, Technology, and Economic Growth: The Case of the Agricultural Experiment Station Scientist, 1875-1914," *Agricultural History*, 44 (January, 1971).

The Managerial Revolution / 98

Ruttan, Vernon W., "Bureaucratic Productivity: The Case of Agricultural Research," *Public Choice*, 35 (1980).

Schumpeter, Joseph A., *Capitalism, Socialism, and Democracy* (New York, 1942).

Smith, C. B., *Cooperative Extension Work, 1924, with Ten-Year Review* (Washington, 1926).

True, Alfred, *Agricultural Experimentation and Research*. reprint, (New York, 1937).

U.S. Bureau of the Census, *Historical Statistics of the United States from Colonial Times to the Present* (Washington, 1961).

U.S. Bureau of the Census, *Historical Statistics of the United States from Colonial Times to the Present* (Washington, 1976).

U.S. Bureau of the Census, *Statistical Abstract of the United States, 1960* (Washington, 1960).

U.S. Bureau of the Census, *Statistical Abstract of the United States, 1981* (Washington, 1981).

U.S. Bureau of the Census, *Statistical Abstract of the United States, 1989* (Washington, 1989).

U.S. Bureau of the Census, *Statistical Abstract of the United States, 1991* (Washington, 1991).

U.S. Bureau of the Census, *Statistical Abstract of the United States, 1992* (Washington, 1992).

U.S. Department of Agriculture, *Agricultural Statistics* (Washington, 1954).

U.S. Department of Agriculture, *Agricultural Statistics* (Washington, 1989).

U.S. Department of Agriculture, *Report of the Secretary of Agriculture, 1890-91* (Washington, 1891).

Vogel, Ezra, *Comeback: Case by Case: Building the Resurgence of American Business* (New York, 1985).

Wade, Robert, *Governing the Market: Economic Theory and the Role of Government in East Asian Industrialization* (Princeton, 1990).

[18]

Japanese Yearbook on Business History — 1992 / 9

The Development of the Producing-Center Cotton Textile Industry in Japan between the Two World Wars

Takeshi ABE

THE PRINCIPAL OBJECTIVE of this study is to show in summary fashion the mechanisms for development in the producing-center cotton textile industry as it existed in Japan from the Panic of 1920 right up to the time immediately prior to the strengthening of cotton-industry controls when the country was put on a war footing (hereafter, this period will be referred to as "between the wars").[1] Perhaps a few words of explanation are needed at the start in regard to this industry.

It is, I believe, a well-established fact that the cotton industry, especially the spinning and weaving segments of it, occupied an important place in Japan's economy before World War II. This was particularly true after it passed through the World War I boom years,[2] when it entered its maturity as an industry and supplied cotton cloth in large quantities not only to the domestic market but also to markets overseas.

---

[1] This study is a revised summary of the main points (supplemented with several observations) I made in my book *Nihon ni okeru sanchi men'orimono gyō no tenkai* [The development of the producing-center cotton textile industry in Japan] (Tokyo University Press, 1989).

[2] This includes the period of approximately one year, beginning from the spring of 1919, that was called "the postwar boom."

The cotton industry in modern Japan is divided into two large business groups: those who combine both spinning and weaving of cloth, and those who specialize in weaving cloth. It is these latter weavers who make up the producing-center cotton textile industry. The former group, which began developing in the 1890s, consisted of large-scale mills equipped from the first with power looms and keen on the latest mechanized technology. The latter group, in contrast, boasted of a history going back into the Tokugawa period; although the creation of "manufacture" is said to have gone ahead in a small fraction of the regions from the late Tokugawa period, the overwhelming majority of weavers were, at least until about the time of the Russo-Japanese War, part of a putting-out-system cottage industry, in which members of farming households, using hand looms and working in their spare time, wove cotton cloth that was collected by merchants.

This system did not seem to lend itself easily to a factory-based industrialization. It was also common for large numbers of cotton cloth producers, merchants, and processers to become concentrated within a relatively small area, thus forming what were called cotton-textile producing centers. The characteristics of the producing-center cotton textile industry, with its concentration in a specific area of small and medium-sized cotton cloth producers along with related businesses, have not changed fundamentally even down to the present day, except that after the Russo-Japanese War and the World War I boom, the industry moved toward a factory structure. In many of the producing centers the construction of small and medium-sized factories equipped with power looms increased markedly from that period; on the other hand, the cottage industry that relied upon hand looms began to decline, as did "manufacture," and these classical representatives of indigenous industry for the most part metamorphosed into small and medium-sized manufacturing industries.

Now, it is held in academic circles in Japan that small industries such as the producing-center cotton textile industry formed the lower stratum of a dual structure from the 1920s on, and that, in stark contrast to the combined spinning-weaving businesses and other such large enterprises that made up the upper stratum, the small industries were characterized by low productivity and low wages.[3] In the

---

[3] For the dual structure of the Japanese economy, see Kōnosuke Odaka, *Rōdō shijō bunseki* [Analysis of the labor market] (Iwanami Shoten, 1984).

cotton textile industry in 1933 very small businesses of fewer than 5 workers made up 91.0% of the total of 53,642 producing premises, with an average total annual output per premise of 13,100 yen; in contrast, the figure for the spinning industry, which was made up principally of large enterprises, came to 2,116,200 yen. Also, the average wages per worker in the cotton textile industry and in the spinning industry, respectively, were 212 yen and 247 yen, with a value-added productivity of 1011 yen and 1900 yen, respectively. Thus it is true that there was a real gap in wages and productivity between the producing-center cotton textile industry and the combined spinning-weaving businesses.[4]

The correctness of the accepted view is, therefore, corroborated by the above data, but that does not lead to the immediate conclusion that the large-enterprise sector developed and the small- and medium-enterprise sector was stagnant or declined. While it is true that the large-enterprise sector in the dual structure did develop, growth in the other sector was marked by diversity and complexity; in the producing-center cotton textile industry, while there were many centers that stagnated or declined, there were also a considerable number of areas that produced a succession of businesses whose output increased remarkably, and in some cases whose scale of operations expanded strikingly.

Now, it is not sufficiently known that the producing-center cotton textile industry on the whole made outstanding progress between the wars. In 1914 "producing-center cotton cloth"[5] ranked sixth in the mining and manufacturing industries in total output, behind cotton yarn, raw silk, military weapons, iron, and coal, at 77,062,000 yen; in 1919 it was third, behind raw silk and cotton yarn, at 595,642,000 yen. And it maintained its high ranking in later years as well: fourth (at 382,039,000 yen) in 1929, after raw silk, cotton yarn, and iron, and still fourth (at 573,221,000 yen) in 1937, after iron, cotton yarn, and military weapons.[6]

[4] The data is based on *Kōjō tōkei hyō* [Factory statistical tables] and *Shokosho tokei hyo* [Ministry of Commerce and Industry statistical tables].

[5] Hereafter I shall refer to cotton cloth produced by producing-center weavers as "producing-center cotton cloth" and that produced by the combined spinner-weavers as "combined cotton cloth."

[6] Abe, *Nihon ni okeru....*, p. 3.

Such progress in the producing-center cotton textile industry owed much to the expansion of new markets both domestically and abroad. It would be no exaggeration to say that prior to World War I the industry relied almost exclusively on domestic demand, the only exception being the weaving of narrow white cotton cloth for the Korean market.[7] Even after the great war the domestic market remained an important basis for the industry's continued existence, but about this time new cotton cloth markets took shape within the country to add to the previous markets. To be specific, because advances in printing techniques made it possible to cut wide cotton cloth into the traditional narrow strips, and because the lifestyles of people in Japan kept moving towards Westernization, the domestic demand for wide cotton cloth—previously hardly ever used within Japan—went on growing.[8]

Another thing: cotton cloth was, obviously, a valuable export item. After outstripping cotton yarn in export totals in 1917, it ranked along with raw silk as one of the two main export items. Led by cotton cloth, the export of other cotton products continued to expand from this point in time, and in 1933 Japan pulled past England in the world market to become the No. 1 cotton-cloth exporting country. Unaffected by the decline (in 1930–1931) in the silk-reeling industry under the influence of the Shōwa Panic, cotton cloth took over as king of export items in 1934. The percentage of "producing-center cotton cloth" among this fast-growing export item was extremely high. While the estimated figure for the amount of "producing-center cotton cloth" in the total amount exported in 1914 is no more than 30%, in 1918 it exceeded 50%. This fell to about 40% in the years between the second half of the 1920s up to the Shōwa Panic, but it went up to 48.2% in 1932 and after that followed an upward trend that saw it around 60% from 1935 on.

What shouldered the main burden of such development in the producing-center cotton textile industry were the few producing centers, alluded to earlier, that continued increasing their output in remark-

[7] The width of the fabrics used in making traditional kimonos in Japan was approximately 36 cm, but textile fabrics several times wider were used in Europe, the United States, and most other countries. The former cloth is called narrow cloth in Japan, and the latter is called wide cloth.

[8] See Takako Sanpei, *Nihon kigyō shi* [History of weaving in Japan] (Yūzankaku, 1961), pp. 296–303.

able fashion. The next sections will explain in detail what they were.

REGIONAL PATTERNS IN THE COTTON TEXTILE INDUSTRY

What I wish to do here is provide an understanding of the national milieu in which the producing-center cotton textile industry developed, from the Russo-Japanese War up to the period between the wars. The positions occupied by the various cotton-textile producing centers within Japan's cotton textile industry, and even in the cotton industry as a whole, and the changes that took place in them, were ascertained by collecting basic data relating to the principal producing centers in the country and then analyzing those figures. Similar attempts have been made in some studies published previously.[9] Yet projects dealing with the period between the wars have not been published, and a considerable number of studies discussing the Meiji and early Taishō periods contain some methodological problems. For example, in most cases they consider the data on the cotton textile industry broken down by prefectures and given in the *Nōshōmu tōkei hyō* [Agriculture and Commerce Ministry statistical tables] as approximately reflecting the true state of the producing-center cotton textile industry, then proceed straightway to an analysis, but because these statistics as a general rule also include figures for "combined cotton cloth," it is dangerous to draw from them any direct conclusions about developments in the producing-center cotton textile industry. Most earlier works also sought the producing centers they would undertake to analyze through introductory outlines of histories of regional industries, and their research ended with descriptions of these centers on the basis of materials such as prefectural statistical papers. On

---

[9] For example, Sadako Nakayasu, "Zairai men'orimono gyō no tenkai to bōseki shihon" [The growth of the indigenous cotton textile industry and spinning capital] (*Tochi seido shigaku* [The Journal of Agrarian History], vol. 14, 1962); Toshio Furushima, *Sangyō shi—III* [History of industry: 3] (*Taikei Nihon shi sōsho* [Systematic history of Japan series], vol. 12, Yamakawa Shuppansha, 1966); Kazuo Yamaguchi, "Orimono gyō no hattatsu to kin'yū" [Progress in the textile industries and finance], in Kazuo Yamaguchi, ed., *Nihon sangyō kin'yū shi kenkyū—orimono kin'yū hen* [Studies in the history of Japan's industrial finance: Textile finance], Introduction (Tokyo University Press, 1974); and Haruki Kandatsu, *Meijiki nōson orimono gyō no tenkai* [The growth of the farming-village textile industry in the Meiji period], chap. 1 (Tokyo University Press, 1974).

the basis of such a method the selection of producing centers tended to become arbitrary, and descriptions of the centers were apt to be inadequate.

With a view to overcoming such problems I adopted as my principal rules of thumb the following procedures.

(1) I decided I would investigate, as a general rule, four years: 1914, which preceded the boom years of World War I; 1919, the year of the "postwar boom"; 1929, which came at the end of the 1920s, when most industries were unable to break out of the recession; and 1937, which immediately preceded the full implementation of wartime controls on all industries.

(2) When I found that "combined cotton cloth" figures had been included in cotton-cloth output totals given in *Nōshōmu tōkei hyō* and *Kōjō tōkei hyō*,[10] I would exclude them before estimating "producing-center cotton cloth" output totals by prefecture, for the top 10 prefectures.[11]

(3) I would select the principal cotton-textile producing centers according to the following plan: a) I would seek, from the statistical papers of the 12 prefectures abstracted by the process described in (2) above, the cotton-cloth output totals, by district and city, for the years 1914 and 1937, taking as a rule only data on pure cotton textiles (hence I would exclude figures for silk-cotton blends); b) from the *Menshi bōseki jijō sankōsho* [Reference work on cotton-yarn spinning] published by Dainippon Bōseki Rengōkai [Japan Cotton Spinners' Association] and statistical papers from all the prefectures, I would search out the proportion of looms the combined spinner-weavers owned out of the total number of looms in operation in the districts and cities in 1914 and 1937, and those regions in which almost all the cotton cloth was produced by the spinner-weavers I would eliminate; c) for the remaining districts and cities I would look for the presence of a weaving industry association in which the principal members were weavers who specialized in weaving, and those regions where I could not find such associations would be excluded; d) the geographical limits of a cotton-textile producing center would be deter-

---

[10] In the case of the *Nōshōmu tōkei hyō* I corrected several mistakes in totals, etc., by revising the figures in the light of data mainly provided by prefectural statistical papers.

[11] A detailed explanation of the elimination procedure is given on pp. 20–22 of Abe, *Nihon ni okeru* ....

mined by taking as norm the jurisdictional area of the above weaving industry association, also taking into consideration district or city mergers or abolitions, and the name customarily given the producing center would be adopted; e) I would exclude any producing centers that did not fulfill one of these two conditions: that their "producing-center cotton cloth" output totals for 1914 were at least 1,000,000 yen, or for 1937 were at least 5,000,000 yen.

The producing centers chosen after the above procedures had been gone through are shown in figure 1. I believe that the principal producing centers in the period that forms the object of this study are almost without exception included in this figure.

(4) In regard to shifts in output totals for the 27 producing centers selected under (3), the markets for their products (in concrete, the ratio between domestic demand and exports), the makeup of their products, their scale of operations (the proportion of total working places with 10 workers or more), and technological level (the proportion of power looms out of total loom numbers), I would try to collect data whose reliability was high.

The results of (4) can be synthesized by saying that cotton-textile production-centers in the period between the wars fall into four types:

I. Producing-centers that moved aggressively into a switch to factories and power looms very quickly after the Russo-Japanese War, during the period between the wars switched their principal product from domestic-oriented narrow white cotton cloth to wide white cotton cloth, and, while producing large quantities of a small variety of cotton fabrics in comparatively large-scale factories, continued to increase their output. Chita in Aichi Prefecture and Sennan in Osaka Prefecture are included in this type; Nagoya in Aichi Prefecture and Senboku in Osaka Prefecture are thought to belong here as well. Hazu in Aichi Prefecture might also be included in this type.

II. Producing-centers that moved into a factory system and into power looms after the Russo-Japanese War or from the boom years of World War I, switched from the weaving of narrow striped cotton cloth for the domestic market to the production of such special products as yarn-dyed cotton cloth for the export market, and, while producing small quantities of a large variety of cotton fabrics in factories of a slightly smaller scale than those in Type I, continued to increase their

Fig. 1. Principal Cotton-Textile Producing Centers

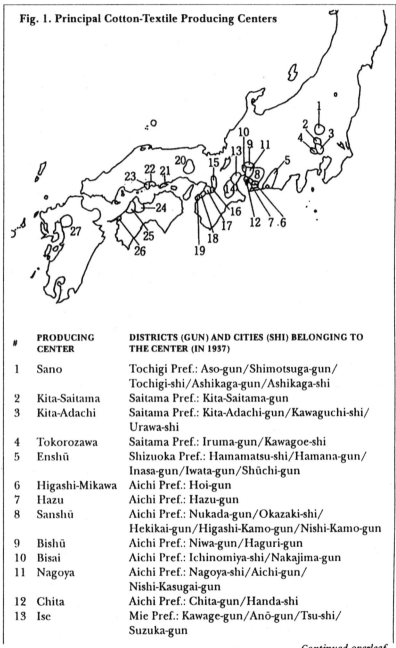

#	PRODUCING CENTER	DISTRICTS (GUN) AND CITIES (SHI) BELONGING TO THE CENTER (IN 1937)
1	Sano	Tochigi Pref.: Aso-gun/Shimotsuga-gun/ Tochigi-shi/Ashikaga-gun/Ashikaga-shi
2	Kita-Saitama	Saitama Pref.: Kita-Saitama-gun
3	Kita-Adachi	Saitama Pref.: Kita-Adachi-gun/Kawaguchi-shi/ Urawa-shi
4	Tokorozawa	Saitama Pref.: Iruma-gun/Kawagoe-shi
5	Enshū	Shizuoka Pref.: Hamamatsu-shi/Hamana-gun/ Inasa-gun/Iwata-gun/Shūchi-gun
6	Higashi-Mikawa	Aichi Pref.: Hoi-gun
7	Hazu	Aichi Pref.: Hazu-gun
8	Sanshū	Aichi Pref.: Nukada-gun/Okazaki-shi/ Hekikai-gun/Higashi-Kamo-gun/Nishi-Kamo-gun
9	Bishū	Aichi Pref.: Niwa-gun/Haguri-gun
10	Bisai	Aichi Pref.: Ichinomiya-shi/Nakajima-gun
11	Nagoya	Aichi Pref.: Nagoya-shi/Aichi-gun/ Nishi-Kasugai-gun
12	Chita	Aichi Pref.: Chita-gun/Handa-shi
13	Ise	Mie Pref.: Kawage-gun/Anō-gun/Tsu-shi/ Suzuka-gun

Continued overleaf

14	Matsuzaka	Mie Pref.: Matsuzaka-shi/Iinan-gun/Ichishi-gun/Taki-gun
15	Naka-/Kita-Kawachi	Osaka Pref.: Naka-Kawachi-gun/Kita-Kawachi-gun/Fuse-shi
16	Minami-Kawachi	Osaka Pref.: Minami-Kawachi-gun
17	Senboku	Osaka Pref.: Senboku-gun
18	Sennan	Osaka Pref.: Sennan-gun/Kishiwada-shi
19	Wakayama	Wakayama Pref.: Wakayama-shi/Kaisō-gun/Kainan-shi
20	Banshū	Hyōgo Pref.: Taka-gun/Katō-gun/Kasai-gun
21	Kojima	Okayama Pref.: Kojima-gun
22	Ibara	Okayama Pref.: Shitsuki-gun/Oda-gun
23	Bingo	Hiroshima Pref.: Numakuma-gun/Ashina-gun/Fukayasu-gun/Fukuyama-shi
24	Imabari	Ehime Pref.: Imabari-shi/Ochi-gun/Shūsō-gun/Nii-gun
25	Matsuyama	Ehime Pref.: Matsuyama-shi/Onsen-gun/Iyo-gun
26	Yawatahama	Ehime Pref.: Yawatahama-shi/Nishi-Uwa-gun
27	Kurume	Fukuoka Pref.: Kurume-shi/Ukeha-gun/Mii-gun/Mitsuma-gun/Yame-gun/Asakura-gun

output. Included in this type are Enshū in Shizuoka Prefecture, Higashi-Mikawa in Aichi Prefecture, Banshū in Hyōgo Prefecture, and Imabari and Yawatahama in Ehime Prefecture. Though Tokorozawa in Saitama Prefecture and Bingo in Hiroshima Prefecture were later in turning to factories or to power looms than the above centers, and Kojima and Ibara in Okayama Prefecture would pour all their efforts into the production of the single variety of cotton cloth called *kokura* (duck cloth), I would be inclined to include them all in this type because they have so many points in common with the above centers.

III. Producing-centers whose alterations in output totals were stagnant in nature, even though they moved to factorization and power looms. Of the 27 centers that make up the total, 9 fall into this category.

IV. Producing-centers that were behind in shifting to factories and power looms even into the 1930s, where cottage industry or very small manufacture were in an overwhelming majority, where traditional products for the domestic market such as *kasuri* (splashed-pattern) or *mekurajima* (blue-stripe cloth), demand for which went on declining, continued to be woven on hand looms and the like, and whose position as a cotton-textile producing center markedly continued to decline. Sano in Tochigi Prefecture, Kita-Saitama in Saitama Prefecture, Matsuyama in Ehime Prefecture, and Kurume in Fukuoka Prefecture are included in this type.

DEVELOPMENT BETWEEN THE WARS

As a result of the above research it would be fairly clear that producing centers in types I and II achieved remarkable development in the period between the wars, but here I would like to push the investigation further and show, with some concrete examples, why development was possible for these two types of producing centers at that time.[12] From figure 2 it can be seen that producing centers belonging to these two types showed a conspicuous increase in output, yet the mechanisms for growth were different for each of them.

1. PRODUCT STRATEGIES

Type II producing centers brought into play an ability to respond quickly to diverse demand from both domestic and overseas markets and to develop products, and they developed by raising their added value. For example, Banshū, a center that produced narrow striped cotton cloth for the domestic market, was stimulated by the drop of the yen exchange rate after the Great Kantō Earthquake in 1923 and the activities of industrial laboratories (to be discussed below) to begin serious production of products for export, and throughout the

---

[12] Historical studies of the cotton textile industry between the wars have at long last been receiving attention. Two recent representative works are Tōru Fukumori, "Momen oroshiuri-shō ni okeru koyō kankei no tenkai" [The development of employment relations in the cotton cloth wholesale trade] (*Keieishigaku,* vol. 25, no. 4, 1991) and Takanori Matsumoto, "Ryōtaisenkanki Senboku kigyō ni okeru orimono kōjō keiei no dōkō" [Trends in textile mill operations within the Senboku textile industry during the 1920s and 1930s] (*Keieishigaku,* vol. 26, no. 4, 1992). In the present discussion I am relying on my own research; for more on Sennan and Banshū, please refer to my work, cited in note 1, *Nihon ni okeru....,* and on Imabari see my article "Senkanki ni okeru chihō sangyō no hatten to kumiai, shikenjō" [The development of regional industries between the wars and associations and laboratories], in Kindai Nihon Kenkyūkai, ed., *Kindai Nihon kenkyū 13—Keizai seisaku to sangyō* [Journal of Modern Japanese Studies 13: Economic policy and industry] (Yamakawa Shuppansha, 1991).

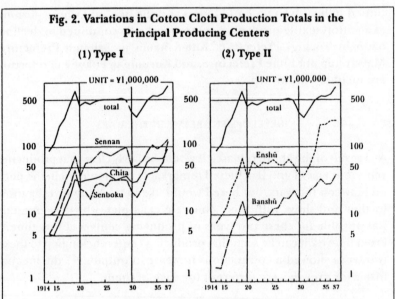

Fig. 2. Variations in Cotton Cloth Production Totals in the
Principal Producing Centers

(1) Type I   (2) Type II

Sources: For Sennan up to 1923, Nōshōmushō [Ministry of Agriculture and Commerce],
Kōmukyoku [Industrial Bureau], *Orimono oyobi meriyasu ni kansuru chosa* [Survey of
woven and knitted goods] (1925), pp. 104–107; for 1924, Sennan-gun Yakusho
[Sennan District office], *Sennan kiyō* [Sennan Bulletin] (1926); for 1926–1927,
Teikoku Shōkō Tsūshinsha [Imperial Commerce and Industry News Service], *Nihon
orimono sōran* [Conspectus of Japan's textiles] (1928); for 1928–1934, Bōshoku
Zasshisha [Spinning and Weaving Journal Publishing Co.], *Bōshoku yoran* [Outline
of spinning and weaving]; for 1935–1937, *Ōsaka-fu tokeisho* [Osaka Prefecture statisti-
cal papers]. For Senboku, *Osaka-fu tokeisho*. For Chita, Chita-gun Shiromomen
Dōgyō Kumiai [Chita District White Cotton Cloth Professional Association] et al.,
eds., *Shōwa 12nen tōkei gaiyō* [1937 statistical summary]. For nationwide figures,
Miyohei Shinohara, *Kokōgyō* [Mining and manufacturing], vol. 10, in Shozaburō
Fujino et al., eds., *Chōki keizai tōkei* [Long-term economic statistics] (Tōyō Keizai
Shinpōsha, 1972), p. 195, and *Sen'i kōgyō* [Textiles], vol. 11, in *Chōki keizai tōkei*
(1979), p. 242.

Note: Nationwide figures = nationwide cotton-cloth production totals minus nationwide
"combined cotton cloth" production totals. For Banshū, Takeshi Abe, *Nihon ni
okeru sanchi men'orimono gyō no tenkai* [The development of the producing-center cotton textile industry in Japan] (Tokyo University Press, 1989), table 5–18. For Enshū,
Hiroaki Yamazaki, "Ryōtaisenkanki ni okeru Enshū men'orimono gyō no kōzō to
undō," *Keiei shirin,* vol. 6, nos. 1/2, 1969, pp. 97, 105, 127–28.

rest of the 1920s it specialized in the production of *shimamitsuaya* (striped
drill); then in the 1930s it developed and continued increasing its output of a huge variety of export-oriented dyed cotton cloth for use in
things such as sarongs, zephyrs, kikois (loincloths for males in
Mombasa, Kenya), saris, and damask tablecloths. Enshū, too, until the

1920s directed its main efforts into the production of narrow striped cotton cloth for the domestic market, but in the 1930s it ranked along Banshū in the field of export-oriented dyed cotton cloth.[13] And Yawatahama is also reported to have turned to extensive weaving of export-oriented dyed cotton cloth.[14]

In contrast to these three producing centers that switched to export-oriented production, there also were producing centers that pushed forward product development in quick response to changes in domestic demand resulting from a more Westernized lifestyle as well as a raising of lifestyle levels. Higashi-Mikawa, for example, began production of kawariaya (twill and cord) in the boom years of World War I, then in the mid-1920s began weaving flannel and interwoven cloth for children's clothes, to become one of the leading producing centers in the country in each of these three categories.[15]

Besides the above, there were centers that carried out slightly special product switches of their own. Kojima had been weaving *Kokura* for sashes and skirts since the late Tokugawa period, as well as *sanada* (tape) and *unsai* (cotton drill), but after the Russo-Japanese War it switched to production of *taitaitsu* for China, and then after the boom of the World War I years and around the time of the 1920 Panic it switched again to producing *kokura* for uniforms for elementary and high-school children, and in these areas it ranked with Ibara as a major producing center.[16] Imabari continued to produce flannel, which had been its main line since the 1890s, in large quantities, but in the 1920s it became as renowned as Banshū as a center of *shimamitsuaya* production, and from the 1920s to the 1930s it also plunged into the

---

[13] Hiroaki Yamazaki, "Ryōtaisenkanki ni okeru Enshū orimonogyō no kōzō to undō" [Structure and movements in the Enshū textile industry between the two great wars] (Hōsei University Faculty of Business Management, *Keiei shirin* vol. 6, nos. 1–2, 1969).

[14] Nagao Tanihara, ed., *Men sufu orimono kōgyō hattatsu shi* [History of progress in the cotton-rayon textile industry] (1958), p. 99.

[15] Tetsuzō Suzuki, "Higashi-Mikawa ni okeru men'orimono gyō no hatten" [The development of the cotton textile industry in Higashi-Mikawa] (Hōsei University Faculty of Economics, *Keizai shirin*, vol. 19, no. 1, 1951).

[16] Kazuhiko Tawa, *Kojima no rekishi—daiikkan: Kojima sangyō-shi no kenkyū* [History of Kojima—vol. 1: Studies of the history of Kojima industries] (1959), and Naokazu Tsunoda, "Tenkanki no Kojima gakudōfuku ōkoku" [The Kojima children's-clothes kingdom in transition], in Nihon Chiiki Shakai Kenkyūjo [Institute of regional society in Japan], ed., *Nihon no kyōdo sangyō* [Local industries in Japan], vol. 5 (Shinjinbutsu Ōraisha, 1975).

production of towels.

Type I producing centers, on the other hand, started out with the production of domestic-oriented narrow white cotton cloth, and in most cases switched in the period between the wars, and especially the 1930s, to the production of such wide cotton cloth as shirting, baft, and coarse cloth. Still, the production techniques for wide white cotton cloth were simple, and many former narrow white cloth production-centers of Type III, such as Sanshū, Bishū, Ise, Matsuzaka, and Minami-Kawachi, were also venturing into it. Also, the principal products among the "combined cotton cloth" weavers in 1929 were shirting (53.7% [of the total production for that year]), coarse cloth (10.3%), and cloth strips (9.9%), while in 1937 they were shirting (64.7%), cotton drill (11.5%), and coarse cloth (9.0%).[17] Thus broad white cotton cloth was a product that had to face competition not only among producing centers but also with the "combined cotton cloth" producers.

There was not as great a demand from Type I producing centers to have the ability to develop products, but they were required to carry out widespread cost-lowering exercises in order to win out over the tough competition. In the case of Sennan, which led the way among other Type I centers in achieving high growth through export initiatives from the 1920s, the important factor in strengthening its cost competitiveness was a rationalization of production in which the key was the use of wide power looms in the weaving process.

Now, one would expect that abundant funds would be necessary in order to effect rationalization. On this point let us look at the case of a representative weaver in Sennan, Obitani Shōten. Obitani had 776 narrow power looms in 1921; its fixed assets including these looms were completely covered by owned capital, of which the nucleus was 500,000 yen of paid-up capital. A huge amount of surplus cash was also produced. The reason why it had such an abundance of owned capital in the early part of the period between the wars is, as the following profit ratios (= current-term pre-depreciation profit divided by {[preceding-term paid-up capital + current-term paid-up capital] divided by 2}) in the boom years of World War I show, that capital accumulation jumped quite sharply. In 1914 it was 14.7%, in 1915 387.3%, in 1916 2,449.1%, in 1917 2,648.5%, in 1918 2118.5%, in 1919

---

[17] Dainippon Bōseki Rengōkai [Japan Cotton Spinners' Association], *Menshibōseki jijō sankōsho.*

1067.6%, and in 1920 a minus 268.4%. Obitani, however, was vigorously trading in futures during the boom period on speculative cotton yarn, and despite the fact that it suffered a heavy blow from the 1920 Panic, it succeeded in scraping through the Panic by imputing a considerable portion of the losses incurred from trading in cotton yarn futures to cotton-yarn merchants in Osaka City, such as Toyoshima Shōten and Iwata Shōji, from whom it had been purchasing large quantities of cotton yarn.

Anyway, between 1922 and 1925 Obitani Shōten abandoned the handling of narrow white cotton cloth for the domestic market and switched to large-scale production of the wide white cotton fabrics of satin and twilled cloth for the export market, repeatedly increasing the number of its wide power looms and continually expanding its scale of operations. The capital needed for equipment investment in the 1920s, being in excess of the range of depreciation that occurred in the process of activating export-oriented production, was being supplied from the large amounts of owned capital; since there was no capital increase during the 1922–1925 period, and increases in reserve funds were also slow, we can say that the returns from the World War I boom years are what supported a considerable portion of equipment investment in the 1920s. The equipment investment that went ahead rapidly from 1931was also financed from owned capital (again having exceeded depreciation limits), but, unlike the 1920s, the replenishment of internal reserves that accompanied the activation of production made such self-financing possible.

Though I have not been able to obtain other examples besides Obitani of profits gained during the World War I boom years and reactions to the 1920 Panic, it is a confirmed fact that most of the comparatively large-scale weavers that belong to Type I were covering equipment investment in the period between the wars with owned capital.[18]

2. SCALE OF OPERATIONS

Next, as opposed to Type II producing-center weavers, who maintained their statuses as small and medium businesses even though they converted to power-driven factories, in Type I producing centers the operating scales of the weavers were as a general rule grander. Thus,

[18] Abe, *Nihon ni okeru...*, pp. 91–93.

for example, the percentages (of the total number of weaving establishments) of those that owned at least 50 power looms in the years 1929 and 1937 were, for Enshū in Type II, 4% and 7% respectively, while for Sennan, in Type I, the percentages were 35% and 37%.[19] In addition, in the case of Type I centers some of the upper-level weavers ("producing-center big weavers")[20] achieved rapid growth, as is shown in table 1.

These differences between the two types could be due mainly to differences in the products made. According to data from around 1950, it is generally held that the appropriate factory scale for wide white cotton cloth is from 150 to 200 power looms.[21] In the Type I producing centers, where the main product was wide white cotton cloth, because the appropriate scale of factory was bigger by reason of production technology, the weavers generally owned large-scale factories, and some of the upper-level weavers, who had abundant capital resources at their disposal, went on increasing their scale of operations quite markedly, though this was done through increasing the number of branch factories. In Type II producing centers, however, because special cotton cloths were being produced that were incompatible with production in large quantities within large factories, the weavers remained small or medium businesses.

3. The Organized Character of the Producing-Centers

In the export-item producing centers of Type II, industrial laboratories[22] and industrial associations became indispensable links within the producing-center structure in the period between the wars, and the organized character of the producing centers was heightened quite conspicuously. Most of the industrial laboratories were organs set up by prefectural governments, but the industrial associations were professional bodies set up throughout the country in accord with the Jūyō Yushutsuhin Kōgyō Kumiai Hō [Important Export Products Industrial Associations Law] of 1925 and the Kōgyō Kumiai Hō [Industrial

---

[19] Ibid., p. 62.

[20] This is a term I have coined.

[21] Kōsei Torihiki Iinkai Jimukyoku [Office of the Fair Trade Commission], *Izumi chihō men'orimono gyō chōsa* [Survey of the cotton textile industry in the Izumi area] (1951), p. 18.

[22] I include within this term the industrial laboratory branches, dyeing and weaving laboratories, and industrial training schools that are mentioned later, as well.

Table 1. "Producing-center Big Weavers" in the Cotton Textile Industry in Japan between the Wars

Producing center	Weaver	About 1923 Power looms A	Plants	About 1936 Power looms B		Plants	B / A
Sennan	Obitani Shōten	866 (300)	—	3,708	(3,708)	6	4.3
	Nakabayashi Menpu	588 (—)	3	2,306	(—)	4	3.9
	Kumatori Orimono	1,000 (500)	5	1,165	(—)	6	1.2
	Kawasaki Menpu	1,158 (124)	3	1,154	(508)	3	1.0
	Minami Orimono	200 (—)	3	911	(911)	3	4.6
Senboku	Morita Shokufu	81a (—)a	1a	1,860	(—)	1	23.0
	Kubosō Shokufu	— —	—	1,758b	(—b)	5b	—
	Ōtori Shokufu	600 (200)	3	1,316	(984)	4	2.2
Chita	Nakashichi Momen	524 (216)	2	1,624	(1,288)	3	3.1
	Okatoku Shokufu	280 (100)	1	1,592c	(1,592c)	6c	5.7
Average no. power looms per each "combined" weaver		1,024 [610]	—	1,339	[808]	—	1.3 [1.3]

1. Compiled from Abe, *Nihon ni okeru…*, table 4-1. Figures for "combined" weavers rely on Dainippon Bōseki Rengōkai, *Menshi bōseki jijō sankōsho.*

2. The weaver company names are those current in 1936. Long dash (—) means the data is not known.

3. Sennan weavers are the top five on the basis of number of power looms about 1936. Senboku and Chita weavers are those that had one thousand or more looms about 1936.

4. Numbers in parentheses ( ) indicate wide-loom numbers.

5. Figures within [ ] brackets indicate loom numbers after figures for Tōyōbō, Kanebō, and Dainihonbō have been subtracted.

6. a = figures for about 1924; b = figures for about 1934; c = figures for about 1934–1935.

Associations Law] of 1931, and they were able to carry on such operations as product inspection, control (concretely, limiting production
of designated products), and joint action (such as collective buying
of raw materials, building of cooperative processing plants, collective
sale of products, and lending of funds to members).

The case of Banshū will help illustrate how things worked. The Nishiwaki branch of the Hyōgo Prefecture Industrial Laboratory (in 1933
this branch became known as the Hyōgo Prefecture Nishiwaki
Dyeing and Weaving Laboratory) was opened in 1921, and within a
couple of years it began encouraging the production of export-oriented cotton cloth. The important stimuli for this course of action
were the fall in the yen exchange rate after the Great Kantō
Earthquake and the switch by Banshū to becoming an export-oriented
producing center. The branch laboratory had hardly been established before it was also pushing for the eradication of slipshod manufacture, something that had become a serious problem in the early
1920s. In 1923, in response to the leap in export-oriented production,
it carried out research on the technique of adjusting the operations
of wide-cloth looms, and in 1925, when the Banshū Ori Seiri Riyō Kumiai
[Banshū Woven Goods Sorting and Use Association] was started for
the purpose of conducting the sorting that was indispensable for
export-oriented cotton cloth, the laboratory was in charge of experimental research on sorting textiles and practical guidance to producers. In all these endeavors the laboratory achieved excellent
results.

For most of the 1920s Banshū weavers continued to specialize in
the production of *shimamitsuaya*, but the head of the Nishiwaki
branch laboratory from 1922, Tarō Yoshida (1885–1938), saw this as
risky, and from November 1929, for over four months, he travelled
in Singapore and the Dutch East Indies to investigate the demand
there for Banshū fabric, and to collect samples of foreign-made cotton cloth. After his return he was convinced that the products that
would be most desired were striped sarongs, textiles of cotton mixed
with rayon, and textiles of rayon, and he urged weavers, through wide
distribution of samples, to move into production of these. In the early
1930s the branch laboratory embarked on the development of
zephyr and kikoi fabrics. From October 1933 Yoshida was sent by the
prefectural government to travel for three and a half months

20 *JAPANESE YEARBOOK ON BUSINESS HISTORY – 1992 / 9*

through Southeast and South Asia and the Middle and Near East: to Singapore, Bangkok, Penang, Rangoon, Calcutta, Madras, Bombay, Aden, Cairo, Suez, Port Said, Alexandria, Izmir, and Istanbul. As a result of this trip, besides collecting samples of textiles, he decided the market in Asia, where import restrictions against Japanese cotton cloth had become notable, ought to be given up as a lost cause, and he pushed for the cultivation of a variety of new products for markets in the Middle and Near East and Africa. Spurred on by Yoshida's firsthand information, Banshū proceeded even further in the direction of a product-diversification strategy. Furthermore, the laboratory increased its efforts in technological guidance to weavers in the late 1920s and through the 1930s, starting in 1928 a year-long training course in dyeing and weaving limited to a quota of 15 males that was continued, with reorganizations and expansions, for the rest of the period between the wars, and the graduates of these courses were warmly welcomed by the weaving companies.

Banshū (like many other textile producing centers) had had, by the way, several professional associations existing within its territory from the earliest years of the twentieth century, as a result of prescriptions of the 1900 Jūyō Bussan Dōgyō Kumiai Hō [Important Products Professional Associations Law]. These associations carried out product inspection, and, during the 1920 Panic, a curtailment of operations, the lowering of wages, and the submission of requests to the Bank of Japan for financing assistance. Banshū Ori Dōgyō Kumiai [Banshū Weavers Association], in particular, was active in the 1920s in the employment of dyeing specialists, the specification to weavers of dyes, the encouragement of bleachers to use pressurized boiling kiers, the establishment of the first industrial association to run a proper sorting plant (Yūgen Sekinin Banshū Ori Seiri Riyō Kumiai [Banshū Woven Goods Sorting and Use Association, Ltd], the encouragement of weavers to adopt electrical power, and so on. Compared to other textile producing centers it was probably far more active. These types of functions were, however, gradually taken over by some industrial associations established around the year 1930.

The biggest project for Banshū's industrial associations in the early years was the *shimamitsuaya* control put into effect from November 1930 with the powerful assistance of the Ministry of Commerce and Industry. While this project, aimed at large numbers of small and medium-sized weavers throughout the country but especially in Banshū, Imabari, Sennan,[23] and Wakayama, ended in failure, the end result was that businesses connected with Banshū weaving that had been specializing in *shimamitsuaya* production were willy-nilly placed under the regulation of the industrial associations. During the favorable conditions that obtained after the reembargo on gold export in late 1931, the industrial associations used their regulatory powers in energetically promoting joint operations, and they strengthened the export competitiveness of the Banshū cotton textile industry. The first thing the associations did was to expand the sorting operations under their direct management that they had been carrying out from almost the start of their existence. Banshū Ori Kōgyō Kumiai [Banshū Weaving Industry Association], which ran the sorting plant that in 1932 employed 300 workers, in that same year closed down the other five businesses engaged in sorting operations within its jurisdictional boundaries and took over exclusive control of the operations. Other associations also strengthened their roles in the dyeing and bleaching industries. Several of the associations directly managed dyeing and bleaching plants as well, but Banshū Ori Kōgyō Kumiai, which did not run these operations, obtained the cooperation of the Nishiwaki Dyeing and Weaving Laboratory in the years 1934 and 1935 to make public the results of tests on the actual costs of the principal dyes, and in this way it was able to check the dyeing businesses that had been making exorbitant profits. This action led to the purchase of dyes and chemicals on consignment from 1935 on. And from the same year the Association signed a special agreement with a leading cotton-yarn merchant in Osaka City, Maruei Shōten, and began buying from them cotton yarn and rayon yarn as requested by members.

The activities of industrial laboratories and industrial associations can be found throughout most of Type II producing centers. In Imabari, for example, the Ehime Prefecture Training School opened in 1922 offered a two-year training course in dyeing and weaving for a maximum of 40 students, as well as short-term in-service training courses aimed at dyers and weavers. In addition, it also provided practical guidance for people in these occupations and conducted experimental research aimed at promoting the production-center.

---

[23] Not all of the Sennan region, but the region from present-day Izumi-Sano City and southwards, which was producing dyed processed cotton cloth and towels for export.

Toshiharu Sugawara (1891–1958), a technician who led the activities of the Training School and later took over as head in 1932, was successful in the 1920s in producing high-grade towels using dobbies and then Jacquard looms, as a result of which Imabari's towel output increased dramatically. After the Training School was reorganized into the Ehime Prefecture Dyeing and Weaving Laboratory in 1934, its significance as a place for nurturing technicians was nearly completely lost, but technological research related to towel production continued, and it came to oversee a whole series of Jacquard-related operations such as patterned designs and the manufacture of pattern sheets. It also promoted the development of new products such as rayon textiles. Obtaining information from trading companies in the large cities in regard to demand for export-oriented wide textiles and towels, and information from large-city department stores and the Nippon Taoru Kōgyō Kumiai Rengōkai [Japan Federation of Towel Industry Associations] in regard to domestic demand for towels, the Dyeing and Weaving Laboratory produced samples accordingly and distributed them to dyers and weavers. The Imabari region had Imabari Orimono Kōgyō Kumiai, which had been established in 1930 to replace the Imabari Orimono Dōgyō Kumiai. While there are many points still unclear about this organization, it is known that it owned processing facilities for cotton cloth and towels, and that it gave powerful support, through financial aid, to the activities of the Dyeing and Weaving Laboratory.

In Enshū, also, from before World War I the Shizuoka Prefecture Hamamatsu Industrial Laboratory was responsible for introducing new technology connected with the textile industry, and after the war it continued its activities over a wide area: setting up textile-industry-related associations; establishing Eikyūsha, a pioneer manufacturing-industry association covering important export products; setting up companies to engage in the processing of textiles; conducting market surveys; and developing products. Then in the 1930s, when the activities of manufacturing-industry associations intensified in all parts of the country, Enshū became involved in joint operations such as nationwide regulation of cloth for sarongs and the like, and joint dyeing, bleaching, sizing, printing, or sorting projects.[24]

[24] See Yamazaki, "Ryōtaisenkanki ni okeru Enshū orimono gyō no kōzō to undō."

As is clear from the above, then, in the period between the wars industrial laboratories in Type II producing centers were much more than organs for experimental research; they were bases for developing new products and sources of a steady supply of technicians. The industrial associations, also, by energetically promoting joint projects, were a second indispensable link in the structures of the producing centers. Their various contributions were all services that individual small and medium-sized weavers could not easily provide themselves, and there is no denying that the activities of these laboratories and associations were strong determinants of the success of Type II producing centers.

In Type I producing centers, however, the situation seems to have been just the opposite. The powerful weavers in this type of producing center concluded separate contracts with cotton-yarn and cotton-cloth merchants and spinning companies that were extremely advantageous as far as accumulating their own capital was concerned, and by carrying out fearless rationalizations to fit their own circumstances they achieved rapid growth.

Obitani Shōten in Sennan is said to have joined in the mid-1920s (during the continuing recession) with Ichitarō Ichihashi of Yagi Shōten, eminent cotton cloth merchant in Osaka City , and with Kiyoshi Inoue of Kanegafuchi Bōseki (Kanebō), one of the leading giant spinning companies in the country, in a division-of-labor scheme in which Obitani used Kanebō yarn to weave five-shaft satin fabric, which Kanebō then processed in its Yodogawa plant, said to have been the biggest in the East, and which Yagi Shōten then exported to East Asia. In this way Obitani became able to produce and sell large quantities of cotton cloth. In Senboku, Kikusaburō Morita [Morita Shokufu] started a similar scheme around 1929; it wove calico using yarn from the large spinning company Kureha Bōseki, and then exported it through the powerful Osaka trading company Itō Chū Shōji, which had close ties with Kureha (Itō Chū is said to have sold 30% of Morita's cloth, and the cooperation between these three companies is said to have continued beyond World War II days).

Large weavers in both Sennan and Senboku made agreements with certain spinning companies from the middle of the 1920s, so that they could have a portion of the spindles of these companies used to make yarn exclusively for their use. What this meant, for example, is that they could have 20-count yarn drawn out to 21 or 22 count, or even sometimes as much as 24 count, and while there would be no appreciable difference in the quantity of raw cotton used when they had 20-count yarn drawn out to 21-count yarn, there would be a substantial lowering of the cost to the weavers of the cotton yarn purchased if, for example, they received 21 meters of yarn instead of the 20 meters they would ordinarily have received. Internal documents confirm that transactions of this sort did in fact take place in Obitani Shōten in the 1930s, but it is said that similar things were done by Nakabayashi Menpu [Nakabayashi Cotton Cloth] and Kawasaki Menpu in Sennan, and Morita Shokufu [Morita Woven Cloth], Kubosō Shokufu, and Ōtori Shokufu in Senboku as well. When one considers the fact that between the wars the price of cotton yarn accounted for over 80% of total expenditure in the production of wide white cotton cloth, it is certain that the acquisition of thinner yarns was a great boost to the growth of the large weavers.

In the 1930s Obitani made another strategic move. While the majority of Sennan weavers were weaving wide cotton cloth on power looms either 36 or 44 inches wide, Obitani ordered large numbers of specially made power looms 34 and 40 inches in width from the Harada-shiki Shokki Kabushiki Kaisha [Harada-type Loom Inc.] and Gōmei Kaisha Hirano Seisakujo [Hirano Manufacturing Plant & Co]. By using these, Obitani was able to weave cloth of the same width as the other weavers, but enjoyed the following advantages: 1) less electric power was used; 2) because a row of these looms took up less space, each woman worker was able to look after more looms; and 3) each loom cost less.

Similarly, in 1929 Nakabayashi Menpu became possibly the first producing-center weaver in the nation to use automatic looms (having purchased 529 from Enshū Loom Inc.), and in 1933 Morita Shokufu followed suit with the introduction of more than 1,000 automatic looms.

Now, these various measures were of their nature individual reforms, not things that could be put into place by the common run of small and medium-sized weavers, who would have only limited funds at their disposal. In Type I producing centers the process of competition within the center itself would have enlarged the gaps among the weavers within that center as far as production conditions and operating scales were concerned. As a result, in these Type I producing centers the emergence of collaboration of any sort among the businesses would have been nearly impossible, and the capacity for guidance of an industrial laboratory or the capacity for regulation of an industrial association would hardly have been able to be of much effectiveness. I think it could be generalized, then, that in the period between the wars, whereas Type II producing centers went on raising their levels of maturity as producing centers, those in Type I on the contrary allowed the organized character of their centers to be progressively lowered.

PRODUCING-CENTER COTTON TEXTILE INDUSTRY WITHIN THE ENTIRE JAPANESE COTTON TEXTILE INDUSTRY

By way of conclusion I would like to say a few things about the place of the producing-center cotton textile industry within the cotton textile industry nationwide during the period between the wars. The dominant school of thought in Japanese scholarly circles on the subject goes something like this: 1) while large enterprises such as those that combined weaving and spinning enlarged their scales of operation and continued to increase production and sales totals, the producing-center cotton textile industry, which was made up of small and medium businesses, could not easily grow in scale and its production totals remained stagnant; 2) the reason there were no prospects of development in the producing-center cotton textile industry is that the weavers were suffering exploitation (in concrete, having high-priced cotton yarn forced on them by the cartel-type activities of the Dainippon Bōseki Rengōkai, or weavers being incorporated into the subcontract factories of the trading companies) or oppression (being forced into fierce competition with "combined cotton cloth" in markets for the same product) at the hands of the large enterprise sector; and 3) the subsistence base of the producing-center cotton textile industry was almost exclusively such poor labor conditions as low wages and long working hours.

This school of thought lumps all the businesses in the producing-center cotton textile industry together as medium/small/tiny businesses, but in fact diverse weavers are found in this industry and at least the distinction must be made between medium businesses and small/tiny businesses. It would be appropriate to refer to Type I and

Type II producing-center weavers as medium businesses, and unlike the Type III small businesses and Type IV tiny businesses, they were extremely prone to development. The commonly accepted school of thought mentioned above might apply to types III and IV. First of all, though, besides the fact that there was, according to my estimated figures, not a great difference in level between the nominal annual growth ratio of 9.3% for the national production totals of "combined cotton cloth" between 1914 and 1937 and the 9.2% figure for national production totals of "producing-center cotton cloth," types I and II producing centers achieved a remarkable growth that exceeded the level of all producing centers in the country. Secondly, there were many weavers in Type I producing centers that were large-scale and had abundant owned capital, and that, moreover, not only were not exploited by the large-business sector but, even as they drew from the latter a variety of free services, crossed beyond the bounds of medium business and enlarged their scale of operations (the "producing-center big weavers"). Thirdly, it should be noted that many of the weavers in Sennan, which belongs to Type I, avoided the fierce competition in the same market with "combined cotton cloth" by changing their main products from plain fabrics to satin and twilled cloth (as we saw in the case of Obitani). Fourthly, even in Type II producing centers, through the joint projects of industrial associations such as joint purchasing of cotton yarn, weavers were able to do business on equal terms with the large-business sector, and aided by the activities of industrial laboratories they succeeded in developing complex and diverse products that could only be made by medium or small business. All these points call for some serious rethinking regarding points 1) and 2) in the accepted theory outlined at the start of this section, and the weavers in the first two types of producing center ought to be seen as in general standing on an equal footing with the large-business sector during the period between the wars, and especially in the 1930s. As far as point 3) goes, this study has no argument with the idea that the producing-center cotton textile industry, including centers from types I and II, subsisted on the poor labor conditions mentioned there. Still, we ought to pay sufficient attention to the fact that during the period between the wars new subsistence bases were being formed, in the expanding export markets, and in the new domestic markets that accompanied changes in the lifestyles of people throughout the nation.

In summary, it is difficult to find any of those controlling, exploitative relations between large business as represented by the combined weaving and spinning companies, and the medium-sized businesses in Type I and Type II, and it would seem that the competition in the marketplace between the two groups was not as fierce as the accepted opinion would have it. It seems that large business gave preferential treatment to medium business as being its biggest customer for cotton yarn, and refrained from making aggressive inroads into the latter's markets. Both groups should be thought of as being in a symbiotic relationship, in which medium business joined with large business to wield stiff competitive power in the world's cotton cloth markets, and this was one of the important factors bringing about the development of Japan's cotton industry in the period between the wars.

Osaka University

[19]

Japanese Yearbook on Business History — 1991 / 8

The Development of Tiered Inter-firm Relationships in the Automobile Industry: A Case Study of Toyota Motor Corporation[1]

Kazuo WADA

THE PROBLEM

Automobile production requires the assembly of a large number of parts. Since the assembler is unable to manufacture internally all the parts required, a certain percentage are normally purchased. When studying automobile production, therefore, it does not suffice to study only the assembler; suppliers also have to be taken into account. Against the background of the Japanese automobile industry's favorable results and high international competitiveness, researchers have been paying increased attention to the multi-tiered and harmonious relationships existing between assemblers and suppliers, relationships that are suspected of being a factor behind the high level of competitiveness.[2]

The present study is limited specifically to Toyota Motor Corpo-

[1] This study was financed in 1990 by the Pache Foundation of Nanzan University. I also wish to express my gratitude to Mr Motohiro Yamada for his assistance in the course of my research.

[2] See James P. Womach, Daniel T. Jones, and Daniel Roos, *The Machine that Changed the World* (Macmillan, 1990).

ration and its past record of relations with suppliers. Why focus on Toyota? Because it is the largest assembler in Japan, and it is reputed to have maintained the best relations with its suppliers, and in the most effective manner. By taking up the case of a trendsetting (thus, an extreme) company instead of an average (in that sense, typical) one, I thought I could put the problem into sharper relief.

The period focussed upon is principally the interval between the end of World War II and the early 1970s, because it was during this time that present relations between Toyota and its suppliers began to take shape and the prototypes virtually established. The principal aspect looked at will be the production side. Therefore, when I speak of "Toyota" in this study, I am referring to Toyota Motor Co., Ltd.[3]

PRELIMINARY CONSIDERATIONS

Before entering the heart of my topic, I think two points need to be cleared up. The first is whether or not the inter-firm relationships between Toyota and its suppliers have actually taken on a multi-tiered structure. The second is whether or not these relationships can be adequately explained in terms of funding and personnel ties.

BRIEF SUMMARY OF SURVEYS ON INTER-FIRM RELATIONSHIPS

An overview of the recent situation can be had from a survey conducted by the Small and Medium Enterprises Agency in 1977, *Bungyō kōzō jittai chōsa (jidōsha)* [Survey of specialization structures (automobile industry)]. The survey focuses on a company it refers to anonymously as "A." (The company is readily identified as

---

[3] Toyota Motor Co., Ltd was established in 1937. To overcome a business crisis after World War II a division occurred in 1950, with Toyota Motor Sales Co. set up separately. The two companies merged again in 1982, taking the name Toyota Motor Corporation, the name by which it is still known.

Toyota, as was done by Shiomi.)[4] According to this survey, there were 168 first-tier subcontractors supplying parts to "A," 4,000 second-tier subcontractors, and 31,600 third-tier subcontractors — a total of 35,768 business establishments hierarchically organized. Yoshirō Kaneko also conducted a questionnaire survey at the end of 1978, principally focused on Toyota's suppliers.[5] He found that each supplier belonging to the first tier used an average of 21.7 companies as its subcontractors or to provide it with goods, and these second-tier suppliers in turn were using an average of 15.5 companies, while these latter in turn were obtaining goods from 3.0 companies on average. If these average values are multiplied, one finds that each first-tier supplier has organized in tiers below it a total of 1,009 companies.[6] Kaneko also confirmed that there were continuous, even firmly fixed, business relations, with very little fluctuation.[7]

Though these two surveys were done by researcers outside Toyota, there is another survey conducted by Toyota itself. It found that 62 of its first-tier suppliers were dealing with 996 second-tier suppliers, who in turn were dealing with 3,497 third-tier suppliers.[8]

---

[4] Haruhito Shiomi, "Seisan rojistikkusu no kōzō: Toyota Jidōsha no keesu" [The structure of production logistics: A case study of Toyota Motors], in Kazuichi Sakamoto, ed., *Gijutsu kakushin to kigyō-kōzō* [Technological innovation and enterprise structure] (Mineruba Shobō, 1985), pp. 97–98.

[5] Yoshirō Kaneko, "Jidōsha kanren chūshō kigyō no jittai to mondaiten" [State of automobile-related small and medium enterprises and their problems], *Aichi keizai jihō* [Aichi Economics Review] no. 120 (1978), and "Jidōsha kanren chūshō kigyō jittai chōsa kekka (dainihō) — Nishi Mikawa chiku o chūshin ni shite" [Results of survey on small and medium automobile-related enterprises (2nd report): With a focus on the western Mikawa region], *Aichi keizai jihō* no. 135 (1982).

[6] Yoshirō Kaneko, "Jidōsha kanren chūshō kigyō jittai chōsa kekka (dainihō)", p. 108.

[7] Ibid., p. 113.

[8] *Toyota manejimento* [Toyota Management] 1969 (December), p. 45.

26   *JAPANESE YEARBOOK ON BUSINESS HISTORY — 1991 / 8*

THE EXTENT OF FUNDING AND PERSONNEL TIES

Are enterprises that have close financial and human ties with Toyota the only enterprise groups involved in the tiered inter-firm relationships that exist between Toyota and its suppliers?

Toyota and the other Japanese assemblers have their first-tier suppliers organized as "*kyōryoku-kai*" [cooperative associations]. In Toyota's case, the group that represents its first-tier suppliers is named the "Kyōhōkai."[9] Toyota normally transacts business directly only with the suppliers that belong to this Kyōhōkai. This results in inter-firm relationships being tiered. Of the fourteen companies referred to as the "Toyota Group,"[10] only ten have direct dealings with Toyota. While it is true that the "Toyota Group" are "united both funding-wise and personnel-wise, and they very decidedly have the character of operation divisions or sectors within a single enterprise body," still, of the 171 companies belonging to the Kyōhōkai only 25 (if you except the ten from the "Toyota Group") can be explained in terms of financial and per-

[9] In 1939, when Toyota came out with its "Purchasing Regulations" (see section 3 below), the suppliers and Toyota held the "First Informal Meeting of Toyota Motor Subcontractors," and it was decided to form an association from this group, giving it the name Kyōryoku-kai. During the war Toyota was dropped to a lower ranking as regards obtaining rations of scarce materials, thus making it difficult to guarantee materials. In order to gain the cooperation of suppliers, Toyota dissolved the Kyōryoku-kai and in December 1943 the Kyōhōkai was inaugurated, with Toyota's vice-president, Hisayoshi Akai, as president of the association, and Hamakichi Kojima, president of Kojima Press Co., as vice-president. See Kyōhōkai Editorial Committee, *Kyōhōkai 25nen no ayumi* [Twenty-five years of the Kyōhōkai] (privately published, 1967), pp. 10 and 13.

[10] The "Toyota Group" consists of: Toyoda Automatic Loom Works, Ltd; Aichi Steel Works, Ltd; Toyoda Machine Works, Ltd; Toyota Auto Body Co., Ltd; Toyoda Tsusho Kaisha, Ltd; Aishin Seiki Co., Ltd; Toyoda Spinning & Weaving Co., Ltd; Kanto Auto Works, Ltd; Towa Real Estate Co., Ltd; Toyota Central Research & Development Laboratories, Inc.; Toyoda Gosei Co., Ltd; Hino Motors, Ltd; Daihatsu Motor Co., Ltd; and Nihon Denso, Ltd.

sonnel ties.[11] Shiomi maintains that we cannot ignore Toyota's ties with the other enterprises in Kyōhōkai, and insists on the need to take into consideration business-transaction relationships as well.[12] Following Shiomi's lead, I shall restrict my analysis to those enterprise groups that have close links with Toyota solely on the basis of business transactions, for it is their existence that is at the heart of the present investigation. Because they have direct business relations with Toyota, they are in the ranks of first-tier suppliers. Yet, from the perspective of enterprise groups that have Toyota at the core of their business activities, they belong to the fringe. In terms of the parts they supply, they are not suppliers of "unit parts" but of subcontracted processed goods.

MANAGEMENT DIAGNOSIS

THE "PERMANENT DEAL" CONCEPT

Toyota's company histories stress that the 1939 "Purchasing Regulations" put its parts enterprises with the framework of "branch factories" and decided that, once a deal was entered into, "a permanent deal would be the rule, and the company would work toward strengthening management abilities and bringing about mutual prosperity."[13] The announcement of such a concept has an important effect on suppliers' operations. It may very well be that business relations in which a high possibility of short-term contracts decided after competitive bids or of changing to another dealer is left open, may, in fact, turn out to be long-term and stable. Still, where both parties to a business relationship know ahead of time that, once the relationship is entered into, it will be long-

[11] H. Shiomi, op. cit., p. 86.

[12] Hirschmeier and Yui also put greater stress on transaction ties than ownership. See J. Hirschmeier and T. Yui, *The Development of Japanese Business*, 2nd ed. (London, 1981), p. 337, and on "Vertical Groups", pp. 336–39.

[13] See, for example, Toyota Motor Company History Editorial Committee, *Sōzō kagiri naku — Toyota Jidōsha 50nen-shi* [Limitless creation: 50 years of Toyota Motors] (privately published, 1987), p. 134.

term one, there will be a difference in business operations. On the one hand, an assembler is positively motivated to give technical guidance to the supplier, while the supplier, on the other hand, is able to invest with the assurance that future orders are guaranteed. Therefore it is safe to say that the very fact of Toyota's announcement of the "permanent deals will be the rule" concept would have played a not inconsiderable role in the formation of inter-firm relationships, with Toyota forming the nucleus.[14]

It must be noted that the permanent deals guaranteed by "Purchasing Regulations" attached a limiting condition, that of the "mutual prosperity" (or "coexistence and coprosperity") of Toyota and of its suppliers. Still, we cannot close our eyes to the historical fact that Toyota's business stability took priority; in its early days, whenever problems arose in regard to the cost or quality of purchased parts, Toyota was quick to move to internal production of those parts.[15] When its business operations were as yet unstable, Toyota did not feel it had room to encourage improvement in the technical level of suppliers, so, despite the rule, if Toyota's operations were in jeopardy it was Toyota's prosperity that took priority. Thus, when Kiichirō Toyota announced at the Kyōhōkai meeting in 1946 that he wanted to foster the specialization of suppliers and establish an automobile parts industry, and joined to this a declaration that Toyota was changing its parts production policy from emphasis on internal production to emphasis on purchasing,[16] he

[14] One cannot ignore the psychological ties that linked those suppliers who staked the fortunes of their businesses on automobile manufacturing when they continued to supply Toyota with parts before and during the war, turning down offers from other firms of prices several times higher than what Toyota was paying them. Toyota's announcement of its "permanent deal" concept surely resulted in large numbers of suppliers willing to pursue their "exclusive dealings with Toyota in high hopes of future reward" and what in the short term might look like an irrational course of action. See *Kyōhōkai nijūgonen no ayumi* [Twenty-five years of the Kyōhōkai], p. 13.

[15] *Toyota Jidōsha nijūnen-shi* [Twenty years of Toyota Motor Co.], pp. 108–109; also, *Sōzō kagiri naku*, p. 145.

[16] Toyota Motor Company History Editorial Committee, *Toyota Jidōsha*

was not simply stating a parts production policy, he was trying to regain the trust of suppliers that had been lost during the war. This declaration by Kiichirō Toyota of a switch in policy led suppliers to have a positive attitude again toward the "Purchasing Regulations" and the concept it enunciated.

Moreover, Toyota shortly after manifested this switch in parts production policy in a very concrete form; by the reorganization of the Kyōhōkai into three regional divisions. The original Kyōhōkai was renamed the Tōkai Kyōhōkai, and the Tokyo (later, Kantō) Kyōhōkai and Kansai Kyōhōkai were newly formed.[17] This organizational change had a symbolic significance that instilled in suppliers confidence in Toyota's policy switch, and at the same time it had an operational meaning for Toyota as well. Suppliers belonging to the Tokyo and Kansai Kyōhōkais were comparatively large-scale businesses, the parts they supplied were mostly specialized, and their dependence on Toyota was low. In contrast, suppliers in the Tōkai Kyōhōkai were for the most part medium and small machine factories doing mostly press and cutting work, whose dependence on Toyota was high. The reorganization thus was not merely because of geographical problems, but also because of the great differences in the makeup of these enterprises.[18] While the Tōkai Kyōhōkai suppliers accounted for no more than 20% of Toyota's total parts purchases, they represented 80% of the total in terms of types of parts.[19] If Toyota was going to "establish an automobile parts industry," it would have to focus on its dealings with its small-scale suppliers in the Tōkai Kyōhōkai, who had no principal sales outlets other than Toyota. It is these suppliers in the Tōkai Kyōhōkai that my study deals with principally.

30nen-shi [The first thirty years of Toyota Motor Company] (privately published, 1967), pp. 253–54.

[17] Ibid.

[18] Toyota Motor Company History Editorial Committee, *Toyota no ayumi* [The history of Toyota] (privately published, 1978), pp. 150–51.

[19] *Kyōhō nyūsu* [Kyōhō News], 19 December 1966.

KEIRETSU DIAGNOSIS

The circumstances that led to Toyota's taking positive steps toward guidance and intervention in the managerial and technical aspects of its suppliers were prompted by a "keiretsu diagnosis" carried out by the Small and Medium Enterprises Agency. The Agency had extended its original management diagnoses from those of individual enterprises (particularly manufacturing plants) to those of groups, among which it included "keiretsu diagnosis", or "diagnosis of groups affiliated with larger firms, including large enterprises."[20] Toyota and twenty-one of its suppliers were subjected to a keiretsu diagnosis in 1952–53, an event that marked a turning point in relations between Toyota and its suppliers.

A party of several people from the Manufacturing Industry Guidance Center and the Industry and Commerce Department of Aichi Prefecture would visit each company, going from factory to factory, spending a few days in each and diagnosing operations. Personnel from Toyota's Purchasing Department also went along. Besides gathering information regarding sales, cost prices, etc., the party also gave concrete advice regarding ways to improve the factory. It assessed each factory in seven categories, grading it so much out of 10,000 points, and added simple comments. The categories and their respective points were: management (3,000 pts); production (2,500 pts); labor (800 pts); marketing & purchasing (1,500 pts); finance (600 pts); accounting (1,200 pts); research (400 pts). Each category had five ranks, beginning with A at the top and ending with E at the bottom, and in each category a certain number of points corresponded to a certain rank. For example, in the category of management, the A rank was 3,000 points, the B rank was 2,400 points, and so on. When the diagnosis was completed, a "Factory Diagnosis Report" was produced for each individual supplier, and for the keiretsu as a whole a "Keiretsu Diagnosis Summary." The contents of this Summary were made public at a meeting in Toyota headquarters attended by represen-

[20] The Ministry of International Trade and Industry, *Shōkō seisaku-shi* [The history of policies for commerce and industry], vol. 12 (1963), p. 646.

tatives from the Small and Medium Enterprises Agency, MITI, Aichi Prefecture, and the suppliers.[21]

Without naming names, the Summary appended a table showing the marks assessed for the twenty-one companies, classified by type of business (see table 1). Since each supplier already knew, from the the "Factory Diagnosis Report" it had received earlier, what its own point score was, the inclusion of the table enabled each supplier to see quite easily where the company stood in relation to other companies in the same line of business and in relation to all the other companies party to the diagnosis. Toyota also was reportedly able to identify individual companies without much difficulty. This ranking of suppliers and its publication at an open meeting in a form that made it easy for suppliers to compare themselves with others had the effect of stimulating a more competitive spirit among the suppliers.

The Summary lists numerous detailed comments on each of the seven categories assessed, and a simple account of these can be found in *Toyota Jidōsha 30nen-shi* (see note 16 above). Because the book's account of the management category contains parts that can easily lead to misunderstanding, however, I would like to make a few observations about that section.[22] The book states that the Summary made the following seven proposals regarding improvement measures:[23]

1) Strengthening of rationalization goals and organs to expedite them;

2) Cooperating factories to seek assistance in managerial rationalization;

3) Reduction in stock and improvement in its turnover rate;

4) Improvement of top management (effective use of meeting system, strengthening of inspections;

---

[21] *Toyota shinbun* [Toyota News], 2 April 1953.

[22] Outside of the 30-year history, accounts of the keiretsu diagnosis are brief in Toyota-published histories, and no mention is made of the matters I raise here.

[23] *Toyota Jidōsha 30nen-shi*, p. 394.

Table 1. Conspectus of Keiretsu Diagnosis Enterprises

Name of Enterprise	1	2	3	4	5	6	7	8	0
Tōkai Rika Denki	A	A	B	C	C	B	B	8680 pts	70
Bannō Kōgyō	B	B	C	B	C	B	C	7640 pts	51
Horie Kinzoku	B	B	B	C	C	B	B	7580 pts	103
Hōjitsu Kōgyō	B	B	B	C	C	B	C	7500 pts	25
Tōyō Radiator (Nagoya)	B	B	B	C	C	C	B	7340 pts	70
Meidō Tekkō	B	B	C	C	B	C	B	7300 pts	47
Ōhashi Tekkōjo	B	C	C	B	C	C	C	6900 pts	78
Kojima Presu Kōgyōsho	B	B	B	C	D	D	C	6900 pts	28
Taihō Kōgyō	B	C	C	B	C	C	D	6820 pts	97
Sango	B	C	D	C	B	C	C	6560 pts	67
Chūtō Springs	C	B	C	B	D	D	C	6440 pts	74
Ishikawa Tekkōjo	C	C	C	B	B	C	C	6420 pts	85
Itō Kinzoku Kōgyō	C	B	C	D	D	B	C	6320 pts	22
Sugiura Seisakusho	C	C	B	C	B	C	C	6280 pts	19
Shinkawa Sangyō	C	C	C	C	C	B	C	6240 pts	195
Koromo Tekkō	C	C	C	C	C	B	C	6240 pts	63
Shin Chūō Hatsujō	C	C	C	B	D	C	C	6180 pts	320
Yutaka Kōgyō	C	C	C	C	C	C	C	6000 pts	20
Wakabayashi Kōgyō	C	C	C	C	C	C	C	6000 pts	21
Shōwa Tankō	C	C	B	D	C	C	C	5860 pts	12
Tsuda Tekkōjo	D	B	C	D	D	B	C	5720 pts	190

Legend: 1 = Management 2 = Production 3 = Labor 4 = Marketing & Purchasing 5 = Finance 6 = Accounting 7 = Research 8 = Total Score 9 = Number of Employees.

Note: This table was compiled from the "Keiretsu Consultation Summary." The names of the companies and the number of employees have been added by myself. In the original document the companies are divided by industries, here I have listed them in the order of their point scores.

5) Adjustment of operational level;
6) Effective use of the convivial get-together (election of executives);
7) Improvement in quality of steel and lowering of price.

The Summary made another proposal, however, and it is omitted from the book's condensed description of proposals: "Increasing the number of personnel in the Purchasing Department and strengthening technical guidance capability." Now, this was not simply just another suggestion for improvement the Summary was giving Toyota; it was a vital point in the enquiry into the relationship between Toyota and its suppliers.

At the time of the keiretsu diagnosis, the places within the Toyota organization that dealt directly with suppliers were the Parts Section and the Chassis Section within the Purchasing Department (see fig. 1). These two sections together had a total of forty employees. The Summary stated that some of these forty "were absent because of illness, and there were too few to carry on well-organized purchasing control," and it accordingly urged Toyota to strengthen its Purchasing Department. It pointed out that Toyota was then purchasing approximately ¥400,000,000 worth of parts every month. On the assumption that the monthly output of each worker on the supplier payrolls was ¥50,000, then, the Summary insisted, the number of supplier personnel dealt with each month would come to 8,000 people, and forty people could not possibly administer that many transactions. Furthermore, though suppliers were clamoring for technical guidance from Toyota, only three people were in charge of technical guidance, and for the most part they were busy handling design changes. The workers in charge of inspection did nothing but inspection. The result was that there was nobody in charge of giving technical guidance to cooperating factories.

Another thing: the 30-year history lists "effective use of the convivial get-together"; this is actually referring to the Kyōhōkai. The Summary, however, quite clearly redefines the Kyōhōkai's activity from that of merely promoting conviviality to that of holding sem-

Figure 1. Organization of Toyota's Purchasing Department

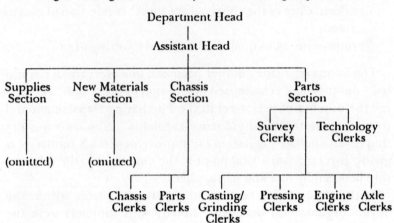

inars and factory visits that would contribute to improving the management abilities of affiliated enterprises.

The above discussion should give some idea of the way in which the Summary set out numerous concrete recommendations based on the observation of members of the diagnosis group. While the contents of these proposals were of valuable assistance to Toyota, probably of more value than anything else was the wonderful opportunity the keiretsu diagnosis gave Toyota to learn how to diagnose factories and assess enterprises.[24]

TOYOTA AND ITS SUPPLIERS AFTER THE DIAGNOSIS

After the keiretsu diagnosis Toyota became more active in contributing to suppliers' work processes. Planning to introduce quality

[24] The words of Shinji Araki, who took part in a diagnosis exercise in the Kantō region after the one carried out in the Tōkai region, are worth noting: "Together with officials from the Small and Medium Enterprises Agency, we visited all the [suppliers'] places, looked through the factories, went around checking on this thing and that. This's how we learned to make a diagnosis, by imitating the way they did it." (Kantō Kyōhōkai, *30nen no ayumi* [Thirty years' progress], p. 32)

control into every step of the manufacturing process, Toyota had Shōichi Saitō, a managing director, address the autumn meeting of the Kyōhōkai, where he requested all suppliers to cooperate in implementing quality control and in rationalizing the receiving and inspecting of purchases. Toyota sent instructors to quality control seminars sponsored by the Kyōhōkai, and followed the seminars up with visits by Toyota staff to suppliers' plants, where they surveyed how quality control was being implemented and gave guidance.

The Kyōhōkai also underwent a great change, from its earlier convivial-association character to a more business-like sponsorship of seminars and visits to the plants of member companies. This revitalizing of the Kyōhōkai was partially prompted by Toyota, but more so by the mutual competitive spirit resulting among suppliers from their being ranked in the Summary. Those suppliers that were not ranked high in the keiretsu diagnosis and did not receive commendations from the Small and Medium Enterprises Agency and Aichi Prefecture, could not help but feel their business capabilities were inferior. It was they who volunteered for factory diagnoses, who took active part in the seminars and visits sponsored by the Kyōhōkai, and who were party to the second keiretsu diagnosis, which was held in 1954. Nor should we forget that these efforts by suppliers to rationalize were being monitored by Toyota, which was not merely sending instructors and supporting Kyōhōkai activities, but also keeping tabs on the extent of individual suppliers' efforts and the results of these efforts. Using the know-how gained from the first keiretsu diagnosis, Toyota was accumulating information on such things as "management indices" regarding suppliers.[25] From Toyota's point of view, ties with suppliers were "becoming more solid than ever."[26] Without this improvement in the management abilities of suppliers,

[25] Yūzō Ichikawa, "Gaichū kanri no kaizen to sono kōka" [Improvement of purchasing control and its effectiveness], *Manejimento* [Management], vol. 33 no. 11 (1954), p. 71.

[26] Ibid., p. 70.

most likely the appearance in 1955 of the first genuine passenger car produced in Japan, the Crown, would not have been possible.

RESTRUCTURING AFTER A SWITCH TO MASS PRODUCTION

UNCOVERING WEAKNESSES

Toyota's monthly automobile production reached the 10,000 mark in late 1959. To cope with trade liberalization and increased demand, it announced in July 1960 plans for a monthly output of 30,000 vehicles. This gives some idea of Toyota's rapid steps in gearing up for mass production. Still, it was having its troubles, both at home and abroad. When it began marketing its Crown model in the U.S. in 1958, they proved to be unsuited to freeway conditions, developing engine noises, losing power, and stalling. This made Toyota management realize how far Japan's technological level lagged behind that of the U.S.[27] At home, problems arose in 1960 when production of the New Corona model began, and then a number of problems arose with the Coronas being used as taxis.[28] To top everything, its competitor, Nissan, was awarded the Deming Prize in 1960, and could thus boast of its technological superiority. Toyota ended up being outstripped by Nissan in the 1960 domestic passenger-car sales race, and from 1960 to 1962 had to be content with second place.[29]

These troubles with its Corona spotlighted a Toyota problem, one that to a certain extent could have been foreseen. People within Toyota were already reporting things like "the office work can't keep up with the increase in production," or "liaison between sections isn't going as smoothly as it used to."[30] The rapid increase

[27] Seishi Katō, *Zakkubaran* [Straight from the shoulder] (Nihon Keizai Shinbunsha, 1981), p. 85.

[28] *Sōzō kagiri naku*, p. 366.

[29] Ibid., p. 367.

[30] Nihon Jinbun Kagaku-kai [The Japanese Association for Cultural Sciences], ed., *Gijutsu kakushin no shakaiteki eikyō* [Social effects of technical innovation] (Tokyo University Press, 1963), p. 58. Also see *Toyota Jidōsha 30nen-shi*, p. 506.

in production also resulted in a relaxing of control over suppliers. Within the Purchasing Department people were already aware that "along with the annual rapid rise in production there has been an increasingly conspicuous number of disruptions to production caused by inferior parts."[31]

The problem came to a head as a result of orders Toyota received in 1958 from the U.S. Army Procurement Agency in Japan (APA), to be filled beginning the next year. Because the U.S. Army required that Toyota put in place a system of quality control over its suppliers as well, Toyota in 1959 presented to its suppliers "a plan for carrying out the promotion of quality control. But once Toyota began the program, it found such great disparity among the various factories in what they considered quality control and in how they practiced it, that the plan was discontinued."[32] Thus at this point it was crystal clear that, in the process of shifting into mass production, concern for guaranteeing the quantity of parts had taken priority over concern for their quality, and problems with the New Corona should have been predictable.

Now, as it turned out, the special procurement orders from the APA had a great impact on Toyota. For Toyota management was astonished at the U.S. Army's high standards of quality. *The First Thirty Years of Toyota Motor Co.* uses the expression "the strict inspections of the APA,"[33] but the following excerpt conveys some idea of the alarm and concern in Toyota circles at the time:

> The receiving of parts [for APA orders] only takes place under extremely rigid control, that is, only after they have been subjected to extraordinarily strict inspection. . . . After the parts . . . have been inspected by our plant inspectors and APA inspection officials, they are moved over to the rustproofing treatment line and packing line, and only after

[31] *Toyota manejimento*, November 1961, p. 39. Also see the report in *Sōzō kagiri naku*, p. 369: "The amount of claims per vehicle, which had been steadily low for a long time, started showing a gradual increase from 1959 on."

[32] *Toyota manejimento*, November 1961, p. 39.

[33] *Toyota Jidōsha 30nen-shi*, p. 464.

they have been inspected for rustproofing and packing are they received. The present contract has detailed instruction as to how the rustproofing and packing is to be done, from the properties of the rustproofing oil right down to the quality of sawdust used for packing.[34]

Toyota's exposure to American-style "strict inspection" because Nissan, which had been filling APA's orders till the previous year but had to stop because of the jump in domestic demand, is considered to have been an important factor in subsequent Toyota development: "There is no getting away from the fact that [the APA orders] were an achievement that had ramifications in many areas as far as the later operations of our company were concerned."[35] Obviously, the contribution of the orders to Toyota's commitment to mass production and to cost cutting was undoubtedly important; but perhaps more important was the realization of the difference between Japanese and American standards of quality, and the acquisition of know-how regarding such things as the paperwork needed for quality control.

COUNTERMEASURES

Toyota sought a solution to its problems through the introduction of a program of Total Quality Control (hereafter, TQC). Vice-president Shōichi Saitō told employees in 1961 that "we shall promote company-wide quality control as the backbone of management control."[36] This should not be understood only as an expression of more than ordinary determination on the part of Toyota management; it was a manifestation of the strong sense of crisis they felt at the time.

While it was spreading TQC within its own walls, Toyota was also trying to instill quality control consciousness among its suppliers. In 1960 the Purchasing Department and a Quality Control Department resumed the quality control program that had been

[34] *Toyota manejimento,* August 1959, p. 28.
[35] *Toyota Jidōsha 30nen-shi,* p. 464.
[36] *Toyota shinbun,* 2 December 1961.

discontinued the year before. Personnel from the Quality Control Department and the Technology Section (of the Purchasing Department) jointly visiting an average of two to three companies a day, gave guidance in quality control to 68 companies between September 1960 and May 1961.[37] They began by attempting to grasp how quality control was being implemented in each supplier visited. Concretely, they calculated marks for each supplier on the basis of the following seven headings: statistical quality control (20 pts) and organization related to quality control (15 pts); internal planning (15 pts); equipment control (10 pts); control during the manufacturing process (15 pts); quality guarantees (15 pts); storage education (10 pts). On the basis of these marks Toyota then divided the suppliers into differing levels and decided which items needed most guidance. Then, between 1961 and 1962 it conducted short training courses for suppliers in accord with their different levels.[38]

At the same time, Toyota aimed at vitalization of the activities of Kyōhōkai, the autonomous supplier organization. One means was to take an active part in the seminars of the Kyōhōkai. It even had its own personnel on each of the eleven committees set up by the Kyōhōkai in 1961. The activity of one committee in particular, the Coordinating Committee for Rationalization, should be noted. Besides carrying out inspection tours of individual factories, this committee, consisting of Toyota director Shinji Araki, Purchasing Department head Shūtarō Mori, and Kyōhōkai officials of section-head level or higher, carried out a survey of the 56 suppliers affiliated with the Tōkai Kyōhōkai. As part of this survey they investigated each supplier's "management indices, owned capital ratio, degree of reliance on the automotive industry, conditions of employees, cost structure, content analysis of added values, labor-equipment ration and sales, processing volume, correlations with personnel costs, etc.," in an operation that was appraised as "a large-scale touring study session that could only described as

[37] *Toyota manejimento*, November 1961, p. 39.
[38] Ibid., pp. 38–39.

epoch-making as far as the Kyōhōkai was concerned."[39] The contents of the survey were similar to the contents of the "factory diagnosis reports" passed on to individual suppliers at the time of the keiretsu diagnosis. Toyota was quick to imitate the diagnostic method it learned during that earlier exercise.[40]

A feature that stands out in Toyota's handling of the sudden increase in production was that, instead of increasing the quantity of parts supplied by increasing the number of suppliers, it managed to increase the former *without* increasing the latter. Not multiplying suppliers needlessly had been a longstanding Toyota policy; also, the problems with those suppliers it did have (problems brought into sharp focus by the Corona fiasco and the APA procurements) had to be solved first. These were two reason why Toyota did not adopt a policy of increasing supplier numbers. To these can be added another one: to cope with trade liberalization, Toyota had as its goal an increase in the operating scales of its present suppliers, with a consequent decrease in the costs of supplies through economies of scale. And, in fact, suppliers who at the time of the keiretsu diagnosis were employing only a few dozen workers reached a level of several hundred workers within five or six years, and their production totals were several times greater. The larger their scale of operations, though, the more necessary it was for them to shed their "back-street factory" type of operating. The purpose of Toyota's factory diagnoses, therefore, was not simply for itself to get to know each supplier, it was also aimed at encouraging suppliers to get an accurate, numerical grasp of their own business operations.

INFLUENCE OF BEING CANDIDATE
FOR THE DEMING APPLICATION PRIZE

ESTABLISHMENT OF A COMPREHENSIVE EVALUATION SYSTEM

Toyota's supplier strategies became clearer when TQC had a firm

[39] *Kyōhōkai 25nen no ayumi*, p. 42.
[40] See note 23 above.

foothold within the company and Toyota took the first steps towards qualifying to be a candidate for the Deming Application
Prize. With a view towards having everyone in the company familiar with its goal of TQC, in 1963 Toyota put it into writing and distributed it to all management personnel from squad leader up;
from the next year the activities of the Kyōhōkai became linked
with Toyota policies. "The annual plans of the Kyōhōkai itself
were determined on the basis of Toyota's purchasing policies, and
people in charge were assigned on the same basis," so that "committees" were set up in the Kyōhōkai that were linked into Toyota's
company-wide policies.[41] Thus, for example, it became the normal
thing that "the basic policy of the Tōkai Kyōhōkai for this year
[1964] became the prioritizing of items required to reach the central target of the three great policies adopted by Toyota for this
year: 'mass production,' 'quality guarantees,' and 'cost reduction,'
and three committees were created: 'Increased Production Strategies,' 'Quality Guarantees,' and 'Cost Reduction Measures'."[42]

That Toyota's company policies and the activities of the
Kyōhōkai were linked is another way of saying that the synchronization of their production schedules was under way. In 1963
Toyota was introducing a "Kanban System" with some of its suppliers. The following year it appealed to its suppliers to institute
systems whereby parts could be received without any inspection
being required. That the "Kanban System" could be introduced
and supplier parts could be received without inspection shows that
the factory diagnoses and quality control education begun in 1961
were bearing fruit. If suppliers were inadequate in their pursuit of
quality control, Toyota's introduction of the "Kanban System" and
attempts at the synchronization of suppliers' production would
only end up in assembly lines being forced to stop because of faulty
parts or in defective vehicles being produced.

While Toyota was upgrading its internal setup and pushing forward the synchronization of production, it also was systematizing

---

[41] *Kyōhōkai 2-hnen no ayumi*, p. 31.
[42] *Kyōhō nyūsu*, 5 June 1964.

its evaluating of suppliers. Although it had carried out evaluations of this or that supplier as need arose following the keiretsu diagnosis, the evaluations had not been done in a uniform or orderly fashion. In May 1965, however, the company took up the task of achieving uniformity in these evaluations, and by September 1966 a comprehensive evaluation system was in place. It included a grade of 100 covering seven items: quality (20 pts), price (30 pts), delivery deadlines (10 pts), finances (15 pts), labor (5 pts), management (10 pts), and future promise (10 pts); to these was added another 100-point evaluation of executives and section heads, to make 200 points in all. When the point score went above a certain number, the amounts ordered from that supplier were increased; when it fell below a certain number, the supplier was given instructions on how to improve control and the amounts ordered stayed a natural increment level.[43] The introduction of this comprehensive evaluation system not only stirred up a competitive spirit among suppliers, it also forced them to pay detailed attention to the management of their businesses.

PURCHASING CONTROL GUIDANCE TO FIRST-TIER SUPPLIERS

In 1965 Toyota was a candidate for, and was awarded, the Deming Application Prize. The Prize Committee indicated, however, that Toyota needed to lift the quality control standards of its suppliers to its own level. To achieve this, Toyota set up a new department in 1966, named Purchasing Control, with Masao Nemoto as head; its goal was the spread of TQC know-how to the principal suppliers.[44] Guidance stressed the lowering of production costs and the advantages to accrue to suppliers. An incentive system was introduced: if a supplier's suggestion on how Toyota could reduce the cost of this or that part actually led to cost savings, Toyota would

[43] *Hinshitsu kanri* [Quality Control], vol. 18 no. 3, pp. 89–90.

[44] Masao Nemoto, *TQC to toppu bukachō no yakuwari* [TQC and the role of middle management] (Nikkagiren, 1983), pp. 151–52. An English version of this book appeared as *Total Quality Control for Management*, translated and edited by David Lu (Prentice Hall, 1987).

return to the supplier half the amount saved.[45] With this incentive, suppliers could be better off if they actually reduced production costs. As a result of this incentive plan, Toyota paid over 20% less for its parts in 1966 than it had the year before. The Kyōhōkai also promoted the cost-reduction scheme through "process-cutting campaign seminars," and after 6 months of these seminars in 1966, Kyōhōkai members in the Tōkai District had eliminated 1.62 million processes and 2,537 workers.[46] The results were so spectacular that in the following year the Tōkai and Kantō branches of the Kyōhōkai jointly sponsored similar seminars. While these "process-cutting campaign seminars" were implanting in suppliers Toyota's ideas about "eliminating waste" and "automating," they were also explaining the "Kanban System," thus acting as very effective media for the diffusion of the "Kanban System" among suppliers.

What eventually became the nucleus of Toyota's countermeasures in regard to suppliers was guidance in purchasing control. The result of Toyota's production expansion had been that suppliers themselves began farming out more and more orders to other suppliers. According to one of Toyota's own surveys, between 1966 and 1967 first-tier suppliers rapidly increased their use of supplier companies.[47] Despite this reaction of its suppliers, Toyota adopted a policy of not dealing directly with second- and third-tier suppliers or exercising active control over them, but of letting the first-tier suppliers control them. In 1968 and 1969, therefore, the Purchasing Control Department sponsored "four-month training courses for purchasing controllers" for 52 first-tier suppliers,

---

[45] *Hinshitsu kanri*, vol. 18 no. 4, p. 78.

[46] *Toyota manejimento*, December 1969, p. 35.

[47] According to internal Toyota surveys, it was from 1960 to 1961, and again from 1966 to 1967, that first-tier suppliers started purchasing from second-tier suppliers in the largest numbers. "Both these periods were when Toyota's increase in the number of vehicles produced showed a big jump over previous trends." (*Toyota manejimento*, December 1969, p. 35)

through which Toyota transferred to them its store of purchasing control know-how.[48]

There are two aspects to consider in looking at the rationale behind the Purchasing Control Department's approach. First of all, Toyota management realized that, the more first-tier suppliers' management abilities improved, the more important it was for Toyota's own quality control system that quality control systems be firmly established among second- and third-tier suppliers. Toyota's earlier surveys had shown how haphazard and primitive were the controls in place among the small-scale firms in the second and third tiers.[49] It had firsthand experience of the deplorable state of controls every time it tracked down troubles involving quality.[50] So the aim of these four-month training courses was to pass on to first-tier supplier purchasing officers the methods of checking on the processing skills of second-tier suppliers and thus eliminating the main cause of their faulty parts.

Secondly, the question can be asked: "Why did Toyota adopt this roundabout way of training first-tier supplier purchasing officers instead of directly checking, itself, the processes of second-tier suppliers?" At this stage it would theoretically still have been possible. Had such a course been adopted, second-tier suppliers would gradually turn into first-tier suppliers, and instead of tiered inter-firm relationships there could have been a flatter structure. Also, the number of Toyota's purchasing personnel would have increased greatly and there would not have been such an extreme gap in 1978 between General Motors' 6,000 purchasing personnel and Toyota's meager 337.[51] Instead, for about six years after the

[48] *Hinshitsu kanri*, vol. 20 no. 8 (1969), p. 64.

[49] *Jidōsha jānaru* [Automobile Journal], November 1968, p. 83.

[50] Ibid. Masao Nemoto describes the situation thus: "More than it being a case of faulty parts increasing among secondary suppliers, it was a case of faulty parts decreasing among primary suppliers, as a result of which secondary suppliers became more conspicuous." See *Hinshitsu kanri*, vol. 20 no. 3 (1969), p. 64.

[51] Massachusetts Institute of Technology Industrial Productivity Research Committee, Naoya Yoda, translator, *Made in America: Amerika saisei*

establishment of the Purchasing Control Department a quota was enforced, and the total personnel of the department was kept at 200.[52] In spite of increases in the volume of parts purchased and sums dealt with, staff numbers were deliberately frozen, and so Toyota did not have the human resources to control second- and third-tier suppliers. Toyota's approach to the problem, therefore, helped bring about multi-tiered inter-firm relationships.

In 1969 Toyota established a "Toyota Quality Control Prize." It was to test the extent to which the know-how relating to management control that Toyota had transferred to first-tier suppliers had actually taken firm hold.[53] In early 1970 this know-how was consolidated in the form of "Criteria for Using Second- and Third-tier Suppliers." The year 1970 is considered to be the year in which the "fundamental ideas and diverse methods" in the "Toyota production system" had become systematized, according to the company's own historians,[54] and the tiered inter-firm relationships built up around Toyota also came into existence around this time.

---

no tame no Bei-Nichi-Ō sangyō hikaku [Made in America: A comparison of American, Japanese, and European industry for the sake of regenerating America] (Sōshisha, 1990), p. 259.

[52] Masao Nemoto, first head of the department, says that the number was fixed at 200 in order to curb sectionalism resulting from the enormous growth of the organization. In spite of the number being fixed, he says, "a considerable amount of new work was added to their responsibilities." (*Toyota manejimento*, May 1970, p. 26)

[53] The purpose of the prize was to spread Toyota's TQC policy to its suppliers, but when it became clear that capital liberalization in the auto industry was in the offing, the need arose for Toyota to show a serious interest in the improvement of the management abilities of its suppliers. Candidates for this prize were assessed zero to five points on company policies, quality guarantees, cost price control, and five other items in the three categories of overall control, on-site inspection, and top-level communication. This was meant to present suppliers with "targets close at hand," but it is obvious it was also used to promote competitiveness between suppliers. (*Hinshitsu kanri*, vol. 23 no. 3, pp. 18–19)

[54] *Sōzō kagiri naku*, pp. 586–87. The same year Toyota became the first recipient of the newly established "Japan Quality Control Prize." We can

CONCLUSION

My answer, then, to the question of when tiered inter-firm relationships were formed would be: "The early 1970s." But this does
not mean simply that the suppliers involved in Toyota's production of automobiles were divided into different levels. First-tier
suppliers were using second- and third-tier suppliers as sources of
goods from quite an early point in Toyota's history. It means the
relationships in which Toyota had a tight grip on first-tier management and had the latter control the second-tier suppliers basically dated from this time.[55] You could almost say the first-tier
suppliers were made into miniature Toyotas. The "structure of
parts transactions" that Banri Asanuma discusses — that is, the introduction into inter-firm relations of the incentive plan returning
to suppliers a portion of the costs saved by following suggestions
for improvement — also took place in the early 1970s.[56]

Why did such relationships come into being? There is no inevitability about relationships between assembler and suppliers taking on a tiered structure, for an assembler could produce all parts
internally, and even if it purchased parts externally its suppliers
need not form tiers: the assembler can form ties with each supplier
individually. When considering the formation of tiered relationships, one needs to investigate the percentage of internal production, first of all, and, secondly, whether or not the assembler sets a
limit on the number of suppliers it will deal with. In the case of

assume this contributed to Toyota's making 1970 the year the "Toyota production system" was systematized.

[55] In 1970 Toyota went so far as to declare that, "as far as guidance of second-tier suppliers goes, we consider it the responsibility of the first-tier
suppliers, and we have adopted the principle of not being directly involved." (*Hinshitsu kanri*, vol. 21 no. 1 [1970], pp. 43–44)

[56] Banri Asanuma, "Jidōsha sangyō ni okeru buhin torihiki no kōzō —
chōsei to kakushinteki tekiō no mekanizumu" [The structure of parts
transactions in the automobile industry: Mechanisms of adjustment and re-
formist adaptation], *Kikan gendai keizai* [Contemporary Economics Quar-
terly], Summer 1984.

Toyota, the restriction of personnel in the Purchasing Department led to the transfer of Toyota's know-how on supplier control to first-tier suppliers, and this promoted the formation of multi-tiered relationships. In addition, the "permanent deal" concept created a situation in which Toyota could not easily terminate dealings with suppliers, which in turn worked to limit the number of first-tier suppliers, with tiered relationships the result.

A low percentage of internal production is considered one of the prerequisites for the formation of tiered inter-firm relationships. The percentage in Toyota is put at approximately 30%; in General Motors it is put at about 70%. Why is it so high in one assembler, so low in another? Monteverde and Teece, studying the levels of vertical integration (internal production) in General Motors and Ford, have come up with an interesting suggestion: that one reason for a high percentage of internal production of parts is an institutional step to reduce exposure to opportunistic exploitation by suppliers. They go on to surmise that such opportunism is not found in Japan because of the close cooperative relationships between assemblers and suppliers.[57] As this study of Toyota, which is reputed to be the assembler with the closest cooperative relationships with its suppliers, has shown, these close cooperative relationships were realized under a system of evaluations of suppliers by Toyota, which stimulated a competitive spirit among suppliers. It is not that Toyota was not liable to opportunistic exploitation, but that close cooperative relationships in themselves contain the means for preventing the occurrence of opportunism. The evaluation system brought into the close cooperative relationships is the important factor that raised the percentage of Toyota's reliance on external production and that brought about the tiered inter-firm relationships.

[57] Kirk Monteverde and David J. Teece, "Supplier switching costs and vertical integration in the automobile industry," *Bell Journal of Economics*, vol. 13 no. 1 (1982), p. 212.

[20]

TRANSPLANTED ORGANIZATIONS: THE TRANSFER OF JAPANESE INDUSTRIAL ORGANIZATION TO THE U.S.[*]

RICHARD FLORIDA
Carnegie Mellon University

MARTIN KENNEY
University of California, Davis

Industrial sociology and organization theory suggest that it is difficult to transfer organizations from one environment to another and that organizations that are transferred will take on characteristics of the new environment. We hypothesize that the organization/environment relation works in both directions and that organizations have the resources to alter their environments in light of their functional requirements. We explore these issues in light of recent debates over new models of production organization and interfirm production networks. Japanese automotive assembly plants and their suppliers in the United States provide an ideal case to explore such questions because they represent organizations that are being transferred from a supportive to a foreign environment. We find that these Japanese automotive transplants have effectively transferred both intra- and interorganizational characteristics, e.g., team-based work organization and "just-in-time" supplier relations to the United States. Thus, they have actively transformed their environments to suit their needs.

Organization theory and industrial sociology suggest that organizations are closely tied to their environments. Both imply that it is difficult to transfer organizations from one environment to another and suggest that organizations that are transferred will gradually take on characteristics of the new environment. Japanese organizations are closely tied to their environment and thus may be particularly difficult to transfer.

We explore the cross-national transfer of organizational forms and practices and hypothesize that such forms and practices can be taken from their original environments and implanted into new ones. We contend that certain types of organizations (e.g., large, resource-rich, powerful organizations) have sufficient resources to alter the new environment in light of their functional requirements. Therefore, we suggest that the organization/environment relation is reciprocal. We address these issues in light of the recent debate over new forms of production and work organization, production subcontracting, and interfirm

production networks (Piore and Sabel 1984; Sabel 1989; Perrow 1990; Kenney and Florida 1988; Florida and Kenney 1990a, 1990b; Lazonick 1990; Womack, Jones, and Roos 1990).

Japanese automobile manufacturing plants in the United States, which we refer to as the "transplants," provide an ideal test of these hypotheses because they have been transferred from a supportive to a nonsupportive environment. The U.S. environment is typically characterized in terms of "diversity," "individualism," and unrestrained market forces, while Japan is characterized in terms of "homogeneity," "familism," "paternalism," and/or "welfare corporatism" (Dore 1973). The ideal-typical large U.S. industrial organization is distinguished by high levels of functional specialization, large numbers of job classifications, extensive internal labor markets (Edwards 1979), adversarial labor-management relations (Kochan, Katz, and McKersie 1986; Katz 1985) and "arm's length" relations between corporations and their suppliers (Altshuler, Anderson, Jones, Roos, and Womack 1984; Womack et al.

[*] Direct all correspondence to Richard Florida, School of Urban and Public Affairs, Carnegie Mellon University, Pittsburgh, PA 15213. This research was funded in part by the Economic Research Service of the U.S. Department of Agriculture and the Ohio Board of Regents. The authors would like to thank Nicole Biggart, Robert Cole, Norman Glickman, Akio Kida and Shoko Tanaka as well as the editor and four anonymous reviewers for their comments. We gratefully acknowledge the collaboration of the Ritsumeikan University Automobile Industry Research Group of Katsuji Tsuji, Akio Kida, Terje Gronning, Bunji Murakami, and Katsuo Nakagawa on site visits and interviews conducted in summer 1990 and the assistance provided by James Curry, W. Richard Goe, James Gordon, Marshall Feldman, and Andrew Mair at various phases of the research. The authors are equally responsible for this article; the order of their names reflects their long-standing policy of rotation.

1990), whereas the ideal-typical large Japanese manufacturing firm is characterized by small numbers of job classifications (Aoki 1988), team-based work organization (Koike 1988), consensual relations between labor and management (Shirai 1983), and long-term supplier relations (Dore 1983, 1986, 1987).[1]

We examine the transfer of Japanese intraorganizational practices, such as work and production organization, and interorganizational characteristics, such as just-in-time supplier relations, to the United States in light of three related research questions: (1) Are organizations derivative of the environments in which they are embedded, or can they be removed from an original environment and successfully implanted in a new one? (2) What strategies do organizations devise to adapt, respond, and/or cope with a new environment? (3) Do they take on characteristics of the environment, or do they act on the new environment to bring it into line with their needs?

THEORETICAL CONTEXT

Organization theory suggests that organizations that are transferred from one environment to another will take on characteristics of the new environment. A few researchers would argue for a tight, deterministic connection between environment and organizations; most suggest that organizations gradually take on characteristics of the new environment and/or of organizations with which they interact (DiMaggio and Powell 1983; Meyer and Rowan 1977; Zucker 1977; Granovetter 1985; Hannan and Freeman 1977; McKelvey and Aldrich 1983).

A few theorists focus explicitly on organizational influences on the environment. In his classic studies of innovation in capitalism, Schumpeter (1947) differentiated between "creative" responses that alter social and economic situations and the more typical "adaptive" responses of firms and economic organizations. Pfeffer and Salancik (1978) suggested that while organizations tend to adapt to their environments, they will sometimes alter the environment in line with their needs. Weick (1979) argued that the ability of an organization to influence, construct or "enact" its environment is a function of size. Young

(1988) suggested that organizations can change their environments by strategic use of resources.

The literature on Japanese development is generally pessimistic regarding the transfer of Japanese organization. It suggests that Japanese organizations derive from cultural factors such as homogeneity, familism, and group loyalty (Nakane 1970; Benedict 1946). For Abegglen (1958), Japanese organizational characteristics like team-based work organization and long-term tenure reflect a general close alignment between persons and groups. Dore (1973) contrasted Japanese model of "welfare corporatism" with the Anglo-American model of "market individualism." Cole (1971) suggested that Japan's cultural legacy informs unique organizational solutions to general development problems. Recent research continues to be pessimistic about the transfer of Japanese organization (Cool and Legnick-Hall 1985).

Recent work (Shimada 1986; Shimada and MacDuffie 1986; Aoki 1988; Koike 1988) has concluded that Japanese work organization is a set of organizational forms that are relatively autonomous from culture and the environment. Several historical studies support this view. Taira (1961, 1964, 1970) documented the emergence of permanent employment from Japanese industrialists' need to cope with high rates of labor mobility and a desire to exert more effective control over the labor force. Gordon (1985) indicated that team-based work organization is the product of postwar industrial unrest over worker control of production (also see Kenney and Florida 1988). Empirical research (Lincoln and Kalleberg 1985, 1990) supports the view that Japanese organization rather than culture is the source of work-force motivation, control, and commitment.

Currently, there is a general debate over the rise of alternative forms of industrial organization, including new forms of work and production organization (Kenney and Florida 1988; Florida and Kenney 1990a; Lazonick 1990; Best 1990; Morris-Suzuki 1988; Zuboff 1988), new mechanisms for generating work-force control and commitment (Lincoln and Kalleberg 1990), new supplier relations (Dore 1983; Sako 1989), interfirm networks and production subcontracting (Piore and Sabel 1984; Lazerson 1988; Perrow 1990; Florida and Kenney 1990b), and ways of organizing the division of labor inside and outside the firm (Richardson 1972; Williamson 1975, 1981, 1983; Robins 1987; Perrow 1981, 1986). A growing body of work argues that the key to the current

---

[1] These are ideal-typical characterizations of large manufacturing firms, particularly automobile firms, in these countries, designed to focus attention on salient differences highlighted in the literature. In reality, there are significant differences among firms in each country and there may even be "mixed" forms.

transition lies in the emergence of new forms of organization at the point of production, such as work teams, task rotation, the application of workers' intelligence in production, and the integration of innovation and production (Florida and Kenney 1990a; Womack et al. 1990; Lazonick 1990; Best 1990). Taking a different perspective, Piore and Sabel (1984) contend that "flexibly specialized" communities of small firms are supplanting the older model of "fordist" industrial mass production (Aglietta 1979); others suggest that flexible specialization may be a transitory phenomenon (Powell 1987) or even a misreading of current trends (Gertler 1988).

A number of studies explore the role of Japanese organizational forms in this more general process. The flexible specialization school views the Japanese model as part of the global convergence toward small-firm networks (Piore and Sabel 1984; Sabel 1989; Friedman 1988). However, detailed empirical studies of Japanese interorganizational relations suggest that it is a distinctive system centered around large companies (Sayer 1986; Sako 1989; Florida and Kenney 1990b). Others see the Japanese system as an advanced and efficient form of fordist mass production (Dohse, Jurgens, and Malsch 1986; Parker and Slaughter 1988). Still others see Japanese production organization as a unique model. According to Womack et al. (1990), Japanese organizational practices constitute a new form of "lean production" toward which firms all over the world are converging. Kenney and Florida (1988; forthcoming) see the Japanese model as a successor to fordism that uses new organizational forms to harness the intellectual as well as the physical capabilities of workers. Our research explores the "generalizability" of these new organizational forms.

The empirical evidence regarding the transfer of Japanese organization is mixed. Yoshino (1976) suggested that the absence of Japanese sociocultural conditions in other countries is a serious obstacle to transfer. Cole (1979) was guardedly optimistic: "There are those who would argue that they [quality control circles] have their basis in Japanese cultural and institutional conditions, with their unique group orientation, practice of permanent employment, and strong employee commitment to organizational goals. Consequently they are held not to be applicable to the United States. My own judgement is they may well be applicable if appropriate adaptations are made to accommodate the circles to U.S. conditions" (Cole 1979, p. 255). White and Trevor

(1983) concluded that Japanese organizational traits were not transferred to Japanese firms operating in the U.K. However, Oliver and Wilkinson (1989), Kumazawa and Yamada (1989), and Morris (1988) concluded that the Japanese management system has been successfully transferred to Japanese firms in the U.K. A study of Nissan in the U.K. (Crowther and Garrahan 1988) documented the emergence a Japanese-style automobile production complex comprising a main assembly plant and supplier firms.

Research on the transfer of Japanese organization to the U.S. is less extensive and the findings are inconclusive. Case studies of the GM-Toyota joint venture automobile assembly plant, NUMMI, in Fremont, California (Krafcik 1986; Brown and Reich 1989) provide evidence of successful transfer of Japanese organization. Mair, Florida, and Kenney (1988) documented the emergence of a complex of Japanese automotive assemblers and suppliers in the midwestern United States. A University of Tokyo study (Institute of Social Science 1990) concluded that automotive plants have been the most successful in transferring Japanese practices, while consumer electronics firms have tended to adapt or conform to the U.S. environment and semiconductor firms occupy a middle position. Fucini and Fucini (1990) reported interviews with Mazda workers as evidence of adaptation problems, including high rates of injury, worker discontent, and labor-management conflict. Most of these studies suffer from very small sample sizes, reliance on case-specific data, and a narrow conceptual focus on managerial practices. Our research remedies such problems by providing a theoretically-informed empirical study of the transfer of intra- and interorganizational forms and practices to Japanese automotive transplants in the United States.

RESEARCH DESIGN

"Transplants" are defined as firms that are either wholly Japanese-owned or have a significant level of Japanese participation in cross-national joint ventures located in the U.S. We developed a database of Japanese transplant assemblers and suppliers from data provided by the Japan Economic Institute, U.S. government sources, industry trade journals, and newspaper reports. Eight assembly centers were identified in the United States, of which one operated two plants at one site and the rest operated single plants. In addition, 229 transplant suppliers were identified; this number has since grown to approximately 270.

The study population is heavily concentrated in a "transplant corridor" of the lower Midwest and upper South — an area with a legacy of traditional U.S. (fordist) organizational practices. Four of the assembly transplants, Mazda, NUMMI, Diamond-Star, and the Ford-Nissan joint venture are unionized; four others, Honda, Nissan, Toyota, and Subaru-Isuzu (SIA), are not. Three assembly transplants are joint ventures with U.S. producers: NUMMI, a GM-Toyota joint venture managed by Toyota, Diamond-Star, a joint venture between Chrysler and Mitsubishi, and Ford-Nissan.

Site visits were conducted at six of the seven operating transplant assembly plants in the U.S. (Honda, Nissan, Toyota, Mazda, NUMMI, and Subaru-Isuzu) and at various supplier firms including Nippondenso which has the largest investment in the U.S. of any transplant supplier.[2] More than 100 personal interviews were conducted. Interviews with Japanese and American executives focussed on investment strategies, location, production and organization, supplier relations, and interorganizational linkages. To reduce the potential for bias and increase reliability, the interviewees in assembly plants and suppliers were asked similar questions. Interviews with present and former shopfloor workers and engineers, trade union officials, and state and local government officials provided an additional check against respondent bias. A member of the research team visited Honda's main assembly facility in Japan as well as several automotive parts suppliers to provide a comparative context for the analysis.

A mail survey was administered to the universe of Japanese-owned or Japanese-U.S. joint venture suppliers in the United States. Establishments were the unit of analysis (rather than firms) to capture differences among plants owned by the same firm because establishments may make different components and use different management and organizational practices. Moreover, the research required responses from plant management familiar with the actual operations of the plant. The suppliers responding to the survey respondents were relatively evenly distributed by the assemblers they supply, thereby reducing the possibility for the idiosyncratic practices of one or two end-users to significantly affect the survey results.

The survey instrument obtained background information such as start-up date, employment, sales, industry, end-users, information on intraorganizational characteristics such as work organization, number of job classifications, use of teams, rotation, quality control circles, wages and wage determination, employment security and workforce characteristics, and information on interorganizational relationships such as delivery times, frequency of communication, shared personnel, and cooperation in R&D and product design. Addresses were located for 196 of the 229 suppliers in the original database. (Some of the firms for whom addresses were unavailable likely had not yet begun operations). Each establishment was then contacted by telephone to identify the appropriate person to complete the survey.

The survey was mailed in 1988. A series of follow-up post cards and letters resulted in 73 completed surveys for a response rate of 37.2 percent, which is comparable to the rates in other research of this type. Lincoln and Kalleberg (1985), for example, obtained a response rate of 35 percent from U.S. manufacturing firms and 40 percent from Japanese manufacturing firms. Further, Japanese-owned firms in the U.S. may have been reticent to respond because of the highly charged political climate surrounding their activities. We have no reason to believe there was any bias between respondents and nonrespondents.

TRANSFER OF INTRAORGANIZATIONAL FORMS AND PRACTICES

Work and Production Organization

Table 1 summarizes the main characteristics of work and production organization for transplant assemblers and for a representative Big Three automobile company. Table 2 presents similar information for transplant suppliers.[3]

Work teams. In Japan, work is organized on the basis of teams that are responsible for planning and carrying out production tasks (Aoki 1988; Koike 1988). Teams socialize production tasks and assign immediate managerial tasks to shopfloor workers. Table 1 indicates that work teams are used at all of the transplant assemblers. At Honda, Toyota, and NUMMI teams meet daily to discuss production improvements and rede-

---

[2] We were unable to arrange a visit to Diamond-Star and the Ford-Nissan venture was not yet operational.

[3] Here we note that not all Japanese automobile firms are organized the same way; each has its own "personality."

Table 1.   Presence of Japanese Intraorganizational Practices In Transplant Assemblers: U.S., 1990

Assembler	Work Organization		Number of Job Classifications	Worker Quality Control	Average Annual Wages	Hourly Wages for Production Workers	Presence of Union
	Work Teams	Rotation					
Honda	+	+	3	o	$33,685	$14.55	No
Nissan	+	+	4	o	$32,579	$13.95	No
NUMMI	+	+	4	o	$36,013	$16.81	Yes
Toyota	+	+	3	o	$29,598	$14.23	No
Mazda	+	+	2	o	$32,970	$15.13	Yes
Subaru-Isuzu (SIA)	+	+	3	o	$28,995	$13.94	No
Big Three U.S.	−	−	90	−	$36,089	$16.41	Yes

Source: Wage data for each transplant and average for Big Three producers are from Jackson (1990); data on intraorganizational practices of transplant assemblers are from site visits and personal interviews; data on intraorganizational practices of a representative Big Three automaker are from U.S. General Accounting Office (1988).

Note: + = similar to Japan; o = modified; − = different from Japan.

sign of tasks; meetings at the other transplants take place at least once a week. More than three-fourths of transplant suppliers organize production on the basis of work teams (Table 2).

Task rotation. Rotation of workers among tasks within a team is a key feature of Japanese production organization. Rotation functions to train workers in multiple tasks and to reduce the incidence of repetitive motion injuries. While rotation is used by all transplant assemblers, its frequency varies, as it does in Japan. Toyota, Honda, and NUMMI rotate workers in the same team quite frequently. Toyota workers in high stress jobs, e.g., jobs that require the use of a high impact "torque gun" or involve constant bending or lifting, rotate as frequently as once an hour, others rotate at break times, at lunch, or every other day. According to a NUMMI worker: "We would be rotating every time we had a break or change. If we had a break in the morning, we rotated. And then lunchtime, we rotated. And we had a break in the afternoon, we rotated. Every time the line stopped, a break or whatever, we rotated." Rotation is less frequent at Mazda, Nissan, and SIA. While these companies consider rotation a long-term goal, each has slowed or even stopped the use of rotation during production ramp-ups. Our interviews with Mazda workers confirm that infrequent rotation has been a major cause of repetitive motion injury at the Mazda plant. Rotation from team to team is less common both in Japan and in the transplants. In Japan, this type of rotation is typically mandated by management; in the U.S., it is more common for workers to apply for job transfers.

According to the supplier survey, roughly 87 percent of suppliers rotate workers within teams, while approximately 66 percent rotate among teams. Nippondenso rotates workers in high stress jobs every hour or two and encourages workers to apply for rotation from team to team. Both U.S. and Japanese managers at all the transplants we visited, as well as many workers, felt that it was too early for implementation of a full Japanese-style rotation system and that it may be a few years before workers have enough basic skills and knowledge to be moved regularly from team to team.

Inventory control. In Japan, production takes place according to the "just-in-time" system of inventory control in which materials are forwarded as needed and inventory is kept to a minimum (Monden 1982; Cusumano 1985). All the assemblers and over two-thirds of suppliers (68.5 percent) use a just-in-time system of production control.

The supplier survey asked: "How similar is your manufacturing process to one that might be found in Japan?" Eighty-six percent of the respondents said that their U.S. manufacturing practice was either "exactly the same" or "very similar" to one that might be found in Japan; only one supplier said that it was not at all similar.

The Division of Labor

Job classifications. Few job classifications are a key characteristic of the Japanese model. This contrasts sharply with traditional U.S. production organization in which virtually every job has its

Table 2. Percentage of Transplant Parts Suppliers with Selected Japanese Intraorganizational Practices:
U.S., 1988

Characteristic	Percent	Number of Cases
Work Organization		
Work teams	76.7	73
Rotation within teams	87.0	69
Rotation between teams	66.2	68
Just-in-time inventory control	68.5	73
Worker Involvement		
Production workers maintain their own machines	79.5	73
Production workers do routine quality control	98.6	73
Production workers help design their own jobs	60.9	69
Division of Labor		
Number of job classifications:		
1	34.3	67
2	14.9	67
3	16.4	67
4	14.9	67
5	6.0	67

own job classification and job classifications are
seen by workers and unions as a "job ladder" that
provides the basis for wage increases and employment security. Kochan et al. (1986) report
that the unionized plants in a multidivisional U.S.
manufacturing firm had an average of 96 job classifications. Table 1 indicates that transplant assemblers use no more than four job classifications, whereas a representative traditional U.S.
Big Three auto maker had 90. The implementation of few job classifications might seem especially difficult at transplants which employ a large
number of managers and workers that were originally socialized to traditional Big Three practices, e.g. NUMMI which has a large percentage of
former GM workers. However, our interviews
with NUMMI officials and workers indicated few
adaptation problems.

More than 85 percent of transplant suppliers
use five or fewer job classifications for production workers; and one-third use only one job classification. Several indicate that they have instituted more job classifications than would be ideal (as many as ten) to keep American workers
happy by providing the appearance of an internal
career ladder.

Team leaders. Japanese production organization includes a class of workers, referred to as

"team leaders," who are members of shopfloor
work groups but also have managerial responsibility for immediate production activities. There
are no foremen or low-level managers whose job
is to supervise shopfloor workers. Team leaders
are used at all the transplant assemblers we visited, and 84 percent of suppliers use them as well.
At Honda, Toyota, NUMMI, Nissan, and SIA
team leaders are the first line of supervision and
play a crucial role in the organization, design, and
allocation of work on a daily basis. At some transplants, team leaders are selected by management,
while at others, especially the unionized transplants, team leaders are selected by joint labor-
management committees. All the transplants consider the input of workers to be an important criterion for the selection of team leaders.

Status distinctions. Overt status distinctions between management and blue-collar workers are
less evident in Japan than in the U.S. For example, in Japan workers and managers eat in the
same cafeteria; middle level managers wear the
same uniforms as shopfloor workers. Managers
typically do not have enclosed offices but sit at
desks on a large open floor adjacent to the production facility. All transplants we visited had
single cafeterias. At Nippondenso, all executives
including the President work at desks on the floor.
Nissan is the only transplant in which status distinctions are more visible, e.g., a separate park-
ing lot for top managers' cars and plush "American-style" offices. This may be because Nissan
has a much higher percentage of former American automobile executives than other transplants.
All the transplants provide uniforms, although
some give workers the option of wearing street
clothes. Transplant officials we interviewed suggested that uniforms create an identification between workers and the company. Most top executives wear company uniforms, although Nissan
is again the exception. In fact, the transplants
tend to have greater visible status equality than
obtains in Japan where top executives have chauf-
feured company automobiles and wear suits and
ties rather than work uniforms.

Hierarchy. Lincoln, Hamada, and McBride
(1986) indicated that management hierarchies are
taller in Japan than in the U.S. Our findings suggest that management hierarchies in the automotive transplants are relatively flat. At Honda, there
are nine levels in the internal hierarchy: associate, team leader, coordinator, department manager, plant manager, assistant vice president, senior vice president, executive vice president, and
president. This structure is typical of the other

transplants as well. At Honda, the various vice presidents do not form separate levels in the reporting structure, but are part of Honda's senior management team, which includes the plant manager and the president of Honda of America Manufacturing. This senior management team makes decisions as a group and thus functions to some extent as a single reporting level. The president of Honda America is a member of and reports to the Board of Directors for Honda Japan. A number of shopfloor workers have risen to management ranks at Honda and the company actively encourages such mobility. Toyota officials indicate that shopfloor workers are recruited for middle-level management positions in the factory and the front office.

Worker Participation and Quality Control

It is important to distinguish between the form of Japanese organization and its substance, i.e., its effects on worker behavior. A main objective of the Japanese system of work and production organization is to harness the collective intelligence of workers for continuous product and process improvement (Kenney and Florida 1988, 1989). This stands in sharp contrast to traditional American automobile industry practices in which there are formal and informal organizational barriers and norms that inhibit the use of worker intelligence (Braverman 1974). In Japan, workers actively participate in company suggestion programs and quality control circles as well as informal, everyday "*kaizen*," or continuous improvement activities. In Japan, different automobile corporations emphasize different aspects of *kaizen* activity. Toyota places greater emphasis on team activities, like quality circles, whereas Honda emphasizes individual initiative and innovation. Japanese scholars use the concept of "voluntarism" to explain the extraordinary initiative of workers in Japan. However, Japanese automobile companies vary significantly in their ability to generate "voluntaristic" behavior — with Toyota being the most effective.

Worker initiative. Transplants encourage worker initiative through the delegation of managerial authority and responsibility to shopfloor workers. Workers at the transplants, especially Honda and Toyota, have significant input into the design of their jobs. More than 60 percent of respondents to the supplier survey indicate that workers are involved in the design of their tasks. At Toyota and Nippondenso, work teams actually design standardized task descriptions for their

work units and post them in the form of drawings and photographs with captions at their work stations. Roughly 80 percent of suppliers indicate that workers are responsible for routine maintenance on their own machines.

Japanese corporations use suggestion systems to harness workers' knowledge and ideas. Honda and Toyota have fairly well-developed suggestion systems. Although Mazda has a suggestion system, Mazda workers have occasionally boycotted it to express their dissatisfaction with management policy. SIA does not yet have a suggestion system, although management indicates that the company will institute one in the future. Thirty percent of transplant suppliers provide cash awards for worker suggestions, and two-thirds report that "willingness to suggest new ideas" is a key criterion for evaluating production workers for wage increases.

Quality circles. Quality circles are an important element of the Japanese system (Cole 1989a; Lillrank and Kano 1989). In Japan, quality circles are groups of workers who devote effort outside regular working hours to improving an element of the production process. According to Lincoln et al. (1986, p. 354), 76 percent of employees in a sample of Japanese plants participated in quality circles compared to 27 percent of workers in U.S. plants. The transplants vary in the extent and intensiveness with which they employ quality circles. Toyota and Honda use quality circles extensively, Mazda and NUMMI "moderately," and SIA not at all. Slightly less than half of suppliers use quality circles, and 68 percent of those who do not use quality control circles plan to do so in the future.

Transplant assemblers pay workers for quality circle activity. Of suppliers that use quality circles, 83 percent pay workers for hours spent working on quality circles. In both transplant assemblers and suppliers, participation in quality circles usually occurs immediately before or after shift work. Several transplants conduct competitions between quality control circles and use prizes, plaques, and cash awards as additional incentives for quality circle participation. Some transplants have sent American quality circles to Japan to participate in annual company competitions. All the transplant assemblers and suppliers that we visited indicated that they will devote significant effort to establishing quality control circles on a par with Japan. We thus agree with Cole's assessment (1989, pp. 111-12) that it is still too early in the transfer process to expect full use of quality control circles. Such activity will likely increase as the transplants complete the process of implanting organizational forms and move on to more subtle techniques of shaping and motivating worker initiative.

We also asked Japanese managers to tell us how much, in percentage terms, Japanese *kaizen* or continuous improvement activity they have been able to replicate in their American work force. Honda executives feel they have completely replicated Japanese practice in their Marysville, Ohio plant. A Toyota manager who has worked in numerous Toyota plants in Japan as well as at NUMMI and Georgetown, Kentucky, indicated the Georgetown plant is at 60 percent of Japanese practice and NUMMI at 40 to 50 percent. Management is actively trying to implement greater *kaizen* activities. Nippondenso, a Toyota group member, has also closely replicated Japanese practice. Mazda and Nissan have had more difficulty implementing *kaizen* activity, and stand at roughly 50 percent of Japanese practice. Executives of SIA, which is the most recent transplant, estimate that the plant is currently at about 30 percent of Japanese practice. Still, the progress of the transplants on this dimension is remarkable, given the limited time they have had to socialize American workers to the requirements of Japanese production.

The central role played by worker initiative and the use of workers' knowledge contradicts the view that the Japanese model is simply an extension of fordist mass production. It lends support to the alternative conceptualization that it is a new and potential successor model based upon harnessing workers' intellectual and physical capabilities.

Transplants recognize this deficit and are working hard to replicate the worker initiative and voluntaristic behavior of Japanese firms. Numerous Japanese executives see the lack of independent initiative of American workers as a product of previous attitudes and socialization, and suggest that it can be changed by education and socialization to Japanese practices. According to the Japanese president of a transplant supplier, education and effort is required to "remove American barriers to worker initiative." Managers at the transplants indicate that they will concentrate on this issue in the next few years. Going even further, Toyota is working with the local school system to redesign curriculum and other socialization mechanisms to impart group-oriented behavior, problem solving, and initiative to students. SIA has also sent local school officials to Japan so that they can learn more about Japanese group-oriented educational practice.

Work Force Selection and Socialization

Japanese corporations do not simply impose Japanese production organization and manufacturing practice on their American work forces. Instead, they use a number of selection and socialization mechanisms to ensure effective transfer.

Selection. Recruitment and selection processes identify workers who possess initiative, are dedicated to the corporation, work well in teams, and do not miss work. The process differs from the recruitment policies of Japanese corporations in Japan (Rosenbaum and Kariya 1989) but serves a similar function. Moreover, the process differs markedly from the typical U.S. practice of hiring "off the street." The transplants subject potential workers to cognitive and psychological tests and other screening procedures to identify workers who "fit" the Japanese model. Previous job records or high school records are scrutinized for absenteeism. Potential employees go through extensive interviews with personnel officials, managers, and even members of their potential work teams to rate their initiative and group-oriented characteristics. While theorists have generally treated the so-called "loyalty" of the Japanese work force as a product of Japanese culture, the screening and selection process constitutes an organizational mechanism that selects potentially "loyal" workers from a large, diverse population. Simply put, this long held "cultural" effect is also a product of organizational practice.

Socialization. Prior to start-up, all the assembly transplants sent key employees (e.g., managers and team leaders) to Japanese sister plants for three to six months. There they received both formal training and informal socialization to Japanese practice (e.g., team work and *kaizen*). They worked closely with veteran Japanese "trainers," who transfer formal and tacit knowledge of production and who function as role models to some extent. Workers and trainers also spent time together outside work to continue the socialization process. These trainers then came to the U.S. for periods from three months to two years to work alongside the same U.S. employees and their teams. The supplier survey indicates that 33 percent of American managers were sent to Japan for training. According to workers at different transplants, "trainers" provided the most substantial and significant exposure to Japanese practices.

The transplants use ongoing training and socialization programs to acclimate workers to Japanese production. Most employees begin with a six- to eight-week introductory session that includes an overview of automotive assembly and fairly rigorous socialization in the Japanese model. After this, workers are assigned to teams where they continue to learn from senior employees. According to the survey, suppliers provide an average of eight days of training for factory workers before they assume shopfloor activities (range = 0-180 days); assemblers have longer training periods. This is supplemented by an average of 61 days additional training on the shopfloor (range = 1-302 days).

Adaptation. Shopfloor workers in the U.S. have experienced few problems adapting to the Japanese system. NUMMI workers who previously worked for GM indicate that they prefer the Japanese model to U.S. fordist practice. According to one: "I was at GM and the part I didn't like — which I like now — is that we had a lot of drug and alcohol problems. It was getting to the point, even with me, when it got around lunchtime I had to go out . . . and take down two or three beers." Mazda has had the most adaptation problems including significant worker discontent and the recent election of a new union local that is less conciliatory toward management. However, Mazda workers indicate that such adaptation problems are largely due to management's failure to fully implement Japanese production organization, e.g., by not rotating workers to prevent repetitive motion injury.

Management has been the source of recurring adaptation problems at the transplants. During site visits and interviews, we were told repeatedly that American middle managers, especially those recruited from U.S. automobile corporations, have experienced great difficulty adapting to Japanese production organization and management. Honda officials indicate that the previously formed attitudes and prejudices of U.S. middle managers toward factory workers are a serious problem. White and Trevor (1983) documented a similar problem in U.K. transplants. NUMMI workers complain that American managers still operating in the GM style are a major obstacle to implementation of a full-blown Japanese system that they see as more favorable to workers than the old fordist system. According to a NUMMI worker: "A lot of things have changed. But see, you hear people talk. You hear them saying once in a while: 'Oh, we're going back to the GM ways.' I hope not. That was rough. . . . I think to completely bring back the Japanese way, Japan would have to take over the plant completely and have nothing to do with General Motors at all." Japanese transplant managers indicate that problems with American middle managers have encouraged them to promote shopfloor workers to supervisory positions.

Wages and Labor-Management Relations

In any industrial system, the immediate organization of production is reflected in rules, regulations, and norms that form the context in which production takes place. This broader production environment includes wage rates, wage determination, the organization and function of the internal labor market, degree of tenure security, type of unionization, and pattern of labor relations. These factors create incentives for work effort, establish the context for labor-management relations, and form the framework for mobilizing employee demands and mediating disputes. In Burawoy's (1979) terminology, they provide the social context for the "manufacture of consent."

Wages and bonuses. The Japanese *"nenko"* system of wage determination is based on a combination of seniority, job-related performance, and the ability to work in a group context (Suzuki 1976; Gordon 1985; Kagono, Nonaka, Sakikabara, and Okumura 1985). Semiannual bonuses constituting roughly 30 percent of total remuneration are used to supplement regular pay (Aoki 1988).

As in Japan, transplant assemblers and suppliers pay relatively high wages. Transplant assemblers pay average annual wages between $28,598 and $36,013 dollars, compared to an average of $36,089 for Big Three auto makers (Table 1). Workers in transplant assembly plants can earn over $50,000 when overtime is included. Hourly wages for regular production workers in transplant assembly plants range between $13.94 and $16.81 per hour, compared to an average of $16.41 at Big Three firms (Table 1). Transplant suppliers also pay relatively high wages, $7.21 per hour to start and $8.00 after a year on the job for "low skill" workers, to more than $11.00 for "high skill" workers — a rate which is slightly below the wage levels at U.S. parts suppliers (U.S. International Trade Commission 1987). Total annual compensation at the transplant suppliers averages $21,200 per year. This wage differential between assemblers and suppliers is roughly similar to that in Japan.

The wage levels and wage determination policies of the transplants are more standardized and uniform than in Japan. This is somewhat striking because academic studies and conventional wisdom contrast American "individualism" to Japanese "familism." Transplant assemblers pay uniform wages for each class of workers, with raises at regular intervals. Transplant suppliers report that work effort, absenteeism, "willingness to work in teams," and "willingness to suggest new ideas" are the major criteria used to evaluate workers for wage increases and promotions.

Bonuses are not as common in the transplants as they are in Japan, and they are not an important component of employee wages. Bonuses at the transplants tend to be across-the-board, equal-percentage wage supplements to all workers. Honda provides a monthly bonus of $100 for perfect attendance. Bonuses represent only 1 percent of total compensation for transplant suppliers. However, 49 percent of transplant suppliers provide small cash awards for attendance, 30 percent provide small cash awards for suggestions, and 18 percent provide small cash awards for participation in quality circles.

Job security. "Permanent employment," or more appropriately, long-term employment tenure, is a much discussed feature of the Japanese system (Abegglen 1958; Taira 1970; Dore 1973; Cole 1979; Lincoln and Kalleberg 1985). The pattern of employment security differs between unionized and nonunionized assembly transplants, and between assemblers and suppliers. Our review of the labor-management agreements for the unionized assembly transplants indicates that all of them have formal contractual agreements that stipulate tenure security, "guaranteeing" jobs except under conditions that jeopardize the financial viability of the company. Both NUMMI and Mazda have fulfilled their commitment to no layoffs. NUMMI has kept full employment during periods of up to 30 percent reduction in output by eliminating overtime, slowing the work pace, offering workers voluntary vacation time, placing workers in special training programs, or transferring them to other jobs. Mazda workers have been loaned to local governments during slowdowns. The nonunionized transplants provide informal assurance of tenure security, although this is not reflected in contractual agreements with workers. Nissan and Toyota have redeployed workers to other jobs to avoid layoffs. However, it is impossible to know at this stage whether the nonunionized transplants will remain committed to tenure security in the event of a severe economic downturn.

Transplant suppliers do not offer formal guarantees of tenure security. However, more than two-thirds of the supplier respondents indicate that the Japanese long-term employment system

should be transferred to the U.S. Nevertheless, they offered a wide range of opinions on this issue — some saw long-term employment as a source of long-run productivity increases, others saw the threat of termination as a way to motivate American workers.

Unionization. The Japanese system of unionization is one of enterprise or "company" unions (Taira 1961; Shirai 1983), which differs markedly from the prevailing U.S. practice of industrial unionism. However, Levine (1958), Taira (1961), and Koike (1988) observed that the U.S. has always had a system of decentralized plant-specific "locals" that operate in a way that is similar to enterprise unions by aggregating worker demands and establishing the context of labor-management relations at the plant level.[4]

The transplants have developed two basic strategies to cope with U.S. labor relations and to recreate some elements of Japanese industrial relations. Most automobile transplants have simply chosen to avoid unionization. Only 4 of the 71 supplier respondents were unionized. The four nonunionized assemblers — Honda, Toyota, Nissan and SIA — have chosen rural "greenfield locations" at least in part to avoid unionization. Nissan went to great lengths to defeat a unionization drive. SIA has implemented an in-plant video system to communicate messages to workers in anticipation of a unionization campaign. Nonunionized transplants, notably Nissan and Toyota, use employee "handbooks" that provide plant rules and regulations and have formed "employee associations" that collect employee input and create a stable structure through which work-related grievances can be addressed. The unionized transplants, Mazda, NUMMI, and Diamond-Star, have established independent agreements with their respective union locals that enlist the union in the implementation of Japanese work organization. These agreements allow fewer job classifications and more flexible work rules and utilize pay systems that differ markedly from the typical U.S. assembly plant.

Work force segmentation. The transplants are recreating aspects of Japan's highly segmented or "dual" labor markets (see Koike 1988; Kalleberg and Lincoln 1988). In Japan, for example, a large manufacturing facility will typically have nonunionized temporary workers or lower-paid

---

[4] The U.S. industrial relations system is experiencing a general decentralization of such functions to the local level. For example, the new GM Saturn plant in Tennessee has instituted an agreement with unique provisions.

workers from subcontractors working side-by-side with regular employees. The transplants use part-time or temporary employees to provide flexibility. At both Mazda and Diamond-Star, temporary employees were laid off during a downturn in the automobile market in early 1990 (Guiles and Miller 1990). The use of temporary workers has been a source of ongoing labor-management conflict at Mazda where (in contrast to Japan) union leaders see temporary workers as a threat to labor solidarity.

Gender is the most common basis of work force segmentation in Japan. Japanese women are prohibited from working in assembly plants by Japanese laws that make it illegal for women to work the night shift. The transplants do not show the extreme pattern of gender-based segmentation that is common in Japan. The supplier survey indicates that women comprise 34 percent of production workers. However, women are only 10 percent of the management work force.

Race is a typical line of work force segmentation in the U.S. Earlier research (Cole and Deskins 1988) inferred racial bias from the site selection and work force composition of Japanese transplants. We did not see large or even representative numbers of minorities in site visits. According to the supplier survey, minorities fill 11 percent of production positions and 9 percent of management slots. Recent data indicate that the transplant assemblers are hiring relatively more minority workers in production jobs. For example, Honda has increased minority employment from 2.8 percent in 1989 to 10.6 percent in 1990. Similarly, Toyota in Kentucky reports that 15 percent of its employees are nonwhite (also see Cole 1989b). In all likelihood, this is a response to the political pressure that resulted from publicizing earlier hiring practices.

Effects and implications. The Japanese transplants have been successful in economic terms. In 1990, the transplants produced nearly 20 percent of all U.S. cars and are projected to increase this to between 40 and 50 percent of the U.S. market over the next five to ten years (Wharton Econometric Forecasting Associates 1990). Productivity comparisons done by the International Motor Vehicle Program at the Massachusetts Institute of Technology indicate that the transplants have productivity ratings that are as good as or better than U.S.-owned automobile assembly plants and comparable to their Japanese sister plants (Krafcik 1989; Womack et al. 1990).

The combined economic and organizational success of the transplants is exerting a powerful demonstration effect on U.S. automobile corporations, resulting in the imitation and diffusion of Japanese practices. The diffusion process has been accelerated by joint ventures with Big Three auto makers, some of which (e.g., NUMMI) were organized explicitly to educate U.S. managers. Furthermore, union leadership is pressing to apply transplant job security provisions to U.S. firms. Each of the Big Three auto makers currently operates plants (e.g., GM's Saturn) that use the "team concept," few job classifications, pay-for-performance, and other organizational practices that have been influenced by the Japanese. However, a recent study (Kochan and Cutcher-Gershenfeld 1988) suggests that U.S. reforms are essentially "hybrid forms" in which workers are grouped in teams but not given decentralized decision-making authority. Whereas the literature predicts convergence of Japanese transplants toward the U.S. model, the reverse is occurring as U.S. producers adopt elements of the Japanese model. This further reinforces the contention that the Japanese model is a potentially generalizable successor to fordist mass production.

Summary. Our findings indicate that both transplant assemblers and suppliers have been remarkably successful in implanting the Japanese system of work organization in the U.S. environment. The basic form of Japanese work organization has been transferred with little if any modification. There are differences in the extent to which the transplants have been able to replicate Japanese behavior in *kaizen*, quality circles and other such activity, but they are working hard to increase the participation of U.S. workers in these activities. Japanese wage determination and labor relations practices have been somewhat modified to fit the U.S. context. However, these practices still resemble Japanese more than U.S. traditions. In sum, our findings are in line with the hypothesis that the Japanese model is a set of organizational practices that can be removed from the Japanese environment and successfully implanted elsewhere. However, we do not imply that the transfer process has occurred automatically. Japanese firms have taken great care to select and even to alter the environment to make it conducive to new organizational forms.

TRANSFER OF INTERORGANIZATIONAL RELATIONS

The Japanese system of interorganizational relations differs markedly from that of the U.S. The Japanese "just-in-time" system of supplier relations is characterized by close geographic proximity of producers, long-term relationships, and tight interfirm linkages characterized by personnel sharing, joint participation in product development, and regular communication and interaction (Asanuma 1985; Odaka, Ono and Adachi 1988). In Japan, suppliers provide as much as 70 percent of a car's components, while U.S. automobile assemblers rely on suppliers for 30 to 50 percent of inputs (Mitsubishi Research Institute 1987; U.S. International Trade Commission 1987). The Japanese supplier system is organized in a pyramidal structure with 500 first-tier suppliers, a few thousand second-tier suppliers and more than 20,000 tertiary automotive parts suppliers (Sayer 1986; Nishiguchi 1987; Sheard 1983). The parent or "hub" company plays a key role by structuring linkages and coordinating flows within the network (Florida and Kenney 1990b). The Japanese supplier system is embedded in a set of organizational relationships that structure economic behavior. Dore (1983) advanced the concept of "relational contracting" to capture elements of the Japanese system and to contrast it with the "arm's length" system of the U.S. (Altshuler et al. 1984).

Japanese assembly transplants initially located facilities in the lower Midwestern region of the United States to take advantage of the indigenous infrastructure of domestic automobile parts suppliers. However, indigenous supplier firms were unable to adapt to the delivery and quality requirements of Japanese just-in-time system. Dismayed by the performance of U.S. suppliers, assembly transplants encouraged their first-tier Japanese suppliers to locate in the U.S. The Japanese suppliers, in turn, found it in their interest to expand overseas. In effect, the creation of a Japanese system of interorganizational relations in the U.S. was a "creative response" (Schumpeter 1947) to the deficiencies of the U.S. environment.

Transplant assemblers have played an active role in the creation of this new production environment by financing and helping to set up U.S. branches for key suppliers. For example, Honda encouraged two of its Japanese suppliers to form Bellemar Parts to supply it with seat subassemblies. In another instance, Honda provided technical and financial assistance to a group of Japanese suppliers to form KTH Parts Industries, a company that took over U.S. production of chassis parts that were once produced in-house by Honda at Marysville. Nearly half of Honda's main suppliers in Japan now operate U.S. plants. The

supplier survey indicates that 12 of 73 suppliers are partially owned by the assemblers they supply.

Furthermore, assemblers played a key role in influencing both the original decision of transplant suppliers to relocate production in the U.S. and their choice of locations in the U.S. According to the supplier survey, more than 75 percent set up U.S. operations to maintain close ties to a major Japanese customer, and 90 percent chose their specific locations to be close to a major customer. Traditional environmental factors like the local labor market or local labor costs have had relatively little impact on locational choices. Recently, other Japanese parts suppliers have opened U.S. plants on their own initiative to access the growing market for their products. Most of the supplier plants are located in states with transplant assembly plants. The strong role played by large assemblers in orienting and structuring the transplant supplier complexes contradicts the claim (Sabel 1989; Friedman 1988) that the Japanese model is converging toward small-firm flexible specialization.

Supplier Relations

Table 3 summarizes data from the supplier survey on the main characteristics of relations among transplant assemblers and suppliers. This table reports the responses of 73 transplant suppliers on their supply relationships with transplant assemblers and with their own "second-tier" suppliers. Geographic proximity is a basic characteristic of the Japanese supplier relations (Sayer 1986). Among transplant suppliers, 40 percent are located within a two-hour shipping radius of end-users, and almost 90 percent are located within an eight-hour radius. Eighty percent make just-in-time deliveries. Still, the distances separating end-users from suppliers are somewhat greater in the United States than in Japan. Transplant complexes are essentially "stretched out" versions of Japan's geographically concentrated just-in-time system of interorganizational linkages. This is likely due to the greater availability of land, well-developed highway systems, larger trucks, and greater storage capacity in the U.S.

Interaction and information exchange. Table 3 reveals a continuous exchange of information between transplant assemblers and suppliers. Approximately 97 percent of transplant suppliers are contacted immediately by phone when they deliver a defective product. Eighty-two percent indicate that engineers from their major customer came on-site while they were setting up

Table 3.   Percentage of Transplant First-Tier Suppliers with
           Selected Japanese Interorganizational Linkages:
           U.S., 1988

Characteristic	Linkages to Assemblers		Linkages to Second-Tier Suppliers	
	%	N	%	N
Transit time				
1/2 hour	6.9	72	—	—
1/2 hour-2 hours	33.3	72	—	—
2-8 hours	38.9	72	—	—
8-24 hours	9.7	72	—	—
Deliver according to just-in-time schedule	80.0	70	43.1	72
Immediate feedback on defective parts	97.2	72	97.2	72
Customers' engineers visit plant site				
For quality control problems	96.8	62	96.9	65
For production problems	74.2	62	83.1	65
Interaction in design				
Close interaction between supplier and customer	50.0	72	33.8	71
Supplier bids on customer design	31.9	72	62.0	71
Supplier can alter customer design	22.2	72	11.3	71
Supplier designs subject to customer approval	15.3	72	11.3	71
Supplier designs but customer can alter	6.9	72	8.5	71

U.S. operations, three-quarters report that engineers from their major customer make ongoing site visits to deal with production problems, and 97 percent indicate that engineers from their major customer make ongoing site visits to deal with quality control problems.

Joint product development. Joint participation in design and development is another key characteristic of Japanese supplier relations. Fifty percent of suppliers said they participate closely with assemblers in the development of new products. This includes interaction with U.S.-owned firms as well. Honda engineers, for example, developed new production techniques for a small Ohio plastics firms that became a Honda supplier. Honda, Toyota, and SIA send teams of engineers and shopfloor workers to consult with sup-

pliers on new product designs and production machinery. Honda intends to use its Marysville R&D center to integrate both transplant and U.S. suppliers into the future design of cars. We thus conclude that Japanese interorganizational practices like high levels of interaction, joint development, and long-term contracts, which typically have been viewed as a function of Japan's sociocultural environment, are actually a product of the organizational relation itself.

Supplier tiers. In Japan, first-tier suppliers play a critical role in organizing and coordinating supply flows between lower-level suppliers and main assembly plants. They are located close to assemblers, interact frequently with them, and often are at least partially owned by them (Asanuma 1985). First-tier suppliers are probably more important in transplant complexes. For example, the windshields for Honda's American-made vehicles originate at PPG, an American producer. PPG supplies windshields to a Japanese supplier, AP Technoglass, twice a week. AP Technoglass screens them for defects, cuts and grinds them, and delivers them to a Honda subsidiary, Bellemar Parts, twice a day. Bellemar, which is located one mile from the Honda plant, applies rubber seals to the windshields and makes just-in-time deliveries to Honda every two hours. Bellemar also screens for defects, so that Honda receives much higher quality windshields than it would without its suppliers. In this way, suppliers serve as a "buffer" between assemblers and the environment.

Table 3 reveals the pyramidal nature of transplant supplier relations. Second-tier suppliers, who supply to the first-tier suppliers, have less interaction in design or development of new products. One-third of first-tier suppliers integrate second-tier suppliers in new product development. Just 43 percent of the first-tier suppliers receive just-in-time deliveries from their second-tier suppliers, whereas in Japan, tight interorganizational relations extend to second- and third-tier suppliers. However, this may be due to the fact that the transplant complex is still in the process of formation so linkages are at an early stage of development. Other evidence indicates that linkages are being extended down through the hierarchy to producers of basic inputs like steel, rubber and tires, and automotive plastics (Kenney and Florida 1991).

Integration of and diffusion to U.S. suppliers. Transplant assemblers are forging interorganizational linkages to U.S. producers, leading to the rapid diffusion of Japanese practices among U.S. producers. Over half of Mazda's U.S. suppliers are U.S.-owned firms: 43 of Mazda's 96 suppliers are independent U.S.-owned firms, 10 are owned by Ford, and 43 are Japanese-owned or Japanese-U.S. joint ventures (*Automotive News* 1989). Helper (1990) indicated that 41 percent of 437 U.S. automotive suppliers surveyed supplied at least one component to the transplants.

Transplant assemblers work with U.S. suppliers to accelerate the diffusion of Japanese practices. As in Japan, Toyota has set up an organization of its Kentucky suppliers, the Bluegrass Automotive Manufacturers Association (BAMA), and has held meetings with U.S. suppliers in Las Vegas and Japan to encourage diffusion of Japanese practices. NUMMI has organized a supplier council of 70 mostly U.S.-owned suppliers to share information and facilitate product improvement (Krafcik 1986). SIA has organized teams of engineers, purchasing representatives, and manufacturing people who work with suppliers to improve quality. Johnson Controls, an American-owned automotive supplier in Georgetown, Kentucky, is now the sole source supplier of seats for the Toyota Camry. Toyota has worked with the company to implement a full-blown Japanese production system. Johnson Controls delivers completed subassemblies to Toyota according to just-in-time requirements every four hours. We visited a ten-person small machine shop in rural Ohio that formerly rebuilt tractor engines, but now rebuilds robot heads for Honda and Honda suppliers.

The emergence of a new system of Japanese supplier relations in the U.S. is exerting a sizable demonstration effect on U.S. practice. Helper (1989) provided empirical evidence of U.S. convergence toward the Japanese model. Rather than taking on characteristics of U.S. suppliers or the broader environment of U.S. supplier relations, the Japanese transplants are transforming existing patterns of interorganizational relations in the U.S.

Summary. Our research indicates that the Japanese system of interorganizational relationships has been successfully transferred to the U.S. The Japanese transplants show little sign of conforming to the prevailing U.S. model of organization. Instead, the transplants have acted on the environment to create the resources and conditions they need to function. Furthermore, our findings reveal considerable symmetry or congruence between intra- and interorganizational relations. The Japanese transplants replicate in their external relations with suppliers the long-term relations, high levels of interaction, and joint problem-solv-

ing typical of their internal relations. Features such as mutual dependence, shared problem solving, and continuous interaction, which are thought to be a function of Japan's sociocultural environment, can be better explained as part of the interorganizational relationship itself.

CONCLUSION

Our findings may come as a surprise, given the legacy, conceptual orientation, and predictions of industrial sociology and organization theory. These theories imply that the environment has a strong effect on organizations, that it is difficult to transfer organizations between dissimilar environments, and that once transferred, organizations tend to take on characteristics of the new environment. At the intraorganizational level, however, the transplants have effectively recreated the basic Japanese system of production organization and are working hard to implant it fully. At the interorganizational level, the transplants have recreated the Japan's "relational contracting" system, establishing a new production environment for automobile manufacture. Thus, our findings suggest that too much explanatory power has been given to cultural factors in organizational development. Outside the plant as well as inside, the Japanese model forms a set of organizational practices that has been effectively transferred to the U.S.

On a more general level, our research suggests a general symmetry between intra- and interorganizational characteristics. The Japanese transplants have replicated long-term, interactive, participative, and/or mutually dependent relations at both the intra- and interorganizational levels. These findings are not specific to the transplants but are reflected in comparative institutional research — the U.S. pattern of short-term adversarial labor-management relations is reflected in the short-term "arm's length" pattern of U.S. supplier relations. We believe that there may be an underlying rationale for such symmetry. Organizational pressures and incentives may lead to increasing continuity in the governance structures inside and outside the firm. Firms that effectively organize intraorganizational activity are likely to replicate it in dealings with external firms as well. More research and theory-building are needed on this crucial issue, using other sectors, industries, and types of organizations.

Our research indicates that organizations can and do shape their environments. Thus, the concept of environmental "embeddedness" should be revised to incorporate measures of the power, intentions, and purposeful activities of organizations. Transferring organizational practices and forms from one society to another means that they must be uncoupled from the environment in which they are embedded and recreated in the new environment. The transplants provide clear evidence that organizational forms can be effectively lifted from an originally supportive context and transferred to a foreign environment. Furthermore, they show that organizations can mold the new environment to their needs and to some degree create the conditions of their own embeddedness. In general terms then, organizations have the resources to alter the environment. Large powerful firms, for example, can control the machines, the organization of production, the hiring of employees, and the establishment of interorganizational connections. These organizational resources can be used to offset and transform the "social matrix" of the environment.

We do not wish to imply that any type of organization can be made to fit any environment. The German automobile manufacturer, Volkswagen, failed to implement its production organization in the U.S. context — its U.S. plant experienced high levels of worker discontent, serious strikes, and was closed after less then ten years of operation. Successful organizational transfer is neither natural nor automatic; it hinges on the strategic actions organizations take to shape the environment to meet their requirements. Based on our findings, we conclude that the organizational-environmental tie works in both directions.

Finally, our research provides useful insights for the debate over new forms of production and industrial organization. The findings resonate with the general notion of a movement toward new models of production organization; the transplants reflect the more general restructuring of production organization, supplier relations, and industrial networks. However, we find little evidence to support the claim made by Sabel (1989) that the Japanese model, as manifested by the transplants, is converging toward flexible specialization. In fact, the evidence clearly suggests that U.S. firms are converging toward the Japanese model. By focussing on what is or can be transferred, our research reveals three defining features of the Japanese model: (1) high levels of task integration, (2) integration of workers' intelligence as well as physical capabilities, and (3) tightly networked production complexes. In organizational terms, the transplants, and the Japanese model in general, display a high degree of *functional integration*

that differs markedly from previous forms of functional (and/or flexible) specialization. Based on our findings here and related research on U.S. high-technology industrial organization (Florida and Kenney 1990a, 1990b), we believe that these features may be the underlying and defining elements that will determine the success, survival, and diffusion of the competing models of production organization that are emerging around the world. It remains for future research to further assess the broad generality of these trends.

Richard Florida is Associate Professor of Management and Public Policy at Carnegie Mellon University's School of Urban and Public Affairs. For the past seven years, he has been working with Martin Kenney on a cross-national project investigating the rise and decline of technological-organizational systems. He is co-author (with Kenney) of a book on the development of U.S. technological-organizational system, The Breakthrough Illusion: Corporate America's Failure to Move from Innovation to Mass Production *(Basic Books, 1990).*

Martin Kenney is an Associate Professor in the Department of Applied Behavioral Science at the University of California, Davis. He and Richard Florida are completing a book on the political economy of Japanese technological-organizational system and its transfer to the United States. The book will be published by Oxford University Press.

REFERENCES

Abeggglen, James. 1958. *The Japanese Factory*. Cambridge, MA: MIT Press.

Aglietta, Michel. 1979. *A Theory of Capitalist Regulation: The U.S. Experience*. London: New Left Books.

Altshuler, Alan, Martin Anderson, Daniel Jones, Daniel Roos, and James Womack. 1984. *The Future of the Automobile*. Cambridge: MIT Press.

Aoki, Masahiko. 1988. *Information, Incentives and Bargaining in the Japanese Economy*. Cambridge: Cambridge University Press.

Asanuma, Banri. 1985. "The Organization of Parts Purchases in the Japanese Automotive Industry." *Japanese Economic Studies* 13:32-53.

Automotive News. 1989. "Mazda: $1 Billion to Suppliers." 23 Oct., p. E29.

Benedict, Ruth. 1946. The *Chrysanthemum and the Sword*. Boston: Houghton-Mifflin.

Best, Michael. 1990. *The New Competition: Institutions of Industrial Restructuring*. Cambridge: Harvard University Press.

Braverman, Harry. 1974. *Labor and Monopoly Capital*. New York: Monthly Review Press.

Brown, Clair and Michael Reich. 1989. "When Does Union-Management Cooperation Work: A Look at NUMMI and GM-Van Nuys." *California Manage-*

ment Review 31:26-44.

Burawoy, Michael. 1979. *Manufacturing Consent.* Chicago: University of Chicago.

Cole, Robert. 1971. *Japanese Blue Collar.* Berkeley: University of California Press.

———. 1979. *Work, Mobility and Participation.* Berkeley: University of California Press.

———. 1989a. *Strategies for Learning.* Berkeley: University of California Press.

———. 1989b. "Reflections on Japanese Corporate Citizenship: Company Reactions to a Study of Hiring Practices in the United States." *Chuo Koron* 10:122-135

Cole, Robert and Donald Deskins. 1988. "Racial Factors in Site Location and Employment Patterns of Japanese Automobile Firms in America." *California Business Review* 31:9-22.

Cool, Karel and Cynthia Legnick-Hall. 1985. "Second Thoughts on the Transferability of the Japanese Management Style." *Organization Studies* 6:1-22.

Crowther, Stuart and Philip Garrahan. 1988. "Invitation to Sunderland: Corporate Power and the Local Economy." *Industrial Relations Journal* 19:51-59.

Cusumano, Michael. 1985. *The Japanese Automobile Industry.* Cambridge: Harvard University Press.

DiMaggio, Paul and Walter Powell. 1983. "The Iron Cage Revisited: Institutional Isomorphism and Collective Rationality in Organizational Fields." *American Sociological Review* 48:147-60.

Dohse, Knuth, Ulrich Jurgens and Thomas Malsch. 1986. "From Fordism to Toyotism? The Social Organization of the Labor Process in the Japanese Automobile Industry." *Politics and Society* 14:45-66.

Dore, Ronald. 1973. *Japanese Factory, British Factory.* Berkeley: University of California Press.

———. 1983. "Goodwill and the Spirit of Market Capitalism." *British Journal of Sociology* 34:459-82.

———. 1986. *Flexible Rigidities.* Stanford: Stanford University Press.

———. 1987. *Taking Japan Seriously.* Stanford: Stanford University Press.

Edwards, Richard. 1979. *Contested Terrain.* New York: Basic Books.

Florida, Richard and Martin Kenney. 1990a. *The Breakthrough Illusion: Corporate America's Failure to Move from Innovation to Mass Production.* New York: Basic Books.

Florida, Richard and Martin Kenney. 1990b. "High-Technology Restructuring in the USA and Japan." *Environment and Planning A* 22:233-52.

Freidman, David. 1988. *The Misunderstood Miracle: Industrial Development and Political Change in Japan.* Ithaca: Cornell University Press.

Fucini, Joseph and Suzy Fucini. 1990. *Working for the Japanese: Inside Mazda's American Auto Plant.* New York: Free Press.

Gertler, Meric. 1988. "The Limits to Flexibility: Com-

ments on the Post-fordist Vision of Production and Its Geography." *Transactions of the Institute of British Geographers* 13:419-32.

Gordon, Andrew. 1985. *The Evolution of Labor Relations in Japan: Heavy Industry, 1853-1955.* Cambridge: Harvard University Press.

Granovetter, Mark. 1985. "Economic Action and Social Structure: The Problem of Embeddedness." *American Journal of Sociology* 91:481-510.

Guiles, Melinda and Krystal Miller. 1990. "Mazda and Mitsubishi-Chrysler Venture Cut Output, Following Big Three's Lead." *Wall Street Journal,* 12 Jan., pp. A2, A12.

Hannan, Michael and John Freeman. 1977. "The Population Ecology of Organizations." *American Journal of Sociology* 82:929-64.

Helper, Susan. 1989. "Changing Supplier Relationships in The U.S.: Results of Survey Research." Department of Economics, Case Western Reserve University, Cleveland. Unpublished manuscript.

———. 1990. "Selling to Japanese Automobile Assembly Plants: Results of a Survey." Department of Economics, Case Western Reserve University, Cleveland. Unpublished manuscript.

Institute of Social Science. 1990. "Local Production of Japanese Automobile and Electronic Firms in The United States: The 'Application' and 'Adaptation' of Japanese Style Management." University of Tokyo, Tokyo, Japan.

Jackson, Kathy. 1990. "Transplant Wages Will Rise to Match Any Gains at Big 3," *Automotive News,* 2 July, p. 60.

Kagono, Tadao, Ikujiro Nonaka, Kiyonori Sakakibara, and Akihiro Okumura. 1985. *Strategic vs. Evolutionary Management.* Amsterdam: North Holland.

Kalleberg, Arne and James Lincoln. 1988. "The Structure of Earnings Inequality in the United States and Japan." *American Journal of Sociology* 94:S121-53.

Katz, Harry. 1985. *Shifting Gears.* Cambridge: MIT Press.

Kenney, Martin and Richard Florida. 1988. "Beyond Mass Production: Production and the Labor Process in Japan." *Politics and Society* 16:121-58.

Kenney, Martin and Richard Florida. 1989. "Response to the Debate Over 'Beyond Mass Production'" (in Japanese). *Mado* no. 2:210-13.

———. 1991. "How Japanese Industry Is Rebuilding the Rustbelt." *Technology Review* 94:24-33.

———. Forthcoming. *Mass Production Transformed: The Japanese Industrial Transplants in the United States.* New York: Oxford University Press.

Kochan, Thomas and Joel Cutcher-Gershenfeld. 1988. "Institutionalizing and Diffusing Innovation in Industrial Relations." U.S. Department of Labor, Bureau of Labor-Management Relations and Cooperative Programs, Washington, DC.

Kochan, Thomas, Harry Katz and Robert McKersie. 1986. *The Transformation of American Industrial*

Relations. New York: Basic Books.

Koike, Kazuo. 1988. *Understanding Industrial Relations in Modern Japan*. New York: St. Martin's.

Krafcik, John. 1986. "Learning From NUMMI." Massachusetts Institute of Technology, International Motor Vehicle Program. Unpublished manuscript.

———. 1989. "A New Diet for U.S. Manufacturers." *Technology Review* 92:28-38.

Kumazawa, Makoto and Jun Yamada. 1989. "Jobs and Skills Under the Lifelong Nenko Employment Practice." Pp. 102-26 in *The Transformation of Work*, edited by Stephen Wood. London: Unwin Hyman.

Lazerson, Mark. 1988. "Organizational Growth of Small Firms: An Outcome of Markets and Hierarchies?" *American Sociological Review* 53:330-42.

Lazonick, William. 1990. *Competitive Advantage on the Shopfloor*. Cambridge: Harvard University Press.

Levine, Solomon. 1958. *Industrial Relations in Postwar Japan*. Urbana: University of Illinois Press.

Lillrank, Paul and Noriaki Kano. 1989. "Continuous Improvement: Quality Control Circles in Japanese Industry." Center for Japanese Studies, The University of Michigan, Ann Arbor.

Lincoln, James and Arne Kalleberg. 1985. "Work Organization and Workforce Commitment: A Study of Plants and Employees in the U.S. and Japan." *American Sociological Review* 50:738-760.

———. 1990. *Culture, Control and Commitment: A Study of Work Organization and Work Attitudes in the United States and Japan*. New York: Cambridge University Press.

Lincoln, James, Mitsuyo Hanada, and Kerry McBride. 1986. "Organizational Structures in Japanese and U.S. Manufacturing." *Administrative Science Quarterly* 31:338-64.

Mair, Andrew, Richard Florida and Martin Kenney. 1988. "The New Geography of Automobile Production: Japanese Transplants in North America." *Economic Geography* 64:352-73.

McKelvey, Bill and Howard Aldrich. 1983. "Populations, Natural Selection and Applied Organizational Science." *Administrative Science Quarterly* 28:101-28.

Meyer, John and Brian Rowan. 1977. "Institutionalized Organizations: Formal Structure as Myth and Ceremony." *American Journal of Sociology* 83:340-63.

Mitsubishi Research Institute. 1987. *The Relationship Between Japanese Auto and Auto Parts Makers*. Tokyo: Japanese Automobile Manufacturers Association, Inc.

Monden, Yasuhiro. 1982. *Toyota Production System*. Norcross, GA: Industrial Engineering and Management Press.

Morris, Jonathan. 1988. "The Who, Why and Where of Japanese Manufacturing Investment in the U.K." *Industrial Relations Journal* 19:31-40.

Morris-Suzuki, Tessa. 1988. *Beyond Computopia:*

Information, Automation and Democracy in Japan. London: Kegan Paul International.

Nakane, Chie. 1970. *Japanese Society*. Berkeley: University of California Press.

Nishiguchi, Toshihiro. 1987. "Competing Systems of Automotive Components Supply: An Examination of the Japanese 'Clustered Control' Model and the 'Alps' Structure." International Motor Vehicle Program, Massachusetts Institute of Technology, Cambridge, MA. Unpublished manuscript.

Odaka, Konosuke, Keinosuke Ono, and Fumihiko Adachi. 1988. *The Automobile Industry In Japan: A Study of Ancillary Firm Development*. Tokyo: Kinokuniya. Distributed by Oxford University Press.

Oliver, Nick and Barry Wilkinson. 1989. "Japanese Manufacturing Techniques and Personnel and Industrial Relations Practice in Britain: Evidence and Implications." *British Journal of Industrial Relations* 27:73-91.

Parker, Mike and Jane Slaughter. 1988. "Management by Stress." *Technology Review* 91:36-44.

Perrow, Charles. 1981. "Markets, Hierarchies and Hegemony: A Critique of Chandler and Williamson." Pp. 371-386 in *Perspectives on Organization Design and Behavior*, edited by Andrew Van de Ven and William Joyce. New York: Wiley Interscience.

———. 1986. "Economic Theories of Organization." *Theory and Society* 15:11-45.

———. 1990. "Small Firm Networks." Paper presented at the Harvard University Conference on Networks, August, Cambridge, MA.

Pfeffer, Jeffery and Gerald Salancik. 1978. *The External Control of Organizations: A Resource Dependence Perspective*. New York: Harper and Row.

Piore, Michael and Charles Sabel. 1984. *The Second Industrial Divide*. New York: Basic Books.

Powell, Walter. 1987. "Hybrid Organizational Arrangements: New Form or Transitional Development." *California Management Review* 30:47-87.

Richardson, G.B., 1972. "The Organization of Industry." *Economic Journal* 82:883-96.

Robins, James. 1987. "Organizational Networks: Notes on the Use of Transaction Cost Theory in the Study of Organizations." *Administrative Science Quarterly* 32:68-86.

Rosenbaum, James and Takehiko Kariya. 1989. "From High School to Work: Market and Institutional Mechanisms in Japan." *American Journal of Sociology* 94:1334-65.

Sabel, Charles. 1989. "Flexible Specialization and the Re-emergence of Regional Economies." Pp. 17-70 in *Reversing Industrial Decline? Industrial Structure and Policies in Britain and Her Competitors*, edited by Paul Hirst and Jonathan Zeitlin. New York: St. Martin's.

Sako, Mari. 1989. "Neither Markets nor Hierarchies: A Comparative Study of the Printed Circuit Board Industry in Britain and Japan." London School of

Economics. Unpublished manuscript.

Sayer, Andrew. 1986. "New Developments in Manufacturing: The Just-in-Time System." *Capital and Class* 30:43-72.

Schumpeter, Joseph. 1947. "The Creative Response in Economic History." *Journal of Economic History* 7:149-59.

Sheard, Paul. 1983. "Auto Production Systems in Japan: Organizational and Locational Features." *Australian Geographical Studies* 21:49-68.

Shimada, Haruo. 1986. "Japanese Industrial Relations in Transition" (Working Paper No. 1854-88). Sloan School of Management, Massachusetts Institute of Technology, Cambridge, MA.

Shimada, Haruo and John MacDuffie. 1986. "Industrial Relations and 'Humanware'" (Working Paper No. 1855-88). Sloan School of Management, Massachusetts Institute of Technology, Cambridge, MA.

Shirai, Taishiro, ed. 1983. *Contemporary Industrial Relations in Japan.* Madison: University of Wisconsin Press.

Suzuki, H. 1976. "Age, Seniority and Wages." *International Labour Review* 113:67-83.

Taira, Koji. 1961. "Japanese Enterprise Unionism and Inter-Firm Wage Structure." *Industrial and Labor Relations Review* 15:33-51.

_____. 1964. "The Labour Market in Japanese Development." *British Journal of Industrial Relations* 2:209-27.

_____. 1970. *Economic Development and the Labor Market in Japan.* New York: Columbia University Press.

U.S. General Accounting Office. 1988. *Foreign Investment: Growing Japanese Presence in the U.S.*

Auto Industry. Washington, DC: U.S. General Accounting Office.

U.S. International Trade Commission. 1987. *U.S. Global Competitiveness: The U.S. Automotive Parts Industry.* Washington, DC: U.S. Government Printing Office.

Wharton Economic Forecasting Associates. 1990. *North American Light Vehicle Outlook.* Philadelphia, PA.

Weick, Karl. 1979. *The Social Psychology of Organizing.* New York: Random House.

White, Michael and Malcolm Trevor. 1983. *Under Japanese Management.* London: Heinemann Educational Books.

Williamson, Oliver. 1975. *Markets and Hierarchies.* New York: Free Press.

_____. 1981. *The Economic Institutions of Capitalism.* New York: Free Press.

_____. 1983. "Organizational Innovation: The Transaction Cost Approach." Pp. 101-33 in *Entrepreneurship,* edited by Joshua Ronen. Lexington, MA: Lexington Books.

Womack, James, Daniel Jones, and Daniel Roos. 1990. *The Machine That Changed the World.* New York: Rawson Associates.

Yoshino, M. 1976. *Japan's Multinational Enterprises.* Cambridge: Harvard University Press.

Young, Ruth. 1988. "Is Population Ecology a Useful Paradigm for the Study of Organizations." *American Journal of Sociology* 94:1-24.

Zuboff, Shoshana. 1988. *In the Age of the Smart Machine.* New York: Basic Books.

Zucker, Lynne. 1977. "The Role of Institutionalization in Cultural Persistence." *American Sociological Review* 42:726-43.

[21]

Richard N. Langlois

External Economies and Economic Progress: The Case of the Microcomputer Industry

The following article provides a thorough chronicle of the microcomputer industry. That industry is a striking case, in which industrial growth took place through the creation of "external" capabilities—that is, capabilities produced by and residing in a specialized market network rather than in large organizations enjoying internal economies of scale and scope. In the microcomputer industry, the most successful products were those that took the greatest advantage—and allowed users to take the greatest advantage—of the market; and the greatest failures occurred when business enterprises bypassed the external network and attempted to rely significantly on internal capabilities.

In a passage that mocked the neoclassical theory of competition as much as the anti-business sentiments of non-economists, Joseph Schumpeter singled out the large business enterprise as the dominant source of economic progress in modern times.

As soon as we go into the details and inquire into the individual items in which progress was most conspicuous, the trail leads not to the doors of those firms that work under conditions of comparatively free competition but precisely to the doors of the large concerns—which, as in the case of agricultural machinery, also account for much of the progress in the competitive sector—and a shocking suspicion dawns upon us that big business may have had

RICHARD N. LANGLOIS is professor of economics at the University of Connecticut, Storrs.

I would like to thank Brian Loasby, Paul Robertson, and two anonymous referees for helpful comments and discussions, and Fadi Abusamra, Laszlo Csontos, Michael Everett, and Donald Vandegrift for research assistance.

Business History Review 66 (Spring 1992): 1–50. © 1992 by The President and Fellows of Harvard College.

Richard N. Langlois / 2

more to do with creating that standard of life than with keeping it down.[1]

The reason for the dominance of the large-scale enterprise lies, in Schumpeter's view, in the superior ability of large firms to generate technological and organizational innovation.

It is not surprising that business historians should be sympathetic to Schumpeter's argument. Indeed, Alfred D. Chandler, Jr., the dean of present-day business historians, paints a similar picture of the large firm as an engine of progress. In Chandler's story, however, the large enterprise comes across less as a generator of innovation than as an "institutional response" to innovation and growth whose superiority lies in its ability to create massive internal economies of high-volume production. "The visible hand of management," Chandler writes, "replaced the invisible hand of market forces where and when new technology and expanded markets permitted a historically unprecedented high volume and speed of materials through the process of production and distribution." More recently, Chandler has extended his analysis to British and German industry, concluding that it was the "large enterprises that were most responsible for the economic growth of the world's three largest industrial nations [and that] have provided a fundamental dynamic or force for change in capitalist economies since the 1880s." And William Lazonick has proposed a theory of the entrepreneurial firm that connects Chandler and Schumpeter. In this view, the large collective enterprise supplants a decentralized market system in an act of innovation; but the innovation necessarily consists in the creation of capabilities within the organization that yield the potential for massive economies of large-scale production and distribution.[2]

Schumpeter, Chandler, and Lazonick are all arguably working within an approach that is coming to be called the dynamic capabilities theory of business organization.[3] Unlike the neoclassical theory of industrial organization, this approach is concerned not with the efficient allocation of known resources but with the ways

---

[1] Joseph A. Schumpeter, *Capitalism, Socialism, and Democracy*, 2d ed. (New York, 1950), 82.

[2] Alfred D. Chandler, Jr., *The Visible Hand: The Managerial Revolution in American Business* (Cambridge, Mass., 1977), 12; Alfred D. Chandler, Jr., *Scale and Scope: The Dynamics of Industrial Capitalism* (Cambridge, Mass., 1991), 4; William Lazonick, *Business Organization and the Myth of the Market Economy* (New York, 1991).

[3] For an elaboration of this idea, and the themes in this introduction, see Richard N. Langlois, "Transaction-Cost Economics in Real Time," *Industrial and Corporate Change* 1 (1991): 99–127.

External Economies and Economic Progress / 3

in which social institutions and organizational forms generate (and sometimes fail to generate) economic growth. The centerpiece of the analysis is the concept of economic capabilities—embodied in human and organizational knowledge that enables business institutions to produce goods and services. The issues are comparative ones. Which forms of business organization are most effective in creating economic capabilities and, withal, economic growth? Chandler's historical cases focus on the creation of *internal* capabilities.[4] Building such organizational capabilities required an investment in the capital equipment necessary for high-volume production. It meant investing in regional, national, or international networks of marketing and distribution. And it also meant turning over the reins of management to a hierarchy of salaried professionals. This, essentially, is the model that Lazonick projects into the future. He believes that to prosper nations must take advantage of substantial economies of scale in major industries, and that this requires a high degree of centralized coordination to overcome market deficiencies.[5]

Yet there is another important tradition in economics that sees the sources of economic growth in a slightly different light. Though never denying the importance to economic progress of internal economies, Alfred Marshall and his followers also highlighted the systemic interactions among a large number of competing and cooperating firms. For Marshall, such interaction could yield "external economies" that play an important role in economic progress quite in addition to that played by the economies internal to particular business organizations.[6] As Lazonick suggests, economic progress requires the development of economic capabilities. But all such capabilities need not reside within the boundaries of the organization, however generously defined. Some important economic capabilities—including perhaps the capability of generating certain kinds of technological and organizational innovation—can reside within a network of interacting firms whose primary—if by no means exclusive—nexus of coordination is the price system.

[4] For a more careful analysis of *Scale and Scope*, see Richard N. Langlois, "The Capabilities of Industrial Capitalism," *Critical Review* 5 (1991): 513–30.

[5] These are in fact popular views within the present-day debate on "industrial policy." See also, for example, Richard Florida and Martin Kenney, *The Breakthrough Illusion* (New York, 1990).

[6] Alfred Marshall, *Principles of Economics*, 8th ed. (London, 1949): book IV, chaps. 9–13.

Richard N. Langlois / 4

I do not wish to argue Marshall against Chandler. Indeed, to see any one set of business institutions as universally superior under all circumstances is a peculiarly ahistorical—not to say historically false—view.[7] It is clear, as Marshall certainly understood, that some types of innovation take place more readily within the organizational structure of a firm. I myself have argued elsewhere for "dynamic" transaction-cost explanations of vertical integration, in which the difficulties of coordinating some types of innovative activity across market boundaries can make internal organization a cheaper alternative. And Paul Robertson and I have explored one important case in which innovation—and rapid declines in product price—took place within the framework of internal economies and large-scale production: the moving assembly line and the Ford Model T.[8] But we also found episodes in the history of the automobile industry in which the existence of a variety of competing firms spurred innovation and even forced some vertical disintegration on the large firms. Moreover, a number of other cases come to mind in which rapid progress—rapid declines in product price and improvements in product quality—took place within a highly disintegrated structure.

One of the most striking examples of this phenomenon is the microcomputer industry.[9] By looking in some detail at the history of this industry, I hope to be able to shed some light on the circumstances under which economic growth proceeds through the generation of external rather than internal capabilities.[10] For it is certainly clear that this industry did not—and does not—fit the Chandlerian model.

[7] Paul L. Robertson and Richard N. Langlois, "Innovation, Networks, and Vertical Integration," Economics and Management Working Paper No. 3, University College, University of New South Wales, Canberra, Australia.

[8] Richard N. Langlois, "Economic Change and the Boundaries of the Firm," *Journal of Institutional and Theoretical Economics* 144 (1988): 635–57; Langlois and Paul L. Robertson, "Explaining Vertical Integration: Lessons from the American Automobile Industry," *Journal of Economic History* 49 (June 1989): 361–75.

[9] Although this may be too recent an episode to count in some minds as business history, it is nonetheless a more interesting case for analytical purposes than one lying further removed in time. The microcomputer industry arose after the managerial revolution chronicled by Chandler; moreover, the industry thrives on mass production and high demand. It thus provides a sharper comparison than would a case from earlier history.

[10] By external capabilities I mean capabilities created within a network of competing and cooperating firms rather than within the boundaries of large vertically integrated organizations.

External Economies and Economic Progress / 5

The Microcomputer: A History

Antecedents and Sources • The microcomputer is a product that came out of nowhere, at least in the sense that established firms initially misunderstood its uses and underappreciated its importance. But no product springs Athena-like, full-blown from the head of Zeus. The microcomputer, in hindsight, is the child of two technological traditions: the mainframe and minicomputer industries and the integrated circuit industry.

Although the history of computers dates back at least to the mechanical tinkerings of Charles Babbage in the nineteenth century, the electronic digital computer was the product of the Second World War.[11] In November 1945, J. Presper Eckert and John W. Mauchly of the Moore School at the University of Pennsylvania produced the ENIAC (Electronic Numerical Integrator and Computer), the first all-electronic digital computer, under contract with the U.S. Army. The machine took up 1,800 square feet, boasted 18,000 tubes, and consumed 174 kilowatts. Collaboration with the mathematician John von Neumann led a few years later to the idea of a stored-program—that is, a programmable rather than a special-purpose—computer, an approach called the von Neumann architecture and used almost universally today in computers of all sizes. By 1951, Eckert and Mauchly had joined Remington Rand, where they produced the UNIVAC (Universal Automatic Computer), the first commercial computer using von Neumann architecture. By 1956, the lead in computer sales had passed from Remington Rand to the International Business Machines Corporation (IBM). Unlike its erstwhile competitors, including electronics plants like General Electric (GE) and Radio Corporation of America (RCA), IBM's strengths lay in the production of mechanical office equipment. These capabilities proved useful in the manufacture of all-important computer peripherals like printers, tape drives, and magnetic drums.[12] IBM cemented its dominance with a bold move in the 1960s. Betting on a high non-military demand for computers, and pushing its advantage in production costs, IBM introduced the 360 system. This was a fam-

---

[11] For brief economic histories of the mainframe computer industry, see Barbara Katz and Almarin Phillips, "The Computer Industry," in *Government and Technical Progress: A Cross-Industry Analysis*, ed. Richard R. Nelson (New York, 1982), and Kenneth Flamm, *Creating the Computer* (Washington, D.C., 1988).

[12] Flamm, *Creating the Computer*, 83.

Richard N. Langlois / 6

Partial View of ENIAC • This early computer, developed at the Moore School, was one hundred feet long, ten feet high, and three feet deep. In 1955, it became part of a permanent exhibit at the Smithsonian Institution in Washington, D.C. (Photograph courtesy of the Smithsonian Institution.)

ily of computers and peripherals from which buyers could tailor a configuration suited to their needs. All pieces of the system, including software, were internally compatible but were proprietary with respect to the systems of other manufacturers. The idea of a proprietary system became a hallmark of the industry, and

External Economies and Economic Progress / 7

IBM's attempts to prevent third parties from selling so-called plug-compatible peripherals led to a famous antitrust case.[13]

By the 1960s, computers had become fully solid state—that is, they used transistors rather than tubes. Nonetheless, a computer with significant power remained physically imposing. More important, computers were imposing in their ways. They required large trained staffs of operators and programmers, and access to the machines was typically guarded closely. As late as the early 1970s, most users communicated with their mainframe via punch cards laboriously typed out and fed in. But the technology for smaller, easier-to-use computers was at hand, and a new industry seized on it. In December 1959, a two-year-old company called Digital Equipment Corporation (DEC) unveiled the prototype of the PDP (Programmed Data Processor)-1.[14] A commercial extension of the early interactive solid-state computers on which DEC's founders, Ken Olsen and Harlan Anderson, had worked at MIT, the machine sold for $120,000, contained 4K bytes of memory, was the size of a refrigerator, and included a cathode ray tube (that is, a television-like video display) built into the console. This was the first commercial minicomputer. In 1964, DEC introduced the PDP-6, the first commercial product designed to support a network of interactive users on time-sharing terminals. Like IBM, DEC built its strategy around a proprietary family of machines— the PDP and later the VAX (Virtual Address Extension) lines— with allied peripherals and software. Also like IBM, DEC became highly integrated vertically and not only assembled equipment, but also manufactured many of its own inputs, from semiconductors to equipment cases, and handled its own sales. Among other firms that entered the minicomputer market were Scientific Data Systems, Data General (founded in 1968 by defectors from DEC), Prime Computer, Hewlett-Packard (HP), Wang, and Tandem.[15]

For reasons explored later in this article, however, the minicomputer did not lead directly to the microcomputer. Nevertheless, technological advance did of course pave the way for that development. In particular, the invention of the integrated circuit

---

[13] United States v. International Business Machines Corporation, 1956 Trade Case, #68, 245 (S.D.N.Y. 1956).

[14] Glenn Rifkin and George Harrar, *The Ultimate Entrepreneur: The Story of Ken Olsen and Digital Equipment Corporation* (Chicago, Ill., 1988), esp. 38–41.

[15] Flamm, *Creating the Computer*, 128, 129–31.

Richard N. Langlois / 8

created a trajectory of miniaturization, culminating in high-density memory chips and microprocessors—the heart of the microcomputers.

In 1958, a decade after three scientists at Bell Labs developed the transistor, Fairchild Semiconductor developed the planar process, a way of making transistors cheaply.[16] Initially, this process was used to make single, or discrete, semiconductors. But within a few months, Jack Kilby at Texas Instruments (TI) and Robert Noyce at Fairchild had taken the next logical step, etching several transistors—an entire circuit—into silicon.[17] The early integrated circuits set the paradigm for the development of the semiconductor industry, and technological change has taken the form primarily of process improvements leading to increased miniaturization and lower production costs.

There are two types of integrated circuit crucial for the microcomputer. One is the random-access memory (RAM) chip, which allows the computer temporarily to remember programs and other information. With each new stage in miniaturization, the price of memory (in dollars per K) has declined steadily, a result not only of the miniaturization itself but also of learning-by-doing economies in production.[18] The microcomputer industry has thus certainly benefited from one important external economy that is internal to a related industry.

The other type of integrated circuit is, of course, the microprocessor. In 1969, a Japanese calculator manufacturer asked Intel, a Fairchild spin-off firm, to design the chips for a new electronic calculator.[19] Marcian E. Hoff, Jr., the engineer in charge of the project, thought that the Japanese design was too complicated to produce. Influenced by the von Neumann architecture of minicomputers, he reasoned that he could simplify the design enormously by creating a programmable chip rather than the single-purpose device that the Japanese had sought. The result was the

---

[16] For a discussion of the history of semiconductors, see Ernest Braun and Stuart Macdonald, *Revolution in Miniature* (New York, 1978), and Richard C. Levin, "The Semiconductor Industry," in Nelson, ed., *Government and Technical Progress*. See also Richard N. Langlois et al., *Microelectronics: An Industry in Transition* (London, 1988), esp. 8–25.

[17] T. R. Reid, *The Chip: How Two Americans Invented the Microchip and Launched a Revolution* (New York, 1984).

[18] See, generally, Langlois et al., *Microelectronics.*

[19] The authoritative account of the history of the microprocessor is Robert N. Noyce and Marcian E. Hoff, Jr., "A History of Microprocessor Development at Intel," *IEEE Micro* 1 (Feb. 1981): 8–21.

External Economies and Economic Progress / 9

Intel 4004, the first microprocessor. One-sixth of an inch long and one-eighth of an inch wide, the 4004 was roughly equivalent in computational power to the ENIAC. It also matched the power of a 1960s IBM computer whose central processing unit (CPU) was about the size of a desk.[20] The 4004 processed information in 4-bit words, that is, four bits at a time. In 1972, Intel introduced the 8008, the first 8-bit microprocessor. This design was later improved and simplified to create the Intel 8080 in 1974. Capable of addressing 64K bytes of memory, the 8080 became the standard 8-bit microprocessor and was widely produced by second sources. It was also the device at the center of the earliest commercial microcomputers. Other important early microprocessors included the Zilog Z80, an improved but compatible version of the 8080 built by an Intel spin-off, and the Motorola 6800, an 8-bit device of a different—and many argue superior—design.

The Hobbyists, 1975–1976 • It is conventional to date the beginning of the microcomputer at January 1975, when that month's issue of *Popular Electronics* carried a cover story on the MITS/Altair computer.[21] MITS (Micro Instrumentation Telemetry Systems), run out of an Albuquerque, New Mexico, storefront by one Ed Roberts, began life making remote-control devices for model airplanes and then entered the electronic calculator business in time to be engulfed by the price wars of the early 1970s. An electronics tinkerer familiar with the hobbyist market, Roberts decided to build a kit computer as a way to save his beleaguered enterprise. He persuaded his bank to loan him an additional $65,000 on the strength of the promised *Popular Electronics* cover, and he negotiated a volume deal for Intel 8080 microprocessors—$75 apiece instead of the usual $360 each. The machine he and his coworkers put together was little more than a box with a microprocessor in it. Its only input/output devices were lights and toggle switches on the front panel, and its memory was a minuscule 256 bytes (not kilobytes). But the Altair was, at least potentially, a fully capable computer. Like a microcomputer, it possessed a number of "slots" that allowed for expansion—for additional memory, various kinds of input/output devices, and so forth. These slots hooked into the microprocessor by a system of

---

[20] Gene Bylinsky, "Here Comes the Second Computer Revolution," in *The Microelectronics Revolution*, ed. Tom Forester (Oxford, U.K., 1980), 7.

[21] Paul Freiberger and Michael Swaine, *Fire in the Valley* (Berkeley, Calif., 1984), 31–44.

Richard N. Langlois / 10

JANUARY, 1975

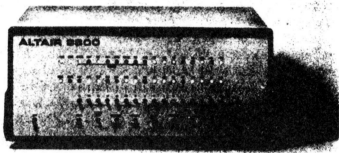

EXCLUSIVE!

ALTAIR 8800
The most powerful minicomputer
project ever presented—can be built
for under $400

ALTAIR 8800

BY H. EDWARD ROBERTS AND WILLIAM YATES

Cover Story on the Altair 8800 • The *Popular Electronics* January 1975 feature on the Altair launched the microcomputer era, although the machine was essentially a box with lights and toggle switches, lacking both software and input-output devices. (Reproduced from *Popular Electronics*, Jan. 1975, p. 33, © 1975, Ziff-Davis Publishing Company and reprinted with permission.)

wires called a "bus"; the Altair bus, which came to be known as the S-100 bus because of its one hundred–line structure, was the early industry standard of compatibility.[22]

Roberts sold the Altair for $379 stripped down and in kit form. Even though it could do almost nothing without add-ons—none of which was yet available—the machine sold beyond all expectation. MITS was besieged with orders after the *Popular Electronics* article appeared and found itself unable to ship in any volume until the summer of 1975. The company concentrated on getting the base model out the door, postponing development of add-ons.[23]

---

[22] Ibid., 49. The S-100 bus was in fact adopted, with some changes and improvements, as the IEEE 696 bus by the Institute of Electrical and Electronics Engineers. Noyce and Hoff, "History of Microprocessor Development at Intel," 16.

[23] Freiberger and Swaine, *Fire in the Valley*, 38.

External Economies and Economic Progress / 11

MITS managed to ship about two thousand machines that year.[24] Although the Altair's impoverished capabilities did not deter buyers, it did give rise to two phenomena: third-party suppliers of add-ons and "user groups," organizations of hobbyists who shared information and software. The most famous group, the Homebrew Computer Club in northern California, actually began meeting before the Altair appeared. The third-party suppliers were also typically enterprising hobbyists: Processor Technology set up shop in a garage in Oakland, and Cromemco took its name from its founders' tenure in Crothers Memorial Hall, the graduate engineering dormitory at Stanford. The products that these firms supplied—such as memory boards—filled the gap left by MITS's tardy and low-quality add-ons.

In a sense, then, the Altair was quickly captured by the hobbyist community, and it became a modular technological system rather than a self-contained product. To accomplish anything, one needed not just the box itself, but also the know-how, add-on boards, and software provided by a large network of external sources. The network character of the microcomputer was fostered by Roberts's design decisions, themselves a reflection of hobbyist attitudes toward information-sharing. More important, however, the capabilities of MITS were tiny compared to those of the larger community; those larger capabilities were necessary to take full advantage of a product with such high demand and so many diverse and unforeseen uses.

The inability of MITS to meet demand led to the emergence not only of complementary activities but also of competitive ones. Within a few months of the introduction of the Altair, the microcomputer industry had its first clone, the IMSAI 8080.[25] An automobile dealer named Phillip Reed approached entrepreneur Bill Millard with the idea of computerizing automobile dealerships. Millard looked into using a microcomputer, but that proved too expensive. Alerted to the MITS/Altair, he approached Ed Roberts, who was unable to fill existing orders, let alone envisage volume sales (and a volume discount) to Millard. So, with the help of engineers Joseph Killian and Bruce Van Natta, Millard set about build-

[24] Adam Osborne, *Running Wild: The Next Industrial Revolution* (Berkeley, Calif., 1979), 28–30.

[25] Jonathan Littman, *Once Upon a Time in ComputerLand* (Los Angeles, 1987); Freiberger and Swaine, *Fire in the Valley*, 59–78; Robert Slater, *Portraits in Silicon* (Cambridge, Mass., 1987), 331–40; Robert Levering, Michael Katz, and Milton Moskowitz, *The Computer Entrepreneurs* (New York, 1984), 340–53.

Richard N. Langlois / 12

ing an 8080 machine of his own.[26] Soon the computer eclipsed the automobile project that inspired it, and Reed was enlisted to help fund IMSAI Manufacturing. The company sold kits for what was essentially an improved version of the Altair and by 1976 began shipping assembled machines. IMSAI quickly outpaced MITS and became for a time the world's leading microcomputer manufacturer, selling 13,000 machines between 1975 and 1978.[27]

Unlike Roberts and most other figures in the early industry, Millard was primarily interested in business, not technology. He went where the winds of profit took him. To help market IMSAI computers, he and others got involved in the franchising of computer stores. This business—ComputerLand—soon came to dwarf the manufacturing operation and made Millard a millionaire many times over. IMSAI fared less well. Because of Millard's early unwillingness to take on financial partners, IMSAI collapsed in a cash-flow crisis, was bought out of bankruptcy by a couple of employees, and faded into oblivion. MITS did no better. Acquired by Pertec, a maker of peripherals for larger computers, the company withered and disappeared.[28]

Nonetheless, the early success of MITS and IMSAI cemented the popularity of the S-100 standard, especially among hobbyists, who were still the primary buying group. Indeed, proponents of the S-100 and the 8080—including Lee Felsenstein, ad hoc leader of the Homebrew Computer Club—felt that their standard had reached "critical mass" and that competing chips and buses were doomed.[29] Part of the reason was the availability of software. Before the Altair even appeared, Gary Kildall, founder of Digital Research, had written CP/M (Control Program for Microcomputers), an operating system for 8080/Z80 microcomputers.[30] An operating system is a master-of-ceremonies program that is especially

---

[26] Freiberger and Swaine, *Fire in the Valley*, 62. Littman, *Once Upon a Time*, 11, reports the story differently. In his account, Bruce Van Natta phoned MITS and ordered a few kits. But MITS would not accept a 30-day purchase order, and IMSAI (then called IMS Associates) did not have the money to pay up front. Van Natta and Killian then conceived the idea of making a clone.

[27] Levering, Katz, and Moskowitz, *The Computer Entrepreneurs*, 351.

[28] Freiberger and Swaine, *Fire in the Valley*, 51–53.

[29] A survey of members of the Homebrew Computer Club in January 1977 found that, of the 181 computers owned, 43 were IMSAIs and 33 were Altairs. Michael Moritz, *The Little Kingdom: The Private Story of Apple Computer* (New York, 1984), 191, 123.

[30] Slater, *Portraits in Silicon*, 251–61; Freiberger and Swaine, *Fire in the Valley*, 136–39; Levering, Katz, and Moskowitz, *The Computer Entrepreneurs*, 204–12.

External Economies and Economic Progress / 13

important for controlling the computer's disk drives. The earliest machines typically used paper-tape readers and ordinary cassette recorders to retrieve and store programs. In 1972, IBM invented the floppy disk drive, and by 1973 Shugart was offering a relatively inexpensive model for 5.25-inch disks. Using a larger computer to simulate the 8080, Kildall wrote CP/M as a way to control such drives. He began selling it through advertisements in the Homebrew Club's newsletter and eventually licensed it to IMSAI for inclusion with all their machines.[31]

In short order, CP/M became the dominant operating system for microcomputers. Also using a simulation rather than the real thing, William Gates and Paul Allen, founders of Microsoft, wrote a version of the programming language BASIC (Beginner's All-Purpose Symbolic Instruction Code) for the Altair.[32] When Roberts tried to tie the sale of MBASIC—as the Gates and Allen version came to be called—to the purchase of inferior MITS memory boards, software pirates raised the Jolly Roger for the first time by copying one another's paper tapes.[33] This prompted a now-famous angry letter from Gates in the Homebrew newsletter. But Gates was bucking the tide. Free software, like other kinds of information-sharing, was part of the hobbyist ethic.[34] And software for CP/M machines proliferated.

The Industry Begins, 1977 • The predicted dominance of CP/M and the S-100 never materialized, however. In 1977, a little more than two years after the Altair's debut, three important new machines entered the market, each with its own incompatible operating system, and two based around a different microprocessor. The almost simultaneous introduction of the Apple II, the Commodore PET, and the Tandy TRS-80 Model I began a new regime of technological competition, moving the industry away from the hobbyists into an enormously larger and more diverse market.

In early 1976, Stephen Wozniak worked as an engineer for Hewlett-Packard. Steven Jobs did work on contract for Atari.[35]

---

[31] Freiberger and Swaine, *Fire in the Valley*, 69.

[32] Slater, *Portraits in Silicon*, 265–68; Freiberger and Swaine, *Fire in the Valley*, 140–43; Levering, Katz, and Moskowitz, *The Computer Entrepreneurs*, 154–59.

[33] Freiberger and Swaine, *Fire in the Valley*, 45.

[34] Moritz, *The Little Kingdom*, 160.

[35] On the early history of Apple, see ibid., passim; Freiberger and Swaine, *Fire in the Valley*, 203–28; Slater, *Portraits in Silicon*, 309–14; Levering, Katz, and Moskowitz, *The Computer Entrepreneurs*, 54–61.

Richard N. Langlois / 14

The two were college dropouts and electronics tinkerers whose previous major collaboration had been the fabrication and sale of "blue boxes" for making long-distance calls without charge (and illegally). Of the two, Wozniak was the gifted engineer. Like most members of the Homebrew Computer Club, he wanted a computer of his own, so he set about designing what became the Apple I. Because the Intel 8080 and its variants were too expensive, Wozniak turned to the 6502, a clone of the Motorola 6800, which he could get for $25 rather than about $175 for a 6800 or an 8080. (The 6502 was designed by Chuck Peddle, who had helped design the 6800 at Motorola, and was produced by Peddle's company, MOS Technology.) Wozniak wrote a version of BASIC for the 6502, then designed a computer. Instead of lights and toggles on the front panel, the machine had a keyboard and loaded from information stored on chips. It had 4K bytes of memory and could drive a black-and-white television. None of these capabilities was significant enough to draw much interest from fellow Homebrew members.[36] But friends asked for schematics, and Jobs became convinced that he and Wozniak could make money selling the device. They scrounged together $1,300 and set about assembling circuit boards in—yes—the garage at Jobs's parents' house.

Seeing a commercial future for the microcomputer, the pair went to their employers—Atari and HP—with the idea. Both were rebuffed. "HP doesn't want to be in that kind of a market," Wozniak was told.[37] So Apple Computer formed as a partnership on 1 April 1976. As Wozniak worked to refine the design, Jobs looked beyond sales to hobbyist friends. He persuaded Paul Terrell, owner of the Byte Shop—perhaps the first computer store and the progenitor of a chain—to order fifty Apples. Soon the pair acquired funding and a new partner in Mike Markkula, a former Intel executive. Apple Computer Corporation supplanted the partnership in early 1977. Meanwhile, Jobs enlisted the Regis McKenna advertising agency to represent Apple for a share of the sales revenue.

The Apple II made its debut at the First West Coast Computer Faire in spring 1977. The machine came in a plastic case with a built-in keyboard, could be expanded from 4K to 48K of memory, drove a color monitor, connected to a cassette recorder, and had a version of BASIC stored in a chip. The Apple also had

---

[36] Moritz, *The Little Kingdom*, 127.
[37] Ibid., 126.

External Economies and Economic Progress / 15

eight expansion slots, the result of the hobbyist Wozniak's winning an argument with Jobs, who tended to see the computer as a narrowly focused product rather than as an open-ended system.[38] Although the Apple II was not necessarily the hit of the Faire, Apple kept a high profile and a professional appearance quite distinct from the hobbyist firms displaying their wares. Almost immediately, sales began to take off. The company took in $750,000 in revenues by the end of fiscal 1977; almost $8 million in 1978; $48 million in 1979; $117 million in 1980 (when the firm went public); $335 million in 1981; $583 million in 1982; and $983 million in 1983.[39] The lion's share of these revenues, especially in the early years, reflects sales of the Apple II.

What accounts for the Apple II's phenomenal success? Industry guru Adam Osborne believes that the machine was in fact "technologically inferior." People bought it, he wrote, "because they were not inconvenienced by its limitations. Technology had nothing to do with Apple Computer Corporation's success; nor was the company an aggressive price leader. Rather, this company was the first to offer real customer support and to behave like a genuine business back in 1976 when other manufacturers were amateur shoe-string operations."[40] Certainly Jobs's drive to create a successful company—not a technologically successful computer—had much to do with the firm's success. Moreover, Apple received good business advice from the venture capitalists who also helped bankroll the company.

In one area, however, technological superiority did help Apple out-distance its competitors. In 1977, tape cassette decks were still the standard for data storage. Floppy drives were available, but they required expensive controller circuits. In what all regard as his most brilliant piece of engineering, Wozniak designed a wholly novel approach to encoding data on a disk and a vastly simplified controller circuit. The design not only won him belated kudos from the Homebrew Club but, more important, it helped Apple beat Commodore and Tandy to market. "It absolutely changed the market," said Chuck Peddle, designer of the rival Commodore

---

[38] Ibid., 157.

[39] Data from Apple Computer, cited in "John Sculley at Apple Computer (B)," Harvard Business School Case no. 9-486-002, revised May 1987, 26.

[40] Adam Osborne and John Dvorak, *Hypergrowth: The Rise and Fall of Osborne Computer Corporation* (Berkeley, Calif., 1984), 11.

Richard N. Langlois / 16

PET.[41] Another event that changed the industry—and helped Apple—was software. Daniel Bricklin, a Harvard MBA and former DEC employee, wanted to buy a microcomputer-like DEC intelligent terminal in order to develop a programming idea: the spreadsheet. Rebuffed by salespeople interested only in volume sales to businesses, he acquired an Apple II instead and created VisiCalc.[42] For a full year, the program was available only in an Apple version, allowing the company to make early inroads into the business market.

In the end, what made the Apple II so successful was its compromise between technology and marketing. Under Jobs's influence, the machine was compact, attractive, and professional in appearance. Under Wozniak's influence, it was elegantly designed, easy both to use and to manufacture. Compared with earlier hobbyist machines like the Altair or the IMSAI, the Apple II was an integrated and understandable product. Yet, thanks to Wozniak's slots, it was also still a system, able to draw on the large crop of external suppliers of software and add-ons that quickly sprang up. Indeed, Apple relied heavily on external suppliers for almost everything. Like the IBM PC a few years later, the Apple II was almost completely "outsourced." Apple president Mike Scott, who was in charge of production, did not believe in automated manufacturing and expensive test equipment. "Our business was designing, educating, and marketing. I thought that Apple should do the least amount of work that it could and that it should let everyone else grow faster. Let the subcontractors have the problems."[43] The company handled board-stuffing (attaching the chips to the circuit boards) on a putting-out system before turning to a contract board-stuffing firm in San Jose; Scott even used a contractor for the firm's payroll.[44]

[41] For Wozniak's own account, see Gregg Williams and Rob Moore, "The Apple Story. Part 2: More History and the Apple III," *Byte*, Jan. 1985, 167–80. Peddle quoted in Moritz, *The Little Kingdom*, 210; see also Levering, Katz, and Moskowitz, *The Computer Entrepreneurs*, 101.

[42] Rifkin and Harrar, *The Ultimate Entrepreneur*, 194–95. On VisiCalc, see also Slater, *Portraits in Silicon*, 285–94, and Levering, Katz, and Moskowitz, *The Computer Entrepreneurs*, 128–33.

[43] Moritz, *The Little Kingdom*, 200–201.

[44] As of 1982, this firm, General Technology Corporation (GTC), remained the principal source of stuffed boards for the Apple II and III. In that year, Apple bought its floppy drives from Shugart and Alps; its hard drives from Seagate; its RAM and ROM chips from Mostek, Synertek, and NEC; and its monitors from Sanyo. The components that Apple made in-house included floppy and hard-drive controllers, the

External Economies and Economic Progress / 17

The Commodore PET, also introduced at the 1977 West Coast Computer Faire, shared with Apple the 6502 microprocessor. This is not entirely surprising, as the designer of the PET was Chuck Peddle, who was also the designer of the 6502. Commodore, a maker of calculators, had acquired Peddle's company, MOS Technology. Jack Tramiel, Commodore's aggressive founder, believed strongly in internal sourcing, and he wanted his own chip-making capability.[45] In a corridor one day in 1976, Peddle suggested to Tramiel that Commodore get into the computer business. Tramiel agreed, and Peddle readied a design based on the KIM-1, a 6502 machine he had designed to train microprocessor engineers. The result was the Commodore PET, which had much the same capabilities as the Apple, including a keyboard built into the case. Commodore never rivaled Apple, however, in part because the company was slow in shipping reliable product. Tramiel's insistence that Commodore use only internal MOS Technology chips caused delays and put him at odds with Peddle, who finally prevailed. More important, Tramiel chose to aim at the low or "home computer" end of the market. Commodore was, however, the most successful protagonist in that market, besting the likes of Texas Instruments, Atari, and Timex.[46]

The third important entrant in 1977 was Tandy Corporation. In 1962 Charles Tandy took the retail chain started by his father in a new direction: he purchased a small Boston-based chain of electronics stores called Radio Shack. By the early 1970s, Radio Shack had come to dominate the market for retail electronics. Although the company had begun some production of its own in 1966,

---

power supply, and the case—all legacies of capabilities that the company developed in its earliest years. These components were assembled into finished machines in plants in California, Texas, Ireland, and Singapore. (See Scott Mace, "Assembling Micros: They Will Sell No Apple before Its Time," *Infoworld*, 8 March 1982, 16.) Not until the Macintosh did Apple begin automated manufacturing (on which, see below), which essentially means an integration of the board-stuffing and other subcomponent-assembly stages into the final assembly stage. This approach was pioneered by Commodore, which had it in place by 1982. (Scott Mace, "Commodore Gives Assembly Plant Tour: Automatic Insertion Equipment Plays Major Manufacturing Role," *Infoworld*, 26 April 1982, 18.) Commodore was, however, an outlier in its adherence to a strategy of vertical integration.

[45] Susan Chace and Michael W. Miller, "Calculating Rival: Commodore's Tramiel Sharpens Competition in Small Computers," *The Wall Street Journal*, 18 Aug. 1983, 1.

[46] See, for example, David Stipp and G. Christian Hill, "Texas Instruments' Problems Show Pitfalls of Home-Computer Market," *The Wall Street Journal*, 17 June 1983, 29.

Richard N. Langlois / 18

Tandy was initially wary of making microcomputers.[47] A Radio Shack buyer named Don French became enamored of the Altair and began developing the idea of a computer for Radio Shack. In December 1976, he received a tentative go-ahead, with the injunction to "do it as cheaply as possible." With the help of Steve Leininger, an engineer who had worked for National Semiconductor, French designed the TRS-80 Model I, which appeared in August 1977. The machine used a Z80 microprocessor, but it ran a proprietary operating system rather than CP/M. It was also slow, lacked lower-case letters, and was genuinely cut-rate in other ways. Nonetheless, Radio Shacks sold 10,000 of the $399 machines in little more than a month.[48] In 1979, Tandy introduced the TRS-80 Model II, which overcame many of the limitations of the original; the TRS-80 Model III followed in 1980.

Growth and Technological Competition, 1978–1981 • For the next few years, Apple, Radio Shack, and Commodore became the top three makers of microcomputers. CP/M was not dead, however; smaller companies like Processor Technology and North Star continued to sell S-100 computers, and add-on boards soon became available to allow users of Apples, PETs, and TRS-80s to run CP/M software on their machines. This period was thus one of strong technological competition, with four major incompatible operating systems vying for position in the market.

The major arena of competition was software. VisiCalc, the first spreadsheet program, gave Apple a boost when it appeared in 1979 in an Apple version. The word processor was another important innovation, giving the microcomputer powers nearly equal to those of expensive stand-alone word processors. By the end of 1976, Michael Shrayer had created Electric Pencil, one of the very earliest word processors. It ran first on S-100 machines, but versions for the other major machines appeared quickly. In 1979, a group of former IMSAI employees at a company called MicroPro introduced WordStar. Unlike Electric Pencil, WordStar was a WYSIWYG (what you see is what you get) word processor. It

---

[47] Tandy had approached Millard of IMSAI about the possibility of selling the IMSAI 8080 in Radio Shack stores. About to start ComputerLand, Millard was not interested (Freiberger and Swaine, *Fire in the Valley*, 74). According to Levering, Katz, and Moskowitz, *The Computer Entrepreneurs*, 101, the Commodore PET was originally to be designed in cooperation with Radio Shack, but the deal fell through.

[48] Freiberger and Swaine, *Fire in the Valley*, 196–99; quote on 198. L. R. Shannon reports that the Model I sold for $599.95 and that Radio Shack shipped 3,000 by the end of 1977 ("A Decade's Progress," *The New York Times*, 6 Sept. 1987, C7).

External Economies and Economic Progress / 19

quickly became a bestseller and the industry standard.[49] In January 1981, Ashton-Tate introduced dBase II, a database management program that National Aeronautics and Space Administration engineer Wayne Ratliff had written in his spare time. It also soon became the industry leader.[50]

By mid-1981, then, the uses of the microcomputer were becoming clearer than they had been only a few years earlier, even if the full extent of the product space lay largely unmapped. A microcomputer was a system comprising a number of more-or-less standard elements: a microprocessor unit with 64K bytes of RAM memory; a keyboard, usually built into the system unit; one or two disk drives; a monitor; and a printer. The machine ran operating-system software and applications programs like word processors, spreadsheets, and database managers. The market was no longer primarily hobbyists but increasingly comprised businesses and professionals. Total sales were growing rapidly. CP/M, once the presumptive standard, was embattled, but no one operating system reigned supreme.

The Paradigm Emerges, 1981 • The emerging outline of a paradigmatic microcomputer gave Adam Osborne an idea: no frills computing.[51] Rather than pushing the technological frontier, he would create a package that was technologically adequate but also inexpensive. In this way, he could seek out, as it were, a local maximum in the product space. "The philosophy was that if 90 percent of users' needs were adequately covered, the remaining ten percent of the market could be sacrificed." Osborne wanted a machine integrated into one package that users could simply plug into the wall, "as they might a toaster."[52] Moreover, he wanted the machine to be portable and small enough to fit under an airline seat. And he wanted to ship a package of basic software "bundled" with the computer so that novice users would have most of what they needed immediately available.

Osborne set about attracting venture capital, and he engaged Lee Felsenstein, the organizer of the Homebrew Club and a consultant for recently defunct Processor Technology, to design the hardware. He acquired an unlimited license for CP/M from Digi-

[49] Freiberger and Swaine, *Fire in the Valley*, 147–48, 152–54.

[50] Levering, Katz, and Moskowitz, *The Computer Entrepreneurs*, 232–33.

[51] Freiberger and Swaine, *Fire in the Valley*, 259–63; Slater, *Portraits in Silicon*, 323–29; Levering, Katz, and Moskowitz, *The Computer Entrepreneurs*, 86–96. For Osborne's own account, see Osborne and Dvorak, *Hypergrowth*, passim.

[52] Osborne and Dvorak, *Hypergrowth*, 11.

Richard N. Langlois / 20

tal Research for $50,000, swapped stock with Microsoft for MBASIC, negotiated a deal with MicroPro for WordStar, and arranged for the development of a VisiCalc clone called Super-Calc. When the Osborne I appeared at the West Coast Computer Faire in March 1981, it had a five-inch screen, two low-density disk drives, a Z80 processor with 64K of memory, and bundled software. It sold for $1,795.

The Osborne I was the hit of the show. The company went from $6 million in sales in its first year to $70 million in its second and to $93 million in 1983. Osborne sold 10,000 units a month at the peak, and some 100,000 people owned one of its machines by 1984. This fantastic growth was matched, however, by an equally dramatic collapse and bankruptcy in 1984, the result of poor management decisions. A contributing factor was the quick rise of competitors. Morrow and Cromemco introduced Z80 machines for about the same price. And Non-Linear Systems, a southern California maker of sensing devices, introduced the Kaycomp II (later the Kaypro II) at the 1982 West Coast Faire. Conceived independently by Andrew Kay, Non-Linear's founder, the Kaypro, like the Osborne, was a Z80 portable with bundled software. Kay also shared Osborne's philosophy. "We don't sell half a computer and call it a computer and then ask a person to come back and buy the rest of it later," he is quoted as saying. "It's like selling an automobile without wheels or seats and saying, 'Those are options.' IBM, Apple, and Tandy play that kind of game. But we don't." Unlike the Osborne, however, the Kaypro had a sturdy metal case and a nine-inch screen with a full eighty-column display. Kaypro Corporation—as the company was rechristened—stepped in when Osborne stumbled and became the fourth largest seller of intermediate-price computers in 1984, reaching sales of $150–175 million that year.[53]

But the signal event of 1981 was not the advent of the cheap bundled portable. On 12 August 1981, IBM introduced the computer that would become the paradigm for most of the 1980s. Like the Osborne and the Kaypro, it was not technologically sophisticated, and it incorporated most of the basic features users expected. But, unlike the bundled portables, the IBM PC was a system, not an appliance: it was an incomplete package, an open box ready for expansion, reconfiguration, and continual upgrading.

[53] Levering, Katz, and Moskowitz, *The Computer Entrepreneurs*, 66, quote on 68.

External Economies and Economic Progress / 21

In July 1980, William Lowe met with IBM's Corporate Management Committee (CMC). John Opel, soon to become IBM's president, had charged Lowe with getting IBM into the market for desktop computers. Lowe's conclusion was a challenge to IBM's top management. "The only way we can get into the personal computer business," he told the CMC, "is to go out and buy part of a computer company, or buy both the CPU and software from people like Apple or Atari—because we can't do this within the culture of IBM."[54] The CMC knew that Lowe was right, but they were unwilling to put the IBM name on someone else's computer. So they gave Lowe an unprecedented mandate: go out and build an IBM personal computer with complete autonomy and no interference from the IBM bureaucracy. Lowe hand-picked a dozen engineers, and within a month they had produced a prototype. The committee approved and gave Lowe a deadline of one year to market.

The timing was critical. IBM sensed that Apple and its competitors were vulnerable: they were failing to capitalize on the developing business market for personal computers. But to get a machine to market quickly meant bypassing IBM's cumbersome system of bureaucratic checks and its heavy dependence on internal sourcing. Philip Donald Estridge, who succeeded Lowe as director of the project, put it this way: "We were allowed to develop like a startup company. IBM acted as a venture capitalist. It gave us management guidance, money, and allowed us to operate on our own."[55]

Estridge knew that, to meet the deadline, he would have to design a machine that was not at the cutting edge of technology. Moreover, IBM would have to make heavy use of outside vendors for parts and software. The owner of an Apple II, Estridge was also impressed by the importance of expandability and an open architecture.[56] He insisted that his designers use a modular bus system that would allow expandability, and he resisted all suggestions that the IBM team design any of its own add-ons.

The only decision implying anything like a technical advance in the IBM PC (personal computer) was the choice of the Intel

[54] James Chposky and Ted Leonsis, *Blue Magic: The People, Power and Politics behind the IBM Personal Computer* (New York, 1988), quote on 9.

[55] "How the PC Project Changed the Way IBM Thinks," *Business Week*, 3 Oct. 1983, 86.

[56] Chposky and Leonsis, *Blue Magic*, 34, 71; Freiberger and Swaine, *Fire in the Valley*, 274.

Richard N. Langlois / 22

8088 microprocessor. Although touted as a 16-bit chip—and thus an advance over the 8-bit 8080, Z80, and 6502—the 8088 processed data internally in 16-bit words but used 8-bit external buses.[57] The IBM team decided against the 8086, a full 16-bit chip, because they feared its power would raise the hackles of turf-protectors elsewhere in the company.[58] Moreover, the 8088 was perhaps the only 16-bit microprocessor for which there already existed a full complement of support chips.[59]

Choosing the 8088 microprocessor meant that the IBM PC could not use existing operating systems designed for 8-bit chips. Here again, IBM chose not to write its own proprietary system but to go on the market for a system. Estridge's group approached Digital Research, where Gary Kildall was working on a 16-bit version of CP/M. But IBM and Digital were unable to come to terms, probably because of Digital's initial unwillingness to sign the non-disclosure agreements on which IBM insisted.[60] So IBM turned instead to Microsoft, which they were already soliciting to supply a new version of MBASIC. Gates jumped at the chance. He bought an operating system for the 8088 created by a local Seattle software house, put the finishing touches on it, and sold it to IBM as MS-DOS (disk operating system).[61] IBM called its version PC-DOS, but it allowed Microsoft to license MS-DOS to other computer makers. Although this allowed competitors to enter, it also helped IBM to force its operating system as a standard on the industry.

Another radical departure from IBM tradition was the marketing of the PC. Shunning IBM's staff of commission sales agents, the PC group turned to retail outlets to handle the new machine: Sears Business Centers and ComputerLand. Here again, the project philosophy was to do things in keeping with the way they were done in the microcomputer industry—not with the way they were done at IBM. The PC group even solicited input from Com-

---

[57] Noyce and Hoff, "A History of Microprocessor Development at Intel," 15.

[58] Chposky and Leonsis, *Blue Magic*, 24.

[59] Robert X. Cringely, *Accidental Empires* (Reading, Mass., 1992), 131.

[60] Chposky and Leonsis, *Blue Magic*, 43–44; Freiberger and Swaine, *Fire in the Valley*, 272; Slater, *Portraits in Silicon*, 258–59; Levering, Katz, and Moskowitz, *The Computer Entrepreneurs*, 210.

[61] Chposky and Leonsis, *Blue Magic*, 50–53; Freiberger and Swaine, *Fire in the Valley*, 269–75; Slater, *Portraits in Silicon*, 268–69; Levering, Katz, and Moskowitz, *The Computer Entrepreneurs*, 159–60.

External Economies and Economic Progress / 23

puterLand dealers, flying a few to group headquarters in Boca Raton, Florida, for top-secret consultations.[62]

Perhaps the most striking way in which IBM relied on external capabilities, however, was in the actual fabrication of the PC. All parts were put up for competitive bids from outside suppliers. When internal IBM divisions complained, Estridge told them to their astonishment that they could submit bids like anyone else. With a little prodding, some IBM divisions did win contracts. The Charlotte, North Carolina, plant won a contract for board assembly, and the Lexington, Kentucky, plant made the keyboard. But an IBM plant in Colorado could not make quality disk drives, so Estridge turned to Tandon as the principal supplier. Zenith made the PC's power supply, SCI Systems stuffed the circuit boards, and Epson made the printer.[63] The machine was assembled from these components on an automated line at Boca Raton that by 1983 could churn out a PC every 45 seconds.[64]

The IBM PC was an instant success, exceeding sales forecasts by some 500 percent. The company shipped a mere 13,533 machines in the last four months of 1981, an amount far behind demand. Order backlogs became intolerable.[65] By 1983, the PC had captured 26 percent of the market, and an estimated 750,000 machines were installed by the end of that year.

The First Era of the Clones, 1982–1987 • The IBM PC called forth a legion of software developers and producers of add-on peripherals. Its early phenomenal success also generated competitors producing compatible machines. The first era of the clones falls into two distinct periods. The early manufacturers of clones fed on the excess demand for PCs, and, with one brilliant exception, these manufacturers disappeared when IBM began catching up with demand and lowered prices in 1983 and 1984. A second wave of clones began a few years later, when IBM abandoned 8088 technology in favor of the PC AT, which was built around the faster Intel 80286 chip.

IBM did have one trick up its sleeve to try to ward off cloners, but it turned out not to be a very powerful trick. The PC-DOS that Microsoft designed for the IBM PC differed slightly in its memory architecture from the generic MS-DOS that IBM allowed

---

[62] Littman, *Once Upon a Time*, 126.
[63] Chposky and Leonsis, *Blue Magic*, 88, 68.
[64] "Personal Computers: And the Winner Is IBM," *Business Week*, 3 Oct. 1983, 78.
[65] Chposky and Leonsis, *Blue Magic*, 24; Littman, *Once Upon a Time*, 156–57.

Richard N. Langlois / 24

Microsoft to license to others.[66] IBM chose to write some of the BIOS (basic input/output system, a part of DOS) into a chip and to leave some of it in software. They then published the design of the chip in a technical report, which, under copyright laws, copyrighted part of the PC-DOS BIOS. To make matters more difficult for cloners, many software developers, especially those using graphics, chose to bypass DOS completely and to access the PC's hardware directly. IBM sued Corona, Eagle, and a Taiwanese firm for infringing the BIOS copyright in their earliest models. These companies and all later cloners responded, however, with an end run. They contracted with software houses like Phoenix to create a software emulation (or sometimes a combination of hardware and software emulation) that does what the IBM BIOS does, but in a different way. The emulation is also able to intercept the hardware calls and to process them through the BIOS. This removed the last proprietary hurdle to copying the original PC.

Among the early cloners were Compaq, Corona, and Eagle. Compaq, which by the early 1990s had grown to become the third largest American seller of microcomputers, started out by combining the idea of Adam Osborne and Andrew Kay—transportability —with strict IBM compatibility and good quality control.[67] Started by two former Texas Instruments engineers, the company achieved $100 million sales in its first year, a plateau that Apple had taken four years to reach. Corona and Eagle fared less well, and they failed to survive the relative downturn in the computer market after 1984.[68]

Although IBM had become the dominant force in the personal computer industry, its dominance was by no means complete. In fact, by 1986 more than half of the IBM-compatible computers sold did not have IBM logos on them.[69] By 1988, IBM's worldwide market share of IBM-compatible computers was only 24.5 per-

[66] Lori Valigra, "Hardware Differences Can Make or Break the 50 IBM PC-Compatible Manufacturers," *Mini-Micro Systems* 17 (July 1984): 97.

[67] "How Compaq's Portable Leaped Ahead of the Pack," *Business Week*, 15 Aug. 1983, 89.

[68] After several years of growth rates for PCs and related products (like peripherals and software) averaging 62 percent per year, growth slowed to 15 percent in 1985 and to 18 percent in 1986. Brenton R. Schendler, "Bouncing Back: Personal Computers Lead Strong Rebound from Industry Slump," *The Wall Street Journal*, 24 April 1987, 1.

[69] IBM's share, in unit terms, of all MS-DOS computers shipped worldwide by vendors based in the United States fell to 48 percent in 1986 from 65 percent in 1985. Standard and Poor's Industry Surveys, 1 Oct. 1987, C91.

External Economies and Economic Progress / 25

cent.[70] The clones had returned. Part of the reason was price. IBM never practiced learning-curve pricing, preferring instead to take some of the premium that its name could command. It thus sacrificed potential market share for revenues. Some have also argued that IBM abandoned the 8088 technology prematurely.[71] But others contend that even IBM's moves upscale from the original PC—the PC XT in 1983 and the 80286 PC AT in 1984—represented no technological breakthroughs and left IBM a "sitting duck."[72] It is surely the case that IBM's choice of an open modular system was a two-edged sword that gave the company a majority stake in a standard that had grown well beyond its control.

What is especially interesting is the diversity of sources of these compatible machines. Many come from American manufacturers who sold under their own brand names. These included Compaq, Zenith, Tandy, and Kaypro, the latter two having dumped their incompatible lines in favor of complete IBM compatibility.[73] Another group consists of foreign manufacturers selling under their own brand names; the largest sellers among these are Epson and NEC of Japan and Hyundai of Korea.[74] But there is also a large OEM (original-equipment manufacturer) market, in which firms—typically Taiwanese or Korean, but sometimes American or European—manufacture PCs for resale under another brand name. The popular Leading Edge computer, for example, is made by Daewoo of Korea, which bought its American distributor out of bankruptcy.[75] Until recently, the AT&T PC was

[70] Dataquest, cited in William M. Bulkeley, "Clone Computer Business Is Booming," *The Wall Street Journal*, 7 Oct. 1988, B1.

[71] In 1984, Estridge made a controversial decision to focus IBM's attention exclusively on technology built around the Intel 80286 chip. The IBM PC AT, the IBM 286 machine, came out in August of that year. Chposky and Leonsis, *Blue Magic*, 171–72.

[72] Geoff Lewis et al., "The PC Wars: IBM Versus the Clones," *Business Week*, 28 July 1986, 64.

[73] Zenith has since been acquired by Groupe Bull of France, though its operations continue to be based in Illinois.

[74] Roberta Faletra, "NEC, Epson Seen Vying for Second-Tier Spot," *PC Week*, 26 Dec. 1988, 60.

[75] Richard March, "Daewoo Signs Deal to Take Over Leading Edge's PC Distribution," *PC Week*, 8 May 1989, 69.

Richard N. Langlois / 26

manufactured by Olivetti in Italy; the contract has now gone to Intel's Systems Division, which maintains a lively OEM business.[76]

But perhaps the most interesting phenomenon is the no-name clone—the PC assembled from an international cornucopia of standard parts and resold, typically through mail orders or storefronts. Because of the openness and modularity of the IBM PC and the dominance of its bus and software standards, a huge industry has emerged to manufacture compatible parts. The resulting competition has driven down prices in almost all areas. Most manufacturers, even the large branded ones, are really assemblers, and they draw heavily on the wealth of available vendors. But the parts are also available directly, and it is in fact quite easy to put together one's own PC from parts ordered from the back of a computer magazine. By one 1986 estimate, the stage of final assembly added only $10 to the cost of the finished machine—two hours' work for one person earning about $5 per hour.[77] Because the final product could be assembled this way for far less than the going price of name brands—especially IBM—a wealth of backroom operations sprang up. One such operation, begun from Michael Dell's dormitory room at the University of Texas, has grown into a business with revenues in the tens of millions of dollars.[78]

The parts list is truly international. Most boards come from Taiwan, stuffed with chips made in the United States (especially microprocessors and ROM BIOS), Japan, or Korea (especially memory chips). Hard disk drives come from the United States, but floppy drives come increasingly from Japan. A power supply might come from Taiwan or Hong Kong. The monitor might be Japanese, Taiwanese, or Korean. Keyboards might come from the United States, Taiwan, Japan, or even Thailand. Although Japan has been an ever-present fear in the American microcomputer industry, that country's success in PCs has not paralleled its well-known success in some other areas of electronics. Apart from laptop computers, the biggest Japanese sellers are NEC at the high end, with a 5.1 percent market share in 1988, and low-end Epson, with a 4.1

[76] Richard L. Hudson and Laura Colby, "AT&T, Olivetti End Partnership Dating Since 1983," *The Wall Street Journal*, 17 July 1989, A3. On Intel, see Lawrence M. Fisher, "Intel: Supplier Rising As a Big Competitor," *The New York Times*, 14 Feb. 1990, D1.

[77] Lewis et al., "The PC Wars," 64.

[78] Geoff Lewis, "The Hottest Little Computer Maker in Texas," *Business Week*, 2 Feb. 1987, 71.

External Economies and Economic Progress / 27

percent share.[79] The biggest foreign players are in fact Taiwan and Korea, countries with dramatically different industry structures.

Taiwan entered the computer business much earlier than Korea. By the late 1970s, the island had become the manufacturing epicenter of a network of low-cost—and illegal—clones.[80] The principal target was the Apple II; but, fed with Taiwanese and other parts, the computer bazaars of Hong Kong could also supply S-100 machines and, in the early 1980s, IBM PC clones. Although there were attempts to export these clones outside the Far East— attempts that met with swift legal action from American firms— most of the clone buyers were local amateurs and business people who could not have afforded the real thing. A side-effect of this industry, then, was to open up the Far East, and especially Taiwan, to the microcomputer and to microcomputer technology. In effect, the years of piracy built up capabilities in the Taiwanese economy that soon could be—and were—directed toward making legal IBM clones and related equipment for export to the Far East, Europe, and the United States. As is apparently traditional in Taiwan, firms like Acer (formerly Multitech) and Mitac are closely held companies that draw for engineering talent on American-trained Taiwanese. Although frequently heavy-handed, the Taiwanese government in this case restricted itself to offering a few generic research and development and coordination services.[81] The leading Taiwanese firm is Acer, which uses the same automated assembly techniques as American firms like Compaq to produce OEM clones for the likes of Unisys, Canon, Siemens, and Philips. Acer also sells under its own brand name; in fact, Texas Instruments makes Acer machines under license in the United States. The company pours about 5 percent of revenues back into R&D, is making a move into high-end work stations, and has begun investing in American firms.[82]

In sharp contrast to the decentralized and entrepreneurial Taiwanese industry, Korea has entered the microcomputer

---

[79] Faletra, "NEC, Epson Seen Vying."

[80] "High-Tech Entrepreneurs Create a Silicon Valley in Taiwan," *Business Week*, 1 Aug. 1983, 34; Daniel Burstein, "The Asian Micro Pirates," *Datamation*, 15 May 1984, 123.

[81] Danny K. K. Lam and Ian Lee, "Guerilla Capitalism and the Limits of Statist Theory: Comparing the Chinese NICs," in *The Evolving Pacific Basin in the Global Political Economy*, ed. Cal Clark and Steve Chan (Boulder, Colo., 1992), 107–124.

[82] David E. Sanger, "PC Powerhouse (Made in Taiwan)," *The New York Times*, 28 Sept. 1989, D1.

Richard N. Langlois / 28

business—as so many other businesses—within the context of a handful of large, vertically integrated firms. Impressed by the model of Japan's industrialization, Korea has attempted to build capabilities in a conscious, directed way within large organizations. The large conglomerates—Hyundai, Daewoo, Samsung, and Gold Star—have all invested heavily in technology to fabricate their own DRAMs and some other chips, with considerable help from the Korean government.[83] The firms have waited until the technology matured and have gone after the low end in microcomputers. The most successful has probably been Daewoo, which provided the OEM machines for Michael Shane's Leading Edge Hardware Products. The combination of Shane's marketing with the Koreans' low-cost manufacture and competent design made the Leading Edge the single most popular clone of the original IBM PC for most of the 1980s. Recently, however, Hyundai, which is the only Korean firm to sell under its own name rather than on an OEM basis, has edged Daewoo in the American market. Korean success has not been universal, however. In some areas Korean firms have been hampered by the lack of (external) technical capabilities. In printers, for example, the inability to manufacture critical parts (notably the printhead) and certain key chips has forced the firms to import most of the printer's components and robbed them of any cost advantage. Another area is disk drives. Because of its strategy of developing internal capabilities, and "unlike Taiwan, which has a large number of small specialized firms, Korea lacks an industrial base necessary to make electromechanical parts, such as disk drive mechanisms."[84]

The Victory of the Clones • The era of the clones is by no means over. Clone makers quickly followed IBM upscale to copy machines using Intel's 80286 and 80386 chips. Indeed, manufacturers of compatibles have begun beating IBM to the punch in introducing new technology. It was Compaq, for example, that introduced the first machine based around the Intel 80386 chip;

---

[83] Langlois et al., *Microelectronics*, 45.

[84] Richard March, "Hyundai, Samsung Stalk Retail Market, Wielding 8088, '286 PCs, DRAM Chips," *PC Week*, 5 Dec. 1988, 55. This ignores Tandy's Korean subsidiary, which was the largest Korean exporter of PCs to the United States in 1985. Quote from Minora Inabu, "Korea to Supply IBM-Like 16-Bit PCs to U.S. OEMs," *Electronic News*, 15 April 1985. On the differences between Taiwan and Korea, see also Brian Levy and Wen-Jeng Kuo, "The Strategic Orientations of Firms and the Performance of Korea and Taiwan in Frontier Industries: Lessons from Comparative Studies of Keyboard and Personal Computer Assembly," *World Development* 19 (April 1991): 363–74.

External Economies and Economic Progress / 29

they also produced a machine using the 80486 chip before IBM did.[85] IBM's response, after a record with more failures than successes, was to begin making the PC proprietary again.[86]

In April 1987, IBM announced its PS/2 line of computers. These machines offered a streamlined design, smaller high-density disk drives, and integrated functions, like high-resolution graphics, that had previously required add-on boards. The higher-end machines, based around the 80286 and the 32-bit 80386 chips, used a new proprietary bus called the Micro Channel Architecture (MCA). The original IBM PC had established an 8-bit industry bus standard, and the PC AT had established a new standard 16-bit bus called the Industry Standard Architecture (ISA). Though still serviceable for most uses, the AT standard was no longer optimal for high-speed 386 and 486 machines. In announcing the Micro Channel, IBM was attempting not only to set the standard, but also to prevent others from taking advantage of it. Nine of the major clone makers, with some nudges from Intel and Microsoft, quickly banded together to announce development of a competing 32-bit bus to be called the Extended Industry Standard Architecture (EISA) bus.[87]

This development led many to expect a protracted, and perhaps fierce, battle of the standards. Essentially, however, no such battle has emerged. The ISA (and to a lesser extent the EISA) standard is perhaps even stronger today than in its early years. IBM continues to sell MCA machines almost exclusively, but has lost market share in doing so. Very few MCA clones appeared,

[85] Bro Uttal and Christopher Knowlton, "Compaq Bids for PC Leadership," *Fortune*, 29 Sept. 1986, 30; Peter H. Lewis, "Compaq Redefines the High End," *The New York Times*, 7 Nov. 1989, C14; Andy Zipser, "Compaq Rolls Out Personal Computers, Claims They Challenge Minicomputers," *The Wall Street Journal*, 7 Nov. 1989, B4. IBM did offer a 486 add-on board for its PS/2 Model 70 a few months earlier.

[86] The successes were the PC XT in 1983 and the PC AT in 1984. The failures include the infamous PC Jr., an attempt at the home computer market; the PC portable in 1984; a work station called the RT PC in 1986; and the PC convertible, a laptop, also in 1986. For a chronology of IBM product introductions, see Chposky and Leonsis, *Blue Magic*, 220–22. Some have described this move as resulting from the pull of IBM's mainframe legacy, which outweighed the lessons learned in the development of the original PC. (William Zachmann, "IBM Is Pulling the PC Back to Mainframe Legacy," *PC Week*, 19 Dec. 1988, 9.)

[87] Paul B. Carroll and Michael W. Miller, "High-Tech War: Nine Firms That Make Personal Computers Gang Up Against IBM," *The Wall Street Journal*, 14 Sept. 1988, 1. The "gang of nine" are Compaq, AST, Epson, Hewlett-Packard, NEC, Olivetti, Tandy, Wyse, and Zenith. EISA is compatible with existing AT add-on cards, but the Micro Channel is not.

Richard N. Langlois / 30

although most manufacturers had the capabilities to make them. IBM's attempt to take the PC proprietary was at best a mixed success. The company was able to trade on its name and reputation to take rents for awhile, selling high-priced machines to corporate customers and others seeking reliability over price and performance. But the passage of time, along with an increasing price-performance gap between IBM and its competitors, soon persuaded more and more corporate customers to buy clones. Newcomers like Dell, AST, Packard Bell, CompuAdd, Gateway 2000, Northgate, and Zeos have gained sales through aggressive pricing—increasingly including sales to corporate buyers.[88] The thickness and competitiveness of the market for components not only drove down PC prices, but also increased reliability. Now a mail-order clone house could credibly offer better service than a big-name manufacturer simply by shipping overnight replacement parts to be swapped by the PC owner. This reduced the rents to a name brand. Moreover, experience with clones diffused through the user population, further reducing the advantages of a brand.[89]

IBM's response has been to cut prices. IBM is undergoing a massive restructuring in response to problems that go well beyond its PC business. The company is selling off divisions and turning others into autonomous units. In effect, IBM is attempting to respond to a changing market with large-scale vertical disintegration.[90]

Ironically, one of the major victims in the victory of the low-cost clones has been Compaq, one of the first clones. Compaq had developed a strategy of competing against IBM on price and performance. Like IBM, Compaq targeted the corporate customer who was willing to pay a premium for reputation, the latest technology, and a hand-holding sales force of exclusive dealers. By 1991, Compaq had been badly wounded by its lower-priced com-

[88] "Dell Aims for the Big Leagues," *The New York Times*, 21 July 1991, F5; Paul M. Eng, "Businesses Are Buying More Clones," *Business Week*, 29 July 1991, 68D; Neal Templin, "PC Price Dive Drags Down Big Players," *The Wall Street Journal*, 8 Nov. 1991, B1; "Cut to the Quick," *The Economist*, 27 March 1992, 76; Michael Allen, "Low-Cost PC Makers Have Come on Strong But Difficulties Loom," *The Wall Street Journal*, 11 May 1992, A1.

[89] Peter H. Lewis, "Personal Computers: Behind the Price Cuts," *The New York Times*, 28 May 1991, C9.

[90] Laurence Hooper, "IBM Plans Revamps, Hints at Price Cuts," *The Wall Street Journal*, 19 April 1991, B1; John Markoff, "I.B.M. Will Change in Effort to Keep Market Dominance," *The New York Times*, 27 Nov. 1991, A1; Evelyn Richards, "Turning IBM Around," *The Washington Post*, 24 Nov. 1991.

External Economies and Economic Progress / 31

petitors. What had been a small start-up firm found itself weighed down by high-cost internal production and bureaucratic purchasing.[91] Compaq's response has been to reorient itself toward the external economies of the market—in a way, indeed, that bears a remarkable similarity to IBM's strategy for the original PC. Compaq's chairman, Benjamin Rosen, sent executives incognito to Comdex, the computer trade fair, and discovered that the company could buy parts in the market and assemble a PC for far less than Compaq's own internal production costs. Taiwanese circuit boards, for example, cost some 30 percent less than Compaq's production cost. The company set up an independent business unit—called the Ruby project—to make a low-cost machine and gave the unit autonomy and the right to bypass internal purchasing procedures. Compaq's internal divisions were not guaranteed contracts and won the rights to produce some components only after lowering their costs substantially—drawing in part on lessons learned by Compaq executives while touring the facilities of outside suppliers.[92]

Apple, with its incompatible line of computers, has also felt price pressure recently.[93] In order to appreciate Apple's position today, we need to back up in time.

Thriving on continued strong sales of the Apple II, Apple survived some disastrous product development efforts in the late 1970s and early 1980s. I will treat these, especially the Apple III, in more detail later. In the late 1970s, Steven Jobs, who had left the Apple III project and was spearheading development of another new machine, paid a reluctant visit to the Xerox Palo Alto Research Center (PARC), where researchers had been developing advanced new ideas for microcomputers.[94] There Jobs saw bit-mapped graphics, overlapping windows, and a pointing control device called a mouse. He went back to Apple and incorporated much of what he saw into the Lisa, which appeared in January 1983. The new machine was expensive ($10,000), slow, and lacked software; it was not in fact much more of a success commercially than the disastrous Apple III. But it set Apple on a new strategic

---

[91] Peter H. Lewis, "Why Compaq Is Getting Down in the Trenches," *The New York Times,* 17 Nov. 1991, sec. 3, 8.

[92] Michael Allen, "Developing New Line of Low-Priced PCs Shakes Up Compaq," *The Wall Street Journal,* 15 June 1991, 1.

[93] "Apple and Dell Cut Prices of Computers," *The New York Times,* 5 Feb. 1992, D4.

[94] Moritz, *The Little Kingdom,* 289–301.

Richard N. Langlois / 32

course: the technological high road. In January 1984, the Macintosh appeared, containing most of the Lisa's features in a less expensive package. The Mac still was not much of a business machine, lacking software and the large memory that IBM users expected. But its novelty won it a following, and John Sculley, who became president of Apple in 1983 and eventually ousted Jobs in 1985, worked to upgrade the Mac into a capable business machine.[95] The company introduced the Macintosh Plus in January 1986 and the Macintosh SE and a high-end machine called the Macintosh II in 1987. By pushing the Mac's desktop publishing capabilities, Apple insinuated itself into the large and medium-sized corporations it had previously neglected. Employees impressed with the Mac's ease of use soon began using the machine for tasks beyond desktop publishing in competition with IBM-compatible machines.

Sculley's reorientation of the Mac line toward business had the effect of spurring a partial convergence toward the IBM standard. The Mac can now read and write to IBM-formatted diskettes, and the Mac II is a modular machine that can use some of the same kinds of parts—such as high-resolution color monitors—as the IBM-compatibles. From their side, IBM and its cohorts have been moving in Macintosh directions as well. Newer IBM-compatibles increasingly sport a mouse, and software writers routinely use overlapping windows and icons. In the summer of 1990, Microsoft introduced version 3.0 of its Windows software, a "graphical user interface" that gives IBM-compatibles some of the "look and feel" of a Mac. And dual-version software, like the word-processing program Microsoft Word, make for "portability" between, for example, an IBM at work and a Mac at home.

One effect of this partial convergence of the Macintosh and IBM standards is that the decreasing cost and increasing power and reliability of ISA clones have drawn Apple away from its niche strategy and into mainstream price competition. In late 1990, Apple introduced a low-priced version of the Mac called the Classic, priced at under $1,000. On the whole, Apple has fared well, holding market share over the years and occasionally eclipsing IBM's share.[96]

[95] Brenton R. Schendler, "Calculated Move: Apple Computer Tries to Achieve Stability but Remain Creative," *The Wall Street Journal*, 16 July 1987, 1.

[96] Andrew Pollack, "A Quirky Loner Goes Mainstream," *The New York Times*, 14 July 1991, sec. 3, 1. In 1988, Apple held a 12.9 percent share of the market, edging

External Economies and Economic Progress / 33

Table 1 presents a portrait of the microcomputer industry from 1980 through 1991. Market shares are based on units sold rather than on dollar value, and the table includes makers of low-end "home" computers as well as business-oriented PCs. Nonetheless, the table suggests both the rapid change in the industry and the declining market share of the leading producers. Table 2 presents the top PC manufacturers for various years, with their (declining) share of the market.

Toward a Standard, Modular Future? • Underlying the partial convergence of the Macintosh and the IBM standard is the trend toward greater power—faster execution and more RAM and disk memory. A typical high-end configuration today might be an IBM-compatible machine using an Intel 80486 microprocessor running at 33 or 50 megahertz.[97] The machine might have eight megabytes of internal memory and a 150-megabyte hard drive. Such computers are beginning to challenge the power of scientific work stations made by the likes of Sun Microsystems and Hewlett-Packard, who have themselves greatly eroded the business of traditional mini-computer makers like DEC and Data General.[98] It seems clear that the future of the personal computer lies in higher-power chips, probably 64-bit microprocessors using the reduced instruction set (RISC) architecture, which is incompatible with the Intel and Motorola chips now in use. The standard for the future is thus up for grabs, and coalitions of players are already positioning themselves for battle.

Perhaps the most significant development is the alliance between IBM and Apple signed on 3 October 1991.[99] In the short run, these two former adversaries will develop both a common hardware platform and an operating system. The hardware will revolve around an inexpensive version of IBM's RS/6000 chip, to be produced by Motorola in a joint venture. These chips will power the next generation of Macintosh computers. The operating

---

IBM's 12.5 share. (Dataquest, cited in "Who Sells the Most PCs in the U.S.? Not Whom You Think," *Business Week*, 5 June 1989, 118E.) These are U.S. shares, not worldwide shares, and are thus not directly comparable to the data in Table 1.

[97] The original IBM PC ran at 4.77 MHz. Clock speed does not translate directly into the functional speed of a machine for particular tasks, but it is a good proxy.

[98] John Markoff, "In an Age When Tiny Is All, Big Computers Are Hurting," *The New York Times*, 4 April 1989, 1; Allan R. Gold, "Computer Changes Jolt Route 128," *The New York Times*, 11 Aug. 1989, D1.

[99] Andrew Pollack, "I.B.M. Now Apple's Main Ally," *The New York Times*, 13 Oct. 1991, sec. 3, 8.

Richard N. Langlois / 34

Table 1
Worldwide Market Share of Personal Computers by Company, 1980-1991
(percent of units shipped)

Company	1980	1981	1982	1983	1984	1985	1986	1987	1988	1989	1990	1991
Acer	0.00	0.00	0.00	0.00	0.00	0.00	0.00	0.72	1.32	0.94	0.68	1.23
ALR	0.00	0.00	0.00	0.00	0.00	0.00	0.00	0.00	0.00	0.00	0.61	0.37
AST	0.00	0.00	0.00	0.00	0.00	0.00	0.00	0.49	0.90	1.46	1.14	1.63
AT&T	0.00	0.00	0.00	0.00	0.19	1.20	1.46	1.00	0.57	0.41	0.65	0.40
Acorn	0.00	0.00	2.94	1.97	2.97	2.00	0.73	0.32	0.28	0.16	0.25	0.20
Amstrad	—	—	—	—	—	—	5.91	8.00	3.93	2.57	1.32	1.02
Apple	13.55	13.55	7.25	6.95	8.94	7.87	7.82	9.05	9.22	7.42	7.45	9.05
Apricot	0.00	0.00	0.00	0.03	0.36	0.50	0.80	0.12	0.15	0.12	0.20	0.12
Atari	4.19	4.54	4.95	6.43	5.36	2.64	3.73	5.13	4.49	4.24	3.06	2.05
Commodore	12.99	12.82	18.39	23.94	19.41	13.23	11.44	9.69	8.46	8.07	7.06	8.32
Compaq	0.00	0.00	0.00	0.49	0.95	1.53	1.84	2.40	2.75	3.05	3.91	3.99
CompuAdd	0.00	0.00	0.00	0.00	0.00	0.00	0.00	0.00	0.49	0.46	0.58	0.57
Corona	0.00	0.00	0.00	0.10	0.47	0.60	0.00	0.00	0.00	0.00	0.00	0.00
Dell	0.00	0.00	0.00	0.00	0.00	0.00	0.00	0.54	0.58	0.56	0.56	0.99
Digital (DEC)	0.00	0.00	0.16	0.77	0.65	0.76	0.43	0.12	0.09	0.13	0.19	0.19
Epson	0.00	0.06	0.16	0.47	0.38	0.86	1.57	1.68	2.06	2.58	2.47	1.17
Everex	0.00	0.00	0.00	0.00	0.00	0.00	0.00	0.00	0.19	0.41	0.48	0.81
Fujitsu	0.00	2.15	2.07	1.58	1.95	2.43	2.18	1.03	0.83	0.61	0.58	0.78
HP	1.26	1.41	0.81	0.48	0.86	1.10	0.82	0.92	1.19	1.18	1.22	1.10
Hyundai	0.00	0.00	0.00	0.00	0.00	0.00	0.00	0.12	0.63	0.62	1.10	1.08
IBM	0.00	1.06	3.23	5.34	12.03	16.10	12.32	12.82	11.24	11.15	11.85	11.38[a]
IBM Japan	0.00	0.00	0.00	0.09	0.25	1.21	0.60	0.48	0.50	0.66	0.59	—
Kaypro	0.00	0.00	0.29	0.83	0.70	0.81	0.66	0.65	0.18	0.09	0.07	0.00
Leading Edge	0.00	0.00	0.00	0.00	0.14	0.28	1.42	1.63	0.36	0.07	0.32	0.39

Continued overleaf

Table 1 continued

Mitac	0.00	0.00	0.00	0.00	0.00	0.00	0.00	0.15	0.63	0.62	0.77	0.75
NCR	0.00	0.00	0.00	0.07	0.36	0.59	0.71	0.84	0.71	0.44	0.55	0.46
NEC	4.60	4.49	5.27	3.90	3.25	4.10	5.30	5.01	4.81	5.37	5.61	5.81
North Star	0.67	0.41	0.29	0.17	0.17	0.13	0.01	0.00	0.00	0.00	0.00	0.00
Olivetti	0.00	0.00	0.39	0.54	0.83	0.89	1.74	2.29	2.29	2.50	1.90	1.73
Osborne	0.00	0.48	2.36	0.33	0.11	0.13	0.03	0.00	0.00	0.00	0.00	0.00
Packard Bell	0.00	0.00	0.00	0.00	0.00	0.00	0.00	0.66	0.83	2.06	2.16	2.46
Panasonic	0.14	0.24	0.33	0.31	0.43	0.65	1.11	0.19	0.34	0.39	0.37	0.33
Philips	0.00	0.18	0.17	0.17	0.32	0.53	0.18	0.05	0.69	0.82	0.78	0.55
Samsung	0.00	0.00	0.00	0.00	0.00	0.00	0.00	0.00	0.14	0.17	1.17	1.15
Sanyo	0.00	0.00	0.64	0.61	1.12	1.54	1.85	0.97	0.73	0.67	0.69	0.17
Sharp	4.89	4.29	2.28	1.30	1.21	1.31	1.52	0.55	0.86	0.56	0.56	0.39
Sinclair	14.67	23.89	11.60	7.56	10.23	8.33	1.78	0.00	0.00	0.00	0.00	0.00
Tandon	0.00	0.00	0.00	0.00	0.00	0.00	0.37	0.86	1.09	1.13	0.87	0.74
Tandy	23.05	12.76	5.92	4.09	6.39	6.51	3.95	4.13	3.20	2.66	2.65	1.91
Texas Instr.	2.10	1.81	13.88	13.24	0.55	0.40	0.26	0.03	0.02	0.00	0.07	0.21
Timex	0.00	0.00	4.45	1.45	0.35	0.00	0.00	0.00	0.00	0.00	0.00	0.00
Toshiba	0.84	1.15	0.70	0.57	0.63	0.84	0.56	1.44	1.22	2.77	3.68	2.03
Unisys (Sperry)	0.00	0.00	0.00	0.00	0.35	0.46	0.63	0.78	0.46	0.60	0.52	0.36
Victor	0.00	0.00	0.71	1.03	0.28	0.34	0.42	0.53	0.64	0.58	0.54	0.37
Wang	0.00	0.00	0.06	0.26	0.57	0.69	0.88	0.48	0.44	0.39	0.36	0.46
Wyse	0.00	0.00	0.00	0.00	0.00	0.00	0.05	0.44	0.86	0.60	0.56	0.39
Xerox	0.00	1.39	0.60	0.25	0.13	0.20	0.19	0.00	0.00	0.00	0.00	0.00
Zenith												
(Groupe Bull)	1.54	1.03	0.54	0.36	0.53	0.75	1.37	2.68	2.93	2.86	1.84	1.87
Others	15.51	12.29	9.56	14.32	16.58	18.49	23.36	22.22	28.92	30.25	30.44	45.63

Source: Dataquest
*Includes IBM Japan

Richard N. Langlois / 36

Table 2
Market Leaders, Selected Years
(percent of units shipped worldwide)

1981		1983		1985		1987		1989		1991	
Sinclair	23.89	Com.	23.94	IBM	16.10	IBM	12.82	IBM	11.15	IBM	11.38
Apple	13.55	TI	13.24	Com.	13.23	Com.	9.69	Com.	8.07	Apple	9.05
Com.	12.82	Sinclair	7.56	Sinclair	8.33	Apple	9.05	Apple	7.42	Com.	8.32
Tandy	12.76	Apple	6.95	Apple	7.87	Amstrad	8.00	NEC	5.37	NEC	5.81
Atari	4.54	Atari	6.43	Tandy	6.51	Atari	5.13	Atari	4.24	Compaq	3.99
NEC	4.49	IBM	5.34	NEC	4.10	NEC	5.01	Compaq	3.05	Packard B	2.46
Sharp	4.29	Tandy	4.09	Atari	2.64	Tandy	4.13	Zenith	2.86	Atari	2.05
Fujitsu	2.15	NEC	3.90	Fujitsu	2.43	Zenith	2.68	Toshiba	2.77	Toshiba	2.03
TI	1.81	Fujitsu	1.58	Acorn	2.00	Compaq	2.40	Tandy	2.66	Tandy	1.91
HP	1.41	Timex	1.45	Sanyo	1.54	Olivetti	2.29	Epson	2.58	Zenith	1.87
Others	12.29	Others	14.32	Others	18.49	Others	22.22	Others	30.25	Others	45.63

Source: Dataquest

External Economies and Economic Progress / 37

system will be a version of IBM's AIX operating system (a version of the UNIX system developed by AT&T for minicomputers and work stations), adapted to the Macintosh user interface. Thus both the Mac and IBM's RS/6000 work stations could run the same software. For the longer run, IBM and Apple have formed a joint venture called Taligent to develop an object-oriented operating system based on an Apple project called Pink. The goal is to write an operating system to be called Power Open that will allow the RS/6000 PC—as it is now being touted—to run software written for any operating system, including the Mac, Windows, or IBM's OS/2.[100]

The IBM-Apple alliance is in many ways a response to the dominance of Intel chips and the Microsoft standard in the current PC market. In most minds, it is Microsoft, not IBM, that is the dominant force in microcomputers today.[101] Microsoft banded together with DEC, Compaq, and a large number of smaller PC makers in the Advanced Computing Environment (ACE) consortium to develop next-generation hardware and software standards. The hardware was to be built around RISC chips from Mips Computer Systems, and the operating system was to allow "interoperability" between Intel-based PCs and MIPS RISC work stations. The consortium has felt the difficulties of collective action, however, and its ability to forge a standard is not clear. DEC has developed its own RISC chip, the Alpha, and Microsoft has endorsed it. Other consortium members are attracted to Intel's P5 chip.[102]

Whatever happens, however, it is clear that all players have abandoned a proprietary strategy. All recognize that an open standard, for both hardware and software, is inevitable, and the strategic issues are ones of placement within a mostly nonproprietary world.

[100] Peter H. Lewis, "The Brave New World of I.B.M. and Apple," *The New York Times*, 13 Oct. 1991, sec. 3, 8.

[101] John Markoff, "An Unlikely Underdog," *The New York Times*, 31 March 1992, D1.

[102] "New Alliances Promise to Reshape Desktop," *Electronic Business*, 8 July 1991, 28; Robert D. Hof, "Why ACE May Be in the Hole: The Attempt at a Computer Standard Has Grown Unwieldy," *Business Week*, 17 Feb. 1992, 132; Glenn Rifkin, "Digital's Chip of the Next Century," *The New York Times*, 25 Feb. 1992; Craig Stedman, "DEC, Microsoft Ink PC Software Deal," *Electronic News*, 27 April 1992, 6; Cate Corcoran, "Intel's P5 Erodes Support for RISC: Key ACE Members Abandon MIPS Platform in the Face of Intel Challenge," *InfoWorld*, 11 May 1992, 23.

Richard N. Langlois / 38

External Economies and the Microcomputer Industry

Although dependent on, and in many ways driven by, economies internal to the semiconductor industry, the rapid growth and development of the microcomputer industry is largely a story of external economies. It is a story of the development of capabilities within the context of a decentralized market rather than within large vertically integrated firms. Indeed, the microcomputer industry represents, in many ways, a case quite exactly opposite to the picture of economic progress that Chandler paints in *Scale and Scope*.

In Chandler's story, a small number of prime movers—who are not necessarily the industry pioneers—seize a dominant, oligopolistic position by making large investments in high-volume production and marketing and in a managerial hierarchy. But it is not clear that there were any such Chandlerian prime movers in the microcomputer industry.[103] One candidate is Apple. With its effective compromise between technology and marketing—a combination typical of prime movers—Apple helped define the personal computer and staked an early dominant position. That position was soon eroded, of course, by IBM and the standard it created—also a situation not atypical for prime movers. IBM might be another candidate. It also combined adequate technology and marketing, aided by its enormous reputation, which was probably the only internal economy of scope IBM brought to bear in the making of the original PC. But IBM's position in the microcomputer industry, though arguably dominant, is scarcely oligopolistic, and it is certainly not dominant in the way most of Chandler's prime movers became dominant. Moreover, as I have argued, internal economies of mass production were never important in this industry, and IBM did not maintain a cost advantage, if it ever had one. What about Microsoft? One could easily argue that Microsoft is indeed the dominant first mover in the microcomputer industry. The firm did invest heavily in marketing and distribution. And it probably does benefit from internal economies of

---

[103] This is contrary to what Chandler implies in "Organizational Capabilities and the Economic History of the Industrial Enterprise," *Journal of Economic Perspectives* 6 (Summer 1992): 97.

External Economies and Economic Progress / 39

scope in software development.[104] But, although it certainly has a managerial hierarchy, it is still managed by its founder, who by all accounts practices what is clearly a form of personal capitalism. Moreover, Microsoft does not have anything like high-volume throughput, nor is it vertically integrated in any degree. It would be odd indeed for the only Chandlerian first mover in the microcomputer industry to produce no microcomputers.

There are, I think, a number of reasons for the relative unimportance of internal economies in the microcomputer industry.

1) The size, diversity, rapid development, and unknown character of the market for microcomputers meant that no single organization could develop the necessary capabilities with anything like the speed that those capabilities could develop in a decentralized market. Henry Ford was forced to integrate vertically because the external markets could not create new capabilities as fast as he could.[105] But IBM was forced to disintegrate almost completely to make the original PC because the company could not create capabilities nearly as fast as the market could. Moreover, the existing level of mass production capabilities available through the market in the worldwide electronics industry is extremely high. It is significant that much of Chandler's story takes place in the nineteenth and early twentieth centuries, precisely as mass production was being developed by the very first movers that Chandler discusses. Once the idea of mass production has had time to diffuse into the economy, however, firms no longer need to develop those capabilities themselves and therefore need far less vertical integration.[106]

2) Microcomputers are not appliances—in the way toasters are appliances—but are modular systems. This is not because of any technological necessity, but because modularity allows for a minute and well-coordinated division of labor in the market, which in turn allows for the rapid creation of new capabilities. The most successful machines—like the Apple II and the IBM PC—were the most modular.

3) The decentralized network of firms and users in the microcomputer industry allowed for a diversity of approaches and led to

[104] On the concept of economies of scope in software development, see Michael A. Cusumano, *Japan's Software Factories: A Challenge to U.S. Management* (New York, 1991), esp. 8.

[105] Langlois and Robertson, "Exploring Vertical Integration."

[106] Langlois, "Transaction Costs"; Morris Silver, *Enterprise and the Scope of the Firm* (London, 1984).

Richard N. Langlois / 40

rapid trial-and-error learning. This decentralized learning system was in many ways a substitute for the government-sponsored university research—another kind of learning system—that had spawned the earlier mainframe and minicomputer industries. Moreover, the modularity of the microcomputer made such innovation autonomous and thus allowed the division of labor to focus and drive innovation.

Internal Versus External Capabilities • We have already examined the case of the original IBM PC in some detail. It is tempting to attribute the success of that machine merely to the power of IBM's name. Although the name was no doubt of some help, especially in forcing MS-DOS as a standard operating system, there are enough counterexamples to suggest that it was the machine itself—and IBM's approach to developing it—that must take the credit. Almost all other large firms, many with nearly IBM's prestige, failed miserably in the PC business. The company that Apple and the other early computer makers feared most was not IBM but Texas Instruments, a power in integrated circuits and systems (notably electronic calculators).[107] But TI flopped by entering at the low end, seeing the PC as akin to a calculator rather than as a multipurpose professional machine. When TI did enter the business market in the wake of the IBM PC, its TI Professional also failed, because the company refused to make the machine fully IBM-compatible. Xerox entered the market with a Z80 machine that—in 1981—was too little too late. Hewlett-Packard was also slow, offering an expensive closed-system machine with a 32-column display and cassette drive as late as 1980.[108] But the two cases on which I want to focus are the failures of DEC and Apple.

The similarities in the histories of the ill-fated DEC Professional series and the Apple III are striking. Both projects were pushed by a charismatic company founder with perfectionist demands and an intense interest in the aesthetics of the computer's design, even down to its case. Both companies tried to design from scratch a machine that was idiosyncratic, incompatible, and proprietary. And both companies neglected third-party capabilities, especially software developers.

DEC is the second largest computer maker in the world, and the largest maker of minicomputers. The company was committed

---

[107] Moritz, *The Little Kingdom*, 228.
[108] On Xerox and HP, see Freiberger and Swaine, *Fire in the Valley*, 264–68.

External Economies and Economic Progress / 41

to a strategy of filling out its line of VAX minicomputers and, more broadly, to the idea of terminal-based time-share computing. In 1980, however, DEC president Ken Olsen became persuaded that the company should enter the personal computer business.[109] He set the company to work on a three-pronged development effort that would lead to the Professional, the Rainbow 100, and the DECmate. The Professional was to be the company's principal entry into the fray. It would have a proprietary operating system based on that of the PDP-11, bit-mapped graphics, and multitasking capabilities. The Rainbow was considered a lower-end alternative. It looked much like the Professional but, rather than a proprietary DEC microprocessor, it had both an 8088 and a Z80 and thus could run both 8-bit CP/M software and 16-bit CP/M-86 or MS-DOS software. It was in no way IBM-compatible, however. The DECmate was essentially a stand-alone word processor.

The Professional was the bellwether of the effort, forecast to attract 90 percent of the profit. The DEC team was confident of the machine's technical superiority—and that such superiority would be the key to its success. This feeling was reinforced when the first IBM PC arrived at DEC headquarters. "If you ever built me something like this," Olsen told the project manager, "you wouldn't be here anymore." Indeed, the perfectionist Olsen not only took a personal interest in the project, but also became part of the design team, focusing on the case, floor stand, and monitor. But, despite winning design awards, the computer was a commercial flop. Most of the 300,000 PCs that DEC sold were Rainbows, and many of those at fire-sale prices. All told, the company lost about $900 million on the three low-end machines.[110]

One might be tempted to see this as a matter of strategic mistakes. But the real mistake was the company's unwillingness to

---

[109] Rifkin and Harrar, *The Ultimate Entrepreneur*, 194ff. My account follows this source.

[110] Olsen quote, ibid., 203; "Digital Equipment Decides to Let the Rainbow Fade," *The Wall Street Journal*, 22 April 1987, 4. DEC discontinued the Rainbow in 1987. By then the firm was selling the VAXmate, an expensive IBM-compatible with the ability to hook easily to a DEC minicomputer network. DEC later contracted to buy OEM clones from Tandy, but has recently announced plans to manufacture its own PCs in Taiwan. William M. Bulkeley, "Digital to Buy and Resell under Its Label Personal Computers Produced by Tandy," *The Wall Street Journal*, 7 Oct. 1988, B4; "Digital Plans to Make PCs," *The New York Times*, 11 Feb. 1992, D15. DEC has also begun emulating the marketing tactics of the successful mail-order clones. Peter H. Lewis, "Digital Returns to PC Wars," *The New York Times*, 2 Feb. 1992, sec. 3, 8; Rifkin and Harrar, *The Ultimate Entrepreneur*, 238.

Richard N. Langlois / 42

take advantage of external economies. A technical perfectionist, Olsen believed that DEC could be successful by creating a superior product. This tactic had worked in minicomputers, where the goal is to put together a machine that will solve a particular problem for a particular application. The PC is not, however, a machine for a particular application; it is a machine adaptable to many applications—including some that its users have not imagined when they buy their machines. Moreover, Olsen underrated the value of software. In minicomputers, DEC could generate adequate software in-house, and users, who are highly skilled technically, could write their own applications. But this was not the case in the wide-open computer market. And, unlike IBM, DEC chose to ignore existing third-party capabilities. Except for the hard disk and the line cord, DEC designed and built every piece of the Professional. The company tooled the sheet metal and the plastics, manufactured the floppy drive, and even developed the microprocessor.[111]

In 1979, Apple was the largest manufacturer of personal computers. The advent of VisiCalc had turned the Apple II from a hobbyist's machine into a small business computer. Apple felt that it needed to develop a new machine with more capabilities to capture the business market more securely.[112] The Apple III would have a built-in drive, a new operating system, an eighty-column display, and lower- as well as upper-case characters. The machine would also be able to run most Apple II software in an "emulation" mode. The result was a machine designed by committee. Afraid of cannibalizing its Apple II revenues, Apple actually added extra chips to make sure that, in emulation mode, the Apple III could not take advantage of its advances over the Apple II. Using the new abilities would require new software, and Apple was trying to write the bulk of this software in-house. In line with this strategy, the company would not release any technical specifications for or information on the machine, thus angering outside software firms.

As head of research and development, Steve Jobs pushed the project relentlessly and set unrealistic deadlines.[113] Unlike the Apple II, which was designed, figuratively speaking, in a garage,

---

[111] Rifkin and Harrar, *The Ultimate Entrepreneur*, 208.

[112] Moritz, *The Little Kingdom*, 291–97; Williams and Moore, "The Apple Story," 177–80; Freiberger and Swaine, *Fire in the Valley*, 231–35.

[113] Despite this, the Apple III took longer to develop than the IBM PC and was priced higher. Moritz, *The Little Kingdom*, 309.

External Economies and Economic Progress / 43

The Apple III • Developed in an attempt to expand Apple's share of the business market, the Apple III represented a basic misunderstanding of the computer's function. It was designed as a closed system, like an appliance, whereas users wanted open-ended architecture and flexibility. (Photograph reproduced courtesy of Apple Computer.)

the Apple III was a test of Apple's ability to develop a new machine as a company. Obsessed by technical elegance, Jobs insisted that all the circuitry fit on one board, even when that proved impossible. Because of this—and poor quality control—almost all of the first units shipped in 1980 failed and had to be returned. The resulting bad reputation, coupled with the lack of software, effectively killed the product. Only 65,000 Apple IIIs

Richard N. Langlois / 44

were sold, fewer than the number of Apple IIs sold in 1980 alone.[114] Total development costs were about $100 million for a product that in the end generated only about 3 percent of Apple's revenues.[115]

Apple has never been as integrated vertically as DEC, but the smaller company created its own internal sourcing problems. Apple attempted to develop its own disk drive, code-named Twiggy, to be used on the Apple III. Shugart drives were proving unreliable, and, since drives were in short supply, the company decided to try its hand at internal production rather than to secure another supplier. The project turned into a disaster, and the drive was never used on the III. Wendell Sander, the Apple III project manager, saw the matter this way: "The company didn't realize it was taking on a project that wasn't really a computer system. There's a closer affiliation between disk drives and integrated circuits than there is between disk drives and computers. They didn't realize it was going to be so big. They didn't appreciate the difficulty."[116] Apple's existing capabilities were not similar to those necessary for making disk drives, and creating dissimilar internal capabilities proved costly.

Modularity • The Apple III—as well as the Lisa and the Macintosh—also reflects the victory of Steve Jobs over Steve Wozniak. Wozniak, with his hobbyist's attitude intact, always believed that the computer should be open in its architecture and open-ended in its uses. He grew increasingly annoyed as the company, in his view, turned its back on the Apple II and the philosophy behind it. In January 1985, he put it this way:

> The right way for one person is not the right way for another. We closed that machine [the Apple III] up to where somebody could have a very difficult time finding out how to add their own I/O drivers. We did not make it easy for the outside world. We thought we wanted all the markets for ourselves.

> You have to let the end users develop their own standards. You've got to give them the freedom to discover how they're going to use an operating system, what sort of things they're going to buy. And

[114] Moritz, *The Little Kingdom*, 297; Freiberger and Swaine, *Fire in the Valley*, 234. Apple sold 78,000 IIs in the 1980 fiscal year.

[115] This is Wozniak's estimate. Williams and Moore, "The Apple Story," 180.

[116] The drive was used on the Lisa, but it would have been cheaper to use an outside drive. In 1983, John Sculley, the new Apple president, killed the internal drive and bought more compact units from Sony. Moritz, *The Little Kingdom*, 323; Sander quote, 302.

External Economies and Economic Progress / 45

if you're right and have provided a good solution, that's where they're going to settle. The thinking on the III was very much like *Grandchildren:* a religion in that it could be done one way—our way. We made it very difficult for outside developers, instead of providing all the information as we did with the Apple II. . . . I think that when a new market evolves, like personal computers did, there's a period of time when you've got to let the world go in random directions, and eventually it will subside because it wants standardization. Then, once it's obvious what the standards are, they should be heavily supported by the manufacturer. You can't try to dictate the standard.

Wozniak described the proprietary attitude as "the most negative thing in our whole company, and it will be for years."[117] Within a few months, he had handed in his resignation.

But the essence of Jobs's view lay not so much in the proprietary character as in the basic nature of the machine. Jobs saw himself as designing not open-ended modular systems but "closed geographical systems."[118] This was evident perhaps even more in the Lisa and early Macintosh computers, which bore Jobs's personal stamp. As Jef Raskin, the original Mac project director, put it, "Apple II is a system. Macintosh is an appliance."[119] On the Mac's introduction in 1984, Apple decided it should be known as "the second desk appliance after the telephone."[120] In large part,

---

[117] Williams and Moore, "The Apple Story," 178.

[118] Lee Butcher, *Accidental Millionaire: The Rise and Fall of Steve Jobs at Apple Computer* (New York, 1988), 142.

[119] Moritz, *The Little Kingdom*, 130. Raskin was the progenitor of the Macintosh, the first prototypes of which appeared in December 1979. Significantly, Raskin's original vision was essentially similar to that of Osborne—a cheap bundled portable built around existing 8-bit technology. Jobs became "intrigued by the concept of an appliance computer that was as easy to use as a toaster," and began meddling in the project, which he eventually took over. Jeffrey S. Young, *Steve Jobs: The Journey Is the Reward* (Glenview, Ill., 1988), 201. It was at Jobs's insistence that the Macintosh used the 16-bit Motorola 6800 chip and incorporated the mouse, icons, and other features developed at the Xerox Palo Alto Research Center.

[120] Moritz, *The Little Kingdom*, 326. A memorandum from Mike Murray, the Macintosh marketing manager, put it this way:

> Think of Mac as an appliance. A thing applied as a means to an end. Like a Cuisinart in the kitchen, one could live without a Macintosh on the desk. Yet the increased personal productivity combined with the opportunity for personal and creative expression will hit hard at our customers' psychic drives. Perhaps only 15–20 percent of a person's working time will be spent using a Mac, but as with the Cuisinart, it will make all the difference in the world. Our customers will find it difficult to return to the "old way" of doing things. Macintosh will become an integral part of life at a desk. In fact, we would like to see the day when a freshly hired product manager for a *Fortune* 500 company walks up to his new

Richard N. Langlois / 46

the non-systemic character of the later machines was simply a reflection of the fact that they were bounded in conception by a single mind: Jobs's. His approach was visionary, personal, and aesthetic. He wanted to design the ideal machine that he would himself like to own. Alan Kay, himself a visionary who had worked at Xerox PARC and became an Apple Fellow, describes Jobs and the Macintosh in this way: "Take a look at the Mac. If you look at it from the front, it's fantastic. If you look at it from the back, it stinks. Steve doesn't think systems at all. Different kind of mentality. . . . Looking at the original Mac, you can see Steve. It's like Steve's head in a sense because it has the good parts of Steve and the bad parts. It has this super quality control and the parts where his brain didn't function."[121]

Although the Apple III and Lisa machines were both dismal failures, the Mac provided the cornerstone of Apple's current strategy: a technological lead, especially in user-friendliness. But the original Mac was an underpowered toy, likened to a Maserati with a one-gallon gas tank.[122] It was only under the administration of John Sculley that the Macintosh took off, and the key to this success was moving the Mac closer to the IBM paradigm of the business computer. This included increased modularity and accessibility to the after-market. Under Sculley, Apple has also begun a process of spinning off unrelated projects into separate companies, beginning with a spin-off designed to create software capabilities at arm's length so as not to discourage third-party suppliers.[123]

Why were the most successful machines—the Apple II and the IBM PC—also the most modular? It is misleading to think of a computer as an end-product. A computer is a means to an end—or to a variety of ends. We thus need to think of computers in hedonic or Lancasterian terms.[124] Computer makers offer a mixture of attributes among which consumers can choose to produce

desk and finds a telephone, a couple of pens, a tablet of paper, a company magazine, and a Mac.
Butcher, *Accidental Millionaire*, 145–46.

[121] Quoted in John Sculley with John A Byrne, *Odyssey: Pepsi to Apple . . . the Journey of a Marketing Impresario* (New York, 1987), 238.

[122] Moritz, *The Little Kingdom*, 326.

[123] Sculley, *Odyssey*, 391.

[124] For an extension and generalization of this idea, see Richard N. Langlois and Paul L. Robertson, "Networks and Innovation in a Modular System: Lessons from the Microcomputer and Stereo Component Industries," *Research Policy* 21 (1992): 277–313.

External Economies and Economic Progress / 47

their favored combinations. For most kinds of products—toasters or automobiles, say—manufacturers offer preset packages. One can choose from a multiplicity of packages, but one cannot choose the engine from one kind of car, the hood ornament from another, and the front suspension from a third. Not only are there transaction costs of such picking and choosing, but there are also economies of scale in assembling the parts into a finished package.[125] In microcomputers, however, both the transaction costs of knowing the available parts and the scale economies of assembling the package are low for a wide segment of the user population. Although firms like Osborne and Kaypro were successful for a time by choosing a preset package that appealed to a large body of users, the real winners in the evolutionary process were the firms that offered protean machines that could be tailored to specific user demands—and could be upgraded easily as new end-uses and technological possibilities emerged.[126]

Innovation • The evolutionary benefits of modularity appear on the producer's as well as on the consumer's side. A modular system is open to innovation of certain kinds in a way that a closed system—an appliance—is not.

As I have already argued, a decentralized and fragmented system can have advantages in innovation to the extent that it involves the trying out of many alternate approaches simultaneously, leading to rapid trial-and-error learning. This kind of innovation is especially important when technology is changing rapidly and there is a high degree of both technological and market uncertainty. And this kind of innovation certainly characterized the microcomputer industry.

In the case of the mainframe and minicomputer industries, innovation was sparked by government—usually military—funding

---

[125] Steven N. S. Cheung, "The Contractual Nature of the Firm," *Journal of Law and Economics* 26 (April 1983): 6–7. Indeed, these economies of scale more than transaction costs explain the tendency of assemblers to offer preset packages. If there were only transaction costs, as Cheung, "Contractural Nature," suggests, of discovering which parts are available and what their prices are, we would expect to see not preset packages but a proliferation of intermediaries who specialize in packaging components tailored to buyers' specific tastes. Indeed, we see such intermediaries in the computer industry; they are called value-added resellers, and they package hardware and software systems to the tastes of particular non-expert buyers. For most appliance-like products, however, the economies of scale of assembly lead to integration of the packaging and assembly functions.

[126] By gradually adding or swapping third-party add-ons, a buyer of the original IBM PC in 1981 could by today have created a machine with all the capabilities of the latest 386 system.

Richard N. Langlois / 48

of university research.[127] Projects like the SAGE computer at MIT, from which both IBM and DEC borrowed, allowed researchers to try out new ideas and approaches. To the extent that multiple projects were funded, often by competing branches of the military at competing universities, there was scope for parallel paths. But, although the uses of the large computer were enormously greater in number than first believed, the product space was relatively small compared with that of the microcomputer. The end-user of the mainframe was the technical computer specialist or systems analyst who stood between the large installation and its non-technical clientele. The principal users of minicomputers were scientists who were not only strong technically, but who also often had computer specialists at their disposal.

That the microcomputer industry partook of external economies of learning and innovation is in many ways a familiar story that need not be retold. Popular accounts of Silicon Valley sound very much like Marshall's localized industry in which the "mysteries of the trade become no mysteries; but are as it were in the air, and children learn many of them unconsciously."[128] Compare, for example, Michael Moritz's discussion of the effect of Silicon Valley culture on one particular child: Steve Wozniak. "In Sunnyvale in the mid-sixties, electronics was like hay fever: It was in the air and the allergic caught it. In the Wozniak household the older son had a weak immune system."[129] One could easily multiply citations. This learning effect went beyond the background culture, however. It included the proclivity of engineers to switch jobs and to start spin-offs, creating a pollination effect and a tendency to biological differentiation that Marshall would have appreciated. Moreover, the external economies of ideas were not in fact restricted to the physical realm of Silicon Valley—or even to Silicon Valley plus Massachusetts's Route 128. As Austin Robinson anticipated long ago, external economies in a developed economy are increasingly intangible and therefore, in his phrase, mobile.[130]

This is a familiar tale but nonetheless an important one. It is not, however, directly related to the issue of modularity, except insofar as the modularity of the product allows more entry points

---

[127] The definitive source here is Kenneth Flamm, *Targeting the Computer* (Washington, D.C., 1987).

[128] Marshall, *Principles*, IV.x.3, 225.

[129] Moritz, *The Little Kingdom*, 29.

[130] E. A. G. Robinson, *The Structure of Competitive Industry* (1935; Chicago, Ill., 1958), 142.

External Economies and Economic Progress / 49

for new firms and thus adds to the diversity in the system. But there is a more specific sense in which innovation proceeds differently in a modular system than in a closed one. The important implication of modularity is that innovation in such a system is potentially autonomous—one part of the system can change without all the other parts having to change at the same time. As long as it maintains its ability to connect to a standard bus, for example, an add-on board can gain in capabilities over a range without any other parts of the system changing. Graphics boards can become more powerful, modems faster, software more user-friendly, and pointing devices more clever.

Nathan Rosenberg has suggested that bottleneck stages in a production process can become focal points for innovation.[131] The same is true in the case of product innovation when the product is a modular one and each element is a "stage" in the "production" of consumer utility. The lack of reliable memory boards was a bottleneck to the usefulness of the early Altair. The forty-column display and the inability to run CP/M software were bottlenecks for the Apple II. The IBM PC's 8088 could address only a limited amount of internal memory. All of these problems—and many more—were the targets of innovation by third-party suppliers, from Cromemco and Processor Technology to Microsoft and Intel. Sometimes a bottleneck is not strictly technological, as when IBM's copyrighted ROM BIOS became the focus of inventing-around by firms like Phoenix and AMI. "Innovations" of this sort may not directly yield improvements in performance (though many firms do in fact improve the products that they have reverse-engineered), but they do help to keep the system open. In a wider sense, we can also include as bottleneck-breakers those innovations that extended the system's abilities in new directions—such as modems, machinery-controller boards, facsimile boards, and graphics scanners. A modular system is also compatible with certain types of integrative innovations—that is, with innovations that allow a single device to perform functions that had previously required several devices. A good example of this would be the chip set designed by Chips and Technologies to integrate into one

---

[131] Nathan Rosenberg, *Perspectives on Technology* (New York, 1976), 125. See also Thomas P. Hughes, *Networks of Power: Electrification in Western Society, 1880–1930* (Baltimore, Md., 1983). Hughes refers to bottlenecks as "reverse salients."

Richard N. Langlois / 50

set of integrated circuits sixty-three of the ninety-four circuits on the original IBM AT, thus greatly facilitating the making of clones. [132]

Conclusion

The microcomputer industry provides a striking example of "organic" growth—that is, growth that takes place through the creation of economic capabilities by and within a network of specialized firms whose major nexus of coordination is the market. In this example, there are lessons for the present-day debates about industrial competitiveness and the forms of economic organization conducive to it. I do not offer this industry as a model for all times and places, however; I do not even want to suggest that the future will see a general trend toward modularity and disintegration in industry, [133] even if the arguments for that vision are at least as good as those for a historical trend toward collective enterprise. [134] Instead, I offer the case of the microcomputer industry as representative of one still-important pattern of industrial growth—a pattern to which both business historians and policymakers ought to pay attention.

[132] John Gantz, "Chips and Technologies: Driving in the Fast Lane," *InfoWorld*, 15 Feb. 1988, 34.

[133] But for a suggestion that modularity and external economies can be important elsewhere—including in process technology—see Richard N. Langlois, "Capabilities and Vertical Disintegration in Process Technology: The Case of Semiconductor Fabrication Equipment," Working Paper 92-10, Consortium on Competitiveness and Cooperation, Haas School of Business, University of California, Berkeley, Nov. 1992.

[134] Notably those in Lazonick, *Business Organization and the Myth of the Market Economy.*

[22]

INSTITUTIONS
AND THE GROWTH OF SILICON VALLEY

AnnaLee Saxenian

Abstract

The success of Silicon Valley is generally explained with reference to free-market competition or to government contracts. Proponents of these explanations overlook the critical role of informal and formal relationships among the region's engineers and executives and among its firms. This article describes the growth and evolution of Silicon Valley as an industrial district, from an early phase characterized by private networks to one characterized by more formal organizations. The existing institutional infrastructure, however, is found to be inadequate in the face of emerging threats to the region's industry. New collective institutions and public forums are required if local companies are to meet the growing challenge of international competition, if they are to secure a skilled work-force, and if they are to solve the transportation, housing, and environmental problems which affect them.

"Fathers of Silicon Valley Reunited," proclaimed *The New York Times*, referring to the eight middle-aged engineers gathered on a stage in Palo Alto, California, on April 14, 1988. The eight had founded the Fairchild Semiconductor Corporation three decades earlier. Honoring them were more than 1,000 "Fairchildren"—former employees of the company who had gathered to celebrate the sale of Fairchild to National Semiconductor, to one of its own offspring.

It might seem odd that this gathering of entrepreneurs was referred to as "fathers" and "children." Pioneers of some of the century's most significant scientific breakthroughs, they are also industrialists who won fame and considerable fortune for pioneering one of the most dynamic and innovative industrial regions in the world.

Yet it is appropriate that these eight men should be referred to as the fathers of a family. In existing stories of the origins of Silicon Valley, the region's early growth is generally attributed either to the dynamism of competitive free markets or to the propulsive role of government markets. Theorists focus either on how Stanford University, its science park, and the local supply of venture capital fostered entrepreneurship and innovation, or they stress the extensive role of the U.S. Department of Defense and NASA in promoting the early development of the semiconductor industry.

The relationships among the region's engineers, referred to here metaphorically as familial, have generally been overlooked. Yet the

The Growth of Silicon Valley, Saxenian

informal cooperation and networking between firms in Silicon Valley were as important to the region's early successes as other, more commonly identified factors. Engineers and scientists developed a commitment to one another, to the region, and to the project of advancing technology which transcended their commitments to individual firms. This culture fostered the rapid diffusion of technology, skill, and know-how within the region and encouraged a continual process of new firm formation and innovation.

Thus, the activities of local and national institutions, including Stanford University and the U.S. Department of Defense (DOD), are generally acknowledged to have contributed to Silicon Valley's early development. Equally important, but almost universally overlooked, is the way that both fostered collaboration and the rapid diffusion of market information, technology, and skill which enabled small firms to survive and constantly innovate in an uncertain and rapidly changing environment. This distinguishes Silicon Valley from most other aspiring high-tech regions—those with universities, science parks, and venture capital, on one hand, and those which receive large quantities of defense dollars, on the other.[1]

This paper suggests that Silicon Valley is best understood as an industrial district, comparable to the 19th century regions described by Alfred Marshall and to their contemporary variants being rediscovered in the technologically dynamic regions of Europe and Japan.[2] Like these European and Japanese districts, Silicon Valley's agglomeration of high-technology producers and highly skilled workers is characterized by the specialization of its producers and their ability to adapt flexibly to changing competitive conditions.

The enterprises which make up Silicon Valley's decentralized industrial structure are embedded in a social structure which supports a complex balance of cooperation and competition. While local firms compete fiercely to be first to the market with new products and processes, they simultaneously rely on dense networks of social and commercial relationships for information, technology, and contacts.[3] This decentralized, region-based pattern of industrialization distinguishes Silicon Valley from other high-technology regions in the U.S. Lacking comparable traditions of informal cooperation and networking, these regions have failed to generate the sustained growth and technological dynamism associated with Silicon Valley.[4]

The paper divides the history of Silicon Valley into three periods. It begins by reviewing the region's development during the 1950s and 1960s, highlighting the role of both Stanford and the U.S. military in creating a social and technical infrastructure which fostered innovative risk-taking and experimentation. It then describes the institutions,

37

largely private and uncoordinated, which emerged during the 1970s to support a highly decentralized industrial structure during the region's most spectacular growth phase.

During the 1980s, Silicon Valley flourished as local firms adapted successfully to changing competitive conditions; however, the region's weaknesses also became apparent. The paper concludes by suggesting that the main constraint to Silicon Valley's continued dynamism lies in the absence of public-minded institutions to organize the responses of local firms to the shared challenges of intensifying international competition, on one hand, and the deterioration of the regional environment, on the other.

The 1950s and 1960s: Relationships Not Recipes

The experience of Silicon Valley provided the original model for the "high-tech recipe." Policy-makers worldwide assumed that by combining such ingredients as a research university, a science park, and venture capital in an environment free of government regulations or labor unions, they could "grow the next Silicon Valley."[5] The recipe, based on the assumptions of neoclassical economics, suggested that unfettered supplies of highly skilled labor, technology, and capital would automatically generate new firm formation and technology-based regional development. Silicon Valley's rapid growth, in this view, represented a triumph of free markets and entrepreneurial capitalism.

Yet the widespread failure of efforts to "grow the next Silicon Valley" suggests the limits of this interpretation.[6] The high-tech recipe overstates the role of such individual institutions as Stanford, its science park, and the venture capital industry in the development of Silicon Valley because it abstracts them from both the industrial structure and the social and economic environment of the region.

World War II laid the foundations for the industrialization of Silicon Valley, formerly an agricultural region. The hostilities in the Pacific drew large numbers of people to work in war-related industries; the Engineering Laboratory at Stanford University received substantial Pentagon funding for electronics research and development (which continued during the post-war period); and large, established electrical and electronics firms began to locate in the region to gain access to the technological watershed emerging at Stanford and to growing aerospace markets in the west.[7]

The war thus created the technological and industrial infrastructure which supported Stanford's first electronics spin-offs during the 1940s and 1950s. The contribution of Stanford's engineering dean, Frederick Terman, lay less in the formal linkages he forged between the university and local industry, as commonly assumed, than in his active support

The Growth of Silicon Valley, Saxenian

for aspiring entrepreneurs like William Hewlett and David Packard. Terman pursued his vision of a "community of technical scholars" in the region not only by building up the University's engineering department but also by supporting the entrepreneurial efforts of his students.[8] He thus initiated a culture of informal cooperation in the region which his proteges in turn replicated in their relationships with other emerging enterprises. In the words of a local analyst commemorating the fiftieth anniversary of the Hewlett-Packard Company:

> As their company grew, both [Hewlett and Packard] became very involved in the formation and growth of other companies. They encouraged entrepreneurs, went out of their way to share what they had learned and were instrumental in getting electronics companies to work together on common problems. Largely because of them, there's an unusual spirit of cooperation in the local electronics industry.[9]

One of Stanford's most significant, but overlooked, contributions to the development of Silicon Valley was thus in fostering these informal practices of inter-firm cooperation.

By the early 1960s, Silicon Valley was distinguished by a now-legendary process of high-tech entrepreneurship and industrial recombination. Between 1963 and 1972, a new firm entered the Silicon Valley electronics industry an average of every two weeks—and most were started by engineers leaving other small technology firms in the region. These entrepreneurs drew upon the assistance of colleagues and friends in the area to put new technical ideas into practice, just as Hewlett and Packard had relied on Terman's support.

This recombination process was initiated by the prodigious Fairchild Semiconductor Corporation. The majority of the semiconductor ventures started in Silicon Valley between 1960 and 1970, or close to forty ventures, trace their lineage to Fairchild Semiconductor.[10] The symbolic significance of this pattern of entrepreneurship to the region is reflected in the Fairchild family tree, a poster-sized genealogy of the firm's scores of spin-offs. This family tree hangs on many walls in Silicon Valley and underscores the quasi-familial nature of the bonds among the region's engineers.

Fairchild also served, in the words of one local executive, as a "corporate vocational school" for its employees. Many of the region's most prominent industrialists gained business and technical experience at Fairchild. At an industry conference in Sunnyvale in 1969, for example, less than two dozen of the 400 people present had never worked for Fairchild. In the early days, it seemed that "everyone knew everyone" in the region. The shared experience of working at Fairchild created a sense of loyalty and trust among Silicon Valley engineers that lasted even as individuals began to work for competing companies, a loyalty similar to those among university classmates. Thus it is not surprising that the sale of the company, long a technological has-been, drew such a huge crowd in 1988.

Socializing and information-sharing were pervasive in Silicon Valley during this early period.[11] The process of informal collaboration was essential to engineers and former colleagues who were trying to solve the enormous technical problems facing the emerging semiconductor industry. Although the region's firms competed fiercely, striving to be the first to introduce innovative new products and processes, they also cooperated. Geographic proximity facilitated open exchanges of information and the informal networking which created a sense of community among local engineers. According to one executive in the semiconductor industry:

> I have people call me quite frequently and say, "Hey, did you ever run into this one?," and you say, "Yeh, seven or eight years ago. Why don't you try this, that or the other thing?" We all get calls like that.[12]

The Stanford Science Park provided fledgling enterprises a physical environment which facilitated this mutually beneficial interaction. Yet the role of the Science Park is often exaggerated. It was important only in the broader context of a technical and social environment which fostered entrepreneurship. More than a decade of experience has demonstrated that the physical infrastructure of a science park alone does not insure mutually beneficial patterns of networking and collaboration.

By the end of the 1960s, neither Stanford University nor its science park were of real significance to the region's rapidly multiplying technology firms. Virtually all of the start-ups during the 1970s and 1980s were spun off of existing firms like Fairchild, and most had only limited relationships with Stanford or the Science Park. Rather, these firms built on the region's growing technical infrastructure and concentration of specialized skills. Stanford's importance to the region today lies primarily in its role in educating large numbers of engineers and managers.

The role of the venture capital industry in the region's development has similarly been misinterpreted. Silicon Valley's venture capital business was a product of the regional concentration of technology enterprises, not the other way around, as commonly assumed. As local entrepreneurs succeeded, some chose to invest their returns in other technology start-ups. These entrepreneurs-turned-venture-capitalists contributed not only capital to fledgling enterprises, but also their technical and managerial experience and access to networks of contacts. The venture capital industry thus grew out of and in turn helped to

The Growth of Silicon Valley, Saxenian

reproduce the patterns of informal cooperation, networking, and new firm formation in Silicon Valley.[13]

In short, the university, the science park, and the venture capital industry—the key elements of the high-tech recipe—were not simply disarticulated factors of production in Silicon Valley. This dynamic industrial region never resembled the neoclassical economic model of free-flowing resources and atomistic firms. Innovative enterprises were embedded in a broader, regional community of engineers and technology firms. The region's technical and social networks and practices of informal cooperation insured that information, technology, and capital diffused rapidly and fostered entrepreneurial initiative and innovation.

The image of Silicon Valley as a product of free markets and small firms similarly leaves out the contribution of the U.S. government to industrial fragmentation and the rapid diffusion of technical information in Silicon Valley.[14] The Department of Defense (DOD) and the National Aeronautics and Space Administration (NASA) invested close to $300 million in production contracts for semiconductors between 1955 and 1968, a large proportion of which went to Silicon Valley.[15] Yet this money is less significant for the volume of dollars spent in the region than for the way that this money reinforced a decentralized industrial structure and the social and technical relationships which supported it.

The DOD and NASA, in an effort to develop more sophisticated weapon systems rapidly, extended contracts to the region's small new ventures as well as to larger, established electronics firms. Thus, for example, the U.S. government was the largest market for new semiconductor ventures during much of the 1960s, and many of Silicon Valley's 1960s start-ups were directly supported by military contracts.[16] The presence of the military as a potential customer and a potentially lucrative market served as an ongoing inducement for local entrepreneurs to start firms and experiment with new technologies. This willingness to support untried firms contrasted with other U.S. military programs which centralized contracts and research funds in a few well-established firms.[17] The military also promoted the rapid diffusion of technology in the region through its liberal licensing and second-sourcing policies. The Defense Department required, for example, that whenever it contributed funds to the development of a product or process, a comprehensive license of free use be issued, insuring that the invention could be used by anyone in connection with government-funded projects. Scores of small subcontractors as well as prime contractors were thus able to stay abreast of the latest technological breakthroughs through this licensing policy.

Berkeley Planning Journal

Finally, the military actively encouraged the practice of "second-sourcing" parts for complex weapons systems. Using a second source was a means of hedging the risk of relying on a single subcontractor for key components which, if delayed, might slow the progress of an entire system. This served as an important means of transferring technology: second sources were typically provided not only with product specifications but also with the prized details of process technology. Moreover, second-source contracts were used by many start-ups as a means of securing the cash flow and production experience to move into innovative new products.[18]

While the importance of military spending to the Silicon Valley economy diminished significantly during the 1960s, the practices of cooperation and technology-sharing through liberal licensing, second-sourcing, and informal exchange persisted.[19] So too did the pattern of entrepreneurial spin-offs which Pentagon contracts had supported.

The unplanned coincidence of such processes contributed to the emergence of Silicon Valley as a dynamic center of technology industry in the 1960s. The region was characterized by a dense social and technical infrastructure which supported new firm formation and innovation. Other U.S. regions which have attempted to recreate this pattern of technology development, through state financing of research facilities and industrial parks, have failed to generate comparable rates of new firm formation, innovation, or growth. Lacking comparable cultures of collaboration and loyalty, the infrastructure of sophisticated suppliers, and the high rates of entrepreneurship which distinguish Silicon Valley, most high-tech regions in the U.S. are dominated by the branch plants of large, established electronics firms.[20]

Regions which have high levels of military spending have similarly failed to generate self-sustaining and diversified high-technology development.[21] Los Angeles, which may be the exception that proves the rule, has generated a dynamic high-technology base, but it remains heavily defense-dependent and lacks the innovative commercial sector which distinguishes Silicon Valley.[22] Even the Route 128 region foundered during the 1980s, in part due to its lack of a flexible industrial and social structure.

The 1970s: The Creation of a Private Institutional Infrastructure

By the 1970s, Silicon Valley was known as the world's leading center of innovation in microelectronics. It was distinguished by a highly decentralized industrial structure, with both small and large firms embedded in the relationships of a technological community. The federal government no longer played a leading role in the region. Instead, the skill-

The Growth of Silicon Valley, Saxenian

base expanded, the technical infrastructure became more complex, and a variety of institutions emerged to support this regional complex.

High levels of inter-firm mobility and entrepreneurship continued to promote new firm formation and the diffusion of technology and skill in the region. Silicon Valley was, by the mid-1970s, distinguished by the highest levels of job-hopping in the nation.[23] Average annual employee turnover was close to 60 percent in the region's small technology firms during the 1970s as it became both common and acceptable for engineers to shift frequently between firms.[24] One technical recruiter noted:

> Two or three years is about max [in a job] for the Valley because there's always something more interesting across the street. You don't see someone staying twenty years at a job here. If they've been in a small company . . . for 10 or 11 years you tend to wonder about them.[25]

This continual process of recombination strengthened the region's social and technical networks: as engineers left established companies, they took with them the skills, know-how, and experience acquired at their previous jobs, along with an expanding circle of professional and personal relationships. A technical culture developed among the members of the region's predominantly high-skilled engineering and scientific workforce, who saw themselves as different from the rest of American business. These engineers developed loyalties to the industry and the region, rather than to the individual firms where they worked.[26]

This culture accorded the highest status to those who took the risk of starting firms. More than 1,000 net new technology enterprises were established in Silicon Valley during the 1970s. While some of these establishments represented new facilities of firms from outside of the region, or the relocation of such firms, a majority were new-firm start-ups. These new ventures were virtually all started by engineers who had acquired business experience, entrepreneurial skills, and technical know-how by working in other small firms in the region. The typical start-up was formed by friends and former colleagues with an innovative idea who sought funding and advice from local venture capitalists (often former engineers and entrepreneurs themselves). And they relied on an expanding circle of local suppliers, consultants, and market researchers for additional assistance with the process of starting a new enterprise.

A wide range of specialist input suppliers, subcontractors, and service industries for semiconductor production in turn developed in the region. For example, an independent semiconductor equipment and materials industry was created as engineers left semiconductor firms and created spin-out firms to manufacture such capital goods as diffusion ovens, step and repeat cameras, testers, and the specialized materials and

43

components for the rapidly growing chipmakers. The equipment industry was, like the semiconductor industry in the early 1970s, highly fragmented and characterized by unusually high rates of entrepreneurship and innovation among small firms.

The region's industrial structure came to be characterized by extensive vertical as well as horizontal disaggregation.[27] The expanding infrastructure of suppliers and services allowed small, specialized firms to survive in a technically uncertain and rapidly changing environment, to rely on the external economies of a dense regional agglomeration rather than pursuing vertical integration. The existence of an independent semiconductor equipment and materials industry, for example, promoted entry of new semiconductor firms by freeing individual firms from the expense of internal development and by spreading the costs of developing new capital goods across multiple producers.

The process of starting a new firm, defining a new product, or experimenting with new technologies was thus inseparable from the networks of social and commercial relationships among the region's specialized firms. While competitive rivalries were fierce, as evidenced by continually falling prices and technological advances in semiconductors, what appeared to both the actors and the outside world as an individual entrepreneurial process was in fact a social process.

The firms which emerged in this environment proved to be highly resilient. While only 75 percent of American manufacturing firms survive their first two years of business, during the 1970s and 1980s, 95 percent of the technology firms in Silicon Valley survived their first six years of business.[28]

This regional environment also fostered innovation. The decentralization of information flows, the rapid spread of market information and technology, and the availability of technical skill and expertise fostered local technical advance. While many of the major technological breakthroughs in the semiconductor industry during the 1960s and 1970s were achieved in non-Silicon Valley firms, the region's flexible enterprises excelled at exploiting technical advances rapidly and generating incremental innovations and product-engineering improvements. Silicon Valley thus became the nation's leading center of innovative, engineering-intensive forms of semiconductor production.[29]

Local venture capital networks simultaneously expanded to support this ongoing process of entrepreneurial recombination and innovation. The interplay of cooperation and competition which characterized the industrial community was replicated in the venture capital community: as individual venture capitalists rarely had the resource or expertise to evaluate the range of new technologies, they created dense networks

The Growth of Silicon Valley, Saxenian

for the exchange of information and assistance. While they often competed to fund promising start-ups, they also usually created shifting consortia to share the risk of funding companies whose management and technology were untested.

Private institutions such as trade organizations and providers of business services also emerged during the 1970s to support Silicon Valley's decentralized industrial structure. The American Electronics Association (AEA), based in Palo Alto, played a central role in the region during the 1960s and early 1970s. Explicitly focusing its activities on the Valley, it provided services as well as managerial and technical education programs to support new and emerging electronics firms in the area. The AEA's hundreds of breakfasts, lunches, seminars, dinners, and other conferences similarly provided opportunities for networking and information exchange.[30] In the words of one observer:

> Perhaps the AEA's most significant contribution to the electronics industry is what it did to foster networking. Most top executives of young, fast-growing electronics companies are relatively inexperienced in some important management areas. The AEA, with its frequent seminars and monthly meetings of company presidents, provided an excellent opportunity for those executives to meet and learn from their peers.

He goes on to point out the crucial role the AEA played in integrating the specialized firms in a highly fragmented industrial structure:

> . . . electronics companies are uniquely systems-oriented. Almost no firm manufactures from the ground up a stand-alone product. A company either draws on other people's components or makes products that fit with other people's products into a system. Friendships made through the AEA help the companies develop products that work together.[31]

The Semiconductor Equipment and Materials International (SEMI) similarly supported the development of the region's highly fragmented but innovative equipment manufacturing sector. SEMI was formed in 1970 in Silicon Valley to sponsor trade shows and to provide market information to semiconductor equipment and material suppliers. It soon took on the ambitious task of setting standards for the semiconductor industry. These activities allowed the hundreds of small firms which manufactured semiconductor equipment and materials to survive and innovate in an industry characterized by continual technological change.[32]

Consulting firms, market research agencies, training programs, and public relations firms—often started by engineers and former entrepreneurs—became part of the regional infrastructure as well. The market

45

research firm Dataquest, for example, provided not only market data but also held regular conferences and gatherings which brought together the members of the industrial community to exchange information and to network. The Silicon Valley Entrepreneurs Club similarly provided a forum where aspiring entrepreneurs gathered monthly to make contacts, find partners, or learn about legal, financial, and managerial aspects of starting a new firm.

By the late 1970s, the most important institutions supporting the dynamic process of recombination and innovation in Silicon Valley were private business services and trade associations. These local institutions fostered the diffusion of technology and the continual process of information-sharing and networking among the region's hundreds of small firms. The Stanford science park and the Defense Department were no longer active in the process of new firm formation and innovation. Institutionalized forms of cooperation, such as public or private research institutes, were also virtually non-existent.

Nor did the federal government or national institutions play any significant role in Silicon Valley. Military contracts had decreased greatly as a proportion of regional output since the 1960s and had little effect on the dynamics of the commercial high-technology sector.[33] National banks and law firms located branches in the Valley but were rarely significant actors. Finally, city and county governments did little more than provide the physical infrastructure for industrial development.

As Silicon Valley entered the 1980s, the institutions which supported industrial development in the region were overwhelmingly private. Not only were the trade associations, venture capital networks, and most universities and training programs private, but so too were the consulting, market research services, and other forums for networking and technology transfer. Moreover, workers in the region's high-technology firms were not represented by unions.[34] Nor were there forums for collective oversight of this dynamic industrial region.[35]

This lack of public involvement is explained in part by the region's history. Silicon Valley's initial growth was the result of an unplanned historical process of agglomeration. Viewing their own successes as a product of individual entrepreneurial and managerial prowess rather than as the work of a regional community, local entrepreneurs and executives remained fiercely independent and shunned external intervention in their affairs. During the 1970s, they were solely preoccupied with the demands of unprecedented growth, and assumed that their dominance of world markets was unassailable. It was not until the 1980s, when foreign competition became a reality, that their individualistic world-view was challenged.

The 1980s and 1990s: The Need for Collective Institutions

Silicon Valley's technologically dynamic industrial complex continued to expand and diversify during the 1980s. However, the vulnerabilities of the regional economy also became apparent for the first time. The intensification of international competition and the accelerating pace of technological change, on one hand, and the limits of a congested transportation infrastructure and inflated housing and real estate prices, on the other, threatened to slow the region's growth. Yet there was no institutional infrastructure to address such shared problems.

There was ample evidence of Silicon Valley's continued dynamism during the 1980s. Computer systems producers and their suppliers came to dominate the regional economy, replacing the semiconductor industry as the leading sector. Innovative new firms pioneered technological advances in markets ranging from computer workstations, network hardware, and hard disk drives to microprocessors, computer-aided-design, and manufacturing software. In fact, the fastest-growing firms in the region's history, Sun Microsystems and Conner Peripherals, were formed during the decade.

Several local firms—such as Hewlett-Packard, Apple Computers, and Intel Semiconductor—became very large during this period; however, small and medium-sized firms remained prominent in the regional economy. More than 85 percent of the region's high-technology establishments employed less than 100 workers in 1985, in part the result of a dramatic acceleration in the pace of start-ups during the early 1980s.[36] Many of the region's small and medium-sized firms specialized in narrow niche markets and competed on the basis of technology, quality, and service rather than low cost.

Silicon Valley continued to expand geographically as well, with its boundaries extending beyond the traditional boundaries of Santa Clara County to encompass portions of adjacent Santa Cruz County (to the south) and Alameda County (to the northeast).

To speak of regional boundaries is not to imply that the region is a self-contained unit. Silicon Valley firms are tightly linked into the international marketplace. Most are heavily export-oriented, many rely on foreign suppliers for key inputs, and some have located production facilities overseas. At the same time, despite this global orientation, they recognize that the region's agglomeration of skill and suppliers is critical to their ongoing success.

While Silicon Valley remains the nation's leading center of innovation in semiconductors and computer systems, it no longer appears invulnerable. The crisis of the semiconductor industry highlighted this fragility. When the region's leading producers fell into crisis during the mid-1980s, many observers predicted that the region would follow Detroit and Pittsburgh into regional decline. Yet in spite of the loss of some 30,000 jobs, more than 80 new semiconductor ventures were formed in the region during the decade. By 1989, regional employment had rebounded to its pre-recession levels.[37]

Local firms adapted to the intensification of international competition by establishing organizational networks which formalized the informal cooperation of earlier decades. Producers of computer systems and components chose to focus only on the aspects of production where they could add the highest value and began to forge collaborative partnerships with specialist suppliers and subcontractors which allowed them to spread the rising costs and risks of production. In so doing, they increased their own flexibility and institutionalized the capacity for joint problem-solving and reciprocal technological advance.[38]

Despite this successful adjustment, the region remains vulnerable. Silicon Valley's decentralized networks of specialist producers depend on a collective infrastructure of social and technical networks for their flexibility and responsiveness, yet they have failed to created institutions to organize these relationships.[39]

There are several scenarios under which this uncoordinated balance of industrial decentralization and private institutions in Silicon Valley might break down and threaten the region's vitality. First, regional institutions could become increasingly exclusive, inhibiting the open diffusion of technology and skill which fosters innovative recombination. As long as local institutions remain private and beyond collective influence, there is no assurance that they will continue to promote the free exchange upon which the region depends.

The collaborative manufacturing consortium Sematech exemplifies this danger. Sematech was organized by local semiconductor firms in response to the industry's crisis and is jointly funded by the U.S. government and industry members, yet the membership requirements are such that only the largest firms in the industry can join.[40] Only 14 of the some 300 semiconductor producers in the U.S. today are members of Sematech. Cooperative research and manufacturing efforts could play a central role in sustaining the technological dynamism of Silicon Valley, but only if they include the region's highly innovative small firms as well as large producers.

Similar problems of exclusion might result from restrictions on access to venture capital or from lawsuits which undermine the trust that allows for open exchange. Such tendencies can only be avoided through the creation of public forums for explicitly considering the collective good of the region. While inter-firm mobility and technology exchange may

The Growth of Silicon Valley, Saxenian

hurt an individual firm, the process of innovative recombination benefits the region (and industry) as a whole. Such forums could create
institutions to insure the availability of venture capital, foster exhanges
of technical and market information, or provide services to small and
medium-sized firms.

Second, decentralized regional economies remain vulnerable to a
shortage of technical skill and the underprovision of research. In an
environment of high inter-firm mobility, individual firms have little
incentive to invest in training or research because they will not reap
the benefits of their investments. These classic cases of market failure
—which are intensified in a decentralized regional economy—underscore
the need for collective action to ensure that local educational and
training programs provide required amounts of appropriately skilled in
an environment of rapid technological change.[41]

The accelerating pace of technological change also suggests the need
for institutions which spread the high costs and risks of technology and
product development. This might include regional research institutes
which are open to all firms and pool technological expertise and support innovation in particular areas. It might also include the collective
financing of a semiconductor fabrication facility which would allow
start-ups which cannot afford a foundry (or which choose not to have
one) to share space and avoid reliance on foreign manufacturers.

The creation of such public forums would also allow local firms to
respond jointly to shared external threats. External challenges might
take the form of macroeconomic shocks such as unfavorable changes
in exchange rates or changes in tax laws, or they might result from
unanticipated shortages of key inputs or from significant technological
breakthroughs elsewhere.[42] Silicon Valley producers are not organized
to respond collectively to such unexpected events. Thus they face the
danger of either failing to respond or responding too slowly. Worse yet,
they might respond in self-interested ways which subvert rather than
strengthen the long-term foundations of the system.

The U.S.-Japan Semiconductor Trade Agreement, which established
price floors on semiconductor memory devices, might be considered
such an anti-region response. While trade protection temporarily benefitted the large semiconductor firms which were besieged by Japanese
competition, it resulted in severe shortages of memory products and
impaired the competitiveness of local systems producers. The trade
accord thus appears to have served the interests of a narrow segment
of firms at the expense of a broad range of other local producers.[43]

The delayed response of Silicon Valley firms to the resulting shortage
of memories, itself largely a consequence of the trade agreement,

49

underscores this problem. It took more than a year of artificially high prices and near-crisis conditions before serious discussions began among firms to devise solutions to the shortage. Discussions of creating a collective facility for manufacturing memories drew in representatives of local semiconductor and systems firms and venture capitalists; however, the long delay in developing joint solutions, as well as the apparent failure of any solutions to materialize, suggests the need for prior organization. In a world of increasing technological parity, it is essential that the region's firms have the capacity to respond rapidly to such unanticipated external threats.

Finally, such institutions would enhance the ability of local producers and policy-makers to respond to problems of the regional environment. The worsening traffic congestion, strong inflation of housing prices, and mounting environmental hazards are problems which undermine the ability of all local producers to function successfully within the region. Public forums could contribute to the process of improving the public transportation system, insuring provision of affordable housing, and monitoring workplace toxics and other environmental hazards.

In short, there is a need for collective institutions which allow for long-range thinking among Silicon Valley's specialist producers, without undermining the openness of the technological community.[44] These institutions would collaborate with existing private institutions and with local and county governments. While they might represent the region's interests to the federal government, they would be oriented locally, not towards Washington. In periods of stability, such institutions would concern themselves with developing strategies for improving the education and training system, supporting research on emerging technologies, and promoting infrastructure development. In periods of crisis, they would also be available as forums to develop collective responses to shared competitive threats.

Silicon Valley has flourished for more than four decades as a technologically innovative industrial district with virtually no conscious planning. However, the intensification of international competition has exposed the limitations of this fragile balance of industrial decentralization and private institutions. The continued responsiveness and technological dynamism of the region's specialist producers increasingly demands institutional oversight. The secret will be to create forums that allow local actors to respond jointly to shared challenges without sacrificing the individual autonomy that motivates their dynamism.

The Growth of Silicon Valley, Saxenian

NOTES

This is a substantially revised version of "A High Technology Industrial District: Silicon Valley in the American Context," included in the conference proceedings Citta della scienza e della tecnologia, *P. Perulli, ed., Venice: Arsenale Editrice, 1989.*

[1]See the survey of 12 aspiring high-tech regions in J. Mitchell, "Silicon Valley Wannabes," *San Jose Mercury News*, August 25, 1991.

[2]On the contemporary period, see Sabel (1987), Herrigel (1988), Goodman and Bamford (1989), Imai (1989), and Friedman (1988). On the 19th century districts, see Marshall (1919), Sabel and Zeitlin (1985), and Scranton (1983).

[3]Granovetter (1985) theorizes the social embeddedness of economic activity. See also Piore (1990) on the social structures of industrial districts.

[4]Even Route 128, long considered the counterpart of Silicon Valley, does not demonstrate a comparable culture of open information exchange and networking. See Weiss and Delbeq (1987).

[5]The literature is extensive. See, for example, Miller (1985), Office of Technology Assessment (1987), Premus (1982).

[6]The experience of the 1980s clearly demonstrates that science parks are not the universal panaceas they were once seen to be. Mishall (1984), for example, concludes that well over 50 percent of science parks fail. See also Macdonald (1987). The discussion of the experience of Cambridge, England, by Saxenian (1989a) underscores the limits of the high-tech recipe. Cambridge has all of the desired attributes identified in the high-tech recipe but has failed to generate substantial or self-sustaining high-technology development.

[7]See Saxenian (1980) for a more detailed description of this process.

[8]For example, Terman helped Hewlett and Packard locate financing for their firm and he arranged for the Varian brothers' free use of Stanford's physics labs during the early years of their venture, Varian Associates.

[9]Cited in James J. Mitchell, "H-P Sets the Tone for Business in the Valley," *San Jose Mercury News*, January 9, 1989.

[10]Fairchild's first spin-off was representative of a process which continues to the present in Silicon Valley. Four of the firm's original founders—Jay Last, Eugene Kleiner, Jean Hoerni, and Sheldon Roberts—left Fairchild in frustration in 1961 to form Amelco. Of these four, only Last remained at Amelco a decade later. Kleiner left in the late 1960s and in 1972 joined another local engineer, Tom Perkins, to establish Kleiner-Perkins Associates, which is now among the most prominent and successful venture capital firms in Silicon Valley. Hoerni left in 1964 to help another ex-Fairchilder start Union Carbide Electronics. In 1967, Hoerni left with two colleagues from Union Carbide to found Intersil and subsequently went on to found several more firms.

[11]This open information exchange remains pervasive in the region today. Rogers and Larsen (1984), Delbecq and Weiss (1988), and Weiss and

51

Berkeley Planning Journal

Delbeq (1987) document the continued importance of networking and inter-firm mobility in Silicon Valley.

[12]Cited in Braun and Macdonald (1978).

[13]Both Bullock (1983) and Florida and Kenney (1987) conclude that the Silicon Valley venture capital industry grew out of the local concentration of technology enterprises, not vice versa.

[14]Large firms played a role in this process as well. According to industry veterans Linvill and Hogan (1977), for example, IBM was Fairchild's first customer in 1959, and soon became the largest commercial customer of the semiconductor industry.

[15]The data is from Borrus (1988). While $300 million does not seem a huge amount of money now, in the 1960s new semiconductor firms were routinely started with an investment of less than $1 million. The U.S. government spent an additional $930 million on semiconductor R&D between 1958 and 1974, much of which went to large, established firms and research universities.

[16]Tilton (1971) concludes that new firms accounted for 69 percent of semiconductor sales during 1959.

[17]Thus, while DOD programs promoted a highly fragmented industrial structure in semiconductors, in the case of the machine tool industry the Pentagon inhibited the development of spin-offs and contributed to the evolution of a militarily dependent and uncompetitive industry structure. See Stowsky (1986).

[18]For documentation of the influence of defense spending on the diffusion of technology, information, and skill, see Utterbach and Murray (1977). On liberal licensing and second-sourcing policies, see also Borrus (1988).

[19]The military share of the U.S. semiconductor market fell from 50 percent in 1960 to 35 percent in 1968 (Tilton, 1971). By 1979, the share had fallen to below 10 percent, where it remains today. Meanwhile, the emergence of the computer industry and its components suppliers, which are overwhelmingly commercial, has further reduced the region's military dependence.

[20]By the early 1980s, the Research Triangle and Austin regions recorded only 20,000 and 30,000 high-technology employees respectively, compared with close to 200,000 in Silicon Valley, according to Rogers and Larsen (1984).

[21]In an empirical study of the relationship between defense spending and high-technology development, Brown (1988) finds that high levels of defense spending are not generally associated with high levels of commercial high-technology industry. He finds Massachusetts and California unusual in the combination of high levels of defense activity and the development of high-tech industries with a commercial focus.

[22]See, for example, Markusen et al. (1990).

[23]On inter-firm mobility, see Angel (1989), Weiss and Delbecq (1987), and Delbecq and Weiss (1988).

[24]See American Electronics Association (1981). It is not uncommon for an individual to have worked for five or six different firms in twice as many years—and many have worked for twice that number.

The Growth of Silicon Valley, Saxenian

[25]Cited in Gregory (1984), p. 216.

[26]In 1982, managerial, professional, and technical workers represented 56 percent of Silicon Valley's total high-tech workforce, three times more than the 19 percent in the average U.S. manufacturing. The professional and technical culture described here excludes the region's unskilled production workers. As Gordon and Kimball (1985) note, however, that production workers accounted for only 30 percent of the Silicon Valley workforce in 1982, compared to 70 percent in U.S. manufacturing as a whole.

[27]See Scott and Angel (1987).

[28]This is the finding of a 20-year study of 400 Silicon Valley firms between 1967 and 1987 conducted by Albert V. Bruno, University of Santa Clara School of Business. Cited in *The New York Times*, March 7, 1988.

[29]Scott and Angel (1987) document the spatial agglomeration of complex specialized and custom semiconductor production within Silicon Valley and the geographic dispersal of mature, high-volume production, such as discrete devices.

[30]The AEA implicitly recognized the regional basis of Silicon Valley's development when it chose to expand by creating a series of regional councils in other localities in order to replicate this pattern of grassroots organization. Since 1980, however, the AEA has increasingly oriented itself towards Washington D.C. and lobbying. See Saxenian (1990).

[31]From an article on the retirement of E. E. Ferrey, AEA president from 1960 to 1985. J. Mitchell, "A Valley Hero Readies to Retire," *San Jose Mercury News,* January 20, 1985.

[32]In 1986, SEMI represented over 900 U.S. members, of which 66 percent had less than 100 employees. See SEMI Membership Profile (1986). For a more extended discussion of the role of business organizations in Silicon Valley, see Saxenian (1990).

[33]A handful of firms in Silicon Valley still depend heavily on military spending, including Lockheed Space & Missiles, Westinghouse, and FMC. However, in 1985, military contracts accounted for only 15.4 percent of total shipments by Silicon Valley high-technology firms and direct employment by military contractors amounted to only 11.1 percent of the region's manufacturing workforce (Pacific Studies Center, 1987a, 1987b).

[34]Despite sporadic attempts to organize the electronics workforce in Silicon Valley, not a single high-tech firm is unionized except traditional defense contractors such as Lockheed and FMC. This reflects both the success of a progressive (if paternalistic) management culture in Silicon Valley and the limitation of the traditional organizing strategies of American unions for decentralized, high-skill industrial development.

[35]The only exception is infrastructure planning. The Santa Clara County Manufacturing Group was formed in 1978 to address the problems of the regional environment. This business organization works with local and regional governments on such infrastructural issues as transportation and housing.

[36]The increase in start-ups was largely a result of the 1978 capital gains tax reduction (from 49 percent to 28 percent), which produced a ten-fold increase in the amount of venture capital available nationwide. Almost one-

Berkeley Planning Journal

third of the total venture capital pool was invested in Silicon Valley firms during the 1980s.

[37]On the crisis of Silicon Valley's established semiconductor producers and the rise of a new wave of more flexible and specialized producers during the 1980s, see Saxenian (1989b).

[38]On the creation of inter-firm production networks in Silicon Valley, see Saxenian (1991).

[39]This contrasts with the industrial districts of Europe and Japan, where truly regional institutions, including trade associations and research institutes, provide training and market information and foster the diffusion of technology among regional networks of vertically disaggregated producers. See Herrigel (1988), Goodman and Bamford (1989), and Shapira (1991).

[40]Membership costs alone exceed $1 million, and a firm is expected to donate five engineers. These requirements make Sematech inaccessible to most of Silicon Valley's small producers. See Saxenian (1990) for more detail.

[41]The Applied Technology Institute of Microelectronics, created in 1990 at San Jose State University to provide training and applied research in microelectronics and computer technologies, is an example of such an institution. Financed jointly by local firms and by the state of California, the state community college system, and state university system, it is explicitly oriented toward meeting the training needs of the regional economy.

[42]In her case study of the Swiss watch industry, Glasmeier (1991) describes the breakdown of a regional economy due to a radical technological advance external to the system.

[43]On the adverse consequences of the semiconductor trade agreement, see Erdilek (1989) and Mowery and Rosenberg (1989).

[44]Scott and Paul (1990) describe similar institutional weaknesses in their analysis of Southern California's technopoles.

REFERENCES

American Electronics Association. 1981. "Statement of Pat Hill Hubbard." *Technical Employment Projections*, Palo Alto, California: American Electronics Association.

Angel, D. 1989. "The Labor Market for Engineers in the U.S. Semiconductor Industry." *Economic Geography* 65(2):99-112.

Borrus, M. 1988. *Competing for Control: America's Stake in Microelectronics*. New York: Ballinger.

Braun, E., and S. Macdonald. 1978. *Revolution in Miniature: The History and Impact of Semiconductor Electronics*. Cambridge: Cambridge University Press.

Brown, L. 1988. "Defense Spending and High Technology Development: National and State Issues." *New England Economic Review*. Boston, Massachusetts: Federal Reserve Bank of Boston, Sept./Oct.

The Growth of Silicon Valley, Saxenian

Bullock, M. 1983. *Academic Enterprise, Industrial Innovation, and the Development of High Technology Financing in the United States.* London: Brand Brothers.

Delbecq, A., and J. Weiss. 1988. "The Business Culture of Silicon Valley: Is it a Model for the Future?" In *Regional Cultures, Managerial Behavior and Entrepreneurship*, J. Weiss, ed., New York: Quorum Books.

Erdilek, A. 1989. "The U.S.-Japan Semiconductor Trade Agreement in the Globalization of Imperfect and Dynamic Competition." In *Industrial Dynamics*, B. Carlsson, ed., Boston: Kluwer.

Florida, R., and M. Kenney. 1987. "Venture Capital, High Technology, and Regional Development." *Regional Studies* 22(1).

Friedman, D. 1988. *The Misunderstood Miracle: Industrial Development and Political Change in Japan.* Ithaca: Cornell University Press.

Gilder, G. 1988. "The Revitalization of Everything: The Law of the Microcosm." *Harvard Business Review* (March-April).

Glasmeier, A. 1991. "Technological Discontinuities and Flexible Production Networks: The Case of Switzerland in the World Watch Industry." *Research Policy* (forthcoming).

Goodman, E., and J. Bamford, eds. 1989. *Small Firms and Industrial Districts in Italy.* London: Routledge.

Gordon, R., and L. Kimball. 1985. "High Technology, Employment and the Challenges to Education." Silicon Valley Research Group Working Paper No. 1, University of California at Santa Cruz.

Granovetter, M. 1985. "Economic Action and Social Structures: The Prolbem of Embeddedness." *American Journal of Sociology* 91(3).

Gregory, K. 1984. "Signing-Up: The Culture and Careers of Silicon Valley Computer People." Unpublished dissertation, Department of Anthropology, Northwestern University.

Herrigel, G. 1988. "Industrial Order and the Politics of Industrial Change." In *Toward a Third Republic?*, P. Katzenstein, ed., Ithaca: Cornell University Press, forthcoming.

Imai, K. 1989. "Evolution of Japan's Corporate and Industrial Networks." In *Industrial Dynamics*, B. Carlsson, ed., Boston: Kluwer.

Linvill, C., and L. Hogan. 1977. "Intellectual and Economic Fuel for the Electronics Revolution." *Scientific American*.

Macdonald, S. 1987. "British Science Parks: Reflections on the Politics of High Technology." *R and D Management*, January.

Markusen, A., P. Hall, S. Campbell, and S. Dietrick. 1990. *The Rise of the Gunbelt.* New York and London: Oxford University Press.

Marshall, A. 1919. *Industry and Trade.* New York: Macmillan & Co.

Berkeley Planning Journal

Miller, R. 1985. "Growing the Next Silicon Valley." *Harvard Business Review* (August).

Mishall, C. 1984. "An Overview of Trends in Science and High Technology Parks." Economic and Policy Analysis Occasional Paper No. 37, Batelle Institute, Columbus, Ohio.

Mowery, D., and N. Rosenberg. 1989. "New Developments in U.S. Technology Policy: Implications for Competitiveness and International Trade Policy." *California Management Review* 32(1):107-124.

Office of Technology Assessment. 1984. *Technology, Innovation and Regional Economic Development.* OTA-STI-238. Washington. D.C.: U.S. Congress, OTA.

Pacific Studies Center. 1987a. "Pentagon role has declined in Silicon Valley." *Global Electronics*, Mountain View, California: PSC.

_____. 1987b. "Silicon Valley Weapons Employment." *Global Electronics*, Mountain View, California: PSC.

Piore, M. 1990. "Work, labour and action: Work experience in a system of flexible production." In *Industrial Districts and Inter-Firm Co-operation in Italy,* F. Pyke et al., eds., Geneva: International Institute for Labour Studies.

Premus, R. 1982. *Location of High Technology Firms and Regional Economic Development.* Staff study for the Subcommittee on Monetary and Fiscal Policy, U.S. Congress Joint Economic Committee, Washington, D.C.: Government Printing Office.

Pyke, F., G. Beccatini, and W. Sengenberger, eds. 1990. *Industrial Districts and Inter-firm Cooperation in Italy.* Geneva: International Labour Organization.

Rogers, E., and J. Larsen. 1984. *Silicon Valley Fever.* New York: Basic Books.

Sabel, C. 1987. "The Reemergence of Regional Economies: Changes in the Scale of Production." Paper prepared for the SSRC Western Europe Committee.

Sabel, C., and J. Zeitlin. 1985. "Historical Alternatives to Mass Production: Politics, Markets and Technology in Nineteenth Century Industrialization." *Past and Present* 108.

Saxenian, A. 1991. "The Origins and Dynamics of Production Networks in Silicon Valley." *Research Policy*, Special Issue on Networks of Innovators.

_____. 1990. "Contrasting Patterns of Business Organization in Silicon Valley." Working Paper no. 535, Institute of Urban and Regional Development, University of California at Berkeley.

_____. 1989a. "Innovation, Regional Development, and the Case of Cambridge, England." *Economy and Society* 18(1).

_____. 1989b. "Regional Networks and the Resurgence of Silicon Valley." *California Management Review* 33(1).

The Growth of Silicon Valley, Saxenian

_____. 1980. "Silicon Chips and Spatial Structure: The Industrial Basis of Urbanization in Santa Clara County, CA." Working Paper No. 345, Institute of Urban and Regional Development, University of California at Berkeley.

Scott, A., and D. Angel. 1987. "The U.S. semiconductor industry: a locational analysis." *Environment and Planning A* 19.

Scott, A., and A. Paul. 1990. "Collective order and economic coordination in industrial agglomerations: the technopolies of Southern California." *Environment and Planning C* 8.

Scranton, P. 1983. *Proprietary Capitalism: The Textile Manufacturers at Philadelphia, 1800-1885*. New York: Cambridge University Press.

Shapira, P. 1991. "Japan's Kohsetsushi Program of Regional Public Examination and Technology Centers for Upgrading Small and Mid-Size Manufacturing Firms." School of Public Policy, Georgia Institute of Technology.

Stowsky, J. 1986. "Beating Our Plowshares into Double-Edged Swords." Berkeley Roundtable on the International Economy (BRIE), Working Paper No. 17, University of California at Berkeley.

Tilton, J. 1971. *International Diffusion of Technology: The Case of Semiconductors*. Washington, D.C.: The Brookings Institution.

U.S. Bureau of the Census. 1959, 1965, 1970, 1980, 1985. *County Business Patterns: California*. U.S. Government Printing Office, Washington, D.C.

Utterbach, J., and A. Murray. 1977. "The Influence of Defense Procurement and Sponsorship of Research and Development on the Development of the US Civilian Electronics Industry." CPA-77-5, Cambridge, Massachusetts: Center for Policy Alternatives.

Weiss, J., and A. Delbecq. 1987. "High Technology Cultures and Management: Silicon Valley and Route 128." *Group and Organization Studies* 12(1):39-54.

Part IV
Policy Perspectives

[23]

Imperatives for a More Productive America

The best-practice firms discussed in the last chapter demonstrate clearly that some American companies still have what it takes to be the best in the world. But many more still do not seem to have recognized that to achieve this status they will have to make far-reaching changes in the way they do business. They will have to adopt new ways of thinking about human resources, new ways of organizing their systems of production, and new approaches to the management of technology. And as we have seen, for these innovations to spread quickly through the large and diverse American economy, coordinated efforts will be needed by government and academia to supplement the actions of individual firms.

Because of the magnitude of the task, it is tempting to focus exclusively on the present predicament of American industry and on remedies that might be applied immediately. But the nature of industrial competition is changing rapidly, and new challenges are arising. Hence, we must look ahead before formulating recommendations. The Commission did not attempt to make detailed forecasts of technological and institutional changes in the business environment. Such forecasts are vulnerable to large error. (Who would have predicted two decades ago that the main commercial applications of the laser would be in compact-disc players and at supermarket checkout counters?) Yet even without a detailed vision of the future, the Commission did identify three major and pervasive long-term trends with broad implications for the productive performance of tomorrow's firms.

Long-Term Trends

First, it seems overwhelmingly likely that economic activity will continue to become more international. The ownership, location, work force, purchases, and sales of firms will all spread out beyond the boundaries of the nation in which the company originated. Only a major episode of protectionism could reverse this trend, and the main threat of such an episode appears to have passed, at least for the time being.

The further internationalization of business will almost certainly intensify competitive pressures. More and more countries will acquire the capacity to produce and to export sophisticated goods and services. Whenever the Latin American economy improves, Brazil and Mexico and perhaps other countries in the region are likely to emerge as players in world markets. The number of newly industrializing countries will surely increase, and some less developed countries will also participate. In the longer term there is the prospect that China will emerge as a potent force in international commerce. Many of these emerging economies will offer labor costs even lower than those of Taiwan and Korea, and far lower than those of the United States, Japan, and Europe. The obvious implication of this trend is that American firms will not be able to compete on the basis of cost alone. The future of American industry will of necessity lie in specialized, high-quality products; elementary commodities will be made in the United States only if their production is extraordinarily capital-intensive and technologically advanced. At the same time, competition among U.S., Japanese, and European firms in markets for high-value-added products will become increasingly fierce.

Second, partly because of internationalization and partly because of rising incomes around the world, markets for consumer goods and intermediate goods are becoming more sophisticated. In many countries, consumers and commercial buyers are becoming more knowledgeable and quality-conscious. Markets are also becoming more segmented and specialized; not everyone is prepared to accept the same designs and specifications. As this process continues, consumers will expect products progressively more customized to individual tastes.

Third, we expect the rapid pace of technological change to continue. Particularly rapid progress seems likely in three areas: information technology, new materials, and biotechnology. Information technology in particular has already permeated nearly every facet of the production of goods and the delivery of services, and we expect it to affect the business environment in a number of ways in the future. Markets will become more integrated. The matching of buyers and sellers will be less affected by geographical differences as computer networking expands. Manufacturing will be able to respond more quickly to market shifts, which in turn will spread more rapidly. Computer and communications technology will allow products to be tailored more closely to the needs and tastes of individual consumers.

Already the use of versatile workstations, rather than fixed, single-purpose machinery, enables short production runs of specialized products, with rapid switching between product types. In the limiting case of fully computer-integrated factories, a continuous stream of different products may be not much more expensive to produce on the factory floor tomorrow than a stream of identical products is today. (Some industries may combine decentralized computer-aided design with centralized foundrylike production, thus exploiting whatever economies of scale remain.)

In the longer run, the convergence of market forces, consumer preferences, and technological opportunities suggests the possibility of "totally flexible" production systems, in which the craft-era tradition of custom-tailoring of products to the needs and tastes of individual customers will be combined with the power, precision, and economy of modern production technology. In such a world the strategic objective will be to deliver high-quality products tailored to each customer at mass-production prices. Information networks and computer simulation techniques will expedite communications between customer and producer. Both purchasing and market research will be facilitated. Simulations will also reduce the need for creating prototypes and will greatly speed the product-development process. In some industries this trend may lead to a continuous flow of product improvements into the market, replacing the present bundling of many improvements into a discrete new product. To achieve this goal, manufacturers will have to move well beyond today's advanced flexible production systems to flexible but fully integrated product development, manufacturing, and marketing systems.

Five Imperatives

In a market economy it is individual firms that have the primary responsibility for correcting past deficiencies and for finding ways to compete successfully in the future. But for these efforts to bear full fruit and for the United States to succeed in building and sustaining an economy with high productivity growth, all sectors—

business, government, labor, and educational institutions—will have to work cooperatively toward this goal.

In the remainder of this chapter we set forth our vision of a more productive America in terms of five imperatives, each of which must be adopted by industry, labor, government, and the educational community. They are not detailed prescriptions but general goals; the next two chapters present our recommendations for how the goals might be achieved. The imperatives are these:

- Focus on the new fundamentals of manufacturing.
- Cultivate a new economic citizenship in the work force.
- Blend cooperation and individualism.
- Learn to live in the world economy.
- Provide for the future.

These goals are interwoven: each one reinforces the others, and all must be pursued together if they are to be effective. Achieving them will not be easy. In many cases, basic changes in attitude will be necessary. Indeed, accepting that there is a need for a sense of common purpose, of shared national goals, may require the biggest attitudinal change of all.

Focusing on the New Fundamentals of Manufacturing

Manufacturing, as we use the term here, encompasses a great deal more than what happens on a production line. It includes designing and developing products as well as planning, marketing, selling, and servicing them. The technologies and processes used in these functions are also part of manufacturing, and so are the ways in which technology and people come together. The United States needs to make a major new commitment to technical and organizational excellence in manufacturing after years of relative inattention. The focus on fundamentals in manufacturing has several subgoals, to which we now turn.

Put products and manufacturing processes ahead of finance. In the postwar years American managers took the production process largely for granted and ranked it below finance and planning in the hierarchy of managerial concerns. The management profession must now reassess its priorities. Managers can no longer afford to be detached from the details of production; otherwise, they will lose the competitive battle to managers who know their business intimately. Business schools must support this change by putting new curricular emphasis on the management of technology and of production processes.

Establish new measures of productive performance. Corporate management and the financial community must work together to develop indicators that better reflect how well companies are actually doing in developing, producing, and marketing their products. Currently, we believe, too much attention is being paid to indicators of short-term financial performance, such as quarterly earnings. At best, these are imperfect measures of longer-term prospects, and at worst, they preoccupy managers and discourage them from focusing on the basics of manufacturing. New measures might include indicators of quality, productivity, product-development time, and time to market.

Focus on the effective use of technology in manufacturing. Manufacturability, reliability, and low cost should be built into products at the earliest possible stages of design. Practices that can help in achieving these aims include extensive analysis of designs, computer simulation, and teamwork among product-planning and production people. Most important, new technologies should be integrated with, rather than thrown at, the work force that will use them. And technology should be integrated with business strategy, sometimes as servant and sometimes as master.

Embrace product customization and production flexibility. Increasingly sophisticated consumers throughout the world are no longer content with identical, mass-produced goods; they are seeking ever more sophisticated products tailored to individual needs. Both manufacturing and service firms will be forced by competition to learn to satisfy such demands. Developments in computer, communications, and manufacturing technology are pushing in the same direction.

In the longer run, as we have already suggested, the goal of "total flexibility"—high-quality, custom-tailored products at mass-production prices—may eventually come within reach. Such a world is still a long way off. But it is already clear that customizing products and being flexible enough to shift production smoothly and efficiently among a broad range of products are emerging as two of the main competitive arenas of the future for manufacturing firms.

134   Chapter 10

Innovate in production processes. The notion that the United States should be content to dominate the inventive front end of the product life cycle is outdated and must change. Although the U.S. economy is still unmatched in its ability to open up new areas of science and technology for commercial exploitation, new products are more likely to originate overseas than they once were. More important, dominating only the front end of the product cycle is not enough to ensure high growth in productivity. The United States, with a fourth of worldwide production and consumption, cannot live off its research alone, just as most companies can get no more than a few percent of their revenue from research. Individual entrepreneurs may profit handsomely from being the first to bring a new product to market, but the biggest economic returns are generally realized later in the product cycle by firms whose strength is in designing better products, delivering them to the marketplace quicker, maintaining higher quality, and continuously improving both products and processes. Innovation must be applied to the processes of production as enthusiastically as it is now applied to products.

The primary responsibility for this must rest with private firms. But there is also an important role for government. Federal policy for science and technology has traditionally put more emphasis on basic research than on technology transfer and the commercialization of new technologies. That has begun to change lately, but there continues to be relatively little support for the development of advanced manufacturing process technologies and for strengthening downstream technical performance. More could be done through tax policy, procurement strategy, and a variety of other measures, as well as through policies for research and development.

Cultivating a New Economic Citizenship in the Work Force

Education for technological competence is crucial for raising the productivity of American firms. But improving productive performance is not the Commission's only objective. We see an unprecedented opportunity in the new technologies for enabling workers at all levels of the firm to master their own work environment. This marks a major change from even the recent past. The technologies for mass-producing standard goods consigned workers to tasks that made few demands on their mental capacities or skills or on their ability to work with others in planning and executing jobs. In a world of assembly-line workers, coordination and responsibility are located at the top of a steep hierarchical structure. In such a system the intrinsic satisfactions of work are few and material compensation is for many people the only motivator.

Today and in the future, effective use of new technology will require people to develop their capabilities for planning, judgment, collaboration, and the analysis of complex systems. In exercising these skills, workers will come to have a larger responsibility for organizing the production process. If American industry can seize this opportunity, individuals may experience a new measure of mastery and independence on the job that could go well beyond maximizing productivity and extend to personal and professional satisfaction and well-being.

Under the new economic citizenship that we envision, workers, managers, and engineers will be continually and broadly trained, masters of their technology, in control of their work environment, and involved in shaping their firms' objectives. No longer will an employee be treated like a cog in a big and impersonal machine. From the company's point of view, the work force will be transformed from a cost factor to be minimized into a precious asset to be conserved and cultivated.

The new economic citizenship will entail new relationships among companies, employees and technology. Learning, especially on the job, will acquire new importance. Greater employee breadth and responsibility are needed to facilitate the absorption of new and rapidly changing manufacturing technologies that span different processes. On the employer's side, greater caring for employees is essential, since under the rules of their new citizenship, employees will be expected to give so much more of themselves to their work.

Once again primary responsibility for achieving this goal rests with individual firms, but government, labor representatives, and educational institutions all have key roles to play as well.

We proceed to a discussion of three principal subgoals that, in our view, will lead to this new kind of economic citizenship.

Learn for work and at work. No matter how much a company invests in capital equipment, automation cannot replace human mastery of the production process, from conception to market. We have learned from foreign examples and from U.S. firms incorporating best practices that successful adaptation to the new economic environment involves workers, technicians, and managers using technology in ways that require good preparation and continuous learning on the job. Chaparral Steel in Texas, like Kyocera Ceramics in Japan and many other firms we visited, operate on the same two principles: technical knowledge must be broadly spread through the production work force to derive maximum advantage from new technologies, and the enterprise must organize its job rotations, career ladders, and training programs to promote learning.

Beyond the need for good basic schooling, which we discuss at the end of this chapter, education and training for work need major overhauling. The expansion of community colleges and other postsecondary educational institutions is a positive development that offsets the sad state of vocational training; it should be encouraged both by connections with the private sector and by public support. University education in the United States in general compares favorably with education in other countries, although there are opportunities for improvement here too, as we discuss in chapter 12. But if postsecondary education is relatively strong in the United States, on-the-job education is seriously underdeveloped. The Commission's research on America's most powerful foreign competitors shows the strengths of a system that offers large-scale training in the workplace, including training through experience in a range of different work responsibilities and frequent job rotations. As we have seen, the Japanese and the West Germans have demonstrated that in-plant training helps to develop a set of firm-specific skills in the context in which they will be employed, to inculcate in all members of the work force an understanding of the whole operation, and finally, by making learning a regular part of the job, to make retraining a normal part of work life. These assets are crucial to success in mastering the new manufacturing technologies. They are also assets that cannot be developed by schools alone, no matter how good the schools may be.

To improve education both in postsecondary institutions and in companies, a variety of contributions from both the private sector and the public sector will be required. Perhaps the most difficult challenge will be to find ways of encouraging more in-plant training and, in particular, training of the broad, general type that is needed over the course of an employee's entire working life.

The German and Japanese employers whom we interviewed feel they have a stake in maintaining a large national reservoir of highly trained workers. It is unlikely that American employers can individually reach this sense of collective responsibility for training workers. But it should be possible to devise incentives that would treat investment in human resources in ways similar to investment in plant and equipment. An equally important goal is to spread the kinds of partnerships among unions, employers, and state and local governments that, in some parts of this country, have begun to make real progress on providing training for the new technologies.

Increase employee breadth, responsibility, and involvement. The possibilities of flexibility, diversity, quality, and reliability offered by flexible computer-aided manufacturing systems can only be realized when the process of production is understood and controlled at all levels of the work force. Unless the jobs of production workers are broadened in ways that require them to understand and control a larger part of the whole process, the full advantages of this new technology cannot be exploited.

In the most successful firms today the role of production workers is shifting from one of passive performance of narrow, repetitive tasks to one of active collaboration in the organization and fine-tuning of production. Skill and flexibility are the result of work experiences in a variety of assignments, and not only or even primarily of courses taken in school or in the plant. Restructuring job categories, flattening hierarchies, broadening responsibilities, and taking on new tasks in regular job rotations—all of these produce a work force capable of responding rapidly and creatively to new problems. The objective should be continuous learning on the job, so that retraining is a normal part of work life.

Provide greater employment stability and new rewards. If people are asked to give maximum effort and to accept uncertainty and rapid change, they must be full participants in the enterprise. They deserve assurance that their striving to increase the productivity of the firm will not simply result in their becoming unnecessary and expendable commodities. The not-very-successful attempt to introduce the NUMMI pattern without NUMMI job security at the General Motors plant in Van Nuys, California, suggests how important this issue is.

138   Chapter 10

Just as important as job security is a measure of participation in the company. In the best-practice firms we visited, participation took various forms, from profit sharing and bonuses based on overall firm performance to ownership of the firm's stock. Such rewards are important, for they focus employee attention on longer-term objectives.

In the longer term, the trends toward shorter production runs, shorter product cycles, a greater variety of products, and a shorter time to market for new products seem likely to result in profit instability, brought about by shifting demand and shifting productive advantage. A business environment of this kind may favor large, diversified firms. Alternatively, firms may become more viable if the risks of business are shared with workers (and suppliers too). In that case, however, workers and suppliers will insist on, and will be entitled to, compensation for their willingness to absorb some of the risks that used to be borne by the entrepreneurial firm. For suppliers, the adjustment might take the form of flexible pricing practices; workers might accept more of their compensation in the form of profit sharing or bonuses. Both developments will probably lead to some sharing of control as well as risk.

Blending Cooperation and Individualism

The challenge ahead is not to suppress individualism in favor of increased cooperation, but rather to combine these two attitudes into a unique mixture that is economically stronger than either extreme. Is this possible, and if so, how?

Americans have traditionally emphasized individualism, often at the expense of cooperation. The nation tends to see the economy as made up of individual persons competing for recognition within their company and of individual companies competing in the marketplace. This view is linked to deeply held national values of individualism and is reflected in the strength of American antitrust legislation and in a widespread suspicion of government intervention. Yet in the best American companies, as in other societies, values of group solidarity, community, and interdependence have led to important economic advantages. For example, they promote better relations with suppliers and customers, they facilitate agreement on common standards, and within a firm they can increase the quality and speed of production.

The presence of a strong tradition of individualism in the United States does not preclude cooperation. Consider the role of land-grant colleges and the extension services in American agriculture, the importance of support by the Defense Advanced Research Projects Agency in the development of the computer field, or the $(TC)^2$ project (Textile/Clothing Technology Corporation), which was funded by government, textile companies, apparel companies, and labor unions to sponsor research on automating sewing. There are also many examples of cooperation between state governments and local industry, and they seem to be growing in number. Within firms, we can point to examples, such as IBM's Proprinter project, where cooperation among scientists, technologists, and production people yielded tangible increases in productive performance. Thus, in our view there is nothing fundamental in American culture that is inimical to the blend of cooperation and individualism that we envision. We next discuss four ways for achieving this.

Organize for both cooperation and individualism. Deep organizational hierarchies, with their rigidity and compartmentalization, are an obstacle to cooperation. They should be replaced with substantially flatter organizational structures that invite communication and cooperation among different corporate departments. The related organizational change of reducing the number of job categories also promotes cooperation, since broadly skilled workers will generally overlap and share knowledge of manufacturing functions. The nation's best-practice firms are distinguished by such flat structures, which demonstrates their feasibility in the American workplace.

Another tangible step is to reward both cooperation and individualism in school. This could be done with team projects, which might receive two grades: one common to all team members that would measure the success of the overall project and another that would measure and reward individual performance. Companies could take exactly the same approach, using individual *and* team bonuses. This has already been tried by some best-practice companies with good results.

Promote better intra- and interfirm relations. We have already extensively discussed the paramount significance of strong and durable relations with suppliers and customers. Toward that end, companies should put less emphasis on legalistic and often adversarial contractual agreements, and promote business relationships based on mutual trust and the prospects of continued business transactions over the long term. Such a shift would not only enhance productive performance but would also help reduce costs.

U.S. firms must also develop cooperative relationships with their domestic competitors to evolve common standards. The lesson of the fragmented U.S. machine-tool industry and the standards-conscious Japanese has apparently not been fully understood.

Expand partnerships. Despite the many positive examples of partnerships here and abroad, Americans continue to regard cooperation among firms and other private and public agencies with suspicion. The nation is paying heavily for this unwillingness to recognize the potential importance of collaboration among the federal government, business, labor, universities, states, and localities in creating the conditions required for economic growth. Americans need to learn to think of cooperation among economic actors as a way of overcoming the defects of the market, which undersupplies certain collective factors that are essential to economic success.

Partnerships can take the form of research consortia or joint business ventures. They can and should also include collaborative efforts with government to promote the development of technologies for productive performance, much as earlier partnerships with the Department of Defense have stimulated new technologies for military purposes. Finally, partnerships should include consortia—especially among small companies and local governments—devoted to training and educating the work force at all levels.

Strengthen cooperation between labor and management. Innovative and cooperative labor-management relationships have emerged within many union and nonunion firms, but they remain fragile and are still at risk of being aborted by the broader adversarial model that continues to dominate labor relations in America. The prevalence of this adversarial model increases the political risks for union leaders who advocate cooperation, raises doubts among managers about the durability of cooperation, and slows the pace of further innovation.

American management, labor, and government therefore face a crucial strategic choice. Clinging to traditional values will mean an escalation of conflict and a diversion of resources away from productive uses. Endorsement of the new patterns of cooperation would create a climate in which further experimentation and innovation would flourish and expand across the economy. Management must accept workers and their representatives as legitimate partners in the innovation process. Labor leaders must become visible champions of the innovative model. And government must become an active party to the process by amending current laws that limit the scope and variety of employee participation and representation.

Learning to Live in the World Economy

Focusing on the technology of manufacturing, cultivating human resources, and encouraging cooperation are the indispensable first steps that Americans must take at home if the United States is to regain the productive edge. But they are not sufficient. To compete successfully in a world that is becoming more international and more competitive, Americans must also expand their outlook beyond their own boundaries. We list four subgoals that in our view will help foster America's international orientation.

Understand foreign languages, cultures, and practices. The ability to export successfully will call for a range of skills that American firms have not needed in the past (or have not perceived that they needed). Companies will have to cultivate knowledge of other languages, market customs, tastes, legal systems, and regulations: they will need to develop a new set of international sensitivities. The key fact here is that competition strengthens the hand of the customer, whose celebrated voice often speaks in languages other than English.

Much can be done toward the learning of foreign languages, customs, and business practices during primary, secondary, and postsecondary education. But schools are not going to embark unilaterally on such a foreign orientation without a strong signal that it is truly useful and in demand. Toward that end, colleges and industry could help directly by requiring a foreign language of those seeking admission or employment.

Shop internationally. American business and American workers must realize that cost considerations will increasingly dictate whether materials and components are best procured at home or abroad. It follows that not only marketing divisions will have to be knowledgeable about conditions abroad; purchasing agents and production managers will have to as well.

Many commentators, ourselves included, have noticed the damage done to American business by the "not invented here" attitude. Increasingly, things invented "there" will have been invented abroad. Thus, the technological net must be cast worldwide. Americans must learn to look for and shop for the best technologies wherever they happen to be.

Shopping internationally should go beyond materials and turnkey technologies to best practices and, particularly, best production benchmarks. Learning and imitating such practices and meeting or exceeding best standards will ensure the continued health of American productive performance within the world economy.

Enhance distribution and service. The history of foreign penetration of American markets suggests that efficient distribution networks and service facilities can be just as important as price and quality of product in getting customers and holding them. It is perhaps best to think of this as part of the general orientation to quality required by sophisticated consumers with money to spend.

Develop internationally conscious policies. All the evidence tells us that a country the size of the United States cannot help itself in the long run by widespread protectionism. Retaliation by others will only set off struggles between different interests at home. But the United States should also actively insist on open trade practices by others in Europe and Asia. It has been relatively ineffective at that so far, partly because of inexperience and ignorance both inside and outside of government.

We have neither the ability nor the wish to provide a manual for the export-competitive firm; we seek only to sketch the outlines of changes in orientation that seem to be required. Perhaps as important as any specific characteristic is America's general attitude about the surrounding world. Smaller countries have long known that the capacity to export at a profit is necessary for domestic success. With internal markets too small to allow full scope for economies of scale, and with resource bases so narrow that many goods and services can only be supplied by imports, which in turn have to be paid for, the smaller countries of Europe have always treated foreign trade as part of life. Japan, lacking domestic oil, minerals, and other resources, has rapidly acquired the same habit. The United States has never before felt that pinch. When the West German economy was being reconstructed after the war, a common slogan was "Exportieren oder sterben!" (Export or die!). The U.S. economy, because of its large scale and natural diversity, is not in quite the same fix. "Export or see your relative standard of living diminish" is not a slogan to set anyone's heart on fire, but it expresses the truth.

Providing for the Future

Many of the actions recommended in this book will bear fruit only in the future, perhaps the distant future. Changes in the organization of production and in the attitudes of producers will not happen overnight; if and when they do happen, the consequences will show themselves only with a further lag. We are talking, then, about investments. And while every one of the five imperatives presented in this chapter may be viewed as an investment, we focus here on providing for the future through a more conventional yet broad use of the term.

We consider in particular four major kinds of investment we believe are necessary to achieve a higher level of productive performance.

Invest in basic education and technical literacy. Americans must be provided with a fundamentally different education from what they receive today. Basic schooling from kindergarten through high school is seriously deficient to the extent that it leaves large numbers of its graduates without basic skills in reading, writing, and mathematics. Only a tiny fraction of young Americans are technologically literate and have some knowledge of foreign societies. Unless the nation begins to remedy these inadequacies, it can make no real progress on all the rest.

At the moment, responsibility for primary and secondary education falls chiefly on local and state governments. We believe, however, that if Americans are to achieve the breadth and depth of changes in education that they need, the federal government will have to provide leadership and incentives. If not, a few cities and states may move ahead, while many others remain at their current unsatisfactory status quo. The large majority of new entrants into the work force in the coming decades will be women, blacks, and Hispanics—groups with major educational and economic handicaps. This makes it all the more important to diffuse educational improvements widely throughout the country.

The Commission has no single, magical solution to America's educational plight. Numerous studies have analyzed the problem and have made their recommendations. In our view, several actions need to converge on this pressing and crucial national problem. The adoption of more rigorous educational standards; a greater focus on science, technology, and foreign languages; perhaps a longer school year; and greater incentives for teachers are some of the ways to begin work on this complex problem. In the next chapter we discuss some of these possibilities at the K–12 and postsecondary levels, where federal and state governments have a role to play, together with private interests.

Develop long-term business strategies. In chapter 4 we came to the conclusion that the shortsightedness of American business strategy goes beyond what can be explained by inappropriately high interest rates. Our case studies suggest that the internal reward systems in American industry are biased in favor of the quick payoff and against the patient exploitation of long-term investments, even when the latter are intrinsically more profitable. If this were a cultural trait, national economic policy might be helpless. However, we find irresistible the inference that the wave of hostile takeovers and leveraged buyouts encourages or enforces an excessive and dangerous overvaluation of short-term profitability. Limiting takeover activity would have efficiency costs as well as the benefits to which we are attracted. It seems clear from the evidence, however, that takeover activity is not entirely driven by efficiency. We believe that the national interest would be served by tax and credit legislation making it harder and more expensive to raise large sums of money for takeovers and buyouts. Among the more important benefits would be the redirection of entrepreneurial talent toward more productive activities.

The high expertise of certain companies in their own business has always been and will undoubtedly continue to be a source of strong competitive advantage. The acquisition, retention, and enhancement of specific expertise in U.S. companies is becoming even more important now that international competitors exhibit ever greater patience in investing for the long term. Thus, shutting down certain business activities and moving into fresh ones that appear to be more profitable may not be effective over the long run.

Another important way in which American businesses can provide for the long term is through investment in research and development. This type of investment may have the longest and least certain payoff period of all, yet it has been successfully pursued in the past, and it continues to be an important and large component of America's best-practice firms. Government, industry, and academic institutions must ensure not only that R&D investment continues strongly in basic research but also that it expands in the direction of productive manufacturing technologies and that it avoids becoming risk-averse.

Establish policies that stimulate productive investment. Reluctance to invest is one important aspect of the general short-windedness that we have identified as a common failing in American industry. An important goal of American economic policy should be to stimulate productive investment. This can be done in several ways. Investment is favored over consumption by a policy mix that combines a more expansionary monetary policy with "tighter" fiscal policy, rather than the reverse; by a fiscal policy that, other things being equal, taxes consumption more heavily than saving or investment when there is a choice; and by tax and other policies that encourage private and public saving, and thus increase the supply of capital to business. In all three of these directions U.S. policy has been perverse and is getting more so. The task of bringing the federal budget closer into balance should receive the highest priority in economic policy making.

Invest in infrastructure for productive performance. The transportation networks of highways, seaways, and airways and the worldwide telephone system are examples of infrastructures that have served their users well. In addition to preserving existing infrastructures, Americans should also consider investing in new infrastructures for tomorrow's changing businesses. One way of doing this is through partnerships among industry, universities, and government that pool their collective strengths but preserve their individual needs. Regional centers set up by state governments and industry would allow small companies to pool their resources for training and other needs that they cannot handle alone. Another possibility is a network of productive-performance centers that would give advice on best available technologies and foreign needs, supplies, and practices. We further believe that the time is right for American business and government to begin developing a national information infrastructure, which would eventually become a network of communication highways as important for tomorrow's business as the current highway network is for today's flow of goods—a prospect that we discuss in more detail in the following chapter.

To summarize, providing for the future is a matter of investing, in the broadest sense of the term. If Americans want the assets thus created to be owned at home, higher investment has to be accompanied by higher savings. It is (almost) as simple as that.

HBR

JANUARY-FEBRUARY 1990

Who Is Us?

by Robert B. Reich

Across the United States, you can hear calls for us to revitalize our national competitiveness. But wait –

who is "us"? Is it IBM, Motorola, Whirlpool, and General Motors? Or is it Sony, Thomson, Philips, and Honda?

Consider two successful corporations:

☐ Corporation A is headquartered north of New York City. Most of its top managers are citizens of the United States. All of its directors are American citizens, and a majority of its shares are held by American investors. But most of Corporation A's employees are non-Americans. Indeed, the company undertakes much of its R&D and product design, and most of its complex manufacturing, outside the borders of the United States in Asia, Latin America, and Europe. Within the American market, an increasing amount of the company's product comes from its laboratories and factories abroad.

☐ Corporation B is headquartered abroad, in another industrialized nation. Most of its top managers and

directors are citizens of that nation, and a majority of its shares are held by citizens of that nation. But most of Corporation B's employees are Americans. Indeed, Corporation B undertakes much of its R&D and new product design in the United States. And it does most of its manufacturing in the U.S. The company ex-

> **The competitiveness of American-owned corporations is not the same as American competitiveness.**

ports an increasing proportion of its American-based production, some of it even back to the nation where Corporation B is headquartered.

Now, who is "us"? Between these two corporations, which is the American corporation, which the foreign corporation? Which is more important to the economic future of the United States?

As the American economy becomes more globalized, examples of both Corporation A and B are increasing. At the same time, American concern for the competitiveness of the United States is increasing.

Robert B. Reich teaches political economy and management at the John F Kennedy School of Government, Harvard University. He is author of many books on trade competitiveness, industrial policy, and government. His most recent book is The Resurgent Liberal (and Other Unfashionable Prophecies), *published by Random House-Times Books in 1989. This is his fifth article for HBR.*

WHO IS US?

Typically, the assumed vehicle for improving the competitive performance of the United States is the American corporation – by which most people would mean Corporation A. But today, the competitiveness of American-owned corporations is no longer the same as American competitiveness. Indeed, American ownership of the corporation is profoundly less relevant to America's economic future than the skills, training, and knowledge commanded by American workers – workers who are increasingly employed within the United States by foreign-owned corporations.

So who is us? The answer is, the American work force, the American people, but not particularly the American corporation. The implications of this new answer are clear: if we hope to revitalize the competitive performance of the United States economy, we must invest in people, not in nationally defined corporations. We must open our borders to investors from around the world rather than favoring companies that may simply fly the U.S. flag. And government policies should promote human capital in this country rather than assuming that American corporations will invest on "our" behalf. The American corporation is simply no longer "us."

Global Companies

American corporations have been abroad for years, even decades. So in one sense, the multinational identity of American companies is nothing new. What is new is that American-owned multinationals are beginning to employ large numbers of foreigners relative to their American work forces, are beginning to rely on foreign facilities to do many of their most technologically complex activities, and are beginning to export from their foreign facilities – including bringing products back to the United States.

Around the world, the numbers are already large – and still growing. Take IBM – often considered the thoroughbred of competitive American corporations. Forty percent of IBM's world employees are foreign, and the percentage is increasing. IBM Japan boasts 18,000 Japanese employees and annual sales of more than $6 billion, making it one of Japan's major exporters of computers.

Or consider Whirlpool. After cutting its American work force by 10% and buying Philips's appliance business, Whirlpool now employs 43,500 people around the world in 45 countries – most of them non-Americans. Another example is Texas Instruments, which now does most of its research, development, design, and manufacturing in East Asia. TI employs over 5,000 people in Japan alone, making advanced semiconductors – almost half of which are exported, many of them back to the United States.

American corporations now employ 11% of the industrial work force of Northern Ireland, making everything from cigarettes to computer software, much of which comes back to the United States. More than 100,000 Singaporians work for more than 200 U.S. corporations, most of them fabricating and assembling electronic components for export to the United States. Singapore's largest private employer is General Electric, which also accounts for a big share of that nation's growing exports. Taiwan counts AT&T, RCA, and Texas Instruments among its largest exporters. In fact, more than one-third of Taiwan's notorious trade surplus with the United States comes from U.S. corporations making or buying

things there, then selling or using them back in the United States. The same corporate sourcing practice accounts for a substantial share of the U.S. trade imbalance with Singapore, South Korea, and Mexico – raising a question as to whom complaints about trade imbalances should be directed.

The pattern is not confined to America's largest companies. Molex, a suburban Chicago maker of connectors used to link wires in cars and computer boards, with revenues of about $300 million in 1988,

> **U.S. companies haven't lost their competitive edge – they've just moved their base of operations.**

has 38 overseas factories, 5 in Japan. Loctite, a midsize company with sales in 1988 of $457 million, headquartered in Newington, Connecticut, makes and sells adhesives and sealants all over the world. It has 3,500 employees – only 1,200 of whom are Americans. These companies are just part of a much larger trend: according to a 1987 McKinsey & Company study, America's most profitable midsize companies increased their investments in overseas production at an annual rate of 20% between 1981 and 1986.

Overall, the evidence suggests that U.S. companies have not lost their competitive edge over the last 20 years – they've just moved their base of operations. In 1966, American-based multinationals accounted for about 17% of world exports; since then their share has remained almost unchanged. But over the same period, the share of exports from the United States in the world's total trade in manufactures fell from 16% to 14%. In other words, while Americans exported less, the overseas affiliates of U.S.-owned corporations exported more than enough to offset the drop.

The old trend of overseas capital investment is accelerating: U.S. companies increased foreign capital spending by 24% in 1988, 13% in 1989. But even more important, U.S. businesses are now putting substantial sums of money into foreign countries to do R&D work. According to National Science Foundation figures, American corporations increased their overseas R&D spending by 33% between 1986 and 1988, compared with a 6% increase in R&D spending in the United States. Since 1987, Eastman Kodak, W.R. Grace, Du Pont, Merck, and Upjohn have all opened new R&D facilities in Japan. At Du Pont's Yokohama laboratory, more than 180 Japanese scientists and technicians are working at developing new materials technologies. IBM's Tokyo Research Lab, tucked away behind the far side of the Imperial Palace in

downtown Tokyo, houses a small army of Japanese engineers who are perfecting image-processing technology. Another IBM laboratory, the Kanagawa arm of its Yamato Development Laboratory, houses 1,500 researchers who are developing hardware and software. Nor does IBM confine its pioneering work to Japan: recently, two European researchers at IBM's Zurich laboratory announced major breakthroughs into superconductivity and microscopy – earning them both Nobel Prizes.

An even more dramatic development is the arrival of foreign corporations in the United States at a rapidly increasing pace. As recently as 1977, only about 3.5% of the value added and the employment of American manufacturing originated in companies controlled by foreign parents. By 1987, the number had grown to almost 8%. In just the last two years, with the faster pace of foreign acquisitions and investments, the figure is now almost 11%. Foreign-owned companies now employ 3 million Americans, roughly 10% of our manufacturing workers. In fact, in 1989, affiliates of foreign manufacturers created more jobs in the United States than American-owned manufacturing companies.

And these non-U.S. companies are vigorously exporting from the United States. Sony now exports audio- and videotapes to Europe from its Dothan, Alabama factory and ships audio recorders from its Fort Lauderdale, Florida plant. Sharp exports 100,000 microwave ovens a year from its factory in Memphis, Tennessee. Last year, Dutch-owned Philips Consumer Electronics Company exported 1,500 color televisions from its Greenville, Tennessee plant to Japan. Its 1990 target is 30,000 televisions; by 1991, it plans to export 50,000 sets. Toshiba America is sending projection televisions from its Wayne, New Jersey plant to Japan. And by the early 1990s, when Honda annually exports 50,000 cars to Japan from its Ohio production base, it will actually be making more cars in the United States than in Japan.

The New American Corporation

In an economy of increasing global investment, foreign-owned Corporation B, with its R&D and manufacturing presence in the United States and its reliance on American workers, is far more important to America's economic future than American-owned Corporation A, with its platoons of foreign workers. Corporation A may fly the American flag, but Corporation B invests in Americans. Increasingly, the competitiveness of American workers is a more important definition of "American competitive-

How Foreign-Owned Businesses Can

What kind of foreign-owned businesses really contribute to national competitiveness? Actually, there are four models to consider, each doing business at a different level of complexity and local intellectual content: importers, assemblers, plant complexes, and fully integrated business operations. For those complex discrete manufacturing businesses such as electronics and automobiles that are at the heart of trade concerns, it is only fully integrated operations that build the local skill base and infrastructure in ways that increase international competitiveness and consequently raise living standards. They do so by bringing in-country the essential engine of business competitiveness.

The Matsushita consumer electronics complex at Kadoma, Japan demonstrates the importance of a fully integrated operation. All four key intellectual elements of the television and videocassette recorder (VCR) product and production systems – product design, manufacturing, process engineering, and vendor management – take place there. Although many components are outsourced, these key intellectual elements are "insourced" at Kadoma so they can be tightly integrated and optimized. Matsushita even builds most of its manufacturing equipment. Mech decks, the highly complex head and tape transport assemblies for VCRs, are assembled by Matsushita robots.

This tight integration enables Matsushita to raise quality, reduce labor hours, provide a high level of product variety to the market, and rapidly incorporate new technology into new products. The mech decks are designed so that every part can be assembled with a simple vertical motion, which facili-

tates 100% assembly automation and high process reliability. This "producible design," which can only be accomplished when there is close teamwork among product designers, process designers, component vendors, and manufacturing managers, in part explains why Matsushita has been able to maintain a leading competitive position worldwide despite the yen shock.

Typical importing and assembly operations are at the opposite end of the scale. Importing companies limit local economic activity to sales, marketing, and distribution; their aim is to win local market share and broaden the business base for an engine of competitiveness located offshore. (We use the term "local" to mean activity carried out in the host country.) Assemblers, a category that includes the U.S. organizations of many Asian-owned consumer electronics companies, make products locally, using designs, processes, and management approaches developed in the home country. They may buy some components locally, but they are likely to import key components, and all the sourcing decisions are made in the home country. As a result, it is difficult for local companies to become suppliers, and the most important supply positions often go to local subsidiaries of home-country suppliers.

Plant complexes add a further level of value added and begin to add intellectual content. Typically, a complex will fabricate product components, and the amount of local engineering content increases. Examples in the United States include the Nissan complex in Smyrna, Tennessee, which makes its own transmissions and transaxels, and the Sony television complex in San Diego, California, which

ness" than the competitiveness of American companies. Issues of ownership, control, and national origin are less important factors in thinking through the logic of "who is us" and the implications of the answer for national policy and direction.

Ownership is less important. Those who favor American-owned Corporation A (that produces overseas) over foreign-owned Corporation B (that produces here) might argue that American ownership generates a stream of earnings for the nation's citizens. This argument is correct, as far as it goes. American shareholders do, of course, benefit from the global successes of American corporations to the extent that such successes are reflected in higher share prices. And the entire U.S. economy benefits to the extent that the overseas profits of American companies are remitted to the United States.

But American investors also benefit from the successes of non-American companies in which Americans own a minority interest – just as foreign citizens benefit from the successes of American companies in which they own a minority interest, and such cross-ownership is on the increase as national restrictions on foreign ownership fall by the wayside. In 1989, cross-border equity investments by Americans, British, Japanese, and West Germans increased 20%, by value, over 1988.

The point is that in today's global economy, the total return to Americans from their equity investments is not solely a matter of the success of particular companies in which Americans happen to have a controlling interest. The return depends on the total amount of American savings invested in global portfolios comprising both American and

WHO IS US?

Contribute to U.S. Competitiveness

makes its own tubes and (together with other Sony operations in California) has a significant engineering force. Still, a plant complex falls well short of a fully integrated business operation. The key intellectual elements of the product and production system are still in the home country, even if the distinctions are becoming more subtle. High-resolution tubes for computer monitors and jumbo television tubes that drive the product and process technology are made at Sony's lead plant in Inazawa, Japan. The U.S. plant makes more mature products.

Assembly operations and plant complexes (particularly the latter) look good on simple economic measures. They employ many assembly workers and some middle managers and engineers. They also can help with catch-up in weak areas of management skills: the GM-Toyota NUMMI plant in California, for example, has shown U.S. managers that management approach rather than automation accounts for much of the Japanese advantage in assembly productivity. These operations cannot bring the host country to the forefront of competitiveness, however, because the engine of competitiveness remains offshore. Thus they do not upgrade the local skill base and technology infrastructure to world leader status; they won't attract the best young managers and engineers; and they are unlikely to stimulate the creative work that spins off new businesses (the "Silicon Valley effect").

The real payoff from local operations for foreign-owned companies, then, comes in the form of fully integrated business operations – when product design, process design, manufacturing, and vendor management are co-located and tightly integrated in-country and the operation is set up to do business in the global market. In this fully integrated operation, the span of activities closely resembles similar operations in the home country.

Examples of fully integrated operations in the United States include the consumer electronics businesses of Philips and Thomson (which were built from acquired companies) and, increasingly, Honda's automobile business. These companies appear to have made commitments to devolve *whole product lines* to their U.S. subsidiaries. The new Honda Accord Coupe, for example, was designed and is made only in the United States and is exported in small quantities to Japan. Likewise, U.S. multinational companies have built many successful fully integrated operations in other parts of the world, for example, IBM's, TI's, and GE Plastics's operations in Japan, Hewlett-Packard's in Singapore, and Ford's in Europe.

The foreign-owned businesses that benefit national competitiveness most are those that commit their engine of competitiveness to the host country. When foreign-owned companies come only to win local market share, they add little to the host country's competitiveness. When they come to build a platform to compete in global markets, then they contribute to national competitiveness.

– Todd Hixon and Ranch Kimball

Todd Hixon is a vice president and high-tech practice leader with the Boston Consulting Group. Ranch Kimball, a manager with BCG, has worked extensively with consumer electronics and automotive companies. Both worked with the American Electronics Association in its high-definition television initiative.

foreign-owned companies – and on the care and wisdom with which American investors select such portfolios. Already Americans invest 10% of their portfolios in foreign securities; a recent study by Salomon Brothers predicts that it will be 15% in a few years. U.S. pension managers surveyed said that they predict 25% of their portfolios will be in foreign-owned companies within 10 years.

Control is less important. Another argument marshaled in favor of Corporation A might be that because Corporation A is controlled by Americans, it will act in the best interests of the United States. Corporation B, a foreign national, might not do so – indeed, it might act in the best interests of its nation of origin. The argument might go something like this: even if Corporation B is now hiring more Americans and giving them better jobs than Corporation

A, we can't be assured that it will continue to do so. It might bias its strategy to reduce American competitiveness; it might even suddenly withdraw its investment from the United States and leave us stranded.

But this argument makes a false assumption about American companies – namely, that they are in a position to put national interests ahead of company or shareholder interests. To the contrary: managers of American-owned companies who sacrificed profits for the sake of national goals would make themselves vulnerable to a takeover or liable for a breach of fiduciary responsibility to their shareholders. American managers are among the loudest in the world to declare that their job is to maximize shareholder returns – not to advance national goals.

Apart from wartime or other national emergencies, American-owned companies are under no special obligation to serve national goals. Nor does our system alert American managers to the existence of such goals, impose on American managers unique requirements to meet them, offer special incentives to achieve them, or create measures to keep American managers accountable for accomplishing them. Were American managers knowingly to sacrifice profits for the sake of presumed national goals, they would be acting without authority, on the basis of their own views of what such goals might be, and without accountability to shareholders or to the public.

Obviously, this does not preclude American-owned companies from displaying their good corporate citizenship or having a sense of social responsibility. Sensible managers recognize that acting "in the public interest" can boost the company's image; charitable or patriotic acts can be good business if they promote long-term profitability. But in this regard, American companies have no particular edge over foreign-owned companies doing business in the United States. In fact, there is every reason to believe that a foreign-owned company would be even more eager to demonstrate to the American public its good citizenship in America than would the average American company. The American subsidiaries of Hitachi, Matsushita, Siemens, Thomson, and many other foreign-owned companies lose no opportunity to contribute funds to American charities, sponsor community events, and support public libraries, universities, schools, and other institutions. (In 1988, for example, Japanese companies operating in the United States donated an estimated $200 million to American charities; by 1994, it is estimated that their contributions will total $1 billion.)[1]

By the same token, American-owned businesses operating abroad feel a similar compulsion to act as good citizens in their host countries. They cannot afford to be seen as promoting American interests; otherwise they would jeopardize their relationships with foreign workers, consumers, and governments. Some of America's top managers have been quite explicit on this point. "IBM cannot be a net exporter from every nation in which it does business," said Jack Kuehler, IBM's new president. "We have to be a good citizen everywhere." Robert W. Galvin, chairman of Motorola, is even more blunt: should it become necessary for Motorola to close some of its factories, it would not close its Southeast Asian plants before it closed its American ones. "We need our Far Eastern customers," says Galvin, "and we cannot alienate the Malaysians. We must treat our employees all over the world equally." In fact, when it becomes necessary to reduce global capacity, we might expect American-owned businesses to slash more jobs in the United States than in Europe (where

labor laws often prohibit precipitous layoffs) or in Japan (where national norms discourage it).

Just as empty is the concern that a foreign-owned company might leave the United States stranded by suddenly abandoning its U.S. operation. The typical argument suggests that a foreign-owned company might withdraw for either profit or foreign policy motives. But either way, the bricks and mortar would still be here. So would the equipment. So too would be the accumulated learning among American workers. Under such circumstances, capital from an-

> **A nation's most important competitive asset is the skills and learning of its work force.**

other source would fill the void; an American (or other foreign) company would simply purchase the empty facilities. And most important, the American work force would remain, with the critical skills and capabilities, ready to go back to work.

After all, the American government and the American people maintain jurisdiction – political control – over assets within the United States. Unlike foreign assets held by American-owned companies that are subject to foreign political control and, occasionally, foreign expropriation, foreign-owned assets in the United States are secure against sudden changes in foreign governments' policies. This not only serves as an attraction for foreign capital looking for a secure haven; it also benefits the American work force.

Work force skills are critical. As every advanced economy becomes global, a nation's most important competitive asset becomes the skills and cumulative learning of its work force. Consequently, the most important issue with regard to global corporations is whether and to what extent they provide Americans with the training and experience that enable them to add greater value to the world economy. Whether the company happens to be headquartered in the United States or the United Kingdom is fundamentally unimportant. The company is a good "American" corporation if it equips its American work force to compete in the global economy.

Globalization, almost by definition, makes this true. Every factor of production other than work

---

1. Craig Smith, editor of *Corporate Philanthropy Report*, quoted in *Chronicle of Higher Education*, November 8, 1989, p. A-34.

2. Bureau of Economic Analysis, *Foreign Direct Investment in the U.S.: Operations of U.S. Affiliates, Preliminary 1986 Estimates* (Washington, D.C.: U.S. Department of Commerce, 1988) for data on foreign companies; Bureau of the Census, *Annual Survey of Manufactures: Statistics for Industry Groups and Industries, 1986* (Washington, D.C., 1987) for U.S. companies.

force skills can be duplicated anywhere around the world. Capital now sloshes freely across international boundaries, so much so that the cost of capital in different countries is rapidly converging. State-of-the-art factories can be erected anywhere. The latest technologies flow from computers in one nation, up to satellites parked in space, then back down to computers in another nation—all at the speed of electronic impulses. It is all fungible: capital, technology, raw materials, information—all, except for one thing, the most critical part, the one element that is unique about a nation: its work force.

In fact, because all of the other factors can move so easily any place on earth, a work force that is knowledgeable and skilled at doing complex things attracts foreign investment. The relationship forms a virtuous circle: well-trained workers attract global corporations, which invest and give the workers good jobs; the good jobs, in turn, generate additional training and experience. As skills move upward and experience accumulates, a nation's citizens add greater and greater value to the world—and command greater and greater compensation from the world, improving the country's standard of living.

Foreign-owned corporations help American workers add value. When foreign-owned companies come to the United States, they frequently bring with them approaches to doing business that improve American productivity and allow American workers to add more value to the world economy. In fact, they come here primarily because they can be more productive in the United States than can other American rivals. It is not solely America's mounting external indebtedness and relatively low dollar that account for the rising level of foreign investment in the United States. Actual growth of foreign investment in the United States dates from the mid-1970s rather than from the onset of the large current account deficit in 1982. Moreover, the two leading foreign investors in the United States are the British and the Dutch—not the Japanese and the West Germans, whose enormous surpluses are the counterparts of our current account deficit.

For example, after Japan's Bridgestone tire company took over Firestone, productivity increased dramatically. The joint venture between Toyota and General Motors at Fremont, California is a similar story: Toyota's managerial system took many of the same workers from what had been a deeply troubled GM plant and turned it into a model facility, with upgraded productivity and skill levels.

In case after case, foreign companies set up or buy up operations in the United States to utilize their corporate assets with the American work force. Foreign-owned businesses with better design capabilities,

production techniques, or managerial skills are able to displace American companies on American soil precisely because those businesses are more productive. And in the process of supplanting the American company, the foreign-owned operation can transfer the superior know-how to its American work force—giving American workers the tools they need to be more productive, more skilled, and more competitive. Thus foreign companies create good jobs in the United States. In 1986 (the last date for which such data are available), the average American employee of a foreign-owned manufacturing company earned $32,887, while the average American employee of an American-owned manufacturer earned $28,954.[2]

This process is precisely what happened in Europe in the 1950s and 1960s. Europeans publicly fretted about the invasion of American-owned multinationals and the onset of "the American challenge." But the net result of these operations in Europe has been to make Europeans more productive, upgrade European skills, and thus enhance the standard of living of Europeans.

Now Who Is Us?

American competitiveness can best be defined as the capacity of Americans to add value to the world economy and thereby gain a higher standard of living in the future without going into ever deeper debt. American competitiveness is not the profitability or market share of American-owned corporations. In fact, because the American-owned corporation is coming to have no special relationship with Americans, it makes no sense for Americans to entrust our national competitiveness to it. The interests of American-owned corporations may or may not coincide with those of the American people.

Does this mean that we should simply entrust our national competitiveness to any corporation that employs Americans, regardless of the nationality of corporate ownership? Not entirely. Some foreign-owned corporations are closely tied to their nation's economic development—either through direct public ownership (for example, Airbus Industrie, a joint product of Britain, France, West Germany, and Spain, created to compete in the commercial airline industry) or through financial intermediaries within the nation that, in turn, are tied to central banks and ministries of finance (in particular the model used by many Korean and Japanese corporations). The primary goals of such corporations are to enhance the wealth of their nations, and the standard of living of their nations' citizens, rather than to enrich their shareholders. Thus, even though they might employ American citizens in their worldwide operations, they may employ fewer Americans – or give Americans lower value-added jobs – than they would if these corporations were intent simply on maximizing their own profits.[3]

On the other hand, it seems doubtful that we could ever shift the goals and orientations of American-owned corporations in this same direction – away

> **National policies should reward any global corporation that invests in the American work force.**

from profit maximization and toward the development of the American work force. There is no reason to suppose that American managers and shareholders would accept new regulations and oversight mechanisms that forced them to sacrifice profits for the sake of building human capital in the United States. Nor is it clear that the American system of government would be capable of such detailed oversight.

The only practical answer lies in developing national policies that reward *any* global corporation that invests in the American work force. In a whole set of public policy areas, involving trade, publicly supported R&D, antitrust, foreign direct investment, and public and private investment, the overriding goal should be to induce global corporations to build human capital in America.

Trade policy. We should be less interested in opening foreign markets to American-owned companies (which may in fact be doing much of their production overseas) than in opening those markets to companies that employ Americans – even if they happen to be foreign-owned. But so far, American trade policy experts have focused on representing the interests of companies that happen to carry the American flag – without regard to where the actual production is being done. For example, the United States recently accused Japan of excluding Motorola from the lucrative Tokyo market for cellular telephones and hinted at retaliation. But Motorola designs and makes many of its cellular telephones in Kuala Lumpur, while most of the Americans who make cellular telephone equipment in the United States for export to Japan happen to work for Japanese-owned companies. Thus we are wasting our scarce political capital pushing foreign governments to reduce barriers to American-owned companies that are seeking to sell or produce in their market.

Once we acknowledge that foreign-owned Corporation B may offer more to American competitiveness than American-owned Corporation A, it is easy to design a preferable trade policy – one that accords more directly with our true national interests. The highest priority for American trade policy should be to discourage other governments from invoking domestic content rules – which have the effect of forcing global corporations, American and foreign-owned alike, to locate production facilities in those countries rather than in the United States.

The objection here to local content rules is not that they may jeopardize the competitiveness of American companies operating abroad. Rather, it is that these requirements, by their very nature, deprive the American work force of the opportunity to compete for jobs, and with those jobs, for valuable skills, knowledge, and experience. Take, for example, the recently promulgated European Community nonbinding rule on television-program production, which urges European television stations to devote a majority of their air time to programs made in Europe. Or consider the European allegations of Japanese dumping of office machines containing semiconductors, which has forced Japan to put at least 45% European content into machines sold in Europe (and thus fewer American-made semiconductor chips).

Obviously, U.S.-owned companies are already inside the EC producing both semiconductors and television programs. So if we were to adopt American-owned Corporation A as the model for America's competitive self-interest, our trade policy might simply ignore these EC initiatives. But through the lens of a trade policy focused on the American work force, it is clear how the EC thwarts the abilities of Americans to excel in semiconductor fabrication and filmmaking – two areas where our work force already enjoys a substantial competitive advantage.

Lack of access by American-owned corporations to foreign markets is, of course, a problem. But it only becomes a crucial problem for America to the extent that both American and foreign-owned companies must make products within the foreign market – products that they otherwise would have made in the United States. Protection that acts as a domestic content requirement skews investment away from the United States – and away from U.S. workers. Fighting against that should be among the highest priorities of U.S. trade policy.

Publicly supported R&D. Increased global competition, the high costs of research, the rapid rate of change in science and technology, the model of Japan

---

3. Robert B. Reich and Eric D. Mankin, "Joint Ventures with Japan Give Away Our Future," HBR March-April 1986, p. 78.

with its government-supported commercial technology investments – all of these factors have combined to make this area particularly critical for thoughtful public policy. But there is no reason why preference should be given to American-owned companies. Dominated by our preoccupation with American-owned Corporation A, current public policy in this area limits U.S. government-funded research grants, guaranteed loans, or access to the fruits of U.S. government-funded research to American-owned companies. For example, membership in Sematech, the research consortium started two years ago with $100 billion annual support payments by the Department of Defense to help American corporations fabricate complex memory chips, is limited to American-owned companies. More recently, a government effort to create a consortium of companies to catapult the United States into the HDTV competition has drawn a narrow circle of eligibility, ruling out companies such as Sony, Philips, and Thomson that do R&D and production in the United States but are foreign-owned. More generally, long-standing regulations covering the more than 600 government laboratories and research centers that are spread around the United States ban all but American-owned companies from licensing inventions developed at these sites.

> ## Should Sony, Philips, and Thomson be eligible to participate in the HDTV consortium – with their American workers?

Of course, the problem with this policy approach is that it ignores the reality of global American corporations. Most U.S.-owned companies are quite happy to receive special advantages from the U.S. government – and then spread the technological benefits to their affiliates all over the world. As Sematech gets under way, its members are busily going global: Texas Instruments is building a new $250 million semiconductor fabrication plant in Taiwan; by 1992, the facility will produce four-megabit memory chips and custom-made, application-specific integrated circuits – some of the most advanced chips made anywhere. TI has also joined with Hitachi to design and produce a super chip that will store 16 million bits of data. Motorola, meanwhile, has paired with Toshiba to research and produce a similar generation of futurist chips. Not to be outdone, AT&T has a commitment to build a state-of-the-art chip-

making plant in Spain. So who will be making advanced chips in the United States? In June 1989, Japanese-owned NEC announced plans to build a $400 million facility in Rosedale, California for making four-megabit memory chips and other advanced devices not yet in production anywhere.

The same situation applies to HDTV. Zenith Electronics is the only remaining American-owned television manufacturer, and thus the only one eligible for a government subsidy. Zenith employs 2,500 Americans. But there are over 15,000 Americans employed in the television industry who do not work for Zenith – undertaking R&D, engineering, and high-quality manufacturing. They work in the United States for foreign-owned companies: Sony, Philips, Thomson, and others (see the accompanying table). Of course, none of these companies is presently eligible to participate in the United States's HDTV consortium – nor are their American employees.

Again, if we follow the logic of Corporation B as the more "American" company, it suggests a straightforward principle for publicly supported R&D: we should be less interested in helping *American-owned companies* become technologically sophisticated than in helping *Americans* become technologically sophisticated. Government-financed help for research and development should be available to any corporation, regardless of the nationality of its owners, as long as the company undertakes the R&D in the United States – using American scientists, engineers, and technicians. To make the link more explicit, there could even be a relationship between the number of Americans involved in the R&D and the amount of government aid forthcoming. It is important to note that this kind of public-private bargain is far different from protectionist domestic content requirements. In this case, the government is participating with direct funding and thus can legitimately exact a quid pro quo from the private sector.

Antitrust policy. The Justice Department is now in the process of responding to the inevitability of globalization; it recognizes that North American market share alone means less and less in a global economy. Consequently, the Justice Department is about to relax antitrust policy – for American-owned companies only. American-owned companies that previously kept each other at arm's length for fear of prompting an inquiry into whether they were colluding are now cozying up to one another. Current antitrust policy permits research joint ventures; the attorney general is on the verge of recommending that antitrust policy permit joint production agreements as well, when there may be significant economies of scale and where competition is global – again, among American-owned companies.

But here again, American policy seems myopic. We should be less interested in helping American-owned companies gain economies of scale in research, production, and other key areas, and more interested in helping corporations engaged in research or production within the United States achieve economies of scale – regardless of their nationality. U.S. antitrust policy should allow research or production joint ventures among any companies doing R&D or production within the United States, as long as they can meet three tests: they could not gain such scale efficiencies on their own, simply by enlarging their investment in the United States; such a combination of companies would allow higher levels of productivity within the United States; and the combination would not substantially diminish global competition. National origin should not be a factor.

Foreign direct investment. Foreign direct investment has been climbing dramatically in the United States: last year it reached $329 billion, exceeding total American investment abroad for the first time since World War I (but be careful with these figures, since investments are valued at cost and this substantially understates the worth of older invest-

ments). How should we respond to this influx of foreign capital?

Clearly, the choice between Corporation A and Corporation B has important implications. If we are most concerned about the viability of American-owned corporations, then we should put obstacles in the way of foreigners seeking to buy controlling shares in American-owned companies, or looking to build American production facilities that would compete with American-owned companies.

Indeed, current policies tilt in this direction. For example, under the so-called Exon-Florio Amendment of the Omnibus Trade and Competitiveness Act of 1988, foreign investors must get formal approval from the high-level Committee on Foreign Investments in the United States, comprising the heads of eight federal agencies and chaired by the secretary of the treasury, before they can purchase an American company. The expressed purpose of the law is to make sure that a careful check is done to keep "national security" industries from passing into the hands of foreigners. But the law does not define what "national security" means: thus it invites all sorts of potential delays and challenges. The actual effect is

U.S. TV Set Production, 1988

Company Name	Plant Type	Location	Employees	Annual Production
Bang & Olufsen	Assembly	Compton, Calif.	n.a.†	n.a.
Goldstar	Total*	Huntsville, Ala.	400	1,000,000
Harvey Industries	Assembly	Athens, Tex.	900	600,000
Hitachi	Total	Anaheim, Calif.	900	360,000
JVC	Total	Elmwood Park, N.J.	100	480,000
Matsushita	Assembly	Franklin Park, Ill.	800	1,000,000
American Kotobuki (Matsushita)	Assembly	Vancouver, Wash.	200	n.a.
Mitsubishi	Assembly	Santa Ana, Calif.	550	400,000
Mitsubishi	Total	Braselton, Ga.	300	285,000
NEC	Assembly	McDonough, Ga.	400	240,000
Orion	Assembly	Princeton, Ind.	250	n.a.
Philips	Total	Greenville, Tenn.	3,200	2,000,000+
Samsung	Total	Saddle Brook, N.J.	250	1,000,000
Sanyo	Assembly	Forrest City, Ark.	400	1,000,000
Sharp	Assembly	Memphis, Tenn.	770	1,100,000
Sony	Total	San Diego, Calif.	1,500	1,000,000
Tatung	Assembly	Long Beach, Calif.	130	17,500
Thomson	Total	Bloomington, Ind.	1,766	3,000,000+
Thomson	Components	Indianapolis, Ind.	1,604	n.a.
Toshiba	Assembly	Lebanon, Tenn.	600	900,000
Zenith	Total	Springfield, Mo.	2,500	n.a.

*Total manufacturing involves more than the assembling of knocked-down kits. Plants that manufacture just the television cabinets are not included in this list. †Not available.

Source: Electronic Industries Association, HDTV Information Center, Washington, D.C.

to send a message that we do not look with favor on the purchase of American-owned assets by foreigners. Other would-be pieces of legislation send the same signal. In July 1989, for instance, the House Ways and Means Committee voted to apply a withholding capital gains tax to foreigners who own more than 10% of a company's shares. Another provision of the committee would scrap tax deductibility for interest on loans made by foreign parents to their American subsidiaries. A third measure would limit R&D tax credits for foreign subsidiaries. More re-

> **The federal government has been cutting back on the investments that are critical for America's competitive future.**

cently, Congress is becoming increasingly concerned about foreign takeovers of American airlines. A subcommittee of the House Commerce Committee has voted to give the Transportation Department authority to block foreign acquisitions.

These policies make little sense – in fact, they are counterproductive. Our primary concern should be the training and development of the American work force, not the protection of the American-owned corporation. Thus we should encourage, not discourage, foreign direct investment. Experience shows that foreign-owned companies usually displace American-owned companies in just those industries where the foreign businesses are simply more productive. No wonder America's governors spend a lot of time and energy promoting their states to foreign investors and offer big subsidies to foreign companies to locate in their states, even if they compete head-on with existing American-owned businesses.

Public and private investment. The current obsession with the federal budget deficit obscures a final, crucial aspect of the choice between Corporation A and Corporation B. Conventional wisdom holds that government expenditures "crowd out" private investment, making it more difficult and costly for American-owned companies to get the capital they need. According to this logic, we may have to cut back on public expenditures in order to provide American-owned companies with the necessary capital to make investments in plant and equipment.

But the reverse may actually be the case – particularly if Corporation B is really more in America's competitive interests than Corporation A. There are a number of reasons why this is true.

First, in the global economy, America's public expenditures don't reduce the amount of money left over for private investment in the United States. Today capital flows freely across national borders – including a disproportionately large inflow to the United States. Not only are foreign savings coming to the United States, but America's private savings are finding their way all over the world. Sometimes the vehicle is the far-flung operations of a global American-owned company, sometimes a company in which foreigners own a majority stake. But the old notion of national boundaries is becoming obsolete. Moreover, as I have stressed, it is a mistake to associate these foreign investments by American-owned companies with any result that improves the competitiveness of the United States. There is simply no necessary connection between the two.

There is, however, a connection between the kinds of investments that the public sector makes and the competitiveness of the American work force. Remember: a work force that is knowledgeable and skilled at doing complex things attracts foreign investment in good jobs, which in turn generates additional training and experience. A good infrastructure of transporation and communication makes a skilled work force even more attractive. The public sector often is in the best position to make these sorts of "pump priming" investments – in education, training and retraining, research and development, and in all of the infrastructure that moves people and goods and facilitates communication. These are the investments that distinguish one nation from another – they are the relatively nonmobile factors in the global competition. Ironically, we do not ordinarily think of these expenditures as investments; the federal budget fails to distinguish between a capital and an operating budget, and the national income accounts treat all government expenditures as consumption. But without doubt, these are precisely the investments that most directly affect our future capacity to compete.

During the 1980s, we allowed the level of these public investments either to remain stable or, in some cases, to decline. As America enters the 1990s, if we hope to launch a new campaign for American competitiveness, we must substantially increase public funding in the following areas:

☐ *Government spending on commercial R&D.* Current spending in this critical area has declined 95% from its level two decades ago. Even as late as 1980, it comprised .8% of gross national product; today it comprises only .4% – a much smaller percentage than in any other advanced economy.

☐ *Government spending to upgrade and expand the nation's infrastructure.* Public investment in critical highways, roads, bridges, ports, airports, and waterways dropped from 2.3% of GNP two decades ago to

WHO IS US?

1.3% in the 1980s. Thus many of our bridges are unsafe, and our highways are crumbling.

□ *Expenditures on public elementary and secondary education.* These have increased, to be sure. But in inflation-adjusted terms, per pupil spending has shown little gain. Between 1959 and 1971, spending per student grew at a brisk 4.7% in real terms – more than a full percentage point above the increase in the GNP – and teachers' salaries increased almost 3% a year. But since then, growth has slowed. Worse, this has happened during an era when the demands on public education have significantly increased, due to the growing incidence of broken homes, unwed mothers, and a rising population of the poor. Teachers' salaries, adjusted for inflation, are only a bit higher than they were in

1971. Despite the rhetoric, the federal government has all but retreated from the field of education. In fact, George Bush's 1990 education budget is actually smaller than Ronald Reagan's in 1989. States and municipalities, already staggering under the weight of social services that have been shifted onto them from the federal government, simply cannot carry this additional load. The result of this policy gap is a national education crisis: one out of five American 18-year-olds is illiterate, and in test after test, American schoolchildren rank at the bottom of international scores. Investing more money here may not be a cure-all – but money is at least necessary.

□ *College opportunity for all Americans.* Because of government cutbacks, many young people in the United States with enough talent to go to college cannot afford it. During the 1980s, college tuitions rose 26%; family incomes rose a scant 5%. Instead of filling the gap, the federal government created a vacuum: guaranteed student loans have fallen by 13% in real terms since 1980.

□ *Worker training and retraining.* Young people who cannot or do not wish to attend college need training for jobs that are becoming more complex. Older workers need retraining to keep up with the demands of a rapidly changing, technologically advanced workplace. But over the last eight years, federal investments in worker training have dropped by more than 50%.

These are the priorities of an American strategy for national competitiveness – a strategy based more on the value of human capital and less on the value of financial capital. The simple fact of American ownership has lost its relevance to America's economic future. Corporations that invest in the United States, that build the value of the American work force, are more critical to our future standard of living than are American-owned corporations investing abroad. To attract and keep them, we need public investments that make America a good place for any global corporation seeking talented workers to set up shop.   ☐

Reprint 90111

[25]

They Are Not Us
Why American Ownership Still Matters
Laura D'Andrea Tyson

Like "Engine" Charlie Wilson, the colorful chief executive of General Motors in the years after World War II, most Americans intuitively assume that what is good for American companies like GM is good for the nation. The competitiveness of the U.S. economy, most Americans believe, means the competitiveness of corporations based in the United States. This identity of interests has been so widely taken for granted that only a few theoreticians of the obvious, like Engine Charlie and Calvin Coolidge ("The business of America is business"), have ever seen a need to express it.

The tradition of identifying nations and corporations extends far back into the past when corporations served the monarchs who gave them special charters. But whether that premise makes sense today is not at all clear. The actual behavior of many American corporations shows that they do not always act as if national loyalty were their guiding motivation. Corporations are quick to relocate to remote countries with lower wages, less demanding social standards, or national laws requiring local production.

Indeed, some are now suggesting that national corporations are entirely a thing of the past. In several articles and an upcoming book that have crystallized the issue, Robert B. Reich warns that as American companies have become ever more global in their operations, the links between them and the U.S. economy are rapidly disappearing, and so policymakers must distinguish sharply between American economic interests and the economic interests of American companies.[1] Whether the U.S. can provide high-wage jobs and support rising living standards depends, in Reich's view, less on the strength of American companies than on the strength and competitiveness of the economic activities located within our borders.

On this fundamental insight, Reich's logic is persuasive. He has framed precisely the right question: How are we to disentangle the interest of the nation-based corporation from that of the nation and its citizens? But the specifics of his analysis and his policy inferences can be challenged in two key respects.

First, his picture is, at best, premature. The economic fate of nations is still tied closely to the success of their domestically based corporations. Second, he assumes that globalization implies a symmetry of national economic policies, when in reality there are wide disparities. Many foreign markets are highly regulated, often to

1. Robert B. Reich, "Who Is Us?" *Harvard Business Review* (Jan.-Feb. 1990), 53-64, and *The Work of Nations: Preparing Ourselves for 21st-Century Capitalism* (Alfred A. Knopf, 1991).

America's disadvantage. Consequently America cannot just foster the best possible workforce and then rely on market forces to bring high-wage jobs to our shores.

Reich argues his case by contrasting two hypothetical corporations. Corporation A, headquartered in the United States and owned by American investors, is an American company. But it is also a global one: Most of its employees are non-Americans, and it undertakes much of its research and development and product design and most of its complex manufacturing outside of the United States.

Corporation B, headquartered in a foreign country and owned primarily by

> *Despite globalization, the competitiveness of the U.S. economy remains tightly linked to the competitiveness of U.S. companies.*

foreign investors, is a foreign company. But like Corporation A, it is also a global company: Much of its R&D and product design and most of its employment and manufacturing are located abroad—in the U.S.

Which of these two corporations is more important to the economic future of the United States? Or, as Reich asks, "Who is Us?"— Corporation A, the American company, or Corporation B, the foreign company? The answer seems obvious and counter to conventional wisdom.

But is the question fair? Have a significant number of American companies really globalized to such an extent that most of their economic activities are located abroad? And have foreign companies increased their investment in the United States so much that they now contribute as much or more to national economic com-

petitiveness than American companies? Although both American and foreign companies are indeed becoming more global, as Reich suggests, the answer to both questions, for now and for the foreseeable future, is "no."

We Are Us

Despite several decades of substantial foreign direct investment by U.S. multinationals, the competitiveness of the U.S. economy remains tightly linked to the competitiveness of U.S. companies. U.S. multinationals still locate the lion's share of their worldwide operations within the U.S. In 1988, the last year for which data are available, U.S. parent operations accounted for 78 percent of the total assets, 70 percent of the total sales, and 74 percent of the total employment of U.S. multinationals.[2] All of these shares were actually higher in 1988 than they were in 1977, the reverse of what one would expect if the links between the domestic economy and U.S. multinationals were precipitously disappearing, as Reich argues.

Within manufacturing, U.S. parent operations accounted for 78 percent of the total assets, 70 percent of the total sales, and 70 percent of the total employment of U.S. multinationals in 1988. The data reveal, moreover, that parent operations provided more productive jobs than affiliate operations. Assets per employee in the manufacturing parent operations were about 20 percent higher than in affiliate operations in developed countries and almost 200 percent higher than in affiliate operations in the developing countries. Similarly, compensation per employee in parent operations was about 17 percent higher than in affiliate operations in developed countries and about 360 percent higher than in affiliate operations in the developing countries. In short, American firms locate their "higher-end" jobs and operations at home.

2. My calculations are based on data in Raymond Mataloni, Jr., "U.S. Multinational Companies: Operations in 1988," *Survey of Current Business* 70 (June 1990), 31-44.

Although American companies may have increased their overseas R&D spending by 33 percent between 1986 and 1988, compared with a 6-percent increase in R&D spending at home, the companies continue to spend the bulk of their R&D budgets within the United States. Between 1966 and 1982, the last year for which data are available, the share of R&D spending by U.S. multinationals in their overseas operations increased from 6.5 percent to only 8.8 percent. This overseas share was far lower than comparable shares for sales (29.4 percent) and assets (26.4 percent).

By 1988 the proportion of the total R&D spending by all U.S. companies that took place overseas had slipped to 8.6 percent, down from 9.4 percent in 1980. Again the trend does not support the notion of increasing globalization. In fact, according to John Dunning, a scholar who has done extensive research on multinationals, the available evidence suggests that except for some European firms and a few U.S. companies, such as IBM, the average share of R&D activity undertaken by global companies outside their home countries is quite small. For Japanese firms it is negligible.[3] Outside of their home environments, global companies mainly produce goods and services, not innovations.

The leadership of American companies also remains overwhelmingly American. Despite innumerable speeches by American corporate leaders on the globalization of American business, most large American companies do not have any foreigners on their boards of directors. According to a recent survey of directors by the executive search firm Korn Ferry reported in *The Economist*, the proportion of the top 1,000 firms with a non-American on the board has declined from a recent peak of 17 percent in 1982 to only 12 percent in 1990.

So, overall, despite globalization, a disproportionate share of the activity of U.S.

multinationals, especially their high-wage, high-productivity, research-intensive activity, remains in the U.S. Of course, many American companies have made huge investments overseas. But these investments have not necessarily weakened domestic economic competitiveness. Indeed, the presumption should run the other way. Since American multinationals continue to locate the bulk of their high-quality productive activities in the U.S., the beneficial competitive effects of their overseas operations spill over into more and better jobs, higher profits, lower prices, and improved products at home.

For the foreseeable future, there are likely to be very few American corporations with a type-A personality—headquartered at home, but with most of their employees and complex manufacturing located abroad. U.S. multinational companies remain "us" in significant ways.

But Are "They" Also Us?

But what about the foreign multinationals that have established affiliate operations in the U.S.? Are they also us? In some industries, such as consumer electronics, U.S. national competitiveness now depends largely on foreign affiliates. In other industries, such as computers, U.S. competitiveness depends almost entirely on American companies, most of which have substantial overseas operations.

Instead of a simple yes or no answer to Reich's question, I suggest five propositions for assessing the contributions of foreign affiliates to national competitiveness.

Proposition 1."They are becoming like us, but they have a long way to go."

Growing evidence indicates that, in certain ways, the affiliates of foreign companies operating in the U.S. resemble the domestic operations of American companies. Foreign affiliates are, on average, virtually indistinguishable from domestic firms in value-added per worker, compensation per worker, and R&D spending per worker, according to a recent study by Ed-

3. J. H. Dunning, "Multinational Enterprises and the Globalization of Innovatory Capacity." University of Reading, Department of Economics, Sept. 1990.

ward M. Graham and Paul R. Krugman, *Foreign Direct Investment in the United States*, published by the Institute for International Economics.

The only significant difference found by Graham and Krugman is that the affiliates of foreign firms apparently import significantly more than do the parent operations of U.S. multinationals—almost two and one half times as much. Because many foreign affiliates were established recently—especially in the 1977-1981 period when foreign direct investment in the U.S. grew rapidly—their dependence on imports will quite likely decline over time, as affiliates begin to rely on networks of local suppliers in the U.S. Affiliates of U.S. companies abroad have followed this pattern.

While on average they look increasingly like domestic companies, foreign affiliates differ sharply among themselves. At one extreme are foreign affiliates that are little more than assembly operations for foreign products. The Ricoh copier operation in California, for example, is an assembly plant with little domestic content.

At the other end of the spectrum are the extensive American operations of Honda and Sony. Honda sells more cars in the United States than in Japan and has set up largely independent design, production, and sales facilities in North America. The American content of the automobiles it produces in the U.S. is fast approaching the American content of the automobiles made by Chrysler.

Foreign affiliates, whatever their character, still represent a relatively small fraction of total economic activity within the United States, accounting for only 4.3 percent of all U.S.-business gross product in 1987, up from 2.3 percent in 1977. The comparable figure for manufacturing was 10.5 percent in 1987, up from 5.0 percent in 1977.[4] In 1988, the last year for which data are available, foreign affiliates accounted for 4.1 per-

cent of U.S. nonbank employment, and 8.5 percent of manufacturing employment.

In light of figures such as these, the proposition that foreign firms are as important to national competitiveness as domestic firms is more a prediction of the future than a reflection of the present. In most areas—such as trade, output, employment, and R&D spending—domestic firms still dominate domestic economic activity.

And there are virtually no examples of Corporation B—a foreign-owned firm with most of its employment and manufacturing in the U.S. Nor do current trends indicate that there will be many examples in the near future. Indeed, after a rapid expansion of foreign affiliate operations in the U.S. in 1987 and 1988, foreign direct investment has tapered off. For the foreseeable future, the fate of the U.S. economy in most industries will remain tied to the fate of U.S.-owned businesses.

Proposition 2. "Where they are most like us, our policies have encouraged them to be so."

In certain sectors of the economy, however, foreign-owned firms represent a substantial share of domestic economic activity. Foreign companies now control roughly one-half of the U.S. consumer electronics industry, one-third of the U.S. chemical industry, and one-sixth of the U.S. automobile industry.

Why have foreign firms gained such large shares of domestic production in these industries? Both U.S. and other multinationals invest abroad primarily to improve their shares of foreign markets. When protectionist trade barriers block access to markets, or even when barriers are only being discussed, foreign firms often respond by making direct investments in local production facilities. Protectionism is not a *sufficient* condition to explain foreign direct investment; foreign firms must be able to compete with domestic firms after incurring the higher costs of establishing local production to serve the domestic market. But protectionism may be a *neces-*

---

4. Jeffrey H. Lowe, "Gross Product of U.S. Affiliates of Foreign Companies, 1977-87," *Survey of Current Business* 70 (June 1990), 45-53.

sary condition to explain such investment, since when they have no reason to fear import barriers, foreign firms typically prefer to supply markets through trade rather than local production.

Trade friction between the U.S. and its trading partners is a major reason for the substantial foreign investment in America's consumer electronics and automobile industries. Honda's extensive operations in the U.S., for example, were largely stimulated by U.S. trade policy. Among Japan's automakers Honda stood the most to lose from the restrictions on Japanese auto exports to the U.S. that were in force between 1981 and 1985 (the so-called "voluntary export restraints"). In Japan itself, Honda's market share had been held in check by Toyota and Nissan, and while the U.S. was Honda's largest and fastest growing over-

> Trade friction is a major reason for the substantial foreign investment in America's electronics and automobile industries.

seas market, its share of the auto export quota to the United States was small. Honda responded by becoming the first Japanese automaker to produce cars in the United States, and by 1985 it was producing more cars than American Motors, making it the fourth largest automaker in the U.S.[5]

The fact is that most governments—including many state governments in the U.S.—regularly negotiate with global companies to get production facilities and jobs located within their borders. And although the U.S. has no explicit federal policies for attracting foreign investment, it often does so through the back door by the threat or actual practice of import protection.

Nations have long used both restrictive and preferential policies to control foreign investment. Indeed, such policies were instrumental in bringing about much of the global reach of American companies into Europe, Japan, and the developing world. The heads of many American companies argue convincingly that they went global because the countries where they sold their products insisted on it, or because they were offered more attractive terms by foreign governments than by our own.

For both the U.S. and other governments, the most desirable foreign production is not the kind of "screwdriver assembly" plant that Ricoh set up in California, but extensive production facilities like those of Honda. Governments compete most vigorously for the parts of a firm's production that provide high-wage jobs and technological advance.

As an illustration of what is at stake, one need only look at a recent "clarification" by the European Community of its rules regarding integrated circuits. The EC has sought to nurture European suppliers by adopting rules against the dumping of cheap imports. But it will now define the origin of an integrated circuit, not by the national ownership of the corporation that makes it, but by the country where the "process of diffusion" takes place. In short, if Europeans are learning the technology, they will overlook who owns the plant. The decision set in motion a number of investment decisions by Japanese and American firms to establish or expand semiconductor fabrication facilities in Europe. As the chairman of Intel says, "You can't pick up a piece of paper that says why Intel has got to manufacture in Europe. The rules don't exist. But customer decisions are driving important decisions right now."[6]

And you can't pick up a piece of paper

---

5. Dennis J. Encarnation, "Cross-Investment: A Second Front of Economic Rivalry," in Thomas McCraw, ed., *The U.S. Versus Japan* (Boston: Harvard University Press, 1988).

---

6. Quoted in Sylvia Ostry, *Governments and Corporations in a Shrinking World* (New York: Council on Foreign Relations, 1990), 49. The European Community in fact has no explicit restrictions on foreign direct investment, except in broadcasting and government procurement.

indicating that Japanese automobile firms need to have substantial operations in the United States to serve the U.S. market. Continued trade friction on automobiles and auto parts, however, clearly sends a message to the Japanese that, in the long run, the best guarantee of access to the U.S. market is to locate a substantial share of production in the U.S. The Japanese have also received the same message more directly and clearly from the Europeans.

In short, there is nothing inevitable about the globalization of industry. Advances in production techniques, transportation, and communications have certainly made it more feasible and attractive for multinational companies to disperse their production around the globe. But government policies have also played an important role in shaping corporate decisions. As flows of investment become ever more important relative to flows of trade, the rivalry between the U.S. and its trading partners will increasingly take the form of locational competition—vying with one another for shares of the world's high-technology production base regardless of ownership.

In the long run, rules to regulate exactly when and how nations can either restrict or encourage foreign direct investment are needed. Without multilateral discipline, each nation is tempted to act on its own, but if each does, the danger is that all will be worse off.

Ideally, an internationally negotiated framework would call for symmetrical national policies on foreign investment. In the absence of such a framework, which is likely to be a long time coming, I agree with Reich that a high priority for U.S. trade policy should be discouraging other governments from invoking domestic content rules, explicitly or by threat of trade protection. At the same time, however, it makes no sense for the U.S. to disarm unilaterally. We must not sacrifice our ability to use trade and other policies to attract foreign investment as long as other

nations continue to do so. If we disarm unilaterally, we leave decisions about the future composition of our economy and its trade, not to the free market, but to the policy decisions of other governments.

Proposition 3. "They are good for us in the short run, but the long-run dynamic effects may be different."

From a static point of view, a foreign firm operating in the United States may look like a domestic firm on such traditional indicators as wages per worker, value-added per worker, R&D per worker, or trade per worker. But the long-run implications may be very different.

First, over time the foreign firm may actually displace or deter the entry or expansion of American companies that might normally be expected to locate more of their production in the United States, thereby generating better jobs, more R&D, closer linkages with local suppliers, and more local technological spillovers.

Second, the foreign firm and the domestic firm may have different long-term effects on industry structure. Suppose, for example, that the foreign firm knocks out one or more domestic competitors, buying them out directly or gradually squeezing them out. The final result may be a more oligopolized industry, where the remaining firms exercise significant market power.

The dangers to national economic welfare from relying on a small number of foreign suppliers in an oligopolistic market are nowhere more apparent than in the semiconductor industry. (Our dependence on a limited number of foreign suppliers of oil also illustrates the point.) Today the dominant global suppliers of DRAMs—the memory chips that are key inputs in all electronic products—are six vertically integrated Japanese companies, which still have the bulk of their operations in Japan. In the Japanese market, a complex web of business and government practices limit access by foreign firms, antitrust regulations are lenient or largely unenforced, and most R&D is financed and executed in proprietary channels that limit the diffusion of technological knowledge to foreign competitors and users.

The Japanese companies, moreover, have substantial and growing shares in systems products, like computers and sophisticated telecommunications equipment. The markets for such products are also highly oligopolized, offering significant potential for the exercise of market power, and the Japanese companies are clearly focused on increasing their penetration into these markets at the expense of American and European producers.

One way for the Japanese companies to pursue this objective is to control the terms and availability of semiconductor supplies to American and European computer companies. There is compelling evidence that the Japanese firms used such techniques in 1987 and 1988, when the worldwide market for DRAMs was extremely tight. And more recent evidence indicates that many of the same Japanese firms have been trying to control the terms and availability of advanced display technologies—such as the liquid crystal displays on laptop computers—to strengthen further their positions in computers and other products.

The practices employed by the Japanese firms to control the prices or deliveries of DRAMs or displays to foreign users are not necessarily illegal or unfair. Indeed, U.S. firms have often done the same when they had comparable market power in input industries. But when they reduce competition in important industries, such practices can be detrimental to the long-term interests of the U.S. and the world economy. Under these circumstances, American policies aimed at maintaining viable domestic producers as a counterweight to the Japanese may make sense as a kind of anti-cartel insurance.

Once we consider the effects of foreign direct investment on industry structure, the "who is us" debate becomes more complicated. It may be prudent, for example, for policy makers to prevent a merger or acquisition by a foreign firm that poses a significant anticompetitive threat. Or it may make sense for policymakers to finance projects, like Sematech, that foster a more competitive supply base in a key input, even if such projects are not commercially viable, and to exclude foreign suppliers—in this case Japanese suppliers—if they exercise significant market power.

From this perspective, the U.S. should be using trade policy to open the Japanese semiconductor market to U.S. and other non-Japanese companies, including American affiliates operating in Japan. Semiconductors produced by Texas Instruments in Japan may promote more competition in the worldwide semiconductor industry than do semiconductors produced by Fujitsu in the United States. In that respect, we might legitimately favor an American company's operations abroad over a foreign company's operations in the U.S.

Proposition 4. "They are allowed to compete with us here, but we are not allowed to compete with them there."

Foreign operations that look like domestic operations in the U.S. economy may be treated differently in their home markets. For example, Motorola, a U.S. company with significant domestic operations, has needed the support of U.S. trade law to penetrate the Japanese market. But, obviously, no Japanese company would find it necessary to get U.S. government assistance to help sell products in Japan that were made in America. Non-Japanese firms have trouble selling to Japan, whether their operations are located in Japan or abroad, but Japanese firms have no trouble selling to Japan from either their domestic or foreign operations.

Japanese import trade is dominated by Japan's own companies. In fact, shipments from Japanese subsidiaries abroad to their parent companies at home represent most of Japanese imports. In 1986, for example, intra-firm trade accounted for 72 percent of U.S. exports to Japan, compared to 48.5 percent of U.S. exports to Europe.[7] In short, Japan's import trade, as well as its export trade, is conducted to a distinctive degree by its own multinationals.

In addition, because of the control of distribution channels in Japan, foreign companies remain highly dependent on Japanese distributors for the sale of their products in Japan. If foreign goods compete directly with domestic products, they have trouble entering Japan. Imports that are complementary with the interests of domestic companies, on the other hand, get in easily.[8] In both cases, corporate control over Japan's trade rests in the hands of Japanese companies.

The same is certainly not the case in the United States. Japanese firms in America can easily distribute their products through their own channels, and most big Japanese firms do. Foreign direct investment in wholesale and retail trade in the U.S. is so substantial, in fact, that by 1986 foreign affiliates accounted for 75 percent of total U.S. imports and nearly 70 percent of U.S. exports. So while Japanese firms control Japanese trade with the rest of the world, foreign firms dominate America's trade.

The barriers to sales by foreign companies in Japan are another justification for America's emphasis in its negotiations with Japan on market-opening for all foreign-owned companies, not just American ones. Trade negotiations between the U.S. and

---

7. See Dennis Encarnation, *Investing to Trade: American and Japanese Multinationals in the Pacific Basin,* unpublished manuscript, Harvard Business School, February, 1990; and Robert Z. Lawrence, "How Open Is Japan?" paper presented to the Conference on the U.S. and Japan: Trade and Investment, National Bureau of Economic Research, Cambridge, Mass. October 1989.

8. John Zysman and I describe this pattern as a "moving band of protection." See Laura D'-Andrea Tyson and John Zysman, "The Politics of Productivity: Developmental Strategy and Production Innovation in Japan," in Chalmers Johnson, Laura Tyson, and John Zysman, eds., *Politics and Productivity: The Real Story of How Japan Works* (Cambridge, Mass. Ballinger Press, 1989).

Japan on specific industries known as the MOSS ("market-oriented, sector-specific") talks, the U.S.-Japan Semiconductor Trade Agreement, and the U.S.-Japan talks on beef, citrus, and more recently rice imports, have all demanded market access for all foreign companies, including the affiliates of foreign companies inside Japan.

In Japan, as in most other parts of the world, a wide variety of factors may favor indigenous over American firms. Some of these factors involve discriminatory policies, the traditional subject matter of trade disputes. Other factors involve policies or institutions that, even if not designed as barriers, effectively block access by American firms. Some examples are product standards and testing, laws regarding intellectual property rights, health and safety rules, and consumer product regulations.

In a world of deep and persistent structural differences among nations, competition is unlikely to be perfect—or perfectly fair. To contain the inevitable friction between nations and between global companies, the U.S. and the other developed countries must achieve two goals.

First, they must scale back policies and dismantle institutions that intentionally discriminate between domestic and foreign companies. Second, they must agree either to harmonize structural differences that hurt foreign producers or to recognize the persistence of such differences and accept them as fair.

Achieving both goals is the best approach to freer and fairer world trade. But neither will be easily or quickly accomplished. In the meantime, what should the U.S. do when national policy differences "slant the playing field" against American producers? Should foreign firms be allowed to compete with us in the relatively open U.S. marketplace, while American firms are precluded from competing with them abroad? Should the American government treat foreign firms exactly like domestic firms in our home market even though foreign governments are discriminating against American firms in their home markets?

The principles of broad-based reciprocity, most favored nation treatment, and national treatment on which U.S. policy has traditionally been based suggest affirmative answers to these questions. These principles imply three conditions: First, overall access to the U.S. market across a broad range of goods and trading partners should be comparable to overall access to foreign markets (comparable access in particular products and with particular trading partners is not required). Second, whatever rights of access the U.S. accords to one of its trading partners should be accorded to all such partners. And third, all foreign-owned firms operating in the U.S., regardless of ownership, should be treated like domestically owned firms.

When American companies are discriminated against by particular foreign partners in particular industries, however, the principle of selective reciprocity may sometimes be a more appropriate guide to U.S. policy. According to this principle, access to the U.S. market by particular foreign firms through trade or investment should depend on comparable access of American firms to the home markets of these firms. Unlike the traditional approach, the selective reciprocity approach focuses on particular industries and trading partners. Selective reciprocity implies that foreign companies will not have access to the U.S. market unless their home countries provide U.S. companies comparable access. Under selective reciprocity there is no guarantee that a right of access accorded by the U.S. to a particular trading partner would be extended to all trading partners, nor is there any guarantee of national treatment. If a foreign country does not accord national treatment to an American company, selective reciprocity might lead U.S. policymakers to act reciprocally toward companies based in that country.

The selective reciprocity principle is a serious and dangerous departure from normal U.S. policy. A world in which market access arrangements were negotiated on a bilateral, sector-specific basis would be a world in which the benefits of broad-based reciprocity, most-favored-nation treatment, and national treatment would be lost. Selective reciprocity encourages preferential trading blocs, retaliation, and bilateral trade deals that carve up national markets to achieve "reciprocal" outcomes in particular industries. Consequently, selective reciprocity should be invoked sparingly and only under exceptional circumstances.

But reciprocity should be the principle behind U.S. policy when there is a long history of foreign restrictions on the sales and investments of U.S. companies, when there is clear evidence of promotional industrial targeting policies that have benefited foreign producers at the expense of American producers, and when the industry in question is particularly important to our future living standards. Under such circumstances, there should be no presumption—and certainly no simple rule—that "they are us."

Proposition 5. *"They are not us."*

For purposes of national security, foreign companies may not be interchangeable with American companies even if they have never benefitted from preferential policies in their home markets and their U.S. operations look exactly like those of American companies.

What, if anything, should be done to regulate foreign ownership and control of production in industries or products that are critical to national security? (Here I define national security in the classic, restricted military sense.) Are foreign affiliates equivalent to domestically owned operations for such purposes?

In a global world economy, a sensible economic strategy for national defense should have three goals.

First, it should use requirements for national ownership, or local production by foreign suppliers, to enhance national control over suppliers regardless of their nationality.

Second, it should seek to stimulate a diversity of suppliers to maintain an honest or competitive supply base.

And, third, it should avoid condemning the nation to mediocre technologies and unnecessarily high costs in the process.[9]

The U.S. cannot rely on a wholly owned U.S. industrial base for military purposes. Such a strategy is simply too expensive and keeps out foreign technology. Many military technologies are dual-use technologies in which U.S. companies no longer have the leading positions or are no longer the low-cost, high-quality producers. Where foreign commercial technology essential to defense has a distinct lead, the U.S. should actively seek foreign investors and encourage them to invest in manufacturing and research facilities within the U.S.

To maintain a strong national defense, control of production is sometimes more important than ownership. What matters may not be the extent of our dependence on foreign suppliers for a critical technology but whether that dependence is concentrated on a few suppliers. In military technologies, an honest, competitive supply base is especially important. Consequently, defense-related activities should be subject to more stringent antitrust supervision than industries unrelated to defense, and this supervision should apply to domestic firms as well as to foreign firms.[10]

If an activity deemed vital to the national defense is subject to excessive market control by foreign producers, we have a num-

9. These objectives are suggested by Theodore Moran, "The Globalization of America's Defense Industries: Managing the Threat of Foreign Dependence," *International Security* 15 (Summer 1990), 57-99.

10. For more on the significance of an honest supply base, see Michael Borrus, "Power, Wealth and Technology: Industrial Decline and American National Security," in Wayne Sandholtz et al., eds. *The Highest Stakes: Economic Change and International Security* (Oxford, England: Oxford University Press, forthcoming.)

ber of possible remedies. As Edward Graham and Paul Krugman suggest, we can, first, require licensing of the capability to provide the good or service to domestic producers; second, pass local content requirements, including provisions that R&D capabilities be maintained in laboratories and plants within the U.S. and that their facilities employ American citizens; and, third, enact policies to promote the entry or deter the exit of U.S. suppliers.

When defense goods and technologies are involved, the assumption that foreign firms are "us" must be subject to careful scrutiny. And sometimes domestic policies may be required to make them more like us or to protect and promote our domestically owned competitors.

U.S. national security law now, in fact, does distinguish between "them and us." Under the Exon-Florio amendment, the president can block mergers, acquisitions, or takeovers of U.S. companies by foreign interests when those actions might threaten national security. All of the other advanced industrial countries have similar national security provisions in their laws on foreign investment. In the U.S., as elsewhere, such a provision may be misused as a protectionist device. But not to recognize legitimate security concerns posed by foreign takeovers would be a great mistake.

Us, Them, and National Economic Competitiveness

Unlike Reich, I read the evidence as proving a strong, continuing link between American companies and the vitality of the U.S. economy. Who is us? American companies still are. And while foreign firms represent bigger shares of the domestic economy, especially in a few major industries, they are still not as important as American firms. "They are not yet us, although they are beginning to bear a strong family resemblance. And for national defense purposes, they will never be just like us."

But although my assessment of the current situation differs from Reich's assessment, I do not disagree with him on the trend. Globalization is here to stay. Over time, U.S. companies are likely to send larger shares of their operations abroad, while foreign companies are likely to bring more of their economic activity here.

There is no evidence, however, to suggest that this trend is accelerating. Indeed, the most recent numbers suggest a slowdown of foreign direct investment. The surge of foreign investment into the U.S. during the 1980s may have been an aberration, encouraged by special factors such as restrictions on auto imports, the boom in mergers and acquisitions, and changes in the dollar's value.

As I agree with Reich about the long-term trend, so I agree with him about what the overarching goal of U.S. policy should be. According to Reich, the goal should be American competitiveness, which he defines as the capacity of Americans to add value to the world economy and thereby gain a higher standard of living in the future without going into ever deeper debt. With this goal in mind, national economic policies should be formulated to make the U.S. an attractive production location for the high-productivity, high-wage, research-intensive activities of both domestic and foreign firms.

Not surprisingly, Reich and I share a policy agenda that gives priority to enhancing the education and skills of the American work force, to building America's economic infrastructure, and to fostering research and development. The nation's human capital, infrastructure, and research base are its most important immovable assets.

We also agree that as a general rule, the U.S. should continue to welcome foreign direct investment, which can bring technology, jobs, greater efficiency, and other benefits. Nonetheless, in some circumstances, these benefits carry attendant risks—in particular, the risk of a more concentrated industrial structure with less competition or the risk of excessive dependence on foreign suppliers for national defense. It is

prudent, therefore, to monitor foreign direct investment for antitrust and national security purposes, as other nations do.

It is also sensible to invoke the principle of reciprocity under some circumstances. If American firms are kept out of foreign markets by overt discriminatory trade or investment barriers, the U.S. may legitimately demand those barriers be reduced as the price for access to the American marketplace.

The judicious use of the reciprocity principle in U.S. negotiations with its trading partners in the second half of the 1980s has had some beneficial results. The U.S. has successfully used the reciprocity idea to get foreign governments to revise their treatment of intellectual property to conform to U.S. standards. The principle of reciprocity has also been behind U.S. efforts to reduce market access barriers in Japan in a variety of products, including telecommunications and supercomputers.

Reciprocity is also a useful principle in thinking about mergers and acquisitions. The advanced countries differ sharply in their rules regarding foreign acquisitions of domestic companies. At one extreme are the U.S. and Great Britain, where foreigners can make acquisitions easily. At the other extreme are Japan and Germany, where mergers and acquisitions are more limited and dominated by domestic companies and domestic financial institutions. These differences are the result chiefly of structural patterns in financial markets, rather than overt discrimination. Consequently, reciprocity implies a gradual harmonization of financial institutions to make markets equally accessible. In the meantime, the U.S. should continue to contest overt barriers to foreign investment in bilateral negotiations.

The principle of reciprocity is also applicable to public support for research and development. As a general rule, the U.S. might want to make publicly funded R&D programs available on the same terms to any company regardless of national origin, provided the home country of a foreign company reciprocates. Foreign firms perceived to hold significant market power might be excluded from such programs on antitrust grounds, particularly where the objective of government funding is to stimulate a more competitive supply.

As companies become more footloose in their location decisions, policies to contain scientific and technical knowledge within national boundaries become increasingly ineffective. And as foreign direct investment in U.S. high-technology industries grows, policies to restrict R&D support to domestic companies become increasingly outdated. For example, U.S. policies to support generic R&D related to high-definition television should be open to both domestic and foreign companies, as long as they agree to do the research here and similar programs in their home countries are open to U.S. firms. In high-definition TV, as in other high-technology pursuits, the U.S. cannot afford the price of relying on national champions and excluding foreign ones,

especially those like Sony, Phillips, and Thomson, that have substantial R&D facilities in the United States.

Nevertheless, America's strength in high-technology industries still depends disproportionately on American firms, even those with large overseas operations that have contributed to the growing high-tech strength of America's major trading partners. Moreover, America's ability to compete with other nations for the investment and R&D activities of foreign multinationals depends in part on the health of its own multinationals. Foreign firms want to be near their healthy American competitors to key into their knowledge and the network of skilled people who carry that knowledge with them. The major attraction to foreign investors is the health of the domestic economy; that in turn depends on the health of domestic companies.

Engine Charlie Wilson may have been right for the 1950s, and Robert Reich may well be right for the next century. But, for now, we need to improvise in a world that fits no ideal model.

Who Do We Think They Are?

Robert B. Reich

Ever since I argued in the *Harvard Business Review* last year that we should pay less attention to corporate nationality and more attention to whether our nation's work force was gaining the skills and competences it needed to compete, I've had the curious sense of being shoved—quite against my will—to the conservative side of the older debate over American industrial policy. My first inkling of this transmigration came when *The Wall Street Journal* praised me and my argument

in its editorial pages. If this were not cause enough for alarm, I found myself the recipient of expressions of shock and outrage from several fellow industrial-policy travelers who accused me of abandoning the worthy cause. And now, to deepen my gloom, comes Laura Tyson.

Anyone wishing to probe my detailed views on all this has only to buy my upcoming book on the subject, *The Work of Nations*. (Under the circumstances, the editors of this journal surely have no objection to a little blatant book promotion.) But for now, to set the record absolutely straight: I am as committed as ever to the notion that the U.S. government has a crucial role to play in the nation's economic development. Yet I no longer have great confidence in the American-owned corporation as its partner. American firms—especially firms engaged in tradeable goods and services (more on this in a moment)—are rapidly becoming global entities with no special relationship to the American economy. Thus, the object of American industrial policy should be to enhance the value that American workers can add to the world economy, not to increase the profitability or global market share of these errant American-owned companies. There is a crucial, and growing, difference between the two.

In the early part of her rebuttal, Tyson takes issue with me on this last point, arguing that there isn't much difference between the American work force and American companies—at least for now. Having (she assumes) disposed of this issue, she then goes on to argue why the U.S. government should promote and defend the interests of the nation in international commerce. As to these latter points, I'm in complete agreement—except that, in pursuing these initiatives, she still assumes that the interests of American firms are good approximations for the interests of Americans, and I don't. In my view, American industrial policymakers should not treat American firms any differently than they treat other global corporations.

"Us" is the American Worker in Global Commerce

First, Tyson's assertion that corporate nationality still matters a great deal: To make her case, she shows that U.S. multinationals have most of their assets, sales, and employment in the United States. But this fact is entirely tautological. Firms are *defined* as U.S. multinationals precisely *because* they have most of their assets, sales, and employment in the United States. Tyson's point that

a larger percentage of the assets, sales, and employment of American "multinationals" was in the United States in 1988 than in 1977 is misleading. During that period, a great many American firms that had been entirely domestic (and therefore not classified as "multinational") began to venture abroad—but cautiously.

Similarly, no one should be surprised by Tyson's argument that domestic firms still dominate domestic economic activity—relegating foreign firms to a small fraction of the American economy. Since most of what's made or serviced in the United States is not traded in international commerce, there is no particular reason why foreign-based corporations would have the expertise or the interest to undertake these activities—particularly when the foreign firms would have to compete with Americans who live here. Few taxicab companies, softdrink bottlers, greeting card factories, or hairdressers are owned by foreign-based corporations.

The globalization of the American economy is most evident—and most important to the future standard of living of Americans—in those sectors of the economy that are *tradeable* internationally, or, more precisely, where the labors of Americans compete in global commerce with the labors of other nations' work forces. Here Tyson reveals very little. She acknowledges that foreign-owned firms now control one-half of the United States consumer electronics industry, one-third of the American chemical industry, and 20 percent of the U.S. automobile industry. She might have added: 70 percent of the American tire industry, and almost 50 percent of the U.S. film and recording industry. And if "control" applies to any foreign ownership in excess of 10 percent of the outstanding shares of stock (a measure used by several federal government agencies), foreign-owned firms now "control" vast segments of America's banking, steel, machine tool, robotics, and telecommunications industries. Clearly, by this measure, foreign-owned firms have established a significant presence in the United States.

What about American corporations as *they* relate to the internationally tradeable skills of Americans? One measure is how much of the value of products sold by American corporations around the world actually derives from American workers. The answer is less and less. In each of the last three years the foreign operations of American-owned firms have accounted for more than $1 trillion in sales—or roughly four times the total export of goods made in the United States, and about seven to eight times the value of the nation's recent trade deficit. In fact, the trade deficit turns into a net surplus when the foreign sales of American-owned firms are included, compared to the total purchases by Americans of the products of foreign-owned firms.

American firms are making large profits overseas, even as their American profits wither. While profits earned by American firms in the United States dropped by 19 percent in 1989, the overseas profits of American-owned firms surged by 14 percent. In the first half of 1990, the foreign affiliates of American corporations accounted for a record 43 percent of their parents' total profits. General Motors, Ford, IBM, DEC, and Coca-Cola, among many others, earned most of their 1990 profits outside the United States. Largely for this reason, the overseas capital spending of American-owned firms has mushroomed—by 17 percent in 1990, on top of 13 percent in 1989, and 24 percent in 1988— even as their capital investments in America have slowed to under 7 percent a year. The trend is clear. American firms aren't exactly abandoning America; it is more accurate to say that they are joining the world, and spreading their production across many continents, as they become truly global firms. It's the same with the siting of high value-added production—research and development, sophisticated design and manufacturing engineering, complex fabrication. Tyson argues that U.S. multinationals are still allocating most of

their R&D budgets to America. But she acknowledges that the trend toward global siting is gathering remarkable speed— American firms increased their overseas R&D spending by 33 percent between 1986 and 1988, compared with a 6-percent increase in R&D spending back home.

Actually, all these data understate the extent of global economic integration. Foreign citizens who are on the payrolls of the far-flung affiliates of American corporations contribute only a small fraction of the total "foreign" value added to these firms' products; the same goes for Americans on the payrolls of foreign firms. The greater share is added through cross-border supply contracts, licensing agreements, and joint ventures. And a large and growing number of high-paid professional workers within every advanced nation are contracting with foreign-owned firms—conveying their services (legal, financial, research, engineering, advertising, management consulting) directly to the foreign company for a fee. These tasks, performed by Americans and purchased by foreign-owned corporations, represent some of the most lucrative ways in which Americans engage in global commerce. Here, as before, the key question is: Who is hiring Americans to add what value to world markets? How can this value be increased? My point, which Tyson has not disproven, is that the profitability and world market share of American firms have less and less to do with the answers.

Industrial Policy Lives

We need a government willing to take an active role in helping American workers add more value to global markets. In fact, my argument about the disengagement of the American corporation from America underscores this need. For if we can't count on the American-owned corporation to take special responsibility for improving the competitiveness of the American work force, then the job necessarily falls to government. Tyson and I both want an activist industrial policy. But she wants government to promote American firms; I want government to promote American workers, regardless of the nationality of the corporation they work for.

For example, Tyson argues that the federal government should encourage foreign firms to invest in the United States—either by quietly threatening to keep them out of the American market if they don't or by luring them here with subsidies and tax breaks. "Where they are most

> *By all means, let's keep pressure on Japan to open its markets to our goods. Our primary goal should not be to open Japan to the sales of American companies, but to open Japan's borders to the work products of Americans.*

like us," she notes, correctly, "our policies have encouraged them to be so." Agreed. But by *my* definition of "us," American-owned firms should be treated no differently. Whatever pressure tactics we apply to foreign-owned firms to induce them to invest in the United States (according to international rules that define fair practices) should be applied in equal measure to those that are American-owned.

Tyson points out that the European Community no longer cares about corporate ownership in examining whether a firm has "dumped" integrated curcuits in Europe; the Community looks instead to whether the technology underlying the circuits in question has been developed and diffused within Europe. This in precisely my point. In seeking to lure certain kinds of investments to America, corporate nationality should be irrelevant. The important issue is whether, and to what extent, the global corporation (of whatever nationality) helps American workers add value.

American governors and mayors, bidding for global capital regardless of the form it takes, have been among the most active proponents of this view.

Tyson next warns that "[t]hey are good for us in the short run, but the long-run dynamic effects may be different." She worries in particular that, unless we're careful, foreign firms will monopolize an industry—displacing or detering the expansion of American companies, or buying American firms and closing them down. But as history has revealed, the desire to monopolize is not exclusively a foreign urge. American companies, from time to time, have sought to do precisely the same thing. Our antitrust laws were enacted to prevent firms operating in the United States from engaging in such practices. The Antitrust Division of the Justice Department and the Federal Trade Commission have been moribund for almost a decade, but at other times in the nation's history they have policed the market vigorously—blocking proposed mergers, disenboweling entire corporate empires, even preventing foreign firms from selling their wares in the United States. (There are signs of a reawakening. At this writing, the Antitrust Division of the Justice Department is investigating whether certain Japanese companies have attempted to monopolize.) Tyson may feel that these laws are not up to the job of preventing foreign-owned firms from monopolizing our market, but she has not made her case.

Next: Should policymakers finance projects, like Sematech, designed to ensure that America has access to the technologies we need? Tyson says yes, and I agree. But why limit membership in such consortia to U.S. companies? The original American members of Sematech have all gone global in the meantime—parceling out the fruits of Sematech's research around the world. Government should impose conditions without regard to corporate nationality. Any global firm ought to be invited to participate in a publicly funded research consortium so long as the firm thereafter applies what it learns within the United States.

Here again the Europeans point the way: Europe's semiconductor research project, nicknamed "Jessi," has just admitted IBM to membership. Meanwhile, Jessi's board has voted to reconsider whether British International Computers Ltd. (ICL) should remain a member, in light of its recent purchase by Fujitsu. In other words, what seems to be emerging in Europe is not only a pro-European R & D policy, but also an anti-Japan-cartel policy, aimed at preventing the Japanese from amassing too much power over microelectronic technologies. Corporate nationality doesn't matter as long as Europeans are developing their own technological capabilities, and no set of firms is monopolizing the world market. These are the sorts of criteria that should guide America's high-technology policies as well.

Tyson also complains that "[t]hey are allowed to compete with us here, but we are not allowed to compete with them there." Her ire is directed particularly at Japan, and I agree that Japan has been slow to open itself to global competition. By all means, let's keep the pressure on Japan to open its market to our goods, but in doing so let's be sure to define "us" correctly. Tyson is concerned about Japan's barriers to sales by American companies. I'm not. Our primary goal should not be to open Japan to the sales of American companies, but to open Japan's borders to the work products of Americans. Our trade representative in Washington has spent considerable time and energy of late trying to force Japan to accept cellular telephones and pagers made by Motorola (mostly in Kuala Lumpur) and to allow Toys-R-Us to sell its wares (mostly produced in Southeast Asia and Latin America). These priorities make no sense from the standpoint of the American work force.

How do we pry open foreign markets? Tyson argues for a system of "selective reciprocity," through which foreign firms in a particular industry would be barred from investing in America so long as American firms in that industry were barred from investing in the country where the foreign firm was based. Tit for tat. This strategy might work if the goal is to enhance the profitability and global market share of American firms, but it may backfire if the goal is to improve the productivity of American workers. My goal is the latter. Thus, I don't want to bar foreign firms from operating in the United States—particularly if they'll spend more money training American workers than is spent by American firms in the same industry, pay American workers higher salaries, give them more job security, and make them far more productive than American firms do— even if the country where they have their worldwide headquarters prohibits American firms from investing there. Studies have shown that Japanese firms, in particular, fulfill all these criteria.

Tyson's analysis of the nation's security needs is unobjectionable—that is, until she starts fretting once again about the nationality of corporate ownership. It makes sense to diversify our sources of critical military supplies and technologies across many nations and firms, to subject defense contractors to more stringent antitrust supervision, and to require that certain critical R&D capabilities be maintained in laboratories and factories within the Unites States, employing American citizens. But why should American firms be subject to any less stringent requirements?

Tyson and I agree on many things. But we don't agree on the difference between global capital and national labor. Money is unpatriotic; these days, investment dollars are speeding to wherever on earth they can get the highest return. People, however, are relatively immobile, and they belong to societies with particular cultures and histories and hopes. It is up to governments to represent people, to respond to their needs and fulfill their hopes—not to represent global money.

[26]

Industry Clusters versus Global Webs: Organizational Capabilities in the American Economy

WILLIAM LAZONICK

(Professor of Economics, Barnard College, Columbia University, and Research Associate, Harvard Institute for International Development)

The Japanese challenge in manufacturing has compelled Americans to think about how enterprises and industries should be organized to be effective in global competition. Many observers of Japanese industry have identified, for example, permanent employment practices within major enterprises and *keiretsu* relations that bind together a number of firms as critical elements of the 'organizational capabilities' that have permitted Japan's phenomenal competitive success. What types of organizational capabilities must enterprises and industries in the United States put in place to meet the Japanese challenge? A debate on this issue of business organization is emerging that is likely to receive considerable attention as we near the century's end.

At the beginning of the 1990s two important books appeared with somewhat similar titles, but very different perspectives, on how US industry should be organized to compete globally. *The Competitive Advantages of Nations* is Michael Porter's third in a series of books on how business enterprises can attain and sustain competitive advantage. This book speaks much more to business enterprises as parts of national or 'domestic' industries than the previous two (see Porter 1980, 1985, and 1990). *The Work of Nations* is Robert Reich's latest book on what the public sector can do to aid business enterprises in contributing to the wealth of the nation (see Reich, 1983, 1987, and 1991a; see also Magaziner and Reich, 1982).

Trained as an economist, Porter is a professor at the Harvard Business School, and a prominent business consultant. Trained as a lawyer, Reich is a lecturer at Harvard's Kennedy School of Government, and a prominent cabinet member in the Clinton administration. The two men have worked in

Industrial and Corporate Change Volume 2 Number 1 1993

——————————— *Industry Clusters versus Global Webs* ———————————

close proximity to one another at Harvard: separated by the narrow Charles River, the geographical distance between the Harvard Business School and the Kennedy School can be covered in a few minutes on foot. But anyone who knows Harvard University knows that the intellectual distance between the two professional schools can be great. When someone at *either* the Business School or the Kennedy School refers to what is going on 'across the river', one gets the distinct impression that he or she is referring to a remote academic outpost that one only visits to observe peculiar native rituals.

The intellectual distance is evident in these books. Porter argues that, for a national (or domestic) industry, the building of a 'home base' within a nation, or within a region of a nation, represents the organizational foundation for global competitive advantage. Quite in contrast, Reich argues that the globalization of industrial competition has led to a global fragmentation of industry, thus making national industries and the national enterprises within them less and less important entities in attaining and sustaining global competitive advantage. For Porter, the key to the future prosperity of a nation is the improvement of productive capabilities by building 'industry clusters' within its borders. For Reich, the key to the future prosperity of a nation is the creation of a work force that can find high-paid employment in the 'global webs' of enterprise that are currently being spun around the world. Industry clusters versus global webs: who is right?

1. *Industry Clusters*

For Porter, the major determinants of global competitive advantage are (1) factor conditions, (2) demand conditions, (3) related and supporting industries, and (4) firm strategy, structure, and rivalry. He conceptualizes these determinants as four corners of a mutual reinforcing 'diamond' of productive activity. What determines the competitive advantage of nations are, first, 'the *pressures* on firms to invest and innovate', and, second, 'the institutional mechanisms for specialized factor creation' (Porter, 1990, p. 71 and p. 80).

By 'pressures', Porter means the social forces that motivate enterprise participants to develop and utilize productive resources. 'The central concern', says Porter, 'is whether [managers and workers] are motivated to develop their skills as well as expend the effort necessary for creating and sustaining competitive advantage' (Porter, 1990, p. 113). Within a national 'diamond', pressures to invest and innovate are generated by factor scarcities, sophisticated demand, and domestic rivalry. Of these pressures, Porter clearly views 'domestic rivalry' as the most critical. 'In global competition,' he tells the reader, 'successful firms compete vigorously at home and pressure each

——————————— *Industry Clusters versus Global Webs* ———————————

other to improve and innovate'. 'Only intense domestic rivalry (or the threat of entry)', he adds later, 'can pressure such behavior' (Porter, 1990, p. 162). And further on, he warns that 'loss of domestic rivalry is a dry rot that slowly undermines competitive advantage by slowing the pace of innovation and dynamism' (Porter, 1990, p. 170).

By 'factor creation', Porter means the development of higher quality productive inputs that can be embodied in innovative products and processes. The most important form of factor creation in the advanced economies, Porter asserts, is the creation of knowledge. For example, in explaining Germany's historical advantage in chemical manufacture, Porter states that 'Germany was the home of the finest university chemistry programs, the Kaiser Wilhelm (later Max Planck) Institutes, the most advanced scientific journals in chemistry, and numerous factor creation investments undertaken by firms, including several apprenticeship programs for workers' (Porter, 1990, p. 133).

Porter emphasizes that 'factor creation is perhaps most strongly influenced by *domestic rivalry*' (Porter, 1990, p. 134). He asserts that 'the single greatest determinant of Japanese success, based on our research, is the nature of domestic rivalry', that 'the real driver of Italian success in many industries (as in Japan) . . . is extraordinary rivalry', and that an 'essential underpinning of Korean competitive advantage is the fierce and even cut-throat rivalry that characterizes every successful Korean industry' (Porter, 1990, pp. 416, 447 and 473).

He recognizes that the domestic rivalry hypothesis does not appear to fit the case of Sweden. Many Swedish industries that are successful in global competition have only two main rivals or even just one dominant enterprise (Porter, 1990, p. 350). But, claims Porter, Sweden has not been successful in industries that require frequent and rapid responses to changed conditions, and Swedish companies tend not to remain innovative when challenged by external competition (Porter, 1990, p. 351). 'The general lesson', he argues from the Swedish case, 'is that it appears to be difficult to fully compensate for the absence of active domestic rivalry' (Porter, 1990, p. 351).

How does domestic rivalry promote factor creation? Porter explains (with my emphases):

> A number of local competitors in vigorous competition stimulates the rapid development of skilled human resources, related technologies, market-specific knowledge, and specialized infrastructure. Firms invest in factor creation themselves, singly or via trade associations, under pressure not to fall behind. As important, however, is that *a group of domestic rivals* also *triggers* special programs in local schools and universities, government-

——————————— 3 ———————————

──────────────── *Industry Clusters versus Global Webs* ────────────────

supported technical institutes and training centers, specialized apprenticeship programs, industry-specific trade journals and other information providers, and other types of investment in factors by government and other
institutions (Porter, 1990, p. 134).

If one accepts Porter's evaluation that domestic rivalry is the driving force in
the national 'diamond', one might be tempted to assume that cooperation
among enterprises plays little, if any, role in the competitive advantage of
nations. Indeed, his reference to 'a group of domestic rivals' that 'triggers'
investments in value-creating infrastructures might lead one to believe that,
even when factor creation benefits many enterprises, interfirm competition as
distinct from interfirm cooperation is solely responsible for generating the
improvements in productive resources.

Porter's own documentation and analysis of the determinants of global
competitive advantage reveal, however, that an emphasis on competition to
the exclusion of cooperation is unwarranted. A closer consideration of Porter's
own evidence suggests that domestic cooperation rather than domestic competition is the *key* determinant of global competitive advantage. For a
domestic industry to attain and sustain global competitive advantage
requires continuous innovation, which in turn requires domestic cooperation. Domestic rivalry is an important determinant of enterprise strategies.
But the substance of these competitive strategies—specifically whether
they entail continuous innovation or cut-throat price-cutting—depends on
how and to what extent the enterprises in an industry cooperate with one
another.

In Porter's analytical framework, 'groups of domestic rivals' are integral to
the operation of industry clusters. These industry clusters are, in turn, at the
core of his analysis of the institutional mechanisms for specialized factor creation and the sources of global competitive advantage (Porter, 1990, pp. 148–
152). Again and again in his theoretical elaborations and empirical illustrations
of the ways in which industry clusters contribute to global competitive
advantage, Porter articulates the centrality of domestic cooperation.

An industry cluster is, on the most general level, defined as 'industries
related by links of various kinds' (Porter, 1990, p. 131). These links are both
vertical (connecting users and suppliers) and horizontal (connecting enterprises that have common customers, employ related technologies, and use
the same channels of communication) (Porter, 1990, p. 149). As institutional mechanisms of factor creation, clusters function most effectively when
rival enterprises as well as related and supporting industries are geographically
concentrated, because then rapid interchanges of technological and market
information among vertically and horizontally related enterprises can take
place.

──────────────── 4 ────────────────

———————————— *Industry Clusters versus Global Webs* ————————————

Interchange implies cooperation, not competition. As Porter puts it:

> Mechanisms that facilitate interchange within clusters are conditions that
> help information to flow more easily, or which unblock information as well
> as facilitate coordination by creating trust and mitigating perceived differ-
> ences in economic interest between vertically and horizontally linked firms
> (Porter, 1990, pp. 152–153).

He then goes on to list a number of 'facilitators of information flow':
'personal relationships due to schooling, military service', 'ties through the
scientific community or professional associations', 'community ties due to
geographic proximity', 'trade associations encompassing clusters' and 'norms
of behavior such as belief in continuity and long-term relationships' (Porter,
1990, p. 153). He also lists a number of 'sources of goal congruence or
compatibility within clusters' that involve family ties, common ownership,
interlocking directors, and national patriotism, and that also facilitate information exchange (Porter, 1990, pp. 153, 790 n. 17).

'Mechanisms that facilitate interchange within clusters', Porter reports,
'are generally strongest in Japan, Sweden, and Italy, and generally weakest in
the United Kingdom and the United States' (Porter, 1990, p. 154). In the
United States, the best-functioning clusters appear to be in health care and
computing, sectors that contain some of America's premier global competitors. 'Here,' Porter observes, 'scientific ties often overcome the natural
reticence of American management toward interchange' (Porter, 1990,
p. 154).

But, Porter, argues, such cooperation should not go so far as to blunt
competition in any particular industry within the cluster. When 'the exchange and flow of information about the needs, techniques, and technology
among buyers, suppliers, and related industries . . . occurs at the same time
that active rivalry is maintained in each separate industry, the conditions for
competitive advantage are most fertile' (Porter, 1990, p. 152).

The rapid and effective interchange of knowledge within the cluster is
clearly the prime contribution that the cluster makes to global competitive
advantage. But are we to conclude that enterprises that compete directly
with one another in a particular industry within the cluster do not engage in
such cooperative activity? Or could it be that individual enterprises that
compete vigorously for global market shares nevertheless see it as in their
interests, as participants in a domestic industry, to share new knowledge
with one another as it becomes available?

For (as all well-behaved children are taught at nursery school), it may well
be that each enterprise in a domestic industry recognizes that if it does not
share with others, then others will not share with it. Such horizontal sharing

——————— *Industry Clusters versus Global Webs* ———————

of information is most likely to occur in industries in which, because of a lack of potential scale economies or the more or less equal access of all firms to vertically related resources, it is difficult for any one enterprise to achieve a dominant market share. Each individual enterprise in a domestic industry knows that it has more to gain from being part of the network than from going it alone (on the 'informal trading of technical know-how', see Von Hippel, 1988; ch. 6; see also Allen, 1983). In the development and utilization of productive resources (although probably not in terms of price), the enterprises in a domestic industry compete vigorously with each other. Domestic rivalry may well, as Porter argues, create the *incentive* for individual enterprises to engage in continuous innovation. But, even then, the fundamental source of the domestic industry's global competitive advantage may well be domestic cooperation that ensures the collectivization of knowledge—a process that gives those individual enterprises within the domestic industry that share knowledge the *ability* to engage in continuous innovation.

In his case study of the Italian ceramic tile industry, Porter provides a prime example of how horizontal cooperation among domestic competitors centered around the town of Sassuolo has contributed to the global competitive advantage attained by the industry over the past four decades. Indeed, it appears to me that Porter's analysis of 'Sassuolo Rivalry' (a subheading in his text) reveals the importance of intra-industry cooperation to the industry's ability to develop and utilize productive resources. I quote the three paragraphs in Porter's 'Sassuolo Rivalry' section in their entirety:

> Rivalry among Italian ceramic tile companies was intense. The sheer number of Sassuolo-area firms led to a fluid situation in which firms constantly sought to gain an edge on the others in technology, design and distribution. News of product and process innovations spread rapidly. Innovations were usually known in days or weeks and copied in a few months. Firms seeking technical leadership had to improve constantly to stay ahead. Similarly, firms specializing in aesthetic design had to turn over their product line rapidly to stay ahead of imitators. This was especially true because copyrights and patents were generally hard to enforce. (In Germany, where the tile firms were not so concentrated, firms were able to protect company secrets longer and were under less pressure to improve continuously.)
>
> Competition among Italian tile producers was intensely personal. All of the producers were located close together. Virtually all were privately held, and most were family run. The owners were committed to their businesses and the community. They lived in the area, knew each other, and were the leading citizens of the same towns.
>
> Assopiastrelle, the ceramic tile industry association, with membership

───────────── *Industry Clusters versus Global Webs* ─────────────

concentrated in the Sassuolo area, gradually began offering services of common interest including bulk purchasing, foreign market research, and consulting on fiscal and legal matters. The association also took the lead in government and union relations. The growing Italian tile cluster stimulated wider mechanisms for factor creation. In 1976, a consortium of the University of Bologna, regional agencies, and various ceramic industry associations founded the *Centro ceramico di Bologna*. Its functions included research on ceramic materials, production processes, and chemical and mechanical analyses of finished products (Porter, 1990, p. 216).

Given this succinct analysis of the dynamic interaction of organization and technology in Sassuolo, it seems difficult (to me at least) to conclude that the rapid interfirm diffusion of product and process innovations that Porter describes can be attributed to intense domestic rivalry rather than the existence of cohesive industrial and technological communities. The last two paragraphs of the passage just quoted speak of cooperation, not competition. The first paragraph is about how domestic firms compete with one another through continuous innovation. But one wonders to what extent the ability of domestic rivals to learn of innovations 'in days or weeks' and to copy them 'in a few months' was the result of the *willingness* of innovative competitors to share information rather than pirate from one another. Was the absence of 'company secrets' in Sassuolo inherent simply in the geographic concentration of the industry, or was it because each Sassuolo enterprise recognized that if it tried to keep innovations secret, it would be shut out of the intense information networks that geographic concentration made possible? And to what extent was 'the sheer number of Sassuolo-area firms' the result of the success of an industry based on extensive external economies made possible by the cooperative investment strategies of, and the sharing of knowledge through, the local industrial and technological communities?

Porter's own analysis as well as research by others on the Third Italy suggest that cooperation, not competition, was the root cause of Sassuolo success (see Best, 1990, ch. 7). For example, Sebastiano Brusco (1982; p. 179) reports that 'in the [Sassuolo] ceramic tile industry, the machines which move the tiles uninterruptedly along the glazing lines, or which detect breakages through the use of sonic waves, were not the product of formal research, but were rather developed through the collaboration of the tile firms with a number of small engineering firms'. As Porter himself sums up the Italian ceramic tile case:

> Foreign firms must compete not with a single firm, or even a group of firms, but with an entire subculture. The organic nature of this system is the hardest to duplicate and therefore the most sustainable advantage of Sassuolo firms (Porter, 1990, p. 225).

───────────── 7 ─────────────

————————————— *Industry Clusters versus Global Webs* —————————————

Let me stress that my argument is not that domestic rivalry was absent or that it did not create pressures on individual enterprises to respond to the innovations of their competitors. Rather my argument is that rivalry in and of itself cannot explain the ability of an enterprise to respond innovatively to competitive challenges. Moreover, in the absence of the capability to be innovative, it is not clear that individual enterprises, pressured by intense domestic (or international) rivalry, will have an unambiguous incentive to make an innovative response. Porter recognizes that 'lack of pressure means there is rarely progress, but too much adversity leads to paralysis' (Porter, 1990, p. 83).

In my book, *Business Organization and the Myth of the Market Economy*, I have emphasized the distinction between innovation and adaptation in the theory of business enterprise. A challenged enterprise that does not have the organizational capabilities to succeed through an innovative investment strategy has an incentive instead to adapt on the basis of its existing capabilities (see Lazonick, 1991, chs. 1–3). Such an adaptive response will enable the enterprise to survive economically in the short run while rendering it even more incapable of remaining competitive in the long run. Too much pressure from competitors can (quite rationally from the perspective of the individual enterprise) lead to adaptive rather than innovative investment behavior.

It is also likely, moreover, that the balance between domestic rivalry and domestic cooperation that yields global competitive advantage will change when a domestic industry faces a new competitive challenge from abroad. As evidenced by the problems that many once-dominant US industries have faced in the late twentieth century, it seems that the appearance of formidable new competitors creates the need for the domestic industry to lessen domestic rivalry and build domestic cooperation in order to respond effectively. In the absence of such a shift of the balance from rivalry to cooperation, it may be that none of the individual enterprises within the domestic industry can mount a sufficient innovative response.

To quote Porter: 'American companies flee tough competition with foreign rivals rather than fight them' (Porter, 1990, pp. 528–529). To fight foreign rivals [as Charles Ferguson (1990) has argued in the case of Silicon Valley] requires a suspension of rivalry in order to build value-creating industrial and technological communities. Unless social organizations are put in place that can engage in innovation, heightened domestic rivalry [as advocated for example by George Gilder (1988)] will lead to decline. As a general rule, more *domestic* rivalry will not result in global competitive advantage when *foreign* rivals, innovating on the basis of their own industry clusters, have already acquired a sustainable competitive advantage.

————————————————————— 8 —————————————————————

―――――――――― *Industry Clusters versus Global Webs* ――――――――――

However much Porter espouses the importance of domestic rivalry for global competitive advantage, much of his own analysis supports the view that the basic problem that US industry faces in international competition is not insufficient rivalry but insufficient cooperation. In Porter's words: 'Employees [in the United States] are not committed to their profession or to their company, partly because they have invested less in training for their profession and partly because their company is not committed to them' (Porter, 1990, p. 528). 'More broadly', states Porter

> the whole concept of strengthening the national cluster is not truly under-stood in America. The focus of US firms is still largely parochial. They rarely invest in building up suppliers, sponsoring specialized research insti-tutes or universities, or working to improve the pool of human resources available to them and their entire domestic industry. US industry associa-tions are little help to their members compared to associations in other nations. They rarely see their role as that of factor creation, which is perhaps the most important role an association can play. With a more international outlook, US industry associations would work to further the common interests of their members, as foreign associations do (Porter, 1990, p. 527).

2. *Global Webs*

Porter's analytical framework and evidence support the view that domestic cooperation has been, and remains, essential to attaining and sustaining global competitive advantage. Especially in high-technology, capital-intensive industries that require the planning and coordination of complex specialized divisions of labor, the most fundamental community-building occurs among the participants of the enterprise itself (see Lazonick 1991; ch. 1). But, as a value-creating social organization, the enterprise does not work on its own. Increasingly, global competitive advantage requires the building of supportive business communities within a domestic industry that extend beyond the enterprise as well as the shaping of domestic professional and labor communities whose goals and activities complement the innovative strategies of the business communities. In providing such support to the innovative enterprise, these business, professional, and labor communities contribute to the process of value creation.

There are, of course, those who beg to differ—and they are not only conservative, free-market economists. In *The Work of Nations*, Robert Reich argues articulately and provocatively against the proposition that the social organization of national industries and national economies matters in global competition. Reich contends that '"American" corporations and "American"

───────── *Industry Clusters versus Global Webs* ─────────

industries are ceasing to exist in any form that can meaningfully be distinguished from the rest of the global economy.'

> The standard of living of Americans, as well of the citizens of other nations, is coming to depend less on the success of the nation's core corporations and industries, or even on something called the 'national economy,' than it is on the worldwide demand for their skills and insights (Reich, 1991a, p. 77).

Although his main concern is with what is happening in the United States, Reich asserts that the separation of the enterprise from the nation is not a uniquely American phenomenon.

> The trend is worldwide. National champions everywhere are becoming global webs with no particular connection to any single nation. As American corporations increasingly produce or buy from abroad, and foreign-owned firms increasingly produce or buy from America, the two sets of global webs are coming to resemble each other—regardless of their nominal nationality (Reich, 1991a, p. 131).

Contrast Reich's view of the emerging 'global webs' with Porter's perspective on the increasing importance of localized 'industry clusters' in global competition. As Porter (1990, p. 158) states:

> Competitive advantage in advanced industries is increasingly determined by differential knowledge, skills, and rates of innovation which are embodied in skilled people and organizational routines. The process of creating skills and the important influences on the rate of improvement and innovation are intensely local. Paradoxically, then, more open global competition makes the home base more, not less, important.

I have already argued that the essence of Porter's argument is that the competitive advantage of nations requires cooperation at the level of the domestic industry to develop superior productive resources, and particularly superior human resources. Reich agrees that superior human resources are central to the wealth of nations. But he claims that, far from industry becoming (to use Porter's words) 'intensely local' around a 'home base' for the sake of 'factor creation', the key to global competitive advantage is the employment of superior human resources wherever one can find them around the world (for Reich on Porter, see Reich, 1990a). Reich sees a shift from a high-volume to a high-value economy because of more flexible production technology and more variegated and sophisticated demand. This shift to high-value production has made economies of scale and hence central location unimportant (Reich, 1991a, ch. 7).

> In the emerging high-value economy, which does not depend on large-scale production, fewer products have distinct nationalities. Quantities can be

―――――――――― *Industry Clusters versus Global Webs* ――――――――――

> produced efficiently in many different locations, to be combined in all sorts
> of ways to serve customer needs in many places. Intellectual and financial
> capital can come from anywhere, and be added instantly (Reich, 1991a,
> p. 112).

Permitting the 'instant addition' of intellectual and financial capital to the
process of production are changes in technology. The results are Reich's
global webs: 'The threads of the global web are computers, facsimile machines,
satellites, high-resolution monitors, and modems—all of them linking
designers, engineers, contractors, licensees, and dealers worldwide' (Reich,
1991a, p. 111). The 'instant addition' of intellectual and financial capital
implies that the relations of the providers of specialized intellectual and
financial services to enterprises in the global web are market, rather than
organization, oriented. As Reich asserts: 'what is traded between nations is
less often finished products than specialized problem-solving (research, product design, fabrication), problem-identifying (marketing, advertising,
customer consulting), and brokerage (financing, searching, contracting) services' (Reich, 1991a, p. 113). What Reich is writing about is the rise of a
global *market* economy, not only in high-value products but also in specialized factors of production.

There exist a variety of business arrangements among and within enterprises, but 'all such variations' Reich contends, 'are differing legal formula-
tions of essentially the same global web'.

> Closely examine each and you begin to see a similar pattern: high-volume,
> standardized production occurs mainly in low-wage countries . . .; high-
> value problem-solving, -identifying, and brokering occurs wherever useful
> insights can be found around the world. This is the high-value global
> enterprise evolving into an international partnership of skilled people whose
> insights are combined with one another and who contract with unskilled
> workers from around the world for whatever must be standardized and
> produced in high volume (Reich, 1991a, p. 132).

The principals in these 'global insight partnerships' are the bearers of
intellectual and financial capital—the highly educated problem-solvers,
-identifiers, and brokers (Reich, 1991a, pp. 132–133). Reich calls these
high-value contributors to the economy 'symbolic analysts', as distinguished
from two classes of low-value contributors whom he calls 'routine producers'
and 'in-person servers' (Reich, 1991a, ch. 14). The high-value contributions of symbolic analysts derive from their education, experience, and
expertise, and enable them to command high levels of remuneration. Lacking such accumulations of human capital, routine producers, who do repetitive and boring work in plants and offices, and in-person servers, who cater

―――――――――――――― 11 ――――――――――――――

—————————— *Industry Clusters versus Global Webs* ——————————

largely to the personal needs of symbolic analysts at work and at home, must accept relatively low pay (Reich, 1991a, ch. 14).

In the high-value global economy, the economic prosperity of any particular geographic region depends on the quantity and quality of symbolic analysts who live and work within that region. Reich calculates that symbolic analysts now hold about 20% of jobs in the United States, up from 8% in 1950. Routine producers hold about 25% of US jobs, but, as high-volume production shifts to lower wage regions of the world, their numbers are declining and their remuneration is falling. In-person servers represent about 30% of jobholders in the United States, and their numbers are growing rapidly in tandem with the growth of the symbolic analyst class whom they serve (Reich, 1991a, pp. 176–179).

Given the propensity of enterprises to spin global webs by searching worldwide for high-paid, but high-value, symbolic analysts and lower paid, but lower value, routine producers, the prosperity of a high-income nation such as the United States depends on increasing the quantity and quality of symbolic analysts available for employment within its borders. What matters less and less are the national origins of the enterprises that employ these symbolic analysts.

Yet the appeal to the ideology of the 'national industry' and (worse yet) the 'national enterprise' is used to justify government support of 'national champions' despite the rapidly diminishing attachment of these enterprises to the nation in which they grew to maturity. Placed at a competitive disadvantage within US borders are those 'foreign' enterprises that are eager to employ US citizens. Foreign enterprises are especially eager to employ US symbolic analysts because their superior value-creating capabilities justify their relatively high paychecks. Hence for an already rich nation such as the United States, the quantity and quality of its symbolic analysts are its prime sources of global competitive advantage and future prosperity.

Reich insists that the need for government intervention in the economy is not at issue. What is at issue is the form that 'industrial policy' should take. 'We need a government', says Reich (1991b, p. 51) in a response to a critique of his globalization argument by Laura Tyson (1991), 'willing to take an active role in helping American workers add more value to global markets.' In an economic world of global webs and insight partnerships, the prime role for a national government is to upgrade the education of the domestic workforce, thus increasing the quantity and quality of symbolic analysts. A secondary role for the government is, within limits, to provide some inducements to enterprises of whatever national origins to bring their capital to the United States and provide employment to Americans (Reich, 1991a, pp. 163, 313).

———————————————————— 12 ————————————————————

——————————— *Industry Clusters versus Global Webs* ———————————

More generally, Reich contends, 'in modern nations, government is the principal agency by which society deliberates, defines, and enforces the norms that organize the market' (Reich, 1991a, pp. 186–187). For Reich, the emergence of global webs of enterprise, with their attendant international divisions of labor, has made the organization of the market in symbolic analysts the top priority for an already rich nation such as the United States.

3. *Is Globalization an Emerging Trend?*

Reich makes his case in a somewhat repetitive but extremely compelling fashion, reminiscent of John Kenneth Galbraith in his prime (see Galbraith, 1967). At the beginning of the 1990s, Reich's analysis of the economic prospects for the United States is the most coherent perspective that liberal America has. Unfortunately, in its characterizations of both the globalization of enterprise and the evolution of American society in the late twentieth century, Reich's argument has serious flaws.

In emphasizing how global webs permit the 'instant addition' of intellectual and financial capital on a worldwide basis, Reich portrays the strategies and structures of global enterprises as a free-market competition to secure the services of the best available symbolic analysts. There is no doubt that, as Reich argues, enterprises around the world are pursuing global strategies that involve new international divisions of labor and the tapping of expertise in many centers. But what determines which enterprises are most successful in the globalization process? Is the national environment really becoming irrelevant as a determinant of the competitive advantage of enterprises on global markets?

Globalization *per se* is not, of course, an entirely new phenomenon. US multinational enterprises have been pursuing global strategies for more than a century (Carstensen, 1984; Wilkins, 1970, 1974; Chandler, 1990). Already by 1914, one-third of the largest 200 enterprises in the United States had built marketing and manufacturing facilities abroad (Chandler 1990, p. 84). Indeed, over the subsequent decades, many US multinational enterprises made such significant and sustained investments in foreign operations—including investments in the productive capabilities of foreign citizens—that overseas divisions eventually found that they had begun to build their *own* home bases, thus transforming them from high-volume extensions of the parent company to high-value innovators in their own right. By investing in home bases abroad, overseas divisions became less dependent on the parent company—some so much so that, apart from corporate ownership, they became for all intents and purposes independent enterprises with their own distinctive investment strategies and organizational

───────────── *Industry Clusters versus Global Webs* ─────────────

structures. Prime examples of such evolution are Ford in Britain and IBM in Japan (see Tolliday, 1991; Abegglen and Stalk, 1985, ch. 9). Conversely, a common complaint by Canadians about the long-standing dominance of their manufacturing sector by US multinational corporations has been that the proximity of the United States has meant that the building of such home bases in Canada has not gone far enough (see Levitt, 1970; Laxer, 1973). Instead, they argue, Canada has become a 'branch plant' economy, with the nation's best and brightest brains draining south across the forty-ninth parallel.

Reich, however, writes as if the global corporation is something new. 'American firms are making large profits overseas,' says Reich (1991b, p. 51) in his reply to the critique by Tyson, 'even as their American profits wither.' He continues:

> General Motors, Ford, IBM, DEC, and Coca-Cola, among many others, earned most of their 1990 profits outside the United States. Largely for this reason, the overseas capital spending of American-owned firms has mushroomed—by 17% in 1990, on top of 13% in 1989, and 24% in 1988—even as their capital investments in America have slowed to under 7% a year. The trend is clear. American firms aren't exactly abandoning America; it is more accurate to say that they are joining the world, and spreading their production across many continents, as they become truly global firms.

For those of us who study history, the notion that companies such as Ford, General Motors, IBM, and Coca-Cola are, in the late twentieth century, 'joining the world' and *becoming* 'truly global firms' does not ring true. Ford constructed its first assembly plant in Britain in 1911–1912, and when it built its integrated factory at Dagenham in the late 1920s, it possessed the world's largest automobile facility outside the United States. During the 1920s General Motors took control of Vauxhall in Britain and Opel in Germany, and quickly became the dominant mass producer of automobiles for the German market. Building factories in Germany and France in the mid-1920s, the Computer-Tabulating-Recording Company saw fit to change its name to International Business Machines (Wilkins, 1970, p. 97, 1974, pp. 72–75, 79). And if there is one US enterprise that has long epitomized a global enterprise it is Coca-Cola, a company that deliberately followed the troops during World War II to become a household name around the world (Wilkins, 1974, p. 268n; Tedlow, 1990, ch. 2). Of the companies to which Reich specifically refers in the passage just quoted, only DEC, founded in 1957, is a relatively recent entrant into global operations.

Are these and many other US multinationals, therefore, really examples of an *emerging* trend? Or, given the relative profit and investment figures that

───────────── 14 ─────────────

————————— *Industry Clusters versus Global Webs* —————————

Reich cites, is it possible that a *problem* for the US economy is that some of these corporations are no longer 'truly global' in the sense that superior organizational capabilities that their overseas 'divisions' have developed abroad are not being transferred back, and replicated at, home? Is it not more reasonable to argue that the superior performance of the overseas divisions derives from superior organizational capabilities created in foreign home bases and the inferior performance of the US divisions derives from an erosion of the value-creating capabilities of the home bases in the United States? Might it not even be possible (as is again suggested by the profit and investment figures that Reich cites) that the economic viability of US divisions of US multinational corporations that have been losing global competitive advantage might be dependent on the value that they can extract as owners of these overseas divisions that, through the development of superior value-creating capabilities in different national environments, have sustained competitive advantage abroad?

To find emerging trends in the globalization of industry, one must look for the emergence of 'truly global firms' from *new home bases* outside the United States, and one must then try to understand how the social organization of the enterprises and industries in both the original home bases and the new home bases have generated global competitive advantage. Take, for example, the movement of Japanese automobile enterprises into manufacturing in the United States during the 1980s. As Richard Florida and Martin Kenney (1991) show, after less than a decade of manufacturing operations in the United States, Japanese companies such as Honda, Nissan, Mazda, and Toyota have effectively transplanted to the United States the organizational innovations that they developed in Japan and that had already made them the world's premier automobile producers. As Kenney and Florida (1991, p. 26) describe the re-creation of the Japanese system of automobile production in the United States:

> Japanese companies operating in this country are providing the steel, parts, tires, glass, and even some of the machines used to manufacture automobiles. And while US firms continue to move manufacturing to low-wage areas of the Sun Belt or Third World, the transplants have located virtually all elements of the production spectrum in a concentrated geographic space—namely, the traditional Rust Belt states of Ohio, Indiana, Illinois, and Michigan, extending southward into Kentucky and Tennessee. They are now bringing in their R&D and design units to solidify this complex.
>
> Consider the following example from Michigan. Mazda assembles cars in Flat Rock. Finished fenders, quarter panels, hoods, roofs, and dashboards are shipped 'just in time' to Mazda from a Japanese-owned metal-stamping plant 40 miles away in Howell. The steel is processed in stamping presses produced by a Michigan branch of Hitachi Zosen. The steel coils come from

————————— 15 —————————

─────────────── *Industry Clusters versus Global Webs* ───────────────

ProCoil, a joint venture of Japan's Marubeni and the US company National Steel located just outside Detroit. ProCoil, in turn, gets its raw steel from a nearby mill owned 70% by another Japanese company, NKK. Both Mazda and NKK have set up R&D centers in the Detroit area.

What is particularly significant about the extent to which Mazda has built a home base in the United States is the fact that, unlike Toyota, Nissan, and Honda that built 'greenfield' plants in rural areas of the Midwest, financial constraints compelled Mazda to enter into US production in a 'brownfield' site in the traditional center of the US automobile industry where it could get immediate access to experienced labor, suppliers, and transportation facilities (see Fucini and Fucini, 1990).

In contrast, Honda, a relatively minor producer of automobiles in Japan, used its successes in exporting automobiles and motorcycles to the US market in the 1970s to finance the building of greenfield capacity in Marysville, Ohio in the 1980s (see Sakiya, 1987, pp. 235–240). During the 1990s, Honda, whose Accord has been the most popular car in the United States, may well come to be viewed as an 'American' company more than a 'Japanese' company, whatever the nationality of its owners. Reich quite rightly argues that such investment by foreigners is good for the American people. But, contrary to Reich, Honda has not sustained its competitive advantage in the United States by operating through a global web in which labor and capital are added instantaneously wherever and whenever they are needed. Rather it has sustained its competitive advantage by investing, and reinvesting, in a new home base in the United States.

As a critical element of 'factor creation' in these new home bases, the Japanese enterprises that are revitalizing the US Rust Belt are investing in the productive capabilities of American blue-collar workers in ways that US automobile enterprises and their suppliers have never done. These Japanese employers are making these investments, not because they feel a social responsibility to upgrade the skills of the workers of Marysville, Ohio or Georgetown, Kentucky, but because they have an economic interest in replicating in the United States the shop-floor capabilities developed in Japan that first permitted them to capture US markets (Lazonick, 1990; ch. 9). In the process, they are creating employment opportunities for workers whom Reich calls 'routine producers' precisely by upgrading their skills so that the contributions that these workers can make to the value-creation process can become more analytical and less repetitive.

While Reich's contention that the home base is no longer important for global competitive advantage can be seriously questioned, the success of the Japanese automobile producers in the United States supports his argument that US government policy should not favor US-owned enterprises over

—————————— *Industry Clusters versus Global Webs* ——————————

foreign-owned enterprises (see also Reich, 1990b). On this policy position, I am in qualified agreement with Reich. Americans are certainly better off working for enterprises with their origins abroad that invest heavily in the United States than relying for employment on enterprises with their origins in the United States that are failing to make the domestic investments in plant, equipment, and personnel required to compete globally. But to adopt the position that the fate of enterprises of US origin is of no consequence to the wealth of the nation is to avoid asking why, over a broad range of industries over the past few decades, enterprises that have grown up in the United States have been losing global competitive advantage. Reich not only fails to pose this question, but also chastises the MIT Commission on Industrial Productivity (see Dertouzas *et al.*, 1989) and 'other commissions, study groups, task forces, advisory committees, caucuses, boards, delegations, and blue-ribbon panels', that have delved into the causes of US industrial decline (Reich, 1991a, pp. 76–77; see also Reich, 1990a).

The question of the loss of global competitive advantage must be asked because the employment of millions of Americans—not only 'routine producers' but also 'symbolic analysts' and 'in-person servers'—depends directly and indirectly on the investment strategies of *existing* industrial enterprises that in the past have built organizations capable of competing globally but that are unable, or unwilling, to do so any longer. Given his conception of the emerging global market in symbolic analysts, however, Reich appears to believe that the high-value labor markets that characterize 'the global webs of enterprise' will quickly re-employ those symbolic analysts left momentarily unemployed by the decline of US industry. Hence the goal of government policy should not be to ensure the competitive viability of existing enterprises but to encourage the upgrading of the skills of routine producers and in-person servers so that they are in the same enviable labor-market position as their fellow citizens who have already attained symbolic-analyst status.

4. Symbolic Analysts: Creators or Extractors of Value?

The logic of Reich's argument is that the 'have-nots' among Americans—the bottom 80% of the income distribution—can view the relatively high incomes of the symbolic analysts as evidence of the economic opportunity that awaits those who acquire the requisite skills. As more Americans, aided by government-supported education and training, gain access to the skills required to be symbolic analysts, they will find employment in the global webs of enterprise and attain the high standards of living enjoyed by Americans who have already acquired symbolic analyst status.

The prospect of joining the ranks of the symbolic analysts is all the more enticing when one considers how well those at the top of the income distribution did during the 1980s. Between 1977 and 1988, average family incomes rose *only* for those in the top 20% of the income distribution, with the average incomes for those in the lower half of the top 20% rising by 1.0% and for those in the top half by 16.5%. Over this period, the average incomes of the top 5% of American families rose by 23.4% and the average incomes of the top 1% by 49.8% (Phillips, 1990, p. 17).

But what if the very ability of many of the top 20%, and even more so the top 1%, to reap high incomes is contributing to US competitive decline? For example, how did it happen that there were 244 000 tax returns reporting incomes of $200 000 or more in 1984 but 739 000 only four years later? (Hinds, 1990). Were the richest Americans generating their high incomes by creating new sources of value in the economy? Or were they finding new ways to extract value that others had created?

Among those who saw their incomes grow dramatically during the 1980s were the top managers of the major US corporations (see Phillips, 1990, pp. 178–181; Crystal, 1991). Reich himself notes that, on average, in 1960 after-tax income of a CEO of one of the hundred largest US corporations was 12 times that of a shop-floor worker whereas by 1988 this ratio had risen to 70 (Reich, 1991a, pp. 204–205). Reich also recognizes that top managers in Germany and Japan saw no such gains (Reich, 1991a, p. 205n). Are we to conclude that during the 1980s the top managers of US corporations found new ways to create value that justified their burgeoning levels of compensation? Or might it not be more reasonable to inquire whether, during the 1980s, these top managers availed themselves of new ways of extracting value from their companies and from the economy more generally?

The emergence of a powerful market for corporate control, beginning with the conglomeration movement of the 1960s and becoming most manifest with the gargantuan leveraged buyouts of the mid-1980s, encouraged and enabled America's top corporate executives to use their existing positions of corporate control to turn from creating to extracting value. Empowered by the existence of, and often their direct participation in, a financial system structured to extract as much value as possible from the economy, many top managers of major US industrial corporations ceased to see themselves as members of their enterprises (for an elaboration of this argument, see Lazonick, 1992). Rather top managers began to identify with a financial community that sought to live off the rents of previous value creation, and that, through the concentration of shareholding in the economy and the transformation of Wall Street from investing to trading, became increasingly able to extract these rents (for accounts of this transformation, see Brooks,

——————————— *Industry Clusters versus Global Webs* ———————————

1973; Auletta, 1986; Carrington, 1987; Lowenstein, 1988; Bruck, 1989; Burrough and Helyar, 1990; Stewart, 1991).

It had been the organizational capabilities of these managerial communities that formed the foundation of US global competitive advantage from the late nineteenth century into the second half of this century. But when, for the sake of their own personal gain, top managers began to act as if they owned the enterprises that employed them and redirected their attention from value creation to value extraction, the superior organizational capabilities of these industrial enterprises could no longer be sustained. This at a time, moreover, when competitive challenges by foreign enterprises with superior value-creating capabilities demanded more, not less, commitment of financial resources to the building of value-creating business organizations in the United States.

5. *Corporate Governance as a National Phenomenon*

From this perspective, contrary to Reich, nationality does matter in the ownership of enterprises because norms concerning, and constraints on, the relation between ownership and control vary markedly across the advanced capitalist economies. The governance of corporate investment strategies is a national phenomenon. Over the past few decades, a market for corporate control has arisen in the United States and Britain, but not in Germany and Japan. During the first half of this century, with ownership of the major US industrial corporations widely distributed and fragmented, and with, for the most part, value-creating managers in control of enterprise resources, it was relatively harmless for Americans to cling to the ideology that individuals as shareholders 'owned' the industrial giants. Now, however, with the concentration of ownership in the hands of a value-extracting financial community and the alliance of top managers of US industrial corporations with that community, the ideology that shareholders are owners who, as such, should control the corporation has become an instrument of industrial decline and an impediment to industrial regeneration.

It is consistent with this ideology of ownership, as well as with the alliance between top managers and value-extracting financiers in the market for corporate control, that Reich appears to make no distinction between corporate shareholders and corporate executives in terms of either their economic interests or economic impacts. For, in proclaiming that the national identity of owners does not matter to the wealth of the nation, Reich simply assumes that owners and managers are as one. In Reich's words: 'The nationality of a firm's dominant shareholders and of its top executives has less and less to do with where the firm invests and [more and more?] with whom

——————————— 19 ———————————

—————————————— *Industry Clusters versus Global Webs* ——————————————

it contracts around the world' (Reich, 1991a, p. 120). And later in the book: 'All global webs—regardless of the nationality of the majority of share-holders or of top executives—are busily investing money, developing technologies, and contracting with workers all over the world' (Reich, 1991a, p. 285; see also p. 313).

In the early 1980s, Reich (1983, p. 157) warned that 'paper entrepreneurialism is supplanting product entrepreneurialism as the most dynamic and innovative business in the American economy'. In *The Work of Nations*, Reich does not ignore the phenomenon of 'paper entrepreneurialism', although he no longer uses the term. He tells the reader that 'the symbolic analysts who headed the savings and loans had everything to gain and nothing to lose from speculating wildly'; that 'symbolic analysts who sell financial and legal services can accumulate great fortunes by rapidly out-maneuvering one another'; that 'legal and financial symbolic analysis has thus become a major source of income for a growing number of Americans, as well as a national pastime for many others'; that 'by the 1990s, lawyers, financiers, and speculators stood ready to earn even larger sums undoing the damage they had wrought during the 1980s' (Reich, 1991a, pp. 189, 190, 192, 193).

But, in *The Work of Nations*, all of these statements are contained in a chapter entitled, 'A Digression on Symbolic Analysts and Market Incentive' (ch. 15). Reich introduces the chapter by stating:

> One final point about symbolic analysts bears mention, although the reader eager for the plot to thicken may skip to the next chapter [entitled 'American Incomes'] without peril. Here I pause to examine the public benefits of symbolic analysis, and how the considerable skills and insights of symbolic analysts can be harnessed for the public good (Reich, 1991a, p. 185).

In the analysis of the prosperity of any nation in the late twentieth century, the harnessing of the skills and insights of the most highly educated segments of the labor force for the public good cannot be treated as a side issue. If, following Porter, one accepts that the organization of business enterprises in the 'home base' is a prime determinant of global competitive advantage, a major challenge facing the United States in the last decade of the twentieth century is to build business organizations that ensure that 'the best and the brightest' within the business community devote their skills and efforts to value creation rather than value extraction. At issue, moreover, is not just how existing human resources are utilized but also how new human resources are developed. The more the interests of the most prosperous Americans become bound up with value extraction, the less likely are they to have an interest in providing the financial resources for the next generation to develop the technological and organizational capabilities required to attain and sustain global competitive advantage in industrial pursuits. Moreover, the high returns on education and experience that can be reaped by participating in the process of value extraction combined with the insecurity of careers in value-creating enterprises and organizations create incentives for young symbolic analysts to see value-extracting activity, rather than value-creating activity, as the route to their own individual success.

In the penultimate chapter of his book, entitled 'The Politics of Secession', Reich does make the case that the interests of the symbolic analysts—the top fifth of the US income distribution—do not include developing the productive capabilities of the bottom four-fifths.

> To improve the economic position of the bottom four-fifths will require that the fortunate fifth share its wealth and invest in the wealth-creating capacities of other Americans. Yet as the top becomes ever more tightly linked to the global economy, it has less of a stake in the performance and potential of its less fortunate compatriots. Thus our emerging dilemma, and that of other nations as well (Reich, 1991a, p. 301).

Confronted by this dilemma, Reich concludes his book by appealing to Americans on a higher moral plane: 'We can, if we choose, assert that our mutual obligations as citizens extend beyond our economic usefulness to one another and act accordingly' (Reich, 1991a, p. 315).

I see the American dilemma differently. The reluctance of the richest Americans to share the wealth and invest in the capabilities of the rest of the population is not because of their participation in the global economy, but because of their participation in value-extracting activities that do not require the development and utilization of masses of managers and workers with technological and organizational skills. If anything, the turn from value creation to value extraction over the past three decades has entailed a withdrawal of many Americans from participation in the global economy (T. Boone Pickens' celebrated voyages to Japanese shareholder meetings a few years back notwithstanding) to focus instead on gaining control of existing resources at home. Conversely, I venture to assert that, as is the case in enterprises in nations such as Japan, Germany, and Sweden, those enterprises operating in the United States that are seeking to remain globally competitive are investing more than ever in the value-creating capabilities of an ever-widening array of their employees at home (for excellent case studies of such investment strategies from around the world, see Magaziner and Patinkin, 1989).

These value-creating enterprises are making these investments, moreover,

———————————— Industry Clusters versus Global Webs ————————————

not out of the goodness of their hearts but because global competition demands that they make long-term investments in technological and organizational skills over which they can subsequently maintain control. One role of the national government is to provide, where necessary, the infrastructure to support such enterprises. But the national government must also be concerned with how business corporations within its boundaries allocate the often considerable surpluses that they control (see Ferleger and Lazonick, 1992). By establishing norms, regulations, and institutions for the governance of corporate investment, the national government must ensure that, both individually and collectively, the business 'leaders' of the nation invest for the future rather than merely reap the rewards of investments made in the past. Only then can the United States build the new industrial 'home bases' that must form the foundations for competing on global markets.

Reich's vision of 'global webs' creates an excuse for ignoring the problem of corporate governance in the United States. For Americans, the governance of the major US-based corporations is a critical issue for the 1990s. The prosperity of the American economy continues to depend on the investments in organization and technology that these business corporations are able and willing to make within the United States. Without these investments within the private sector, much-needed complementary public-sector investments in educating the labor force simply will not occur. To expect that industrial corporations based in foreign lands will compensate for the erosion of organizational capabilities that have occurred within the United States over the past quarter century will only foster further inaction, both public and private, to deal with America's long-term industrial decline.

References

Abegglen, J. C. and G. Stalk, Jr. (1985), *Kaisha: The Japanese Corporation*. Basic Books: New York.

Allen, R. C. (1983), 'Collective Invention'. *Journal of Economic Behavior and Organization*, 4, 1–24.

Auletta, K. (1986), *Greed and Glory on Wall Street*. Warner: New York.

Best, M. (1990), *The New Competition: Institutions of Industrial Restructuring*. Harvard University Press: Cambridge, MA.

Brooks, J. (1973), *The Go-Go Years*. Dutton: New York.

Bruck, C. (1989), *The Predator's Ball*. Penguin: New York.

Brusco, S. (1982), 'The Emilian Model: Productive Decentralisation and Social Integration'. *Cambridge Journal of Economics*, 6, 167–184.

Burrough, B. and J. Helyar. (1990), *Barbarians at the Gate*. Harper: New York.

Carrington, T. (1987), *The Year They Sold Wall Street*. Dutton: New York.

Carstensen, F. W. (1984), *American Enterprise in Foreign Markets: Studies of Singer and International Harvester in Imperial Russia*. University of North Carolina Press: Chapel Hill.

Chandler, A. D. Jr. (1990), *Scale and Scope: The Dynamics of Industrial Capitalism*. Harvard University Press: Cambridge, MA.

——————————— *Industry Clusters versus Global Webs* ———————————

Crystal, G. S. (1991), *In Search of Excess: The Overcompensation of U.S. Executives*. Norton: New York.

Dertouzos, M. L., R. M. Solow and R. K. Lester (1989), *Made in America: Regaining the Productive Edge*. MIT Press: Cambridge, MA.

Ferguson, C. H. (1990), 'Computers and the Coming of the U.S. Keiretsu'. *Harvard Business Review*, 68, 55–70.

Ferleger, L. and W. Lazonick (1992), 'Organizational Revolution Needed'. *Boston Globe*, October 27, 42.

Florida, R. and M. Kenney (1991), 'Transplanted Organizations: the Transfer of Japanese Industrial Organization to the U.S.' *American Sociological Review*, 56, 1–18.

Fucini, J. J. and S. Fucini (1990), *Working for the Japanese: Inside Mazda's American Auto Plant*. Free Press: New York.

Galbraith, J. K. (1967). *The New Industrial State*. Houghton Mifflin: New York.

Gilder, G. (1988). 'The Revitalization of Everything: The Law of the Microcosm'. *Harvard Business Review*, 66, 49–61.

Hinds, M. deC. (1990), 'Reading the Lips of the Rich: Spending, Not Taxes, Is the Problem.' *New York Times*, October 20, 8.

Kenney, M. and R. Florida (1991). 'How Japanese Industry is Rebuilding the Rust Belt'. *Technology Review*, 25–33.

Laxer, J. (1973), 'Canadian Manufacturing and U.S. Trade Policy', in R. M. Laxer, (ed.), *(Canada) Ltd.: The Political Economy of Dependency*. McClelland and Stewart: Toronto.

Lazonick, W. (1990), *Competitive Advantage on the Shop Floor*. Harvard University Press: Cambridge, MA.

Lazonick, W. (1991), *Business Organization and the Myth of the Market Economy*. Cambridge University Press: Cambridge.

Lazonick, W. (1992), 'Controlling the Market for Corporate Control: The Historical Significance of Managerial Capitalism'. *Industrial and Corporate Change*, 1, 445–488.

Levitt, K. (1970), *Silent Surrender: The Multinational Corporation in Canada*. Macmillan: Toronto.

Lowenstein, L. (1988), *What's Wrong with Wall Street?* Addison Wesley: Reading, MA.

Magaziner, I. and M. Patinkin (1989), *The Silent War: Inside the Global Business Battles Shaping America's Future*. Vintage: New York.

Magaziner, I. and R. B. Reich (1982), *Minding America's Business*. Harcourt Brace Jovanovich: New York.

Phillips, K. (1990), *The Politics of Rich and Poor: Wealth and the American Electorate in the Reagan Aftermath*. Random House: New York.

Porter, M. E. (1980), *Competitive Strategy*. Free Press: New York.

Porter, M. E. (1985), *Competitive Advantage*. Free Press: New York.

Porter, M. E. (1990), *The Competitive Advantage of Nations*. Free Press: New York.

Reich, R. B. (1983), *The Next American Frontier*. Penguin Books: New York.

Reich, R. B. (1987), *Tales of a New America*. Time Books: New York.

Reich, R. B. (1990a), 'Reviews of Michael E. Porter, *The Competitive Advantage of Nations*, and Michael L. Dertouzos, Robert M. Solow, and Richard K. Lester, *Made in America: Regaining the Productive Edge*'. *Times Literary Supplement*, August 31–September 6, 1–5.

Reich, R. B. (1990b), 'Who Is Us?' *Harvard Business Review*, 68, 53–64.

Reich, R. B. (1991a), *The Work of Nations: Preparing Ourselves for 21st-Century Capitalism*. Knopf: New York.

Reich, R. B. (1991b), 'Who Do We Think They Are?' *The American Prospect*, 4, 49–53.

Sakiya, T. (1987), *Honda Motor: The Men, the Management, the Machines*. Updated paperback edition, Kodansha: Tokyo.

Stewart, J. B. (1991), *Den of Thieves*. Simon and Schuster: New York.

Tedlow, R. (1990), *New and Improved: The Story of Mass Markets in America*. Basic Books: New York.

——————————— 23 ———————————

——————————— *Industry Clusters versus Global Webs* ———————————

Tolliday, S. (1991), 'Ford and Fordism in Postwar Britain: Enterprise Management and the Control of Labour, 1937–1987,' in S. Tolliday and J. Zeitlin, (eds.), *The Power to Manage?: Employers and Industrial Relations in Comparative-Historical Perspective.* Routledge/St. Martin's Press: London.

Tyson, L. D'A. (1991), 'They Are Not Us: Why American Ownership Still Matters'. *The American Prospect,* 4, 37–49.

Von Hippel, E. (1988), *The Sources of Innovation.* Oxford University Press: New York.

Wilkins, M. (1970), *The Emergence of Multinational Enterprise.* Harvard University Press: Cambridge, MA.

Wilkins, M. (1974), *The Maturing of Multinational Enterprise: American Business Abroad from 1914 to 1970.* Harvard University Press: Cambridge, MA.

Name Index

Abegglen, James 477, 485, 629
Adahi, Fumihiko 487
Adams, John Quincy 291
Aglietta, Michel 478
Aitken, Hugh G.J. 92–3
Alchian, Armen A. 60–62, 64–5, 67
Aldrich, Howard 477
Allen, Paul 506
Altshuler, Alan 476, 487
Amsden, Alice 164, 394
Anderson, Harlan 500
Anderson, Martin 476
Anderson, P. 203, 209
Aoki, Masahiko 477, 479, 484
Araki, Shinji 467
Arnold, Thurman 354
Asanuma, Banri 474, 487–8
Ashby, Eric 145
Auerbach, Jerold S. 90
Auletta, K. 634

Babbage, Charles 498
Bagnasco, A. 223
Baker, Gladys 407, 412–13
Ballou, Adin 292
Bancroft, Eben D. 330
Bancroft, Joseph 295, 330–31
Barksdale, Hamilton 345–6
Barney, J.B. 218
Baumol, W. 196, 198
Becker, Gary 255
Becker, William H. 86
Benedict, Ruth 477
Benger, Ernest 353
Berkhofer, Robert 74
Berle, Adolf 164
Best, Michael 477–8, 622
Bilzern, Paul A. 116
Blackford, Mansel G. 84
Blackman, S. 196, 198
Bledstein, Burton J. 89
Bolton, Elmer K. 351, 353–4
Boorstin, Daniel J. 79
Botta, P. 231
Boulding, Kenneth 55, 66
Braverman, Harry 482
Bricklin, Daniel 509

Brooks, Jennifer 402, 633
Brown, Clair 478
Brown, E. Richard 91
Bruck, C. 634
Brusco, S. 226, 229–30, 235–6, 622
Bucharin 53
Burawoy, Michael 484
Burch, Philip 143
Burgelman, R. 200, 219
Burns, T. 216
Burrough, B. 634
Bush, George 598

Cameron, K. 218, 220
Cantwell, J. 200
Capecchi, V. 223, 238
Carnegie, Andrew 267
Carothers, Wallace H. 351, 353–4, 366
Carrington, T. 634
Carstensen, F.W. 628
Chakravarthy, B.S. 216, 220
Chandler, Alfred D. 74–78, 127–8, 130,
    132–72, 196–7, 199–200, 202–5, 270–71,
    345, 397, 402, 417, 495–7, 531–2, 628
Church, Roy 127, 129, 140
Clark, K. 204, 209, 215, 220
Clarke, Sally 396, 404, 417–18
Clinton, Bill 616
Cohen, W. 200
Cole, Robert 477–8, 482, 485–6
Collins, Robert M. 85
Cool, Karel 477
Coolidge, Calvin 599
Corbusier, Le 136
Cramer, Stuart 314
Crowther, Stuart 478
Crystal, G.S. 633
Cuff, Robert D. 85
Cusumano, Michael 480
Cutcher-Gershenfeld, Joel 486
Cyert, R. 200

Daems, Herman 77
Danbom, David B. 412
Darwin, Charles 59, 62
David, P. 231
de Castro, Edson 109

Dell, Michael 519
de Lupus, Hugo 5
Dertouzas, M.L. 632
Deskins, Donald 486
DiMaggio, Paul 477
Doezema, William 83
Dohse, Knuth 478
Dore, Ronald 476–7, 485, 487
Dosi, G. 200–201
Downs, A. 145
Draper, Clare 329–30, 335, 338
Draper, Eben S. 301, 329, 332
Draper, Ebenezer D. 291–4, 296
Draper (family) 287–90, 295–9, 301–7,
    309–24, 340
Draper, George 293–6, 298
Draper, George A. 301, 329
Draper, George Otis 307, 318, 329–30, 340
Draper, Ira 291
Draper, James 291
Draper, William F. 296, 301, 305, 307, 318,
    329–30, 335
Duisburg, Carl 103
Dunning, John 602
Du Pont, Alfred I. 342–3
Du Pont, Francis I. 343–4
Du Pont, Irenee 348
Du Pont, Pierre S. 342, 344–5, 359
Du Pont, T. Coleman 342–3, 345
Durkheim, E. 252–3
Dutcher, Elihu 294–7
Dutcher, Frank 330–32
Dutcher, Warren 294, 298, 306

Eckert, J. Presper 498
Eddy, Edward D. 407, 409
Edison, Thomas 78, 104–5
Edwards, Richard 79, 476
Eisenhower, Dwight D. 83, 85
Enke, Stephen 61
Enright, Michael J. 191
Estridge, Philip Donald 514–16
Evenson, Robert E. 403, 413, 416, 418–19

Fairchild (family) 547
Farben, I.G. 350
Felsenstein, Lee 505, 512
Ferguson, Charles 623
Ferleger, Lou 405, 407, 637
Filene, Edward A. 83
Filippi, E. 234
Filuppucci, C. 223
Fishlow, Albert 128–9, 163
Fletcher, S.W. 407

Fligstein, Neil 128–9, 167
Florida, Richard 204, 476–8, 482, 487–8,
    490, 630
Ford, Henry 30, 107–8, 133, 136, 164, 228,
    532
Foster, R. 220
Freeman, C. 205
Freeman, John 477
French, Don 511
Frey, L. 226
Friedman, David 478, 487
Fucini, Joseph 478, 631
Fucini, Suzy 478, 631
Fujimoto, T. 204, 209, 220
Furner, Mary O. 90

Galambos, Louis 73
Galbraith, John K. 628
Galvin, Robert W. 592
Garrahan, Philip 478
Gates, William 506, 515
Gee, Edwin 358–61
Gerschenkron, Alexander 164
Gertler, Meric 478
Giddens, A. 211
Gilbert, R. 198
Gilder, George 623
Ginsburg 242
Giovannetti, E. 230
Gordon, Andrew 477, 484
Gordon, R.A. 48
Graebner, William 83
Graham, Edward M. 603, 609
Granovetter, Mark 477
Gras, N.S.B. 77
Greenewalt, Crawford 359
Griffith, Robert 85
Griliches, Zvi 417
Gropius, Walter 136
Guglielmi, M. 234
Guiles, Melinda 486

Hamada, Mitsuyo 481
Hamel, G. 200, 208–9
Hammond, Seth 327
Hannan, Michael 477
Harding, T. Swann 415–16
Haskell, Thomas L. 89
Hawley, Ellis, W. 84–5
Hayes, R.H. 209, 215, 220
Heckert, Richard 361
Heilbroner, Robert L. 79
Helper, Susan 489
Helyar, J. 634

Henderson, R. 200, 209
Hertz, Heinrich 92
Hewlett, William 547
Hightower, James 404, 421
Hinds, M. de C. 633
Hirsch, Fred 262
Hirschman, Albert 260
Hitler, Adolf 110
Hitt, M. 209
Hixon, Todd 591
Hobhouse, L.T. 242, 251, 253, 259, 263
Hofer, C.W. 209
Hoff, Marcian E. Jr 501
Hogan, Michael J. 86
Holmstrom, B. 198
Hounshell, D.A. 204, 368
Houston, David F. 419
Howard, Robert P. 401, 420
Hrebiniak, L.G. 209
Huber, G. 222
Huffman, Wallace E. 403, 413, 419
Hughes, Agatha 129
Hughes, Jonathan R.T. 81
Hughes, Thomas Parke 76–8, 127, 129, 135, 205

Ireland, R.D. 209
Itami, H. 209, 220

Jefferson, Edward G. 362–3
Jenkins, Resse V. 76–77
Jobs, Steven 506–9, 524–5, 535–9
Johnson, Chalmers 394
Johnson, James P. 83
Johnson, Thomas 112
Jones, Daniel 204, 476
Jordan, David Starr 410
Jurgens, Ulrich 478

Kagono, Tadao 484
Kalleberg, Arne 477, 479, 485
Kaneko, Yoshirō 453
Kano, Noriaki 482
Kanter, R.M. 219–20
Kaplan, Robert 112
Kariya, Takehiko 483
Katz, Harry 476
Kay, Alan 539
Kay, Andrew 513, 517
Kennedy, John F. 85
Kenney, Martin 204, 476–8, 482, 487–8, 490, 630
Kerr, Norwood A. 405, 408–10, 412–15
Key, V.O. 414

Keynes, John M. 85
Kilby, Jack 501
Kildall, Gary 505–6, 515
Kile, Orville M. 401, 420
Killian, Joseph 504
Kimball, Ranch 591
Kimberly, J.R. 211
Kirkendall, Richard S. 420–21
Knoblauch, H.C. 408, 410–11, 415, 419
Kochan, Thomas 476, 481, 486
Kocka, Jürgen 127, 129, 148
Kogut, B. 200
Kohler, Robert E. 93
Koike, Kazuo 477, 479, 485
Krafcik, John 478, 486, 489
Krugman, Paul R. 603, 609
Kuehler, Jack 592
Kumazawa, Makoto 478
Kuznets, Simon 97

Langlois, R. 200
Laxer, J. 629
Layton, Edwin T. Jr 91–2
Lazerzon, Mark 477
Lazonick, William 200, 202, 204, 396, 405, 422, 476–8, 495–6, 623–4, 631, 633, 637
Legnick-Hall, Cynthia 477
Leibenstein, Harvey 255–6
Leibnitz 46
Leininger, Steve 511
Leonard-Barton, D. 209, 214–15, 218
Leslie, Stuart W. 92
Levin, R. 200
Levine, Solomon 485
Levitt, K. 629
Lewchuk, Wayne 143–4
Lieberman, M. 209
Lillrank, Paul 482
Lincoln, James 477, 479, 481–2, 485
Locke, Robert 146
Lodge, Oliver 92
Lord, Russell 419–21
Lowe, William 514
Lowenstein, L. 634

Macaulay, Stewart 258
MacDuffie, John 477
Macfarlane, A. 251
MacGregor, I. 255
Magaziner, I. 616, 636
Mair, Andrew 478
Malagoli, W. 226, 230
Malsch, Thomas 478
March, J. 200

Marconi, Guglielmo 92
Marcus, Alan I. 405
Markkula, Mike 507
Marous, John C. 118
Marris, Robin 145
Marshall, Alfred 27, 54–5, 496–7, 541, 545
Martin, Albro 80
Marx, Karl 169, 243, 276
Mather, Sir William 105
Matusow, Allen J. 85
Mauchly, John W. 498
McBride, Kerry 481
McConnell, Grant 400–401, 420–21
McCraw, Thomas K. 83
McKelvey, Bill 477
McKersie, Robert 476
Means, Gardiner 164
Meinhard, A. 211
Mengoli, P. 230
Messori, M. 223
Meyer, John 477
Mill, J.S. 48
Millard, Bill 504–5
Miller, Krystal 486
Mintzberg, H. 214
Mitchell, S.Z. 138
Mitchell, W. 209
Monden, Yashuhiro 480
Monsen, K.J. 145
Monteverde, Kirk 475
Montgomery, David 79, 209
Moore, Ernest G. 407, 412, 415, 417
Morgan, J.P. 243
Mori, Shūtarō 467
Morikawa, Hidemasa 128–9, 153
Morison, Elting G. 79
Moritz, Michael 541
Morris, Jonathan 478
Morris-Suzuki, Tessa 477
Moxham, A.J. 343
Muller, J. 229
Mumford, Lewis 129

Nakane, Chie 477
Nakatani, I. 251
Navin, Thomas R. 298, 301, 303
Nelson, Richard R. 418
Nemoto, Masao 470
Nishiguchi, Toshihiro 487
Nitobe 253
Nixon, Richard 187
Noble, David F. 91
Nonaka, Ikujiro 484
Northrop, James H. 305–6, 318, 330, 333

Northrop, Jonas 330, 335, 337
Noyce, Robert 501

Odaka, Konosuke 487
Ohno, Taiichi 340
Okimura, Akihiro 248, 484
Okun, Arthur 261
Oliver, Nick 478
Olsen, Ken 108, 500, 534–5
Ono, Keinosuke 487
Opel, John 514
Ordover, J. 198
Osborne, Adam 508, 512, 517

Paci, M. 233
Packard, David 547
Palgrave, R.H.I. 242
Pareto, V. 40
Parker, Mike 478
Parsons, T. 253
Passer, Harold 134
Patinkin, M. 636
Pattarin, E. 231
Pavitt, K. 200, 209, 217, 220
Peddle, Chuck 507–8, 510
Penrose, E. 200
Perkin, William 102
Perrow, Charles 476–7
Pettigrew, A. 211
Pfeffer, Jeffery 219, 477
Phillips, K. 633
Pickens, T. Boone 636
Piore, Michael 476–8
Pisano, G. 200, 209
Porter, Michael E. 176, 185, 196–7, 616–25, 635
Powell, Walter 477–8
Power, D.J. 222
Prahalad, C.K. 200, 208–9
Pugliese, E. 238

Quant, Mary 239
Quinn, J.B. 209, 218, 220

Raskin, Jef 538
Rasmussen, Wayne D. 400, 412, 419
Rathenau, Emil 138
Rathenau, Walther 138
Ratliff, Wayne 512
Reagan, Ronald 187, 598
Reed, Phillip 504–5
Reese, Dr Charles L. 343, 346–9, 351
Reich, Leonard S. 91–2, 204
Reich, Michael 478

Reich, Robert B. 599–600, 602, 605, 609–11, 616–17, 624–37
Reinganum, J. 198–9
Rhoades, Alonzo E. 331, 333
Ricardo, David 178
Richardson, G.B. 477
Ritchie, Donald A. 83
Roberts, Ed 502–6
Roberts, Richard 289
Robertson, Paul 497
Robins, James 477
Robinson, Austin 541
Rockefeller, John D. 100–101, 108
Roehl, T. 209
Roos, Daniel 204, 476
Roosevelt, F.D. 354, 415, 420, 422
Roper, C.F. 318, 330
Roscher 16
Rosen, Benjamin 524
Rosenbaum, James 483
Rosenberg, Charles 412
Rosenberg, Nathan 542
Rosenbloom, R. 200
Rosenthal, R. 217
Rowan, Brian 477
Rubin, D. 217
Rumelt, R.P. 200, 209
Ruttan, Vernon W. 413, 416, 418

Sabel, Charles 235, 476–8, 487, 490
Saito, Shoichi 463, 466
Sakikabara, Kiyonori 484
Sakiya, T. 631
Sako, Mari 477–8
Salancik, Gerald 477
Saloner, G. 198
Samuelson, J. 243
Sander, Wendell 537
Sanderson, J.M. 145–6
Sands, Saul 130
Sawyer, Jacob H. 297–8, 306
Sayer, Andrew 478, 487
Schein, E. 211
Schendel, D. 209
Scherer, Frederic M. 128, 130
Schumpeter, Joseph 197, 199–200, 205, 209, 397, 477, 487, 494–5
Scott, Mike 509
Sculley, John 525, 539
Seltzer, L.H. 144
Senge, P. 220
Senior 29
Shane, Michael 521
Shapiro, Irving 360

Sheard, Paul 487
Shimada, Haruo 477
Shiomi, Haruhito 453, 455
Shirai, Taishiro 477, 485
Shoten, Maruei 444
Shrayer, Michael 511
Shuen, A. 200, 209
Shugart 506
Simon, H. 200
Singh, J. 211
Slaughter, Jane 478
Smith, Adam 29–30, 33, 39, 178, 241–2, 252
Smith, C.B. 400
Smith, J. 204
Smith, J.K. 368
Snow, C.C. 209
Solow, Robert 246
Souder, W.E. 209
Sparre, Fin 347, 350, 357
Spencer 59, 252
Sperry, Elmer 76, 129
Stalk, G. Jr 629
Stalker, G.M. 216
Stewart, J.B. 634
Stimpson, E.S. 318, 331–2
Stimpson, Wallace I. 331–2
Stine, Charles M.A. 351–5
Stinnes, Hugo 138
Stone, Charles 138
Sugawara, Toshiharu 445
Suzuki, H. 484

Taira, Koji 477, 485
Tandy, Charles 510–11
Taylor, Frederick W. 136, 228, 272
Tedlow, Richard S. 128, 629
Teece, David J. 200–201, 204, 209–10, 475
Tenti, Paolo 191
Terman, Frederick 546–7
Terrell, Paul 507
Tirole, J. 198
Tolliday, S. 629
Toyota, Kiichirō 456–7
Tramiel, Jack 510
Trevor, Malcolm 478, 484
True, Alfred 402–3, 407–10, 413, 416
Tucker, D. 211
Tushman, M. 203, 209
Tyson, Laura 611–15, 627, 629

van der Rohe, Mies 136
Van de Ven, A. 209, 220
Van Natta, Bruce 504
Veblen, T. 53

Vogel, Ezra 421
von Hippel, E. 218, 621
von Neumann, John 498, 501

Wade, Robert 394
Waggoner, Paul 416, 418
Wallace, Henry A. 419
Watson, Thomas Jr 108
Weber, Max 153
Webster, Edwin 138
Weick, Karl 220, 222, 477
Wheelwright, S.C. 209
White, Michael 478, 484
Whitney, D. 217
Wiebe, Robert 74, 88–9
Wilkins, M. 628–9
Wilkinson, Barry 478
William the Conqueror 5
Williamson, Oliver 145, 198–9, 202–3,

244–6, 250–51, 256, 477
Wilson, 'Engine' Charlie 599, 611
Wilson, James 407–9, 412, 416
Wilson, James Q. 84
Wilson, M.L. 420–21
Winter, S. 200–202
Wolff, E. 196, 198
Womack, James 204, 476, 478, 486
Wozniak, Stephen 506–9, 537–8, 541
Wright, Carroll D. 410

Yamada, Jun 478
Yoshida, Tarō 442–3
Yoshino, M. 478
Young, Owen D. 83
Young, Ruth 477

Zuboff, Shoshana 477
Zucker, Lynne 211, 218, 477